ALL·IN·ONE

CISM®

Certified Information Security Manager

EXAM GUIDE

ABOUT THE AUTHOR

Peter H. Gregory, CISM, CISA, CRISC, CISSP, CCISO, CCSK, PCI-QSA, is a 30-year career technologist and an executive director at Optiv Security, the largest pure-play cybersecurity solutions provider in the Americas. He has been developing and managing information security management programs since 2002 and has been leading the development and testing of secure IT environments since 1990. In addition, he has spent many years as a software engineer and architect, systems engineer, network engineer, security engineer, and systems operator. Throughout his career, he has written many articles, white papers, user manuals, processes, and procedures, and he has conducted numerous lectures, training classes, seminars, and university courses.

Peter is the author of more than 40 books about information security and technology, including *Solaris Security, CISSP Guide to Security Essentials,* and *CISA Certified Information Systems Auditor All-In-One Study Guide.* He has spoken at numerous industry conferences including RSA, Interop, SecureWorld Expo, West Coast Security Forum, IP3, Society for Information Management, the Washington Technology Industry Association, and InfraGard.

Peter is an advisory board member at the University of Washington's certificate program in information security and risk management, the lead instructor (emeritus) and advisory board member for the University of Washington certificate program in cybersecurity, a former board member of the Washington State chapter of InfraGard, and a founding member of the Pacific CISO Forum. He is a 2008 graduate of the FBI Citizens' Academy and a member of the FBI Citizens' Academy Alumni Association.

Peter resides with his family in the Seattle, Washington, area and can be found at www.peterhgregory.com.

About the Technical Editor

Jay Burke, CISSP, CISM, is a highly accomplished information security professional with more than 20 years of operational and executive experience across a variety of industries.

Mr. Burke has worked with customers of different sizes and types to build, enhance, and manage best-in-class cybersecurity programs. As an executive-level security professional he has led detailed maturity assessments as well as facilitated executive workshops to assist CISOs in maturing their cybersecurity programs. His practical experience includes engagements addressing strategic consulting, project management, regulatory compliance (Sarbanes–Oxley, Payment Card Industry, NERC CIP, HIPAA, SOC 1 and 2), and cybersecurity program development leveraging ISO 27001/2, NIST 800-53, Cloud Security Alliance CCM, Shared Assessments SIG, and Unified Compliance Framework.

Jay currently serves as the director of strategy and governance for Kudelski Security, an independent cybersecurity solutions provider supporting large enterprise and public-sector clients in Europe and the United States.

ALL·IN·ONE

CISM®

Certified Information Security Manager

EXAM GUIDE

Peter H. Gregory

Mc
Graw
Hill
Education

New York   Chicago   San Francisco
Athens   London   Madrid   Mexico City
Milan   New Delhi   Singapore   Sydney   Toronto

Cataloging-in-Publication Data is on file with the Library of Congress

McGraw-Hill Education books are available at special quantity discounts to use as premiums and sales promotions, or for use in corporate training programs. To contact a representative, please visit the Contact Us pages at www.mhprofessional.com.

CISM® Certified Information Security Manager All-in-One Exam Guide

1 2 3 4 5 6 7 8 9 LCR 21 20 19 18

ISBN: Book p/n 978-1-260-02701-3 and CD p/n 978-1-260-02702-0
of set 978-1-260-02703-7

MHID: Book p/n 1-260-02701-5 and CD p/n 1-260-02702-3
of set 1-260-02703-1

Sponsoring Editor	Technical Editor	Production Supervisor
Wendy Rinaldi	Jay Burke	James Kussow
Editorial Supervisor	**Copy Editor**	**Composition**
Jody McKenzie	Kim Wimpsett	MPS Limited
Project Manager	**Proofreader**	**Illustration**
Vivek Khandelwal, MPS Limited	Richard Camp	MPS Limited
Acquisitions Coordinator	**Indexer**	**Art Director, Cover**
Claire Yee	Jack Lewis	Jeff Weeks

To current and aspiring security managers everywhere who want to do the right thing, through professional growth and practicing sound security and risk management techniques, to keep their organizations out of trouble.

CONTENTS AT A GLANCE

CONTENTS

Figure Credits

Figure 2-2 Adapted from The Business Model for Information Security,
    ISACA.
Figure 2-4 Adapted from The University of Southern California, Marshall
    School of Business, Institute for Critical Information Infrastructure
    Protection, USA.
Figure 2-5 Courtesy Xhienne: SWOT pt.svg, CC BY-SA 2.5,
    https://commons.wikimedia.org/w/index.php?curid=2838770.
Figure 2-6 Courtesy High Tech Security Solutions Magazine.
Figure 3-2 Source: National Institute for Standards and Technology.
Figure 4-1 Courtesy The Open Group.
Figure 4-9 Courtesy Bluefoxicy at en.wikipedia.org.
Figure 5-3 Source: NASA.

ACKNOWLEDGMENTS

I am especially grateful to Wendy Rinaldi for affirming the need to have this book published on a tight timeline. My readers, including current and future security managers, deserve nothing less.

Heartfelt thanks to Claire Yee for proficiently managing this project, facilitating rapid turnaround, and equipping me with information I needed to produce the manuscript.

I would like to thank my former consulting colleague, Jay Burke, who took on the task of tech reviewing the manuscript. Jay carefully and thoughtfully scrutinized the entire draft manuscript and made scores of useful suggestions that have improved the book's quality and value for readers.

Many thanks to Jody McKenzie and Vivek Khandelwal for managing the editorial and production ends of the project, and to Kim Wimpsett for copyediting the book and further improving readability. Much appreciation to MPS Limited for expertly rendering my sketches into beautifully clear line art and for laying out the pages. Like Olympic athletes, they make hard work look easy.

Many thanks to my literary agent, Carole Jelen, for diligent assistance during this and other projects. Sincere thanks to Rebecca Steele, my business manager and publicist, for her long-term vision and for keeping me on track.

Despite having written more than 40 books, I have difficulty putting into words my gratitude for my wife, Rebekah, for tolerating my frequent absences (in the home office and away on business travel) while I developed the manuscript. This project could not have been completed without her loyal and unfailing support.

INTRODUCTION

The dizzying pace of information systems innovation has made vast expanses of information available to organizations and the public. Often, design flaws and technical vulnerabilities bring unintended consequences, usually in the form of information theft and disclosure. The result: a patchwork of laws, regulations, and standards such as Sarbanes–Oxley, GDPR, Gramm-Leach-Bliley, HIPAA, PCI-DSS, PIPEDA, NERC CIP, and scores of U.S. state laws requiring public disclosure of security breaches involving private information. Through these, organizations are either required or incentivized to build or improve their information security programs to avoid security breaches, penalties, sanctions, and embarrassing news headlines.

These developments continue to drive demand for information security professionals and information security leaders. These highly sought professionals play a crucial role in the development of better information security programs that result in reduced risk and improved confidence.

The Certified Information Security Manager (CISM) certification, established in 2002, is the leading certification for information security management. Demand for the CISM certification has grown so much that the once-per-year certification exam was changed to twice per year in 2005 and is now offered multiple times each year. In 2005, the CISM certification was awarded accreditation by the American National Standards Institute (ANSI) under international standard ISO/IEC 17024. CISM is also one of the few certifications formally approved by the U.S. Department of Defense in its Information Assurance Technical category (DoD 8570.01-M). In 2017, CISM was a finalist in SC Magazine's Best Professional Certification Program. There are now more than 34,000 professionals with the certification.

Purpose of This Book

Let's get the obvious out of the way: this is a comprehensive study guide for the security management professional who needs a serious reference for individual or group-led study for the Certified Information Security Manager (CISM) certification. The content in this book contains the technical information that CISM candidates are required to know. This book is one source of information to help you prepare for the CISM exam but should not be thought of as the ultimate collection of all the information and experience that ISACA expects qualified CISM candidates to possess. No one publication covers all of this information.

This book is also a reference for aspiring and practicing IT security managers and CISOs. The content that is required to pass the CISM exam is the same content that practicing security managers need to be familiar with in their day-to-day work. This book is an ideal CISM exam study guide as well as a desk reference for those who have already earned their CISM certification.

This book is also invaluable for information security professionals who are not in a leadership position today. You will gain considerable insight into today's information security management challenges. This book is also useful for IT and business management professionals who work with information security leaders and need to better understand what they are doing and why.

This book is an excellent guide for anyone exploring a security management career. The study chapters explain all the relevant technologies, techniques, and processes used to manage a modern information security program. This is useful if you are wondering what the security management profession is all about.

How This Book Is Organized

This book is logically divided into four major sections:

- **Introduction** The "front matter" of the book and Chapter 1 provide an overview of the CISM certification and the information security management profession.

- **CISM study material** Chapters 2 through 5 contain everything a studying CISM candidate is responsible for. This same material is a handy desk reference for aspiring and practicing information security managers.

- **Glossary** There are more than 550 terms used in the information security management profession.

- **Practice exams** Appendix explains the online CISM practice exam and Total Tester software accompanying this book.

Becoming a CISM

In this chapter, you will learn about
- What it means to be a CISM-certified professional
- ISACA, its code of ethics, and its standards
- The certification process
- How to apply for the exam
- How to maintain your certification
- How to get the most from your CISM journey

Congratulations on choosing to become a Certified Information Security Manager (CISM)! Whether you have worked for several years in the field of information security or have just recently been introduced to the world of security, governance, risk management, and disaster recovery planning, don't underestimate the hard work and dedication required to obtain and maintain CISM certification. Although ambition and motivation are required, the rewards can far exceed the effort.

You may not have imagined you would find yourself working in the world of information security (or *infosec,* as it's often called) or looking to obtain an information security management certification. Perhaps the increase in legislative or regulatory requirements for information system security led to your introduction to this field. Or possibly you have noticed that CISM-related career options are increasing exponentially and you have decided to get ahead of the curve. You aren't alone: in the past 15 years, more than 34,000 professionals worldwide reached the same conclusion and have earned the well-respected CISM certification. In its 2016 salary survey, Global Knowledge ranked CISM as one of the top three paying certifications for 2016. CISM was selected as a 2014 SC Magazine Award Finalist for Best Professional Certification Program. The IT Skills and Certifications Pay Index from Foote Partners consistently ranks CISM among the most sought-after IT certifications. In 2017, CISM was a finalist in SC Magazine's Best Professional Certification Program and was a finalist for Best Professional Training or Certification Programme at SC Awards Europe. It's hard to find a professional certification with so many accolades. Welcome to the journey and the amazing opportunities that await you.

I have put together this information to help you further understand the commitment needed, prepare for the exam, and maintain your certification. Not only is it my wish to see you pass the exam with flying colors, but I also provide you with the information and resources to maintain your certification and to proudly represent yourself and the professional world of information security management with your new credentials.

ISACA (formerly known as the Information Systems Audit and Control Association) is a recognized leader in the areas of control, assurance, and IT governance. Formed in 1967, this nonprofit organization represents more than 140,000 professionals in more than 180 countries. ISACA administers several exam certifications, including the CISM, the Certified Information Systems Auditor (CISA), the Certified in Risk and Information Systems Control (CRISC), and the Certified in the Governance of Enterprise IT (CGEIT) certifications. The CISM certification program has been accredited by the American National Standards Institute (ANSI) under International Organization for Standardization and International Electrotechnical Commission standard ISO/IEC 17024:2003, which means that ISACA's procedures for accreditation meet international requirements for quality, continuous improvement, and accountability. If you're new to ISACA, I recommend you tour the web site and become familiar with the guides and resources available. In addition, if you're near one of the 200+ local ISACA chapters in 80+ countries, consider taking part in the activities and even reaching out to the chapter board for information on local meetings, training days, conferences, and study sessions. You may be able to meet other information security professionals who can give you additional insight into the CISM certification and the information security management profession.

The CISM certification was established in 2002 and primarily focuses on security management, security governance, risk management, and business continuity planning. It certifies the individual's knowledge of establishing information security strategies, building and managing an information security program, preparing for and responding to security incidents, and business continuity planning. Organizations seek out qualified personnel for assistance with developing and maintaining strong and effective security programs. A CISM-certified individual is a great candidate for this.

Benefits of CISM Certification

Obtaining the CISM certification offers several significant benefits:

- **Expands knowledge and skills; builds confidence**   Developing knowledge and skills in the areas of security strategy, building and managing a security program, and responding to incidents can prepare you for advancement or expand your scope of responsibilities. The personal and professional achievement can boost confidence that encourages you to move forward and seek new career opportunities.

- **Increases marketability and career options**   Because of various legal and regulatory requirements, such as the Health Insurance Portability and Accountability Act (HIPAA), Payment Card Industry Data Security Standard (PCI-DSS), Sarbanes–Oxley, Gramm Leach Bliley Act (GLBA), Food and Drug Administration (FDA), Federal Energy Regulatory Commission/North American Electric Reliability Corporation (FERC/NERC), and the European General Data Protection Regulation (GDPR), demand is growing for individuals with experience in developing and running security programs. In addition, obtaining your CISM certification demonstrates to current and potential employers your willingness and commitment to improve your knowledge and skills in information systems management. Having a CISM certification can provide a competitive advantage and open up many doors of opportunity in various industries and countries.

- **Meets employment requirements**   Many government agencies and organizations are requiring CISM certifications for positions involving information security management and information assurance. One example is the United States Department of Defense (DoD). DoD Directive 8570 mandates that those personnel performing information assurance activities within the agency are certified with a commercial accreditation approved by the DoD. The DoD has approved the ANSI-accredited CISM certificate program because it meets ISO/IEC 17024:2003 requirements. All Information Assurance Management (IAM) Level III personnel are mandated to obtain CISM certification, as are those who are contracted to perform similar activities.

- **Builds customer confidence and international credibility**   Prospective customers needing security management work will have faith that the quality of the strategies and execution are in line with internationally recognized practices and standards.

Regardless of your current position, demonstrating knowledge and experience in the areas of security strategy and security management can expand your career options. The certification does not limit you to security management; it can provide additional value and insight to those in or seeking the following positions:

- Executives such as chief executive officers (CEOs), chief financial officers (CFOs), and chief information officers (CIOs)
- IT management executives such as chief information officers (CIOs), chief technology officers (CTOs), directors, managers, and staff
- Chief audit executives, audit partners, and audit directors
- Chief privacy officers (CPOs), data protection officers (DPOs), and other privacy professionals
- Compliance executives and management
- Seurity and audit consultants

Becoming a CISM Professional

To become a CISM professional, you are required to pay the exam fee, pass the exam, prove that you have the required experience and education, and agree to uphold ethics and standards. To keep your CISM certification, you are required to take at least 20 continuing education hours each year (120 hours in three years) and pay annual maintenance fees. This is depicted in Figure 1-1.

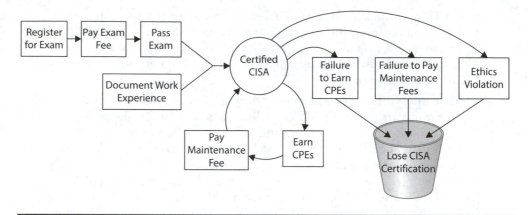

Figure 1-1   The CISM certification life cycle

The following list outlines the major requirements for becoming certified:

- **Experience**   A CISM candidate must be able to submit verifiable evidence of at least five years of experience, with a minimum of three years of professional work experience in three or more of the CISM job practice areas. Experience must be verified and must be gained within the ten-year period preceding the application date for certification or within five years from the date of passing the exam. Substitution and waiver options for up to three years of experience are available.

- **Ethics**   Candidates must commit to adhere to ISACA's Code of Professional Ethics, which guides the personal and professional conduct of those certified.

- **Exam**   Candidates must receive a passing score on the CISM exam. A passing score is valid for up to five years, after which the score is void. This means that a CISM candidate who passes the exam has a maximum of five years to apply for CISM certification; candidates who pass the exam but fail to act after five years will have to take the exam again if they want to become CISM certified.

- **Education**   Those certified must adhere to the CISM Continuing Professional Education Policy, which requires a minimum of 20 continuing professional education (CPE) hours each year, with a total requirement of 120 CPEs over the course of the certification period (three years).

- **Application**   After successfully passing the exam, meeting the experience requirements, and having read through the Code of Professional Ethics and Standards, a candidate is ready to apply for certification. An application must be received within five years of passing the exam.

Experience Requirements

To qualify for CISM certification, you must have completed the equivalent of five years of total work experience. These five years can take many forms, with several substitutions available. Additional details on the minimum certification requirements, substitution options, and various examples are discussed next.

NOTE Although it is not recommended, a CISM candidate can take the exam before completing any work experience directly related to information security management. As long as the candidate passes the exam and the work experience requirements are filled within five years of the exam date and within ten years from the application for certification, the candidate is eligible for certification.

Direct Work Experience

You are required to have a minimum of three years of work experience in the field of security strategy and management. This is equivalent to 6000 actual work hours, which must be related to three or more of the CISM job practice areas, as follows:

- **Information security governance**   Establish and/or maintain an information security governance framework and supporting processes to ensure that the information security strategy is aligned with organizational goals and objectives.

- **Information risk management**   Manage information risk to an acceptable level based on risk appetite to meet organizational goals and objectives.

- **Security program development and management**   Develop and maintain an information security program that identifies, manages, and protects the organization's assets while aligning to information security strategy and business goals, thereby supporting an effective security posture.

- **Information security incident management**   Plan, establish, and manage the capability to detect, investigate, respond to, and recover from information security incidents to minimize business impact.

All work experience must be completed within the ten-year period before completing the certification application or within five years from the date of initially passing the CISM exam. You will need to complete a separate Verification of Work Experience form for each segment of experience.

There is only one exception to this minimum three-year direct work experience requirement: if you are a full-time instructor. This option is discussed in the next section.

Substitution of Experience

Up to a maximum of three years of direct work experience can be substituted with the following to meet the five-year experience requirement.

Two Years

- Certified Information Systems Auditor (CISA) in good standing.

- Certified Information Systems Security Professional (CISSP) in good standing.

- A post-graduate degree in information security or a related field can be substituted for two years of direct work experience. Transcripts or a letter confirming degree status must be sent from the university attended to obtain the experience waiver.

One Year

- One full year of information systems management experience
- One full year of general security management experience
- Skills-based security certifications (e.g., GIAC, MCSE, Security+, CBCP, ESL IT Security Manager)
- Completion of an information security management program at an institution aligned with the Model Curriculum

As noted earlier, there is only one exception to the experience requirements. Should you have experience as a full-time university instructor teaching the management of information security, each two years of your experience can be substituted for one year of required direct work experience, without limitation.

Here is an example CISM candidate whose experience and education are considered for CISM certification: Jane Doe graduated in 2000 with a bachelor's degree in computer science. She spent five years working for a software company managing IT, and in January 2005, she began managing information security. In January 2007, she took some time off work for personal reasons. In 2012, she earned her Security+ certification and rejoined the workforce in December 2013, working for a public company in its enterprise risk management department as a risk manager. Jane passed the CISM exam in June 2014 and applied for CISM certification in January 2015. Does Jane have all of the experience required? What evidence will she need to submit?

- **Skills-based certification** Jane obtained her Security+ certification, which equates to a one-year experience substitution.
- **Two years of direct experience** She can count her two full years of information security management experience in 2005 and 2006.
- **One-year substitution** She cannot take into account one year of IT management experience completed between January 2000 to January 2005, as it was not completed within ten years of her application.
- **One-year direct experience** Jane would want to utilize her new risk manager experience for work experience.

Jane would need to send the following with her application to prove the experience requirements are met:

- Verification of Work Experience forms filled out and signed by her supervisors (or any superior) at the software company and the public company, verifying both the security management and nonsecurity management work conducted
- Transcripts or letter confirming degree status sent from the university

---

NOTE I recommend you also read the CISM certification qualifications on the ISACA web site. From time to time ISACA does change the qualification rules, and I want you to have the most up-to-date information available.

ISACA Code of Professional Ethics

Becoming a CISM professional means you agree to adhere to the ISACA Code of Professional Ethics. The code of ethics is a formal document outlining those things you will do to ensure the utmost integrity and that best support and represent the organization and certification.

Specifically, the ISACA code of ethics requires ISACA members and certification holders to do the following:

- Support the implementation of, and encourage compliance with, appropriate standards and procedures for the effective governance and management of enterprise information systems and technology, including audit, control, security, and risk management.

- Perform their duties with objectivity, due diligence, and professional care, in accordance with professional standards.

- Serve in the interest of stakeholders in a lawful manner, while maintaining high standards of conduct and character and not discrediting their profession or the association.

- Maintain the privacy and confidentiality of information obtained in the course of their activities unless disclosure is required by legal authority. Such information shall not be used for personal benefit or released to inappropriate parties.

- Maintain competency in their respective fields and agree to undertake only those activities they can reasonably expect to complete with the necessary skills, knowledge, and competence.

- Inform appropriate parties of the results of work performed including the disclosure of all significant facts known to them that, if not disclosed, may distort the reporting of the results.

- Support the professional education of stakeholders in enhancing their understanding of the governance and management of enterprise information systems and technology, including audit, control, security, and risk management.

Failure to comply with this Code of Professional Ethics can result in an investigation into a member's or certification holder's conduct and, ultimately, in disciplinary measures.

You can find the full text and terms of enforcement of the ISACA Code of Ethics at www.isaca.org/ethics.

The Certification Exam

The certification is offered throughout the year in several examination windows. You have several ways to register; however, regardless of the method you choose, I highly recommend you plan ahead and register early.

In 2018 the schedule of exam fees in U.S. dollars is

- CISM application fee: $50
- Regular registration: $575 member/$760 nonmember

The test is administered by an ISACA-sponsored location. For additional details on the location nearest you, see the ISACA web site.

Once registration is complete, you will immediately receive an e-mail acknowledging your registration. Next, you will need to schedule your certification exam. The ISACA web site will direct you to the certification registration page where you will select a date, time, and location to take your exam. When you confirm the date, time, and location for your exam, you will receive a confirmation via e-mail. You will need the confirmation to enter the test location—make sure to keep it unmarked and in a safe place until test time.

When you arrive at the test site, you will be required to sign in, and you may be required to sign an agreement. Also, you will be required to turn in your smartphone, wallet or purse, and other personal items for safekeeping. The exam proctor will read aloud the rules you are required to follow while you take your exam. These rules will address matters such as breaks, drinking water, and snacks.

While you take your exam, you will be supervised by the proctor, and possibly you will be monitored by video surveillance to make sure that no one can cheat on the exam.

Each registrant has four hours to take the multiple-choice question exam. There are 150 questions on the exam representing the five job practice areas. The exam is computerized. Each question has four answer choices; test-takers can select only one best answer. You can skip questions and return to them later, and you can also flag questions that you want to review later if time permits. While you are taking your exam, the time remaining will appear on the screen.

When you have completed the exam, you are directed to close the exam. At that time, the exam will display your pass or fail status, with a reminder that your score and passing status is subject to review.

You will be scored for each job practice area and then provided one final score. All scores are scaled. Scores range from 200 to 800; however, a final score of 450 is required to pass.

Exam questions are derived from a job practice analysis study conducted by ISACA. The areas selected represent those tasks performed in a CISM's day-to-day activities and represent the background knowledge required to develop and manage an information security program. You can find more detailed descriptions of the task and knowledge statements at www.isaca.org/CISMjobpractice.

The CISM exam is quite broad in its scope. The exam covers four job practice areas, as shown in Table 1-1.

Independent committees have been developed to determine the best questions, review exam results, and statistically analyze the results for continuous improvement. Should you come across a horrifically difficult or strange question, do not panic. This question may have been written for another purpose. A few questions on the exam are included for research and analysis purposes and will not be counted against your score. The exam includes no indications in this regard.

Domain	CISM Job Practice Area	Percentage of Exam
1	Information security governance	24%
2	Information risk management	30%
3	Information security program development and management	27%
4	Information security incident management	19%

Table 1-1 CISM Exam Practice Areas

Exam Preparation

The CISM certification requires a great deal of knowledge and experience from the CISM candidate. You need to map out a long-term study strategy to pass the exam. The following sections offer some tips and are intended to help guide you to, through, and beyond exam day.

Before the Exam

Consider the following list of tips on tasks and resources for exam preparation. They are listed in sequential order.

1. **Read the candidate's guide**   For information on the certification exam and requirements for the current year, see www.isaca.org/Certification/Pages/Candidates-Guide-for-Exams.aspx.

2. **Register**   If you are able, register early for any cost savings and to solidify your commitment to moving forward with this professional achievement.

3. **Schedule your exam**   Find a location, date and time, and commit.

4. **Become familiar with the CISM job practice areas**   The job practice areas serve as the basis for the exam and requirements. Beginning with the 2017 exam, the job practice areas have changed. Ensure your study materials align with the current list, shown at www.isaca.org/CISMjobpractice.

5. **Know your best learning methods**   Everyone has preferred styles of learning, whether it's self-study, a study group, an instructor-led course, or a boot camp. Try to set up a study program that leverages your strengths.

6. **Self-assess**   Run through practice exam questions available for download (see the appendix for more information). You may also go to the ISACA web site for a free 50-question CISM self-assessment.

7. **Iterative study**   Depending on how much work experience in information security management you have already, I suggest you plan your study program to take at least two months but as long as six months. During this time, periodically take practice exams and note your areas of strength and weakness. Once you have identified your weak areas, focus on those areas weekly by rereading the related sections in this book and retaking practice exams, and note your progress.

8. **Avoid cramming** We've all seen the books on the shelves with titles that involve last-minute cramming. Just one look on the Internet reveals a variety of web sites that cater to teaching individuals how to most effectively cram for exams. There are also research sites claiming that exam cramming can lead to susceptibility to colds and flu, sleep disruptions, overeating, and digestive problems. One thing is certain: many people find that good, steady study habits result in less stress and greater clarity and focus during the exam. Because of the complexity of this exam, I highly recommend the long-term, steady-study option. Study the job practice areas thoroughly. There are many study options. If time permits, investigate the many resources available to you.

9. **Find a study group** Many ISACA chapters and other organizations have formed specific study groups or offer less expensive exam review courses. Contact your local chapter to see whether these options are available to you. In addition, be sure to keep your eye on the ISACA web site. And use your local network to find out whether there are other local study groups and other helpful resources.

10. **Confirmation letter** Check your confirmation letter again. Do not write on or lose it. Put it in a safe place, and take note of what time you will need to arrive at the site. Note this on your calendar. Confirm that the location is the one you selected and located near you.

11. **Logistics check** Check the candidate's guide and your confirmation letter for the exact time you are required to report to the test site. Check the site a few days before the exam—become familiar with the location and tricks to getting there. If you are taking public transportation, be sure you are looking at the schedule for the day of the exam: if your CISM exam is scheduled on a Saturday, public transportation schedules may differ from weekday schedules. If you are driving, know the route and where to park your vehicle.

12. **Pack** Place your confirmation letter and a photo ID in a safe place, ready to go. Your ID must be a current, government-issued photo ID that matches the name on the confirmation letter and must not be handwritten. Examples of acceptable forms of ID are passports, driver's licenses, state IDs, green cards, and national IDs. Make sure you leave food, drinks, laptops, cell phones, and other electronic devices behind, as they are not permitted at the test site. For information on what can and cannot be brought to the exam site, see www.isaca.org/CISMbelongings.

13. **Notification decision** Decide whether you want your test results e-mailed to you. You will have the opportunity to consent to an e-mail notification of the exam results. If you are fully paid (zero balance on exam fee) and have consented to the e-mail notification, you should receive a one-time e-mail approximately eight weeks from the date of the exam with the results.

14. **Sleep** Make sure you get a sound night's sleep before the exam. Research suggests that you avoid caffeine at least four hours before bedtime, keep a notepad and pen next to the bed to capture late-night thoughts that might keep you awake, eliminate as much noise and light as possible, and keep your room a good temperature for sleeping. In the morning, rise early so as not to rush and subject yourself to additional stress.

Day of the Exam

All of your preparation for the CISM certification culminates on the day you scheduled to take your exam. On the day of the exam, follow these tips:

- **Arrive early**   Check the Bulletin of Information and your confirmation letter for the exact time you are required to report to the test site. The confirmation letter or the candidate's guide explains that you must be at the test site *no later* than approximately 30 minutes *before* testing time. The examiner will begin reading the exam instructions at this time, and any latecomers will be disqualified from taking the test and will *not* receive a refund of fees.

- **Observe test center rules**   There may be rules about taking breaks. This will be discussed by the examiner along with exam instructions. If at any time during the exam you need something and are unsure as to the rules, be sure to ask first. For information on conduct during the exam, see www.isaca.org/CISMbelongings.

- **Answer all exam questions**   Read questions carefully, but do not try to overanalyze. Remember to select the *best* solution. There may be several reasonable answers, but one is *better* than the others. If you aren't sure about an answer, you can mark the question and come back to it later. After going through all the questions, you can return to the marked questions (and any others) to read them and consider them more carefully. Above all, don't try to over-analyze questions, and do trust your instincts. Do not try to rush through the exam, as there is plenty of time to take as much as a few minutes for each question. But at the same time, do watch the clock so that you don't find yourself going too slowly that you won't be able to thoughtfully answer every question.

- **Note your exam result**   When you have completed the exam, you should be able to see your pass/fail result. Your results may not be in large, blinking text; you may need to read the fine print to get your preliminary results. If you passed, congratulations! If you did not pass, do observe any remarks about your status; you will be able to retake the exam—there is information about this on the ISACA web site.

If You Did Not Pass

If you did not pass your exam on the first attempt, don't lose heart. Instead, remember that failure is a stepping stone to success. Thoughtfully take stock and determine your improvement areas. Go back to this book's practice exams and be honest with yourself regarding those areas where you need to learn more. Reread the chapters or sections where you need to improve your knowledge. If you participated in a study group or training, contact your study group coach or class instructor if you feel you can get any advice from them on how to study up on the topics you need to master. Do take at least several weeks to study those topics, and refresh yourself on other topics; then give it another go. Success is granted to those who are persistent and determined.

After the Exam

A few weeks from the date of the exam, you will receive your exam results by e-mail or postal mail. Each job practice area score will be noted in addition to the overall final score. All scores are scaled. Should you receive a passing score, you will also receive the application for certification.

Those unsuccessful in passing will also be notified. These individuals will want to take a close look at the job practice area scores to determine areas for further study. They may retake the exam as many times as needed on future exam dates, as long as they have registered and paid the applicable fees. Regardless of pass or fail, exam results will not be disclosed via telephone, fax, or e-mail (with the exception of the consented e-mail notification).

 NOTE You are not permitted to display the CISM moniker until you have completed certification. Passage of the exam is *not* sufficient to use the CISM designation anywhere, including e-mail, resumes, correspondence, or social media.

Applying for CISM Certification

To apply for certification, you must be able to submit evidence of a passing score and related work experience. Keep in mind that once you receive a passing score, you have five years to use this score on a CISM certification application. After this time, you will need to take the exam again. In addition, all work experience submitted must have been within ten years of your new certification application.

To complete the application process, you need to submit the following information:

- **CISM application** Note the exam ID number as found in your exam results letter, list the information security management experience and any experience substitutions, and identify which CISM job practice area (or areas) your experience pertains to.

- **Verification of Work Experience forms** These must be filled out and signed by your immediate supervisor or a person of higher rank in the organization to verify your work experience noted on the application. You must fill out a complete set of Verification of Work Experience forms for each separate employer.

- **Transcript or letter** If you are using an educational experience waiver, you must submit an original transcript or letter from the college or university confirming degree status.

As with the exam, after you've successfully mailed the application, you must wait approximately eight weeks for processing. If your application is approved, you will receive an e-mail notification, followed by a package in the mail containing your letter of certification, certificate, and a copy of the Continuing Professional Education Policy. You can then proudly display your certificate and use the "CISM" designation on your résumé, e-mail and social media profiles, and business cards.

NOTE You are permitted to use the CISM moniker *only* after receiving your certification letter from ISACA.

Retaining Your CISM Certification

There is more to becoming a CISM professional than merely passing an exam, submitting an application, and receiving a paper certificate. Becoming a CISM professional is an ongoing and continuous journey. Those with CISM certification not only agree to abide by the code of ethics but must also meet ongoing education requirements and pay annual certification maintenance fees. Let's take a closer look at the education requirements and explain the fees involved in retaining certification.

Continuing Education

The goal of continuing professional education requirements is to ensure that individuals maintain CISM-related knowledge so that they can better develop and manage security management programs. To maintain CISM certification, individuals must obtain 120 continuing education hours within three years, with a minimum requirement of 20 hours per year. Each CPE hour is to account for 50 minutes of active participation in educational activities.

What Counts as a Valid CPE Credit?

For training and activities to be utilized for CPEs, they must involve technical or managerial training that is directly applicable to information security and information security management. The following list of activities has been approved by the CISM certification committee and can count toward your CPE requirements:

- ISACA professional education activities and meetings.
- If you are an ISACA member, you can take Information Systems Control Journal CPE Quizzes online or participate in monthly webcasts. For each webcast, CPEs are rewarded after you pass a quiz.
- Non-ISACA professional education activities and meetings.
- Self-study courses.
- Vendor sales or marketing presentations (ten-hour annual limit).
- Teaching, lecturing, or presenting on subjects related to job practice areas.
- Publication of articles and books related to the profession.
- CISM exam question development and review.
- Passing related professional examinations.
- Participation in ISACA boards or committees (20-hour annual limit per ISACA certification).

- Contributions to the information security management profession (ten-hour annual limit).
- Mentoring (ten-hour annual limit).

For more information on what is accepted as a valid CPE credit, see the Continuing Professional Education Policy (www.isaca.org/cpe).

Tracking and Submitting CPEs

Not only are you required to submit a CPE tracking form for the annual renewal process, but you also should keep detailed records for each activity. Records associated with each activity should have the following:

- Name of attendee
- Name of sponsoring organization
- Activity title
- Activity description
- Activity date
- Number of CPE hours awarded

It is in your best interest to track all CPE information in a single file or worksheet. ISACA has developed a tracking form for your use, which can be found in the Continuing Professional Education Policy. To make it easy on yourself, consider keeping all related records such as receipts, brochures, and certificates in the same place. Documentation should be retained throughout the three-year certification period and for at least one additional year afterward. This is especially important, as you may someday be audited. If this happens, you would be required to submit all paperwork. So why not be prepared?

For new CISMs, the annual and three-year certification period begins January 1 of the year following certification. You are not required to report CPE hours for the first partial year after your certification; however, the hours earned from the time of certification to December 31 can be utilized in the first certification reporting period the following year. Therefore, should you get certified in January, you will have until the following January to accumulate CPEs and will not have to report them until you report the totals for the following year, which will be in October or November. This is known as the *renewal period*. During this time, you will receive an e-mail directing you to the web site to enter CPEs earned over the course of the year. Alternatively, the renewal will be mailed to you, and then CPEs can be recorded on the hard-copy invoice and sent with your maintenance fee payment. CPEs and maintenance fees must be received by January 15 to retain certification.

Notification of compliance from the certification department is sent after all the information has been received and processed. Should ISACA have any questions about the information you have submitted, it will contact you directly.

Sample CPE Submission

Table 1-2 contains an example of a CPE submission.

Name_____John Jacob_____

Certification Number___67895787_____

Certification Period____1/1/2018_____to____12/31/2018_____

Activity Title/Sponsor	Activity Description	Date	CPE Hours	Support Docs Included?
ISACA presentation/lunch	PCI compliance	2/12/2018	1 CPE	Yes (receipt)
ISACA presentation/lunch	Security in SDLC	3/12/2018	1 CPE	Yes (receipt)
Regional Conference, RIMS	Compliance, risk	1/15–17/2018	6 CPEs	Yes (CPE receipt)
BrightFly webinar	Governance, risk, & compliance	2/16/2018	3 CPEs	Yes (confirmation e-mail)
ISACA board meeting	Chapter board meeting	4/9/2018	2 CPEs	Yes (meeting minutes)
Presented at ISSA meeting	Risk management presentation	6/21/2018	1 CPE	Yes (meeting notice)
Published an article in XYZ	Journal article on SOX ITGCs	4/12/2018	4 CPEs	Yes (article)
Vendor presentation	Learned about GRC tool capability	5/12/2018	2 CPEs	Yes
Employer-offered training	Change management course	3/26/2018	7 CPEs	Yes (certificate of course completion)

Table 1-2   Sample CPE Submission

CPE Maintenance Fees

To remain CISM certified, you must pay CPE maintenance fees each year. These fees are (as of 2018) $45 for members and $85 for nonmembers each year. These fees are in addition to ISACA membership and local chapter dues (neither of which is required to maintain your CISM certification).

Revocation of Certification

A CISM-certified individual may have his or her certification revoked for the following reasons:

- Failure to complete the minimum number of CPEs during the period.
- Failure to document and provide evidence of CPEs in an audit.

- Failure to submit payment for maintenance fees.
- Failure to comply with the Code of Professional Ethics can result in investigation and ultimately can lead to revocation of certification.

If you have received a revocation notice, you will need to contact the ISACA Certification Department at certification@isaca.org for more information.

Summary

Becoming and being a CISM professional is a lifestyle, not just a one-time event. It takes motivation, skill, good judgment, persistence, and proficiency to be a strong and effective leader in the world of information security management. The CISM was designed to help you navigate the security management world with greater ease and confidence.

In the following chapters, each CISM job practice area will be discussed in detail, and additional reference material will be presented. Not only is this information useful for studying prior to the exam, but it is also meant to serve as a resource throughout your career as an information security management professional.

Information Security Governance

In this chapter, you will learn about
- Business alignment
- Security strategy development
- Security governance activities
- Information security strategy development
- Resources needed to develop and execute a security strategy
- Obstacles to strategy development and execution
- Information security metrics

The topics in this chapter represent 24 percent of the Certified Information Security Manager (CISM) examination. This chapter discusses CISM job practice 1, "Information Security Governance."

ISACA defines this domain as follows: "Establish and/or maintain an information security governance framework and supporting processes to ensure that the information security strategy is aligned with organizational goals and objectives."

Security governance should be the wellspring from which security-related strategic decisions and all other security activities flow.

Properly implemented, *governance is a process* whereby senior management exerts strategic control over business functions through policies, objectives, delegation of authority, and monitoring. Governance is management's oversight for all other business processes to ensure that business processes continue to effectively meet the organization's business vision and objectives.

Organizations usually establish governance through a steering committee that is responsible for setting long-term business strategy, and by making changes to ensure that business processes continue to support business strategy and the organization's overall needs. This is accomplished through the development and enforcement of documented policies, standards, requirements, and various reporting metrics.

Introduction to Information Security Governance

Information security governance typically focuses on several key processes. Those processes include personnel management, sourcing, risk management, configuration management, change management, access management, vulnerability management, incident management, and business continuity planning. Another key component is the establishment of an effective organization structure and clear statements of roles and responsibilities. An effective governance program will use a balanced scorecard, metrics, or other means to monitor these and other key processes. Through a process of continuous improvement, security processes will be changed to remain effective and to support ongoing business needs.

Information security is a business issue, and organizations that are not yet adequately protecting their information have a business problem. The reason for this is almost always a lack of understanding and commitment by boards of directors and senior executives. For many, information security is only a technology problem at the tactical level. Recent events have brought the issue of information security to the forefront for many organizations. The challenge is that because of a lack of awareness or cybersecurity savviness, organizations still struggle with how to successfully organize, manage, and communicate about it at the boardroom level.

To be successful, information security is also a people issue. When people at each level in the organization—from boards of directors to individual contributors—understand the importance of information security and their own roles and responsibilities, an organization will be in a position of reduced risk. This reduction in risk or identification of a potential security event results in fewer incidents that, when they do occur, will have lower impact on the organization's ongoing reputation and operations.

Information security governance is a set of activities that are established so that management has a clear understanding of the state of the organization's security program, its current risks, and its direct activities. A goal of the security program is to continue to contribute toward fulfillment of the security strategy, which itself will continue to align to the business and business objectives. Whether the organization has a board of directors, council members, commissioners, or some other top-level governing body, governance begins with the establishment of top-level strategic objectives that are translated into actions, policies, processes, procedures, and other activities downward through each level in the organization.

For information security governance to be successful, an organization must also have an effective IT governance program. IT is the enabler and force multiplier that facilitates business processes that fulfill organization objectives. Without effective IT governance, information security governance will not be able to reach its full potential. The result may be that the proverbial IT bus will travel safely but to the wrong destination. This is depicted in Figure 2-1.

While the CISM certification is not directly tied to IT governance, this implicit dependence of security governance on IT governance cannot be understated. IT and security professionals specializing in IT governance itself may be interested in ISACA's Certified in the Governance of Enterprise IT (CGEIT) certification, which specializes in

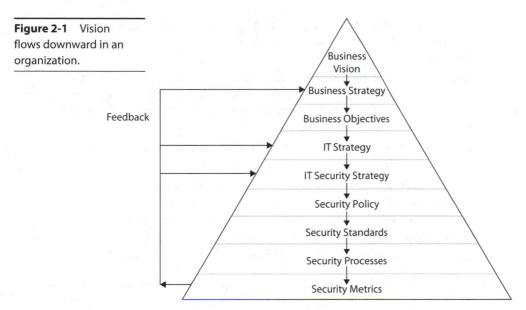

Figure 2-1 Vision flows downward in an organization.

this domain. While IT governance and information security governance may be separate, in many organizations the governance activities will closely resemble each other. Many issues will span both IT and security governance bodies, and a number of individuals will participate actively in both areas. Some organizations may integrate IT and information security governance into a single set of participants, activities, and business records. The most important thing is that organizations figure out how to establish governance programs that are effective for achieving desired and documented business outcomes.

The purpose of security governance is to align the organization's security program with the needs of the business. The term *information security governance* refers to a collection of top-down activities intended to control the security organization (and security-related activities in every part of the organization) from a strategic perspective to ensure that information security supports the business. These are some of the artifacts and activities that flow out of healthy security governance:

- **Objectives** These are desired capabilities or end states, ideally expressed in achievable, measurable terms.
- **Strategy** This is a plan to achieve one or more objectives.
- **Policy** At its minimum, security policy should directly reflect the mission, objectives, and goals of the overall organization.
- **Priorities** The priorities in the security program should flow directly from the organization's mission, objectives, and goals. Whatever is most important to the organization as a whole should be important to information security as well.
- **Standards** The technologies, protocols, and practices used by IT should be a reflection of the organization's needs. On their own, standards help to drive a

consistent approach to solving business challenges; the choice of standards should facilitate solutions that meet the organization's needs in a costeffective and secure manner.

- **Processes**   These are formalized descriptions of repeated business activities that include instructions to applicable personnel. Processes include one or more procedures, as well as definitions of business records and other facts that help workers understand how things are supposed to be done.

- **Controls**   These are formal descriptions of critical activities to ensure desired outcomes.

- **Program and project management**   The organization's IT and security programs and projects should be organized and performed in a consistent manner that reflects business priorities and supports the business.

- **Metrics/reporting**   This includes the formal measurement of processes and controls so that management understands and can measure them.

To the greatest possible extent, security governance in an organization should be practiced in the same way that the organization performs IT governance and corporate governance. Security governance should mimic corporate and/or IT governance processes, or security governance may be integrated into corporate or IT governance processes.

While security governance contains the elements just described, strategic planning is also a key component of governance. Strategy development is discussed in the next section.

Reason for Security Governance

Organizations in most industry sectors and at all levels of government are increasingly dependent on their information systems. This has progressed to the point where organizations—including those whose products or services are not information related—are completely dependent on the integrity and availability of their information systems to continue business operations. As an information security professional, it is imperative that you understand the priority of the business with regard to confidentiality, integrity, and availability (CIA). All three of these should be considered when building out the security governance structure, but the type of information used by the business will drive the priority that is given to confidentiality, integrity, and availability. Information security governance, then, is needed to ensure that security-related incidents do not threaten critical systems and their support of the ongoing viability of the organization.

Among information security professionals, it is a known fact that without adequate safeguards, information technology assets that are Internet accessible would be compromised in mere minutes of being placed online. Further, many if not all information technology assets thought to be behind the protection of firewalls and other control points may also be easily accessed and compromised. The tools, processes, and controls needed to protect these assets are as complex as the information systems they are designed to protect. Without effective top-down management of the security controls and processes protecting IT assets, management will not be informed or in control of these protective measures. The consequences of failure can impair, cripple, and/or embarrass the organization's core operations.

Security Governance Activities and Results

Within an effective security governance program, an organization's senior management team will see to it that information systems necessary to support business operations will be adequately protected. These are some of the activities required to protect the organization:

- **Risk management**   Management will ensure that risk assessments will be performed to identify risks in information systems and supported processes. Follow-up actions will be carried out that will reduce the risk of system failure and compromise.

- **Process improvement**   Management will ensure that key changes will be made to business processes that will result in security improvements.

- **Event identification**   Management will be sure to put technologies and processes in place to ensure that security events and incidents will be identified as quickly as possible.

- **Incident response**   Management will put incident response procedures into place that will help to avoid incidents, reduce the impact and probability of incidents, and improve response to incidents so that their impact on the organization is minimized.

- **Improved compliance**   Management will be sure to identify all applicable laws, regulations, and standards and carry out activities to confirm that the organization is able to attain and maintain compliance.

- **Business continuity and disaster recovery planning**   Management will define objectives and allocate resources for the development of business continuity and disaster recovery plans.

- **Metrics**   Management will establish processes to measure key security events such as incidents, policy changes and violations, audits, and training.

- **Resource management**   The allocation of manpower, budget, and other resources to meet security objectives is monitored by management.

- **Improved IT governance**   An effective security governance program will result in better strategic decisions in the IT organization that keep risks at an acceptably low level.

These and other governance activities are carried out through scripted interactions among key business and IT executives at regular intervals. Meetings will include a discussion of the impact of regulatory changes, alignment with business objectives, effectiveness of measurements, recent incidents, recent audits, and risk assessments. Other discussions may include such things as changes to the business, recent business results, and any anticipated business events such as mergers or acquisitions.

These are two key results of an effective security governance program:

- **Increased trust**   Customers, suppliers, and partners trust the organization to a greater degree when they see that security is managed effectively.
- **Improved reputation**   The business community, including customers, investors, and regulators, will hold the organization in higher regard.

Business Alignment

An organization's information security program needs to fit into the rest of the organization. This means that the program needs to understand and align with the organization's highest-level guiding principles including the following:

- **Mission**   Why does the organization exist? Who does it serve, and through what products and services?
- **Goals and objectives**   What achievements does the organization want to accomplish, and when does it want to accomplish them?
- **Strategy**   What are the activities that need to take place so that the organization's goals and objectives can be fulfilled?

To be business aligned, people in the security program should be aware of several characteristics about the organization, including the following:

- **Culture**   Culture includes how personnel in the organization work, think, and relate to each other.
- **Asset value**   This includes information the organization uses to operate. This often consists of intellectual property such as designs, source code, production costs, and pricing, as well as sensitive information related to not only its personnel but its customers, its information-processing infrastructure, and its service functions.
- **Risk tolerance**   Risk tolerance for the organization's information security program needs to align with the organization's overall tolerance for risk.
- **Legal obligations**   What external laws and regulations govern what the organization does and how it operates? These laws and regulations include the Gramm-Leach-Bliley Act (GLBA), Payment Card Industry Data Security Standard (PCI-DSS), European General Data Protection Regulation (GDPR), Health Insurance Portability and Accountability Act (HIPAA), and the North American Electric Reliability Corporation (NERC) standard. Also, contractual obligations with other parties often shape the organization's behaviors and practices.
- **Market conditions**   How competitive is the marketplace in which the organization operates? What strengths and weaknesses does the organization have in comparison with its competitors? How does the organization want its security differentiated from its competitors?

Security as Business Prevention

The information security profession is still plagued by the reputation of "being the department of 'no'" or as the department of business prevention. This stemmed from overzealous security managers who were more risk-averse than the business itself and who did not understand the organization's need to grow, expand, and establish new products and services. The result of this reputation is the still-present tendency for IT and other parts of the business to avoid involvement with security professionals out of fear that their involvement will hamper their efforts.

This can lead to shadow IT, which in many cases puts the organization at a greater risk of data leakage. Most people within a business want to do the right thing and complete their job activities in a successful manner. They do not intentionally set out to expose sensitive data; many employees are just trying to complete their assigned duties. As an example, the person in the new accounts department receives an e-mail from the external marketing team with a listing of all newly signed-up accounts. What the person fails to recognize is the file contains sensitive card holder data and is being shared over a public connection.

Goals and Objectives

An organization's goals and objectives specify the activities that are to take place in support of the organization's overall strategy. Goals and objectives are typically statements in the form of imperatives that describe the development or improvement of business capabilities. For instance, goals and objectives may be related to increases in capacity, improvements of quality, or the development of entirely new capabilities. Goals and objectives further the organization's mission, helping it to continue to attract new customers or constituents, increase market share, and increase revenue and/or profitability.

Risk Appetite

Each organization has a particular appetite for risk, although few have documented that appetite. ISACA defines risk appetite as the level of risk that an organization is willing to accept while in pursuit of its mission, strategy, and objectives, and before action is needed to treat the risk.

Risk capacity is related to risk appetite. ISACA defines *risk capacity* as the objective amount of loss that an organization can tolerate without its continued existence being called into question.

Generally, only highly risk-averse organizations such as banks, insurance companies, and public utilities will document and define risk appetite in concrete terms. Other organizations are more tolerant of risk and make individual risk decisions based on gut feeling. However, because of increased influence and mandates by customers, many organizations are finding it necessary to document and articulate the risk posture and appetite of the organization. This is an emerging trend in the marketplace but is still fairly new to many organizations.

Risk-averse organizations generally have a formal system of accountability and traceability of risk decisions back to department heads and business executives. This activity is often seen within risk management and risk treatment processes, where individual risk treatment decisions are made and one or more business executives are made accountable for their risk treatment decisions.

In a properly functioning risk management program, the chief information security officer (CISO) is rarely the person who makes a risk treatment decision and is accountable for that decision. Instead, the CISO is a facilitator for risk discussions that eventually lead to a risk treatment decision. The only time the CISO would be the accountable party would be when risk treatment decisions directly affect the risk management program itself, such as the selection of a governance, risk, and compliance (GRC) tool for managing and reporting on risk.

Organizations rarely have a single risk tolerance level across the entire business; instead, different business functions and different aspects of security will have varying levels of risk. For example, a mobile gaming software company may have a moderate tolerance for risk with regard to the introduction of new products, a low tolerance for workplace safety risks, and no tolerance for risk for legal and compliance matters. Mature organizations will develop and publish a statement of risk tolerance or appetite that expresses risk tolerance levels throughout the business.

Roles and Responsibilities

Information security governance is most effective when every person in the organization knows what is expected of them. Better organizations develop formal roles and responsibilities so that personnel will have a clearer idea of their part in all matters related to the protection of systems, information, and even themselves.

In the context of organizational structure and behavior, a *role* is a description of expected activities that employees are obliged to perform as part of their employment. Roles are typically associated with a *job title* or *position title,* which is a label assigned to each person that designates their place in the organization. Organizations strive to adhere to more or less standard position titles so that other people in the organization, upon knowing someone's position title, will have at least a general idea of a person's role in the organization.

Typical roles include the following:

- IT auditor
- Systems engineer
- Accounts receivable manager
- Individual contributor

Often a position title also includes a person's *rank,* which denotes an individual person's seniority, placement within a command-and-control hierarchy, span of control, or any combination of these. Typical ranks include the following in order of increasing seniority:

- Supervisor
- Manager
- Senior manager
- Director

- Senior director
- Executive director
- Vice president
- Senior vice president
- Executive vice president
- President
- Chief executive officer
- Member, board of directors
- Chairman, board of directors

This should not be considered a complete listing of ranks. Larger organizations also include the modifiers *assistant* (as in assistant director), *general* (general manager), and *first* (first vice president).

A *responsibility* is a statement of activities that a person is expected to perform. Like roles, responsibilities are typically documented in position descriptions and job descriptions. Typical responsibilities include the following:

- Perform monthly corporate expense reconciliation
- Troubleshoot network faults and develop solutions
- Audit user account terminations and develop exception reports

In addition to specific responsibilities associated with individual position titles, organizations typically also include general responsibilities in all position titles. Examples include the following:

- Understand and conform to information security policy, harassment policy, and other policies
- Understand and conform to code of ethics and behavior

In the context of information security, an organization assigns roles and responsibilities to individuals and groups so that the organization's security strategy and objectives can be met.

RACI Charts

Many organizations utilize Responsible-Accountable-Consulted-Informed (RACI) charts to denote key responsibilities in business processes, projects, tasks, and other activities. A RACI chart assigns levels of responsibility to individuals and groups. Development of a RACI chart helps personnel determine roles for various business activities. A typical RACI chart follows.

(continued)

Activity	Responsible	Accountable	Consulted	Informed
Request User Account	End user	End user manager	IT service desk End user manager	Asset owner Security team
Approve User Account	Asset owner	COO	End user manager Security team	End user Internal audit IT service desk
Provision User Account	IT service desk	IT service manager	Asset owner	End user End user manager Security team
Audit User Account	Internal auditor	Internal audit manager	Asset owner	IT service desk IT service manager End user manager

The same RACI chart can also be depicted like this second example:

Activity	End User	Manager	IT Service Desk	IT Service Manager	Asset Owner	COO	Internal Audit	Audit Manager	Security Team
Request User Account	R	A	I		I				I
Approve User Account	I	C	I	I	R	A	I		C
Provision User Account	I	I	R	A	C				I
Audit User Account		I	I	I	C		R	A	I

This RACI chart specifies the roles carried out by several parties in the user account access request process.

The meanings of the four roles in a RACI chart are as follows:

- **Responsible**   The person or group that performs the actual work or task.
- **Accountable**   The person who is ultimately answerable for complete, accurate, and timely execution of the work. Often this is a person who manages those in the Responsible role.
- **Consulted**   One or more people or groups who are consulted for their opinions, experience, or insight. People in the Consulted role may be a subject-matter expert for the work or task, or they may be an owner, steward, or custodian of an asset associated with the work or task. Communication with the Consulted role is two-way.

(continued)

- **Informed**   One or more people or groups who are informed by those in other roles. Depending on the process or task, Informed may be told of an activity before, during, or after its completion. Communication with Informed is one-way.

Several considerations must be taken into account when assigning roles to individuals and groups in a RACI chart. These include the following:

- **Skills**   Some or all individuals in a team assignment, as well as specific named individuals, need to have the skills, training, and competence to carry out tasks as required

- **Segregation of duties**   Critical tasks such as the user account provisioning RACI chart depicted earlier must be free of segregation of duties conflicts. This means that there must be two or more individuals or groups required to carry out a critical task. In this example, the requestor, approver, and provisioner cannot be the same person or group.

- **Conflict of interest**   Critical tasks must not be assigned to individuals or groups when such assignments will create conflicts of interest. For example, a user who is an approver cannot approve a request for their own access. In this case, a different person must approve the request—while also avoid a segregation of duties conflict.

There are some variations of the RACI model, including Participant, Accountable, Review Required, Input Required, Sign-off Required (PARIS) and Perform, Accountable, Control, Suggest, Informed (PACSI).

Board of Directors

The board of directors in an organization is a body of people who oversee activities in an organization. Depending on the type of organization, board members may be elected by shareholders or constituents, or they may be appointed. This role can be either paid or voluntary in nature.

Activities performed by the board of directors, as well as directors' authority, are usually defined by a constitution, bylaws, or external regulation. The board of directors is typically accountable to the owners of the organization or, in the case of a government body, to the electorate.

In many cases, board members have *fiduciary duty*. This means they are accountable to shareholders or constituents to act in the best interests of the organization with no appearance of impropriety, conflict of interest, or ill-gotten profit as a result of their actions.

In nongovernment organizations, the board of directors is responsible for appointing a chief executive officer (CEO) and possibly other executives. The CEO, then, is accountable to the board of directors and carries out their directives. Board members may also be selected for any of the following reasons:

- **Investor representation**   One or more board members may be appointed by significant investors to give them control over the strategy and direction of the organization.

- **Business experience**   Board members bring outside business management experience, which helps them develop successful business strategies for the organization.

- **Access to resources**   Board members bring business connections, including additional investors, business partners, suppliers, or customers.

Often, one or more board members will have business finance experience in order to bring financial management oversight to the organization. In the case of U.S. public companies, the U.S. Sarbanes-Oxley Act requires board members to form an audit committee; one or more audit committee members are required to have financial management experience. External financial audits and internal audit activities are often accountable directly to the audit committee in order to perform direct oversight of the organization's financial management activities. As the issue of information security becomes more prevalent in discussions at the executive level, some organizations have added a board member who is technically savvy or have formed an additional committee, often referred to as the Technology Risk Committee.

Boards of directors are generally expected to require that the CEO and other executives implement a corporate *governance* function to ensure that executive management has an appropriate level of visibility and control over the operations of the organization. Executives are accountable to the board of directors to demonstrate that they are effectively carrying out the board's strategies.

Many, if not most, organizations are highly dependent upon information technology for their daily operations. As a result, information security is an important topic to boards of directors. Today's standard of due care for corporate boards requires that they include information security considerations in the strategies they develop and the oversight they exert on the organization. In its publication *Cyber-Risk Oversight*, the National Association of Corporate Directors has developed five principles about the importance of information security:

- Principle 1: Directors need to understand and approach cybersecurity as an enterprise-wide risk management issue, not just an IT issue.

- Principle 2: Directors should understand the legal implications of cyber risks as they relate to their company's specific circumstances.

- Principle 3: Boards should have adequate access to cybersecurity expertise, and discussions about cyber-risk management should be given regular and adequate time on board meeting agendas.

- Principle 4: Boards should set the expectation that management will establish an enterprise-wide cyber-risk management framework with adequate staffing and budget.

- Principle 5: Board management discussions about cyber risk should include identification of which risks to avoid, which to accept, and which to mitigate or transfer through insurance, as well as specific plans associated with each approach.

Executive Management

Executive management is responsible for carrying out directives issued by the board of directors. In the context of information security management, this includes ensuring that there are sufficient resources for the organization to implement a security program and to develop and maintain security controls to protect critical assets.

Executive management must ensure that priorities are balanced. In the case of IT and information security, these functions are usually tightly coupled but sometimes in conflict. IT's primary mission is the development and operation of business-enabling capabilities through the use of information systems, while information security's mission includes security and compliance. Executive management must ensure that these two sometimes-conflicting missions are successful.

Typical IT and security-related executive position titles include the following:

- **Chief information officer (CIO)**   This is the title of the topmost leader in a larger IT organization.

- **Chief technical officer (CTO)**   This position is usually responsible for an organization's overall technology strategy. Depending upon the purpose of the organization, this position may be separate from IT.

- **Chief information security officer (CISO)**   This position is responsible for all aspects of data-related security. This usually includes incident management, disaster recovery, vulnerability management, and compliance. This role is usually separate from IT.

To ensure the success of the organization's information security program, executive management should be involved in three key areas:

- **Ratify corporate security policy**   Security policies that are developed by the information security function should be visibly ratified or endorsed by executive management. This may take different forms, such as formal minuted ratification in a governance meeting, a statement for the need for compliance along with a signature within the body of the security policy document, a separate memorandum to all personnel, or other visible communication to the organization's rank and file that stresses the importance of, and need for compliance to, the organization's information security policy.

- **Leadership by example**   With regard to information security policy, executive management should lead by example and not exhibit behavior suggesting they are "above" security policy—or other policies. Executives should not be seen to enjoy special privileges of the nature that suggest that one or more security policies do not apply to them. Instead, their behavior should visibly support security policies that all personnel are expected to comply with.

- **Ultimate responsibility**   Executives are ultimately responsible for all actions carried out by the personnel who report to them. Executives are also ultimately responsible for all outcomes related to organizations to which operations have been outsourced.

Security Steering Committee

Many organizations form a security steering committee, consisting of stakeholders from many (if not all) of the organization's business units, departments, functions, and principal locations. A steering committee may have a variety of responsibilities, including the following:

- **Risk treatment deliberation and recommendation**   The security steering committee may discuss relevant risks, discuss potential avenues of risk treatment, and develop recommendations for said risk treatment for ratification by executive management.

- **Discussion and coordination of IT and security projects**   The security steering members may discuss various IT and security projects to resolve any resource or scheduling conflicts. They might also discuss potential conflicts between various projects and initiatives and work out solutions.

- **Review of recent risk assessments**   The security steering committee may discuss recent risk assessments in order to develop a common understanding of their results, as well as discuss remediation of findings.

- **Discussion of new laws, regulations, and requirements**   The committee may discuss new laws, regulations, and requirements that may impose changes in the organization's operations. Committee members can develop high-level strategies that their respective business units or departments can further build out.

- **Review of recent security incidents**   Steering committee members can discuss recent security incidents and their root causes. Often this can result in changes in processes, procedures, or technology changes to reduce the risk and impact of future incidents.

Reading between the lines, the main mission of a security steering committee is to identify and resolve conflicts and to maximize the effectiveness of the security program, as balanced among other business initiatives and priorities.

Business Process and Business Asset Owners

Business process and asset owners are typically nontechnical personnel in management positions in an organization. While they may not be technology experts, in many organizations their business processes are enhanced by information technology in the form of business applications and other capabilities.

Remembering that IT and information security serve the organization and not the other way around, business process and business asset owners are accountable for making business decisions that sometimes impact the use of information technology, the organization's security posture, or both. A simple example is a decision on whether an individual employee should have access to specific information. While IT or security may have direct control over which personnel have access to what assets, the best decision to make is a business decision by the manager responsible for the process or business asset.

The responsibilities of business process and business asset owners include the following:

- **Access grants**   Asset owners decide whether individuals or groups should be given access to the asset, as well as the level and type of access. Example access types include combinations of read only, read-write, create, and delete.

- **Access revocation**   Asset owners should also decide when individuals or groups no longer require access to an asset, signaling the need to revoke that access.

- **Access reviews**   Asset owners should periodically review access lists to see whether each person and group should continue to have that access. Access reviews may also include access activity reviews to determine whether people who have not accessed assets still require access to them.

- **Configuration**   Asset owners determine the configuration needed for assets and applications, ensuring their proper function and support of applications and business processes.

- **Function definition**   In the case of business applications and services, asset owners determine which functions will be available, how they will work, and how they will support business processes. Typically, this definition is constrained by functional limitations within an application, service, or product.

- **Process definition**   Process owners determine the sequence, steps, roles, and actions carried out in their business processes.

- **Physical location**   Asset owners determine the physical location of their assets. Factors influencing choices of location include physical security, proximity to other assets, proximity to relevant personnel, and data protection and privacy laws.

Often, business and asset owners are nontechnical personnel, so it may be necessary to translate business needs into technical specifications.

Custodial Responsibilities

In many organizations, asset owners are not involved in the day-to-day activities related to the management of their assets, particularly when those assets are information systems and the data stored within them. Instead, somebody in the IT organization (or several people in IT) acts as a proxy for asset owners and makes access grants and other decisions on their behalf. While this is a common practice, it is often carried too far, resulting in the asset owner being virtually uninvolved and uninformed. Instead, asset owners should be aware of, and periodically review, activities carried out by people, groups, and departments making decisions on their behalf.

The most typical arrangement is that people in IT make access decisions on behalf of asset owners. Except in cases where there is a close partnership between these IT personnel and asset owners, these IT personnel often do not adequately understand the business nature of assets or the implications when certain people are given access to them. Most often, far too many personnel have access to assets, usually with higher privileges than necessary.

Chief Information Security Officer

The CISO is the highest-ranking security person in an organization. A CISO will develop business-aligned security strategies that support present and future business initiatives and be responsible for the development and operation of the organization's information risk program, the development and implementation of security policies, security incident response, and perhaps some operational security functions.

In some organizations, the CISO reports to the chief operating officer (COO) or the CEO, but in some organizations the CISO may report to the CIO, chief legal counsel, or other person in the organization.

Other similar titles with similar responsibilities include the following:

- **Chief security officer (CSO)**   This position generally has the responsibilities of a CISO plus responsibilities for non-information assets such as business equipment and work centers. A CSO often is responsible for workplace safety.

- **Chief information risk officer (CIRO)**   Generally this represents a change of approach to the CISO position, from being protection-based to being risk-based.

- **Chief risk officer (CRO)**   This position is responsible for all aspects of risk including information risk, business risk, compliance risk, and market risk. This role is separate from IT.

Many organizations do not have a CISO but instead have a director or manager of information security who reports further down in the organization chart. There are several possible reasons for organizations not having a CISO, but generally it can be said that the organization does not consider information security as a strategic function. This will hamper the visibility and importance of information security and often results in information security being a tactical function concerned with basic defenses such as firewalls, antivirus, and other tools. In such situations, responsibility for strategy-level information security implicitly lies with some other executive such as the CIO. This type of situation often results in the absence of a security program and the organization's general lack of awareness of relevant risks, threats, and vulnerabilities.

The one arena where a CISO may not be required is in small to medium-sized organizations where a full-time strategic leader may not be cost effective. In these situations, it is advisable to contract with a virtual CISO (vCISO) to assist with strategy and planning. The benefit of taking this type of approach for organizations that may not require or cannot afford a full-time person is that it allows the organization to benefit from the knowledge of seasoned security professional to assist in driving the information security program forward.

Rank Sets Tone and Gives Power

A glance at the title of the highest-ranking information security position in an organization reveals much about executive management's opinion of information security in larger organizations. Executive attitudes about security are reflected in the security manager's title and may resemble the following:

- **Security manager**   Information security is tactical only and often viewed as consisting only of antivirus software and firewalls. The security manager has no visibility into the development of business objectives. Executives consider security as unimportant and based on technology only.

- **Security director**   Information security is important and has moderate decision-making capability but little influence on the business. A director-level person in a larger organization may have little visibility to overall business strategies and little or no access to executive management or the board of directors.

- **Vice president**   Information security is strategic but does not influence business strategy and objectives. The vice president will have some access to executive management and possibly the board of directors.

- **CISO/CIRO/CSO/vCISO**   Information security is strategic, and business objectives are developed with full consideration for risk. The C-level security person has free access to executive management and the board of directors.

Chief Privacy Officer

Some organizations, typically those that manage large amounts of sensitive data on customers, will employ a chief privacy officer (CPO). Some organizations have a CPO because applicable regulations such as HIPAA, the Fair Credit Reporting Act (FCRA), and GLBA require it, while others have a CPO because they store massive amounts of personally identifiable information (PII).

The roles of a CPO typically include the safeguarding of PII, as well as ensuring that the organization does not misuse PII at its disposal. Because many organizations with a CPO also have a CISO, the CPO's duties mainly involve oversight into the organization's properly handling and use of PII.

The CPO is sometimes seen as a customer advocate, and often this is the role of the CPO, particularly when regulations require a privacy officer.

Software Development

Positions in software development are involved in the design, development, and testing of software applications.

- **Systems architect**   This position is usually responsible for the overall information systems architecture in the organization. This may or may not include overall data architecture and interfaces to external organizations.

- **Systems analyst**   A systems analyst is involved with the design of applications, including changes in an application's original design. This position may develop technical requirements, program design, and software test plans. In cases where organizations license applications developed by other companies, systems analysts design interfaces to other applications.

- **Software engineer/developer**   This position develops application software. Depending upon the level of experience, people in this position may also design programs or applications. In organizations that utilize purchased application software, developers often create custom interfaces, application customizations, and custom reports.

- **Software tester**   This position tests changes in programs made by software engineers/developers.

While the trend to outsourcing applications has resulted in organizations infrequently developing their own applications from scratch, software development roles persist in organizations. Developers are needed for the creation of customized modules within software platforms, as well as integration tools to connect applications to each other. Still, most organizations have a smaller number of developers than they did a decade or two ago.

Data Management

Positions related to data management are responsible for developing and implementing database designs and for maintaining databases. These positions are concerned with data within applications, as well as data flows between applications.

- **Data manager**   This position is responsible for data architecture and data management in larger organizations.

- **Database architect**   This position develops logical and physical designs of data models for applications. With sufficient experience, this person may also design an organization's overall data architecture.

- **Big data architect**   This position develops data models and data analytics for large, complex data sets.

- **Database administrator (DBA)**   This position builds and maintains databases designed by the database architect and those databases that are included as part of purchased applications. The DBA monitors databases, tunes them for performance and efficiency, and troubleshoots problems.

- **Database analyst**   This position performs tasks that are junior to the database administrator, carrying out routine data maintenance and monitoring tasks.

- **Data scientist**   This position applies scientific methods, builds processes, and implements systems to extract knowledge or insights from data.

 EXAM TIP   The roles of data manager, big data architect, database architect, database administrator, database analyst, and data scientist are distinct from data owners. The former are IT department roles for managing data models and data technology, whereas the latter role governs the business use of, and access to, data in information systems.

Network Management

Positions in network management are responsible for designing, building, monitoring, and maintaining voice and data communications networks, including connections to outside business partners and the Internet.

- **Network architect**   This position designs data and voice networks and designs changes and upgrades to networks as needed to meet new organization objectives.

- **Network engineer**   This position implements, configures, and maintains network devices such as routers, switches, firewalls, and gateways.

- **Network administrator**   This position performs routine tasks in the network such as making configuration changes and monitoring event logs.
- **Telecom engineer**   Positions in this role work with telecommunications technologies such as telecomm services, data circuits, phone systems, conferencing systems, and voice-mail systems.

Systems Management

Positions in systems management are responsible for architecture, design, building, and maintenance of servers and operating systems. This may include desktop operating systems as well. Personnel in these positions also design and manage virtualized environments as well as microsegmentation.

- **Systems architect**   This position is responsible for the overall architecture of systems (usually servers), in terms of both the internal architecture of a system and the relationship between systems. This position is usually also responsible for the design of services such as authentication, e-mail, and time synchronization.
- **Systems engineer**   This position is responsible for designing, building, and maintaining servers and server operating systems.
- **Storage engineer**   This position is responsible for designing, building, and maintaining storage subsystems.
- **Systems administrator**   This position is responsible for performing maintenance and configuration operations on systems.

Operations

Positions in operations are responsible for day-to-day operational tasks that may include networks, servers, databases, and applications.

- **Operations manager**   This position is responsible for overall operations that are carried out by others. Responsibilities will include establishing operations and shift schedules.
- **Operations analyst**   This position may be responsible for developing operational procedures; examining the health of networks, systems, and databases; setting and monitoring the operations schedule; and maintaining operations records.
- **Controls analyst**   This position is responsible for monitoring batch jobs, data entry work, and other tasks to make sure they are operating correctly.
- **Systems operator**   This position is responsible for monitoring systems and networks, performing backup tasks, running batch jobs, printing reports, and other operational tasks.
- **Data entry**   This position is responsible for keying batches of data from hard copy or other sources.
- **Media manager**   This position is responsible for maintaining and tracking the use and whereabouts of backup tapes and other media.

Security Operations

Positions in security operations are responsible for designing, building, and monitoring security systems and security controls to ensure the confidentiality, integrity, and availability of information systems.

- **Security architect**   This position is responsible for the design of security controls and systems such as authentication, audit logging, intrusion detection systems, intrusion prevention systems, and firewalls.

- **Security engineer**   This position is responsible for designing, building, and maintaining security services and systems that are designed by the security architect.

- **Security analyst**   This position is responsible for examining logs from firewalls and intrusion detection systems, as well as audit logs from systems and applications. This position may also be responsible for issuing security advisories to others in IT.

- **Access administrator**   This position is responsible for accepting approved requests for user access management changes and performing the necessary changes at the network, system, database, or application level. Often, this position is carried out by personnel in network and systems management functions; only in larger organizations is user account management performed in security or even in a separate user access department.

Security Audit

Positions in security audit are responsible for examining process design and for verifying the effectiveness of security controls.

- **Security audit manager**   This position is responsible for audit operations, as well as scheduling and managing audits.

- **Security auditor**   This position is responsible for performing internal audits of IT controls to ensure that they are being operated properly.

 CAUTION   Security audit positions need to be carefully placed in the organization so that people in this role can be objective and independent from the departments, processes, and systems they audit.

Service Desk

Positions at the service desk are responsible for providing frontline support services to IT and IT's customers.

- **Service desk manager**   This position serves as a liaison between end users and the IT service desk department.

- **Service desk analyst** This position is responsible for providing frontline user support services to personnel in the organization. This is sometimes known as a help-desk analyst.
- **Technical support analyst** This position is responsible for providing technical support services to other IT personnel and perhaps also to IT customers.

Quality Assurance

Positions in quality assurance are responsible for evaluating IT systems and processes to confirm their accuracy and effectiveness.

- **QA manager** This position is responsible for facilitating quality improvement activities throughout the IT organization.
- **QC manager** This position is responsible for testing IT systems and applications to confirm whether they are free of defects.

Other Roles

Other roles in IT organizations include the following:

- **Vendor manager** This position is responsible for maintaining business relationships with external vendors, measuring their performance, and handling business issues.
- **Project manager** This position is responsible for creating project plans and managing IT projects.

General Staff

The rank and file in an organization may or may not have explicit information security responsibilities, determined in part by executive management's understanding of the broad capabilities of information systems and the personnel who use them and determined also in executives' understanding of the human role in information security.

Typically, general staff security-related responsibilities include the following:

- Understanding and compliance to organization security policy
- Acceptable use of organization assets, including information systems and information
- Proper judgment, including proper responses to people who request information or request that staff members perform specific functions (the primary impetus for this is the phenomenon of social engineering and its use as an attack vector)
- Reporting of security-related matters and incidents to management

Better organizations have standard language in job descriptions that specify general responsibilities for the protection of assets.

Monitoring Responsibilities

The practice of monitoring responsibilities helps an organization confirm that the correct jobs are being carried out in the right way. There is no single approach, but several activities provide information to management, including the following:

- **Controls and internal audit**   Developing one or more controls around specific responsibilities gives management greater control over key activities. Internal audit of controls provides objective analysis on control effectiveness.
- **Metrics and reporting**   Developing metrics for repeated activities helps management better understand work output.
- **Work measurement**   This is a more structured activity used to carefully measure repeated tasks to better understand the volume of work performed.
- **Performance evaluation**   This is a traditional qualitative method used to evaluate employee performance.
- **360 feedback**   Soliciting structured feedback from peers, subordinates, and management helps subjects and management better understand characteristics related to specific responsibilities.
- **Position benchmarking**   This technique is used by organizations that want to compare job titles and people holding them with those in other organizations. There is no direct monitoring of responsibilities, but instead this helps an organization determine whether they have the right positions in place and that they are staffed by competent and qualified personnel. This may be useful for organizations that are troubleshooting employee performance.

Information Security Governance Metrics

Metrics are the means through which management can measure key processes and know whether their strategies are working. Metrics are used in many operational processes, but in this section, metrics as related to security governance are the emphasis. In other words, there is a distinction between tactical IT security metrics and those that reveal the state of the overall security program. The two, however, are often related, as discussed in the sidebar "Return on Security Investment."

Security metrics are often used to observe technical IT security controls and processes and to know whether they are operating properly. This helps management better understand the impact of past decisions and can help drive future decisions. Examples of technical metrics include the following:

- **Firewall metrics**   Number and types of rules triggered
- **Intrusion detection/prevention system (IDPS) metrics**   Number and types of incidents detected or blocked, and targeted systems
- **Anti-malware metrics**   Number and types of malware blocked, and targeted systems

- **Other security system metrics**   Measurements from data loss prevention (DLP) systems, web content filtering systems, cloud access security broker (CASB) systems, and so on

While useful, these metrics do not address the bigger picture of the effectiveness or alignment of an organization's overall security program. They do not answer key questions that boards of directors and executive management often ask, such as the following:

- How much security is enough?
- How should security resources be invested and applied?
- What is the potential impact of a threat event?

These and other business-related questions can be addressed through the right metrics, addressed in the remainder of this section.

Security strategists sometimes think about metrics in simple categorization, including the following:

- **Key risk indicators (KRIs)**   These are metrics associated with the measurement of risk.
- **Key goal indicators (KGIs)**   These metrics portray the attainment of strategic goals.
- **Key performance indicators (KPIs)**   These metrics are used to show efficiency or effectiveness of security-related activities.

Return on Security Investment

An ongoing debate has been raging for years on the return on investment (ROI) of information security safeguards, known as *return on security investment* (ROSI— pronounced "rosy"). The problem with investments in information security is that significant events such as highly impactful security attacks are infrequent (occurring far less than once per year for many organizations). Therefore, investments in information security controls may not have a noticeable effect.

An organization may well ask itself, if there were no break-ins prior to implementing new security systems and no break-ins afterward, was the investment in new security systems warranted? Could the resources spent on security systems have been better spent in other ways to increase service delivery capacity or increase production efficiency, resulting in increased revenues or profits? Additionally, if an investment is made, it may well uncover new risks that were previously unknown to the organization. So, the return on investment is diminished, but the benefit is that a previously unknown risk was identified. This can be found in areas such as security monitoring and vulnerability management solutions.

(continued)

It is easier to compute ROSI for events that occur more frequently. For example, lost and stolen laptop computers and mobile devices occur frequently enough in many organizations, so investments in security controls of various types have a more obvious benefit.

Security managers do keep in mind, however, that ROSI is only one of several means for helping justify the expenditure of resources on security capabilities. Other means include the following:

- **Fiduciary responsibility**   Many types of security controls are considered part of an organization's fiduciary responsibility to implement, regardless of the organization's actual history of related incidents.

- **Regulation**   Some types of security controls are required by applicable regulations such as HIPAA, the Canada Personal Information Protection and Electronic Documents Act (PIPEDA), and PCI-DSS.

- **Competitive differentiation**   In many industries, organizations that compete for business include claims of superior security controls as part of their marketing messages.

Security managers, of course, need to employ appropriate means for justifying or explaining security expenditures in various situations.

Effective Metrics

For metrics to be effective, they need to be measurable. A common way to ensure the quality and effectiveness of a metric is to use the SMART method. A metric that is SMART is

- Specific
- Measurable
- Attainable
- Relevant
- Timely

Additional considerations for good metrics, according to *Risk Metrics That Influence Business Decisions* by Paul Proctor (Gartner, Inc., 2016), include the following:

- **Leading indicator**   Does the metric help management to predict future risk?
- **Causal relationship**   Does the metric have a defensible causal relationship to a business impact, where a change in the metric compels someone to act?
- **Influence**   Has the metric influenced decision-making (or will it)?

You can find more information about the development of metrics in NIST Special Publication 800-55 Revision 1, *Performance Measurement Guide for Information Security*, available at www.nist.gov.

Strategic Alignment

For a security program to be successful, it must align to the organization's mission, strategy, and goals and objectives. A security program strategy and objectives should contain statements that can be translated into key measurements—the key performance and risk metrics of the program.

Here is an example: The organization CareerSearchCo, which is in the online career search and recruiting business, has the following as its mission statement:

> *Be the best marketplace for job seekers and recruiters*

Here are its most recent strategic objectives:

> *Integrate with leading business social network LinkedIn*

> *Develop an API to facilitate long-term transformation into a leading career and recruiting platform*

To meet these objectives, CareerSearchCo has developed a security strategy that includes the following:

> *Ensure Internet-facing applications are secure through developer training and application vulnerability testing*

Security and metrics would then include these:

> *Percentage of software developers not yet trained*

> *Number of critical vulnerabilities identified*

> *Time to remediate critical and high vulnerabilities*

Based on these criteria, these metrics are all measurable, they align to the security strategy, and they are all leading indicators. The higher these metrics, the more likely a breach would occur that would damage CareerSearchCo's reputation and ability to earn new business contracts from large corporations.

Risk Management

Effective risk management is the culmination of the highest-order activities in an information security program; these include risk analyses, the use of a risk ledger, formal risk treatment, and adjustments to the suite of security controls.

While it is difficult to effectively and objectively measure the success of a risk management program, it is possible to take indirect measurements—much like measuring the shadow of a tree to gauge its height. Thus, the best indicators of a successful risk management program would be improving trends in metrics involved with the following:

- Reduction in the number of security incidents
- Reduction in the impact of security incidents
- Reduction in the time to remediate security incidents
- Reduction in the time to remediate vulnerabilities
- Reduction in the number of new unmitigated risks

Regarding the previous mention of the reduction of security incidents, a security program improving its maturity from low levels should first expect to see the number of incidents increase. This would be not because of lapses in security controls but because of the development of—and improvements in—mechanisms used to detect and report security incidents.

Similarly, as a security program is improved and matures over time, the number of new risks will, at first, increase and then later decrease.

Performance Measurement

Metrics on the performance of information security provide measures of timeliness and effectiveness. Generally speaking, performance measurement metrics provide a view of tactical security processes and activities. As discussed earlier in this section, performance measurements are often the operational metrics that need to be transformed into executive-level metrics for those audiences.

Performance measurement metrics can include any of the following:

- Time to detect security incidents
- Time to remediate security incidents
- Time to provision user accounts
- Time to deprovision user accounts
- Time to discover vulnerabilities
- Time to remediate vulnerabilities

Nearly every operational activity that is security-related and measurable is a candidate for performance metrics.

Convergence

Larger organizations with multiple business units, geographic locations, or security functions (often as a result of mergers and acquisitions) may be experiencing issues related to overlapping or underlapping coverage or activities. For instance, an organization that recently acquired another company may have some duplication of effort in the asset management and risk management functions. In another example, local security personnel in a large, distributed organization may be performing security functions that are also being performed on their behalf by other personnel at headquarters.

Metrics in the category of convergence will be highly individualized, based on specific circumstances in an organization. Some of the categories of metrics may include the following:

- Gaps in asset coverage
- Overlaps in asset coverage
- Consolidation of licenses for security tools
- Gaps or overlaps in skills, responsibilities, or coverage

Value Delivery

Metrics on value delivery focus on the long-term reduction in costs, in proportion to other measures. Examples of value delivery metrics include the following:

- Controls used (seldom used controls may be candidates for removal)
- Percentage of controls that are effective (ineffective controls consume additional resources in audit, analysis, and remediation activities)
- Program costs per asset population or asset value
- Program costs per employee population
- Program costs per revenue

Organizations are cautioned against using *only* value delivery metrics—doing so will risk the security program spiraling down to nothing since a program that costs nothing will produce the best possible metric.

Resource Management

Resource management metrics are similar to value delivery metrics; both convey an efficient use of resources in an organization's information security program. But because the emphasis here is program efficiency, these are areas where resource management metrics may be developed:

- Standardization of security-related processes—because consistency drives costs down
- Security involvement in every procurement and acquisition project
- Percentage of assets protected by security controls

Developing Metrics in Layers for Audience Relevance

When embarking on the quest of security metrics development, a common pitfall is the development of a one-dimensional metrics framework that publishes a set of metrics to all audiences. For instance, a metrics program might publish figures on vulnerabilities discovered, vulnerabilities remediated, security incidents, and internal audits and their exceptions. Publishing this or a similar set of metrics to various stakeholders will add little value to some audiences and no value to others.

A better approach is the development of operational metrics, which are usually easily discovered and measured. The next step is to transform those operational metrics into different metrics, stated in business terms, for business audiences. In a given organization, a security program might employ two, three, or more layers of metrics, usually related to each other, and stated in relevant technical or business terms for each respective audience.

While it may be a good starting point to ask business leaders what kinds of metrics they want to see, in many cases security practitioners will be asked what

(continued)

metrics they want to see. This can be a challenge at times, but by understanding the business, culture, compliance climate, and individuals involved at the stakeholder level, the security practitioner can start with a set of metrics that show success in investments made or use them as a call to action by the leadership team.

The Security Balanced Scorecard

The balanced scorecard (BSC) is a management tool that is used to measure the performance and effectiveness of an organization. The balanced scorecard is used to determine how well an organization can fulfill its mission and strategic objectives and how well it is aligned with overall organizational objectives.

In the balanced scorecard, management defines key measurements in each of four perspectives:

- **Financial**   Key financial items measured include the cost of strategic initiatives, support costs of key applications, and capital investment.
- **Customer**   Key measurements include the satisfaction rate with various customer-facing aspects of the organization.
- **Internal processes**   Measurements of key activities include the number of projects and the effectiveness of key internal workings of the organization.
- **Innovation and learning**   Human-oriented measurements include turnover, illness, internal promotions, and training.

Each organization's balanced scorecard will represent a unique set of measurements that reflects the organization's type of business, business model, and style of management.

The balanced scorecard should be used to measure overall organizational effectiveness and progress. A similar scorecard, the security balanced scorecard, can be used to specifically measure security organization performance and results.

Like the balanced scorecard, the security balanced scorecard (security-BSC) has the same four perspectives, mapped to key activities as depicted in Table 2-1.

The security balanced scorecard should flow directly out of the organization's overall balanced scorecard and its IT balanced scorecard (IT-BSC). This will ensure that security will align itself with corporate objectives. While the perspectives between the overall BSC and the security BSC vary, the approach for each is similar, and the results for the security-BSC can "roll up" to the organization's overall BSC.

Business Model for Information Security

Developed by ISACA in 2009, the Business Model for Information Security (BMIS) is a guide for business-aligned, risk-based security governance. The use of BMIS helps security leadership ensure that the organization's security program continues to address emerging threats, developing regulations, and changing business needs.

	Financial	Customer	Internal Processes	Innovation and Learning
Awareness and Education	Lower cost of incidents	Increase confidence	Improve processes	Improve awareness
Access Control	Control access	Provide access	Ensure proper access	Improve communication
Vulnerability Management	Reduce vulnerabilities	Protect against vulnerabilities	Manage risks	Learn from incidents
Business Continuity	Ensure continuity	Provide core services	Test continuity	Ensure awareness
Compliance	Comply with regulations	Ensure compliance	Ensure compliance	Review compliance
Program Management	Ensure efficiency	Include customer input	Reduce reactive processes	Continue improvement

Table 2-1   Security Balanced Scorecard Domains

BMIS is a three-dimensional, three-sided pyramid, depicted in Figure 2-2. The three foundation elements of the pyramid are people, process, and technology, while the apex element of the pyramid is the organization.

The BMIS model includes the three traditional elements found in IT, which are people, process, and technology, and adds a fourth element, organization. The elements are connected by dynamic interconnections (DIs), which are culture, governing, architecture, emergence, enabling and support, and human factors. The elements and dynamic interconnections are described in more detail in the following sections.

Figure 2-2   The BMIS model
(Adapted from The Business
Model for Information
Security, ISACA)

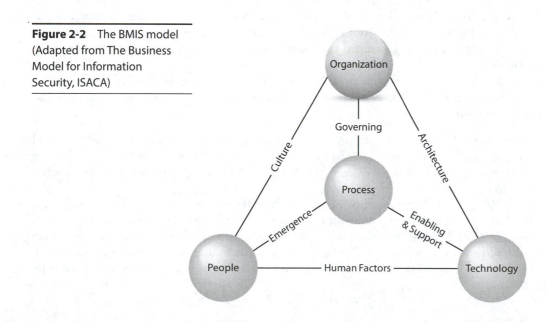

BMIS is described fully in the document *The Business Model for Information Security* from ISACA, available at https://www.isaca.org/bmis.

The BMIS is derived from the Systemic Security Management Framework, developed by the University of Southern California (USC) Marshall School of Business in 2006.

BMIS Elements and Dynamic Interconnections

The elements and dynamic interconnections are the major pieces of the BMIS model and are described in detail in this section.

Organization The organization element in the BMIS model makes the model unique. Most other models focus on people, process, and technology—or other aspects of an organization without considering the organization itself.

BMIS defines the organization as "a network of people interacting, using processes to channel this interaction." This is not unlike the executive management perspective that views the organization as a set of elements that act together to accomplish strategic objectives. The organization includes not only the permanent staff but also temporary workers, contractors, and consultants, as well as third-party organizations that also play roles in helping the organization achieve its objectives.

Organizations are formally structured through organization charts, command-and-control hierarchy, policies, processes, and procedures.

But organizations also have their informal, undocumented organization, which can be viewed like additional synapses that connect people or groups across the organization in ways not intended, nonetheless helping the organization achieve its objectives. This is often seen in distributed organizations, where expediency and pragmatism often rule over policy and process, particularly in locations farther away from corporate headquarters.

People The people element in the BMIS model represents all of the people in an organization, whether full-time employees or temporary workers, contractors, or consultants. Further, as an organization outsources its operations to other organizations, the people in those organizations are also part of the people in the people element in BMIS.

Like the other elements in the BMIS model, people cannot be studied by themselves but instead must be considered alongside the other elements of process, technology, and organization.

Process The process element in the BMIS model represents the formal structure of all defined activities in the organization, which together help the organization achieve its strategic objectives. Process defines practices and procedures that describe how activities are to be carried out.

ISACA's Risk IT framework defines an effective process as a reliable and repetitive collection of activities and controls to perform a certain task. Processes take input from one or more sources (including other processes), manipulate the input, utilize resources according to the policies, and produce output (including output to other processes). Processes should have clear business reasons for existing, accountable owners, clear roles and responsibilities around the execution of each key activity, and the means to undertake and measure performance.

Individual processes have the attribute of *maturity*, which qualitatively describes how well the process is designed, as well as how it is measured and improved over time.

Technology   The technology element in the BMIS model represents all of the systems, applications, and tools used by practitioners in an organization. Technology is a powerful enabler of an organization's processes and of its strategic objectives, although unless tamed with process and by people, technology by itself can accomplish little for an organization.

As the BMIS model illustrates, technology in an organization does not run by itself. Instead, people and processes are critical to any successful use of technology. Technology can be viewed as a process enabler and as a force multiplier, helping the organization accomplish more work in less time, for less cost, and with greater accuracy.

Culture   The culture DI connects the organization and people elements. Culture as part of a governance model makes BMIS unique, as most other models do not consider culture with strategic importance. BMIS defines culture as "a pattern of behaviors, beliefs, assumptions, attitudes, and ways of doing things."

Culture is the catalyst that drives behavior, with as much or more influence than formal directives such as policies and standards. Culture determines the degree to which personnel strive to conform to security policy and contribute to the protection of critical assets or whether they behave contrary to policy and put critical assets in jeopardy.

An organization's culture is considered one of the most critical factors in the success or failure of an information security program. By its nature, culture cannot be legislated or controlled directly, but instead it reflects the attitudes, habits, and customs adopted by the people in the organization.

The civil culture of the community in which the organization resides plays a large role in shaping the organization's culture. For this reason, establishing a single culture in an organization with many regional or global locations is not feasible.

Of utmost importance to the security strategist is the development of a productive security culture. Like other aspects of organizational culture, a desired security culture cannot simply be legislated through policy but must be carefully curated and grown. Steps to create a favorable security culture include the following:

- Involve personnel in discussions about the protection of critical assets.
- Executive leadership must lead by example and follow all policies.
- Include security responsibilities in all job descriptions.
- Include security factors in employees' compensation—for example, merit increases and bonuses.
- Link the protection of critical assets to the long-term success of the organization.
- Integrate messages related to the protection of assets, and other aspects of the information security program, into existing communications such as newsletters.

- Incorporate "secure by design" into key business processes so that security is part of the organization's routine activities.

- Reward and recognize desired behavior; similarly, admonish undesired behavior privately.

Changing an organization's security culture cannot be accomplished overnight, and it cannot be forced. Instead, every individual needs to understand consistent messaging that reiterates the importance of sound security practices.

For individuals and teams who don't "get it," the organization must be willing to take remedial action, not unlike that which would be undertaken when other undesired behavior is witnessed. Individuals who are teachable need to be coached on desired behavior. Those who prove to be unteachable may be dealt with in other ways.

Governing   The governing DI connects the organization and process elements. Per the definition from ISACA, "governance is the set of responsibilities and practices exercised by the board and executive management with the goal of providing strategic direction, ensuring that objectives are achieved, ascertaining that risks are managed appropriately and verifying that the enterprise's resources are used responsibly."

This means that processes are influenced, even controlled, by the organization's mission, strategic objectives, and other factors. In other words, the organization's processes must support the organization's mission and strategic objectives. When they don't, governance is used to change them until they are.

The tools used in governing include the following:

- Policies
- Standards
- Guidelines
- Process documentation
- Resource allocation
- Compliance

These tools are used by management to exert control over the development and operation of business processes, ensuring desired outcomes.

Communications is vital in the governing DI. Information flows down from management in the form of directives to influence change in business processes.

When the governing DI fails, processes no longer align with organization objectives and take on a life of their own.

Architecture   The architecture DI connects the organization and technology elements. The purpose of the DI between organization and technology signifies the need for the use of technology to be planned, orderly, and purposeful.

The definition of architecture, according to ISO/IEC 42010, "Systems and software engineering — Architecture description," is fundamental concepts or properties of a system in its environment embodied in its elements, in its relationships, and in the principles of its design and evolution. The practice of architecture ensures the following:

- **Alignment**   Applications and infrastructure will support the organization's mission and objectives.

- **Consistency**   Similar or even identical practices and solutions will be employed throughout the IT environment.

- **Efficiency**   The IT organization as well as its environment can be built and operated more efficiently, mainly through consistent designs and practices.

- **Low cost**   With a more consistent approach, acquisition and support costs can be reduced, through economy of scale and less waste.

- **Resilience**   Purposeful architectures and designs with greater resilience can be realized.

- **Flexibility**   Architectures must have the desired degree of flexibility to accommodate changing business needs and external factors such as regulations and market conditions.

- **Scalability**   Sound architectures are not rigid in their size but can be made larger or smaller to accommodate various business needs, such as growth in revenue, various size branch offices, and larger data sets.

- **Security**   With the development of security policies, standards, and guidelines, the principle of "secure by design" is more certain in future applications and systems.

The Zachman framework

The Zachman enterprise architecture framework, established in the late 1980s, continues to be the dominant enterprise architecture standard today. Zachman likens IT enterprise architecture to the construction and maintenance of an office building: at a high (abstract, not number of floors) level, the office building performs functions such as containing office space. As you look into increasing levels of detail in the building, you encounter various trades (steel, concrete, drywall, electrical, plumbing, telephone, fire control, elevators, and so on), each of which has its own specifications, standards, regulations, construction and maintenance methods, and so on.

In the Zachman architecture model, IT systems and environments are described at a high, functional level and then, in increasing detail, encompassing systems, databases, applications, networks, and so on. The Zachman framework is illustrated in Table 2-2.

While the Zachman model allows an organization to peer into cross sections of an IT environment that supports business processes, the model does not convey the relationships between IT systems. Data flow diagrams are used instead to depict information flows.

Data flow diagrams (DFDs) are frequently used to illustrate the flow of information between IT applications. Like the Zachman model, a DFD can begin as a high-level diagram, where the labels of information flows are expressed in business terms. Written specifications about each flow can accompany the DFD; these specifications would

	Data	Functional (Application)	Network (Technology)	People (Organization)	Time	Strategy
Scope	List of data sets important in the business	List of business processes	List of business locations	List of organizations	List of events	List of business goals and strategy
Enterprise Model	Conceptual data/object model	Business process model	Business logistics	Workflow	Master schedule	Business plan
Systems Model	Logical data model	System architecture	Detailed system architecture	Human interface architecture	Processing structure	Business rule model
Technology Model	Physical data/class model	Technology design	Technology architecture	Presentation architecture	Control structure	Rule design
Detailed Representation	Data definition	Program	Network architecture	Security architecture	Time definition	Rule speculation
Function Enterprise	Usable data	Working function	Usable network	Functioning organization	Implemented schedule	Working strategy

Table 2-2   The Zachman Framework Shows IT Systems in Increasing Levels of Detail

describe the flow in increasing levels of detail, all the way to field lengths and communication protocol settings.

Similar to Zachman, DFDs permit nontechnical business executives to easily understand the various IT applications and the relationships between them. Figure 2-3 shows a typical DFD.

Emergence   The emergence DI connects the people and process elements. The purpose of the emergence DI is to bring focus to the way people perform their work. Emergence is seen as the arising of new opportunities for organizations, new processes, new practices, and new ways of doing things. Emergence can be a result of people learning how to do things better, faster, more accurately, or with less effort.

Emergence can be seen as a two-edged sword. The creativity and ingenuity of people can lead to better ways of doing things, but on the other hand, this can lead to inconsistent results including errors or lapses in product or service quality.

Organizations that want to reduce work output deviation caused by emergence have a few potential remedies.

- **Increase automation**   Removing some of the human factors from a process through automation can yield more consistent outcomes.

- **Enact controls**   Putting key controls in place can help management focus on factors responsible for outcome deviation. This can lead to process improvements later.

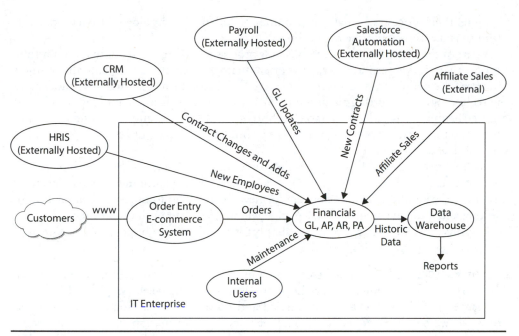

Figure 2-3 A typical DFD shows the relationship between IT applications.

- **Increase process maturity** Organizations can enact changes in business process to increase the maturity of those processes. Examples include adding key measurements or producing richer log data so that processes can be better understood and improved over time.

Organizations need to understand which activities can benefit from automation and which require human judgment that cannot be programmed into a computer. This sometimes involves human factors because there may be times when people prefer to interact with a person versus a machine, even if the machine is faster or more accurate. Automation does not always equal improvement to all parties concerned.

Enabling and Support The enabling and support DI connects the process and technology elements. The purpose of the enabling and support DI is the enablement and support of business processes by technology. Put another way, information technology makes business processes faster and more accurate than if they were performed manually.

In an appropriate relationship between business processes and technology, the structure of business processes determines how technology will support them. Unfortunately, many organizations compromise their business processes by having capabilities in poorly selected or poorly designed technology determine how business processes operate. While it is not always feasible for technology to support every whim and nuance in a business process, many organizations take the other extreme by selecting technology that does not align with their business processes or the organization's mission and objectives and changing their processes to match capabilities provided by technology. This level of compromise is detrimental to the organization.

A part of the disconnect between business processes and technologies that do not fully support them is that technology experts often do not sufficiently understand the business processes they support, and business owners and users do not sufficiently understand the technologies supporting them. To paint with a broad brush, technology people and businesspeople think differently about technology and business and often find it difficult to understand each other enough to make technology's support of business processes as successful as they could be.

The tool that is used to fill this gap is the requirements document. Often developed at the onset of a major project (and often a minor one), business people endeavor to develop charts listing required and desired functionality for new technologies to improve their chances of selecting and implementing a technology that will support their business processes.

The BMIS model for enabling and support is a life cycle, as opposed to a do-it-once approach, as depicted in Figure 2-4.

Human Factors   The human factors DI connects the people and technology elements. The purpose of the human factors DI is the interaction between people and information systems. This is an extensively studied and researched topic, sometimes known as *human–computer interaction (HCI)*. The elements of information systems that people interact with are often known as *user interfaces (UIs)*; considerable research is devoted to the improvement of UIs to make software and systems easier to use and more intuitive.

From an information security perspective, information systems need to implement security requirements in ways that do not impede users' interaction wherever possible. Where users have choices to make while interacting with a system, security features and functions need to be easy to use and intuitive. Further, users should not be able to easily circumvent security controls put in place to protect systems and data. Finally, systems should be designed so that they cannot be abused or that their use permit abuse of other assets.

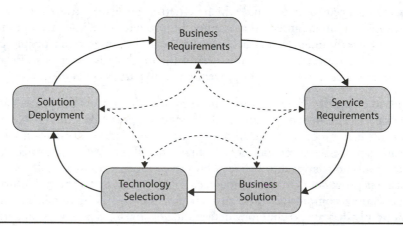

Figure 2-4   BMIS enabling and support life cycle (Adapted from The University of Southern California, Marshall School of Business, Institute for Critical Information Infrastructure Protection, USA)

There are many considerations that need to be included in the design of information systems (both hardware and software), including the following:

- **Consistency**   Operating an information system should resemble other commonly used systems. For instance, keyboard arrangement should be consistent with other products in use.

- **Typing and data entry**   Entering text should be straightforward and simple. The method for entering data should be commensurate with the interface. For instance, a small touchscreen keyboard would be a poor choice for entering large amounts of data (e.g., sentences and paragraphs). Further, pointing methods should be easy to use and intuitive.

- **Display and readability**   Users should be able to easily read text and images.

- **Error recovery**   Users should be able to repeat a step when they have recognized that they have made an error.

- **Sound**   Sounds as part of interaction should be adjustable and loud enough to be heard. The system should not emit prolonged loud noise, such as banks of cooling fans, if users are expected to work in proximity without hearing protection.

- **Voice and biometric recognition**   Technologies used to recognize voice commands and various types of biometrics should be easy to use and accurate as well.

- **Ergonomics**   Whether portable or stationary, devices should be easy to use without inducing strain or requiring contortions to use.

- **Environment**   Information systems should be designed to operate in a variety of environments where they would typically be used. For instance, ruggedized laptops for use at construction sites should withstand dust, dirt, water, and sunlight, while small portable devices should be water resistant and not break when dropped.

Using BMIS

Organizations employ BMIS to better understand how their people, processes, and technologies help to protect the overall organization. BMIS helps the strategist better understand the holistic relationships between various aspects (the *elements*) in the organization and the factors that influence them (the *dynamic interconnections*).

The structure of BMIS itself is a key factor in its success. Equally important, however, is the ability for holistic thinking rather than detailed thinking. It is vital to understand that BMIS shows how everything is connected to everything else. A change introduced at any element or DI will affect other elements and DIs and most likely affect the adjacent elements and DIs the most.

Considering, again, the structure of BMIS, refer to Figure 2-2.

When a security analyst or strategist is pondering an incident, problem, or situation, they identify the element or DI in the BMIS that corresponds to the subject of the matter. Next, they identify the adjacent elements or DIs and think about the relationships:

these represent aspects in the organization that would be related or affected. Examining one element, noting the DI connecting it to another element, helps identify the nature of the connecting factor.

Examples are covered next, which should make these concepts clearer.

Example 1: Adverse Effects of a Policy Change

A security manager wants to enact a new policy regarding the use of personally owned mobile devices for corporate use including e-mail. Policy is a part of the governing DI, and the adjacent elements are organization and process.

The organization element here means that a new policy affects the organization in some way, by altering how it does things. The process element means that one or more processes or procedures may be affected.

But what if the new mobile device policy adversely affects other processes? One would then follow the DIs from process and see where they lead and how they lead. First, the emergence DI connects to people. In the case of this policy, emergence includes ways in which people follow—or don't follow—the process. Next, following the enabling and support DI to technology, this could indicate how other technologies may be affected by the policy change.

Example 2: Examining Causes for Process Weakness

An organization hired a security consulting company to perform security scans of its internal network. The consulting company found numerous instances of servers being several months behind in their security patches. The organization uses a vulnerability scanning tool and is wondering why patches are so far behind.

Thinking that technology is the problem, the investigator examines the scanning tool to see whether it is operating properly. This would be the technology element. The tool is seen to be operating correctly and is running up-to-date software. The investigator next examines the BMIS model to see what DIs are connected to technology.

First, the architecture DI is examined. This prompts the investigator to think about whether the scanning tool is able to reach all systems in the network. The investigator confirms that it is.

Next, the human factors DI is examined. The investigator contacts the engineer who runs the scanning tool and asks to observe his use of the tool. The investigator is wondering whether the engineer understands how to use the tool properly (there has been a history of problems because the scanning tool is not easy to use). The engineer is using the scanning tool correctly, so the investigator needs to keep looking.

Finally, the enabling and support DI is examined. This prompts the investigator to ponder whether there are any business processes related to the use of the scanning tool that might be a factor. When interviewing engineers, the investigator discovers that there are several new networks in the organization that are not included in the scanner's configuration.

By using the BMIS tool to understand how things relate to each other, the investigator was able to determine the cause of the problem: the failure of a network change process to notify security personnel caused those security personnel to *not* configure the scanning tool to include them. Thus, for some time, security scans did not identify vulnerabilities present in systems in the new network segments. The security consulting company's scans included all of the organization's networks, including those that the organization did not scan itself.

Security Strategy Development

Among business, technology, and security professionals, there are many different ideas about what exactly a strategy should entail and which techniques are best used to develop it, as well as general confusion on the topic. While a specific strategy itself may be complex, the concept of a strategy is quite simple. It can be defined as follows:

> *The plan to achieve an objective.*

The effort to build a strategy requires more than saying those six words. Again, however, the idea is not complicated. The concept is this: understand where you are now and where you want to be. The strategy is the path you much follow to get from where you are (current state) to where you want to be (strategic objective).

The remainder of this section explores strategy development in detail.

Strategy Objectives

As stated earlier in this section, a strategy is the plan to achieve an objective. The objective (or objectives) is the desired future state for the organization's security posture and level of risk.

There are, in addition, objectives *of* a strategy. These objectives are as follows:

- **Strategic alignment**   The desired future state, and the strategy to get there, must be in alignment with the organization and *its* strategy and objectives.

- **Effective risk management**   A security program must include a risk management policy, processes, and procedures. Without risk management, decisions are made blindly without regard to their consequences or level of risk.

- **Value delivery**   The desired future state of a security program should include a focus for continual improvement and increasing efficiency. No organization has unlimited funds for security; instead, organizations need to reduce risk for the lowest reasonable cost.

- **Resource optimization**   Similar to value delivery, strategic goals should efficiently utilize available resources. Among other things, this means having only the necessary staff and tools to meet strategic objectives.

- **Performance measurement**   While it is important for strategic objectives to be SMART, the ongoing security and security-related business operations should themselves be measurable, giving management an opportunity to drive continual improvement.

- **Assurance process integration**   Organizations typically operate one or more separate assurance processes in silos that are not integrated. An effective strategy would work to break down these silos and consolidate assurance processes, reducing hidden risks.

All of these should be developed in a way that makes them measurable. This is why these six topics were discussed earlier when discussing governance metrics. These components were made to fit together in this way.

Control Frameworks

While every organization may have its unique missions, objectives, business models, tolerance for risk, and so on, organizations need not invent governance frameworks from scratch to manage their IT objectives.

In the context of strategy development, some organizations may already have a suitable control framework in place, while others might not. While it is not always necessary for an organization to select an industry control framework, it is advantageous to do so. Industry-standard control frameworks have been in use in thousands of companies, and they are regularly updated to reflect changing business practices, emerging threats, and new technologies.

It is often considered a mistake to select a control framework because of the presence or absence of a small number of specific controls. Usually such selection is made on the assumption that control frameworks are rigid and inflexible. Instead, the strategist should take a different approach: select a control framework based on industry alignment and then institute a process for developing additional controls based on the results of risk assessments. Indeed, this is exactly the approach described in ISO/IEC 27001, as well as in the NIST Cybersecurity Framework. Start with a well-known control framework and then create additional controls, if needed, to address risks specific to the organization. When assessing the use of a specific framework, there may be occasions where a specific control area may not be applicable. In those cases, do not just ignore the section. Document both the business and technical reasons why the organization chose not to use the control area. This will assist when a question is raised at a point in the future as to why the decision was made to not implement the control area. The date and those involved in the decision should also be documented.

Several standard frameworks are discussed in the remainder of this section:

- COBIT
- ISO/IEC 27001
- ISO/IEC 38500
- ITIL / ISO/IEC 20000
- HIPAA
- NIST SP 800-53
- NIST CSF
- CIS 20
- PCI-DSS

COBIT

Developed in 1996, Control Objectives for Information and Related Technologies (COBIT) is an IT management framework developed by the IT Governance Institute and ISACA. COBIT's four domains are Plan and Organize, Acquire and Implement, Deliver and Support, and Monitor and Evaluate.

COBIT is not primarily a security control framework but an IT process framework that includes security processes that are interspersed throughout the framework. COBIT contains 37 processes; the security- and risk-related processes are as follows:

- Ensure risk optimization
- Manage risk
- Manage security
- Manage security resources
- Monitor, evaluate, and assess compliance with external requirements

COBIT is available from https://www.isaca.org/COBIT/Pages/Product-Family.aspx (registration and payment required).

ISO/IEC 27001

ISO/IEC 27001, "Information technology — Security techniques — Information security management systems — Requirements," is an international standard for information security and risk management. This standard contains a requirements section that outlines a properly functioning information security management system (ISMS), as well as a comprehensive control framework.

ISO/IEC 27001 is divided into two sections: requirements and controls. The requirements section describes required activities found in effective ISMSs. The controls section contains a baseline set of controls that serve as a starting point for an organization. The standard is updated periodically; the latest version was released in 2015 and is known as ISO/IEC 27001:2015.

The requirements in ISO/IEC 27001 are described in these seven sections:

- Context of the organization
- Leadership
- Planning
- Support
- Operation
- Performance evaluation
- Improvement

The 14 control categories in the ISO/IEC 27001 standard are as follows:

- Information security policies
- Organization of information security
- Human resource security
- Asset management
- Access control

- Cryptography
- Physical and environmental security
- Operations security
- Communications security
- System acquisition, development, and maintenance
- Supplier relationships
- Information security incident management
- Information security aspects of business continuity management
- Compliance

While ISO/IEC 27001 is a highly respected control framework, its adoption has been modest, partly because the standard costs about $117. Unlike NIST standards, which are free of charge, it is unlikely that students or professionals will pay this much for a standard to learn more about it. Despite this, ISO/IEC 27001 is growing in popularity in organizations throughout the world.

ISO/IEC 27001 is available from https://www.iso.org/standard/54534.html (registration and payment required).

ISO/IEC 38500

ISO/IEC 38500, "Governance of IT for the Organization," is an international standard on the corporate governance of information technology, suitable for small and large organizations in the public or private sector.

ISO/IEC 38500 is available from https://www.iso.org/standard/62816.html (registration and payment required).

ITIL / ISO/IEC 20000

Known as the IT Infrastructure Library, ITIL is a framework of processes for IT service delivery and IT service management. ITIL was originally developed by the UK Office of Government Commerce in order to improve its IT management processes. The international standard, ISO/IEC 20000, is adapted from ITIL.

ITIL is not a security framework but instead a process framework for IT service management. However, it is often said that an organization will have a difficult time building a successful information security program with effective controls in the absence of a service management framework such as ITIL.

ITIL is available from https://www.axelos.com/best-practice-solutions/itil (registration and payment required).

HIPAA

The U.S. Health Insurance Portability and Accountability Act established requirements for the protection of electronic protected health information (EPHI). These requirements apply to virtually every corporate or government entity (known as a *covered entity*) that stores or processes EPHI. HIPAA requirements fall into three main categories.

- Administrative safeguards
- Physical safeguards
- Technical safeguards

Several controls reside within each of these three categories. Each control is labeled as Required or Addressable. Controls that are labeled as Required must be implemented by every covered entity. Controls that are labeled as Addressable are considered optional in each covered entity, meaning the organization does not have to implement an Addressable control if it does not apply or if there is negligible risk if the control is not implemented.

HIPAA is available from https://www.gpo.gov/fdsys/pkg/CRPT-104hrpt736/pdf/CRPT-104hrpt736.pdf.

NIST SP 800-53

Developed by the U.S. National Institute for Standards and Technology, NIST Special Publication (SP) 800-53, "Security and Privacy Controls for Federal Information Systems and Organizations," is one of the most well-known and adopted security control frameworks. NIST SP 800-53 is required for all U.S. government information systems, as well as all information systems in private industry that store or process information on behalf of the U.S. federal government.

NIST controls are organized into 18 categories:

- Access control
- Awareness and training
- Audit and accountability
- Security assessment and authorization
- Configuration management
- Contingency planning
- Identification and authentication
- Incident response
- Maintenance
- Media protection
- Physical and environmental protection
- Planning
- Personnel security
- Risk assessment
- System and services acquisition
- System and communications protection
- System and information integrity
- Program management

Even though the NIST 800-53 control framework is required for U.S. federal information systems, many organizations that are not required to employ the framework have utilized it, primarily because it is a high-quality control framework with in-depth implementation guidance and also because it is available without cost.

NIST SP 800-53 is available from http://csrc.nist.gov/publications/PubsSPs.html.

NIST Cybersecurity Framework

The NIST Cybersecurity Framework (NIST CSF) is a risk-based life-cycle methodology for assessing risk, enacting controls, and measuring control effectiveness that is not unlike ISO/IEC 27001. The components of the NIST CSF are as follows:

- **Framework Core**   These are a set of functions—Identify, Protect, Detect, Respond, Recover—that make up the life cycle of high-level functions in an information security program. The Framework Core includes a complete set of controls (known as *references*) within the four activities.
- **Framework Implementation Tiers**   These are maturity levels, from least mature to most mature: Partial, Risk Informed, Repeatable, Adaptive.
- **Framework Profile**   This is an alignment of elements of the Framework Core (the functions, categories, subcategories, and references) with an organization's business requirements, risk tolerance, and available resources.

Organizations implementing the NIST CSF would first perform an assessment by measuring its maturity (Implementation Tiers) for each activity in the Framework Core. Next, the organization would determine desired levels of maturity for each activity in the Framework Core. The differences found would be gaps that would need to be filled through several means, including the following:

- Hiring additional resources
- Training resources
- Adding or changing business processes or procedures
- Changing system or device configuration
- Acquiring new systems or devices

The NIST CSF is available from https://www.nist.gov/cyberframework.

Center for Internet Security Critical Security Controls

The Critical Security Controls (CSC) framework from the Center for Internet Security (CIS), known as CIS CSC 20, is a well-known control framework that traces its lineage back to the SANS organization. The framework is still commonly referred to as the "SANS 20" or "SANS 20 Critical Security Controls."

The CIS CSC control categories are as follows:

- Inventory of Authorized and Unauthorized Devices
- Inventory of Authorized and Unauthorized Software
- Secure Configurations for Hardware and Software on Mobile Devices, Laptops, Workstations, and Servers
- Continuous Vulnerability Assessment and Remediation
- Controlled Use of Administrative Privileges

- Maintenance, Monitoring, and Analysis of Audit Logs

- E-mail and Web Browser Protections

- Malware Defenses

- Limitation and Control of Network Ports, Protocols, and Services

- Data Recovery Capability

- Secure Configurations for Network Devices such as Firewalls, Routers, and Switches

- Boundary Defense

- Data Protection

- Controlled Access Based on the Need to Know

- Wireless Access Control

- Account Monitoring and Control

- Security Skills Assessment and Appropriate Training to Fill Gaps

- Application Software Security

- Incident Response and Management

- Penetration Tests and Red Team Exercises

CIS CSC controls available from https://www.cisecurity.org/critical-controls/(registration required).

PCI-DSS

The Payment Card Industry Data Security Standard is a control framework specifically for the protection of credit card numbers and related information when stored, processed, and transmitted on an organization's networks. The PCI-DSS was developed by the PCI Standards Council, a consortium of the world's dominant credit card brands, namely, Visa, MasterCard, American Express, Discover, and JCB.

The PCI-DSS has 12 control objectives:

- Install and maintain a firewall configuration to protect cardholder data.

- Do not use vendor-supplied defaults for system passwords and other security parameters.

- Protect stored cardholder data.

- Encrypt transmission of cardholder data across open, public networks.

- Protect all systems against malware and regularly update antivirus software or programs.

- Develop and maintain secure systems and applications.

- Restrict access to cardholder data by business need to know.

- Identify and authenticate access to system components.

- Restrict physical access to cardholder data.
- Track and monitor all access to network resources and cardholder data.
- Regularly test security systems and processes.
- Maintain a policy that addresses information security for all personnel.

PCI-DSS is mandatory for all organizations that store, process, or transmit credit card data. Organizations with larger volumes of card data are required to undergo annual on-site audits.

Many organizations use the controls and the principles in PCI-DSS to protect other types of financial and personal data such as account numbers, Social Security numbers, and dates of birth.

PCI-DSS is available from https://www.pcisecuritystandards.org/ (registration and license agreement required).

Risk Objectives

A vital part of strategy development is the determination of desired risk levels. One of the inputs to strategy development is the understanding of the current level of risk, and the desired future state may also have a level of risk associated with it.

It is quite difficult to quantify risk, even for the most mature organizations. Getting risk to a reasonable "high/medium/low" is simpler, though less straightforward and difficult to do consistently across an organization. In specific instances, the costs of individual controls can be known, and the costs of theoretical losses can be estimated, but doing this across an entire risk-control framework is tedious and yet uncertain because the probabilities of occurrence for threat events amounts to little more than guesswork.

Still, in a general sense, a key part of a security strategy may well be the reduction of risk (it could also be cost reduction or compliance improvement). When this is the case, the strategist will need to employ a method for determining before-and-after risk levels that are reasonable and credible. For the sake of consistency, a better approach would be the use of a methodology—however specific or general—that fits with other strategies and discussions involving risk.

Strategy Resources

Before a strategy can be developed, it is first necessary to understand everything that is in place currently. A strategy describes how goals and objectives are to be met. Without knowing the starting place in a journey, it is not possible to chart a course to the journey's destination. Before future security capabilities can be mapped out, it's first necessary to understand an organization's current capabilities. The differences can be seen as a gap that needs to be filled, whether that means technologies, skills, policies, or practices.

More than simply defining point A in a journey to point B, existing resources also paint a picture of an organization's current capabilities, including behavior, skills, practices, and security posture.

There are two types of inputs that must be considered: those that will influence the development of strategic objectives and those that define the current state of the security program and protective controls. The following are inputs that must be considered before objectives are developed:

- Risk assessments
- Threat assessments

When suitable risk and threat assessments have been completed, the security strategist can then develop strategic objectives or, if they have been created already, validate that strategic objectives will satisfactorily address risks and threats identified in those assessments.

Next, security strategists can examine several other inputs that help them understand the workings of the current security program, including the following:

- Policy
- Standards
- Guidelines
- Processes and procedures
- Architecture
- Controls
- Skills
- Metrics
- Assets
- Risk ledger
- Vulnerability assessments
- Insurance
- Critical data
- Business impact analysis
- Security incident log
- Outsourced services
- Audits
- Culture
- Maturity
- Risk appetite

All of the focus areas listed here are described in the rest of this section.

Risk Assessment

A strategist should choose to have a risk assessment performed to reveal risks present in the organization. This helps the strategist understand threat scenarios and their estimated impact and frequency of occurrence. The results of a risk assessment give the strategist valuable information on the types of resources required to bring risks down to acceptable levels. This is vital for developing and validating strategic objectives.

Any historical record of risk assessments may give the strategist a better idea of the maturity of the security program, as well as an indication of whether risks in the past had been mitigated. If older risk assessments indicate significant risks that are still present in newer risk assessments or if risk assessments are performed only for compliance purposes and not for making actual improvements in the organization's security posture, you could wonder whether the organization places much credence in those risk assessments.

Risk assessments should drive the actual creation of strategic objectives. Otherwise, there is a danger that strategic objectives might not include changes to an organization's security program and the protective measures needed to reduce significant risks.

Threat Assessment

Strategists should have a threat assessment performed so that they can better understand relevant threats. This gives the strategist information about the types of threats most likely to have an impact on the organization, regardless of the effectiveness of controls.

Performing a threat assessment provides an additional perspective on risk. This is because a threat assessment focuses on external threats and threat scenarios, regardless of the presence or effectiveness of preventive or detective controls. While vulnerabilities may change frequently, threats are considered to be more constant. Because of this, security policies need to reflect threats that have been identified.

A threat assessment is an essential element of strategy development. Without a threat assessment, there is a possibility that strategic objectives may fail to address important threats. This would result in a security strategy that will not adequately protect the organization.

A history of threat assessments gives the strategist insight into the maturity of the security program: an absence of threat assessments may be an indication of low maturity or scarce resources. Details in threat assessment records may reveal remediation trends if key threats are not appearing repeatedly, which would be an indication they have not been mitigated.

Policy

An organization's security policy, as well as its practices in relation to its policy, may say a great deal about the organization's desired current state.

Security policy can be thought of as an organization's internal laws and regulations with regard to the protection of important assets (as well as personnel safety). Examination of current security policy can reveal a lot about what behaviors are required in the organization. The following are a few aspects of security policy:

- **Breadth of coverage**   What subject areas are covered by the policy? Does it include expected computer and mobile device usage behavior? Are other topics such as vulnerability management, third-party risk, or software development are included in security policy?

- **Relevance**   Does the policy include content on new technologies and practices?

- **Policy strictness**   Does the policy broadly prohibit certain behaviors such as the occasional personal use of corporate e-mail or limit or prohibit the use of external USB data storage devices?

- **Accountability and consequences**   Does the policy specify expectations for adherence to policy or the consequences of willingly violating policy? For instance, do policy violations include the prospect of suspension or termination of employment?

- **Compliance**   It is important to understand the degree to which the organization is in compliance with its policy, including the margin of compliance. Does the organization's security policy reflect good practices, and does the organization meet most or all of them? Or does its policy appear to be more of a vision statement of how things could be in the future?

- **Last management review** It is important to know when an organization's security was last updated, reviewed, and approved by management. This speaks to more than just the organization's policy but also to how active its security program has been in the recent past.

Standards

An organization's security standards describe, in detail, the methods, techniques, technologies, specifications, brands, and configurations to be used throughout the organization.

Like security policy in the preceding section, for the organization's standards it is important to understand the breadth of coverage, strictness, compliance, and last review and update. These all tell the security manager the extent to which an organization's security standards are used—if at all.

In addition to the aforementioned characteristics, it is important to know how the organization's standards were developed and how good they are. For instance, are there device-hardening standards, and are they aligned to or derived from industry-recognized standards such as Center for Internet Security, National Institute for Standards and Technology (NIST), European Union Agency for Network and Information Security (ENISA), Defense Information Systems Agency Security Technical Implementation Guides (DISA STIG), or another?

Similarly, it is important to know whether standards are highly detailed (configuration item by configuration item) or whether they are principle based. If they are the latter, then engineers may exercise potentially wide latitude when implementing these standards. You should understand that highly detailed standards are not necessarily better than principle-based standards; it depends on the nature of the organization, its risk tolerance, and its maturity.

Guidelines

While an organization's guidelines are not "the law" per se, the presence of guidelines may signal a higher-than-average maturity. Many organizations don't get any further than creating policies and standards, so the presence of proper guidelines means that the organization may have (or had in the past) sufficient resources or prioritization to make documenting guidance on policies important enough to do.

According to their very nature, guidelines are typically written for personnel who need a little extra guidance on how to adhere to policies.

Like other types of security program documents, guidelines should be reviewed and updated regularly. Because guidelines bridge rarely changing policy with often-changing technologies and practices, a strategist examining guidelines should find them being changed frequently—or they may be found to be irrelevant. But that, too, is possibly evidence of an attempt to improve maturity or communications (or both) but with the absence of long-term commitment.

Processes and Procedures

An organization's processes and procedures may speak volumes about its level of discipline, consistency, risk tolerance, and maturity of not only its security program but of IT and the business in general. Like other types of documents discussed in this section, the relevance, accuracy, and thoroughness of process and procedure documents are indicators of maturity and commitment to a solid security program.

Relying on process documentation is not sufficient. Strategists need to examine more than process and procedure documents. Additionally, they must interview personnel, examine business records, and observe processes in action to ensure that they are being carried out as designed.

Further evidence of process and procedure effectiveness can be found in risk assessments and audits. Those topics are discussed later in this section.

Architecture

An organization's architecture—that is, its documentation of systems, networks, data flows, and other aspects of its environment—gives the security strategist a lot of useful information about how the organization has implemented its information systems.

While it's good to look for and examine network diagrams, system diagrams, data flow diagrams, and so forth, it's nearly as valuable to find good and consistent designs even if they aren't documented anywhere. I'd rather see an organization's infrastructure as modern, effective, and consistent versus a collection of outdated diagrams or, worse yet, inconsistent uses of technologies and techniques throughout an organization. Whether architecture diagrams exist or not is a concern that is similar to that regarding policies, standards, guidelines, and other artifacts.

Equally important here is whether the architecture of technology effectively supports the organization. Does an organization's technology and the way that the technology has been implemented adequately support the organization's goals, objectives, and operations? Like so many other aspects of information security and information technology, alignment with the business and its goals and objectives is critical and cannot be disregarded. Making key changes in this regard may need to be part of an overall strategy.

Another aspect of architecture is known as *technical debt*. This is a term that represents two characteristics of an organization's infrastructure:

- **Poor design**   Lack of an overall design, or a poor design, causes subsequent additions and changes to the environment to be done in a less than optimal manner, further degrading the environment in terms of performance, resilience, or simplicity.

- **Outdated and unsupported components**   In this instance, major hardware or software components of the environment have exceeded their service life, are no longer supported by their manufacturers, or have subcomponents that cannot be easily replaced.

The concept of technical debt is a metaphor for financial debt in two aspects. First, "interest payments" come in the form of additional effort every time the environment requires attention. Next, "retiring the debt" requires major architectural changes and/or replacement of many components.

Technical debt is accumulated when organizations lack personnel capable of creating good architectural designs and also when an organization fails to upgrade end-of-life components.

Controls

The presence of controls—and the control framework—speaks volumes about the organization's security program. However, controls may exist only on paper and not in practice. It is useful to read about the organization's controls, but by themselves we know very little. The strategist needs to understand whether the controls are actually implemented. More than that, it's important to know whether they are effective.

When examining control documentation, the strategist should look for details such as control owners, the purpose and scope of controls, related process and procedure documents, and other metadata that will help the strategist understand their purpose.

Next, the strategist should look for artifacts or interview personnel to see whether specific controls are in place. Again, the presence of documentation alone may not indicate they are actually being carried out or whether documentation is just more shelf-ware. Interviewing personnel and observing controls in action is a better way to see whether controls are in place.

Internal and external audits, discussed later in this section, are another way to understand control effectiveness. See the "Audits" section.

A strategist will want to understand whether the controls in place are part of a control framework such as ISO27001, NIST 800-53, HIPAA, or PCI. But more than that, are all controls in the control framework implemented, or have some been omitted? The reason for omission may vary from irrelevance to irresponsible avoidance.

Finally, the strategist should look for additional controls that have been implemented. This may be a sign of regulatory requirements or the result of an effective risk management program where identified risks compelled management to enact additional controls to mitigate risk.

Skills

An inventory of skills provides the strategist with an idea of what staff members are able to accomplish. This is useful on a couple of levels.

- **Tenure**   This includes how many years of different types of experience a staff member may have.
- **Behavioral**   This includes leadership, management, coordination, and logistics.
- **Disciplines**   This includes fields such as systems engineering, network engineering, controls development, audit, risk management, and risk analysis.
- **Technologies**   This includes skills with specific technologies such as Palo Alto Networks firewalls, CentOS operating systems, Logrhythm, and AppScan.

Understanding skills at all of these levels helps the strategist understand the types of work that the current staff is able to perform, where minor skills gaps are, and where the strategist may recommend adding additional staff through hiring, contracting, or professional services.

A key consideration a strategist needs to keep in mind is the potential for a major shift in technologies. A good example is if the organization has been using products from a particular vendor for many years, but because of a change in leadership and a good deal by a different vendor, the decision was made to migrate to a different vendor's products. Without fully understanding the skills and capabilities of the team, an organization can create significant risks because of the lack of ability to effectively manage the new products. This could lead to outages, departure of key resources, increased cost associated with consulting, and a loss of trust from the end-user community.

Metrics

Metrics indicate the state of an information security program over time. Effective metrics help personnel see how effectively the security program is protecting the organization; this is a key consideration for the people developing long-term strategies.

If metrics were properly established, they'll serve as a guide for the long-term effectiveness of security controls. This helps the strategist understand what works well and where improvement opportunities are. The strategist can then design end states with more certainty and confidence than if metrics didn't exist.

When examining metrics, a strategist needs to understand the audience. For example, were security metrics developed for internal security operations' use only, or were the metrics developed for consumption by other audience, such as internal users, senior management, or the board of directors? Next, the strategist will want to look for evidence that metrics were delivered to these other audiences and whether metrics were ever used as a reason for making tactical or strategic changes in the security program.

Assets

It is often said among information security professionals, "You cannot protect what you cannot find." This saying refers to assets in an organization, namely, servers, network devices, end-user workstations, and mobile devices—but also application software and software tools. Because many security incidents involve the exploitation of a vulnerability (usually with malware), this necessitates that organizations have effective vulnerability management programs in place. The life-cycle process in a vulnerability management program is as follows:

- Identify the environment to be scanned.
- Scan assets for vulnerabilities.
- Identify and categorize vulnerabilities.
- Remediate vulnerabilities (often through applying security patches but sometimes through configuration changes or increased monitoring and alerting).

Depending on an organization's tools and methods, it's typical that only known identified assets are scanned. Unknown or unidentified assets may or may not get scanned, but even if they do, they might get lost in the process later. Intruders are familiar with this and use this to their advantage: by performing scans of their own, they can identify unpatched systems and use them as a beachhead from which to infiltrate the organization.

Risk Ledger

A risk ledger can give the strategist a great deal of insight into risk management and risk analysis activities in the organization. Depending on the detail available in the risk ledger, a strategist may be able to discern the following:

- Scope, frequency, quality, and maturity of risk assessments
- Presence or absence of risk treatment
- Security incidents

A risk ledger is the business record reflecting the history and findings from risk assessments, threat assessments, vulnerability assessments, security incidents, and other activities. Its content reflects the types of activities occurring in the information security program and the significant results of those activities.

The lack of a risk ledger would indicate that the organization's security management program is not taking a risk-based approach. Instead, the organization may be compliance based or, worse yet, asset based or ad hoc. These approaches are signs of lower maturity where the organization's security personnel are mainly reactive and do little planning.

Vulnerability Assessment

Strategists may choose to have a vulnerability assessment performed so that they may better understand the current security posture of the organization's infrastructure. The vulnerability assessment may target network devices, appliances, operating systems, subsystems such as web servers and database management system, and applications—or any suitable combination thereof.

The results of a vulnerability assessment will tell the strategist several things about the organization, including the following:

- **Operational maturity**   The consistency of vulnerabilities among targets will reveal whether the organization has configuration standards or automated tools for managing the configuration across targets. When a vulnerability assessment finds variations in vulnerabilities among similar systems, you may assume that the organization is not using automated tools to distribute patches to its systems but instead appears to be installing patches in an ad hoc manner. On the other hand, when the vulnerability assessment shows consistency in vulnerabilities among similar systems, this is an indication of greater operational maturity and possibly the presence and use of automated tools for system management.

- **Security maturity**   The range of vulnerabilities among targets will reveal the maturity of the organization's vulnerability management program. If the presence or absence of security patches is inconsistent or if there are numerous older vulnerabilities found, this may indicate that vulnerability management is given a low priority or insufficient resources. When a vulnerability assessment identifies large numbers of vulnerabilities—particularly "high" and "critical" vulnerabilities dating back many months or longer—this is an indication that the organization is not placing emphasis on basic security hygiene.

Insurance

The security strategist may want to know whether the organization has cybersecurity insurance or any general insurance policy that covers some types of cyber events and incidents.

As important as having cyber insurance is, equally important is the reason the organization purchased it. A strategist will want to explore possible reasons.

- **Compliance**   The organization may have purchased a cyber-insurance policy to be compliant with a law, regulation, or standard.

- **Customer requirement**   The organization may have a cyber-insurance policy because a key customer required it.

- **Prior incidents**   Perhaps the organization has a cyber-insurance policy because a costly incident occurred in the past. Similarly, a company known to the organization's management may have suffered an incident, prompting the organization to purchase cyber insurance in case a similar event could happen to them.

- **Risk treatment**   The organization may have purchased cyber-insurance because risks were identified that the organization chose to have transferred to another organization.

It is vitally important to understand the terms of any cyber-insurance policy. While the amounts of benefits are important, the most important aspects of a cyber-insurance policy are its terms and conditions. Many organizations have been known to purchase cyber-insurance policies only to find out that they receive little or no relief from them because of one or more exclusions. Cyber-insurance policies vary quite a lot, and many require policyholder organizations to have many policies and controls in place. Interestingly enough, organizations that have the required components in their security programs are much less likely to experience significant security incidents—but this is the whole point of developing an information security strategy and the use of cyber insurance: risk reduction. This is similar to automobile insurance, homeowners' insurance, and renters' insurance: it is important to read and fully understand insurance policies in detail.

Critical Data

Most organizations do not have an accurate notion regarding the location and use of their critical data. Organizations have their key business applications that store and process their critical data, but in most organizations, copies of parts of their critical data also reside in many other places, including internal file servers, sanctioned data storage services such as Box and Dropbox, and unsanctioned data storage services and unsanctioned cloud-based applications.

While this section is not about the cloud and cloud services, it is precisely the existence and ease of use of cloud services that make it so easy for individuals and groups in an organization to upload critical data to these services. The fact that many cloud-based services offer low-cost and zero-cost services encourages this phenomenon all the more. This has given rise to the colloquial phrase "bring your own app" as a way of labeling this growing problem. Sanctioned or not, most organizations have lost sight of all the locations and uses of their critical data.

Another component of critical data is the bring-your-own-device (BYOD) phenomenon, which results in sensitive business information residing on personally owned devices, outside of the organization's direct control. The ubiquity and openness of IT services makes it all but impossible for organizations to prevent staff members from using personally owned devices as part of their work.

The cloud and BYOD underscore the lack of visibility and control over critical and sensitive data. Understanding this is important for strategists when determining the current state of security, which, as stated before, is required if a viable strategy is to be developed to take the organization to a desired future state. This is one of many categories where a strategist will be unable to gather all desired facts about the state of security and where experience and judgment is required to tread on without knowing all that should be known.

Business Impact Analysis

A business impact analysis (BIA) is used to identify an organization's business processes, the interdependencies between processes, the resources required for process operation, and the impact on the organization if any business process is incapacitated for a time.

A BIA is a cornerstone of a business continuity and disaster recovery (BCDR) program because the BIA indicates which business processes and underlying resources are the most vital to the organization. The most critical processes are those that receive the most attention during the development of disaster recovery and business continuity plans.

The BIA is also useful for information security professionals aside from business continuity purposes. Again, the BIA indicates the most critical processes (and underlying resources such as information systems and other IT infrastructure), giving the security strategist a better idea of which business processes and systems warrant the greatest protection.

The presence of a BIA provides a strong indication of the organization's maturity, through its intention to protect its most critical processes from disaster scenarios. Correspondingly, the absence of a BIA suggests that the organization does not consider BCDR as having strategic importance.

Security Incident Log

A security incident log provides the strategist with a history of security incidents in the organization. Depending on the information that is captured in the incident log, the strategist may be able to discern the maturity of the organization's information security program, especially its incident response program. For instance, a highly mature organization will perform post-mortem analysis on significant incidents and direct changes to take place in people, processes, and technology to reduce the probability, impact, or scope of similar incidents in the future.

Like other business records and activities, the strategist needs to understand the reason for the existence of the security incident log. Is it in place merely for compliance purposes (in which case the incident log may be sparsely populated and there may be an absence of corrective actions), or does the organization really want to learn from and even anticipate security incidents? These are the deeper questions that the security strategist needs to discover and know.

An organization with a sparsely populated incident log may be an indication of several things, including the following:

- **Lack of/deficient SIEM**   A security information and event management (SIEM) is a system that collects log data from servers, endpoints, network devices such as firewalls, and other sources such as antivirus consoles; correlates this log data; and produces security alerts when actionable security-related activities are taking place. An organization without a SIEM may have little way of knowing whether security incidents such as break-ins are occurring. Similarly, an organization with a SIEM that is not well maintained may also have many blind spots and be unaware of incidents occurring in its environment.

- **Training**   Personnel may not be trained in the recognition of security incidents. Security incidents might be occurring but go unrecognized, resulting in incidents with greater impact and the loss of learning opportunities.

Outsourced Services

Most organizations outsource a good portion of their IT systems and services. Unlike earlier eras when organizations had their own data centers and when most or all applications were running in-house (usually called on-premise), today the model has almost completely flipped: organizations are moving the bulk of their business applications to cloud-based infrastructure as a service (IaaS), platform as a service (PaaS), and software as a service (SaaS) environments.

The degree to which any particular organization has outsourced its business applications to the cloud is not the concerning matter. Instead, what's important is the amount of due care exercised in the process of outsourcing.

The practice of determining and managing risks associated with outsourcing is called *third-party risk*. In lawyer-speak, these external organizations are called third parties (and the organizations *they* outsource to are called *fourth parties*).

The third-party risk practices that the strategists are looking for include the following:

- **Up-front due diligence**   This is an assessment of risk performed on a service provider prior to the organization electing to use the service. This initial risk assessment gives the organization an opportunity to enforce security-related terms and conditions on the service provider in the legal agreement. An up-front risk assessment may include one or more of the following:
  - **Relationship risk assessment**   Here, the organization analyzes the strategic importance of the service provider in terms of contract value and service criticality.
  - **Inherent risk assessment**   This is an analysis of the service provider's financial health and geopolitical risk.
  - **Control risk assessment**   This is an analysis of the controls that the organization would like the service provider to use to protect the organization's data.

- **Site visit**   The organization may elect to visit one or more of the service provider's processing sites and perhaps corporate offices.

- **Risk tiering**   This is the practice of establishing tiers of service provider risk. Each service provider, based on the nature of services provided to the organization, is assigned a risk level, or *tier*. The due diligence activities performed for each tier are commensurate with the risk level. For example, services providers at the highest risk tier may be issued a lengthy questionnaire annually, required to undergo annual penetration tests, as well as an on-site visit to confirm the presence of key controls. Service providers at a middle tier of risk may be issued a shorter questionnaire annually, and service providers at the lowest tier may be issued a brief questionnaire annually. Response to questions in questionnaires answered negatively will also vary according to risk tier. For top-tier services providers, this may involve a detailed mitigation plan; at lower tiers, there is lower concern.

- **Ongoing due diligence**   Throughout the duration of a service provider relationship, the organization will periodically assess each service provider to ensure that risks discovered at the start of the relationship have not significantly changed. An organization will carry out a number of activities, as outlined for up-front due diligence.

Audits

Internal and external audits can tell the strategist quite a bit about the state of the organization's security program. A careful examination of audit findings can potentially provide significant details on control effectiveness, vulnerabilities, disaster preparedness, or other aspects of the program—depending on the objectives of those audits.

When examining audit results, a security strategist needs to understand several things.

- **Objective**   The objective or purpose of the audit tells the reader why the audit took place. This often provides additional insight on why certain people, processes, or technologies were examined while others were apparently omitted. For example, was an audit performed because it is required by regulation or another requirement, or was it performed voluntarily as another means of self-improvement?

- **Scope**   The scope of an audit tells the reader which technologies, business processes, business locations, or other aspects of the organization were examined.

- **Qualifications of auditors**   An audit is going to be only as effective as its auditors are skilled and experienced in performing audits, as well as their familiarity with the things being audited. An IT auditor with little operational IT experience is not going to be as effective and insightful as an IT auditor with a background in some aspect of IT engineering or operations.

- **Audit methodologies**   It is important for the reader to understand the audit methodologies used in any particular audit. For instance, did the auditor interview personnel, examine systems and records, observe personnel performing their tasks, or perform tasks of their own? Equally important are sampling methodologies, including how samples are selected and who performs the selection.

The security strategist needs to consider the bigger picture. Mainly, is the organization taking audit results and driving improvements into the organization, or are audit reports merely shelfware to show to regulators on their annual visit?

Culture

The culture of an organization can tell the strategist a lot about the state of security. Many people mistakenly believe that information security is all about the technology. While technology is part of security, the most important aspect of information security is people. No amount of technology can adequately compensate for the wrong attitude and understanding about protecting an organization's information assets. People are absolutely key.

A strategist will want to explore a few aspects of an organization's culture, including the following:

- **Leadership** It is important to understand the actions of executive management, mainly to see whether they abide by company policies and lead by example. A classic example is on the topic of "no personal devices for company business" policy, but the CEO wants his personal iPad connected to corporate e-mail.

- **Accountability** The strategist will look for evidence that the organization enforces company policies and requires employees to be accountable for violations. Equally important is the observation of outcomes of bad decisions—are decision-makers held accountable?

- **Empowerment** Organizations are sometimes measured by employee empowerment and whether employees are implicitly given the go-ahead to act and "ask for forgiveness" if something goes wrong versus organizations that do not empower employees, requiring them to "ask for permission" before acting. There is not so much about good versus bad but rather to have an understanding of how the organization behaves. Also important is the organization's behavior when things go wrong. Does the organization seek to punish the guilty, learn from its mistakes, or somewhere in between?

- **Security awareness** Even now, people seem to lack much Internet safety common sense and seem willing to click anything arriving in their inboxes. While this may seem a discouraging point of view, many organizations do an inadequate job of informing their personnel about the various risks associated with Internet and computer usage. A strategist will want to investigate the organization's security awareness program to see how engaging the program is, how rigorous any training is, and whether there are rewards for good behavior and penalties for risky behavior. The other aspects in this section—leadership, accountability, and empowerment—are all related to security awareness because they help the strategist understand whether executives lead by example, whether empowered personnel make good decisions that impact security, and whether personnel are accountable for their actions.

These and other aspects of an organization's culture help the strategist better understand the organization's present state.

Maturity

The characteristics of a security management program discussed in this section all contribute to the overall maturity of the organization's program. By itself, the maturity level of the program doesn't tell the strategist anything about the program's details. But the strategist's observations of the overall program will provide a "thumb in the air" feeling for its overall maturity.

The strategist will probably find that the maturity levels of various aspects of the organization's security program vary widely. For instance, the organization may have mature asset management and vulnerability management programs but be lacking in other areas such as internal audit and security awareness.

The levels of maturity are discussed in greater detail in the next section, "Strategy Development." Maturity also plays a part during a gap assessment, also discussed in the next section.

Strategy Development

After the security strategist has performed risk and threat assessments and carefully reviewed the state of the security program through the examination of artifacts, the strategist can develop strategic objectives. Generally speaking, strategic objectives will fall into one of these categories:

- Improvements in protective controls
- Improvements in incident visibility
- Improvements in incident response
- Reductions in risk, including compliance risk
- Reductions in cost
- Increased resiliency of key business systems

These categories all contribute to strategic improvements in an organization's security program. Depending on the current and desired future state of security, objectives may represent large projects or groups of projects implemented over several years to develop broad new capabilities, or they may be smaller projects focused on improving existing capabilities.

Examples of broad, sweeping objectives for developing new security capabilities include the following:

- Define and implement a SIEM to provide visibility into security and operational events.
- Define and implement a security incident response program.
- Define and implement a security awareness learning program.

Examples of objectives for improving existing capabilities include the following:

- Integrate vulnerability management and GRC systems.
- Link security awareness and access management programs so that staff members must successfully complete security awareness training to retain their system access.

Once one or more objectives have been identified, the security strategist will undertake several activities that are required to meet the objectives. These activities are explained in the remainder of this section.

The strategist must consider many inputs before developing objectives and strategies to achieve them. These inputs serve a critical purpose: to help the strategist understand the organization's current state. The journey to developing and achieving a strategy is not possible without understand the journey's starting point. These are discussed in the previous section, "Strategy Resources."

Gap Assessment

To implement a security strategy and accomplish objectives, security professionals often spend too much time focusing on the end goal and not enough time on the starting point. Without sufficient knowledge of the starting point, accomplishing objectives will be more difficult, and achieving success will be less certain.

A gap assessment will need to focus on several aspects of a security program, including one or more of these:

- **Existing/previous strategy** Understanding prior strategies can reveal much about the security program in the past. Several aspects of prior strategies to consider include the following:
  - Was the prior strategy actually a strategy, or was it an objective, a road map, or something else?
  - Was the strategy achievable?
  - Was the strategy achieved, or was reasonable progress made?
  - Was the strategy business aligned?
  - Was the strategy measurable?
  - Were sufficient resources made available to achieve the strategy?
- **Security charter** The organization may have a charter that defines a strategy, roles and responsibilities, objectives, or other matters.
- **Security policy** Existing security policy needs to be carefully studied to understand alignment between security policy and the strategy. The security manager should review security policy enforcement as well as exceptions and related incidents.
- **Security standards** Existing security standards should be examined to understand what emphasis has been placed on proven and consistent methods

for hardening systems. The security manager will want to look at the approach. Are security standards a set of principles only, or do they include configuration details?

- **Security procedures**   This includes security procedures, as well as IT and other business procedures that have security subject matter or implications.

- **Security guidelines**   While security guidelines are considered optional, it is important to understand what they say about implementing security policies and procedures. Content in security guidelines may provide important clues on organizational culture and its views about policy.

- **Security controls**   While it is necessary to review control objectives and control narratives, it is equally important to understand control effectiveness and how well controls support existing objectives.

- **Risk assessments**   Available risk assessments may provide insight into risks observed in the organization. This would provide a valuable, risk-based perspective on the state of the organization in the recent—or not so recent—past.

- **Internal and external audit results**   Audit reports are generally seen as an in-depth view of the effectiveness of internal controls in the organization. A security manager needs to understand how to read the audit report—as well as be able to read in between the lines—to understand specific audit methodologies used to examine controls and report on them. Note that for some audits, auditors are examining specific controls, whether or not they actually exist in the organization. Understanding the scope of an audit is also important, as it may in some cases be quite narrow and not provide a broad view of control risk.

- **Security metrics**   Examining security metrics over time should give a security manager some important information. Not only can certain details of the security program be seen, but the bigger picture is also important: the metrics that the organization chose to measure. If metrics have been in place long enough, there may be trends that can be observed.

- **Risk ledger**   An organization's risk ledger can provide insight into the issues that are considered important security issues. Depending on the details are available in the risk ledger, a security manager may be able to discern the various activities and methods in place to capture content for the risk ledger.

- **Risk treatment decision records**   When available, risk treatment records reveal what issues warranted attention, discussion, and decisions. Coupled with the risk ledger, information here can provide a record of issues tackled by the organization's risk management process.

- **Security incident program**   This includes program objectives, processes, procedures, records, tools, and practices. Further, the presence of playbooks indicates a desire to respond quickly and effectively when an incident occurs.

- **Security incident records**   The record of security incidents can reveal a lot about the capabilities and attitudes in the security program. A sparse record might indicate gaps in capabilities or skills. A rich record is probably an indication of a more mature program and personnel intent on identifying issues so that improvements can be made.

- **Third-party risk**   Vendor risk, also known as third-party risk, is a near-universal problem for organizations, given the trend in outsourcing line-of-business applications and the use of cloud-based services. Here, the security manager needs to understand the degree of attention the organization places on third-party risk, including the completeness of business records, the frequency of risk and control assessments, the history of site visits, and the organization's practice of following up on risk issues discovered in key third parties.

- **Business continuity and disaster recovery program**   The presence of business continuity planning (BCP) and/or disaster recovery planning (DRP) activities is a good indication (although not a certain one) that the organization cares enough about its long-term viability that it wants to minimize the impact of natural and man-made disasters. A security manager needs to understand whether BCP/DRP records and procedures are up-to-date and to what extent the organization elects to train its personnel and conduct tests of its plans.

- **Security awareness training program**   A security awareness training and communications program says a lot about an organization, namely, the extent to which the organization acknowledges that people are a critical aspect to the success of a program and its ability to protect itself from harm. The variety of messaging techniques used, as well as their frequency, are important aspects of a security awareness program, but they are not as important as the program's alignment with the organization.

- **IT and security projects**   Business records for recent projects speak volumes about the organization's value and emphasis on security. The security manager will want to look through the list of project participants to see whether security personnel are included. Equally important are the presence (or absence) of security requirements—if requirements are part of bigger projects.

When examining all of this and other information about an organization's security program, the security strategist should bring the right measure of skepticism. There is much to know about what information is found, but the absence of information may speak volumes as well. Here are some considerations:

- **Absence of evidence is not evidence of absence**   This time-honored quote applies to artifacts in any security program. For instance, a sparse or nonexistent security incidents log may be an indication of several things: the organization may not have the required visibility to know when an incident has taken place, the organization's staff may not be trained in the recognition of incidents, or the organization may only be watching for "black swan" events and be missing the routine incidents.

- **Freshness, usefulness, and window dressing**   When it comes to policy, process, and procedure documentation, it is important to find out whether documents are created for appearances only (in which case they may be well-kept secrets except by their owners) or whether they are widely known and utilized. A look at these documents' revision histories tells part of the story, while interviewing the right personnel completes the picture by revealing how well their existence is known and whether they are really used.

- **Scope, turf, and politics**   In larger organizations, the security manager needs to understand current and historical practices with regard to roles and responsibilities for security and security-related activities. For example, records for a global security program might instead reflect only what is occurring in the Americas, even though there may not be anything found in writing to the contrary.

- **Reading between the lines**   Depending upon the organization's culture and the ethics of current or prior security personnel, records may not accurately reflect goings-on in the security program. There may be overemphasis, underemphasis, distortions, or simply "looking the other way" situations that may result in records being incomplete.

- **Off the books**   For various reasons, certain activities and proceedings in a security program may not be documented. For example, certain incidents may conveniently *not* be present in the incident log—otherwise, external auditors might catch the scent and go on a foxhunt, causing all manner of unpleasantries.

- **Regulatory requirements**   When examining each aspect of a security program, the security manager needs to understand one thing: Is that activity there because it is required by regulations (with hell and fury from regulators if absent) or because the organization is managing risk and attempting to reduce the probability and/or impact of potential threats?

When performing a gap assessment, a strategist is examining the present condition of processes, technologies, and people. But by definition, a gap assessment is the study of the difference between the present condition of something and the desired future state. A common approach to determining the future state is to determine the current maturity of a process or technology and compare that to the desired maturity level. Continue reading in the next section for a discussion on maturity levels.

Strengths, Weaknesses, Opportunities, Threats Analysis

Strengths, weaknesses, opportunities, and threats (SWOT) analysis is a tool used in support of strategy planning. SWOT involves introspective analysis where the strategist asks four questions about the object of study:

- **Strengths**   What characteristics of the business give it an advantage over others?

- **Weaknesses**   What characteristics of the business put it at a disadvantage?

- **Opportunities**   What elements in the environment could the business use to its advantage?

- **Threats**   What elements in the environment threaten to harm the business?

SWOT analysis uses a matrix, as shown in Figure 2-5.

Figure 2-5 A SWOT matrix with its four components (Courtesy of Xhienne)

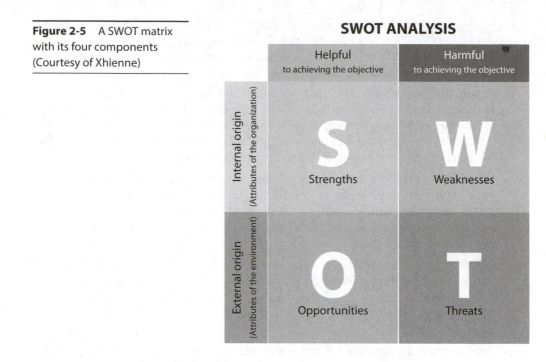

Capability Maturity Models

The Software Engineering Institute (SEI) at Carnegie Mellon University accomplished a great deal with its development of the Capability Maturity Model Integration for Development (CMMi-DEV). Capability maturity models are useful tools for understanding the maturity level of a process. Maturity models in other technology disciplines have been developed, such as the Systems Security Engineering Capability Maturity Model (SSE-CMM).

The CMMi-DEV uses five levels of maturity to describe the formality of a process.

- **Level 1: Initial**   This represents a process that is ad hoc, inconsistent, unmeasured, and unrepeatable.

- **Level 2: Repeatable**   This represents a process that is performed consistently and with the same outcome. It may or may not be well-documented.

- **Level 3: Defined**   This represents a process that is well-defined and well-documented.

- **Level 4: Managed**   This represents a quantitatively measured process with one or more metrics.

- **Level 5: Optimizing**   This represents a measured process that is under continuous improvement.

Not all security strategists are familiar with maturity models. Strategists unaccustomed to capability maturity models need to understand two important characteristics of maturity models and how they are used:

- *Level 5 is not the ultimate objective.* Most organizations' average maturity level targets range from 2.5 to 3.5. There are few organizations whose mission justifies level 5 maturity. The cost of developing a level 5 process or control is often prohibitive and out of alignment with risks.

- *Each control or process may have its own maturity level.* It is neither common nor prudent to assign a single maturity level target for all controls and processes. Instead, organizations with skilled strategists can determine the appropriate level of maturity for each control and process. They need not all be the same. Instead, it is more appropriate to use a threat-based or risk-based model to determine an appropriate level of maturity for each control and process. Some will be 2, some will be 3, some will be 4, and a few might even be 5.

The common use of capability maturity models is the determination of the current maturity of a process, together with analysis, to determine the desired maturity level process by process and technology by technology.

Road Map Development

Once strategic objectives, risk and threat assessments, and gap analyses have been completed, the security strategist can begin to develop road maps to accomplish each objective.

A road map is a list of steps required to achieve a strategic objective. The term *road map* is an appropriate metaphor because it represents a journey that, in the details, may not always appear to be contributing to the objective. But in a well-designed road map, each task and each project gets the organization closer to the objective.

A road map is just a plan, but the term *road map* is often used to describe the steps that an organization needs to take to undertake a long-term, complex, and strategic objective. Often a road map can be thought of as a series of projects—some running sequentially, others concurrently—that an organization uses to transform its processes and technology to achieve the objective.

Figure 2-6 depicts a road map for an 18-month identity and access management project.

Policy Development

The execution of a security strategy may result in additions or improvements in its security-related capabilities. These additions or improvements might require that one or more security policies be updated to reflect these new or improved capabilities.

While security policies are designed to be durable and not tied to specific technologies, significant changes in technologies might put security policy at odds with them. Here is an example:

> The Fast Car Company recently implemented its first security incident and event monitoring system that produces alerts whenever actionable security events occur. Prior to implementing the SIEM, IT and security personnel would examine security logs every day to see whether any security events had occurred in the past 24 hours.
>
> Before implementing the SIEM, Fast Car Company's security policy stated that appropriate personnel were required to examine security logs daily and log any actions taken. Now that Fast Car Company has a SIEM, IT and security personnel no longer need to examine logs. The company's policy needs to be changed so that 1) personnel are required to respond to security alerts, and 2) personnel are required to periodically examine the SIEM's configuration so that it will produce alerts for relevant events.

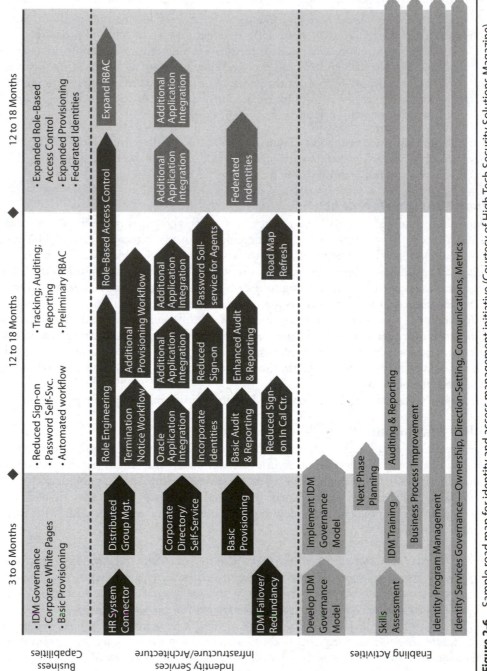

Figure 2-6 Sample road map for identity and access management initiative (Courtesy of High Tech Security Solutions Magazine)

Security policies are supposed to align with current capabilities and not be a vision statement describing future capabilities. This is the case whether policies are addressing the use of technologies or business processes. It's generally considered unwise to develop a security policy that requires an activity that the organization is incapable of performing.

Industries generally consider security policies as being out-of-date if they are not examined and updated annually. This is not saying that security policies are required to be updated annually but that they be examined annually and updated as needed.

While not generally required in most industries, it is nonetheless a common practice to structure the organization's security policy with one or more relevant standards or frameworks. Common standards and frameworks used in this way include

- NIST SP 800-53
- ISO 27001
- HIPAA/HITECH
- PCI-DSS
- CIS CSC 20

Because security frameworks are moderately to highly technical, some organizations develop a shorter information security policy focused in Internet hygiene and data protection for all of its workers (often called an *acceptable-use policy*) and a separate technical security policy for its technology workers who design, implement, and manage information systems and applications. This pragmatic approach helps to avoid, for instance, nontechnical office workers trying to understand and comply with cryptography and access management policy; with such unintelligible content, workers are more likely to "tune out" the security policy in its entirety and not benefit from the relevant parts of policy that really matter, such as recognizing phishing scams.

The goal of a good security policy is to define the "rules of the road" for an organization's employees. Policies should be clear, concise, and applicable to the organization. The policies should be developed in a collaborative manner to reduce prevent situations like the previous example. Additionally, if policies are written without the involvement or buy-in of the different stakeholders, an organization risks deploying policies that it cannot adhere to or will cause significant investment to comply to the policy.

Controls Development

When an organization executes a security strategy, often this means that the organization has made changes to its security-related capabilities. This, in turn, may necessitate changes to one or more aspects of existing controls, as well as the development of new control and the retirement of controls that are no longer necessary.

Controls are generally changed as a result of a risk assessment, where some unacceptable risk was identified and a decision made to implement a control to ensure better outcomes. Quite possibly, a risk assessment may have compelled the organization to make some changes in the form of security projects that were part of a strategy. When these projects are executed and completed, controls related to the processes or technologies involved need to be changed accordingly. Here are some of the possible outcomes:

- **Changes to control narrative** Changes to processes, procedures, or technologies will undoubtedly impact control narratives, which often describe controls in detail. Project deliverables will include these changes.

- **Changes to scope** Changes in processes, procedures, or technologies may require that the scope of one or more controls be changed. For instance, if an organization replicates sensitive data to another data center as part of a business continuity strategy, the scope of controls related to the protection of sensitive data may need to be expanded to include the additional data center.

- **Changes in control testing** New or different processes, procedures, or technologies will often mean that the procedures for testing a control will have changed. One of the project deliverables will be updates to control testing procedures. For example, the implementation of a new single sign-on (SSO) tool will require new instructions for control testing so that internal auditors and others will know what steps to perform to view information related to access controls.

- **Entirely new control** Sometimes a new or changed security capability provides an opportunity (or possibly a mandate) to create a new control. For instance, the acquisition of a new identity and access management auditing tool brings an entirely new capability, that of auditing various aspects of user accounts, roles, and accesses. Prior to the tool, performing the work manually was infeasible, so there was no control. And this absence may have been documented in a risk assessment, which gave way to the project that enables this capability. When the new capability is finally implemented, a new control is developed to ensure the user audits are regularly performed.

Selecting a Control Framework

Organizations that desire to raise their security maturity often start by selecting a control framework. Organizations often spend an excessive amount of time selecting a control framework, typically struggling to decide between CIS CSC, ISO/IEC 27002, and NIST 800-53. An organization lacking a control framework typically spends too much time stuck at this point, arguing the finer points of each control framework without realizing that there is not a great deal of difference between them. This is like a person accustomed to walking everywhere shopping for an automobile and getting hung up on two-door versus four-door or gas-powered versus diesel or hybrid, all the while ignoring the fact that any of these choices is going to result in a significant shift in travel time.

Standards Development

An organization executing a security strategy may find that one or more of its standards are impacted or that new standards need to be developed.

While policies define *what* is to be done, standards define *how* policies are to be carried out. For instance, a policy may stipulate that strong passwords are to be used for end-user authentication. A password standard, then, would be more specific by defining the length, complexity, and other characteristics about a strong password.

Where policies are designed to be durable and long-lasting, they do so at the expense of being somewhat unspecific. Standards take on the burden of being more specific but also that they change more frequently because they are closer to the technology and are concerned with the details of the implementation of policy.

Standards need to be developed carefully, for several reasons:

- They must properly reflect the intent of one or more corresponding policies.
- They will have to be able to be successfully implemented.
- They need to be unambiguous.
- Their directives will need to be able to be automated, where large numbers of systems, endpoints, devices, or people are involved, leading to consistency and uniformity.

There are several types of standards in use, including the following:

- **Protocol standards**   Examples include TLS 1.2 for web server session encryption, AES-256 for encryption at rest, 802.11ac for wireless networking, and SAML 2.0 for authentication.
- **Vendor standards**   For example, tablet computers are to be Apple iPad and iPad Pro, perhaps with specific model numbers.
- **Configuration standards**   For instance, a server-hardening standard would specify all of the security-related settings to be implemented for each type of server operating system in use.
- **Programming language standards**   Examples include C++, Java, and Python. Organizations that do not establish and assert programming language standards may find themselves with programs written in dozens of different languages, which may drive up the cost of maintaining them.
- **Methodology standards**   Examples include the use of factor analysis of information risk (FAIR) risk analysis techniques; Operationally Critical Threat, Asset, and Vulnerability Evaluation (OCTAVE) for security assessments: and SMART for the development of strategic objectives.
- **Control frameworks**   These include NIST SP800-53, PCI-DSS, HIPAA, COBIT, and ISO 27002.

Because technologies change so rapidly, standards are often reviewed and updated more frequently than policies. New security strategies are not the only reason that standards are reviewed and updated; other reasons include the release of new versions of hardware and software, new techniques for data protection, and the acquisition of new network devices and applications.

Processes and Procedures

Processes and procedures describe the steps to be followed when carrying out functions and tasks. They exist so that these activities may be performed more consistently, in the right sequence, and in the right way.

Implementation of a security strategy means that new things will be done, some things will be done differently, and other things will no longer be done. All of these have a direct impact on processes and procedures.

Often, the purpose of a new security strategy is the increase in maturity of security-related technologies and activities in an organization. And because many organizations' security maturity levels are low, often this means that many important tasks are poorly documented or not documented at all. The desired increase in maturity might compel an organization to identify undocumented processes and procedures and assign staff to document them. An organization in such a state might also consider developing document management procedures and standards so that there is consistency among all processes, procedures, and their written documents, as well as consistent development and review.

Roles and Responsibilities

The implementation of a new security strategy often impacts the way people work. When the strategy involves changes in technologies or processes (as they usually do), this may in turn impact the roles and responsibilities for security personnel, IT workers, and perhaps other staff. Where business processes are added or changed, this often means that changes need to be made to the roles and responsibilities of personnel.

In organizations without documented roles and responsibilities, this is an opportunity to document them. This can be done in a number of different ways, including the following:

- Job descriptions
- Department charter documents
- Department policy documents
- Roles and responsibility sections of process documents

Training and Awareness

Execution of a new security strategy often has broad reach, impacting technology as well as policies, standards, processes, and procedures. The result of this is new information, in many forms and for several audiences, including the following:

- General security awareness
- New and updated processes and procedures
- New and updated technologies

Each of these may necessitate additions or updates to training content.

Recent studies indicate that more than 90 percent of breaches begin with phishing attacks. Arguably, security awareness training is one of the most important defenses available for an organization, given that with even the best spam filters, some phishing attacks do successfully penetrate even the best organizations' defenses. The next line of defense is sound judgment on the part of every worker with an e-mail account. Organizations implementing new security strategies often do so to improve their defenses; it makes sense, then, to include a review and perhaps an upgrade in security awareness training for all personnel. Some of the new features available in security awareness training include the following:

- **Engaging, multimedia content**   Rather than just text on a screen, audio and video content, including playback of computer sessions, will better hold viewers' attention, ensuring they will retain content.

- **Opportunities to learn and practice skills**   Better training programs, even online varieties, provide opportunities to practice skills such as creating strong passwords, spotting phishing messages, and understanding how to recognize other threats.

- **Quizzes at the end of each topic**   Short quizzes throughout training sessions hold a viewer's interest and keep them engaged. Better training programs don't let a participant proceed until previous learning has been proven.

- **Built-in acknowledgment of organization security policy**   Online and in-person awareness training can incorporate acknowledgment of security policy. This helps raise awareness of corporate security policy and its content, as well as driving the point that all staff members are expected to comply with it.

- **A permanent record of quiz scores and completion**   Modern learning management systems (LMSs) keep a permanent record of test and quiz scores. This helps to reinforce the notion that an employer is holding staff members responsible for complying with policy.

When new technologies are introduced into the organization, often there are individuals and even entire teams that need to be trained so that they will better understand how to operate and maintain the new programs and products. Unfortunately, many organizations skimp on training, and this often results in organizations underutilizing new products or not using them correctly.

Developing a Business Case

Many organizations require the development of a business case prior to approving expenditures on significant security initiatives. A business case is a written statement that describes the initiative and describes its business benefits. The typical elements found in a business case include the following:

- **Problem statement**   This is a description of the business condition or situation that the initiative is designed to solve. The condition may be a matter of compliance, a finding in a risk assessment, or a capability required by a customer, partner, supplier, or regulator.

- **Current state**   This is a description of the existing conditions related to the initiative.

- **Desired state**   This is a description of the future state of the relevant systems, processes, or staff.

- **Success criteria**   These are the defined items that the program will be measured against.
- **Requirements**   This is a list of required characteristics and components of the solution that will remedy the current state and bring about the desired future state.
- **Approach**   This is a description of the proposed steps that will result in the desired future state. This section may include alternative approaches that were considered, with reasons why they were not selected. If the initiative requires the purchase of products or professional services, business cases may include proposals from vendors. Alternatively, the business case may include a request for proposal (RFP) or request for information (RFI) that will be sent to selected vendors for additional information.
- **Plan**   This will include costs, timelines, milestones, vendors, and staff associated with the initiative.

Mature organizations utilize an executive steering committee that evaluates business cases for proposed initiatives and makes go/no-go decisions for initiatives. Business cases are often presented to a steering committee in the form of an interactive discussion, providing business leaders with the opportunity to ask questions and propose alternative approaches.

Characteristics of business cases should include the following:

- **Alignment with organization**   The business case should align with the organization's goals and objectives, risk appetite, and culture.
- **Statements in business terms**   Problem statements, current state, and future state descriptions should all be expressed in business terms.

Establishing Communications and Reporting

Effective communications and reporting are a critical element of a successful security program. Because success depends mainly on people, in the absence of effective communications, they won't have the required information to make good security-related decisions. Without regard for information security, the results of decisions may include harmful incidents.

These are common forms of communications and reporting that are related to information security:

- **Board of directors meetings**   Discussions of strategies, objectives, risks, incidents, and industry developments keep board members informed about security in the organization and elsewhere.
- **Governance and steering committee meetings**   Discussions of security strategies, objectives, assessments, risks, incidents, and developments guide decision-makers as they discuss strategies, objectives, projects, and operations.
- **Security awareness**   Periodic communications to all personnel help keep them informed on changes in security policy and standards, good security practices, and risks they may encounter, such as phishing and social engineering attacks. New hires often get a healthy dose of security-related information that includes current security policies and practices, acceptable use, security tools, and where to go for help.

- **Security advisories**   Communications on potential threats helps keep affected personnel aware of developments that may require them to take steps to protect the organization from harm.

- **Security incidents**   Communications internally as well as with external parties during an incident keep incident responders and other parties informed. Organizations typically develop security incident plans and playbooks in advance, which include business rules on internal communications as well as with outside parties, including customers, regulators, and law enforcement.

- **Metrics**   Key metrics are reported upward in an organization, keeping management, executives, and board members informed as to the effectiveness and progress in the organization's security program.

When building or expanding a security program, it's best to utilize existing communications channels and add relevant security content to those channels, as opposed to building new, parallel channels. An effective security program makes the best use of existing processes, channels, and methods in an organization.

Obtaining Management Commitment

The execution of a security strategy requires management commitment. Without that commitment, the security strategist will be unable to obtain funding and other resources to implement the strategy.

Getting management commitment is not always straightforward. Often, executives and board members are unaware of their fiduciary responsibilities as well as the potency of modern threats. Many organizations mistakenly believe they are an unlikely target of hackers and cyber-criminal organizations because they are small or uninteresting. Further, the common perception of executives and senior managers is that information security is a tactical problem solved with "firewalls and antivirus software" and that information security is in no way related to business issues and business strategy.

A security strategist in a situation where top management lacks a strategic understanding about security will need to embark on efforts to inform top management on one or more aspects of modern information security management. When success is elusive, it may be necessary to bring in outside experts to convince executives that their security manager is not attempting to build a kingdom but instead is just trying to build a basic program to keep the organization out of trouble. As part of developing an effective communication approach, the security strategist should not use fear, uncertainty, and doubt (FUD) in an attempt to move the leadership team toward adopting the strategy. The better approach, as noted in this section, is to relate it to the leadership team in business terms and as opportunities to improve business functions.

Normalcy Bias

People at all levels can suffer from *normalcy bias,* a pattern of thinking in which people believe that because a disaster or breach has never occurred, it will never occur. Normalcy bias manifests itself in many situations, the common theme being a general lack of preparedness for disastrous events. This may be part of the reason that organizations do not take information security seriously—because they have never had a breach before. Experienced information security professionals understand that an organization claiming to have not suffered from security breaches in the past may simply be unaware of them because of a lack of visibility into events in their environment. A common saying in the information security profession is, "There are two types of organizations: those that have been breached and those that do not yet realize they have been breached."

Strategy Constraints

While the development of a new security strategy may bring hope and optimism to the security team, there is no guarantee that changes in an organization can be implemented without friction and even opposition. Instead, there are many constraints and obstacles that the security manager should anticipate and be prepared to maneuver around, over, or through.

No security manager plans to fail. However, the failure to anticipate obstacles and constraints may result in the failure to execute even the best strategy. The presence of an excellent strategy, even with executive support, does not mean that obstacles and constraints will simply get out of the way. Instead, obstacles and constraints represent the realities of human behavior, as well as structural and operational realities that may present challenges to the security manager and the organization as a whole. There is apt meaning to the phrase "the devil's in the details."

Typical constraints, obstacles, and other issues are discussed in this section.

Basic Resistance to Change

It is our basic human nature to be suspicious of change, particularly when we as individuals have no control over it and have no say about it. Change is bad, or so we tend to think.

For this reason, organizations need to consider methods of involving management and staff members about anticipated changes, such as town-hall meetings, surveys, and cross-functional committees. Organizations are cautioned to ensure these efforts are not merely window dressing but serious efforts to better understand staff points of view.

Culture

Organizational culture, according to the Business Dictionary (www.businessdictionary .com), is the collection of values and behaviors that "contribute to the unique social and psychological environment of an organization." In other words, it's the way that people think and act in an organization and how people feel as employees.

Aspects of organizational culture that are important for the security strategist to understand include the following:

- **Strong culture**   The culture reflects and aligns with stated organizational values. Personnel understand and support organizational goals and objectives and need little prodding to figure out how to be productive and provide value to the organization and its constituents.

- **Weak culture**   The culture is not well-aligned with the organization. As a result, management must spend more time managing staff who are not motivated and feel micromanaged.

- **Culture of fear**   Workers are distrustful of management who act as tyrants, resulting in pervasive feelings of fear and doubt.
- **Healthy culture**   Workers and management value and respect each other, have a strong sense of accountability, and cooperate to be successful and accomplish organizational goals and objectives.

One might consider organizational culture as the collective consciousness of all workers, regardless of rank. The security strategist should not expect to significantly change the culture but instead should work with the culture when developing and executing the information security strategy.

Organizational Structure

The security strategist must understand the organization's command-and-control structure, which is often reflected by the organizational chart. However, there may be an undocumented aspect to the org chart, which is actually more important: who is responsible for what activities, functions, and assets. In other words, security strategists must understand "who owns what turf" and develop collaborative relationships with those individuals and groups if they want the strategy to be successful.

Like other considerations in a security strategy, alignment with written and unwritten organizational structures is key to success.

Staff Capabilities

A security strategy generally represents the introduction of new capabilities, as well as changes or upgrades to existing capabilities. A strategy cannot be expected to succeed if the new or changed capabilities do not align with what staff members are able to do. A gap analysis to understand the present state of the organization's security program (discussed earlier in this chapter) needs to include staff knowledge, skills, and capabilities. Where gaps are found, the strategy needs to include training or other activities to impart the necessary skills and language to staff.

This is not limited to technical workers who design, build, and manage information systems and application. To the extent that all staff members are impacted by some change introduced by the strategy, those staff members need to be informed or trained so that they too will be successful.

For example, an organization that needs to better protect its sensitive data includes the development of a data protection program in its strategy. The strategy for data protection includes the development of a data classification scheme with data-handling policies and procedures for data at each classification level and in each use case. This is a high-impact endeavor that will require that many, if not all, workers in the organization be trained in data classification and handling procedures. If there are new security systems in place that augment manual tasks, personnel will need to be trained in the use of those tools as well.

When an organization lacks staff with specific knowledge on security techniques or tools, organizations may look to external resources to augment internal staff. The security strategist needs to consider the costs and availability of with these resources. Consultants and contracts in many skill areas are difficult to find; even larger firms may have backlogs of several months as a result.

Budget and Cost

A security strategy is a statement of changes to take place in the organization to better protect critical or sensitive information and systems. These changes will have hard and soft costs associated with them that represent expenditures for hardware, software, and cloud services, as well as consultants, contractors, and the value of existing workers' time.

The security strategist must determine, with a high degree of precision, all of the hard and soft costs associated with each element of a strategy. Often, executive management will want to see alternative approaches; for example, if additional labor is required, the security strategist may want to determine the costs of hiring additional personnel versus the retention of consultants or contractors.

Every organization has a core business to run, with budgeted costs for all associated activities. A security strategy almost always represents added costs, which must also be funded. While it is possible to obtain out-of-budget money for unbudgeted activities, usually it is necessary to take security strategy initiatives and attempt to get those activities budgeted in future fiscal cycles. For initiatives in future budget cycles, the security strategist needs to determine the price increases that may occur that will impact the strategy. A key project that will cost $100,000 this year may cost $105,000 to $110,000 a year from now and be even more expensive in future years.

Time

As security strategies take shape, each initiative will have its own project plan with associated timelines for executing various tasks. Realistic project planning is needed so that everyone will know when project and strategy milestones will be completed. Project and strategy timelines need to take into account all business circumstances, including peak period and holiday production freezes (where IT systems are maintained in a more stable state), external events such as regulatory audits, and other significant events that may impact schedules.

Time constraints may also involve legal and regulatory obligations, discussed next.

Legal and Regulatory Obligations

An organization may be including items in its strategy that may represent business capabilities that are required to exist for legal or regulatory reasons. For example, a public company may be compelled to complete a key identity and access management project before its next public audit cycle begins to ensure a favorable audit outcome. In another example, an organization may be undertaking implementation of an intrusion prevention system (IPS) to meet a contractual obligation with a customer that has a hard deadline. In a final example, an organization may be implementing a web application firewall (WAF) in order to maintain its PCI-DSS compliance.

As seen in these examples, legal and regulatory obligations often have time components. New laws and contracts require organizations to have specific capabilities in place by established deadlines. For organizations that have failed to meet a deadline, the obligation still exists, and its completion has a greater sense of urgency.

Legal and regulatory requirements often have international considerations. What is legal and required in one country may be forbidden in another. For instance, an international organization may have, as a part of its strategy, key improvements in its pre-employment and post-employment background checks. The organization needs to understand that some countries such as the United States are quite permissive with background checks, while other countries such as France do not permit background checks for most positions. In another example, a security project that is improving its endpoint protection capabilities with cloud-based web proxy filters will find that users' Internet access activities may not be observed or logged in some countries.

Acceptable Risk

A security strategist who develops an information security policy needs to be familiar with the organization's current risk appetite or threshold for acceptable risk.

Risk is, by its nature, difficult to quantify. Most organizations, then, have a cultural "feel" for risk appetite that may or may not be documented. The security strategist must be familiar with the organization's risk appetite, in whatever formal or informal sense, and keenly understand two important aspects of the strategy:

- **Its alignment with risk appetite** Initiatives in the security strategy need to align with executive management's risk appetite. For example, implementation of a data loss prevention (DLP) system together with restricting the use of USB-attached external storage may help to better protect data but may be seen as excessive in some organizations. A common mistake made by security strategists is the incorporation into strategies of new capabilities that may not be urgently needed. This can happen, especially if a strategy is developed without soliciting input from key stakeholders in the organization.

- **Its impact on risk appetite** Specific initiatives within the security strategy may, by design, "push the envelope." A typical organization's security strategy probably contains initiatives that improve security capabilities that better align capabilities with risk appetite. But because many organizations are deficient in their security practices, the perception is that the organization is becoming less tolerant of risk, when in fact it's just trying to get its practices into alignment with its risk tolerance. The appearance of lowering risk appetite may more of a "catchup."

The Obstacle of Organizational Inertia

Every organization has a finite capacity to undergo change. This is a fact that is often overlooked by overly ambitious security strategists who want to accomplish a great deal in too short a time. I have coined the term *organizational inertia* to represent an analogy to Newton's laws of motion: an object either remains at rest or continues to move at a constant velocity, unless acted upon by a force. In an organization, this means that things will be done in the same way until change is exerted upon the organization to change what is done or how things are done.

The nature of organizational inertia, or its resistance to change, is threefold:

- **Operational people performing change** For an organization to make major changes, some of the people making the change are the same people who perform the work. Because business processes undergoing change must continue operation, changes must be enacted slowly and carefully so that operational and quality levels are not adversely affected.

- **Learning curve** Any time there is significant change to a system or process, affected personnel need to learn the new systems, processes, or procedures. This involves a learning curve and possibly training that will take them offline for hours or even days.

- **Human resistance to change** Left alone, people have a tendency to want to do things the same way, even if new and better ways are developed. People, particularly when they have no influence, tend to resist change, which makes adoption take longer.

Chapter Review

Information security governance is the top-down management and control of security and risk management in an organization. Governance is usually undertaken through a steering committee that consists of executives from throughout the organization. The steering committee is responsible for setting overall strategic direction and policy, ensuring that security strategy is in alignment with the organization's IT and business strategy and objectives. The wishes of the steering committee are carried out through projects and tasks that steer the security organization toward strategic objectives. The steering committee can monitor progress through metrics and a balanced scorecard.

For an information security program to be successful, it must align with the business and its overall mission, goals and objectives, and strategy. The security program must take into account the organization's notion of asset value, culture, risk tolerance/appetite, legal obligations, and market conditions. A successful and aligned security program does not lead the organization but enables and supports it as it carries out its mission and pursues its goals.

Risk appetite is the level of risk that an organization is willing to accept while in the pursuit of its mission, strategy, and objectives. Risk treatment and risk acceptance decisions should be assigned to and made by associated business owners and executives who are accountable for those decisions. The chief information security officer is there to facilitate and communicate the information and only in specific instances will own a risk item.

Security governance is accomplished using the same means as IT governance: it begins with board-level involvement that sets the tone for risk appetite and is carried out through the chief information security officer, who develops security and privacy policies, as well as strategic security programs, including software assurance, change management, vendor management, configuration management, incident management, vulnerability management, security awareness training, and identity and access management.

Security governance is used to establish roles and responsibilities for security-related activities throughout all layers of the organization, from the board of directors to individual staff. Roles and responsibilities are defined in job description, in policy and process documents, and in RACI charts.

The board of directors in the defined team is responsible for overseeing all activities in an organization. Boards select and manage a chief executive officer who is responsible for developing a governance function to manage assets, budgets, personnel, processes, and risk.

The security steering committee is responsible for security strategic planning. The security steering committee will develop and approve security policies and appoint managers to develop and maintain processes, procedures, and standards, all of which should align with each other and with the organization's overall mission, strategy, goals, and objectives.

The chief information security officer develops business-aligned security strategies that support the organization's overall mission and goals and is responsible for the organization's overall security program, including policy development, risk management, and perhaps some operational activities such as vulnerability management, incident management, access management, and security awareness training. In some organizations, the topmost security executive has a title of chief security officer or chief information risk officer.

The chief privacy officer is responsible for the protection and proper use of sensitive personal information (often referred to as personally identifiable information). The CPO's information protection responsibilities are sometimes shared with the CISO who has overall information protection responsibilities.

Virtually all other roles in IT have security responsibilities, including software development and integration, data management, network management, systems management, operations, service desk, internal audit, and all staff members.

A formal metrics program provides both qualitative and quantitative data on the effectiveness of many elements of an organization's security program and operations. Metrics can be developed via the SMART method: specific, measurable, attainable, relevant, and timely. Metrics must align to the organization's mission, strategy, and objectives. Some metrics can be used to report on results in the recent past, but there should be some metrics that serve as leading indicators or drive a call to action by the leadership team.

A common shortcoming of a metrics program is its failure to provide relevant metrics for various audiences. For instance, reporting the number of packets dropped by a firewall or the number of viruses detected by antivirus to the board of directors provides no value for that audience. As an organization develops its metrics program, it must take care to develop metrics that matter for each audience. A security balanced scorecard can also be used to depict the high-level effectiveness of an organization's security program.

The business model for information security, developed by ISACA, is a guide for business-aligned, risk-based security governance. BMIS consists of four elements: organization, people, process, and technology. It consists of six dynamic interconnections: culture (connecting organization and people elements), governing (connecting organization and process elements), architecture (connecting organization and technology elements), emergence (connecting people and process elements), enabling and support (connecting process and technology elements), human factors (connecting people and technology elements). BMIS helps the strategist understand the dynamics between the four elements and how they may be manifested. The key takeaway from BMIS is that everything is connected to everything else.

A strategy is a plan to achieve a defined set of objectives to enable the vision of the organization to be successfully achieved. Objectives are the desired future states in an organization and, in the context of information security, in the organization's information security program. A strategy should be business-aligned, deliver value, optimize resources, and be measurable.

The development of an overall security strategy includes the adoption of or alignment with a control framework. Most organizations select an industry-standard control framework such as COBIT, NIST 800-53, ISO/IEC 27001, HIPAA, or PCI-DSS. Then, as part of the organization's risk management processes, additional controls are added as identified risks warrant.

Strategy development may include establishing desired risk levels. This may be expressed in qualitative or quantitative terms, depending upon an organization's maturity.

Many resources are needed for the development of a strategy. These resource include several types of information that reveal the current state of the organization, including risk assessments, vulnerability assessments, business impact analysis, metrics, risk ledger, and incident log. Several other inputs are required that define the structure of the security program, including policy, standards, guidelines, processes and procedures, insurance, and outsourced services.

To develop a strategy, the security strategist first must understand the organization's present state and then define one or more desired future states. A gap analysis helps the strategist understand missing capabilities. The development of a road map defines the steps to develop missing capabilities and augment existing capabilities so that the strategy will be realized.

The security strategist may choose to use the strengths, weaknesses, opportunities, threats (SWOT) analysis model in support of strategy planning. The strategist may also employ capability maturity models to help determine appropriate future states of key security processes.

Often it is necessary to build a business case so that executive management will agree to support and fund a strategy. A business case typically includes a problem statement, followed by a description of the current state, the desired future state, requirements, an approach, and a plan to achieve the strategy. Often a business case is reviewed by a business or IT steering committee consisting of business stakeholders.

A security strategist must be aware of potential obstacles to achieving strategic objectives, including culture, organizational structure, existing staff capabilities, budgets, time, and legal and regulatory obligations. A business-aligned strategy should take these obstacles into account and minimize them if the strategy is to be approved and achieved.

Notes

- The addition of information security as part of fiduciary duty by board members and executives is an important and growing trend in business today.

- Security executives and the board of directors are responsible for implementing a security governance model encompassing information security strategy and mandates. As such, the industry is seeing a shift from a passive to a more active board when it comes to cybersecurity issues.

- A security program should be in alignment with the organization's overall mission, goals, and objectives. This means that the chief information security officer and others should be aware of, and involved in, strategic initiatives and the execution of the organization's strategic goals.

- Risk appetite is generally expressed in qualitative terms such as "very low tolerance for risk" and "no tolerance for risk." Different activities in an organization will have differing risk appetites.

- An organization's definitions of roles and responsibilities may or may not be in sync with its culture of accountability. For instance, an organization may have clear definitions of responsibilities documented in policy and process documents and yet may rarely hold individuals accountable when preventable security events occur.

- Ideally, an organization's board of directors will be aware of information security risks and may direct that the organization enact safeguards to protect the organization. However, in many organizations the board of directors is still uninvolved in information security matters; in these cases, it is still possible to have a successful risk-based information security program, provided it is supported by senior executives.

- While the use of security steering committees is not required, organizations find it helpful to implement single-level or multilevel security steering groups as a cross-functional vehicle for discovering security risks and disseminating security organization.

- Information security is the responsibility of every person in an organization; however, the means for assigning and monitoring security responsibilities to individuals and groups varies widely.

- At present, there are no well-known frameworks for information security metrics. Instead, it is up to every organization to develop metrics that are meaningful and applicable to various audiences with interest in receiving them.

- The methodology for calculating return on security investment is widely discussed but not widely practiced, mainly because it is difficult to calculate the benefit of security controls designed to detect or prevent incidents that occur infrequently.

- Security managers developing an information security strategy in an organization without a program will need to rely on their past experiences, anecdotal accounts of practices, and policies in the organization.

- Security strategists should be mindful of each organization's tolerance for change within a given period of time. While much progress may be warranted, the amount of change that can be reasonably implemented within a year's time is limited.

- The business model for information security is a useful model for understanding the qualitative relationships among various aspects of an organization, as well as the types of activities that relate to these aspects.

- Many organizations ruminate over the selection of a control framework. Instead, the organization should select a framework and then make adjustments to its controls to suit the business. A control framework should generally be considered a starting point, not a rigid and unchanging list of controls—except in cases where regulations stipulate that controls may not be changed.

- While it is important for the security strategist to understand the present state of the organization when developing a strategic road map, the strategist must proceed, knowing that there can never be a sufficient level of understanding. Besides, if even the most thorough snapshot has been taken, the organization is slowly (or perhaps quickly) changing anyway. Execution of a strategic plan is to accelerate changes in certain aspects of an organization that is slowly changing anyway.

- Capability maturity models are useful tools for understanding the maturity level of a process and developing desired future states. The maturity of processes in the organization will vary, as it is appropriate for some processes to have high maturity while it is acceptable for others to have lower maturity. The right question to ask about each separate process is, what is the appropriate level of maturity for this process?

- Each organization has its own practice for the development of business cases for the presentation, discussion, and approval for strategic initiatives.

- A security strategist must anticipate obstacles and constraints affecting the achievement of strategic objectives and consider refining those objectives so that they can be realized.

Questions

1. Security governance is most concerned with:

   A. Security policy

   B. IT policy

   C. Security strategy

   D. Security executive compensation

2. A gaming software startup company does not employ penetration testing of its software. This is an example of:

   A. High tolerance of risk

   B. Noncompliance

   C. Irresponsibility

   D. Outsourcing

3. An organization's board of directors wants to see quarterly metrics on risk reduction. What would be the best metric for this purpose?

   A. Number of firewall rules triggered

   B. Viruses blocked by antivirus programs

   C. Packets dropped by the firewall

   D. Time to patch vulnerabilities on critical servers

4. Which of the following metrics is the best example of a leading indicator?

   A. Average time to mitigate security incidents

   B. Increase in the number of attacks blocked by the intrusion prevention system (IPS)

   C. Increase in the number of attacks blocked by the firewall

   D. Percentage of critical servers being patched within service level agreements (SLAs)

5. What are the elements of the business model for information security (BMIS)?

   A. Culture, governing, architecture, emergence, enabling and support, human factors

   B. People, process, technology

   C. Organization, people, process, technology

   D. Financial, customer, internal processes, innovation, and learning

6. The best definition of a strategy is:

   A. The objective to achieve a plan

   B. The plan to achieve an objective

   C. The plan to achieve business alignment

   D. The plan to reduce risk

7. The primary factor related to the selection of a control framework is:

   A. Industry vertical

   B. Current process maturity level

   C. Size of the organization

   D. Compliance level

8. As part of understanding the organization's current state, a security strategist is examining the organization's security policy. What does the policy tell the strategist?

   A. The level of management commitment to security

   B. The compliance level of the organization

   C. The maturity level of the organization

   D. None of these

9. While gathering and examining various security-related business records, the security manager has determined that the organization has no security incident log. What conclusion can the security manager make from this?

   A. The organization does not have security incident detection capabilities.

   B. The organization has not yet experienced a security incident.

   C. The organization is recording security incidents in its risk register.

   D. The organization has effective preventive and detective controls.

10. The purpose of a balanced scorecard is to:

    A. Measure the efficiency of a security organization

    B. Evaluate the performance of individual employees

    C. Benchmark a process in the organization against peer organizations

    D. Measure organizational performance and effectiveness against strategic goals

11. A security strategist has examined a business process and has determined that personnel who perform the process do so consistently, but there is no written process document. The maturity level of this process is:

    A. Initial

    B. Repeatable

    C. Defined

    D. Managed

12. A security strategist has examined several business processes and has found that their individual maturity levels range from Repeatable to Optimizing. What is the best future state for these business processes?

    A. All processes should be changed to Repeatable.

    B. All processes should be changed to Optimizing.

    C. There is insufficient information to determine the desired end states of these processes.

    D. Processes that are Repeatable should be changed to Defined.

13. In an organization using PCI-DSS as its control framework, the conclusion of a recent risk assessment stipulates that additional controls not present in PCI-DSS but present in ISO 27001 should be enacted. What is the best course of action in this situation?

    A. Adopt ISO 27001 as the new control framework.

    B. Retain PCI-DSS as the control framework and update process documentation.

    C. Add the required controls to the existing control framework.

    D. Adopt NIST 800-53 as the new control framework.

14. A security strategist is seeking to improve the security program in an organization with a strong but casual culture. What is the best approach here?

    A. Conduct focus groups to discuss possible avenues of approach.

    B. Enact new detective controls to identify personnel who are violating policy.

    C. Implement security awareness training that emphasizes new required behavior.

    D. Lock users out of their accounts until they agree to be compliant.

15. A security strategist recently joined a retail organization that operates with slim profit margins and has discovered that the organization lacks several important security capabilities. What is the best strategy here?

    A. Insist that management support an aggressive program to quickly improve the program.

    B. Develop a risk ledger that highlights all identified risks.

    C. Recommend that the biggest risks be avoided.

    D. Develop a risk-based strategy that implements changes slowly over an extended period of time.

Answers

1. **C.** Security governance is the mechanism through which security strategy is established, controlled, and monitored. Long-term and other strategic decisions are made in the context of security governance.

2. **A.** A software startup in an industry like gaming is going to be highly tolerant of risk: time to market and signing up new customers will be its primary objectives. As the organization achieves viability, other priorities such as security will be introduced.

3. **D.** The metric on time to patch critical servers will be the most meaningful metric for the board of directors. The other metrics, while potentially interesting at the operational level, do not convey business meaning to board members.

4. **D.** The metric of percentage of critical servers being patched within SLAs is the best leading indicator because it is a rough predictor of the probability of a future security incident. The other metrics are trailing indicators because they report on past incidents.

5. **C.** The elements of BMIS are organization, people, process, and technology. The dynamic interconnections (DIs) are culture, governing, architecture, emergence, enabling and support, and human factors.

6. **B.** A strategy is the plan to achieve an objective. An objective is the "what" that an organization wants to achieve, and a strategy is the "how" the objective will be achieved.

7. **A.** The most important factor influencing a decision of selecting a control framework are the industry vertical. For example, a healthcare organization would likely select HIPAA as its primary control framework, whereas a retail organization might select PCI-DSS.

8. **D.** By itself, security policy tells someone little about an organization's security practices. An organization's policy is only a collection of statements; without examining business processes, business records, and interviewing personnel, a security professional cannot develop any conclusions about an organization's security practices.

9. **A.** An organization that does not have a security incident log probably lacks the capability to detect and respond to an incident. It is not reasonable to assume that the organization has had no security incidents since minor incidents occur with regularity. Claiming that the organization has effective controls is unreasonable, as it is understood that incidents occur even when effective controls are in place (because not all types of incidents can reasonably be prevented).

10. **D.** The balanced scorecard is a tool that is used to quantify the performance of an organization against strategic objectives. The focus of a balanced scorecard is financial, customer, internal processes, and innovation/learning.

11. **B.** A process that is performed consistently but is undocumented is generally considered to be Repeatable.

12. **C.** There are no rules that specify that the maturity levels of different processes need to be the same or at different values relative to one another. In this example, each process may already be at an appropriate level, based on risk appetite, risk levels, and other considerations.

13. **C.** An organization that needs to implement new controls should do so within its existing control framework. It is not necessary to adopt an entirely new control framework when a few controls need to be added.

14. **A.** Organizational culture is powerful, as it reflects how people think and work. In this example, there is no mention that the strong culture is bad, only that it is casual. Punishing people for their behavior may cause resentment, a revolt, or people to leave the organization. The best approach here is to better understand the culture and to work with people in the organization to figure out how a culture of security can be introduced successfully.

15. **D.** A security strategist needs to understand an organization's capacity to spend its way to lower risk. In an organization with profit margins, it is unlikely that the organization is going to agree to an aggressive improvement plan. Developing a risk ledger that depicts these risks may be a helpful tool for communicating risk, but by itself there is no action to change anything. Similarly, recommending risk avoidance may mean discontinuing the very operations that bring in revenue.

Information Risk Management

In this chapter, you will learn about

- Benefits and outcomes from an information risk management perspective
- Risk assessment and risk management frameworks
- Developing a risk management strategy
- The risk management life-cycle process
- Integrating risk management into an organization's practices and culture
- The components of a risk assessment: asset value, vulnerabilities, threats, and probability and impact of occurrence
- Risk treatment options: mitigate, accept, transfer, avoid
- The risk register
- Monitoring and reporting risk

This chapter covers CISM Domain 2, "Information Risk Management." The topics in this chapter represent 30 percent of the Certified Information Security Manager (CISM) examination.

Information risk management is the practice of balancing business opportunity with potential information security–related losses. Information risk management is largely a qualitative effort since it is difficult to know the probability and costs of significant loss events. Still, several methods for measuring risk have been established that help organizations better understand risks and how they can be handled. These methods include both qualitative and quantitative techniques that are used to contribute to business decisions.

Risk Management Concepts

Risk management is the fundamental undertaking for any organization that desires to be reasonably aware of risks that, if not identified or monitored, could result in unexpected losses and even threaten the survival of the organization. The purpose of risk management is the identification of credible threats and the means to decide what to do about those threats. Organizations using effective risk management processes experience fewer security incidents; those that do occur have lower impact, and the organization is better prepared to deal with them.

The Importance of Risk Management

Risk management is the cornerstone of any information security program. Risk management represents time-proven methods and techniques used to identify risks, understand their probability of occurrence and potential impact to the organization, make decisions about those risks based on established decision criteria, and measure key attributes of security and risk for long-term trending and for reporting to executive management.

Risk management provides key information that enables the security manager to prioritize scarce resources in a way that results in the greatest possible risk reduction. Without risk management techniques, security managers would be making prioritization decisions based on gut feel or other arbitrary means.

The effectiveness of a risk management program is largely dependent on two factors: support from executive management, and an organization's culture with respect to security awareness and accountability. Additionally, an effective risk management program can serve as a catalyst to make subtle but strategic changes to an organization's culture.

No two risk management programs are alike; instead, each is uniquely different, based on several factors:

- Culture
- Mission, objectives, and goals
- Management structure
- Management support
- Industry sector
- Market conditions
- Applicable laws, regulations, and other legal obligations
- Stated or unstated risk tolerance
- Financial health

Outcomes of Risk Management

An organization that implements an effective risk management program will have heightened awareness about the business use of technology, as well as how technology can impact the business. The greatest benefit that an organization will derive is a lower probability for security incidents, and for those incidents that do occur, the organization will be better prepared, and the impact from the incident will be reduced.

An organization with the risk management program will develop a culture of risk-aware planning, thinking, and decision-making. Executives in the organization will be more aware of information risk, resulting in a more realistic view of the risks associated with the use of information technology and the Internet. Executives and other decision-makers will begin to develop an instinct for the risk levels of different kinds of business activities.

Risk Management Technologies

Throughout the risk management process, an organization will identify specific risks and will often choose to mitigate those risks with specific process and technology solutions. The categories and types of solutions include the following:

- Access governance systems
- Access management systems
- Advanced anti-malware software (often touted as a replacement for antivirus)
- Antivirus software
- Cloud access security brokers (CASBs)
- Dynamic application security testing tools (DASTs)
- File activity monitoring systems (FAMs)
- File integrity monitoring systems (FIMs)
- Firewalls (including so-called next-generation firewalls)
- Forensics tools
- Governance, risk, and compliance (GRC) systems
- Intrusion detection systems (IDSs)
- Intrusion prevention systems (IPSs)
- Network access controls
- Phishing assessment
- Privileged access management systems (PAMs)
- Public key infrastructure (PKI)
- Security information and event management system (SIEM)
- Single sign-on (SSO) systems
- Static application security testing tools (SASTs)
- Spam filters
- Third-party risk management systems (TPRMs)
- User behavioral analytics systems (UBAs)
- Unified threat management systems (UTMs)
- Virtual private network (VPN) systems
- Vulnerability scanning tools
- Web application scanning tools
- Web filtering
- Wireless access controls
- External monitoring and intelligence services

Organizations without effective risk management programs often acquire many of these capabilities but do so without first identifying specific, relevant risks to their organizations. Instead, they are purchasing these solutions for other reasons, including the following:

- Salespeople who claim their solutions will solve the organization's security risks (without actually knowing what those specific risks are)

- Security managers in other organizations who purchase the same or similar solutions (again, in the presence or absence of sound risk management)

- Articles in trade publications that explain the merits of security solutions

 NOTE The security solutions portfolio should be based on supporting the business objectives and have defined success criteria, business requirements, and technical requirements prior to the purchase of specific technologies.

Implementing a Risk Management Program

The implementation of a risk management strategy is not a straightforward undertaking. There are several risk management frameworks to choose from, and they share common principles, including the concept of risk management being a life-cycle process, periodic assessment, and continuous improvement.

Both internal and external factors will influence what risk management framework should be adopted and how it will be implemented. Applying a risk management framework in an organization requires a keen understanding of the organization's mission, objectives, strategies, cultures, practices, structure, financial condition, risk appetite, and level of executive management support.

External factors that will influence the selection and implementation of a risk management framework include market and economic conditions, applicable regulations, geographical operations, customer base/type, and the social and political climates. Specific frameworks are discussed later in this section.

Once a framework has been selected, the security manager can then start to develop a sound risk management strategy. Security managers will need to perform one or more gap analyses to better understand the current state so that they can develop adequate plans to define, document, and highlight the desired future state. Because no security manager has a complete repertoire of knowledge and skill, many outside resources are available to supplement their knowledge, as well as to provide direct assistance.

Risk Management Strategy

The objectives of a risk management strategy are to identify all credible risks and to reduce them to a level that is acceptable to the organization. The acceptable level of risk is generally related to these factors:

- Executive management's risk appetite

- The organization's ability to absorb losses, as well as its ability to build defenses

- Regulatory and legal requirements

As the organization establishes its acceptable level of risk (also known as *risk tolerance*), this will drive the implementation and refinement of controls. Then, over time, risk assessments and risk treatment will drive adjustments to its controls. This is because controls are the primary means for mitigating risks by ensuring desired outcomes, whatever they might be.

For organizations with other instances or pockets of risk management, it is important to consider merging these functions, or at least aligning them so that they are more consistent with each other. For organizations with enterprise risk management (ERM) functions, this may represent an opportunity to feed information risk into the ERM system so that its overall depiction of all business risk will include information risk.

It should be noted that in many small to midsize organizations, risk management programs originate from the IT group. This can be an opportunity for the IT team and security manager to increase the awareness and visibility of issues that could have a negative impact on the organization. An added benefit is the fostering of relationships with business leaders and moving away from the view of IT and security being seen as the "no" group and instead being viewed as a business enabler.

Several internal and external factors will govern the implementation of risk management objectives, including the following:

- Culture
- Organizational maturity
- Management structure
- Management support
- Market conditions
- Regulatory and legal requirements

Possibly the most important factor that will enable or constrain security managers as they develop a risk management strategy is the development of key relationships throughout the organization. When a security manager develops and implements a risk management strategy, the security manager is acting as a change agent in the organization. The security manager is subtly but intentionally driving key changes in the organization through changes in people, processes, and technologies. This role as a security catalyst is an ongoing journey that will become a way of life as the organization becomes a risk-aware culture.

Risk Communication

Risk management cannot be a business function kept as a secret; instead, it must be introduced to the organization's key stakeholders in a way that helps them understand the role of risk management in the organization. Stakeholders need to understand how the risk management program will work and the role they will play in it being an effective program in achieving business objectives. An important factor in the process is helping stakeholders understand the impact that the risk management program will have on their relationships with each other, on their autonomy, and on how the program will improve the organization, including their own jobs.

Successful information risk management requires that the channels of communication be open at all times and operate in all directions. Successful information risk programs operate through transparency so that all stakeholders understand what is happening in the program and why. For sure, there are some matters in information security that need to be kept confidential, but generally, information about risks should be readily available to all board members, executives, stakeholders, and risk owners.

Risk Awareness

Risk awareness refers to activities whose objective is to make business leaders, stakeholders, and other personnel aware of the organization's information risk management program. Similar to security awareness programs, the goal of risk awareness is to ensure that business leaders and decision-makers are aware of the idea that all business decisions have a risk component and that many decisions have implications on information risk. Further, they need to be aware of the presence of a formal information risk management program, which includes a process and techniques for making risk-aware decisions.

There is some overlap in the content and audience of security awareness and risk awareness programs. Primarily, security awareness applies to an entire organization, whereas risk awareness encompasses senior personnel who are involved in the risk management process. Also, the methods for communicating this information in these two programs are the same. Ideally, security awareness and risk awareness programs are developed side by side, ensuring that all audiences receive useful and actionable information when needed.

Risk Consulting

Security managers often play the role of a security and risk consultant in their organizations. As they develop trusted relationships throughout the business, security managers are regarded as technology risk experts who are available to consult on a wide variety of issues. While this may seem like an ad hoc activity, security managers should treat these mini-consulting engagements as formal service requests, even in the absence of a service request system or formal capability. This includes being mindful of responsiveness and service levels. Here are some of the key attributes that make a good information risk consultant:

- Ability to listen to business leaders
- Ability to assess the information and how it may impact a process or business unit, as well as identify other areas in the business the issue may cascade to
- Have a good understanding of the business, not just the technology supporting the business

Risk Management Frameworks

When building an information risk program, the security manager needs to develop processes and procedures, roles and responsibilities, and templates for business records. This can be a lengthy and laborious undertaking that lacks assurance for success. Instead of building a program from scratch, it is suggested that security managers refer to the multitude of high-quality risk management frameworks, including the following:

- ISO/IEC 27001, "Information technology — Security techniques — Information security management systems — Requirements." Requirements 4 through 10 in this standard describe the structure of an entire information security management system (ISMS) including risk management.

- ISO/IEC 27005, "Information Technology — Security Techniques — Information security risk management."

- ISO/IEC 31010, "Risk management — Risk assessment techniques."

- NIST Special Publication 800-37, "Guide for Applying the Risk Management Framework to Federal Information Systems: A Security Life Cycle Approach."

- NIST Special Publication 800-39, "Managing Information Security Risk."

- COBIT 5.

- RIMS Risk Maturity Model.

- Facilitated Risk Assessment Process.

There are two main approaches that risk managers can choose when considering existing frameworks. First, they can select the single framework that has the best alignment with the organization's practices. Second, the security manager can select elements from one or more frameworks to build the organization's risk management program. As noted earlier in the chapter, there are several things that influence the decision.

Framework Components

Risk management frameworks have a common core of components, including the following:

- Program scope
- Information risk objectives
- Information risk policy
- Risk appetite/tolerance
- Roles and responsibilities
- Risk management life-cycle process
- Risk management documentation
- Management review

Security managers in regulated industries need to understand legal and regulatory requirements so that they might select a framework and build a program that has all the required activities and characteristics. Second, if an enterprise risk management program is in place within the organization, then the security manager should consult with the ERM team to understand how the frameworks will support each other.

Integration into the Environment

To be efficient and effective, the organization's risk management program needs to fit neatly and easily into the organization's existing policies, processes, and systems. The risk management program should complement existing structures instead of building separate structures. For instance, a security manager should consider acquiring risk management modules in an existing GRC platform used to manage policies and external vendors, as opposed to purchasing a separate GRC platform for managing risk—even if a new, separate platform might do a better job. In another example, the security manager should consider supplementing an existing security awareness program platform with additional information for information risk, as opposed to building or acquiring a completely separate learning system.

The principle at work here is one of utilizing existing structures and minimizing impact on the organization. A new or improved risk management program will already be disruptive on an organization in need of such a program—there is no point in making the componentry of a program disruptive as well.

Risk management programs need to integrate into the organization's culture. To the greatest extent possible, a new or improved risk management program should leverage current thinking, vocabulary, customs, and practices to fit seamlessly into the organization. But as stated previously, an organization's culture may be in need of minor adjustments with regard to information risk and information security. If so, the new risk management program should be "eased into" the culture as opposed to being haphazardly imposed upon the organization.

The most important part of integrating an information risk program into an existing environment has little to do with the organization's existing systems or even its processes. Instead, integrating into the organization's culture is the most important consideration. By nature, people oppose change since change that is out of one's control is instinctively seen as bad and may be subconsciously or even consciously opposed. A better way is to introduce a program in a way that feels less intrusive and disruptive to the organization but instead feels like a welcome and needed addition that will improve the organization's fortunes.

Risk Management Context

When designing and establishing a risk management program, the security manager needs to understand the business context on which the risk management program will exist. This includes the scope of the program, as well as the entire business environment in which the program will operate, including the organization's policies, processes, practices, and culture.

The context is not simply the whole of the organization, although in some cases it may be. Instead, the security manager, together with executive management, needs to define the boundaries within which the risk management program will operate. These definitions may include the following:

- Business units, lines of business, locations/regions
- Participants and stakeholders in the information risk program
- Roles and responsibilities for participants and stakeholders
- Risk appetite/tolerance

Internal Environments

While designing an information risk program, the security manager must understand many key aspects of the organization's internal environment. If a security manager fails to take these considerations into account, the program may be less effective or fail altogether. Key aspects include the following:

- Organization mission, goals, and objectives
- Existing business strategies, including major initiatives and projects in flight
- Financial health and access to capital
- Existing risk practices
- Organizational maturity
- Formal and informal communication protocols/relationships
- Culture

External Environments

It is critical that the security manager and executive management understand the organization's external environment. While the external environment cannot be in scope in a risk management program, many aspects of the external environment must be well understood if the organization and its risk management program are to be successful. These aspects include the following:

- Market conditions
- Economic conditions
- Applicable laws and regulations
- Social and political environments
- External stakeholders including regulators, business partners, suppliers, and customers
- External threats and threat actors
- Geopolitical factors

Knowing these will help the organization better understand external influences on the organization, which in turn may influence various aspects of the risk management program, including considerations to include when making risk decisions and overall risk tolerance.

Gap Analyses

As security managers design the organization's information risk management program, they have a vision for the desired end state, often based on one or more information risk frameworks as discussed earlier in this section. But when it comes to developing actual plans for implementing components of the program, the security manager must understand the current state of the program, even if there is no formal program at all. To do this, the security manager should conduct a gap analysis.

A *gap analysis* is defined as an examination of a process or system to determine differences between its existing state and a desired future state. This helps the security manager better understand the current state and how it is different from the desired future state. In further detail, the gap analysis will reveal what characteristics of the current state can remain, what should be discarded, what should be replaced, and what should be added.

For example, a security manager examines an organization's existing change control process. All that can be found is a log of changes and e-mail attachments containing management approvals for changes. The gap analysis reveals the lack of a change request procedure, change advisory board (CAB) calls, and roles and responsibilities. The existing business record is usable but needs additional fields and annotations. With this information, the security manager now can undertake (or direct) the work required to get the change control process improvements implemented.

A second example would be a security manager who identifies that the current risk program is done annually with no input from the business and process leaders. The information is kept by the internal audit team and updated by the chief executive officer (CEO). In this case, a gap analysis would identify several opportunities for improvement with the program through the involvement of senior leaders.

External Support

Setting up a new information risk management program involves a great deal of knowledge and details. Even the most experienced security managers will often find themselves lacking in a few areas. For instance, a new security manager may have worked previously in an organization without an existing risk management program, or the security manager may have worked in a different industry sector in the past. Or, the organization may have tools, technologies, or processes in place that the security manager may not be fully familiar with.

Fortunately, there's a wealth of information available to security managers, which will help to supplement the knowledge and skills that they already have so that they can proceed with building and running their information risk management program with more confidence and with better assurances of positive outcomes.

Here are some of these information sources:

- **Security round tables**   Many cities have informal security round tables whose members include chief information security officers (CISOs) and security managers. These local networks of information risk professionals are invaluable for networking and getting advice from other professionals.

- **Organization chapters**   There are several professional organizations with local chapters, where security professionals can congregate and learn from each other and from event speakers. These organizations are as follows:

  - Information Systems Security Association (ISSA)

- International Information Systems Security Certification Consortium, known as (ISC)^2
- ISACA (formerly known as the Information Systems Audit and Control Association)
- Society for Information Management (SIM)
- Society of Information Risk Analysts (SIRA)
- Cloud Security Alliance (CSA)
- InfraGard
- International Association of Privacy Professionals (IAPP)

- **Published risk management practices**   Several organizations publish standards and/or articles describing risk management practices, techniques, and case studies. Here are some of the organizations that publish them:
  - (ISC)^2
  - ISACA
  - SANS Institute (formerly known as Systems Administration, Network, and Security Institute)

- **Sources for security industry news**   Many organizations publish articles and white papers on various information security and risk management topics. These sources include the following:
  - Information Security Magazine
  - SC Magazine
  - CSO Magazine
  - CIO Magazine
  - Dark Reading
  - TechTarget
  - (ISC)^2
  - ISACA
  - SANS

- **Reports from research organizations**   Several organizations conduct research and publish reports on many security-related topics. These organizations include the following:
  - Ponemon Institute
  - Verizon Business
  - Symantec
  - PricewaterhouseCoopers (PWC)
  - Ernst and Young (EY)

- **Advisory services**   Several advisory firms publish articles, studies, and advice for security and risk managers, including the following:
  - Gartner
  - Forrester
  - IDC
  - Ovum
  - Frost Sullivan
- **Consulting firms**   Many large and numerous smaller security professional services firms are equipped to provide professional advice on the establishment of a security strategy, as well as doing the actual work of designing and implementing a risk management program.
- **Training**   Education and training courses tailored for established security and risk professionals are available from many universities, community colleges, and vocational schools, as well as ISACA and SANS.
- **Books**   Some of the titles listed in the Cybersecurity Canon are focused on risk management and go deeper into the topic than is needed for the CISM certification. The Cybersecurity Canon is available from https://cybercanon .paloaltonetworks.com.
- **Conferences**   Regional, national, and international conferences on security and risk management attract large numbers of security and risk professionals and include speakers, workshops, and training. Like other events listed here, these conferences provide numerous professional networking opportunities. Some of these conferences include the following:
  - RSA
  - BlackHat
  - Defcon
  - Gartner Risk
  - ISSA
  - SecureWorld Expo
  - Evanta
  - Security Advisor Alliance
- **Intelligence services**   Several organizations publish advisories on threat actors, threats, and vulnerabilities. Some are designed to be human readable, while others are designed as machine readable and intended to be fed into an organization's SIEM. A word of caution: there are many organizations promoting and selling threat intelligence services today. The security manager should fully vet the services and the specific value they will add to the organization.

The Risk Management Life Cycle

Like other life-cycle processes, risk management is a cyclical, iterative activity that is used to acquire, analyze, and treat risks. This book focuses on information risk, but overall the life cycle for information risk is functionally similar to that for other forms of risk: a new risk is introduced into the process, the risk is studied, and a decision is made about its outcome.

Like other life-cycle processes, risk management is formally defined in policy and process documents that define scope, roles and responsibilities, workflow, business rules, and business records.

There are several frameworks and standards from U.S. and international sources that define the full life-cycle process. Security managers are generally free to adopt any of these standards, use a blend of different standards, or develop a custom framework.

Information risk management relies upon risk assessments that consider valid threats against the organization's assets, considering any present vulnerabilities. There are several standards and models for risk assessments that can be used. The results of risk assessments are placed into a risk register, which is the official business record containing current and historic information risk threats.

Risk treatment is the activity where decisions about risks are made after weighing various risk treatment options. Risk treatment decisions are typically made by a business owner associated with the affected business activity.

The Risk Management Process

The risk management process consists of a set of structured activities that enable an organization to systematically manage risks. Like other business processes, risk management processes vary somewhat from one organization to the next, but generally they consist of the following activities:

- **Scope definition** The organization defines the scope of the risk management process itself. Typically, scope definitions include geographical or business unit parameters. Scope definition is not part of the iterative portion of the risk management process, although scope may be redefined from time to time.

- **Asset identification and valuation** The organization uses various means to discover and track its information and information system assets. A classification scheme may be used to identify risk and criticality levels. Asset valuation is a key part of asset management processes, and the value of assets is appropriated for use in the risk management processes.

- **Risk appetite** Developed outside of the risk management life-cycle process, risk appetite is an expression of the level of risk that an organization is willing to accept. A risk appetite that is related to information risk is typically expressed in qualitative means; however, organizations in financial services industries often express risk in quantitative terms.

- **Risk identification** This is the first step in the iterative risk management process. Here, the organization identifies a risk that comes from one of several sources, including the following:
  - **Risk assessment** This includes an overall risk assessment or a focused risk assessment.
  - **Vulnerability assessment** This may be one of several activities, including a security scan, a penetration test, or a source code scan.
  - **Threat advisory** This is an advisory from a product vendor, threat intelligence feed, or news story.
  - **Risk analysis** This is an analysis of risk focused on some other matter may uncover additional risks that require attention.
- **Risk analysis** This is the second step in a typical risk management process. After the risk has been identified, it is then analyzed to determine several characteristics, including the following:
  - **Probability of event occurrence** Here, the risk analyst studies event scenarios and calculates the likelihood that an event associated with the risk will occur. This is typically expressed in the number of likely events per year.
  - **Impact of event occurrence** The risk analyst studies different event scenarios and determines the impact of each. This may be expressed in quantitative terms (dollars or other currency) or qualitative terms (high/medium/low or a numeric scale of 1 to 5 or of 1 to 10).
  - **Mitigation** The risk analyst studies different available methods for mitigating the risk. Depending upon the type of risk, there are many techniques, including changing a process or procedure, training staff, changing architecture or configuration, or applying a security patch.
  - **Recommendation** After studying a risk, the risk analyst may develop a recommended course of action to address the risk. This reflects that fact that the individual performing risk analysis is often not the risk decision-maker.
- **Risk treatment** This is the last step in a typical risk management process. Here, an individual decision-maker or committee makes a decision about a specific risk. The basic options for risk treatment are as follows:
  - **Accept** Here, the organization elects to take no action related to the risk.
  - **Mitigate** The organization chooses to mitigate the risk. This takes the form of some action that serves to reduce the probability of a risk event or reduce the impact of a risk event. The actual steps taken may include business process changes, configuration changes, the enactment of a new control, or staff training.
  - **Transfer** The practice of transferring risk is typically achieved through an insurance policy, although other forms are available, including contract assignment.

- **Avoid**   Here, the organization chooses to discontinue the activity associated with the risk. This choice is typically selected for an outdated business activity that is no longer profitable or for a business activity that was not formally approved in the first place.

- **Risk communication**   This takes many forms, including formal communications within risk management processes and procedures, as well as information communications among risk managers and decision-makers.

In addition to business processes, a risk management process has business records associated with it. The *risk register,* sometimes known as a *risk ledger,* is the primary business record in most risk management programs. A risk register is a listing of risks that have been identified. Typically, a risk register contains many items, including a description of the risk, the level and type of risk, and information about risk treatment decisions.

Figure 3-1 shows the elements of a typical risk management life cycle.

Risk Management Methodologies

Several established methodologies are available for organizations that want to manage risk using a formal standard. Organizations select one of these standards for a variety of reasons; they may be required to use a specific standard to address regulatory or contractual terms, or they may feel that a specific standard better aligns with their overall information risk program or the business as a whole.

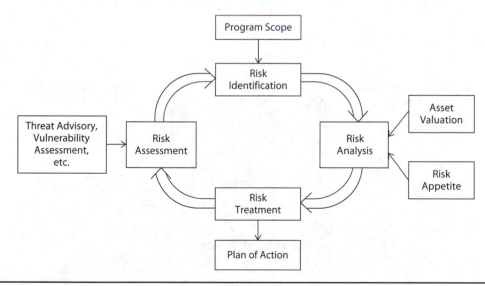

Figure 3-1   The risk management life cycle

NIST Standards

The National Institute for Standards and Technology (NIST) develops standards for information security and other subject matter. NIST Special Publication 800-30, "Guide for Conducting Risk Assessments," is a detailed, high-quality standard that describes the steps used for conducting risk assessments. NIST Special Publication 800-39, "Managing Information Security Risk: Organization, Mission, and Information, System View," describes the overall risk management process.

NIST SP 800-39   The methodology described in NIST Special Publication 800-39 consists of multilevel risk management, at the information systems level, at the mission/business process level, and at the overall organization level. Communications up and down these levels ensures that risks are communicated upward for overall awareness, while risk awareness and risk decisions are communicated downward for overall awareness. Figure 3-2 depicts this approach.

The tiers of risk management are described in NIST SP 800-39 in this way:

- **Tier 1: Organization view**   This level focuses on the role of governance, the activities performed by the risk executive, and the development of risk management and investment strategies.

- **Tier 2: Mission/business process view**   This level is all about enterprise architecture, enterprise security architecture, and ensuring that business processes are risk aware.

- **Tier 3: Information systems view**   This level concentrates on more tactical things such as system configuration and hardening specifications, vulnerability management, and the detailed steps in the systems development life cycle.

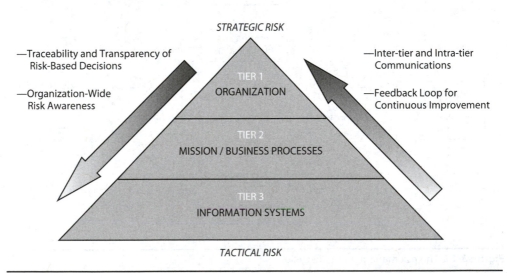

Figure 3-2   Multitier risk management in NIST SP800-39 (Source: National Institute for Standards and Technology)

Other concepts discussed in NIST SP 800-39 include trust, the trustworthiness of systems, and organizational culture.

The overall risk management process defined by NIST SP 800-39 consists of several steps, as shown here:

- **Step 1: Risk framing**   This consists of the assumptions, scope, tolerances, constraints, and priorities, in other words, the business context that is considered prior to later steps taking place.

- **Step 2: Risk assessment**   This is the actual risk assessment, where threats and vulnerabilities are identified and assessed to determine levels and types of risk.

- **Step 3: Risk response**   This is the process of analyzing each risk and developing strategies for reducing it, through appropriate risk treatment for each identified risk. Risk treatment options are *accept, mitigate, avoid,* and *transfer*. This step is defined in more detail in NIST Special Publication 800-30, described later in this section.

- **Step 4: Risk monitoring**   This is the process of performing periodic and ongoing evaluation of identified risks to see whether conditions and risks are changing.

NIST SP 800-30   NIST Special Publication 800-30 describes in greater detail a standard methodology for conducting a risk assessment. The techniques in this document are quite structured and essentially involve setting up a number of worksheets where threats and vulnerabilities are recorded, along with the probability of occurrence and impact if they occur.

In this standard, the steps for conducting a risk assessment are as follows:

- **Step 1: Prepare for assessment**   The organization determines the purpose of the risk assessment. Primarily, it is important to know the purpose of the results of the risk assessment and the decisions that will be made as a result of the risk assessment. Next, the scope of the assessment must be determined and known. This may take many forms, including geographic and business unit boundaries, as well as the range of threat scenarios that are to be included. Also, any assumptions and constraints pertaining to the assessment should be identified. Further, the sources of threat, vulnerability, and impact information must be identified (NIST 800-30 has exemplary lists of threats, vulnerabilities, and impact in its appendixes).

- **Step 2: Conduct assessment**   The organization performs the actual risk assessment. This consists of several tasks.

  A. **Identify threat sources and events**   The organization identifies a list of threat sources and events that will be considered in the assessment. The following sources of threat information are found in the standard and can be used. Organizations are advised to supplement these sources with other information as needed.

    - Table D-1: Threat source inputs
    - Table D-2: Threat sources

- Table D-3: Adversary capabilities
- Table D-4: Adversary intent
- Table D-5: Adversary targeting
- Table D-6: Nonadversary threat effects
- Table E-1: Threat events
- Table E-2: Adversarial threat events
- Table E-3: Nonadversarial threat events
- Table E-4: Relevance of threat events

B. **Identify vulnerabilities and predisposing conditions**   Here, the organization examines its environment (people, processes, and technology) to determine what vulnerabilities exist that could result in a greater likelihood that threat events may occur. The following sources of vulnerability and predisposing condition information are found in the standard and can be used in a risk assessment. Like the catalog of threats, organizations are advised to supplement these lists with additional vulnerabilities as needed.

- Table F-1: Input—vulnerability and predisposing conditions
- Table F-2: Vulnerability severity assessment scale
- Table F-4: Predisposing conditions
- Table F-5: Pervasiveness of predisposing conditions

C. **Determine likelihood of occurrence**   The organization determines the probability that each threat scenario identified earlier will occur. The following tables guide the risk manager in scoring each threat:

- Table G-1: Inputs—determination of likelihood
- Table G-2: Assessment scale—likelihood of threat event initiation
- Table G-3: Assessment scale—likelihood of threat event occurrence
- Table G-4: Assessment scale—likelihood of threat event resulting in adverse impact
- Table G-5: Assessment scale—overall likelihood

D. **Determine magnitude of impact**   In this phase, the risk manager determines the impact of each type of threat event on the organization. These tables guide the risk manager in this effort:

- Table H-1: Input—determination of impact
- Table H-2: Examples of adverse impacts
- Table H-3: Assessment scale—impact of threat events
- Table H-4: Identification of adverse impacts

E. **Determine risk**   Here, the organization determines the level of risk for each threat event. These tables aid the risk manager in this effort:

- Table I-1: Inputs—risk

- Table I-2: Assessment scale—level of risk (combination of likelihood and impact)

- Table I-3: Assessment scale—level of risk

- Table I-4: Column descriptions for adversarial risk table

- Table I-5: Template for adversarial risk table to be completed by risk manager

- Table I-6: Column descriptions for nonadversarial risk table

- Table I-7: Template for nonadversarial risk table to be completed by risk manager

- **Step 3: Communicate results**   When the risk assessment has been completed, the results are then communicated to decision-makers and stakeholders in the organization. The purpose of communicating risk assessment results is to ensure that the organization's decision-makers make decisions that include considerations for known risks. Risk assessment results can be communicated in several ways, including the following:

  - Publishing to a central location

  - Briefings

  - Distributing via e-mail

  - Distributing hard copies

- **Step 4: Maintain assessment**   After a risk assessment has been completed, the organization will then maintain the assessment by monitoring risk factors identified in the risk assessment. This enables the organization to maintain a view of relevant risks that incorporates changes in the business environment since the risk assessment was completed. NIST Special Publication 800-137, "Information Security Continuous Monitoring (ISCM) for Federal Information Systems and Organizations," provides guidance on the ongoing monitoring of information systems, operations, and risks.

NIST 800-30 is available at http://csrc.nist.gov/publications/PubsSPs.html.

ISO/IEC 27005

ISO/IEC 27005 is an international standard that defines a structured approach to risk assessments and risk management. The methodology outlined in this standard is summarized here:

- **Step 1: Establish context**   Before a risk assessment can be performed, a number of parameters need to be established, including the following:

  - **Scope of the risk assessment**   This includes which portions of an organization are to be included, based on business unit, service, line, geography, organization structure, or other means.

- **Purpose of the risk assessment** Reasons include legal or due diligence or support of an ISMS, business continuity plan, vulnerability management plan, or incident response plan.

- **Risk evaluation criteria** Determine the means through which risks will be examined and scored.

- **Impact criteria** Determine how the impact of identified risks will be described and scored.

- **Risk acceptance criteria** Specify the method that the organization will use to determine risk acceptance.

- **Logistical plan** This includes which personnel will perform the risk assessment, which personnel in the organization need to provide information such as control evidence, and what supporting facilities are required such as office space.

- **Step 2: Risk assessment** The risk assessment is performed.

  - **Asset identification** Risk analysts identify assets, along with their value and criticality.

  - **Threat identification** Risk analysts identify relevant and credible threats that have the potential to harm assets, along with their likelihood of occurrence. There are many types of threats, both naturally occurring and man-caused, and they could be accidental or deliberate. Note that some threats may affect more than one asset. ISO/IEC 27005 contains a list of threat types, as does NIST Special Publication 800-30 (in Table D-2) described earlier in this section. Note that a risk analyst may identify additional threats.

  - **Control identification** Risk analysts identify existing and planned controls. Those controls that already exist should be examined to see whether they are effective. The criteria for examining a control includes whether it reduces the likelihood or impact of a threat event. The results of this examination will conclude whether the control is effective, ineffective, or unnecessary. Finally, when identifying threats, the risk analyst may determine that a new control is warranted.

  - **Vulnerability identification** Vulnerabilities that can be exploited by threat events that cause harm to an asset are identified. Remember that a vulnerability does not cause harm, but its presence may permit a threat event to harm an asset. ISO/IEC 27005 contains a list of vulnerabilities. Note that a risk analyst may need to identify additional vulnerabilities.

  - **Consequences identification** The risk analyst will identify consequences that would occur for each identified threat against each asset. Consequences may be the loss of confidentiality, integrity, or availability of any asset, as well as a loss of human safety. Depending on the nature of the asset, consequences may take many forms, including service interruption or degradation, reduction in service quality, loss of business, reputation damage, or monetary penalties including fines. Note that consequences may be a primary result or a secondary result of the realization of a specific threat. For example, the theft of sensitive financial information may have little or no operational impact in the short term, but legal proceedings over the long term could result in financial penalties, unexpected costs, and loss of business.

- **Step 3: Risk evaluation** Levels of risk are determined according to the risk evaluation and risk acceptance criteria established in step 1. The output of risk evaluation is a list of risks, with their associated threats, vulnerabilities, and consequences.

- **Step 4: Risk treatment** Decision-makers in the organization will select one of four risk treatment options for each risk identified in step 3. These options are as follows:

  - **Risk reduction (sometimes known as *risk mitigation*)** In this option, the organization alters something in information technology (e.g., security configuration, application source code, or data), business processes and procedures, or personnel (e.g., training).

    In many cases, an organization will choose to update an existing control or enact a new control so that the risk reduction may be more effectively monitored over time. The cost of updating or creating a control—as well as the impact on ongoing operational costs of the control—will need to be weighed alongside the value of the asset being protected, as well as the consequences associated with the risk being treated. A risk manager remembers that a control can reduce many risks, and potentially for several assets, so the risk manager will need to consider the benefit of risk reduction in more complex terms.

    Chapter 4 includes a comprehensive discussion on the types of controls.

  - **Risk retention (sometimes known as *risk acceptance*)** Here, the organization chooses to accept the risk and decides not to change anything.

  - **Risk avoidance** The organization decides to discontinue the activity associated with the risk. For example, an organization assesses the risks related to the acceptance of credit card data for payments. They decide to change the system so that credit card data is sent instead directly to a payment processor so that the organization will no longer be accepting credit card data.

  - **Risk transfer** The organization transfers risk to another party. The common forms of risk transfer are insurance and outsourcing security monitoring to a third party.

    When an organization transfers risk to another party, there will usually be residual risk that is more difficult to treat. For example, while an organization may have had reduced costs from a breach because of cyber insurance, the organization may still suffer reputational damage in the form of reduced goodwill.

Decision-makers weigh the costs and benefits associated with each these four options and decide the best course of action for the organization.

The four risk treatment options are not mutually exclusive; sometimes a combination of risk treatment options is the best option for an organization. For instance, a business application was found to accept weak passwords; the chosen risk treatment was a combination of security awareness training (mitigation) and acceptance (the organization elected not to modify the application as this would have been too expensive).

Further, some treatments can address more than one risk. For example, security awareness training may reduce several risks associated with end-user computing and behavior.

Often, after risk treatment, some risk—known as *residual risk*—remains. When analyzing residual risk, the organization may elect to undergo additional risk treatment to reduce the risk further, or it may accept the residual risk as is. Note that residual risk cannot be reduced to zero—there will always be some level of risk.

Because some forms of risk treatment (mainly, risk reduction and risk transfer) may require an extended period of time to be completed, risk managers usually track ongoing risk treatment activities to completion.

- **Step 5: Risk communication**   All parties involved in information risk—the CISO (or other top-ranking information security official), risk managers, business decision-makers, and other stakeholders—need channels of communication throughout the entire risk management and risk treatment life cycle. Examples of risk communication include the following:

  - Announcements and discussions of upcoming risk assessments
  - Collection of risk information during risk assessments (and at other times)
  - Proceedings and results from completed risk assessments
  - Discussions of risk tolerance
  - Proceedings from risk treatment discussions and risk treatment decisions and plans
  - Educational information about security and risk
  - Updates on the organization's mission and strategic objectives
  - Communication about security incidents to affected parties and stakeholders

- **Step 6: Risk monitoring and review**   Organizations are not static, and neither is risk. The value of assets, impacts, threats, vulnerabilities, and likelihood of occurrence should be periodically monitored and reviewed so that the organization's view of risk continues to be relevant and accurate. Monitoring should include the following:

  - Discovery of new, changed, and retired assets
  - Change in business processes and practices

- Changes in technology architecture
- New threats that have not been assessed
- New vulnerabilities that were previously unknown
- Changes in threat event probability and consequences
- Security incidents that may alter the organization's understanding of threats, vulnerabilities, and risks
- Changes in market and other business conditions
- Changes in applicable laws and regulations

ISO/IEC 27005 is available at www.iso.org.

Factor Analysis of Information Risk

Factor Analysis of Information Risk (FAIR) is an analysis method that helps a risk manager understand the factors that contribute to risk, as well as the probability of threat occurrence and an estimation of loss.

FAIR is used to help a risk manager understand the probability of a given threat event and the losses that may occur. In the FAIR methodology, there are six types of loss:

- **Productivity**   Lost productivity caused by the incident
- **Response**   The cost expended in incident response
- **Replacement**   The expense required to rebuild or replace an asset
- **Fines and judgments**   All forms of legal costs resulting from the incident
- **Competitive advantage**   Loss of business to other organizations
- **Reputation**   Loss of goodwill and future business

FAIR also focuses on the concept of asset value and liability. For example, a customer list is an asset because the organization can reach its customers to solicit new business; however, the customer list is also a liability because of the impact on the organization if the customer list is obtained by an unauthorized person.

FAIR guides a risk manager through an analysis of threat agents and the different ways in which a threat agent acts upon an asset.

- **Access**   Reading data without authorization
- **Misuse**   Using an asset differently from intended usage
- **Disclose**   Threat agent shares data with other unauthorized parties
- **Modify**   Threat agent modifies asset
- **Deny use**   Threat agents prevent legitimate subjects from accessing assets

FAIR is claimed to be complementary to risk management methodologies such as NIST SP 800-30 and ISO/IEC 27005.

You can obtain FAIR at www.fairinstitute.org.

Asset Identification and Valuation

After a risk assessment's scope has been determined, the initial step in a risk assessment is the identification of assets and a determination of each asset's value. In a typical information risk assessment, assets will consist of information, as well as the information systems that support and protect those information assets.

Hardware Assets

Hardware assets may include server and network hardware, user workstations, office equipment such as printers and scanners, and WiFi access points. Depending on the scope of the risk assessment, assets in storage and replacement components may also be included.

There are some challenges with the accurate identification of hardware assets. Many organizations do a subpar job of building and maintaining inventory information. Accounting may have asset inventory in its accounting system, but this would not account for assets not in use or retired assets reverted to storage. Further, asset inventory in accounting often does not cite the business applications they support. Tools used by IT for security scans or patch management are another source of inventory information, although these are often incomplete for many reasons. Even purpose-made asset inventory systems are plagued with inaccuracies because maintaining the data in them is not always a high priority.

An organization that is responsible for the management of information and information systems must have a means for knowing what all of those assets are. More than that, IT needs to acquire and track several characteristics about every asset, including the following:

- **Identification**   This includes the make, model, serial number, asset tag number, logical name, and any other means for identifying the asset.

- **Value**   Initially, this may signify the purchased value but may also include its depreciated value if an IT asset management program is associated with the organization's financial asset management program.

- **Location**   The asset's location needs to be specified so that its existence may be verified in a periodic inventory.

- **Security classification**   Security management programs almost always include a plan for classifying the sensitivity of information and/or information systems. Example classifications include secret, restricted, confidential, and public.

- **Asset group**   IT assets may be classified into a hierarchy of asset groups. For example, any of the servers in a data center that support a large application may be assigned to an asset group known as "Application X Servers."

- **Owner**   This is usually the person or group responsible for the operation of the asset.

- **Custodian**   Occasionally, the ownership and operations of assets will be divided into two bodies, where the owner owns them but a custodian operates or maintains them.

Because hardware assets are installed, moved, and eventually retired, it is important to periodically verify the information in the asset inventory by physically verifying the existence of the physical assets. Depending upon the value and sensitivity of systems and data, this inventory "true-up" may be performed as often as monthly or as seldom as once per year. Discrepancies in actual inventory must be investigated in order to verify that assets have not been moved without authorization or stolen.

Subsystem and Software Assets
Software applications such as software development tools, drawing tools, security scanning tools, and subsystems such as application servers and database management systems are all considered assets. Like physical assets, these often have tangible value and should be periodically inventoried.

Information Assets
Information assets are less tangible than hardware assets, as they are not easily observed. Information assets take many forms:

- **Customer information**   Most organizations have information about people, whether they are employees, customers, constituents, beneficiaries, or citizens. The information may include sensitive information such as contact information and personal details, transactions, order history, and other details.

- **Intellectual property**   This type of information can take the form of trade secrets, source code, product designs, policies and standards, and marketing collateral.

- **Business operations**   This generally includes merger and acquisition information and other types of business processes and records not mentioned earlier.

- **Virtual assets**   Most organizations are moving their business applications to the cloud, thereby eliminating the need to purchase hardware. Organizations that use infrastructure as a service (IaaS) have virtual operating systems that are another form of information. Even though these operating systems are not purchased but instead are rented, there is nonetheless an asset perspective: they take time to build and configure and therefore have a replacement cost. The value of assets is discussed more fully later in this section.

Cloud-Based Information Assets
One significant challenge related to information assets lies in the nature of cloud services and how they work. An organization may have a significant portion of its information assets stored by other organizations in their cloud-based services. Unless an organization has exceedingly good business records, some of these assets will be overlooked. The main reason for this is because of the ways in which cloud services work; it's easy to sign up for a zero-cost or low-cost service and immediately begin uploading business information to the service. Unless the organization has advanced tools such as a cloud access security broker, it will be next to impossible for an organization to know all of the cloud-based services that are used.

Virtual Assets

Virtualization technology, which allows an organization to employ multiple, separate operating systems to run on one server, is a popular practice for organizations, whether on their own hardware servers located in their own data centers or in hosting facilities. Organizations employing IaaS are also employing virtualization technology.

More discipline is required to properly track and manage virtual server assets. Unlike physical servers, whose purchase involves different stakeholders in order to initiate and approve a purchase, virtual servers can be created at the click of a button, with or without additional cost to the organization and often without approval. The term *virtual sprawl,* or *virtualization sprawl,* reflects this tendency.

The creation/use of virtual servers and other virtual machines is not limited to manual techniques. Virtual machines can also be created through automatic means. A typical example of this is through a cloud services feature known as *elasticity,* whereby additional virtual machines can be automatically created and started during heavy workloads when additional servers are needed.

Software-defined networking (SDN), the class of technologies that facilitate the creation and management of virtual network devices, poses the same challenge to organizations. Additional devices can be created at will or by automatic means. Managing them requires more discipline and potentially greater effort.

While IaaS and virtualization make it far easier to create and manage server assets, maintaining an accurate inventory of virtual server assets is even more challenging than it is for physical assets.

Asset Classification

Asset classification is an activity whereby an organization assigns an asset to a category that represents usage or risk. The purpose of asset classification is to determine, for each asset, its level of criticality to the organization.

Criticality can be related to information sensitivity. For instance, a database of customer information that includes contact and payment information would be considered highly sensitive and in the event of compromise could result in significant impact to present and future business operations.

Criticality can also be related to operational dependency. For example, a database of virtual server images might be considered highly critical. If an organization's server images were to be compromised or lost, this could adversely affect the organization's ability to continue its operations.

These and other measures of criticality form the basis for information protection, system redundancy and resilience, business continuity planning, and access management. Scarce resources in the form of information protection and resilience need to be allocated to the assets that require it the most; it doesn't usually make sense to protect all assets to the same degree but instead to protect the more valuable and critical assets more than those less valuable and critical.

The best approach to asset classification in most organizations is to first identify and classify *information* assets and then follow this with system classification. It should be noted that one area that is often overlooked or not addressed to a satisfactory level is dealing with unstructured data, as well as data that resides outside of the organization's approved systems.

Information Classification

Information classification is a process whereby different sets and collections of data in an organization are analyzed for various types of value, criticality, integrity, and sensitivity. There are different ways to understand these characteristics. These are some examples:

- **Monetary value**   This information may be more easily monetized by intruders who steal this information. Types of information include credit card numbers, bank account numbers, gift certificates or cards, and discount or promotion codes. Loss of this type of information may cause direct financial losses.

- **Operational criticality**   In this category, information must be available at all times, or perhaps the information is related to some factors of business resilience. Examples of information in this category include virtual server images, incident response procedures, and business continuity procedures. Corruption or loss of this type of information may have a significant impact on ongoing business operations.

- **Accuracy or integrity**   Information in this category is required to be highly accurate. If altered, the organization could suffer significant financial or reputational harm. Examples of this kind of information include exchange rate tables, product or service inventory data, machine calibration data, and price lists. Corruption or loss of this type of information impacts business operations by causing incomplete or erroneous transactions.

- **Sensitivity**   This type of information is most commonly associated with individual citizens. Examples of sensitive information include personal contact information, personal financial data including credit card and bank account numbers, and medical records.

Most organizations have information that falls into all of these categories, with degrees of importance within them. While this may result in a complex matrix of information types and degrees of importance or value, the most successful organizations will be those that build a fairly simple information classification scheme. For instance, an organization may develop four levels of information classification as follows:

- Secret
- Restricted
- Confidential
- Public

These levels of information, together with examples of the types of levels that fall into each category and with instructions on handling information at each level, form the heart of a typical information classification program.

Most organizations depend on its personnel to understand the information classification program, including correctly classifying information and then handling that information properly. This is the main reason why better information classification programs have only three or four classification levels. While it may be more desirable to have more classification levels, doing so often results in confusion and misclassification or mishandling of sensitive and critical data.

Drilling into further detail, examples of information at each of these levels of classification include the following:

- **Secret**   Merger and acquisition plans, user and system account password, and encryption keys
- **Restricted**   Credit card numbers, bank account numbers, Social Security numbers, detailed financial records, detailed system configuration, and vulnerability scan reports
- **Confidential**   System documentation, end-user documentation, internal memos, and network diagrams
- **Public**   Marketing collateral, published financial reports, and press releases

The next step in information classification is the development of handling procedures. These instruct users in the proper acquisition, storage, transmission, and destruction of information at every classification level. Table 3-1 shows a sample information-handling procedure matrix.

The previous classification and handling guidelines are meant as an example to illustrate the differences in various forms of information handling for different classification levels. However, the contents of Table 3-1 can serve as a starting point for an actual data classification and handling procedure.

Organizations that develop and implement information classification programs find that personnel will often misclassify information, either because they do not understand the nature of the sensitivity of a particular set of data or because they know that at a higher level of classification, they may feel that they cannot store or transmit the information in a way they feel is needed. This is a classic case of people taking shortcuts in the name of expediency, mainly when they are not aware of the possible harm that may befall the organization as a result.

The Ideal Number of Classification Levels

Would it be easier to simply handle all information in the same way as the most sensitive information in the organization? While it would be easier to remember how to handle and dispose of all information, it might also be onerous, particularly if all information is handled at the level warranted for the organization's most sensitive or critical information. Encrypting everything and shredding everything would be a wasteful use of resources. That said, it is incumbent on an organization to build a simple information classification program that is easy to understand and follow. Too many levels of classification would be as burdensome as a single level.

	Secret	Restricted	Confidential	Public
Example Information Types	Passwords; merger and acquisition plans and terms	Credit card numbers; bank account numbers; Social Security numbers; detailed financial records; detailed system configuration; vulnerability scan reports	System documentation; end-user documentation; internal memos; network diagrams	Brochures; press releases
Storage on Server	Must be encrypted; store only on servers labeled sensitive	Must be encrypted	Access controls required	Access controls required for update
Storage on Mobile Device	Must never be stored on mobile device	Must be encrypted	Access controls required	No restrictions
Storage in the Cloud	Must never be stored in the cloud	Must be encrypted	Access controls required	Access controls required for update
E-mail	Must never be e-mailed	Must be encrypted	Authorized recipients only	No restrictions
Website	Must never be stored on any web server	Must be encrypted	Access controls required	No restrictions
Fax	Encrypted, manned fax only	Manned fax only; no e-mail–based fax	Manned fax only	No restrictions
Courier and Shipment	Double wrapped; signature and secure storage required	Signature and secure storage required	Signature required	No restrictions
Hard-Copy Storage	Double locked in authorized locations only	Double locked	Locked	No restrictions
Hard-Copy Distribution	Only with owner permission; must be registered	To authorized parties only; only with owner permission	To authorized parties only	No restrictions
Hard-Copy Destruction	Cross-cut shred; make specific record of destruction	Cross-cut shred	Cross-cut shred or secure waste bin	No restrictions
Soft-Copy Destruction	Erase with DoD 5220.22-M spec tool	Erase with DoD 5220.22-M spec tool	Delete and empty recycle bin	No restriction

Table 3-1   Example Information-Handling Requirements

With too many levels of classification, there is a greater chance that information will be misclassified and then put at risk when handled at a too low a level. With too few levels, the organization will either have excessive resources protecting all information at a higher level or insufficient resources protecting information inadequately.

System Classification

Once an organization is satisfied that its information classification is in order, the organization can next embark on system classification. Like various types of information assets, information systems also need to be classified, according to various security and operational criteria.

The purpose for system classification is similar to the purpose for information criteria: to identify and categorize system assets, according to the classification of information stored, processed, or transmitted by them, so that an appropriate level of protection can be determined and implemented.

For any given system, once it is classified according to the highest classification level of information stored, processed, or transmitted through it, the measures used to protect the information system may well play a role in protecting the information, or in some cases it will protect only the system. Both means are utilized, and both are essential.

A typical approach to system classification and protection is this: for each level of classification and for each type of system, a system-hardening standard will be developed that specifies the features and configuration settings to be applied to the system. These settings will help to make the system resistant to attack, and in some cases these settings will also help protect the information being stored, processed, or transmitted by the systems.

Some examples will help illustrate these points.

- **Database management server** In this example, a database management server is used to store information at the Restricted level of classification, perhaps credit card data. The system itself will be classified as Restricted, and the organization will develop system-hardening standards for the operating system and database management systems.

- **Demilitarized zone (DMZ) firewall** In this example, a firewall protects servers located in a DMZ from threats on the Internet, as well as protecting the organization's internal assets from the DMZ, in the event that an asset in the DMZ is compromised by an attacker. While the firewall does not store information, it protects information by restricting the types of traffic that are permitted to flow from the Internet to systems upon which the information resides. The organization will develop and implement hardening standards for the firewall.

- **Internet time server** Here, a server provides precise time clock data to other servers, network devices, and end-user workstations in the organization. While the time server itself does not store, process, or transmit sensitive information, it is still classified as Restricted because this server has direct access (via time protocols and possibly other protocols) to assets that are classified as Restricted. This server will be hardened according to hardening standards developed by the organization.

This final example introduces the concept of zones of protection. In the architecture of typical information-processing environments, there are information systems that directly store, process, and transmit information at various classification levels, and the systems themselves are classified accordingly. The other servers and assets in the same environment that access these servers or are accessed by them typically need to be classified at the same level. If one of these support servers were compromised by an attacker, the attacker would then have direct, and perhaps unrestricted, access to one of the assets that stores, processes, or transmits sensitive or valuable data.

In a large, flat network, this logic could result in an organization having to classify many or all of its systems at the same level as the highest classified system. This could require an organization to implement costly and complex protective and administrative measures to large numbers of systems. For this and other reasons, organizations often employ *network segmentation*, which is the practice of dividing a large, flat network into multiple zones, with firewalls and other protective measures implemented at the boundaries between these zones.

Figure 3-3 depicts a typical network segmentation scheme.

Facilities Classification

Data, asset, and systems classification can often be extended to facilities classification in larger organizations. *Facilities classification* is a method for assigning classification or risk levels to work centers and processing centers, based on their operational criticality or other risk factors. The purpose for facilities classification is to develop more consistent security controls for facilities with similar risk levels.

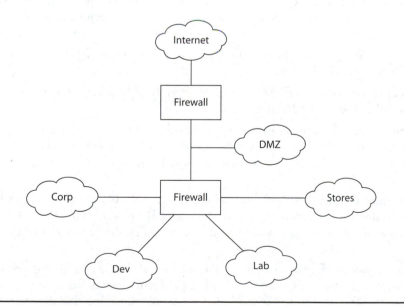

Figure 3-3 Example network segmentation

Asset Valuation

A key part of a risk assessment is the identification of the value of an asset. In the absence of an asset's value, it is more difficult to calculate risks associated with an asset, even when qualitative risk valuation is employed. Without a known valuation, the impact of loss is more difficult to know.

Qualitative Asset Valuation

Because many risk assessments are qualitative in nature (as will be revealed later in this chapter), establishing asset valuation in qualitative terms is common. Instead of assigning a dollar (or other currency) value to an asset, the value of an asset can be assigned to a low-medium-high scale or to a numeric scale such as 1 to 5 or 1 to 10.

The objective of qualitative asset valuation is to establish which assets have more value than others. Qualitative valuation gives an organization the ability to see which assets have greater value and which have less value. This can be highly useful in an organization with a lot of assets, as this can provide a view of its high-value assets without the "noise" of comingled lower-valued assets.

Quantitative Asset Valuation

Many organizations opt to surpass qualitative asset valuation and assign a dollar (or other currency) valuation to its assets. This is common in larger or more mature organizations that want to better understand the actual costs that may be associated with loss events.

In a typical quantitative valuation of an asset, its value may be one of the following:

- **Replacement cost**   If the asset is a hardware asset, its valuation might be determined to be the cost of purchasing (and deploying) a replacement. If the asset is a database, its cost might be determined to be the operational costs to restore it from backup or the costs to recover it from its source such as a service provider.

- **Book value**   This represents the value of an asset in the organization's financial system, typically the purchase price less depreciation.

- **Net present value (NPV)**   If the asset directly or indirectly generates revenue, this valuation method may be used.

- **Redeployment cost**   If the asset is a virtual machine, its valuation might be determined to be the cost of setting it up again. This is typically a soft cost if it is set up by internal staff, but it could be a hard cost if another company is hired to redeploy it.

- **Creation or reacquisition cost**   If the asset is a database, its cost might be determined to be the cost of creating it again. If the asset is intellectual property such as software source code, its valuation might be determined to be the effort for developers to re-create it.

- **Consequential financial cost**   If the asset is a database containing sensitive data, its valuation might be measured in the form of financial costs that result from its theft or compromise. While the cost of recovering that database may be relatively low, the consequences of its compromise could cost hundreds of dollars per record. This is a typical cost when measuring the full impact of a breach.

Security managers need to carefully determine the appropriate method for setting the value of each asset. While some instances will be fairly straightforward, others will not. In many cases, an individual asset will have more than a single valuation category described earlier. For example, a credit card database may primarily be valued on its consequential cost (because of the potential fines plus remediation costs associated with consumers who may have been harmed) and also redeployment costs, although in this case this may be a small fraction of the total valuation.

Security managers should document their rationale and method of valuation, particularly for sensitive information assets whose valuations could vary widely depending on the method used. Better yet, larger and more mature organizations will have guidelines that specify methods and formulas to be used in information asset valuation.

Threat Identification

The identification of threats is a key step in a risk assessment. A *threat* is defined as an event that, if realized, would bring harm to an asset and, thus, to the organization.

In the security industry, the key terms involved with risk assessments are often misunderstood and misused. These terms are distinguished from one another in this way: a *threat* is the actual action that would cause harm, not the person or group (generically called an *actor* or *threat actor*) associated with it. A threat is also *not* a weakness that may permit a threat to occur; that is known as a *vulnerability*.

Threats are typically classified as external or internal, as intentional or unintentional, and also as manmade or natural. The origin of many threats is outside the control of the organization but not necessarily out of their awareness. A good security manager can develop a list of threats that are likely (more or less) to occur to any given asset.

When performing a risk assessment, the security manager needs to develop a complete list of threats for use in the risk assessment. Because it's not always possible for a security manager to memorize all possible threats, the security manager may turn to one or more well-known sources of threats, including the following:

- ISO/IEC 27005's Appendix C, "Examples of Typical Threats"
- NIST Special Publication 800-30's Appendix E, "Threat Events"

Upon capturing threat events from one or both of these sources, the security manager may well identify a few additional threats not found in these lists. These additional threats may be specific to the organization's location, business model, or other factors.

A security manager will typically remove a few of the threats from the list that do not apply to the organization. For instance, an organization located far inland is not going to be affected by tsunamis, so this threat source can be eliminated. Similarly, in an organization located in an area not affected by tornados, volcanos, or earthquakes, for instance, these too can be removed.

Internal Threats

Internal threats are those that would originate within the organization. Internal threats are most often associated with employees of the organization, and quite possibly internal employees may be the intentional actors behind these threats.

Security managers need to understand the nature of internal threats and the interaction between personnel and information systems. A wide range of events can take place that constitute threats, including the following:

- Well-meaning personnel making errors in judgment
- Well-meaning personnel making errors in haste
- Well-meaning personnel making errors because of insufficient knowledge or training
- Well-meaning personnel being tricked into doing something harmful
- Disgruntled personnel being purposefully negligent
- Disgruntled personnel deliberately bringing harm to an asset
- A trusted individual in a trusted third-party organization doing any of these

After understanding all the ways that something can go wrong, security managers may sometimes wonder that things can ever proceed as planned!

An important concept for a security manager to understand is this: while employees are at the top of a short list of potential threat actors, employees are the same people who need to be given broad access to sensitive data in order for each of them to do their job and for the organization to function. While there have been marginal improvements in technologies such as data loss prevention (DLP), employers are in a position where they must trust employees by giving them access to virtually all of the organization's information, with the hope that they will not accidentally or deliberately abuse those privileges with potential to cause the organization great harm. Examples of employees gone rogue include the following:

- A network manager in San Francisco who locked all other network personnel out of the network on the claim that no others were competent enough to manage it
- A securities trader at a UK-based brokerage firm who bankrupted the firm through a series of large unauthorized trades
- A systems administrator at an intelligence agency who acquired and leaked thousands of classified documents to the media

A significant factor in employees going rogue is an access control policy that results in individual employees having access to more information than is prudent. That said, increasing the granularity of access controls is known to be time-consuming and costly, and it increases the friction of doing business; few organizations tolerate this despite identified risks.

Table 3-2 contains man-made threats that may be included in an organization's risk assessment.

It may be useful to build a short list of threat actors (the people or groups that would initiate a threat event), but remember that these are not the threats themselves. However, building such a list may help the security manager identify additional threat events that may not be on the list.

Table 3-3 contains a list of internal and external natural threats.

Table 3-2 Internal and External Man-Made Threats

Man-Made Threat
Leak data via e-mail
Leak data via upload to unauthorized system
Leak data via external USB storage device or medium
Leak information face to face to unauthorized person
Perform a programming error
Misconfigure a system or device
Shut down an application, system, or device
Error perpetrated by any internal staff
Respond to phishing attack
Respond to social engineering attack
Share login credential with another person
Install or run unauthorized software program
Copy sensitive data to unauthorized device or system
Destroy or remove sensitive or critical information
Retrieve discarded, recycled, or shredded information
Conduct security scan
Conduct denial-of-service attack
Conduct physical attack on systems or facilities
Conduct credential-guessing attack
Eavesdropping of a sensitive communication
Impersonate another individual
Obtain sensitive information through any illicit means
Cause data integrity loss through any action
Intercept network traffic
Obtain sensitive information through programmatic data leakage
Perform reconnaissance as part of an attack campaign
Conduct a social engineering attack
Power anomaly or failure
Communications failure
Heating, venting, or air-conditioning failure
Degradation of electronic media
Fire
Smoke damage
Fire retardant damage
Flood due to water main break or drainage failure
Vandalism
Demonstrations/protests/picketing
Terrorist attack
Electromagnetic pulse
Explosion
Bombing

Table 3-3 Internal and External Natural Threats

Natural Threat
Forest fire or range fire
Smoke damage from forest fire or range fire
River flood
Landslide
Avalanche
Tornado
Hurricane
Wind storm
Hailstorm
Earthquake
Tsunami
Lightning
Epidemic
Explosion of naturally occurring substances
Solar storm

External Threats

Threats that originate outside of the organization are typically called *external threats*. Like internal threats, these can include both deliberate and accidental actions; further, it includes those that are man-made and those that are associated with naturally occurring events.

The security manager performing a risk assessment needs to understand the full range of threat actors, along with motivations. This is particularly important for organizations where specific types of threat actors or motivations are more common. For example, certain industries such as aerospace and weapons manufacturers attract industrial espionage and intelligence agencies, and certain industries attract hacktivists

Table 3-4 contains a list of external threat actors, and Table 3-5 lists motivations behind these actors.

In a risk assessment, it is essential to identify all threats that have a reasonable likelihood of occurrence. Those threats that are unlikely because of geographical and other conditions are usually excluded. For example, hurricanes can be excluded for locations far from oceans, and earthquakes and volcanos can be excluded from locations where these are not known to occur. Threats such as meteorites and space debris are rarely included in risk assessments because of the minute chance of occurrence.

Advanced Persistent Threats

Advanced persistent threats (APTs) is a term used to describe a particular type of threat actor. An APT, whether an individual or a cybercrime organization, is known for techniques that indicate resourcefulness, patience, and resolve. Rather than employing a "hit-and-run" or "smash-and-grab" operation, an APT will patiently perform reconnaissance on a target and use tools to infiltrate the target and build a long-term presence there.

Table 3-4 External
Threat Actors

External Threat Actors
Former employees
Current and former consultants
Current and former contractors
Competitors
Hacktivists
Personnel in current and former third-party service organizations, vendors, and suppliers
Government intelligence agencies (foreign and domestic)
Criminal organizations (including individuals)
Terrorist groups (including individuals)
Activist groups (including individuals)
Armed forces (including individuals)

Table 3-5 Threat
Actor Motivations

Threat Actor Motivations
Competitive advantage
Economic espionage
Monetary gain
Political gain
Intelligence
Revenge
Ego
Curiosity
Unintentional errors

APT is defined by NIST SP800-39 as follows:

"An APT is an adversary that possesses sophisticated levels of expertise and significant resources which allow it to create opportunities to achieve its objectives using multiple attack vectors (e.g., cyber, physical, and deception). These objectives typically include establishing and extending footholds within the IT infrastructure of the targeted organizations for purposes of exfiltrating information, undermining or impeding critical aspects of a mission, program or organization; or positioning itself to carry out these objectives in the future. The advanced persistent threat: (i) pursues its objectives repeatedly over an extended period of time; (ii) adapts to defenders' efforts to resist it; (iii) is determined to maintain the level of interaction needed to execute its objectives."

The term APT was developed in the early 2000s to describe a new kind of adversary that worked slowly but effectively to compromise a target organization. Prior to APTs, threat actors were unsophisticated and conducted operations that ran for short periods of time, a few days at most. But as more organizations put more valuable information assets online, threat actors became craftier and more resourceful; they resorted to longer-term campaigns to study a target for long periods of time before attacking it, and once an attack began, it would carry on for months or longer. APTs would compromise multiple systems inside the target organization and use a variety of stealthy techniques to establish and maintain a presence using as many compromised targets as possible. Once an APT was discovered (if it was *ever* discovered), the security manager would clean up the compromised target, often not knowing that the APT had compromised many other targets, with not all of them using the same technique.

This cat-and-mouse game could continue for months or even years, with the adversary continuing to compromise targets and study the organization's systems—all the while searching for specific targets—while the security manager and others would continually chase the adversary around like the carnival game of "whack a mole."

 NOTE The term APT is not used as often nowadays, although its definition is largely unchanged. APTs were discussed more often when their techniques were new. But today, there are a multitude of cybercriminal organizations, along with hundreds if not thousands of talented, individual threat actors, whose techniques resemble the APTs of a dozen years ago. Today APTs are not novel but routine.

Emerging Threats

The theater in which cyberwarfare takes place today is constantly changing and evolving. Several forces are at work, as explained in Table 3-6, that continually "push the envelope" in the areas of attack techniques as well as defense techniques.

The subject of emerging threats should be seen as the phenomenon of new techniques, rather than as a fixed set of techniques. Often, the latest techniques are difficult

Phenomenon	Response
Emerging technologies, including bring your own device (BYOD), cloud computing, virtualization, and Internet of Things (IoT)	New targets of opportunity, many of which are poorly guarded when first implemented
Improved technologies (faster processing time)	More rapid compromise of cryptosystems
Improved technologies (faster network speeds)	More rapid exfiltration of larger data sets; easier transport of rainbow tables used to crack hash tables
Improved anti-malware controls	Attack innovation—techniques evaded anti-malware controls

Table 3-6 The Cascade of Emerging Threats

to detect since they fall outside the span of attack techniques that one expects to observe from time to time.

When viewed as the former, emerging threats will always represent the cutting edge of attack techniques that are difficult to detect and/or remediate when they are discovered.

When viewed as the latter, those emerging threats will soon be routine, and even newer threat techniques will exist.

Security managers need to understand that, even as defensive technologies improve that help prevent and/or detect attacks of increasing sophistication, attack techniques will continuously improve in their ability to evade detection by even the most sophisticated defense techniques.

Vulnerability Identification

The identification of vulnerabilities is an essential part of any risk assessment. A *vulnerability* is any weakness in a system that permits an attack to successfully compromise a target system.

In the security industry, the key terms involved with risk assessments are often misunderstood and misused. These terms are distinguished from one another in this way: a *vulnerability* is the weaknesses in a system that could permit an attack to occur. A vulnerability is not the attack vector or technique—this is known as a *threat*.

Vulnerabilities usually take one of these forms:

- **Configuration fault**   A system, program, or component with configuration settings has one or more settings set incorrectly, which could provide an attacker with additional opportunities to compromise a system. For example, the authentication settings on a system may permit an attacker to employ a brute-force password-guessing attack that will not be blunted by target user accounts being automatically locked out.

- **Design fault**   The relationship between components of a system may be arranged in such a way that makes it easier for an attacker to compromise a target system. For instance, an organization may have placed a database server in its DMZ network instead of in its internal network, making it easier for an attacker to identity and attack.

- **Known unpatched weakness**   A system may have one or more vulnerabilities for which security patches are available but not yet installed. For example, a secure communications protocol may have a flaw in the way that an encrypted session is established, which could permit an attacker to easily take over an established communications session. There may be a security patch available for the security flaw, but until the security patch is installed, the flaw exists and may be exploited by any individual who understands the vulnerability and available techniques to exploit it.

  Sometimes, known weaknesses are made public through a disclosure by the system's manufacturer or responsible third party. While there may not be a patch available, there may be other avenues available to mitigate the vulnerability, such as a configuration change in the target system.

- **Undisclosed unpatched weakness**   A system may have vulnerabilities that are known only to the system's manufacturer and that are not publicized. Until an organization using one of these systems learns of the vulnerability via a security bulletin or a news article, the organization can do little to defend itself, short of employing essential security techniques such as system hardening, network hardening, and secure coding.

- **Undiscovered weakness**   Security managers have long accepted the fact that all kinds of information systems have security vulnerabilities that are yet to be discovered, disclosed, and mitigated. The reason for this is that new techniques for attacking systems are being developed, and some of these techniques can exploit weaknesses no one knew to look for. As new techniques have been discovered that involve examining active memory for snippets of sensitive information, system and tool designers can design defense techniques for detecting and even blocking attacks. For example, techniques were developed that would permit an attacker to harvest credit card numbers from PCI-compliant point-of-sale software programs. Soon, effective attacks were developed that enabled cybercriminal organizations to steal tens of millions of credit card numbers from global retail companies.

Vulnerabilities exist everywhere—in software programs, database management systems, operating systems, virtualization platforms, business processes, encryption algorithms, and personnel. As a rule, security managers should consider that every component of every type in every system has both known and unknown vulnerabilities, some of which, if exploited, could result in painful and expensive consequences for the organization. Table 3-7 contains the places where vulnerabilities may exist, together with techniques that can be used to discover at least some of them.

Third-Party Vulnerability Identification

Most organizations outsource at least a portion of their software development and IT operations to third parties. Mainly this occurs through the use of cloud-based applications and services such as SaaS applications, PaaS, and IaaS environments. Many organizations have the misconception that third parties take care of all security concerns in their services. Instead, organizations need to thoroughly understand the security responsibility model for each outsourced service so that organizations understand which portions of security are their responsibility and which are managed by the outsourced service.

Regardless of whether security responsibilities for any given aspect of operations are the burden of the organization or the outsourcing organization, vulnerabilities need to be identified and managed. For aspects of security that are the responsibility of the organization, the organization needs to employ normal means for identifying and managing them. For aspects of security that are the responsibility of the outsourced organization, that organization needs to identify and manage vulnerabilities, and in many cases the outsourced organization will make these activities available to their customers upon request.

Further discussion on the risks identified with third parties appears later in this chapter.

Vulnerability Context	Detection Technique
Network device	Vulnerability scanning Penetration testing Code analysis Network architecture review
Operating system	Vulnerability scanning Penetration testing System architecture review
Database management system	Vulnerability scanning Penetration testing
Software application	Vulnerability scanning Penetration testing Dynamic application scanning Static code scanning Application architecture review
Physical security	Reviews of physical security controls Social engineering assessments Physical penetration testing
Business process	Process review Internal audit Control self-assessment
Personnel	Social engineering assessments Competency assessments Phishing assessments (continual)

Table 3-7   Vulnerabilities and Detection Techniques

Risk Identification

Risk identification is the activity during a risk assessment where various scenarios are studied for each asset. Several considerations are applied in the analysis of each risk, including the following:

- **Threats**   All realistic threat scenarios are examined for each asset to see which ones are likely to occur.

- **Threat actors**   It is important to understand the variety of threat actors and to know which ones are more motivated to target the organization and for what reasons. This further illuminates the likelihood that a given threat scenario will occur.

- **Vulnerabilities**   For each asset, business process, and staff members being examined, vulnerabilities need to be identified. Then, various threat scenarios are examined to see which ones are made more likely because of corresponding vulnerabilities.

- **Asset value**   The value of each asset is an important factor to include in risk analysis. As described in the earlier section on asset value, there are several ways in which assets may be valued. For instance, a customer database may have a modest recovery cost if it is damaged or destroyed; however, if that same customer database is stolen and sold on the black market, the value of the data may be much higher to cybercriminals, and the resulting costs to the organization to mitigate harm done to customers may be higher still. Other ways to examine asset value is through the revenue derived from its existence or use.

- **Impact**   The risk manager examines vulnerabilities, threats (with threat actors), asset value, and estimates the impact of the different threat scenarios. Impact is considered separately from asset value, as there are some threat scenarios that have minimal correlation with asset value but instead are related to reputation damage. Breaches of privacy data can result in high mitigation costs and reduced business. Breaches in hospitals can threaten patient care. Breaches in almost any IoT context can result in extensive service interruptions and life safety issues.

Qualitative and quantitative risk analysis techniques help to distinguish higher risks from lower risks. These techniques are discussed later in this section.

Risks above a certain level are often transferred to a risk register where they will be processed through risk treatment.

Risk, Likelihood, and Impact

During risk analysis in a risk assessment, the risk manager will perform some simple calculations to stratify all of the risks that have been identified. These calculations generally resemble one or more of these:

$$Risk = threats \times vulnerabilities$$
$$Risk = threats \times vulnerabilities \times asset\ value$$
$$Risk = threats \times vulnerabilities \times probabilities$$

ISO/IEC Guide 73, "Risk management – Vocabulary," defines risk as "the combination of the probability of an event and its consequence." This is an excellent way to understand risk in simple, non-numeric terms.

Likelihood

In risk assessments, likelihood is an important dimension that helps a risk manager understand several aspects related to the unfolding of a threat event. Likelihood of a serious security incident has less to do with technical details and more to do with the thought process of an adversary. The considerations related to likelihood include the following:

- **Hygiene**   This is related to an organization's security operations practices, including vulnerability management, patch management, and system hardening. Organizations that do a poor job in these areas are more likely to suffer incidents simply because they are making it easier for adversaries to break in to systems.

- **Visibility**   This is related to the organization's standing: how large and visible the organization is and how much the attacker's prestige will increase when able to successfully compromise a target.

- **Velocity**   This factor is related to the timing of various threat scenarios and whether there is any warning or foreknowledge.

- **Motivation**   Here, it is important to consider various types of adversaries to better understand the factors that would motivate them to attack the organization. It could be about money, reputation, or rivalry.

- **Skill**   For various threat scenarios, what skill level is required to successfully attack the organization? A higher skill level does not always mean an attack is less likely; other considerations such as motivation come into play as well.

Impact

During risk assessments, *impact* is a key attribute of any threat scenario that a risk manager needs to fully understand. In the context of information security, the definition of impact is the actual or expected result from some action such as a threat or disaster.

Impact is perhaps the most important attribute to understand for a threat scenario. A risk assessment can describe all types of threat scenarios, the reasons behind them, and how they can be minimized, but without understanding the impact of threat scenarios, a risk manager cannot determine how important one threat is from another, in terms of the urgency to mitigate the risk.

A wide range of possible impact scenarios include the following:

- Direct cash losses
- Reputation damage
- Loss of business—decrease in sales
- Drop in share price—less access to capital
- Reduction in market share
- Diminished operational efficiency (higher internal costs)
- Civil liability
- Legal liability
- Compliance liability (fines, censures, etc.)
- Interruption of business operations

Some of these impact scenarios are easier to analyze in qualitative terms than others, and the magnitude of most of these is difficult to quantify except in specific threat scenarios.

One of the main tools in the business continuity and disaster planning world, the business impact analysis (BIA) is highly useful for information security managers. A BIA can be conducted as part of a risk assessment or separate from it.

A BIA differs from a risk assessment in this way: while a risk assessment is used to identify risks and, perhaps, suggested remedies, a BIA is used to identify the most critical business processes, together with their supporting IT systems and dependencies on other processes or systems. The value that a BIA brings to a risk assessment is the understanding on which business processes and IT systems are the most important to the organization. For information security managers, the BIA helps the security manager better understand which processes are the most critical and, therefore, which warrant the most protection, all other considerations being equal.

In qualitative risk analysis where probability and impact are rated on simple numeric scales, a risk matrix is sometimes used to portray levels of risk based on probability and impact. Figure 3-4 shows a risk matrix.

Risk Analysis Techniques and Considerations

In a risk assessment, the security manager examines assets, together with associated vulnerabilities and likely threat scenarios. The detailed examination that takes place here is known as *risk analysis*.

Risk analysis considers many dimensions of an asset, including the following:

- Asset value
- Threat scenarios
- Threat probabilities
- Relevant vulnerabilities
- Existing controls and their effectiveness
- Impact

Risk analysis can also consider business criticality, if a BIA is available.

Various risk analysis techniques are discussed in the remainder of this section.

Figure 3-4
Qualitative risk matrix

Probability		Slightly Harmful	Harmful	Extremely Harmful
	Likely	Medium Risk	High Risk	Extreme Risk
	Unlikely	Low Risk	Medium Risk	High Risk
	Highly Unlikely	Insignificant Risk	Low Risk	Medium Risk
		Slightly Harmful	**Harmful**	**Extremely Harmful**
		Consequences		

Gathering Information

A security manager needs to gather a considerable amount of information so that the risk analysis and the risk assessment are valuable and complete. Several sources are available, including the following:

- Interviews with process owners
- Interviews with application developers
- Interviews with security personnel
- Interviews with external security experts
- Security incident records
- Analysis of incidents that occur in other organizations
- Prior risk assessments (caution is advised, however, to stop the propagation of errors from one assessment to the next)

Qualitative Risk Analysis

Most risk analysis begins with qualitative risk analysis. This technique does not seek to identify exact (or even approximate) asset value or impact or the exact probability of occurrence. Instead, these items are expressed as high, medium, or low.

The purpose of qualitative risk analysis is to quickly understand risks relative to one another so that higher risks can be distinguished from lower risks. This is a valuable pursuit because this gives an organization the ability to focus on risks that are more critical, based on impact in qualitative terms.

Semiquantitative Risk Analysis

In qualitative risk analysis, the probability of occurrence can be expressed as a numeric value, such as in the range 1 to 5 (where 5 is the highest probability), and the impact can also be expressed as a numeric value, also in the range 1 to 5. Then, for each asset and for each threat, risk is calculated as probability times impact.

For example, an organization has identified two risk scenarios. The first is a risk of data theft from a customer database; the impact is scored as a 5 (highest), and probability is scored as a 4 (highly likely). The risk is scored as $5 \times 4 = 20$. The second is a risk of theft of application source code; the impact is scored as a 2 (low), and probability is scored as a 2 (less likely). This risk is scored as $2 \times 2 = 4$.

The security manager understands that the data theft risk is a larger risk (scored as 20) as compared to the source code theft risk (scored as 4). These risk scores do not say that the larger risk is five times as likely to occur, nor does it say that it is five times as expensive. It only determines that one risk is higher than the other.

Note that some security managers consider this a qualitative risk analysis, as the results are no more accurate in terms of costs and probabilities than the qualitative technique described earlier.

Quantitative Risk Analysis

In quantitative risk analysis, risk managers are attempting to determine actual costs and probabilities of events. This technique provides more specific information to executives about the actual costs that they can expect to incur in various security event scenarios.

There are two aspects of quantitative risk analysis that prove to be a continuing challenge:

- **Event probability** It is difficult to come up with even an order-of-magnitude estimate on the probability of nearly every event scenario. Even with better information coming from industry sources, the probability of high-impact incidents are dependent upon many factors, some of which are difficult to quantify.

- **Event cost** It is difficult to put an exact cost on any given security incident scenario. Security incidents are complex events that involve many parties and have unpredictable short- and long-term outcomes. Despite improving information from research organizations on the cost of breaches, these are still rough estimates and may not take into account all aspects of cost.

Because of these challenges, quantitative risk analysis should be regarded as an effort to develop estimates, not exact figures. Partly this is because risk analysis is a measure of events that may occur, not a measure of events that *do* occur.

Standard quantitative risk analysis involves the development of several figures:

- **Asset value (AV)** This is the value of the asset, which is usually (but not necessarily) the asset's replacement value. Depending on the type of asset, different values may need to be considered.

- **Exposure factor (EF)** This is the financial loss that results from the realization of a threat, expressed as a percentage of the asset's total value. Most threats do not completely eliminate the asset's value; instead, they reduce its value. For example, if an organization's $120,000 server is rendered unbootable because of malware, the server will still have salvage value, even if that is only 10 percent of the asset's value. In this case, the EF would be 90 percent. Note that different threats will have different impacts on EF because the realization of different threats will cause varying amounts of damage to assets.

- **Single loss expectancy (SLE)** This value represents the financial loss when a threat scenario occurs one time. SLE is defined as AV × EF. Note that different threats have a varied impact on EF, so those threats will also have the same multiplicative effect on SLE.

- **Annualized rate of occurrence (ARO)** This is an estimate of the number of times that a threat will occur per year. If the probability of the threat is 1 in 50 (one occurrence every 50 years), then ARO is expressed as 0.02. However, if the threat is estimated to occur four times per year, then ARO is 4.0. Like EF and SLE, ARO will vary by threat.

- **Annualized loss expectancy (ALE)** This is the expected annualized loss of asset value due to threat realization. ALE is defined as SLE × ARO.

ALE is based upon the verifiable values AV, EF, and SLE, but because ARO is only an estimate, ALE is only as good as ARO. Depending upon the value of the asset, the risk manager may need to take extra care to develop the best possible estimate for ARO, based upon whatever data is available. Sources for estimates include the following:

- History of event losses in the organization
- History of similar losses in other organizations
- History of dissimilar losses
- Best estimates based on available data

When performing a quantitative risk analysis for a given asset, the ALE for all threats can be added together. The sum of all ALEs is the annualized loss expectancy for the total array of threats. A particularly high sum of ALEs would mean that a given asset is confronted with a lot of significant threats that are more likely to occur. But in terms of risk treatment, ALEs are better off left as separate and associated with their respective threats.

OCTAVE

Operationally Critical Threat Asset and Vulnerability Evaluation (OCTAVE) is a risk analysis approach developed by Carnegie Mellon University. The latest version is known as OCTAVE Allegro and is used to assess information security risks so that an organization can obtain meaningful results from a risk assessment.

The OCTAVE Allegro methodology uses eight steps:

- **Step 1: Establish risk measurement criteria**   Here, the organization identifies the most important impact areas. The impact areas in the model include *reputation/customer confidence, financial, productivity, safety and health, fines/legal penalties,* and *other.* For example, reputation may be the most important impact area for one organization, while privacy or safety may be the most important for others.

- **Step 2: Develop an information asset profile**   The organization identifies its in-scope information assets and develops a profile for these assets that describe its features, qualities, characteristics, and value.

- **Step 3: Identify information asset containers**   The organization identifies all the internal and external information systems that store, process, and transmit in-scope assets. Note that many of these systems may be operated by third-party organizations.

- **Step 4: Identify areas of concern**   This is the start of identifying threats that, if realized, could cause harm to information assets. Typically, this is identified in a brainstorming activity.

- **Step 5: Identify threat scenarios**   This is a continuation of step 4, where threat scenarios are expanded upon (and unlikely ones eliminated). A threat tree may be developed that first identifies actors and basic scenarios and then is expanded to include more details.

- **Step 6: Identify risks**   A continuation of step 5, the consequences of each threat scenario are identified.

- **Step 7: Analyze risks**   This is a simple quantitative measure that is used to score each threat scenario based on risk criteria developed in step 1. The output is a ranked list of risks.

- **Step 8: Select mitigation approach**   A continuation of step 7, the risks with higher scores are analyzed to determine methods available for risk reduction.

The OCTAVE Allegro methodology includes worksheets for each of the steps here, making it easy for a person or team to perform a risk analysis based on this technique.

Further information about OCTAVE Allegro is available at www.cert.org/resilience/products-services/octave/.

Other Risk Analysis Methodologies

Additional risk analysis methodologies provide more complex approaches that may have usefulness for certain organizations or in selected risk situations:

- **Delphi method**   Here, questionnaires are distributed to a panel of experts in two or more rounds. A facilitator will anonymize the responses and distribute them to the experts. The objective is for the experts to converge on the most important risks and mitigation strategies.

- **Event tree analysis (ETA)**   Derived from the fault tree analysis method (described next), ETA is a logic-modeling technique for analysis of success and failure outcomes given a specific event scenario, in this case a threat scenario.

- **Fault tree analysis (FTA)**   This is a logical modeling technique used to diagram all the consequences for a given event scenario. FTA begins with a specific scenario and proceeds forward in time with all possible consequences. A large "tree" diagram can result that depicts many different chains of events.

- **Monte Carlo analysis**   Derived from Monte Carlo computational algorithms, this analysis begins with a given system with inputs, where the inputs are constrained to minimum, likely, and maximum values. Running the simulation provides some insight into actual likely scenarios.

Risk Evaluation and Ranking

Upon completion of a risk assessment when all risks have been identified and scored, the security manager, together with others in the organization, will begin to analyze the results and begin to develop a going-forward strategy.

Risks can be evaluated singly, but the organization will better benefit from analysis of all the risks together. The reason for this is that many risks are interrelated, and the right combination of mitigation strategies can result in many risks having been adequately treated.

The results of a risk assessment should be analyzed in several different ways, including the following:

- Looking at all risks by business unit or service line

- Looking at all risks by asset type

- Looking at all risks by activity type

- Looking at all risks by type of consequence

Because no two organizations (or their risk assessment results) are alike, this type of analysis is likely to identify themes of risk treatment that may have broad implications across many risks. For example, an organization may have several tactical risks all associated with access management and vulnerability management. Rather than treating individual tactical risks, a better approach might be to improve or reorganize the access or vulnerability management programs from the top down, resulting in many identified risks being mitigated in a programmatic fashion. Organizations need to consider not just the details in a risk assessment but the big picture.

Another type of risk to look for is a risk with low probability of occurrence and high impact. This is typically the type of risk treated by transfer. Risk transfer most often comes in the form of cyber-risk insurance but also in security monitoring when it includes indemnification.

Risk Ownership

When considering the results of a risk assessment, the organization needs to assign individual risks to individual people, typically middle- to upper-management leaders. These leaders, who should also have ownership of controls that operate within their span of control, have budget, staff, and other resources used in daily business operations. These are the risk owners and, to the extent that there is a formal policy or statement on risk tolerance or risk appetite, should be the people making risk treatment decisions for risks in their domain. To the extent that these individuals are accountable for operations in their part of the organization, they should also be responsible for risk decisions, including risk treatment, in their operational areas. A simple concept to approach risk ownership is that if nobody owns the risk, then nobody is accountable for managing the risk, which will lead to a great probability of the risk becoming an active issue with negative impacts on the business, along with the possible identification of a scapegoat who will be blamed if an event occurs.

Risk Treatment

After a risk assessment has been completed, management can view reports and other information that lists risks that have been identified and explained. This is the point where the organization has completed identifying risks and begins to determine what should be done about those risks. The decisions and the activities that follow are known as *risk treatment*. A key element in deciding the appropriate risk treatment is ensuring the right people at the right level of the organization are actively involved in deciding upon the risk treatment. This is achieved by having a formalized risk management program in place that includes all the key elements of a good program that are outlined in this chapter.

In a general sense, risk treatment represents the actions that take place that the organization undertakes to reduce risk to an acceptable level. More specifically, for each risk identified in a risk assessment, there are four actions that an organization can take:

- Risk acceptance
- Risk mitigation
- Risk avoidance
- Risk transfer

These four actions are explained in more detail in the following sections.

There is a fifth potential action—or, rather, *inaction*—related to risk treatment, known as *ignoring the risk*. A potentially dangerous undertaking, ignoring a risk amounts to the organization pretending that the risk does not exist. In this case, the organization has unofficially accepted the risk and is responsible if the risk becomes an issue. By unofficially accepting the risk and not assigning a risk owner, the organization is possibly increasing the impact and likelihood of the risk evolving into an incident.

The preceding matter of ignoring a known risk is different from an organization's *ignoring an unknown risk*. This is usually a result of a risk assessment or risk analysis that is not sufficiently thorough to identify all relevant risks. The best solution for these "unknown unknowns" is to have an external, competent firm perform an organization's risk assessment every few years or for such an organization to thoroughly examine an organization's risk assessment for the purpose of discovering opportunities for improvement, including expanding the span of threats, threat actors, and vulnerabilities so that there are fewer or no unknown risks.

Risk Acceptance   Risk acceptance is one of the four choices that the organization may take for any identified risk. *Risk acceptance* is defined as a decision whereby the organization finds the presence of a risk as acceptable and that it requires no reduction or mitigation.

If only risk acceptance were this simple. Further analysis of risk acceptance shows that there are conditions under which an organization will elect to accept risk:

- The cost of risk mitigation is greater than the value of the asset being protected.
- The impact of compromise is low, or the value or classification of the asset is low.

Organizations may elect to establish a framework for risk acceptance, as shown in Table 3-8.

When an organization accepts a risk, instead of closing the matter for perpetuity, the organization should review the risk at least annually. These are reasons for revisiting an accepted risk:

- The value of the asset may have changed during the year.
- The value of the business activity related to the asset may have changed during the year.

Risk Level	Level Required to Accept
Low	Chief information officer (CIO) or manager of information security
Medium	CISO or director of information security
High	CEO, COO, or president
Severe	Board of directors

Table 3-8   Framework for Risk Acceptance

- The potency of threats may have changed during the year, potentially leading to a higher risk rating.

- The cost of mitigation may have changed during the year, potentially leading to greater feasibility for risk mitigation or transfer.

As with other risk treatment activities, detailed record keeping helps the security manager better track matters such as risk assessment review.

Risk Mitigation   Risk mitigation is one of four choices that an organization can take when confronted with a risk. *Risk mitigation* is defined as a decision to reduce the risk through some means, such as by changing a process or procedure, by changing how a security control functions, or by adding a security control.

Risk mitigation is generally chosen when management understands that performing risk mitigation costs less than the value of the asset being protected. Sometimes, however, an asset's value is difficult to measure, or there may be a high degree of goodwill associated with the asset. For example, the value of a customer database that contains sensitive data including bank account or credit card information may itself be low; however, the impact of a breach of this database may be higher than its book value because of the loss of business or negative publicity that may result.

Risk mitigation may, at times, result in a task that can be carried out in a relatively short period of time. However, risk mitigation may also involve one or more major projects that start in the future, perhaps in the next budget year or many months or quarters in the future. Further, such a project may be delayed, its scope may change, or it may be canceled altogether. For this reason, the security manager needs to carefully monitor risk mitigation activities to ensure they are completed as originally agreed so that the risk mitigation is not forgotten.

Risk Avoidance   Risk avoidance is one of four choices that an organization takes to address a risk. *Risk avoidance* is defined as a decision to discontinue that activity that precipitates the risk.

Often, risk avoidance is selected in response to an activity that was not formally approved in the first place. For example, a risk assessment may have identified a department's use of an external service provider that represented measurable risk to the organization. The service provider may or may not have been formally vetted in the first place. Regardless, after the risk is identified in a risk assessment (or by other means), if risk avoidance is selected, the organization chooses to cease activities with that service provider.

Risk Transfer   Risk transfer is one of the choices available to an organization to address a risk. *Risk transfer* is defined as a decision to employ an external organization to accept the risk.

Risk transfer is selected when an organization does not have the operational or financial capacity to accept the risk and where risk mitigation is not the best choice.

In risk transfer, an organization may have identified a significant financial risk related to a breach of its most sensitive data. The risk transfer decision in this case may involve the purchase of cyber-risk insurance that would offset the costs associated with such a breach. A risk transfer decision may also involve the purchase of an incident response retainer, which is essentially the prepurchase of incident response services in the event of a breach.

A risk assessment may reveal the absence of security monitoring of a critical system. Another form of risk transfer involves the use of an external security services provider to perform monitoring of the critical system.

Residual Risk   When an organization undergoes risk treatment for risks that it identifies, in most cases the risk treatment does not eliminate the risk entirely but instead reduces the risk to some degree. *Residual risk* is defined as the risk that remains after risk treatment is applied.

Some organizations approach risk treatment and residual risk improperly. They identify a risk, employ some risk treatment, and then fail to understand the residual risk, but instead they close the risk matter. A better way to approach risk is to analyze the residual risk as though it were a new risk and apply risk treatment to the residual risk. This iterative process provides organizations with an opportunity to revisit residual risk and make new risk treatment decisions about it. Ultimately, after one or more iterations, the residual risk will be accepted, and finally the matter can be closed.

For instance, a security manager identifies a risk in its access management system where multifactor authentication is not used. This is considered a high risk, and the IT department implements a multifactor authentication solution. When security managers reassess the access management system, they find that multifactor authentication is required in some circumstances but not in others. A new risk is identified, at perhaps a lower level of risk than the original risk. But the organization once again has an opportunity to examine the risk and make a decision about it. It may improve the access management system further by requiring multifactor authentication in more cases than before, which further reduces risk, which should be examined again for further risk treatment opportunities. Finally, the risk will be accepted as is when the organization is satisfied that the risk has been sufficiently reduced.

In addition to the risk treatment life cycle, subsequent risk assessments and other activities will identify risks that represent residual risk from earlier risk treatment activities. And over time, the nature of residual risk may change, based on changing threats, vulnerabilities, or business practices, resulting in an originally acceptable residual risk that is no longer acceptable.

Controls

A common outcome of risk treatment, when mitigation is chosen, is the enactment of controls. Put another way, when an organization identifies a risk in a risk assessment, the organization might decide to develop (or improve) a control that will mitigate the risk that was found.

For example, an organization found that its procedures for terminating access for departing employees were resulting in a lot of user accounts not being deactivated. The existing control was a simple, open-loop procedure where analysts were instructed to deactivate user accounts. Often they were deactivating user accounts late or not at all. To reduce this risk, the organization modified the procedure (updated the control) by introducing a step where a second person would verify all account terminations on a daily basis.

Controls are measures put in place to ensure a desired outcome. Controls can come in the form of procedures, or they can be implemented directly in a system. There are many categories and types of controls, as well as standard control frameworks. All of this is discussed in great detail in Chapter 4.

Legal and Regulatory Considerations

Organizations in many industries are subject to regulatory and legal requirements. Many organizations are also duty bound through legal agreements between companies. Many of these legal obligations involve the topic of data protection, data privacy, and data usage.

This theme concerning data protection, privacy, and usage manifests itself in so many forms that it would fill volumes of works, and for information security professionals it would not be that interesting to read. But there are some common approaches to these regulations:

- **Mandatory protective measures**   Many laws, regulations, and private legal obligations require organizations to enact a variety of specific measures to protect information. Typically, these measures are required to be in place, regardless of the reduction of actual risk in any specific organization, simply because the law or regulation says so. A good example of this is the Payment Card Industry Data Security Standard (PCI-DSS), which requires any organization that stores, processes, or transmits credit card data to implement a large set of controls. PCI-DSS makes no provision for whether any particular control is actually going to reduce risk in any specific organization. Instead, all the controls are required all of the time in every such organization.

- **Optional protective measures**   Some laws, regulations, and other legal obligations include a number of specific protective measures, which the organization *could* choose not to implement. For example, the U.S. Health Insurance Portability and Accountability Act (HIPAA) lists required controls and "addressable" controls. In most cases, the organization would be required to have a formal, valid business reason why any optional measures are not implemented.

- **Mandatory risk assessments**   Some laws, regulations, and legal obligations require organizations to perform risk assessments, but many do not require specific actions to take place as a result of those risk assessments. For instance, the Payment Card Industry Data Security Standard (PCI-DSS) requires organizations to perform annual risk assessments (in requirement 12.2), but nowhere does PCI-DSS permit an organization to opt out of any PCI-DSS control because of the absence of risk.

Another facet of concern related to laws, regulations, and other legal obligation is the concept of compliance risk. *Compliance risk* is defined as any risk associated with any general or specific consequences of not being compliant with a law, regulation, or private legal obligation. Compliance risk takes on two forms:

- An organization may be out of compliance with a specific law, regulation, or obligation because of the absence of a protective measure, whose absence could lead to a security incident that could bring fines and other sanctions from regulators or other organizations, or civil lawsuits from injured parties.

- An organization that is out of compliance with a specific law, regulation, or obligation could incur fines and other sanctions simply because of the noncompliant condition, regardless of the level of actual risk. Another way to describe this is that an organization can get into trouble with regulators or other bodies simply because they are not in compliance with a specific legal requirement, regardless of the presence or absence of any actual risk.

Security managers sometimes fail to understand a business strategy in which executive management chooses to pay fines instead of bringing their organizations into compliance with a law or regulation. Fines or other sanctions may have a lesser impact on the organization than the cost and effort to be compliant. At times, security managers and other security professionals may feel that they are in an ethical dilemma if their professional codes of conduct require them to obey the law.

Costs and Benefits

As organizations ponder options for risk treatment (and in particular, risk mitigation), they generally will consider the costs of the mitigating steps and the expected benefits they may receive. When an organization understands the costs and benefits of risk mitigation, this helps them develop strategies that are either more cost effective or result in greater cost avoidance.

There are several cost- and benefit-related considerations that an organization needs to understand when weighing mitigation options, including the following:

- **Change in threat probability**   Organizations need to understand how a mitigating control changes the probability of threat occurrence and what that means in terms of cost reduction and avoidance.

- **Change in threat impact**   Organizations need to understand the change in the impact of a mitigated threat in terms of an incident's reduced costs and avoided costs versus the cost of the mitigation.

- **Change in operational efficiency**   Aside from the direct cost of the mitigating control, organizations need to understand the impact on the mitigating control on other operations. For instance, adding code review steps to a software development process may mean that the development organization may complete fewer fixes and enhancements in a given period of time.

- **Total cost of ownership (TCO)**   When an organization considers a mitigation plan, the best approach is to understand its total cost of ownership, which may include costs for the following:
  - Acquisition
  - Deployment and implementation
  - Recurring maintenance
  - Testing and assessment
  - Compliance monitoring and enforcement
  - Reduced throughput of controlled processes
  - Training
  - End-of-life decommissioning

While weighing costs and benefits, organizations need to keep in mind several things:

- Estimating the probability of any particular threat is difficult, particularly infrequent, high-impact events like large-scale data thefts.
- Estimating the impact of any particular threat is difficult, especially those infrequent, high-impact events.

In other words, the precision of cost–benefit analysis is no better than estimates of event probability and impact.

An old adage in information security states that an organization would not spend $20,000 to protect a $10,000 asset. While that may be true in some cases, there is more to consider than just the replacement (or depreciated) value of the asset. For example, loss of the asset could result in an embarrassing and costly public relations debacle, or that asset may play a key role in the organization's earning hundreds of thousands of dollars in revenue each month.

Still, the principle of proportionality is valid and is often a good starting point for making cost-conscious decisions on risk mitigation. The principle of proportionality is described in generally accepted security systems principles (GASSPs) and in section 2.5 of the generally accepted information security principles (GAISPs).

Operational Risk Management

Operational risk management is concerned with financial losses and survival of an organization. *Operational risk* is defined as the risk of loss resulting from failed controls, processes, and systems; internal and external events; and other occurrences that impact business operations and threaten an organization's survival.

Organizations generally establish recovery objectives, which are time intervals associated with business resilience and recovery from security and disaster events. Particular attention is paid to the risks associated with third parties, primarily because it is more difficult to obtain usable risk information.

The key business record in risk management is the risk register, which is a log of historic and newly identified risks. Also known as a *risk ledger,* a risk register contains risk metadata about each risk that helps security managers and executives understand all of the organization's risks, including information that helps them understand which risks are more serious than others, which are associated with various business activities, and other means of categorization that are useful to the organization.

The risk management process is not isolated but instead is integrated into several other business processes throughout the organization.

Risk Management Objectives

Risk managers typically use a variety of risk management objectives that help them determine the resources required to continue business operations in the face of many different types of events that may occur. These objectives mainly represent time intervals related to the availability and recovery of business services after some security incident or disaster has occurred.

Executive management participates in, or has final approval over, the establishment of risk management objectives since the values of those objectives translate directly into one-time and operational costs associated with event readiness. Executives generally seek a balance between the potential costs associated with significant security and disaster events, with the costs required to establish specific levels of business resilience.

Recovery Time Objective

Recovery time objective (RTO) is defined as the period of time from the onset of an outage until the resumption of service. The purpose of an RTO is to establish a measurable interval of time, during which the necessary activities for recovering or resuming business operations must take place.

Various business processes in an organization will have different RTO targets. Further, some business processes will have RTOs that vary according to business cycles on a daily, week, monthly, or annual basis. For instance, point-of-sale terminals may have a short RTO during peak business hours, a longer RTO during less busy hours, and a still longer RTO when the business is closed. Similarly, financial and payroll systems will have RTOs that are shorter during times of critical processing, such as payroll cycles and financial month end.

RTOs, data classification, and asset classification are all interrelated. Business processes with shorter RTOs are likely to have data and assets that are classified as more operationally critical.

When establishing RTOs, security managers typically interview personnel in middle management, as well as senior and executive management. Security managers will observe that personnel at different levels of responsibility will have different perspectives on the criticality of business functions. Ultimately, it is executive management that will prioritize business functions across the entire organization. As a result, any particular business function prioritized at one level by a middle manager may be classified as higher or lower by executives. Ultimately, it is executive prioritization that will prevail. For example, a middle manager in the accounting department may assert that accounts payable is the most critical business activity because external service providers will stop providing service if they are not paid. But executives, who have control over the entire organization, stipulate that customer service is the most critical business function since the organization's future revenue depends on the quality of care they receive every day.

RTOs are established by conducting a business impact analysis. A BIA helps the security manager better understand the criticality of business processes, their resource dependencies and interdependencies, and the costs associated with interruptions in service.

RTOs are a cornerstone objective in business continuity planning (BCP). Once RTOs are established for a particular business function, contingency plans that support the RTO can be established. While shorter RTOs are most often associated with higher costs, organizations generally seek a break-even point where the cost of recovery is the same as the cost of interruption for the period of time associated with the RTO.

Recovery Point Objective

Recovery point objective (RPO) is defined as the period of acceptable data loss due to an incident or disaster. Generally, this equates to the maximum period of time between backups or data replication intervals. RPO is generally measured in minutes or hours, and like RTO, shorter RPO targets typically are associated with higher costs.

RPOs represent a different aspect of service quality, as any amount of data loss represents required rework. For example, if an organization receives invoices that are entered into the accounts payable system, an RPO of four hours means that up to four hours of rekeying would be required in the event of an incident or disaster.

RPOs are a key objective in business continuity planning. When RPOs are established, contingency plans can be developed that will help the organization meet its RPO targets.

Recovery Capacity Objective

Recovery capacity objective (RCapO) is defined as the capacity of a temporary or recovery process, as compared to the normal process. In the event of any incident or disaster that results in the organization switching to a temporary or recovery process or system, the capacity of that temporary or recovery process or system may be less than that used during normal business operations.

For example, in the event of a communications outage, cashiers in a retail location will hand-write sales receipts, which may take more time than the use of point-of-sale terminals. The manual process might mean cashiers can process 80 percent as much work.

Organizations often do not need their temporary processes or systems to work at 100 percent of the capacity as their normal operations processes and systems. Having a backup capacity of 100 percent may cost more and will seldom be used.

Service Delivery Objective

Service delivery objective (SDO) is defined as the level or quality of service that is required after an event, as compared to business normal operations. Depending on the nature of the business process in question, SDO might be measured in transaction throughput, service quality, response time, available capabilities and features, or something else.

SDO, RTO, RPO, and RCapO are all related to each other. Organizations are free to construct recovery target models in ways that work for them. One organization might start with SDOs and derive appropriate RTO, RPO, and RCapO targets, but others might start with RTO and RPO and figure out their SDOs.

Maximum Tolerable Downtime

Maximum tolerable downtime (MTD) is defined as a theoretical time period, measured from the onset of a disaster, after which the organization's ongoing viability would be at risk. Organizations undergoing risk analysis sometimes start with this metric and then derive recovery targets such as RTO, RPO, and RCapO.

Maximum tolerable downtime is also known as *acceptable interruption window (AIW)*.

It would be a mistake to call MTD a target, but sometimes it is referred to as a target. It would be better to consider MTD as an arbitrary "point-of-no-return" time value.

Executives should ultimately determine MTD targets for various critical business functions in their organization; there is often not a single MTD target for the entire organization, but usually an MTD for each major function. For example, an online merchandiser might establish an MTD of 7 days for its online ordering function and 28 days for its payroll function. If the organization's ability to earn revenue is incapacitated for seven days, in the opinion of its executives, its business will suffer so greatly that the organization itself may fail. However, the organization could tolerate an MTD of four weeks for its payroll system, as enough employees are likely to tolerate a lengthy payroll outage that the organization will survive. After four weeks, enough employees may abandon their jobs that the organization will be unable to continue operations.

MTD is generally used for business continuity planning purposes. However, as some operational and security incidents can, when severe enough, become a disaster, MTD is also considered in information risk management planning.

Maximum Tolerable Outage

Maximum tolerable outage (MTO), sometimes known as *maximum acceptable outage (MAO),* is defined as the maximum period of time that an organization can tolerate operating in recovery (or alternate processing) mode. This metric comes into play in situations where an organization's recovery mode is unlike its normal business operations and not viable for long-term business operations.

For instance, an organization produces online advertising that is specially targeted to individual users based on known characteristics about those users. The targeting is a feature that makes the organization competitive in the online ad market. In recovery mode, the organization's system lacks several key targeting capabilities; in the long run, the organization would not be competitive and could not sustain business operations in the long term in such a state. This organization has set its MTO at 48 hours. Running in alternate processing mode for more than 48 hours would result in lost revenue and losses in market share.

Like MTD, MTO is not a target, but when MTO is set, then recovery targets such as RTO, RPO, and RCapO can be established.

Service Level Agreements

A *service level agreement (SLA)* is a written agreement that specifies service levels in terms of the quantity of work, quality, timeliness, and remedies for shortfalls in quality or quantity. Service level agreements are typically established in operational processes and systems. In the context of risk management, SLAs may be established for activities in risk management and risk treatment processes, such as the maximum elapsed time for notifications about new risks, or the timeliness of communications about recent risk treatment decisions.

Risk Management and Business Continuity Planning

The two disciplines, risk management and business continuity planning, are focused on identifying risks that may adversely impact the organization's operations. Risk management and business continuity planning have several common characteristics and goals:

- Risk management and business continuity planning both seek to discover risks and develop remedies for events that threaten business operations and the ongoing viability of an organization.

- Risk management and business continuity planning rely on risk assessments to identify risks that will require mitigation.

- Risk management and business continuity planning can rely on the results of a business impact analysis to better understand the criticality of business processes and the interdependency of processes and assets.

- Risk management identifies threats that, if unchecked, could unfold into disaster scenarios.

- Many of the threat scenarios in a risk assessment are disaster situations used in business continuity planning.

Third-Party Risk Management

Third-party risk management (TPRM) refers to activities used to discover and manage risks associated with external organizations performing operational functions for an organization. Many organizations outsource some of their information processing to third-party organizations, often in the form of cloud-based software as a service (SaaS) and platform as a service (PaaS), for economic reasons: it is less expensive to pay for software in a leasing arrangement as opposed to developing, implementing, and maintaining software internally.

Third-party risk management is the extension of techniques used to identify and treat risk within an organization to include risks present in third parties that represent risks within the organization itself. The discipline of third-party risk exists because of the complexities associated with identifying risks in third-party organizations, as well as risks inherent in doing business with specific third parties. At the core, third-party risk is like other risk management, but the difference lies in the solicitation of information to identify risks outside of the organization's direct control.

Cloud Service Providers

Organizations moving to cloud-based environments often assumed that those cloud service providers took care of many or all information security functions, when often this is not the case at all. The result has been innumerable breaches, often a result of each party believing that the other was performing key data protection tasks. The cause of this is that most organizations are unfamiliar with the shared responsibility model that delineates which party is responsible for which operations and security functions. Tables 3-9 and 3-10 depict shared responsibility models in terms of operations and security, respectively.

Component	On-Premise	IaaS	PaaS	SaaS
Applications	Org	Org	Org	Provider
Data	Org	Org	Org	Provider
Runtime	Org	Org	Provider	Provider
Middleware	Org	Org	Provider	Provider
Operating system	Org	Org	Provider	Provider
Virtualization	Org	Provider	Provider	Provider
Servers	Org	Provider	Provider	Provider
Storage	Org	Provider	Provider	Provider
Networking	Org	Provider	Provider	Provider
Data center	Org	Provider	Provider	Provider

Table 3-9 Cloud Services Operational Shared Responsibility Model

Activity	On-Premise	IaaS	PaaS	SaaS
Human resources	Org	Shared	Shared	Provider
Application security	Org	Org	Shared	Provider
Identity and access management	Org	Org	Shared	Provider
Log management	Org	Org	Shared	Provider
System monitoring	Org	Org	Shared	Provider
Data encryption	Org	Org	Shared	Provider
Host intrusion detection	Org	Org	Shared	Provider
Host hardening	Org	Org	Shared	Provider
Asset management	Org	Org	Shared	Provider
Network intrusion detection	Org	Org	Provider	Provider
Network security	Org	Org	Provider	Provider
Security policy	Org	Shared	Shared	Provider
Physical security	Org	Provider	Provider	Provider

Table 3-10 Cloud Services Security Shared Responsibility Model

Note that the values in Tables 3-9 and 3-10 are not absolutely consistent across different service providers. Instead, these tables serve to illustrate the nature of shared responsibilities between an organization and its service providers. The specific responsibilities for operations and security between an organization and any specific service provider may vary somewhat from these tables. It is vital that an organization clearly understand its precise responsibilities for each third-party relationship so that no responsibilities are overlooked or neglected; doing so may introduce risks to the organization's operations and/or security. The organization is ultimately responsible for ensuring that specific areas are addressed, as it will be the organization that will be held responsible in the eye of shareholders, board of directors, and customers if a breach occurs.

TPRM has been the subject of many standards and regulations that compel organizations to proactively discover risks present in the operations of their critical third parties. Historically, many organizations were not voluntarily assessing their critical third parties. Statistical data about breaches over several years have revealed that more than half of all breaches have a nexus in third parties. This statistic has illuminated the magnitude of the third-party risk problem and has resulted in the enactment of laws and regulations in many industries that now require organizations to build and operate effective third-party risk programs in their organizations. This has also garnered innovation in the form of new tools, platforms, and services that help organizations manage third-party risk more effectively.

TPRM Life Cycle

The management of business relationships with third parties is a life-cycle process. The life cycle begins when an organization contemplates the use of a third party to augment or support the organization's operations in some way. The life cycle continues during the ongoing relationship with the third party and concludes when the organization no longer requires the third party's services.

Initial Assessment   Prior to the establishment of a business relationship, an organization will assess and evaluate the third party for suitability. Often this evaluation is competitive, where two or more third parties are vying for the formal relationship. During the evaluation, the organization will require that each third party provide information describing its services, generally in a structured manner through a request for information (RFI) or a request for proposal (RFP).

In their RFIs and RFPs, an organization often includes sections on security and privacy so that the organization can better understand how each third party protects the organization's information. This, together with information about the services themselves, pricing, and other information, reveals details that the organization uses to select the third party that will provide services.

Legal Agreement   Before services can commence, the organization and the third party will negotiate a legal agreement that describes the services provided, along with service levels, quality, pricing, and other terms found in typical legal agreements. Based on the details discovered in the assessment phase, the organization can develop a section in the legal agreement that addresses security and privacy. This part of the legal agreement will typically cover these subjects:

- **Security and/or privacy program**   Require the third party to have a formal security and/or privacy program including but not limited to governance, policy, risk management, annual risk assessment, internal audit, vulnerability management, incident management, secure development, security awareness training, data protection, and third-party risk.

- **Security and/or privacy controls**   Require the third party to have a control framework, including linkages to risk management and internal audit.

- **Vulnerability assessments**   Require the third party to undergo penetration tests or vulnerability assessments of its service infrastructure and applications, performed by a competent security professional services firm of the organization's choosing (or a company that the organization and third party jointly agree upon), with reports made available to the organization upon request.

- **External audits and certifications**   Require the third party to undergo annual SOC1 and/or SOC 2 Type 2 audits, ISO 27001 certifications, HITRUST certifications, PCI ROCs, or other industry-recognized and applicable external audits, with reports made available to the organization upon request.

- **Security incident response**   Require the third party to have a formal security incident capability that includes testing and training.

- **Security incident notification**   Require the third party to notify the organization in the event of a suspected and confirmed breach, within a specific time frame, typically 24 hours. The language around "suspected" and "confirmed" needs to be developed carefully so that the third party cannot sidestep this responsibility.

- **Right to audit**   Require the third party to permit the organization to conduct an audit of the third-party organization without cause. If the third party does not want to permit this, one fallback position is to insist on the right to audit in the event of a suspected or confirmed breach or other circumstances. Further, include the right to have a competent security professional services firm perform an audit of the third-party security environment on behalf of the organization (useful for several reasons, including geographic location and that the external audit firm will be more objective). The cost of the audit is usually paid for by the organization, and in some cases the organization will provide credits or compensation to the third parry for the time incurred by the third party's team.

- **Periodic review**   Require the third party to permit an annual on-site review of its operations and security. This can give the organization greater confidence in the third party's security and operations.

- **Annual due diligence**   Require the third party to respond to annual questionnaires and evidence requests as part of the organization's third-party risk program.

- **Cyber insurance**   Require the third party to carry a cyber-insurance policy with minimum coverage levels. Require the third party to comply with all requirements in the policy so that the policy will pay out in the event of a security event. A great option is to have the organization be a named beneficiary on the policy, in the event there is a widespread breach that could result in a large payout to many customers.

Organizations with many third parties might consider developing a standard security clause that includes all of the previous provisions. Then, when a new third-party service organization is being considered, the organization's security team can perform its up-front examination of the third party's security environment and then make adjustments to the security clause as needed.

Organizations vetting third parties will often find one or more shortcomings in the third party's security program that it is unwilling or unable to remediate right away. There are still options: the organization can compel the third party to enact improvements in a reasonable period of time after the start of the business relationship. For example, a third-party service provider might not have an external audit such as a SOC1 or SOC2 audit but could agree to undergo such an audit one year in the future. Or, a third-party service provider that has never had external penetration testing performed could be compelled to begin having penetration testing performed at regular intervals. Alternatively, the third party could be required to undergo a penetration test and be required to remediate all Critical and High issues before the organization will begin using the third party's services.

Classifying Third Parties   Organizations utilizing third parties often find that there is a wide range of risk among the third parties. Some third parties may have access to large volumes of operationally critical or highly sensitive data, while others may have access to small volumes of important data, and still others do not access data or associated with critical operations at all. Because of this wide span of risk levels, many organizations choose to develop a scheme consisting of levels of risk, based on criteria important to the organization. Typically, this risk scheme will have two to four risk levels, with each third party assigned to a risk level.

Organizations need to periodically assess their third parties to ensure that they remain in the right level of classification. Third parties that provide a variety of services may initially be classified as low risk; but in the future, if the third party is retained to provide additional services, this could result in the third party being reclassified at a higher level of risk.

The purpose of this classification is explained in the following sections on using questionnaires and assessing third parties.

Questionnaires and Evidence   Organizations that utilize third parties need to periodically assess those third parties. Generally, this consists of creating a security and/or privacy questionnaire that is sent to the third party with the request to answer all of the questions and return to the organization in a reasonable amount of time.

Often, an organization does not want to rely simply on the answers provided by the third party. The organization can also request that the third party furnish specific artifacts that serve as evidence that support the responses in the questionnaire. Typical artifacts that an organization will request of its third party include the following:

- Security policy
- Security controls
- Security awareness training records
- New-hire checklists
- Details on employee background checks (not necessarily actual records but a description of the checks performed)
- Nondisclosure and other agreements signed by employees (not necessarily signed copies but blank copies)
- Vulnerability management process
- Secure development process
- Copy of general insurance and cyber insurance policies
- Incident response plan and evidence of testing

An organization with many third parties may find that it utilizes various types of third parties, including some that store or process large volumes of critical or sensitive data, others that are operationally critical but do not access data, and other categories. Often it makes sense for an organization to utilize different versions of questionnaires, one or more for each category of third party, so that the majority of questions asked of each third party are relevant. Organizations that don't do this risk having large portions of questionnaires being irrelevant, which could be frustrating to third parties that would rightfully complain of wasted time and effort.

As described previously about the classification of third parties, organizations often use different questionnaires for different risk levels of third parties. For example, the highest-risk third parties would get very extensive questionnaires that include requests for many pieces of evidence, while medium-risk third parties receive shorter question-naires, and low-risk third parties receive very short questionnaires. While it is courteous to send questionnaires of appropriate length to various third parties (mainly to avoid over-burdening low-risk third parties with huge questionnaires), remember that this practice also reduces the burden on the organization since someone has to review the questionnaires and attached evidence. An organization with hundreds of third parties does not want to overburden itself with the task of analyzing hundreds of question-naires, each with hundreds of questions, when most of the third parties are lower risk and deserving of shorter questionnaires.

Assessing Third Parties   To discover risks to the business, organizations need to assess their third parties, not only at the onset of the business relationship (prior to the legal agreement being signed, as explained earlier) but periodically thereafter. Business con-ditions and operations often change over time, which necessitates that third parties be assessed throughout the relationship.

As described earlier on the classification of third parties and on the questionnaires in use, the assessment of third parties can be performed according to risk and the types of services being performed. Generally, higher-risk third parties will be assessed more frequently and more rigorously, including longer questionnaires, requests for more artifacts and evidence, and perhaps other forms of assessments such as vulnerability assessments or on-site reviews and audits. Lower-risk third parties can be assessed less frequently, using shorter questionnaires and fewer requests for evidence. The lowest-risk third parties can be assessed even less frequently and with the shortest questionnaires, with perhaps no requests for evidence.

Organizations assessing third parties often recognize that IT and security controls are not the only form of risk that require examination. Instead, organizations generally will seek other forms of information about the more important third parties, including the following:

- Financial risk
- Geopolitical risk
- Inherent risk
- Recent security breaches
- Lawsuits
- Operational effectiveness/capabilities

These and other factors can influence the overall risk to the organization and manifest itself in various ways, including degradations in overall security, failures to meet production or quality targets, and even going out of business.

Because of the effort required to collect information on these other risk areas, organizations often rely on third-party service organizations that collect information on companies and make it available on a subscription basis. Of course, these themselves are third-party organizations that also require an appropriate measure of due diligence.

Risk Mitigation   When assessing its third parties, organizations that carefully examine the information provided often find that there are matters that the organization will find unacceptable in its third parties. In these cases, the organization will analyze the matter and decide on a course of action.

For instance, a highly critical third party indicates that it does not perform annual security awareness training for its employees, and the organization finds this unacceptable. To remedy this, the organization needs to analyze the risk (in a manner not unlike any risk found internally) and decide on a course of action. In this example, the organization contacts the third party and attempts to compel them to institute annual security awareness training for its employees.

Sometimes, a deficiency in a third party is not so easily solved. For example, a third party that has been providing services for many years indicates in its annual questionnaire that it does not employ encryption of the most sensitive data when stored. At the onset of the business relationship this was not a common practice, but over time it has become a common practice in the organization's industry. The service provider, when confronted with this, explains that it is not operationally feasible to implement encryption of stored data in a manner acceptable to the organization, mainly for financial reasons: because of the significant impact of cost on its operations, the third party would have to increase its prices to cover these costs. In this example, the organization and the third party would need to pragmatically discover the best course of action so that the organization can be satisfied with the level of risk and its own costs.

The Risk Register

A *risk register* is a business record that contains information about business risks and information about their origin, potential impact, affected assets, probability of occurrence, and treatment. A risk register is the central business record in an organization's risk management program, the set of activities used to identify and treat risks.

Together with other records, the risk register serves as the focal point of evidence that an organization is at least attempting to manage risk. Other records include evidence of risk treatment decisions and approvals, tracking of projects linked to risks, and risk assessments and other activities that contribute content to the risk register.

A risk register can be stored in a spreadsheet, database, or within a governance, risk, and compliance tool used to manage risk and other activities in the security program. Table 3-11 shows a typical risk register entry.

Sources of Information for the Risk Register

Awareness of risks can come from many places and through a variety of events. The information in Table 3-11 provides some hints about the potential sources of information that would lead to the creation of a risk register entry. These sources include the following:

- **Risk assessment**   A prime source for risk register entries, a risk assessment identifies risks in the organization's staff (e.g., excessive workload, competency, and training issues), business processes, and technology.

- **Vulnerability assessment**   The high-level results of a vulnerability assessment (or penetration test, code review, social engineering assessment, etc.) may indicate overarching problems in staff, business processes, or technology at a strategic level.

- **Internal audit**   Internal audit and other internal control self-assessments can identify problems in staff, business processes, or technology.

- **Security incident**   The occurrence of a security incident may reveal the presence of one or more risks that require attention. Note that a security incident in another organization may highlight risks in one's own organization.

- **Threat intelligence**   Formal and informal subscriptions or data feeds on threat intelligence may reveal risks that warrant attention.

- **Industry development**   Changes in the organization's industry sector, such as new business activities and techniques, may reveal or magnify risks that require attention.

Item	Description
Entry number	A unique numeric value identifying the entry. This can be in the form of a date, such as 20180127a.
Status	Current status of the entry. • Open • Assigned • Closed
Date entered	The date the risk register entry was created.
Entered by	The person who created the risk register entry.
Source	The activity or event that compelled someone to create this entry. Sources include the following: • Risk assessment • Vulnerability assessment • Security incident • Threat intelligence • External party
Incident number	Reference to an incident record, if applicable.
Title	Short title describing the risk entry.
Description	Description of the risk.
Threat description	Description of the potential threat activity.
Threat actor	Description of the type of threat actor: • Worker • Former worker • Supplier, vendor, or partner • Cybercriminal • Nation-state
Vulnerability description	Description of one or more vulnerabilities that increases the probability or impact of threat realization.
Third-party organization	Name of the third-party organization where the risk is present, if applicable.
Third-party classification	Classification level of the third-party organization, if applicable.
Business impact	Business language description of the impact of threat realization.
Technical impact	Technical language description of the impact of threat realization, if applicable.
Asset	The specific asset, asset group, or asset class affected by the risk.
Asset owner	The owner of the affected asset.
Risk owner	The owner of the risk.
Control group	A reference to the affected control group, if applicable.
Control	A reference to the affected control, if applicable.
Process	A reference to the affected process, if applicable.
Untreated probability of occurrence	An estimate of the probability of occurrence of the threat event associated with the risk. Usually expressed as high, medium, or low or on a numeric scale such as 1 to 5.

Table 3-11   Sample Risk Register Data Structure *(continued)*

Item	Description
Untreated impact of occurrence	An estimate of the impact of occurrence of the threat event associated with the risk. Usually expressed as high, medium, or low or on a numeric scale such as 1 to 5.
Untreated risk score	An overall risk score that is generally a product of probability, impact, and asset value.
Treated probability of occurrence	An estimate of the probability of occurrence of the threat event associated with the risk, after risk treatment. Usually expressed as high, medium, or low or on a numeric scale such as 1 to 5.
Treated impact of occurrence	An estimate of the impact of occurrence of the threat event associated with the risk, after risk treatment. Usually expressed as high, medium, or low or on a numeric scale such as 1 to 5.
Treated risk score	An overall risk score that is generally a product of probability, impact, and asset value, after risk treatment.
Estimated cost of risk treatment	An estimated cost of risk treatment. This is expressed in dollars or the local currency.
Estimated level of effort of risk treatment	An estimated level of effort of risk treatment. This can be expressed as high, medium, or low or on a numeric scale such as 1 to 5 or as an estimate of range of man-hours, as follows: • Less than 1 hour • Less than 10 hours • Less than 100 hours • Less than 1,000 hours • Less than 10,000 hours
Risk treatment	The chosen method of risk treatment: • Accept • Mitigate • Transfer • Avoid
Risk treatment approver	The person or body that approved the risk treatment method.
Risk treatment approval date	The date that the risk treatment method was approved.
Risk treatment owner	The person responsible for carrying out risk treatment.
Risk treatment description	A description of the risk treatment.
Risk treatment planned completion	Date when risk treatment is expected to be completed.
Actual cost of risk treatment	The actual cost of risk treatment, which would be known when risk treatment has been completed. This is expressed in dollars or the local currency.
Actual level of effort of risk treatment	The actual level of effort of risk treatment, which would be known when risk treatment has been completed. This is expressed in man-hours.
Risk treatment closure date	Date when risk treatment is actually completed.

Table 3-11 Sample Risk Register Data Structure

- **New laws and regulations**   The passage of new laws, regulations, and applicable standards and private legal obligations may reveal the presence of risks that require attention. Also note that compliance risk (i.e., the possibility that regulators or others may impose fines or sanctions on the organization) may well be included in one or more risk register entries, if the organization has identified such risks.

- **Consultants**   A visit by, or conversation with, an expert security consultant may reveal risks that were previously unknown. The consultant, who may be an auditor or assessor or may be working in the organization on a project may or may not be expecting to find risks that the organization's security manager would want to be aware of.

Strategic vs. Tactical Risks

When managing the contents of the risk register, an organization may establish business rules related to the types of content that may be included in the risk register. An important distinction is the matter of strategic versus tactical: strategic risks certainly belong in a risk register, but tactical risks often do not.

For instance, an organization that performs vulnerability scans or application scans would not put all of the contents of the vulnerability scan in the risk register. In even modest-sized organizations, there can be hundreds or thousands of entries in a vulnerability scan that warrant attention (and occasionally, immediate action). But these are considered tactical as they are associated with individual assets. However, if in the course of conducting vulnerability scans, the security manager discovers that there are systemic problems with recurring vulnerabilities, this phenomenon may warrant an entry in the risk register. For example, there may be recurring instances of servers that are not being patched or a problem that results in patches being removed. This could be part of a larger problem that incurs significant risk to the organization, deserving of an entry in the risk register.

Risks identified in third parties in the organization's third-party risk management program should be included in the risk register.

Risk Analysis Contribution

Note that, in Table 3-11, there are ratings for mitigated probability, impact, and risk, as well as a description of risk treatment with associated cost and level of effort. The information in those fields should represent the result of more detailed risk analysis for each entry in the risk register.

For example, a security manager may have discovered that the organization's software development team continues to produce code containing numerous security defects. The security manager would analyze the situation and consider many different potential remedies, each with its own costs, levels of effort, and impact on risk. The security manager might consider the following:

- Secure development training
- An incentive program that rewards developers who produce the fewest security defects

- Code scanning tools present in each developer's integrated development environment (IDE)
- Code scanning tools in the organization's software build system
- Periodic application penetration tests performed by a qualified external party
- Web application firewall appliances
- Web application firewall in the organization's content delivery network (CDN) service

In the course of analyzing this situation, the security manager will probably confer with people in various parts of the organization to discuss these and other potential solutions. Depending on the practices and processes that are in place in the organization, the security manager may unilaterally select a decision or bring the array of choices to a security steering committee for discussion.

Ultimately, the ratings in the risk register, as well as the risk mitigation description, will reflect the mitigation technique that is selected.

Also note that, in this example, the security manager may select two or more methods to mitigate the risk. In this case, the security manager may decide to have developers undergo secure development training and also implement a web application firewall.

Residual Risk

Risk treatment rarely eliminates all risk; instead, risk treatment will reduce the probability and/or the impact of a specific threat. The leftover risk, known as *residual risk,* should be entered into the risk register for its own round of risk treatment. Depending upon the nature of the original risk, an individual risk may undergo two or more cycles of risk treatment, until finally the residual risk is accepted and the risk matter closed.

Integration of Risk Management into Other Processes

The risk management life-cycle process is not the only place where risk analysis and risk management is performed in an organization. Instead, the concept of risk should be integrated into several other IT and business processes in an organization. This section describes the incorporation of security and risk into several processes including the following:

- Software development
- Change management
- Configuration management
- Incident and problem management
- Physical security
- Enterprise risk management
- Human resource management
- Project management

Secure Software Development

Developers, in the creation and maintenance of software programs, sometimes introduce software defects (commonly known as *bugs*) in their programs, resulting in unexpected behavior. This unexpected behavior may include calculation errors or errors in the way that information is displayed, read from storage, or written to storage. Sometimes, these defects can be exploited by a user or attacker to trick the software program into performing unexpected or unwanted activities.

Unless software developers are specifically aware of the security implications of the use of specific functions and calculations, they may unknowingly introduce benign to serious security defects in their programs. Some of these defects may be easily discovered with scanning programs or other techniques, while others may lay undiscovered for years. Often, a researcher will find security defects associated with a particular coding technique that is present in many programs; this can result in many organizations discovering for the first time that their programs have a particular exploitable effect.

Without specific software development experience, a security manager in a smaller organization may not have specific knowledge of the pitfalls associated with the use of the programming language in that organization. Oftentimes, an outside security expert with experience in software development and insecure coding is needed to assist such an organization to discover any weaknesses in its coding practices. In a larger organization, there may be one or more experts in secure development with the languages used there who may be able to provide this assistance internally.

In addition to secure coding, organizations need to introduce several security-related steps into their software development process, including the following:

- **Threat modeling**   Implemented during the design phase to anticipate potential threats and incorporate design features to block them.

- **Coding standards**   Standards that specify allowed and disallowed coding techniques, including those more likely to introduce security defects and other defects.

- **Code reviews**   Reviews performed by peers that are part of the program development and maintenance process. A peer is more likely to find defects in security problems than the developer who wrote the code.

- **Code scanning**   Performed in the developer's IDE or executed separately in the developers' central software build environments.

- **Application scanning**   Performed on web applications to discover exploitable defects.

- **Application penetration testing**   Performed periodically by internal personnel or by qualified security advisory firms.

The concept of *security by design* is one in which security and risk are incorporated in every level of product development, from inception to development, testing, implementation, maintenance, and operations. Organizations that incorporate security by design into their development and business processes are less likely to suffer from security incidents than those that do not. They are also less likely to undergo frequent security changes caused by unexpected security incidents.

Security managers need to understand the root cause behind the phenomenon where software developers introduce security defects into their software. Most university computer science programs, where many if not most software developers received their formal education, do not include the concepts of secure programming in their curricula. Many universities do not even offer secure development as an elective course. Instead, developers encounter this subject matter in their jobs, and because secure development was not part of their formal education, the concepts and principles behind secure development are often rejected. We are continuing to churn out new developers from universities who have little or no exposure to security.

Change Management

Change management is the IT function that is used to control changes made to an IT environment. The purpose of change management is to reduce the likelihood that proposed changes will introduce unexpected risks, which could lead to unplanned outages and security incidents.

A basic change management process begins with a formal *request for change,* which includes several specific pieces of information:

- Description of the change
- Reason for the change
- Who will perform the change
- When will the change be performed
- A procedure for making the change
- A procedure for verifying the change
- A back-out procedure in case the change cannot be verified
- Security impact of the change and also of not implementing the change
- Privacy impact
- Dependencies
- Defined change windows

A group of individuals from IT and across the business (collectively known as a *change review board* or *change control board*) can meet periodically to discuss new change requests. The requestor would describe the change, including the elements listed previously, and others on the change review board have an opportunity to ask questions or voice concerns related to the change.

In many organizations, one or more security personnel are permanent members of the change review board and will have a voice in the discussion about each change to ensure that security and privacy issues are properly identified, discussed, and managed.

Security professionals overall are maligned by the few who seek to frequently block proposed changes and other activities on account of the risks that may be introduced.

Generally, this creates a challenge where change review boards need to incorporate security concerns and be sure that security managers are included in all discussions. Also, security managers need to be pragmatic and understand that there is no advancement of business without risk.

Configuration Management

Configuration management is the IT function where the configuration of components in an IT environment is independently recorded. Configuration management is usually supported by the use of automated tools used to inventory and control system configurations, but sometimes manual means are used. A configuration management database (CMDB) is the repository for this information.

Configuration management can be thought of as the creation of a historical record of the configuration of devices and systems. This historical record can sometimes be used during troubleshooting, in support of investigations where the personnel need to understand in detail any changes in configuration that may have occurred in a system that could account for an incident or problem.

Security and risk considerations in configuration management are as follows:

- Protection of configuration management data from unauthorized access
- Inclusion of security-related information in configuration management data

Looking into the content itself in configuration management, this brings to mind the fact that organizations need to develop server, endpoint, and network device–hardening standards to make them more resilient to attack. Once an organization develops a hardening standard, it is implemented in some manner such as a golden server or endpoint image, which should also be managed and protected, whether contained in the CMDB or not.

Incident and Problem Management

The IT service management (ITSM) companion activities, incident management and problem management, are important activities for IT organizations. *Incident management* is the IT function that is used to analyze service outages, service slowdowns, service errors, security incidents, and software bugs, as well as to restore the agreed-on service as soon as possible. *Problem management* is the IT function that is used to analyze chronic and recurring incidents to discover their root cause and prevent further occurrences.

Incident management and problem management need to include the disciplines of security and risk. Four primary security- and risk-related considerations in incident management are these:

- **Security or risk component associated with an incident**   IT personnel analyzing an incident or problem need to understand the security nature of the incident or problem, including whether the incident or problem has an impact on security. For instance, a malfunctioning firewall may be permitting traffic to pass through a control point that should not be permitted. Further, many security incidents are first recognized as simple malfunctions or outages and recognized later as symptoms of an attack. For example, users complaining of slow or unresponsive servers may be experiencing the effects of a distributed denial-of-service (DDoS) attack on the organization's servers, which, incidentally, may be a diversionary tactic to an actual attack occurring elsewhere in the organization. In the context of problem management, a server suffering from availability or performance issues may have been compromised and altered by an attacker.

- **Security or risk implication associated with actions to restore service**   IT personnel analyzing an incident and working to restore service need to understand the security and risk impact that their analysis and corrective actions have on IT systems and associated information. For example, rebooting a security server in an attempt to remedy a situation may result in a loss of visibility and/or protection from events.

- **Security or risk implications associated with root-cause analysis (RCA)**   *Root-cause analysis* is defined as the analysis of a problem in order to identify its underlying origin, instead of merely its symptoms and factors. IT personnel analyzing a problem must be aware of the security and risk considerations while performing root-cause analysis. IT personnel need the skills to recognize the security and risk implications of symptoms and origins. For example, a problem with server availability was traced to some file system permissions that were set improperly; those file system permission changes affected the ability for users to directly access sensitive data that should be accessed only by an application.

- **Security or risk implications associated with corrective action**   IT personnel analyzing a problem must be aware of the security and risk implications of changes being considered within business processes and technology. For instance, an application malfunction that is corrected by elevating its service account to the privileged (administrative) level may solve the underlying access permission error, but it creates significant risks as well.

Physical Security

Physical security is mainly concerned with the development and management of controls to protect physical assets, workplaces, and personnel. There is significant intersection between information security and physical security: information security relies upon physical security controls for the protection of information processing and communications equipment. While some of this equipment resides in data centers, some also resides in workplaces where an organization's personnel also work. These common controls make workplace safety a close relative to information security.

Information security and physical security are frequently managed by separate parts of an organization. Changes in physical security technologies such as video surveillance and building access control systems are bringing information and physical security closer together than they have ever been before. In most organizations, however, they are still managed separately. In these cases, information security and physical security can partner together because they share many technologies, assets, and overall objectives of protecting the organization from harm.

Information and physical security functions can be integrated together in a number of ways, including the following:

- Ensuring that organization-wide risk and threat assessments cover both areas adequately

- Ensuring that business continuity and disaster recovery planning adequately covers information and physical security concerns

- Ensuring that information and physical security risks exist on a common risk register and are managed in a common risk management and risk treatment process

- Ensuring that information systems with high availability requirements are located in facilities with high availability as part of their design

- Ensuring that IP-based physical security assets and systems are incorporated into the organization's overall technology and security architecture, with adequate protection based on risk

- Incorporating physical facilities into the organization's information and asset classification program so that facilities and work centers can also be rated and adequately protected based on classification and risk

- Incorporating physical facility access into the organization's identity and access management program

- Ensuring that supervisory control and data acquisition (SCADA) and industrial control systems (ICS) are supporting, monitoring, and controlling the environmental systems that support information technology such as heating, ventilation, and air-conditioning (HVAC) and that physical access control systems are monitored in a common monitoring platform

Information Risk and ERM

Larger organizations, more mature organizations, and organizations in financial services industries often have an enterprise risk management (ERM) function. Typical ERM programs are developed to identify and manage business-specific risks, and they frequently use a life-cycle process similar (if not identical) to the information risk processes described in this book.

Organizations with ERM and information risk functions have an opportunity to combine or leverage these functions. For example, information risk issues that are placed in the information risk register can also be entered into the ERM risk register. Further, organizations with both functions could decide to use a common risk register for all business and information risks. Often, this makes sense since information risk is just one form of business risk. And organizations that portray all of their risks together will have a more complete view of all business risks, regardless of the context. For organizations that do not come by their risk registers, there are still opportunities for synergy, including having some personnel involved in both risk processes so that there are people in the organization who have a complete picture of all of its risks.

Human Resource Management

The entire life-cycle process of human resource management (HRM or HR) is involved in the acquisition, onboarding, care, and termination of permanent, temporary, and contingency workers in an organization. Many aspects of human resource management are risk related, as well as being related to information security.

An organization's workers are tasked with the acquisition and management of critical and sensitive information. Thus, there are several practices in HR that contribute to the support of information protection, including the following:

- **Background checks**   Prior to hiring an individual, an organization uses various means to verify the background of a candidate and to ensure that they are free of a criminal history and other undesired matters.

- **Legal agreements**   An organization will generally direct new employees to agree to and sign legal documents including nondisclosure, noncompete, and compliance with security and other organization policies.

- **Training**   HR organizations are typically responsible for delivering training of all kinds to its workers, including but not limited to security awareness training. This helps workers in the organization better understand the organization's security policy, the importance of information and asset protection, and practices in place for information protection.

- **Development and management of roles**   HR organizations typically create and maintain job descriptions, which should include security-related responsibilities, and a hierarchy of positions in the organization.

- **Management of the human resource information system (HRIS)**   Most HR organizations today utilize an HRIS for all official records concerning its workers. Many HRIS systems today are integrated with an organization's identity and access management system: when an employee is hired, transferred, or terminated, a data feed from the HRIS to the identity and access management (IAM) platform ensures that axis management information and systems are kept up-to-date. This makes it all the more important that HRIS systems have accurate information in them.

Project Management

Whether a centralized project management office (PMO) is utilized or project managers are scattered throughout an organization, security and risk are an essential element of program management and project planning. There are several ways in which security and risk should be incorporated into projects, including the following:

- Risk analyses should be performed at the onset of a project so that potential risks in the proposed finished project or program can be identified. This gives organizations an opportunity to refine project/program objectives, architecture, and requirements.

- The impact of a project or program on the organization's security, compliance, and privacy must be established prior to any procurement, development, or implementation.

- Security requirements need to be included in any activity where requirements are developed. Like other requirements, security requirements must be verifiable.

Risk Monitoring and Reporting

Risk monitoring is defined as ongoing activities including control effectiveness assessments and risk assessments to observe changes in risk. Security managers perform risk monitoring to report risk levels to executive management and to identify unexpected changes in risk levels.

Typical activities that contribute to risk monitoring include internal audit, control self-assessment, vulnerability assessments, and risk assessments. Because the primary audience of risk monitoring is executive management, the reporting of risk monitoring is often done using dashboards, which may be part of a GRC system's risk management function that permits drill-down when desired.

Information security managers should periodically meet with senior managers and executives to give them an update on key changes in the information security program and on changes to key risk indicators. Further, executives should be notified of key security-related and risk-related events, such as security incidents, and changes in compliance risk.

Key Risk Indicators

A *key risk indicator (KRI)* is a measure of information risk, used to reveal trends related to levels of risk of security incidents in the organization. KRIs are security metrics that are designed to serve as early indicators of rising or falling risk and of the rising or falling probability of various types of security incidents and events.

There is no standard set of KRIs that are used across organizations; rather, each organization develops its own set of keys risk indicators based on specific requirements from regulators, board members, senior executives, and other parties.

KRIs are often derived from operational activities throughout the IT and business environment. On their own, those activities are often meaningless to executives and others, but when properly developed, they can serve as valuable risk signposts that help executives and others better understand information risk in the business over time.

For example, basic operational metrics in an organization's vulnerability management program provide information about vulnerabilities in an organization's business applications. These metrics by themselves are not useful to executives. But when combined with business context, activities that are tactical and transactional can also be portrayed as strategic and in business terms.

Adding remediation information can transform this metric from a number of vulnerabilities identified (which is useless to executives) into a better metric such as the time to remediate critical vulnerabilities. This, however, can be transformed still further into a KRI such as the percentage of vulnerabilities in systems supporting revenue operations that are remediated in less than 30 days. This is a valuable risk indicator for executives, as they will more easily understand how quickly IT is patching critical vulnerabilities in key systems.

Several other KRIs can be developed in various operational areas, including the following:

- Number of security incidents resulting in external notifications
- Changes in attrition rates for IT workers and for key business employees
- Amount of money paid out each quarter in an organization's bug bounty program
- Percentage of employees who have not completed the required security training
- Numbers of critical and high risks identified in risk assessments

The most useful key risk indicators are those that serve as leading indicators, which communicate increases or decreases in the probability of future security incidents and events.

Training and Awareness

The majority of security incidents happen because of human error. Further analysis of security incidents indicates that there are several factors that contribute to security incidents:

- Lack of awareness of the risks associated with general computing and Internet use
- Lack of training and experience in the configuration and operation of systems and applications
- Lack of training and awareness of key business processes and procedures
- Lack of information on workers' responsibilities for reporting problems and incidents

A security awareness program is an essential ingredient in every organization; information on safe computing, security policy, security procedures, and workers' security-related responsibilities can be imported to all workers through training programs, messaging, and other means. Chapter 4 contains more details on establishing and managing a security awareness program.

Risk Documentation

Any business process that warrants the time and effort to execute deserves to be documented so that it can be performed consistently and correctly. An organization's risk management program should be fully documented, including the following:

- Policy and objectives, such as how risk management is run in the organization
- Roles and responsibilities, such as who is responsible for various activities

- Methods and techniques, such as how probability and impact of risks are evaluated and scored
- Locations for data storage and archival, such as where the risk register and risk treatment records reside
- Risk tolerance, such as how acceptable and unacceptable risks are defined
- Business rules for why something is included in the risk register
- Risk treatment procedures and records
- Procedures and methods for the development of metrics and key risk indicators
- Communication and escalation protocols defined
- Review cycle defined to be sure the program is in alignment with the business

Chapter Review

Risk management is the core of an organization's information security program. Through its techniques for identifying risks and understanding their probability of occurrence and impact upon the organization, risk management helps the organization prioritize scarce resources to most effectively reduce risk. The proper application of risk management helps an organization reduce the frequency and impact of security incidents, through improved resilience and preparation.

When implementing a risk management program, it is necessary to consider several characteristics about the organization, including risk tolerance, regulatory and legal obligations, management structure, executive management support, and culture.

A risk management program should include several avenues of communication so that business leaders and stakeholders understand the program and how it is integrated into the organization. The program should be transparent with regard to its procedures and practices.

When building or improving a risk management program, security managers may select one of several industry frameworks, such as ISO/IEC 27001, ISO/IEC 27005, ISO/IEC 31010, NIST SP 800-37, NIST SP 800-39, COBIT 5, or the RIMS Risk Maturity Model. These and other frameworks have similar components including scope, objectives, policy, risk tolerance, roles and responsibilities, the risk management life-cycle process, and management review. To the greatest reasonable extent, a risk management program should be integrated into the business to minimize the impact of the program's activities.

When planning a risk management program, the security manager and executive leadership need to understand—and to some extent, define—the context of the program. This includes the program's scope, participants and stakeholders, and risk tolerance. The security manager needs to consider many aspects of the organization's internal environment, as well as external environments such as market and economic conditions, external stakeholders, customers, and external threats. The security manager may need to perform gap analyses to better understand the current state as compared to the desired future state of the program. Security managers can fill gaps in knowledge and experience by networking with other security and risk professionals, training, periodicals, and conferences.

The risk management life cycle consists of a set of activities that enable the discovery and management of risks. The steps in the process include scope definition, asset identification and valuation, risk identification, risk analysis, risk treatment, and risk communication. Periodic risk assessments and other means contribute to continued risk identification.

Several risk management standards can be used including NIST SP 800-39, NISTSP 800-30, ISO/IEC 27001, and FAIR.

Assets need to be identified and valued in a risk management program. The types of assets to be identified include hardware, subsystem and software, information, cloud-based information, and virtual assets. Assets need to be classified according to a risk-based scheme, similar to that commonly used for data classification. This helps a security manager more easily identify assets that are more critical than others. Methods for valuing assets include qualitative (high, medium, low) and quantitative (either replacement cost, book value, net present value, redeployment cost, or other method).

A key step in risk analysis is the identification and analysis of internal and external threats. Risk management standards such as NIST SP 800-37 contain comprehensive lists of credible threats. Security managers need to recognize that there are often emerging threats that need to be considered in a risk assessment, and some may not yet be included in current standards. Further, there are sometimes threats specific to an industry sector.

Another key step in risk analysis is the identification of vulnerabilities, or weaknesses, in people, business processes, or technology.

The next step in risk analysis is the identification of risk. Risk is calculated using input from threats, threat actors, vulnerabilities, asset value, and impact. In most cases, risk is calculated in a qualitative way, primarily because it is difficult to know the precise (or even an approximate) probability of threat occurrence and somewhat difficult to know the financial impact of a threat.

In quantitative risk analysis, key values are asset value, exposure factor, single loss expectancy, annualized rate of occurrence, and annualized loss expectancy.

Industry-standard techniques are available for performing risk analysis, including OCTAVE Allegro, Delphi, event tree analysis, fault tree analysis, and Monte Carlo analysis.

Risk treatment is the activity in risk management where the organization chooses how to handle an identified risk. The four risk treatment choices are *accept, mitigate, transfer,* and *avoid*. Risk treatment decisions should be made by the affected line of business owner, executive management, or security steering committee empowered by executive management. After risk treatment, leftover risk is known as residual risk. Residual risk should be processed through the risk management process as though it were a new risk.

During risk treatment, the organization needs to consider legal and regulatory issues to ensure that risk treatment decisions and methods of risk mitigation do not themselves create compliance risk.

The costs and benefits of risk treatment should also be considered. While, as the adage goes, it doesn't make sense to spend $20,000 to protect a $10,000 asset, the value and role of an asset need to be considered. As the adage continues, it may be a

$10,000 asset, but it may be a critical component in the earning of $1 million in revenue every month.

When considering risk treatment options, established risk management recovery objectives must also be considered. These objectives may include recovery time objective, recovery point objective, recovery capacity objective, and service delivery objectives. Often, these objectives are derived from two additional figures, which are maximum tolerable downtime and maximum tolerable outage.

Risk management and business continuity planning have several common components and linkages. Both are concerned with business resilience and survival, and both utilize business impact analysis to better understand the organization's most critical processes.

Third-party risk management is growing as a separate subdiscipline of risk management on account of trends where organizations are outsourcing key business systems to SaaS and other cloud-based service providers. The principles of risk management and risk analysis are present in TPRM; however, TPRM is often carried out separately because of the additional effort required to collect information about risks in third-party organizations.

Third parties are assessed mainly through the use of questionnaires and requests for evidence that are sent to third parties. Most organizations have large numbers of third parties, so many organizations employ a risk tier scheme to identify the third parties that are the most critical to the organization. Third parties at a higher level of risk undergo more frequent and rigorous risk assessments, while third parties at lower levels undergo less frequent and less rigorous risk assessments.

The risk register is the central business record in a risk management program. A risk register is a catalog of all current and historical risks, along with many pieces of metadata describing the risk in detail. A risk register may be stored in a spreadsheet, in a database, or in a governance, risk, and compliance tool's risk management module.

Security and risk management are incorporated into many other business activities, including but not limited to software development, change management, configuration management, incident and problem management, physical security, enterprise risk management, and human resource management.

Risk monitoring is the set of ongoing activities to detect changes in risks. Typical risk monitoring activities include risk assessments, vulnerability assessments, internal audit, and control self-assessment.

Key risk indicators are metrics used in a risk management program to communicate risk trends to executive management. KRIs help an organization understand key risks in strategic business terms. The most useful KRIs are leading indicators, which help an organization better understand rising and falling probabilities of security incidents.

Like a security awareness program, training and other forms of information dissemination to affected personnel are essential for the success of a risk management program. A risk awareness program helps the organization better understand the purpose of the risk management program and its part in it.

Like any formal business process, a risk management program needs to be documented. Required documentation includes policy and processes, roles and responsibilities, risk tolerance/appetite, and records such as the risk register.

Notes

- Like other activities in information security, it can be difficult to measure the benefits of an information risk management program, mainly because it is difficult to identify the security events that did not occur because of the program.

- Understanding and changing aspects of an organization's culture is one of the most important success factors in an organization and also one of the most difficult. Culture is the collective way that people in the organization think and work. It is documented everywhere and nowhere.

- Selecting a risk management and risk assessment framework is among the least important decisions in the development of a risk management program. And yet, organizations get hung up on this like they do on the topic of control frameworks.

- The need to minimize the impact of the risk management business process cannot be overstated. Where possible, utilize existing governance, management, control, and communications structures already present in the organization. The impact on decisions made in the risk management program may be significant; the process itself need not be.

- External factors such as market conditions, competition, and the sentiment of clients or customers are as important as internal factors such as access to capital and culture. Organizations in some industry sectors may have an opportunity to make security a competitive differentiator, in which case it will be more important to establish effective security management and risk management programs. Customers and competitors will notice.

- Security managers, when their knowledge or skills fall short on any topic, underestimate the value of networking and getting advice from industry peers. There are a lot of security professionals who are willing to help, and there are plenty of events with networking opportunities to meet them.

- Risk tolerance/appetite is difficult to quantify, and few organizations have defined it for themselves. A lack of a formal risk tolerance statement should not be an impediment to starting or continuing a risk management program. Instead, make risk decisions one at a time.

- Any time an "accept" risk treatment decision is made, the item should remain on the risk register and the matter taken up again, no more than one year later. Conditions may change that will compel the organization to reconsider that decision. "Accept" should never be forever.

- Asset identification is a cornerstone of any risk management and security management program, and yet most organizations do a poor job of it. Asset identification is the first control in the Center for Internet Security (CIS) Controls, and there is a reason for that.

- Enacting a data classification scheme is easy, but implementing the program is hard. Data classification should be extended to include system classification (the classification of a system should be the same as the highest classified data stored or processed on the system), asset classification, and even facilities (work center) classification.

- Qualitative asset valuation is sufficient for qualitative risk assessments. But when it's necessary to calculate figures such as exposure factor or annual loss expectancy, it will be necessary to obtain quantitative valuation for relevant assets. However, the need to be precise is low since it is difficult to know the probability of threat events.

- In a risk assessment while listing credible threat events, first obtain the list of threats from a standard such as NIST SP 800-30 and then add additional threats that may be relevant for the asset, organization, or geographic location.

- The term *advanced persistent threats* was developed when such threats were novel. They no longer are new. Use of the term has diminished, and yet this type of threat has become commonplace.

- Identifying all reasonable vulnerabilities during a risk assessment is not as easy as identifying threats. You must know more about the asset or process being examined.

- In qualitative risk assessments, it's easy to become focused on the risk scores for various risks. Remember that risk scores are the result of basic calculations based on very coarse threat and vulnerability ratings. Risk ratings should only serve to distinguish very high risks from very low ones, and even then, these are just rough approximations.

- Recovery objectives such as recovery time objective and recovery point objective serve as signposts for the development of risk mitigation plans and business continuity plans. Eventually they must be developed and tested, usually in the context of business continuity planning.

- Most organizations' third-party risk management programs are immature, and most organizations admit they do not have a complete list of their service providers. The presence of many free SaaS solutions and the absence of cloud access security broker tools in most organizations results in most organizations not having control over the use of third-party service providers.

- Most organizations that are establishing a risk management program for the first time can use spreadsheets for key business records such as the risk register and the security incident log. As organizations become more mature, they can acquire a governance, risk, and compliance platform that includes risk management modules.

- The mistake that most organizations make in the development of their metrics is that they publish operational metrics to executives. For instance, the number of packets dropped by the firewall or the number of viruses stopped is irrelevant to the business. Security managers need to take care to translate operational metrics (which may indeed be useful in operations) into business-relevant metrics for more senior audiences.

Questions

1. A risk manager is planning a first-ever risk assessment in an organization. What is the best approach for ensuring success?

   A. Interview personnel separately so that their responses can be compared.

   B. Select a framework that matches the organization's control framework.

   C. Work with executive management to determine the correct scope.

   D. Do not inform executive management until the risk assessment has been completed.

2. A security manager has completed a vulnerability scan and has identified numerous vulnerabilities in production servers. What is the best course of action?

   A. Notify the production servers' asset owners.

   B. Conduct a formal investigation.

   C. Place a single entry into the risk register.

   D. Put individual vulnerability entries into the risk register.

3. The concept of security tasks in the context of a SaaS or IaaS environment is depicted in a:

   A. Discretionary control model

   B. Mandatory control model

   C. Monte Carlo risk model

   D. Shared responsibility model

4. The categories of risk treatment are:

   A. Risk avoidance, risk transfer, risk mitigation, and risk acceptance

   B. Risk avoidance, risk transfer, and risk mitigation

   C. Risk avoidance, risk reduction, risk transfer, risk mitigation, and risk acceptance

   D. Risk avoidance, risk treatment, risk mitigation, and risk acceptance

5. Which of the following recovery objectives is associated with the longest allowed period of service outage?

   A. Recovery tolerance objective (RTO)

   B. Recovery point objective (RPO)

   C. Recovery capacity objective (RCapO)

   D. Recovery time objective (RTO)

6. When would it make sense to spend $50,000 to protect an asset worth $10,000?

   A. If the protective measure reduced threat impact by more than 90 percent.

   B. It would never make sense to spend $50,000 to protect an asset worth $10,000.

   C. If the asset was required for realization of $500,000 monthly revenue.

   D. If the protective measure reduced threat probability by more than 90 percent.

7. Which of the following statements is true about compliance risk?

   A. Compliance risk can be tolerated when fines cost less than controls.

   B. Compliance risk is just another risk that needs to be measured.

   C. Compliance risk can never be tolerated.

   D. Compliance risk can be tolerated when it is optional.

8. A security steering committee empowered to make risk treatment decisions has chosen to accept a specific risk. What is the best course of action?

   A. Refer the risk to a qualified external security audit firm.

   B. Perform additional risk analysis to identify residual risk.

   C. Reopen the risk item for reconsideration after one year.

   D. Mark the risk item as permanently closed.

9. A security steering committee has voted to mitigate a specific risk. Some residual risk remains. What is the best course of action regarding the residual risk?

   A. Accept the residual risk and close the risk ledger item.

   B. Continue cycles of risk treatment until the residual risk reaches an acceptable level.

   C. Continue cycles of risk treatment until the residual risk reaches zero.

   D. Accept the residual risk and keep the risk ledger item open.

10. A security manager has been directed by executive management to *not* document a specific risk in the risk register. This course of action is known as:

   A. Burying the risk

   B. Transferring the risk

   C. Accepting the risk

   D. Ignoring the risk

11. A security manager is performing a risk assessment on a business application. The security manager has determined that security patches have not been installed for more than a year. This finding is known as a:

    A. Probability

    B. Threat

    C. Vulnerability

    D. Risk

12. A security manager is performing a risk assessment on a data center. The security manager has determined that it is possible for unauthorized personnel to enter the data center through the loading dock door and shut off utility power to the building. This finding is known as a:

    A. Probability

    B. Threat

    C. Vulnerability

    D. Risk

13. A security manager has developed a scheme that prescribes required methods be used to protect information at rest, in motion, and in transit. This is known as a(n):

    A. Data classification policy

    B. Asset classification policy

    C. Data loss prevention plan

    D. Asset loss prevention plan

14. A security manager is developing a strategy for making improvements to the organization's incident management process. The security manager has defined the desired future state. Before specific plans can be made to improve the process, the security manager should perform a:

    A. Training session

    B. Penetration test

    C. Vulnerability assessment

    D. Gap analysis

15. What is usually the primary objective of risk management?

    A. Fewer and less severe security incidents

    B. No security incidents

    C. Improved compliance

    D. Fewer audit findings

Answers

1. **C.** The best approach for success in an organization's risk management program, and during risk assessments, is to have support from executive management. Executives need to define the scope of the risk management program, whether by business unit, geography, or other means.

2. **A.** Most organizations do not place individual vulnerabilities into a risk register. The risk register is primarily for strategic issues, not tactical issues such as individual vulnerabilities. However, if the vulnerability scan report was an indication of a broken process or broken technology, then that matter of brokenness might qualify as a valid risk register entry.

3. **D.** The shared responsibility model, sometimes known as a shared responsibility matrix, depicts the operational model for SaaS and IaaS providers where client organizations have some security responsibilities (such as end user access control) and service provider organizations have some security responsibilities (such as physical access control).

4. **A.** The four categories of risk treatment are risk mitigation (where risks are reduced through a control or process change), risk transfer (where risks are transferred to an external party such as an insurance company or managed services provider), risk avoidance (where the risk-producing activity is discontinued), and risk acceptance (where management chooses to accept the risk).

5. **D.** Recovery time objective is the maximum period of time from the onset of an outage until the resumption of service.

6. **C.** Ordinarily it would not make sense to spend $50,000 to protect an asset worth $10,000. But sometimes there are other considerations, such as revenue realization or reputation damage, that can be difficult to quantify.

7. **B.** In most cases, compliance risk is just another risk that needs to be understood. This includes the understanding of potential fines and other sanctions in relation to the costs required to reach a state of compliance. In some cases, however, being out of compliance can also result in reputation damage, as well as larger sanctions if the organization suffers from a security breach because of the noncompliant state.

8. **C.** A risk register item that has been accepted should be shelved and considered after a period of time, perhaps one year. This is a better option than closing the item permanently; in a year's time, changes in business conditions, security threats, and other considerations may compel the organization to take different action.

9. **B.** After risk reduction through risk mitigation, the residual risk should be treated like any new risk: it should be reexamined, and a new risk treatment decision should be made. This should continue until the final remaining residual risk is accepted.

10. **D.** The refusal of an organization to formally consider a risk is known as ignoring the risk. This is not a formal method of risk treatment because of the absence of deliberation and decision-making. It is not a wise business practice to keep some risk matters "off the books."

11. **C.** The absence of security patches on a system is considered a vulnerability. A vulnerability is defined as a weakness in a system that could permit an attack to occur.

12. **B.** Any undesired action that could harm an asset is known as a threat.

13. **A.** A data classification policy is a statement that defines two or more classification levels for data, together with procedures and standards for the protection of data at each classification for various use cases such as storage in a database, storage on a laptop computer, transmissions via e-mail, and storage on backup media.

14. **D.** When the desired end state of a process or system is determined, a gap analysis must be performed so that the current state of the process or system can also be known. Then, specific tasks can be performed to reach the desired end state of the process.

15. **A.** The most common objective of a risk management program is the reduction in the number and severity of security incidents.

Information Security Program Development and Management

In this chapter, you will learn about

- Security program frameworks, scope, and charter
- Security program alignment with business processes and objectives
- Information security frameworks
- Security program management administrative activities
- Security operations
- Internal and external audits and assessments
- Metrics that tell the security management story
- Controls

This chapter covers Certified Information Security Manager (CISM) domain 3, "Information Security Program Development and Management," representing 27 percent of the CISM examination.

Security program development represents a wide assortment of activities in an organization. Most of these activities have a direct impact on personnel, business processes, or information technology. Often, security programs are focused on linking many disparate activities in an organization that are all, one way or another, associated with the protection of valuable information assets. Another way of thinking of security program management is that the security manager (and team, if any) acts as a catalyst to ensure that activities throughout the organization are carried out in a way that does not produce unacceptable risk.

The typical sequence for developing an information security program includes these major steps:

- Development of a security strategy (covered in Chapter 2's "Security Strategy Development" section)
- Performing a gap analysis (covered in Chapter 2's "Gap Assessment" section)

- Development of a roadmap (covered in Chapter 2's "Road Map Development" section)
- Development of the security program (covered in this chapter)

Information Security Programs

Information security programs are the collection of activities used to identify, communicate, and address risks. The security program consists of controls, processes, and practices to increase the resilience of the computing environment and ensure that risks are known and handled in an effective manner. These activities might be handled by a single individual in a smaller organization, while larger organizations will have a security leader that leads an internal team that is supported by external partners as needed.

Security program models have been developed that include the primary activities needed in any organization's security program. However, because every organization is different, security managers need to understand their organizations' internal workings so that their security programs can effectively align with the organization's operations, practices, and culture.

The activities in an information security program serve to operationalize the security manager's vision for effective security and risk management in the organization. Generally, a security manager's vision is focused on *how* the security program aligns and supports the business.

Outcomes

The primary outcome of a security program is the realization of its strategy, goals, and objectives, as discussed in Chapter 2. When a strategy is aligned with the business and its risk tolerance and operations, the organization's security program will act as a business enabler, allowing it to consider new business ventures while being fully aware of associated risks that can be mitigated. Like the brakes on a race car that allow it to maneuver more quickly, an effective security program allows the organization to embark on new ventures, knowing that the security program acts as the organization's brakes and allows it to adjust effectively to keep it on the road.

The outcomes that should be part of any information security program include the following:

- **Strategic alignment** The program needs to align with and work in harmony with the rest of the organization. This includes being aware of all new business initiatives under consideration, developing risk tolerance criteria that business leaders agree with, and working day by day with business leaders to establish mutual trust. Better security programs utilize a security council or governance committee consisting of stakeholders from across the business; this helps ensure that information security activities work with the business instead of against it.

- **Risk management** An effective security program includes an effective risk management program that identifies risks and facilitates desired outcomes through appropriate risk treatment.

- **Value delivery**   An effective information security program delivers value to the organization. This is most often achieved through aligning security activities that are directed toward risk reduction in the organization's most critical activities. Reducing risk to an acceptable level effectively and efficiently is another key part of value delivery.

- **Resource management**   An information security program's primary objective is risk management and risk reduction. Doing so requires resources in the form of permanent and temporary staff, external service providers, and tools. These resources must be managed so that they are effectively used to reduce risks in alignment with the risk management program. Additionally, efficiently using resources will assist the security mangers in "rightsizing" the information security budget and spend. This will lead to greater confidence from the business when it comes to "resource requests" from the security manager.

- **Performance management**   As a security program is developed and implemented, key activities need to be measured to ensure that they are operating as planned. Security metrics are used to measure and report key activities to management.

- **Assurance process integration**   An effective information security program is aligned with other assurance processes and programs in an organization, including human resources, finance, legal, audit, enterprise risk management, information technology, and operations. Further, a security program should influence these activities so that they themselves are adequately protected from harm.

Charter

A *program charter* is a formal, written definition of the objectives of a program, its main timelines, the sources of funding, the names of its principal leaders and managers, and the business executives who are sponsoring the program. In many organizations, a program charter is a document that gives authority to the person or group that runs the program. The charter also demonstrates the support from the executive leadership team.

An information security program charter gives authority to the security manager to perform several functions, including the following:

- Develop and enforce security policy.

- Develop and implement the risk management process.

- Develop and manage security governance.

- Develop and direct the implementation and operation of controls across department or business unit boundaries.

- Develop and direct the implementation of key security processes, including vulnerability management, incident management, third-party risk, security architecture, business continuity planning, and security awareness training.

Information security in any size organization is a team sport. The security manager (with or without a staff) does not perform these functions alone; rather, all of these activities involve nearly every other department, business unit, and affiliate in the organization. For this reason, it is important that the security charter be ratified by executive management.

A security charter that designates the security manager as the person responsible for implementing the program does not give the security manager the right to dictate the program to others. As is stated numerous times in this book, an effective and successful security management program may be led and guided by the security manager, but only through collaboration and consensus by stakeholders across the business. For this reason, it may be appropriate to say that a charter empowers the security manager to be a facilitator of security in the organization. Another key element that should be understood is that while the security manager is the facilitator of the program, the ultimate responsibility or ownership for protecting information is at the executive leadership and board of directors level. Another way to think about this is the security charter gives the security manager authority to design and operate the program, but accountability is shared between the security manager and the executive leadership team and board of directors.

Scope

An early step in the creation of an information security program is the definition of its scope. Management needs to define the departments, business units, affiliates, and locations that are to be included in the organization's information security program. The scope of a program is essential because it defines the boundaries and what parts of the organization are to be included and subject to information security governance and policy.

The discussion of scope is generally more relevant in larger organizations with autonomous business units or affiliates. In larger organizations, business units or affiliates may have programs of their own, which may or may not be defined as part of a larger security program, or they may be entirely autonomous.

If the scope of a security program is defined as "headquarters only" in an organization with autonomous business units, this does not mean there is no interaction between the headquarters security program and business unit security programs. For instance, there may be a single set of policies for all entities, but separate processes, personnel, and standards in each business unit.

There is no right or wrong way to define the relationship between two or more security programs in an organization. Rather, management needs to be aware of factors that represent similarities and differences between parts of larger organizations that will help management to define scope in a way that results in effective security management throughout the organization.

Information Security Management Frameworks

Information security management frameworks are business process models that include essential processes and activities needed by most organizations. These frameworks are risk centric because the identification of risk is a key driver for activities in other parts of the framework to reduce risk to acceptable levels.

The following are the three most popular security management frameworks:

- **ISO/IEC 27001:2013**   The well-known international standard ISO/IEC 27001, "Information technology – Security techniques – Information security management systems – Requirements," defines the requirements and steps taken to run an information security management system (ISMS), which is the set of processes used to assess risk, develop policy and controls, and manage all of the typical processes found in information security programs such as vulnerability management and incident management.

- **COBIT 5**   Developed by ISACA, COBIT 5 is a controls and governance framework for managing an IT organization. COBIT 5 for Information Security is an additional standard that extends the view of COBIT 5 and explains each component of COBIT 5 from an information security perspective.

- **NIST CSF**   The U.S. National Institute of Standards and Technology (NIST) developed the Cyber Security Framework (CSF) in 2014 to address the rampant occurrence of security breaches and identity theft in the United States. The NIST CSF is an outcomes-based security management and control framework that guides an organization to understand its existing maturity levels, assess risk, identify gaps, and develop action plans for strategic improvement.

These frameworks are described in greater detail later in this chapter.

 NOTE   Security management frameworks are distinct from control frameworks. Security management frameworks describe the overall activities in an information security program, whereas control frameworks are collections of security controls.

Defining a Road Map

A *road map* is defined as the steps required to achieve a strategy or strategic objective in support of the business vision and mission. In the context of developing or making key improvements to an information security program, a road map will consist of various tasks and projects that will result in the creation and implementation of capabilities that contribute to a reduction of information risk.

The development of a strategy and road map is discussed in detail in Chapter 2's "Security Strategy Development" section.

Information Security Architecture

Enterprise architecture (EA) is both a business function and a technical model. In terms of a business function, the establishment of an enterprise architecture consists of activities that ensure that important business needs are met by IT systems. EA may also involve the construction of a model that is used to map business functions into the IT environment and IT systems in increasing levels of detail so that IT professionals can more easily understand the organization's technology architecture at any level.

Information security architecture can be thought of as a subset or special topic within enterprise architecture that is concerned with two things: the protective characteristics found in many components in an overall enterprise architecture, as well as specific components in an enterprise architecture that provide preventive or detective security functions.

The purpose of enterprise architecture and enterprise security architecture ensures the following:

- All hardware and software components fulfill a stated specific business purpose.
- All components work well together.
- There is overall structure and consistency in infrastructure throughout the organization.
- Infrastructure resources are used efficiently.
- Infrastructure is scalable and flexible.
- Existing elements can be upgraded as needed.
- Additional elements can be added as needed.

Information security architecture exists in two main layers in an organization:

- **Policy**   At this level, security policy defines the necessary characteristics of the overall environment as well as some characteristics of individual components. For example, policy will dictate the existence of centralized authentication and endpoint-based web filtering.
- **Standards**   At this level, there will be several types of standards, including vendor standards (that state the makes and models of hardware and software that will be used), protocol standards (that state the network protocols that will be used), and configuration or hardening standards (that define the detailed configuration of different types of systems, devices, and programs).

Modern information security architecture makes broad use of centralized functions and services that operate more efficiently and effectively than would isolated, local instances. Centralized functions and services help to amplify the workforce so that a relatively small staff can effectively manage hundreds or even thousands of devices. These functions and services include the following:

- **Authentication**   Organizations make use of centralized identity and access management services such as Microsoft Active Directory (AD) and Lightweight Directory Access Protocol (LDAP) so that users' identities, authentication, access controls, and authorization exist on a single, central service, as opposed to existing on individual systems and devices.
- **Monitoring**   Organizations can implement centralized monitoring for operational and security purposes to observe at a central management console the events occurring on systems and devices at all locations.

- **Device management**   Organizations can implement tools to manage large numbers of similar devices such as servers, workstations, mobile devices, and network devices. Central device management helps to make the configuration of systems and devices more consistent.

Two frameworks for enterprise architecture are discussed in this book: the Open Group Architecture Framework (TOGAF) and the Zachman Framework. Note that these are enterprise architecture models, not enterprise *security* architecture models.

The Open Group Architecture Framework

The Open Group Architecture Framework is a life-cycle enterprise architecture framework used for designing, planning, implementing, and governing an enterprise technology architecture. TOGAF could be considered a high-level approach for designing enterprise infrastructure.

The phases used in the TOGAF framework are as follows:

- Preliminary
- Architecture vision
- Business architecture
- Information systems architecture
- Technology architecture
- Opportunities and solutions
- Migration planning
- Implementation governance
- Architecture change management
- Requirements management

TOGAF is a business-driven, life-cycle management framework for enterprise architecture overall, and it certainly can be used for information security architecture as well. Figure 4-1 depicts TOGAF visually.

You can find information on TOGAF at https://togaf.info or http://www.opengroup.org/subjectareas/enterprise/togaf/.

The Zachman Framework

The Zachman enterprise architecture framework, established in the late 1980s, continues to be a dominant EA standard today. Zachman likens IT enterprise architecture to the construction and maintenance of an office building: at an abstract level, the office building performs functions such as containing office space. As you look into increasing levels of detail in the building, you encounter various trades (steel, concrete, drywall, electrical, plumbing, telephone, fire control, elevators, and so on), each of which has its own specifications, standards, regulations, construction and maintenance methods, and so on. Zachman can easily be used to develop enterprise security architecture as part of enterprise architecture.

Figure 4-1 TOGAF components (Courtesy of The Open Group)

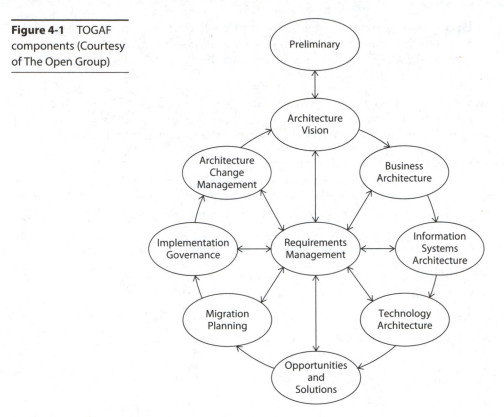

In the Zachman framework, IT systems and environments are described at a high, functional level and then in increasing detail, encompassing systems, databases, applications, networks, and so on. Table 4-1 illustrates the Zachman framework.

While the Zachman framework allows an organization to peer into cross sections of an IT environment that supports business processes, the model does not convey the relationships between IT systems. Data flow diagrams are used instead to depict information flows.

Information about the Zachman framework is available at https://www.zachman.com/about-the-zachman-framework.

Implementing a Security Architecture

Organizations use different means for implementing a security architecture. Because security architecture is both a big-picture pursuit and a detailed plan, different decision makers may be involved, and different business processes are used.

At the enterprise level, the organization will use its policy and governance functions to make decisions about major aspects of security architecture, such as decisions about the brands of servers, workstations, and network devices to be used.

	Data	Functional (Application)	Network (Technology)	People (Organization)	Time	Strategy
Scope	List of data sets important in the business	List of business processes	List of business locations	List of organizations	List of events	List of business goals and strategy
Enterprise Model	Conceptual data/object model	Business process model	Business logistics	Workflow	Master schedule	Business plan
Systems Model	Logical data model	System architecture	Detailed system architecture	Human interface architecture	Processing structure	Business rule model
Technology Model	Physical data/class model	Technology design	Technology architecture	Presentation architecture	Control structure	Rule design
Detailed Representation	Data definition	Program	Network architecture	Security architecture	Time definition	Rule speculation
Function Enterprise	Usable data	Working function	Usable network	Functioning organization	Implemented schedule	Working strategy

Table 4-1 Zachman Framework Showing IT Systems in Increasing Levels of Detail

At the detail level, processes such as configuration management and change management are used to implement device characteristics on individual devices or groups of devices. For instance, an upgrade to an organization's Domain Name System (DNS) infrastructure might result in an increase in the number of name servers in use, necessitating that most or all devices in the organization be updated accordingly.

Over time, organizations will make changes to their architecture models (both at the macro level and at the micro level). For instance, changes and advances in technologies such as software-defined networking (SDN), virtualization, and microservices architectures will compel organizations to revise their enterprise security architecture. However, updating architecture documents is only the beginning. Organizations will also initiate tasks or projects to implement these improvements in their environment. Some of these changes, such as updates to industry device-hardening standards, may result in little more than change management to update a few configuration settings. But other changes may involve multiyear projects to modernize some aspect of an organization's environment.

Security Program Management

Information security program management includes several types of activities to ensure that organizational objectives are met. These activities include resource management (staff, professional services, budget, equipment), decision-making at every level, and coordination of activities through projects, tasks, and routine operations.

Security Governance

Security governance is the assemblage of an organization's management activities that identifies, analyzes, and treats risks to key assets; establishes key roles and responsibilities;

and measures key security processes. Depending upon the structure of the organization and its business purpose, information security governance may be included in IT governance, or security governance may stand on its own. If a stand-alone approach is taken, then security governance should be linked to IT governance so that these two activities are kept in sync. Regardless of how IT and security governance are positioned, they should align and roll up into corporate governance.

From the perspective of governance, personnel in the following roles should have roles and responsibilities to include the following:

- **Board of directors**   The board is responsible for establishing the tone for risk appetite and risk management in the organization. To the extent that the board of directors establishes business and IT security, so, too, should the board consider risk and security in that strategy.

- **Information steering committee**   The information security steering committee should establish the operational strategy for security and risk management in the organization. This includes setting strategic and tactical roles and responsibilities in more detail than was done by the board of directors. The security strategy should align with the strategy for IT and the business overall. The steering committee should also ratify security policy, as well as other strategic policies and processes developed by the chief information security officer (CISO).

- **Chief information security officer**   The CISO should be responsible for developing security policy; conducting risk assessments; developing processes for vulnerability management, incident management, identity and access management, security awareness and training, and compliance management; and informing the steering committee and board of directors of incidents and new or changed risks. In some organizations, this is known as the chief information risk officer (CIRO).

NOTE   Some organizations may employ a chief security officer (CSO) who is responsible for information security as described in the CISO role, as well as physical security, including workplace and personnel safety, physical access control, and investigations.

- **Audit**   The audit function is responsible for examining selected business processes and information systems to verify that they are designed and operating properly.

- **Chief information officer (CIO)**   The CIO is responsible for overall management of the IT organization, including IT strategy, development, operations, and service desk. In some organizations the CISO or other top-ranking security individual reports to the CIO, while in other organizations they are peers.

- **Management**   Every manager in the organization should be at least partially responsible for the conduct of their employees. This approach helps to establish a chain of accountability from the top of the organization all the way down to individual employees.

- **All employees**   Every employee in the organization should be required to comply with the organization's security policy, as well as with security requirements and processes, and all other policies. All senior and executive management should visibly and demonstrably comply with these policies as an example for others.

Security governance is not only for the identification and enforcement of applicable laws, regulations, and other legal requirements, but also for the fulfillment of goals and objectives, as well as management of risk, policies, and processes.

Security governance should also make it clear that compliance with policy is a condition of employment; employees who fail to comply with policy are subject to discipline or termination of employment.

Reasons for Security Governance

Organizations are dependent on their information systems. This has progressed to the point where organizations—including those whose products or services are not information related—are completely dependent on the integrity and availability of their information systems to continue operations. Security governance, then, is needed to ensure that security-related incidents do not threaten critical systems and their support of the ongoing viability of the organization. Ineffective security governance can lead to negligence that may result in a breach that impacts business operations or the organization's reputation.

Security Governance Activities and Results

Within an effective security governance program, the organization's management will see to it that information systems necessary to support business operations will be adequately protected. Some of the activities that will take place are as follows:

- **Risk management**   Management will ensure that risk assessments will be performed to identify risks in information systems. Follow-up actions will be carried out that will reduce the risk of system failure and compromise.

- **Process improvement**   Management will ensure that key changes will be made to business processes that will result in security improvements and reduced risk.

- **Incident response**   Management will put incident response procedures into place that will help to avoid incidents, reduce the probability and impact of incidents, and improve response to incidents so that their impact on the organization is minimized.

- **Improved compliance**   Management will be sure to identify all applicable laws, regulations, and standards and carry out activities to confirm that the organization is able to attain and maintain compliance.

- **Business continuity and disaster recovery planning** Management will define objectives and allocate resources for the development of business continuity and disaster recovery plans.

- **Effectiveness measurement** Management will establish processes to measure key security events such as incidents, policy changes and violations, audits, and training.

- **Resource management** The allocation of manpower, budget, and other resources to meet security objectives is monitored by management.

- **Improved IT governance** An effective security governance program will result in better strategic decisions in the IT organization that keep risks at an acceptable level.

These and other governance activities are carried out through scripted interactions among key business and IT executives at regular intervals. Meetings will include a discussion of effectiveness measurements, recent incidents, recent audits, and risk assessments. Other discussions may include such things as changes to the business, recent business results, and any anticipated business events such as mergers or acquisitions.

The following are two key results of an effective security governance program:

- **Increased trust** Customers, suppliers, and partners trust the organization to a greater degree when they see that security is managed effectively.

- **Improved reputation** The business community, including customers, investors, and regulators, will hold the organization in higher regard.

Steering Committees

A security steering committee is a great way to establish a cross-functional conversation on information security in an organization. With members from various departments, issues on various topics can be discussed in meetings to understand how different leaders feel about things.

Security steering committees can be used to discuss larger projects, make risk decisions, discuss priorities, and in general build consensus on many information security topics.

In larger organizations, steering committees can be organized on several levels, including executive, VP/director, and staff. Each can have its own purpose, with communications connecting the levels together.

Steering committees can exist as part of the formal governance structure, or they can exist as more of a special interest group (SIG) to provide its members with an opportunity to discuss security issues in the organization as well as professional development.

Risk Management

The purpose of risk management is to identify risk and enact changes to bring risks to acceptable levels. Organizations need to understand the internal activities, practices, and systems, as well as external threats, that are introducing risk into their operations. The span of activities that seek, identify, and manage these risks is known as *risk management*. Like many other processes, risk management is a life-cycle activity that has no beginning and no end. It's a continuous and phased set of activities that includes the examination of processes, records, systems, and external phenomena in order to identify risks. This is continued by an analysis that examines a range of solutions for reducing or eliminating risks, followed by formal decision-making that brings about a resolution to risks.

A properly designed and managed risk management program will support and align with overall business objectives. This alignment will include the adoption of a *risk appetite* that reflects the organization's overall approach to risk. For instance, if an organization is a conservative financial institution, then that organization's risk management program will likely adopt a position of being risk averse. Conversely, a high-tech startup organization that, by its very nature, is comfortable with overall business risk will probably be less averse to risks identified in its risk management program.

A key purpose of a risk management program is to maintain the control framework. As new risks are identified (or as existing risks change), new controls will be created or existing controls modified. Occasionally, controls can be reduced or eliminated as a result of risk management.

Regardless of its overall risk appetite, when an organization identifies risks, the organization will take one of four possible actions.

- **Accept**   The organization accepts the risk as is.
- **Mitigate (or Reduce)**   The organization takes action to reduce the level of risk.
- **Transfer (or Share)**   The organization shares the risk with another entity, usually an insurance company.
- **Avoid**   The organization discontinues the activity associated with the risk.

These actions are known as *risk treatments*. Often, a particular risk will be treated with a blended solution that consists of two or more of the actions just listed.

This section explores the details of risk management, risk analysis, and risk treatment.

The Risk Management Program

An organization building and operating a risk management program should follow several principles that will enable the program to succeed. These may include the following:

- **Objectives**   The risk management program must have specific objectives; otherwise, it will be difficult to determine whether the program is successful. Example objectives include the following: reduce the number of industrial accidents, reduce the cost of insurance premiums, or reduce the number or impact of stolen assets. If objectives are measurable and specific, then the individuals who are responsible for the risk management program can focus on its objectives to achieve the best possible outcome.

- **Scope**   Executive management must determine the scope of the risk management program. This is a fairly delicate undertaking because of the many interdependencies found in IT systems and business processes. However, in an organization with several distinct operations, affiliates, or business units (BUs), a risk management program could be isolated to one or more operational arms or BUs. In such a case, where there are dependencies on other services in the organization, those dependencies can be treated like external service providers (or customers).

- **Authority**   Typically, a risk management program is being started and is maintained at the request of one or more executives in the organization. It is important to know who these individuals are and their level of commitment to the program.

- **Roles and responsibilities**   This defines specific job titles, together with their respective roles and responsibilities in the risk management program and its processes and procedures. In a risk management program with several individuals, it should be clear which individuals or job titles are responsible for which activities in the program.

- **Resources**   The risk management program, like other activities in the business, requires resources to operate. This will include a budget for salaries as well as for workstations, tools, and possibly travel.

- **Policies, processes, procedures, and records**   Various risk management activities, such as asset identification, risk analysis, and risk treatment, along with some general activities such as record keeping, should be documented.

NOTE   An organization's risk management program should be documented in a *charter*. A charter is a formal document that defines and describes a business program and becomes part of the organization's record.

Figure 4-2 shows the risk management life cycle.

The Risk Management Process

Risk management is a life cycle set of activities used to identify, analyze, and address risks based on the organization's risk appetite. These activities are methodical and, as mentioned in the previous section, should be documented so that they will be performed

Figure 4-2 The risk management life cycle

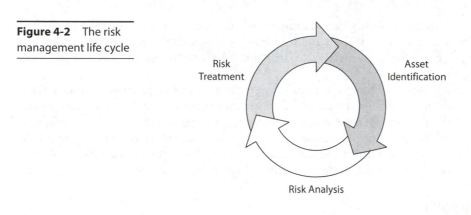

consistently, in support of the program's charter and objectives, and in alignment with the organization.

The risk management process is part of a larger risk framework, such as ISACA's Risk-IT Framework, whose components are as follows:

- **Risk Governance**   This includes integrating with the organization's enterprise risk management (ERM), establishing and maintaining a common risk view, and ensuring that business decisions include the consideration of risk.
- **Risk Evaluation**   This includes asset identification, risk analysis, and the maintenance of a risk profile.
- **Risk Response**   This includes the management and articulation of risks and the response to events.

NOTE CISM candidates are not required to memorize the Risk-IT Framework, but familiarity with its principles are important.

Identifying and Grouping Assets

Risk management can only be effective to the extent that the organization is aware of the assets that it uses in support of organization activities. You may sense an insinuation that organizations are unaware of their assets; this is true of IT assets in many organizations, particularly virtual assets and information assets. Asset management is discussed fully later in this chapter.

For risk management purposes, an electronic inventory of assets will be useful in support of the risk management life cycle. It is not always necessary to list each individual asset. Often, it is acceptable to instead list classes or groups of assets as a single asset entity for risk management purposes. For instance, a single entry for laptop computers may be preferred over listing every laptop computer; this is because the risks for all laptop computers are roughly the same (ignoring behavior differences among individual employees or employees in specific departments). This eliminates the need to list them individually.

Similarly, groups of IT servers, network devices, and other equipment can be named instead of all the individual servers and devices, again because the risks for each of them will usually be similar. However, one reason to create multiple entries for servers might be their physical location or their purpose: servers in one location may have different risks than servers in another location, and servers containing high-value information will have different risks than servers that do not contain high-value information.

Risk Analysis

Risk analysis is the activity in a risk management program where individual risks are examined. A risk consists of the intersection of threats, vulnerabilities, probabilities, asset value, and impact. In its simplest terms, risk is described in the following formula:

$$Risk = Probability \times Impact$$

This equation implies that risk is always expressed in quantitative terms, but risk is equally used in qualitative risk analysis.

Other definitions of risk include the following:

- The combination of the probability of an event and its consequence (source: ISACA Cybersecurity Fundamentals Glossary)

- The probable frequency and probable magnitude of future loss (source: "An Introduction to Factor Analysis of Information Risk [FAIR]," Risk Management Insight, LLC)

- The potential that a given threat will exploit vulnerabilities of an asset or group of assets and thereby cause harm to the organization (according to ISO 27005)

These definitions convey essentially the same message: the amount of risk is directly proportional to the probability of occurrence and the impact that a risk would have if realized.

A risk analysis consists of identifying threats and their impact of realization against each asset. This usually also includes a vulnerability analysis, where assets are studied to determine whether they are vulnerable to identified threats. The sheer number of assets—even in modestly sized organizations—may make this task appear daunting; however, threat and vulnerability analyses can usually be performed against groups of assets. For instance, when identifying natural and human-made threats against assets, it often makes sense to perform a single threat analysis against all of the assets that reside in a given location. After all, the odds of a volcanic eruption (or any other applicable event) are the same for any of the servers in the room—the threat need not be called out separately for each asset.

Threat Analysis   The usual first step in a risk analysis is to identify threats against an asset or group of assets. A threat is an event that, if realized, would bring harm to an asset and, hence, to the organization. A typical approach is to list all of the threats that have some realistic opportunity of occurrence; those threats that are highly unlikely to occur can be left out. For instance, the listing of meteorites, tsunamis in landlocked regions, and wars in typically peaceful regions will just add clutter to a risk analysis.

A more reasonable approach in a threat analysis is to identify all of the threats that a reasonable person would believe could occur, even if the probability is low. For example, include flooding when a facility is located near a river, hurricanes for an organization located along the southern or eastern coast (and inland for some distance) of the United States, or a terrorist attack in practically every major city in the world. All of these would be considered reasonable in a threat analysis.

When conducting a threat assessment, it is important to include the entire range of both natural and human-made threats. The full list could approach or even exceed 100 separate threats. These are the categories of potential threats:

- **Severe storms**   This may include tornadoes, hurricanes, lightning, windstorms, ice storms, and blizzards.

- **Earth movement**   This includes earthquakes, landslides, avalanches, volcanoes, and tsunamis.

- **Flooding**   This can include both natural and human-made inundations of water that disrupt business operations.

- **Disease**   This includes sickness outbreaks and pandemics, as well as the effects of quarantines that result.

- **Fire**   This includes forest fires, range fires, and structure fires, all of which may be natural or human-caused.

- **Labor**   This includes work stoppages, sick-outs, protests, and strikes.

- **Violence**   This includes riots, looting, terrorism, and war.

- **Malware**   This includes all kinds of viruses, worms, Trojan horses, root kits, fileless malware, and associated malicious software.

- **Intrusion**   This includes automated attacks (think of an Internet worm that is on the loose) as well as targeted attacks by employees, former employees, or cybercriminal organizations.

- **Hardware failures**   This includes any kind of failure of IT equipment or related environmental equipment failures, such as heating, ventilation, and air conditioning (HVAC).

- **Software failures**   This can include any software problem that precipitates a disaster. Examples are the software bug that caused a significant power blackout in the U.S. Northeast in 2003 and the Nest home thermostat bug in 2016.

- **Utilities**   This includes electric power failures, water supply failures, and natural gas outages, as well as communications outages.

- **Transportation** This may include airplane crashes, railroad derailments, ship collisions, and highway accidents.

- **Hazardous materials** This includes chemical spills. The primary threat here is direct damage by hazardous substances, casualties, and forced evacuations that occur as a result.

- **Criminal** This includes extortion, embezzlement, theft, vandalism, sabotage, terrorism, and hacker intrusion. Note that company insiders can play a role in these activities; this is a part of the so-called *insider threat*.

- **Errors** This includes mistakes made by personnel that result in harm to the organization's operations.

Tables E-2 (Adversarial Threat Events) and E-3 (Non-Adversarial Threat Events) in the document NIST 800-30, "Guide for Conducting Risk Assessments," contain a good reference of threats.

Security and Business Continuity Planning Common Ground

An analysis of the threats listed in this section should prompt you to think of natural and man-made disasters that, when they occur, invoke business contingency plans to ensure continuity of critical services. It is not an accident that information security and business continuity planning have a lot in common. Risk assessments are often designed to amply serve both efforts. Indeed, one may argue that business continuity planning is just a branch of information security; the common objective for both is the protection and availability of critical assets and functions.

Alongside each threat that is identified, the risk analyst assigns a probability or frequency of occurrence. This may be a numeric value, expressed as a probability of one occurrence within a calendar year. For example, if the risk of a flood is 1 in 100 years, it would be expressed as 0.01, or 1 percent. Probability can also be expressed as a ranking (for example, Low, Medium, and High), or on a numeric probability scale from 1 to 5 (where 5 can be either highest or lowest probability).

There are several approaches for continuing a threat analysis:

- **Perform a geographic threat analysis for each location** This will provide an analysis on the probability of each type of threat against all assets in each location. For example, a hurricane is more likely to occur in areas so affected; a transportation incident is more likely to occur for a location near a railroad or highway, or an operation critically dependent upon transportation may be more likely to be affected by such an event.

- **Perform a logical threat analysis for each type of asset** This provides information on all of the logical (that is, not physical) threats that can occur to each asset type. For example, the risk of malware on all assets of one type is probably the same, regardless of their location. Instead, other factors on malware attacks are probably more important, such as a server's role or location in an environment (in a DMZ, for instance).

- **Perform a threat analysis for each highly valued asset** This will help to identify any unique threats that may have appeared in the geographic or logical threat analysis, but with different probabilities of occurrence.

Threat Forecasting Data Is Sparse

One of the biggest problems with information security–related risk management is the lack of reliable data on the probability of many types of threats. While the probability of some natural threats can sometimes be obtained from local disaster response agencies, the probabilities of most other threats are difficult to accurately predict.

The difficulty in predicting security events sits in stark contrast to volumes of available data related to automobile and airplane accidents, as well as human life expectancy. In these cases, insurance companies have been accumulating statistics on these events for decades, and the variables (for instance, tobacco and alcohol use) are well known. On the topic of cyber-related risk, there is a general lack of reliable data, and the factors that influence risk are not well known from a statistical perspective. It is for this reason that risk analysis still relies on educated guesses for the probabilities of most events. But given the recent surge in popularity for cyber insurance, the availability and quality of cyberattack risk factors may soon be determined.

Vulnerability Identification A vulnerability is a weakness or absence of a protective control that makes the probability of one or more threats more likely. A vulnerability analysis is an examination of an asset to discover weaknesses that could lead to a higher-than-normal rate of occurrence or potency of a threat.

Examples of vulnerabilities include the following:

- Missing or inoperative antivirus or anti-malware software
- Outdated and unsupported software in use
- Missing security patches
- Weak password settings
- Unnecessary services running on a server or workstation
- Misconfigurations in devices, operating systems, or programs
- Missing or incomplete audit logs
- Inadequate monitoring of event logs
- Weak or defective application session management
- Building entrances that permit tailgating

In a vulnerability analysis, the risk manager needs to examine the asset itself as well as all of the protective measures that are—or should be—in place to protect the asset from relevant threats.

Vulnerabilities can be ranked by severity. Vulnerabilities are indicators that show the effectiveness, ineffectiveness, or absence of protective measures. For example, an antivirus program on a server that updates its virus signatures once per week might be ranked as a medium vulnerability, whereas the complete absence (or malfunction) of an antivirus program on the same server might be ranked as a high vulnerability. Severity is an indication of the likelihood that a given threat might be realized. This is different from impact, which is discussed later in this section.

TIP A vulnerability, and its ranking, should not be influenced by the probability that a threat will be realized. Instead, a vulnerability ranking should depend on whether the threat will actually bring about harm to the asset. Also, the ranking of a vulnerability should not be influenced by the value of the asset or the impact of a realized threat. These factors are covered separately in risk analysis and risk management.

Probability Analysis   For any given threat and asset, the probability that the threat will actually be realized needs to be estimated. This is often easier said than done, as there is a lack of reliable data on security incidents. A risk manager still will need to perform some research and develop a best guess based on any available data.

Impact Analysis   A threat, when actually realized, will have some effect on the organization. Impact analysis is the study of estimating the impact of specific threats on specific assets.

In impact analysis, it is necessary to understand the relationship between an asset and the business processes and activities that the asset supports. The purpose of impact analysis is to identify the impact on business operations or business processes. This is because risk management is not an abstract identification of abstract risks related to tangible or intangible IT assets but instead a search for risks that have real impact on business operations.

In an impact analysis, the impact can be expressed as a rating such as H-M-L (High-Medium-Low) or as a numeric scale, and it can also be expressed in financial terms. But what is also vitally important in an impact analysis is the inclusion of a statement of impact for each threat. Example statements of impact include "inability to process customer support calls" and "inability for customers to view payment history." Statements such as "inability to authenticate users" and "failure to block command-and-control traffic" may be technically accurate, but they do not identify the business impact.

NOTE Because of the additional time required to quantify and develop statements of impact, impact analysis is usually performed only on the highest-ranked threats on the most critical assets.

Qualitative Risk Analysis   A qualitative risk analysis is an in-depth examination of in-scope assets with a detailed study of threats (and their probability of occurrence), vulnerabilities (and their severity), and statements of impact. The threats, vulnerabilities, and impact are all expressed in qualitative terms such as High-Medium-Low or in numeric terms such as a 1–5 or 1–10 rating scale.

The purpose of qualitative risk analysis is to identify the most critical risks in the organization based on these rankings.

Qualitative risk analysis does not get to the issue of "how much does a given threat cost my business if it is realized?"—nor does it mean to. The value in a qualitative risk analysis is the ability to quickly identify the most critical risks without the additional burden of identifying precise financial impacts.

The individuals performing risk analysis may want to include threat-vulnerability pairing as well as asset-threat pairing. These are techniques that may help a risk analyst better understand the probability or impact of specific threats.

 NOTE   Organizations that do need to perform quantitative risk analysis often begin with qualitative risk analysis to determine the highest-ranked risks that warrant the additional effort of quantitative analysis.

Quantitative Risk Analysis   Quantitative risk analysis is a risk analysis approach that uses numeric methods to measure risk. The advantage of quantitative risk analysis is the statements of risk in terms that can be easily compared with the known value of their respective assets. In other words, risks are expressed in the same units of measure as most organizations' primary unit of measure: financial.

Despite this, quantitative risk analysis must still be regarded as an effort to develop estimates, not exact figures. Partly this is because risk analysis is a measure of events that may occur, not a measure of events that *do* occur.

A quantitative risk analysis is no more accurate than the accuracy (or inaccuracy) of the probability of occurrence. Often, the probability is no better than a guess. So while the financial impact of a threat can sometimes be known, when coupled with the probability, the end result is just an estimate.

Standard quantitative risk analysis involves the development of several figures:

- **Asset value (AV)**   This is the value of the asset, which is usually (but not necessarily) the asset's replacement value.
- **Exposure factor (EF)**   This is the financial loss that results from the realization of a threat, expressed as a percentage of the asset's total value. Most threats do not completely eliminate the asset's value; instead, they reduce its value. For example, if a construction company's $120,000 earth mover is destroyed in a fire, the equipment will still have salvage value, even if that is only 10 percent of the asset's value. In this case, the EF would be 90 percent. Note that different threats will have different impacts on EF because the realization of different threats will cause varying amounts of damage to assets.

- **Single loss expectancy (SLE)**   This value represents the financial loss when a threat is realized one time. SLE is defined as AV × EF. Note that different threats have a varied impact on EF, so those threats will also have the same multiplicative effect on SLE.

- **Annualized rate of occurrence (ARO)**   This is an estimate of the number of times that a threat will occur per year. If the probability of the threat is 1 in 50, then ARO is expressed as 0.02. However, if the threat is estimated to occur four times per year, then ARO is 4.0. Like EF and SLE, ARO will vary by threat. Obtaining an accurate figure for ARO is often the most challenging part of quantitative risk analysis.

- **Annualized loss expectancy (ALE)**   This is the expected annualized loss of asset value due to threat realization. ALE is defined as SLE × ARO.

ALE is based upon the verifiable values AV, EF, and SLE, but because ARO is only an estimate, ALE is only as good as ARO. Depending upon the value of the asset, the risk manager may need to take extra care to develop the best possible estimate for ARO, based upon whatever data is available. Sources for estimates include the following:

- History of event losses in the organization
- History of similar losses in other organizations
- History of dissimilar losses
- Best estimates based on available data

 TIP   When performing a quantitative risk analysis for a given asset, the ALE for all threats can be added together. The sum of all ALEs is the annualized loss expectancy for the total array of threats. A particularly high sum of ALEs would mean that a given asset is confronted with a lot of significant threats that are more likely to occur. But in terms of risk treatment, ALEs are better off left as separate and associated with their respective threats.

Developing Mitigation Strategies   An important part of risk analysis is the investigation of potential solutions for reducing or eliminating risk. This involves understanding specific threats and their impact (EF) and likelihood of occurrence (ARO). Once a given asset and threat combination has been *baselined* (i.e., the existing asset, threats, and controls have been analyzed to understand the threats as they exist right now), the risk analyst can then apply various hypothetical means for reducing risk, documenting each one in terms of its impact on EF and ARO.

For example, suppose a risk analysis identifies the threat of attack on a public web server. Specific EF and ARO figures have been identified for a range of individual threats. Now the risk analyst applies a range of fixes (on paper), such as an application firewall, an intrusion prevention system (IPS), and a network anomaly detection tool. Each solution will have a specific and unique impact on EF and ARO (these are all estimates, of course, just like the estimates of EF and ARO on the initial conditions); some will have better EF and ARO figures than others. Each solution should also be rated in terms of cost (financial or H-M-L) and effort to implement (financial or H-M-L).

NOTE Developing mitigation strategies is the first step in risk treatment, where various solutions are put forward, each with its cost and impact on risk.

While security analysts may have the responsibility for documenting vulnerabilities, threats, and risks, it is senior management's responsibility (through the security steering committee) to formally approve the treatment of risk. Risk treatment is discussed later in this chapter.

Risk Analysis and Business Continuity Planning Business continuity planning (BCP) utilizes risk analysis to identify risks that are related to application resilience and the impact of disasters. The risk analysis performed for BCP is the same risk analysis that is discussed in this chapter—the methods and approach are the same, although the overall objectives are somewhat different.

Business continuity planning is discussed in detail in Chapter 5.

High-Impact Events The risk manager is likely to identify one or more high-impact events during the risk analysis. These events, which may be significant enough to threaten the very viability of the organization, require risk treatment that warrants executive management visibility and belongs in the categories of business continuity planning and disaster recovery planning. These topics are discussed in Chapter 5.

Risk Analysis Standards

The methodology described in this section of identifying assets, threats, and vulnerabilities are embodied in several industry-standard risk analysis standards, including the following:

- NIST SP 800-30, "Guide for Conducting Risk Assessments"
- ISO/IEC 27005, "Information technology – Security techniques – Information security risk management"

Risk Treatment

When risks to assets have been identified through qualitative or quantitative risk analysis, the next step in the risk management process is to decide what to do about the identified risks. In the risk analysis, one or more potential solutions may have been examined, along with their cost to implement and their impact on risk. In risk treatment, a decision about whether to proceed with any of the proposed solutions (or others) is needed.

Risk treatment pits available resources against the need to reduce risk. In an enterprise environment, not all risks can be mitigated or eliminated because there are not enough resources to treat them all. Instead, a strategy for choosing the best combination of solutions that will reduce risk by the greatest possible margin is needed. For this reason, risk treatment is often more effective when all the risks and solutions are considered together, instead of each one separately. Then they can be compared and prioritized.

When risk treatment is performed at the enterprise level, risk analysts and technology architects can devise ways to bring about the greatest possible reduction in risk. This can be achieved through the implementation of solutions that will reduce many risks for many assets at once. For example, a firewall can reduce risks from many threats on many assets; this will be more effective than individual solutions for each asset.

So far, this discussion focused on risk mitigation as if it were the only option available when handling risk. Rather, there are four primary ways to treat risk: mitigation, transfer, avoidance, and acceptance. And there is always some leftover risk, called residual risk. These four approaches are discussed here.

The Most Important Aspect of Risk Treatment

The aspect of risk treatment of utmost importance to the ongoing success of an organization's security management program is who makes the risk treatment decisions. There are three choices:

- **Security manager**   This may be the person who is most knowledgeable about risk, but this is not the best choice. A security manager who makes risk treatment decisions runs the risk of others in the organization not supporting those decisions.

- **Security steering committee**   A consensus decision is often the best choice, as this allows stakeholders and others to provide input and contribute to a decision. When stakeholders have a say in risk matters, they're more likely to support decisions affecting them.

- **Undefined**   An organization that does not define who makes risk treatment decisions is, by definition, not running an effective security management program.

Risk Mitigation

Risk mitigation, or risk reduction, involves the implementation of some solution that will reduce an identified risk. For instance, the risk of advanced malware being introduced onto a server can be mitigated with advanced malware prevention software or a network-based intrusion prevention system. Either of these solutions would constitute mitigation of this risk on a given asset.

An organization usually makes a decision to implement some form of risk mitigation only after performing some cost analysis to determine whether the reduction of risk is worth the expenditure of risk mitigation.

> ## Risk Mitigation and Control Frameworks
> Controls and risk assessments are tightly coupled in the risk management life cycle. In a typical security program, an organization selects a control framework (such as NIST SP 800-53, ISO/IEC 27001 Annex A, HIPAA, NERC, or PCI-DSS) as a starting point. Then, as the organization conducts risk assessments, from time to time the action taken to mitigate a risk is the creation of a new control. It is important to understand that control frameworks represent a starting point, not the entire journey, in an information security program. Every organization is different, and no experienced information risk professional believes that any of the standard control frameworks will address all risks in an organization.

Risk Transfer

Risk transfer, or risk sharing, means that some or all of the risk is being transferred to some external entity, such as an insurance company or business partner. When an organization purchases an insurance policy to protect an asset against damage or loss, the insurance company is assuming part of the risk in exchange for payment of insurance premiums.

The details of a cyber-insurance policy need to be carefully examined to be sure that any specific risk is transferrable to the policy. Cyber-insurance policies typically have exclusions that limit or deny payment of benefits in certain situations.

Risk Avoidance

In risk avoidance, the organization abandons the risk-inducing activity altogether, effectively taking the asset out of service or discontinuing the activity so that the threat is no longer present. In another scenario, they may decide that the risk of pursuing a given business activity is too great, so they may decide to avoid that particular activity.

NOTE Organizations do not often back away completely from an activity because of identified risks. Generally, this avenue is taken only when the risk of loss is great and when the perceived probability of occurrence is high.

Risk Acceptance

Risk acceptance occurs when management is willing to accept an identified risk as is, with no effort taken to reduce it. Risk acceptance also takes place (sometimes implicitly) for residual risk, after other forms of risk treatment have been applied.

> ### The Fifth Option in Risk Treatment
>
> For decades, risk management frameworks have cited the same four risk treatment options: accept, mitigate, transfer, and avoid. There is, however, a fifth option that some organizations select: *ignore the risk*.
>
> Ignoring a risk is a choice, although it is not considered a wise choice. Ignoring a risk means doing nothing about it, not even making a decision about it. It amounts to little more than pretending the risk does not exist. It's off the books.
>
> Organizations without risk management programs may be implicitly ignoring all risks, or many of them at least. Organizations might also be practicing informal and maybe even reckless risk management—risk management by gut feel. Without a systematic framework for identifying risks, many are likely to go undiscovered. This could also be considered ignoring risks through the implicit refusal to identify them and treat them properly.

Residual Risk

Residual risk is the risk that is left over from the original risk after some of the risk has been removed through mitigation or transfer. For instance, if a particular threat had a probability of 10 percent before risk treatment and 1 percent after risk treatment, the residual risk is that 1 percent left over. This is best illustrated by the following formula:

$$\textit{Original Risk} - \textit{Mitigated Risk} - \textit{Transferred Risk} = \textit{Residual Risk}$$

It is unusual for risk treatment to eliminate risk altogether; rather, various controls are implemented that remove some of the risk. Often, management implicitly accepts the leftover risk; however, it's a good idea to make that acceptance of residual risk more formal by documenting the acceptance in a risk management log or a decision log.

Iterative Risk Treatment

Often it is appropriate to reassess a risk after risk treatment takes place. The proper way to do this is to introduce the residual risk as a new risk to be analyzed in the risk management life cycle. A risk treatment decision will be made on the residual risk, resulting in a new, and probably smaller, residual risk, which will go through the process again. Eventually, when the remaining residual risk is low enough, it will be accepted.

For example, risk analysis identifies a risk of malware attack through web sites containing malicious code (this is typically known as a *watering hole attack*). The first round of risk treatment is risk mitigation, through the introduction of a centralized web filtering device that blocks user access to known malicious web sites. Residual risk is identified: when users are away from office locations, the web filter is not in their Internet data path, and they remain vulnerable. This new risk is treated through mitigation, this time in the form of a proxy agent installed on all workstations that direct their web traffic through a SaaS-based web filtering service. After this second round of risk treatment, residual risk consists of user access to web sites not yet flagged as malicious. Since the organization also has advanced anti-malware software on each workstation, the organization elects to accept the risk introduced through the SaaS web filtering service not knowing about some malicious web sites.

Compliance Risk: The Risk Management Trump Card

Organizations that perform risk management are generally aware of the laws, regulations, and standards they are required to follow. For instance, U.S.-based banks, brokerages, and insurance companies are required to comply with the Gramm–Leach–Bliley Act (GLBA), and organizations that store, process, or transmit credit card numbers are required to comply with the Payment Card Industry Data Security Standard (PCI-DSS).

GLBA, PCI-DSS, and other regulations often state that specific controls are required in an organization's in-scope IT systems. This brings to light the matter of compliance risk. Sometimes, the risk associated with a specific control (or lack of a control) may be rated as a low risk, either because the probability of a risk event is low or because the impact of the event is low. However, if a given law, regulation, or standard requires that the control be enacted anyway, then the organization must consider the compliance risk. The risk of noncompliance may result in fines or other sanctions against the organization, which may (or may not) have consequences greater than the actual risk.

The end result of this is that organizations often implement specific security controls because they are required by laws, regulations, or standards—not because their risk analysis would otherwise compel them to.

The Risk Ledger

A *risk ledger* is a business record used to document risks identified through risk assessments and other means. The purpose of a risk ledger, also known as a risk register, is to record the discovery of risks and track decisions about their disposition. When properly implemented, a risk ledger is a concise summary record of the entire life cycle of any individual risk.

Depending upon its implementation, a risk ledger may contain details, such as risk assessments, risk analysis, and details on decision makers, or the risk ledger or something else in the risk management process may refer to those details in some way.

Typical elements in a risk ledger include these groupings and details:

- **Risk identification** Information about the introduction of the risk into the risk ledger, including a unique ID designation, the date of discovery, how it was discovered, and by whom
- **Risk description** Information about the risk itself, including relevant threats, vulnerabilities, and consequences

- **Affected assets**   Information about assets or asset groups in the organization that are affected by the risk, as well as the business owners of those assets
- **Risk score**   Information about the probability and impact of threat occurrence, expressed in qualitative terms, and possibly quantitative terms
- **Risk treatment analysis**   Information about the potential impact of various risk treatment options
- **Risk treatment**   Information of risk treatment approved by the organization, including the person, group, or asset owner that made the risk treatment decision, the date that the decision was made, and the person or group responsible for carrying out the risk treatment

This summary represents details that may appear in an organization's risk ledger. Each organization's risk management program and methods for risk treatment will govern what additional information may be included in a risk ledger.

Organizations that are just getting started on information risk management may opt to use a spreadsheet program for their first risk ledger. This is often a recommended strategy because a risk ledger can be implemented this way for very little cost. As organizations mature, they may begin to realize that many aspects of their security program record keeping are not scaling up with them. This compels organizations to move their risk ledger and other risk management records to a governance, risk, and compliance (GRC) tool. It should be noted that those risks may also leverage the enterprise risk team's tools, if such a team is in place in the organization.

Audits and Reviews

An essential function in information security management is a set of activities that determine whether security safeguards are in place and working properly. These activities range from informal security reviews to formal and highly structured security audits. Most organizations undergo one or more of these reviews or audits from time to time, either as part of a compliance program or because management realizes that reviews and audits are a necessary part of knowing whether an organization is in fact secure.

The terms *security review* and *security audit* are used in the information risk industry, correctly by many professionals but haphazardly by many others. Generally speaking, a security review is a less formal and less rigorous examination of one or more controls, processes, or systems to determine their state. A security audit is a more formal and more rigorous examination of one or more controls, processes, or systems. An audit generally requires the presentation of evidence of control design and effectiveness, where a review often does not.

Figure 4-3 depicts the relationship between security reviews and security audits.

Audits

An audit is a systematic and repeatable process whereby a competent and independent professional evaluates one or more controls, interviews personnel, obtains and analyzes evidence, and develops a written opinion on the effectiveness of the controls. In an audit of information systems and the processes that support them, an information systems

Figure 4-3 Security reviews and security audits

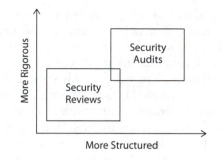

auditor interviews personnel, gathers and analyzes evidence, and delivers a written opinion on the effectiveness of controls implemented in information systems.

There are generally two parties in an audit: the auditor and the auditee. This is true whether the audit is formal or informal and whether it's internal or external. In terms of the context of an audit, there are two types: internal audit and external audit. These only have to do with who performs the audit and why. Otherwise, the methodologies and techniques used in auditing are the same. This section describes audit techniques, which is followed by more detailed discussions on internal and external audits.

For a more complete discussion on audits and auditing, see *CISA Certified Information Systems Auditor All-in-One Exam Guide*.

Audit Techniques   Like most any business undertaking, an audit is a planned event. Formal planning is required so that the organization successfully achieves the objectives for an audit. The types of planning that are required include the following:

- **Purpose**   The auditor and the auditee must establish a *reason* why an audit is to be performed. The purpose for a particular audit could be to determine the level of compliance to a particular law, regulation, standard, or contract. Another reason could be to determine whether specific control deficiencies identified in past audits have been remediated. Still another reason is to determine the level of compliance to a new law, standard, or contract that the organization may be subject to in the future.

- **Scope**   The auditor and the auditee must also establish the *scope* of the audit. Often, the audit's purpose will make the scope evident, but not always. Scope may be multidimensional: it could be a given period, meaning records spanning a start date and end date may comprise the body of evidence, geography (systems in a particular region or locale), technology (systems using a specific operating system, database, application, or other aspect), business process (systems that support specific processes such as accounting, order entry, or customer support), or segment of the organization.

- **Risk analysis**   To know which areas require the greatest amount of attention, the auditor needs to be familiar with the levels of *risk* associated with the domain being audited. Two different perspectives of risk may be needed. First, the auditor needs to know the relative levels of risk among the different aspects of the domain being audited so that audit resources can be allocated accordingly. For example, if the subject of an audit is an enterprise resource planning (ERP) system and the auditor knows that the accounts receivable function has been problematic in the past, the auditor will probably want to devote more resources and time on the accounts receivable function than on others. Second, the auditor needs to know about the absolute level of risk across the entire domain being audited. For example, if this is an audit to determine compliance to new legislation, the overall risk could be very high if the consequences of noncompliance are high. Both aspects of risk enable the auditor to plan accordingly.

- **Audit procedures**   The purpose and scope of the audit may help to define the procedures that will be required to perform the audit. For a compliance audit, for example, there may be specific rules on sample sizes and sampling techniques, and it may require that auditors possess specific qualifications. A compliance audit may also specify criteria for determining whether a particular finding constitutes a deficiency. There may also be rules for materiality and additional steps to follow if material weaknesses are identified.

- **Resources**   The auditor must determine what resources are needed and available for the audit. In an external audit, the auditee (which is a client organization) may have a maximum budget figure available. For an external or internal audit, the auditor needs to determine the number of man-hours that will be required in the audit and the various skills required. Other resources that may be needed include specialized tools to gather or analyze information obtained from information systems—for example, an analysis program to process the roles and permissions in a database management system in order to identify high-risk areas. To a great degree, the purpose and scope of the audit will determine which resources are required to complete it.

- **Schedule**   The auditor needs to develop an audit schedule that will give enough time for interviews, data collection and analysis, and report generation. Additionally, the schedule could also come in the form of a constraint, meaning the audit must be complete by a certain date. If the auditor is given a deadline, he will need to see how the audit activities can be made to fit within that period. If the date is too aggressive, the auditor will need to discuss the matter with the auditee to make required adjustments in scope, resources, or schedule.

Audit Objectives   The term *audit objectives* refers to the specific goals for an audit. Generally, the objective of an audit is to determine whether controls exist and whether they are effective in some specific aspect of business operations in an organization. Generally, an audit is performed as part of regulations, compliance, or other legal obligations. It may also be performed in the aftermath of a serious incident or event to determine whether any additional weaknesses are found elsewhere in the organization that could also suffer an event. Sometimes, an organization will initiate an internal audit of relevant systems if a competitor or other similar organization has suffered an incident; the purpose here is to determine whether the organization is likely to suffer the same fate.

Depending on the subject and nature of the audit, the auditor may examine the controls and related evidence herself, or the auditor may instead focus on the business content that is processed by the controls. In other words, if the focus of an audit is an organization's accounting system, the auditor may focus on financial transactions in the system to see how they affect financial bookkeeping. Or, the auditor could focus on IT processes that support the operation of the financial accounting system. Formal audit objectives should make such a distinction so that the auditor has a sound understanding of the objectives. This tells the auditor where to look and what to look at during the audit. Of course, the type of audit being undertaken helps too; this is covered in the next section.

Types of Audits   The scope, purpose, and objectives of an audit will to a great extent determine the type of audit that will be performed. Auditors need to understand each type of audit, including the procedures that are used for each, so that the correct type of audit will be selected. The following are the types of audits:

- **Operational audit**   This type of audit is an examination of IT controls, security controls, or business controls to determine control existence and effectiveness. The focus of an operational audit is usually the operation of one or more controls, and it could concentrate on the IT management of a business process or on the business process itself.

- **Financial audit**   This type of audit is an examination of the organization's accounting system, including accounting department processes and procedures. The typical objective of a financial audit is to determine whether business controls are sufficient to ensure the integrity of financial statements.

- **Integrated audit**   This type of audit combines an operational audit and a financial audit in order for the auditor to gain a complete understanding of the entire environment's integrity. Such an audit will closely examine accounting department processes, procedures, and records, as well as the business applications that support the accounting department or other financial function. Virtually every organization uses a computerized accounting system for management of its financial records; the computerized accounting system and all of the supporting infrastructure (database management system, operating system, networks, workstations, and so on) will be examined to see whether the IT department has the entire environment under adequate control.

- **IS audit**   This type of audit is a detailed examination of most or all of an information systems (IS) department's operations. An IS audit looks at IT governance to determine whether IS is aligned with overall organization goals and objectives. The audit also looks closely at all of the major IT processes, including service delivery, change and configuration management, security management, systems development life cycle, business relationship and supplier management, and incident and problem management. This audit will determine whether each control objective and control is effective and operating properly.

- **Administrative audit**   This type of audit is an examination of operational efficiency within some segment of the organization.

- **Compliance audit**   This type of audit is performed to determine the level and degree of compliance to a law, regulation, standard, internal control, or legal contract. If a particular law or standard requires an external audit, the compliance audit may have to be performed by approved or licensed external auditors; for example, a U.S. public company's annual financial audit must be performed by a public accounting firm, and a PCI audit must be performed by a licensed qualified security assessor (QSA). If, however, the law or standard does not explicitly require audits, the organization may still want to perform one-time or regular audits to determine the level of compliance to the law or standard. This type of audit may be performed by internal or external auditors and typically is performed so that management has a better understanding of the level of compliance risk.

- **Forensic audit**   This type of audit is usually performed by an auditor or a forensic specialist in support of an anticipated or active legal proceeding. To withstand cross-examination and to avoid having evidence being ruled inadmissible, strict procedures must be followed in a forensic audit, including the preservation of evidence and a chain of custody of evidence.

- **Service provider audit**   Because many organizations outsource critical activities to third parties, often these third-party service organizations will undergo one or more external audits to increase customer confidence in the integrity and security of the third-party organization's services. In the United States, a Statement on Standards for Attestation Engagements No. 18 (SSAE 18) audit can be performed on a service provider's operations and the audit report transmitted to customers of the service provider. SSAE 18 superseded the similar SSAE 16 standard, which replaced the older Statement of Accounting Standards No. 70 (SAS 70) audit in 2011. The SSAE 18 standard was developed by the American Institute of Certified Public Accountants (AICPA) for the purpose of auditing third-party service organizations that perform financial services on behalf of their customers.

TIP   SSAE 18 is closely aligned with the global standard, *International Standard on Assurance Engagements 3402, Assurance Reports on Controls at a Service Organization* (ISAE 3402), from the International Auditing and Assurance Standards Board (IAASB).

- **Pre-audit**   While not technically an audit, a pre-audit is an examination of business processes, information systems, applications, or business records in anticipation of an upcoming audit. Usually, an organization will undergo a pre-audit to get a better idea of its compliance to a law, regulation, standard, or other legal obligation prior to an actual compliance audit. An organization can use the results of a pre-audit to implement corrective measures, thereby improving the outcome of the real audit.

Audit Methodology   An *audit methodology* is the set of audit procedures that is used to accomplish a set of audit objectives. An organization that regularly performs audits should develop formal methodologies so that those audits are performed consistently, even when carried out by different personnel. The phases of a typical audit methodology are described here:

- **Audit subject**   Determine the business process, information system, or other domain to be audited. For instance, an auditor might be auditing an IT change control process, an IT service desk ticketing system, or the activities performed by a software development department.

- **Audit objective**   Identify the purpose of the audit. For example, this may be an audit that is required by a law, regulation, standard, or business contract. Or this may be an audit to determine compliance with internal control objectives to measure control effectiveness.

- **Type of audit**   This may be an operational audit, financial audit, integrated audit, administrative audit, compliance audit, forensic audit, or a security provider audit.

- **Audit scope**   The business process, department, or application that is the subject of the audit. Usually, a span of time needs to be identified as well so that activities or transactions during that period can be examined.

- **Pre-audit planning**   Here, the auditor needs to obtain information about the audit that will enable her to establish the audit plan. Information needed includes locations that need to be visited, a list of the applications to be examined, the technologies supporting each application, and the policies, standards, and diagrams that describe the environment.

This and other information will enable the auditor to determine the skills required to examine and evaluate processes and information systems. The auditor will be able to establish an audit schedule and will have a good idea of the types of evidence that are needed. The IS audit may be able to make advance requests for certain other types of evidence even before the on-site phase of the audit begins.

For an audit with a risk-based approach, the auditor has a couple of options:

- Precede the audit itself with a risk assessment to determine which processes or controls warrant additional audit scrutiny.

- Gather information about the organization and historic events to discover risks that warrant additional audit scrutiny.

Audit Statement of Work   For an external audit, the auditor may need to develop a statement of work or engagement letter that describes the audit purpose, scope, duration, and costs. The auditor may require a written approval from the client before audit work can officially begin.

Establish Audit Procedures   Using information obtained regarding audit objectives and scope, the auditor can now develop procedures for this audit. For each objective and control to be tested, the auditor can specify the following:

- A list of people to interview
- Inquiries to make during each interview
- Documentation (policies, procedures, and other documents) to request during each interview
- Audit tools to use
- Sampling rates and methodologies
- How and where evidence will be archived
- How evidence will be evaluated

Audit Communication Plan   The auditor will develop a communication plan to keep the auditor's management, as well as the auditee's management, informed throughout the audit project. The communication plan may contain one or more of the following:

- A list of evidence requested, usually in the form of a PBC (provided by client) list, which is typically a worksheet that lists specific documents or records and the names of personnel who can provide them (or who provided them in a prior audit)
- Regular written status reports that include activities performed since the last status report, upcoming activities, and any significant findings that may require immediate attention
- Regular status meetings where audit progress, issues, and other matters may be discussed in person or via conference call
- Contact information for both IS auditor and auditee so that both parties can contact each other quickly if needed

Report Preparation   The auditor needs to develop a plan that describes how the audit report will be prepared. This will include the format and the content of the report, as well as the manner in which findings will be established and documented.

The auditor will need to ensure that the audit report complies with all applicable audit standards, including ISACA IS audit standards.

If the audit report requires internal review, the auditor will need to identify the parties that will perform the review and make sure they will be available at the time when the auditor expects to complete the final draft of the audit report.

Wrap-up   The auditor needs to perform a number of tasks at the conclusion of the audit, including the following:

- Deliver the report to the auditee.
- Schedule a closing meeting so that the results of the audit can be discussed with the auditee and so that the auditor can collect feedback.

- For external audits, send an invoice to the auditee.

- Collect and archive all work papers. Enter their existence in a document management system so that they can be retrieved later if needed and to ensure their destruction when they have reached the end of their retention life.

- Update PBC documents if the auditor anticipates that the audit will be performed again in the future.

- Collect feedback from the auditee and convey to any audit staff as needed.

Post-audit Follow-up   After a given period (which could range from days to months), the auditor should contact the auditee to determine what progress the auditee has made on the remediation of any audit findings. There are several good reasons for doing this:

- It establishes a tone of concern for the auditee organization (and an interest in its success) and demonstrates that the auditee is taking the audit process seriously.

- It helps to establish a dialogue whereby the auditor can help auditee management work through any needed process or technology changes as a result of the audit.

- It helps the auditor better understand management's commitment to the audit process and to continuous improvement.

- For an external auditor, it improves goodwill and the prospect for repeat business.

Audit Evidence   *Evidence* is the information collected by the auditor during the audit. The contents and reliability of the evidence obtained are used by the auditor to reach conclusions on the effectiveness of controls and control objectives. The auditor needs to understand how to evaluate various types of evidence and how (and if) it can be used to support audit findings.

The auditor will collect many kinds of evidence during an audit, including observations, written notes, correspondence, independent confirmations from other auditors, internal process and procedure documentation, and business records.

When an auditor examines evidence, he needs to consider several characteristics about the evidence, which will contribute to its weight and reliability. These characteristics include the following:

- Independence of the evidence provider
- Qualifications of the evidence provider
- Objectivity
- Timing

Gathering Evidence   The auditor must understand and be experienced in the methods and techniques used to gather evidence during an audit. The methods and techniques used most often in audits include the following:

- Organization chart review
- Review of department and project charters
- Review of third-party contracts and service level agreements (SLAs)

- Review of IS policies and procedures
- Review of risk register (also known as a risk ledger)
- Review of incident log
- Review of IS standards
- Review of IS system documentation
- Personnel interviews
- Passive observation

Observing Personnel   It is rarely sufficient for an auditor to obtain and understand process documentation and be able to make judgments about the effectiveness of the process. Usually, the auditor will need to collect evidence in the form of observations to see how consistently a system's process documentation is actually followed. Some of the techniques in observing personnel include the following:

- **Real tasks**   The auditor should request to see some functions actually being carried out.
- **Skills and experience**   The auditor should ask each interviewee about his or her career background to determine the interviewee's level of experience and career maturity.
- **Security awareness**   The auditor should observe personnel to see whether they are following security policies and procedures.
- **Segregation of duties**   The auditor should observe personnel to see whether adequate segregation of duties (SOD) is in place.

An experienced auditor will have a well-developed "sixth sense," an intuition about people that can be used to better understand the people who execute procedures.

Sampling   *Sampling* refers to the technique that is used when it is not feasible to test an entire population of transactions. The objective of sampling is to select a portion of a population so that the characteristics observed will reflect the characteristics of the entire population.

There are several methods for sampling:

- **Statistical sampling**   The IS auditor uses a technique of random selection that will statistically reflect the entire population.
- **Judgmental sampling (also known as nonstatistical sampling)**   The IS auditor judgmentally and subjectively selects samples based on established criteria such as risk or materiality.
- **Attribute sampling**   This technique is used to study the characteristics of a given population to answer the question of "how many?" After the auditor has selected a statistical sample, she then examines the samples. A specific attribute is chosen, and the samples are examined to see how many items have the

characteristic and how many do not. For example, an auditor may test a list of terminated user accounts to see how many were terminated within 24 hours and how many were not. This is used to statistically determine the rate at which terminations are performed within 24 hours among the entire population.

- **Variable sampling**   This technique is used to statistically determine the characteristic of a given population to answer the question "how much?" For example, an auditor who wants to know the total value of an inventory can select a sample and then statistically determine the total value in the entire population based on the total value of the sample.

- **Stop-or-go sampling**   This technique is used to permit sampling to stop at the earliest possible time.

- **Discovery sampling**   This technique is used when an auditor is trying to find at least one exception in a population. When he is examining a population where even a single exception would represent a high-risk situation (such as embezzlement or fraud), the auditor will recommend a more intensive investigation to determine whether additional exceptions exist.

- **Stratified sampling**   Here, the event population will be divided into classes, or strata, based upon the value of one of the attributes. Then, samples are selected from each class, and results are developed from each class or combined into a single result. An example of where this could be used is a selection of purchase orders (POs), where the auditor wants to make sure that some of the extremely high-value and low-value POs will be selected to see whether there is any statistical difference in the results in different classes.

NOTE   Part of the body of evidence in an audit is a description of how a sample was selected and why the particular sampling technique was used.

Reliance Upon Third-Party Audit Reports   Another common setting for the reliance of other auditors is the case where an organization may choose to rely upon audit reports for an external service provider rather than audit the external service provider directly. A typical example is a case where an organization outsources payroll to a payroll services provider and the payroll services provider has its own SSAE 18 audit that is performed by qualified audit firms. The organization's own auditors will likely choose to rely on the payroll service provider's SSAE 18 audit rather than audit the payroll service provider directly.

From the service provider's point of view, the costs to commission an SSAE 18 audit and make the audit report available to its clients is less than the cost for even a small percentage of its customers to perform their own audits of the service provider's business.

Reporting Audit Results   The work product of an audit project is the *audit report*, a written report that describes the entire audit project, including audit objectives, scope, controls evaluated, opinions on the effectiveness and integrity of those controls, and recommendations for improvement.

While an auditor or audit firm will generally use a standard format for an audit report, some laws and standards require that an audit report regarding those laws or standards contain specific information or be presented in a particular format. Still, there will be some variance in the structure and appearance of audit reports created by different audit organizations.

The auditor is typically asked to present findings in a closing meeting, where he can explain the audit and its results and be available to answer questions about the audit. The auditor may include an electronic presentation to guide discussion of the audit.

Structure and Contents   While there are often different styles for presenting audit findings, as well as regulations and standards that require specific content, an audit report will generally include several elements:

- Cover letter
- Introduction
- Summary
- Description of the audit
- Listing of systems and processes examined
- Listing of interviewees
- Listing of evidence obtained
- Explanation of sampling techniques
- Description of findings and recommendations

When the auditor is creating the report, he must make sure that it is balanced, reasonable, and fair. The report should not just be a list of everything that was bad; it should also include a list of controls that were found to be operating effectively.

The auditor also needs to take care when describing recommendations, realizing that any organization is capable of only so much change in a given period. If the audit report contains many findings, the auditor needs to realize that the organization may not be able to remediate all of them in an elegant manner. Instead, the organization will need to understand which findings should be remediated first—the audit report should provide this guidance.

NOTE   It is typically *not* the auditor's role to describe *how* an audit finding should be remediated. Deciding the methods used to apply remediation is the role of auditee management.

Evaluating Control Effectiveness   When developing an audit report, the auditor needs to communicate the effectiveness of controls to the auditee. Often, this reporting is needed at several layers; for instance, the auditor may provide more detailed findings and recommendations to control owners, while the report for senior management may contain only the significant findings.

One method that auditors frequently use is the development of a matrix of all audit findings, where each audit finding is scored on a criticality scale. This helps the auditor to illustrate the audit findings that are the most important and those that are less important, in the auditor's opinion. The auditor can also report on cases where an ineffective control is mitigated (fully or partially) by one or more compensating controls. For example, a system may not have the ability to enforce password complexity (e.g., requiring upper- and lowercase letters, plus numbers and special characters), but this can be compensated through the use of longer-than-usual passwords and perhaps even more frequent expiration.

Internal Audit   *Internal audit* is an audit of an organization's controls, processes, or systems, and it is carried out by personnel who are a part of the organization. Many organizations have one or more people in an internal audit function.

Organizations that are serious about their commitment to an effective security program will commit resources to the internal audit function. Recognizing that external resources are far more costly, internal auditors become more familiar with internal processes and systems and can examine them more frequently and provide better feedback to others in the organization.

Some regulations and standards require organizations to conduct internal audits as part of required compliance efforts; examples include Sarbanes–Oxley and ISO/IEC 27001.

In U.S. public companies and in many other organizations, internal audit (IA) departments report to the organization's audit committee or board of directors (or a similar "governing entity"). The IA department often has close ties with and a "dotted line" reporting relationship to finance leadership in order to manage day-to-day activities. An internal audit department will launch projects at the request and/or approval of the governing entity and, to a degree, members of executive management.

Regulations and standards play a large role in internal audit work. For example, public companies, banks, and government organizations are all subject to a great deal of regulation, much of which requires regular information systems controls testing. Management, as part of their risk management strategy, also requires this testing. External reporting of the results of internal auditing is sometimes necessary. Similarly, organizations that are ISO/IEC 27001 certified are required to carry out regular internal audit work to ensure that controls continue to be effective.

A common internal audit cycle consists of several categories of projects:

- Risk assessments and audit planning
- Cyclical controls testing (SOX, ISO/IEC 27001, and A-123, for example)
- Review of existing control structures
- Operational and IS audits

It is common for the IA department to maintain a multiyear plan, in which it maintains a schedule or rotation of audits. The audit plan is shared with the governing entity, and the governing entity is asked to review and approve the IA department's plan. The governing entity may seek to include specific reviews in the IA department's audit plan at this point. When an audit plan is approved, the IA department's tasks for the year (and tentative tasks for future years) are now determined.

Even if the risk assessment is carried out by other personnel, internal auditors are often included in a formal risk assessment process. Specific skills are needed to communicate with an organization's IT personnel regarding technology risks. Internal auditors will use information from management to identify, evaluate, and rank an organization's main technology risks. The outcome of this process may result in IT-related specific audits within the IA department's audit plan. The governing entity may select areas that are financial or operational and that are heavily supported by information systems.

Internal audits may be launched using a project charter, which formalizes and communicates the project to audit sponsors, the auditors, and the managers of the departments subject to the audit.

The Institute of Internal Auditors (IIA) has excellent guidance for audit planning at https://na.theiia.org.

Cyclical Controls Testing

Cyclical controls testing is the practice of an organization conducting internal audits on its internal controls. A great deal of effort has recently been expended getting organizations to execute a controls testing life cycle. Most frequently, these practices are supporting the integrity of controls in financially relevant processes. Public corporations are required to comply with Sarbanes–Oxley Section 404 requirements, and U.S. government organizations have been subject to OMB Circular A-123, compliance with the Federal Information Security Management Act (FISMA), and other similar requirements. Countries outside of the United States have instituted similar controls testing requirements for publicly traded companies and governmental organizations. Many industries, such as banking, insurance, and healthcare, are likewise required to perform control testing because of industry-specific regulations. Organizations that elect to maintain ISO/IEC 27001 certification are required to perform internal control testing.

Organizations often employ GRC tools to assist with tracking controls testing. These systems track the execution and success of control tests performed as part of a testing cycle and can frequently manage archival of supporting evidence.

Establishing Controls Testing Cycles

Young or growing organizations may not have established or documented internal controls testing cycles. Internal auditors, working in conjunction with individuals focused on manual controls, will participate in the establishment of controls testing. The auditor produces documentation of controls through a series of meetings with management. During the process, auditors will develop process and controls documentation and confirm their accuracy with control owners through the performance of control walk-throughs.

These engagements are likely to occur when companies prepare to go public. Such companies need to comply with Sarbanes–Oxley Section 404 requirements, which involve documenting controls and performing a test of existence, also known as a "test set of 1" or a "walk-through," for each identified key control.

Private companies will maintain SOX-equivalent documentation to retain the option of seeking public financing or when lenders or private investors require it. Many organizations will find external resources to assist in the documentation and testing of applicable internal controls.

External Audit   An external audit is an audit that is performed by auditors who are not employees of the organization. There are three principal reasons that an organization will undergo an external audit versus an internal audit:

- **Legal or regulatory requirement**   Various laws and regulations, such as Sarbanes–Oxley and A-123, require periodic external audit of relevant systems and business processes. Additionally, standards such as PCI-DSS and ISO/IEC 27001 require organizations to undergo external audits in some circumstances.

- **Lack of internal resources**   An organization may not have internal staff with skills in auditing, or its internal audit staff may not have enough time to conduct all of the organization's internal audits.

- **Objectivity**   Organizations sometimes opt to have an objective, expert third party perform audits to ensure that audit results are unbiased.

Organizations planning external audits need to understand several aspects of the audit, including the following:

- **Objective**   What is the purpose of the audit? This includes whether it is required by regulations, laws, or standards such as Sarbanes–Oxley, A-123, ISO/IEC 27001, or PCI-DSS.

- **Scope**   What business units, departments, systems, processes, and personnel are the subject of the audit?

- **Time**   What is the time period for the audit? This generally involves the acquisition of evidence in the form of business records associated with controls that auditors will want to examine.

- **Resources**   What resources will be required for the audit? For external audits, this includes office space for one or more auditors, access to workspaces, and access to networks and systems for the acquisition of evidence.

- **Schedule**   Organizations need to understand the schedule for the audit, including when it will start, when specific activities will take place during the audit, and when it is expected to be completed.

- **Audit firm and auditor qualifications**   Organizations should assess the quality of the firm and the people conducting the audit when using external audit firms. Has the firm or auditor conducted the type of audit before? If so, how many audits have they done and in what business segments was the audit conducted?

- **Audit methodology**   What sampling techniques and other details will be used by the auditors?

- **Personnel**   What internal personnel will be needed for the audit? This includes process and system owners that auditors will want to interview, plus any administrators or coordinators who will manage the scheduling of internal personnel as well as meeting spaces.

Organizations undergoing any particular audit for the first time generally plan much further ahead. In many cases, a pre-audit will be performed to get a preliminary idea of the results that will be achieved in the actual audit.

Organizations planning a pre-audit need to ensure that the same techniques will be used in the pre-audit as will be performed in the audit. This is a common mistake in a pre-audit. If the pre-audit is less rigorous and thorough than the audit, the organization may have a false sense of confidence in a favorable audit outcome, and instead there is the unpleasant surprise that the audit went poorly while the pre-audit was seemingly successful.

Organizations need to ensure that personnel are ready for the audit. In particular, personnel who have never worked with external auditors need to be coached as follows:

- Personnel should only answer questions that auditors asked. Personnel should be trained in the skill of *active listening* so that they understand what the auditor is asking, prior to giving an answer.

- Personnel should not express their opinions about the subject matter. Determination of the effectiveness of a control is the auditor's job, not that of the control owner or other person providing information.

- Personnel should not volunteer additional information. Doing so will only cause confusion and potential delays in completion of the audit.

Seeding Audit Results

Management may spend considerable time and energy making sure that personnel understand one thing when dealing with auditors: they should specifically answer the question that the auditor asked, not the question the auditor *should have* asked, and they should not volunteer any information.

There is, however, a useful technique that management (and only management) sometimes uses when working with auditors. I prefer to call this *seeding* the audit results. Similar to the technique of cloud seeding, where rain clouds are seeded with substances to cause them to release rain, management can use audit seeding as a way of ensuring that auditors are aware of specific situations that they are willing to include in their audit report. The purpose of audit seeding is generally the creation of an audit issue that will permit management to prioritize an initiative to improve the business.

For example, external auditors are examining access controls, an area where a security manager has had difficulty obtaining funds to make key improvements. While in a discussion with auditors, the security manager may choose to illuminate particular actions, inactions, or other situations in access control processes or technology that the auditor might not have otherwise noticed.

Persons who are considering audit seeding must have a thorough understanding of the subject matter, the controls being tested, the procedures and technologies in play, the auditing methodology in use, and a bit of grit. Audit seeding may be considered a daring move that may have unforeseen results. Finally, people considering audit seeding must not make auditors feel they are being manipulated, as this could have greater consequences. Instead, management is simply making auditors aware of an important aspect of a control they are auditing.

Control Self-Assessment

Control self-assessment (CSA) is a methodology used by an organization to review key business objectives, risks related to achieving these objectives, and the key controls designed to manage those risks. The primary characteristic of a CSA is that the organization takes initiative to self-regulate rather than engage outsiders, who may be experts in auditing but not in the organization's mission, goals, objectives, and culture.

CSA Advantages and Disadvantages   Like almost any business activity, control self-assessments have a number of advantages and disadvantages that a security manager and others should be familiar with. This will help the organization make the most of this process and avoid some common problems.

The advantages of a control self-assessment include the following:

- Risks can be detected earlier, since subject-matter experts are involved earlier.
- Internal controls can be improved in a timely manner.
- Control self-assessment leads to greater ownership of controls through involvement in their assessment and improvement.
- Control self-assessment leads to improved employee awareness of controls through involvement in their assessment and improvement.
- Control self-assessment may help improve relationships between departments and auditors.

Some of the disadvantages of a control self-assessment include the following:

- Control self-assessment could be mistaken by employees or management as a substitute for an internal audit.
- Control self-assessment may be considered extra work and dismissed as unnecessary.
- Employees may attempt to cover up shoddy work and misdeeds.
- Control self-assessment may be considered an attempt by the auditor to shrug off his or her own responsibilities.
- Lack of employee involvement would translate to little or no process improvement.

The Control Self-Assessment Life Cycle   Like most continuous-improvement processes, the control self-assessment process is an iterative life cycle. The phases in the control self-assessment are as follows:

- **Identify and assess risks**   Operational risks are identified and analyzed.
- **Identify and assess controls**   Controls to manage risks are identified and assessed. If any controls are missing, new controls are designed.
- **Develop questionnaire or conduct workshop**   An interactive session is conducted, if possible, for discussion of risks and controls. If personnel are

distributed across several locations, a conference call can be convened, or a questionnaire may be developed and sent to them.

- **Analyze completed questionnaires or assess workshop**   If a workshop was held, the workshop results are assessed to see what good ideas for remediation emerged. If a questionnaire was distributed, the results are analyzed to see the deficiencies that were identified and the ideas for risk remediation that were identified.
- **Control remediation**   Using the best ideas from the workshop or questionnaire, controls are designed or altered to better manage risk.
- **Awareness training**   This activity is carried out through every phase of the life cycle to keep personnel informed about the activities in the various phases.

Figure 4-4 illustrates the control self-assessment life cycle.

Self-Assessment Objectives   The primary objective of a control self-assessment is to transfer some of the responsibility for oversight of control performance and monitoring to the control owners. The roles of the security manager and IS auditor are not diminished, as an internal or external audit still needs to periodically test control effectiveness, but control owners will play a more active role in the audit of their controls.

Another objective of control self-assessment is the long-term reduction in exceptions. As control owners assume more responsibility for the performance of their controls,

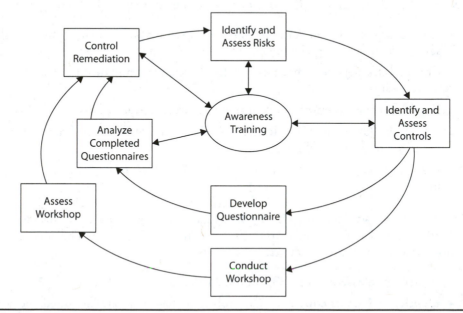

Figure 4-4   The control self-assessment life cycle

they will strive to avoid situations where auditors identify exceptions. The CSA gives control owners an opportunity and a process for cleaning house and improving audit results.

 NOTE The security manager and internal auditor should be involved in control self-assessments to ensure that the CSA process is not hijacked by efficiency zealots who try to remove the controls from processes because they do not understand their purpose or significance.

Auditors and Self-Assessment Auditors should be involved in control self-assessments that various departments conduct. The role of an auditor should be that of an objective subject-matter expert who can guide discussions in the right direction so that controls will receive the right kind of development and improvements over time.

Auditors should resist too large a role in control self-assessments. Responsibility for control development and maturation should lie within the department that owns the CSA. However, if a department is new at conducting a CSA, it may take some time before they are confident and competent enough to take full ownership and responsibility for the process.

Security Reviews

A *security review* is an examination of a process, procedure, system, program, or other object to determine the state of security. A security review may be done as part of an ad hoc request, or it may be part of a repeatable business process.

These are some examples of security reviews:

- Review of a firewall configuration to ensure that all expected rules are present and that there are no unwanted rules such as "any-any"
- Review of source code as part of the software development life cycle to ensure the code in question is free of security defects
- Review of an employee onboarding procedure to make sure that necessary security steps are followed

Organizations sometimes perform security reviews in advance of an audit so that there are no unexpected audit findings during the audit. A security review may also be thought of as a "dry run" prior to an audit so that personnel are familiar with the subject matter that auditors will be asking them about during the audit. This type of review is sometimes known as a *pre-audit*.

Security reviews are generally less rigorous than security audits. Security reviews are generally devoid of rules for evidence collection, types of testing, or sampling techniques. For instance, a security review of a firewall configuration may take more of a glance at its rules, whereas an audit may examine each individual rule: its purpose, its meaning, who approved it, and when it will next be reviewed.

Policy Development

The development of security policy is a foundational component of any organization's security program. Security policy defines the principles and required actions for the organization to properly protect its assets and personnel.

The audience for security policy is the organization's personnel, not only its full-time and part-time employees but also its temporary workers, including contractors and consultants. Security policy must be easily accessible by all personnel so that they can never offer ignorance as an excuse for violating policy. To this point, many organizations require all personnel to acknowledge the existence of, and their understanding of, the organization's security policy at the time of hire and annually thereafter.

Considerations

Security policy cannot be developed in a vacuum. Instead, it needs to align with a number of internal and external factors. The development of policy needs to incorporate several considerations, including the following:

- Applicable laws, regulations, standards, and other legal obligations
- Risk tolerance
- Controls
- Organizational culture

Alignment with Controls

Security policy and controls need to be in alignment. This is not to say that there must be a control for every policy or a policy for every control. However, policies and controls must not contradict each other. For example, if a control states that no personally owned mobile devices may connect to internal networks, then policy cannot state that those devices may be used, provided no corporate information is stored on them.

Alignment with the Audience

Security policy needs to align with the audience. In most organizations, this means that policy statements need to be understood by the majority of workers. A common mistake in the development of security policy is the inclusion of highly technical policies such as permitted encryption algorithms or statements about the hardening of servers. Such topics are irrelevant to most workers. The danger of including policies that are irrelevant to most workers is that they are likely to "tune out" and not pay attention to those policies that *are* applicable to them. In other words, security policy should have a high signal-to-noise ratio.

In organizations with extensive uses of technology, one avenue is to create a general security policy intended for all workers (technical and nontechnical) and a separate policy for technical workers who design, build, and maintain information systems. Another alternative is to create a general security policy for all workers that includes a policy stating that all controls are mandatory. Either approach would be sufficient by aligning messages about policy with various audiences.

Security Policy Structure

There are several different topics that are the subject of security policy. The range of topics may include the following:

- Acceptable use of organization assets
- Mobile devices
- Protection of information and assets
- Access control and passwords
- Personally owned devices
- Security incidents
- E-mail and other communications
- Social media
- Ethics and applicable laws
- Workplace safety
- Visitors
- Consequences of noncompliance
- Cloud computing
- Data exchange with third parties

Security managers are free to choose how to package these and other security policies. For example, they may exist in separate documents or all together in one document. There is no right or wrong here; instead, a security manager should figure out what would work best in the organization by observing how other policies are structured and published.

Security policy statements should be general in nature and not cite specific devices, technologies, or configurations. Policy statements should state *what* is to be done (or not done) but not *how*. This way, security policies will be durable and will need to be changed infrequently. On the other hand, security standards and procedures may change more frequently as practices, techniques, and technologies change.

Policy Distribution and Acknowledgment

Security policy—indeed, all organization policy—should be well known and easily accessible by all workers. This might mean that it's published on a corporate intranet or other online location where workers go to obtain information about internal operations.

All workers need to be informed of the presence of the organization's security policy. The best method in most organizations is for a high-ranking executive to write a memo or an e-mail to all workers stating the importance of information security in the organization and informing them that the information security policy describes required behavior on the part of all workers. Another effective tactic is to have the senior executive record a message outlining the need and importance of security policy. Additionally, the message should state that the executive leadership team has reviewed and fully supports the policies.

Executives need to be mindful that they lead by example. If executives are seen to carve out exceptions for themselves (for example, if an executive insists on using a personal tablet computer for company business when policy forbids it), then other workers are apt to notice and take their own shortcuts wherever they're able. If executives work to visibly comply with security policy, then others will too. Organization culture includes behavior such as compliance to policy or a tendency for workers to skirt policy whenever possible.

Third-Party Risk Management

Third-party risk management (TPRM) is the practice of identifying risks associated with the use of outsourced organizations that perform business processes. Most organizations are moving their internal IT infrastructure to cloud-based organizations, and they are similarly moving their core business applications from on-premise to cloud-based software-as-a-service (SaaS) organizations.

The purpose of TPRM is to identify and remediate risks associated with third parties. The techniques used in TPRM serve to extend an organization's risk management functions to include methods of identifying various types of risks introduced as a result of relationships with third parties.

TPRM practices have advanced significantly in recent years, in response to the wave of outsourcing to cloud-based infrastructure and software services. With so much of corporate IT existing in and being managed by other organizations, TPRM practices have changed so that security and risk managers can continue to have a clear idea of the risks present in their IT operations, much of which is run by other companies.

NOTE Organizations sometimes fail to understand that while operations can be outsourced, accountability cannot be outsourced. Organizations that outsource operations to third parties are responsible for the outcome.

Benefits from Use of Third Parties

Organizations that are considering outsourcing operations to third parties need to carefully weigh the benefits and the costs to determine whether the effort to outsource will result in measurable improvement in their processing, service delivery, or finances. In the 1990s, when many organizations rushed to outsource development and support functions to organizations located in other countries, they did so with unrealistic short-term gains in mind and without adequately considering all the real costs and risks of outsourcing. This is not to say that outsourcing to third parties is bad but that many organizations made outsourcing decisions without fully understanding them.

Outsourcing can bring many benefits:

- **Available skills and experience** Organizations that may have trouble attracting people with specialized skills often turn to third parties whose highly skilled personnel can ply their trade in a variety of client organizations.

- **Economies of scale**   Often specialized third parties can achieve better economies of scale through discipline and mature practices than organizations are able to achieve.

- **Objectivity**   Some functions are better done by outsiders. Personnel in an organization may have trouble being objective about some activities such as process improvement and requirements definition. Also, auditors frequently must be from an outside firm to achieve sufficient objectivity and independence.

- **Reduced costs**   When outsourcing to third parties is done with offshore personnel, an organization may be able to lower its operating costs and improve its competitive market position, usually through currency exchange rates and differences in the standards of living in headquarters versus offshore countries.

When an organization is making an outsourcing decision, it needs to consider these advantages together with risks that are discussed in the next section.

Risks from Use of Third Parties

While outsourcing to third parties can bring many tangible and intangible benefits to an organization, it is not without certain risks and disadvantages. Naturally, when an organization employs third parties to perform some of its functions, it relinquishes some control to those third parties. The risks of outsourcing to third parties include the following:

- **Higher-than-expected costs**   Reduced costs were the main driver for offshore outsourcing in the 1990s. However, many organizations failed to fully anticipate the operational realities and/or the cost savings. For instance, when outsourcing to overseas operations, IT personnel back in U.S.-based organizations had to make many more expensive trips than expected. Also, changes in international currency exchange rates can transform this year's bargain into next year's high cost.

- **Poor quality**   The work product produced by a third party may be lower than was produced when the function was performed in-house.

- **Poor performance**   The third-party service may not perform as expected. The capacity of networks or IT systems used by third parties may cause processing delays or longer-than-acceptable response times.

- **Loss of control**   An organization that is accustomed to being in control of its workers may feel loss of control. Making small adjustments to processes and procedures may be more time-consuming or increase costs.

- **Employee integrity and background**   It may be decidedly more difficult to determine the integrity of employees in a third party, particularly when the third party is located offshore. Some countries, even where outsourcing is popular, lack nationwide criminal background checks and other means for making a solid determination on an employee's background and integrity.

- **Loss of competitive advantage**   If the services performed by the third party are not flexible enough to meet the organization's needs, this can result in the organization losing some of its competitive advantage. For example, an organization outsources its corporate messaging (e-mail and other messaging) to a third-party service provider. Later, the organization wants to enhance its customer communication by integrating its service application with e-mail. The e-mail service provider may be unable or unwilling to provide the necessary integration, which will result in a loss of competitive advantage.

- **Errors and omissions**   The third party may make serious errors or fail to perform essential tasks. For instance, a third party may suffer a data security breach that may result in the loss or disclosure of sensitive information. This can be a disastrous event when it occurs within an organization's four walls, but when it happens to a third party, the organization may find that the lack of control will make it difficult to take the proper steps to contain and remedy the incident. If a third party has a security breach or other similar incident, it may be putting its interests first and only secondarily watching out for the interests of its customers.

- **Vendor failure**   The failure of a third party may result in increased costs and delays in service or product delivery.

- **Differing mission and goals**   An organization's employees are going to be loyal to its mission and objectives. However, the employees in a third party usually have little or no interest in the hiring organization's interests; instead, they will be loyal to the third party's values, which may at times be in direct conflict. For example, a third party may place emphasis on maximizing billable hours, while the hiring organization emphasizes efficiency. These two objectives conflict with each other.

- **Difficult recourse**   If an organization is dissatisfied with the performance or quality of its third party, contract provisions may not sufficiently facilitate a remedy. If the third-party operation is in a foreign country, applying remediation in the court system may also be futile.

- **Lowered employee morale**   If part of an organization chooses to outsource operations to a third party, those employees who remain may be upset because some of their colleagues may have lost their jobs as a result of the outsourcing. Further, remaining employees may feel that their own jobs may soon be outsourced or eliminated. They may also feel that their organization is more interested in saving money than in taking care of its employees. Personnel who have lost their jobs may vent their anger at the organization through a variety of harmful actions that may threaten assets or other workers.

- **Audit and compliance**   An organization that outsources part of its operation that is in scope for applicable laws and regulation may find it more challenging to perform audits and achieve compliance. Audit costs may rise, as auditors need to visit the third parties' work centers. Requiring the third party to make changes to achieve compliance may be difficult or expensive.

- **Applicable laws**   Laws, regulations, and standards in headquarters and offshore countries may impose requirements on the protection of information that may complicate business operations or enterprise architecture.

- **Cross-border data transfer**   Governments around the world are paying attention to the flow of data, particularly the sensitive data of its citizens. Many countries have passed laws that attempt to exert control over data about its citizens when it is transferred out of their jurisdiction.

- **Time zone differences**   Communications will suffer when an organization outsources some of its operations to offshore third parties that are several time zones distant. It will be more difficult to schedule telephone conferences when there is very little overlap between workers in each time zone. It will take more time to communicate important issues and to make changes.

- **Language and cultural differences**   When outsourcing crosses language and cultural barriers, it can result in less-than-optimal communication and results. The outsourcing customer will express its needs through its own language and culture, but the third party will hear those needs through its own language and culture. Both sides may be thinking or saying, "They don't understand what we want" and "We don't understand what they want." This can result in unexpected differences in work products produced by the outsourcing firm. Delays in project completion or delivery of goods and services can occur as a result.

 CAUTION   Some of the risks associated with outsourcing to third parties are intangible or may lie outside the bounds of legal remedies. For instance, language and time zone differences may introduce delays in communication, adding friction to the business relationship in a way that may not be easily measurable.

Third-Party Risk Had a Bad Start

Years ago, when organizations began the migration to cloud-based infrastructure and cloud-based applications, organizations mistakenly believed that those third-party organizations took care of security. This has resulted in numerous breaches, both because organizations believed their third parties were taking care of security and because organizations that knew they had to take care of security did not do so properly.

   As a result, the discipline of third-party risk received a bit of a jolt, as there were many organizations who had not been practicing TPRM that suddenly wanted to do so right away.

Identifying Third Parties

Because the topic of third-party risk is relatively new, many existing organizations are still just getting started with third-party risk management programs in their organizations. Thus, "the metaphorical third-party horse is already out of the barn." In other words, many organizations today do not have a firm grasp on the identity of all of its third parties. Indeed, stakeholders from around an organization may each have a few critical third parties that they are aware of, but often there is a total lack of central organization of all of an organization's third parties. An early step in an organization's third-party risk program may involve conducting an initial inventory of its third-party vendors.

There is no single place where information on all third-parties may be found. Partly this is because of the varying nature of third parties and the types of goods or services they provide to the organization. It is suggested, then, that the security manager consult with several stakeholders in the organization, where a subset of third parties can be identified. These stakeholders may include the following:

- **Legal**   One of the most important allies to the security manager, legal negotiates purchase and service contracts with third parties. Thus, legal will have a collection of contracts that can be identified. Security managers need to understand, however, that legal does not handle contracts for every third party. Some suppliers and vendors do not use contracts. Many online service providers have a simple "click-through" agreement that legal is frequently unaware of.

- **Procurement**   The procurement function is a critical party in an organization's third-party risk program. Larger purchases are frequently negotiated by a procurement function or team. Like the legal team, procurement may have a collection (and perhaps even a list) of third parties it has negotiated business deals with.

- **Accounts payable**   Sometimes the only way to learn about some third parties is to find out what third parties are being paid for products or services. Typically, the accounts payable function will remit funds only to organizations that are registered as vendors in the organization's financial accounting system. The security manager may find that some third parties are found only here.

- **Information technology (IT)**   The IT department is another good source of third parties. IT may have established data connections to certain third parties; IT may have specific firewall rules associated with access that some third parties are given to internal systems; and IT may have logical connections between its internal identity and access management (IAM) system and some third parties. Finally, information systems including firewalls, intrusion detection systems and intrusion prevention systems (IDSs and IPSs), and cloud access security broker (CASB) systems can provide a wealth of information, particularly about third-party services that are offered free of charge. Free online services are so numerous that many organizations are challenged to identify them until they utilize a CASB system (and even then, there may still be a few that go unnoticed).

- **Facilities**   The facilities department will probably be aware of third parties not found by other means. This is because of facilities' function: maintaining and supplying processing center locations and work locations. The facilities department likely has several third-party relationships with organizations that do not access IT systems. This is one reason why facilities needs to be involved in the initial search.

- **Department heads and business unit leaders**   An organization's department heads and business unit leaders are certainly going to be aware of key third-party relationships, including key suppliers, service providers, and sources of temporary workers.

- **Location-specific leaders**   The saying goes, "The further away one is from corporate headquarters, the more that business is conducted by expediency than by policy." In other words, workers in satellite offices are more apt to conduct business with unique, local-to-them third parties that may not be identified otherwise. Security managers may need to tread lightly here so that their quest for information about third parties does not represent a threat to their ongoing relationships.

When conducting an initial inventory, a security manager will, along the way, discover other sources of third parties or other ways to identify them. Security managers should realize that an initial effort at identifying third parties will probably not identify every last active third party, but it should suffice that most will be identified and that personnel should be on the lookout for those that have not yet been identified so that they may be brought into the third-party risk program.

When building an initial inventory of third parties, the security manager may opt to use a spreadsheet program to track them. Columns can be added that help the security manager remember how each third party was identified, and other columns can include criteria that can be used to classify third parties, using the criteria discussed in the prior section. However, security managers may soon learn that managing third parties by spreadsheet may quickly become burdensome. There are several vendors and service providers that have purpose-built applications used to manage third parties, including the following (in alphabetical order):

- Allgress
- CyberGRX
- KY3P
- Lockpath
- Optiv
- Prevelant
- RSA Archer
- RSAM
- Service Now

Because third-party risk is a rapidly growing and changing field, the number and type of service vendors to help manage third parties will itself change frequently.

Risk Tiering and Vendor Classification

Most companies have a large number of third-party vendors—so many that they cannot possibly perform all of the due diligence on every vendor. For this reason, it makes sense to take a risk-based approach to third-party risk management and apply a level of due diligence to vendors according to the level of risk. The approach to this is to classify vendors according to risk level and then perform a level of due diligence in proportion to their classification.

To achieve this, an organization needs to establish a few simple criteria by which a vendor can be classified into the right risk level. These are some of the criteria used by organizations to classify their vendors:

- **Volume of sensitive customer data**   The amount of sensitive customer data that the vendor stores on its systems. Sensitive customer data can include their contact information, financial information, healthcare information, transaction history, and location. The greater the amount of data or the longer that this data resides on a vendor's information systems, the higher the risk. Generally, organizations use a simple numeric scale that reflects their operations. For example, the criteria might be less than 10,000 records, between 10,000 and 1,000,000 records, or greater than 1,000,000 records.

- **Volume of sensitive internal data**   The amount of sensitive internal data that the vendor stores on its systems. Internal data can mean employee information, intellectual property, customer lists, marketing plans, and other data. The greater the amount of data or the longer that the vendor stores this data on its information systems, the higher the risk.

- **Operational criticality**   The degree to which the organization depends upon the day-by-day, hour-by-hour, minute-by-minute, or even second-by-second readiness and operation of the vendor on the organization's product or services output. For example, a movies-on-demand service may store its content and serve movies to customers via a third-party infrastructure-as-a-service (IaaS) vendor. The movies-on-demand service depends upon this IaaS vendor for continuous availability; even a few seconds of downtime would interrupt the playing of movies to all of its customers. Incidentally, in this example, the IaaS vendor would be rated as high risk because of the movie's content stored in its systems.

- **Physical access**   The degree to which a vendor has access to the organization's information processing centers or work centers. These two could even be rated separately. For instance, there may be technical support vendors with physical access to information systems in a data center. Also, there may be service vendors with physical access to work centers, such as freight delivery, janitorial, plant care, office supplies replenishment, or IT service vendors who maintain copiers, scanners, and other office equipment.

- **Access to systems**   Whether the vendor has the ability to access information systems accessed by the organization. For example, there may be tech support organizations that have occasional or 24/7 access to specific information systems so that they may perform routine maintenance or help troubleshoot problems. Further, ratings might vary depending on the type of systems that these third parties have access to (those with large amounts of critical or sensitive data, or systems that are operationally critical, as described in prior criteria).

- **Contractual obligations**   Whether the vendor is required to establish and maintain a security program, security controls, vulnerability management, incident response, or other activities. Third parties may be rated as higher risk if there are few or no security requirements imposed upon them in a contract. While effective third-party risk management seeks to have appropriate security clauses in contracts, security managers may occasionally encounter contracts with third parties where no clauses were used.

No matter what the criteria are, organizations typically use these criteria to identify the most critical vendors and other third parties. Generally, organizations will classify their third parties into three levels of criticality. Table 4-2 depicts a typical third-party risk classification scheme. Based on what is important to them, each organization will construct this risk tiering scheme differently.

Organizations can use Table 4-2 in a number of ways. First, each third-party can be scored based on how many of the low, medium, or high categories are met. Or, each third-party can be assigned to a risk level if any single criteria are met at that level. Organizations are cautioned to refrain from making any tiering or scoring too complicated since the final objective is to arrive at no more than three, or perhaps four, tier classifications for each vendor. The reason for this is related to third-party assessments, discussed next.

In most organizations, a minority of third parties will be assigned to the top risk level, perhaps 0.5 percent to 2 percent. A few more will be assigned to the second risk level, perhaps another 5 percent to 10 percent. The remainder of third parties will be assigned to the third risk level. The purpose of assigning third parties to risk levels is explained in the next section.

Organizations need to realize that, from time to time, some third parties will need to be reclassified from one risk level to another. For example, a third-party service provider is initially hired to perform low-risk services, and its initial risk classification is low. However, that third party might earn more business that represents high risk; unless there is some triggering mechanism (such as the negotiation of an additional legal contract), organizations would need to actively analyze the relationship with each of its third parties annually (or more often) to confirm their risk rating. Similarly, if a third party is originally classified as high risk but later discontinues performing high-risk services, the third party should be reclassified at a lower risk tier; otherwise, the organization is spending too much effort assessing the third party.

Criteria	High	Medium	Low
Customer data volume	<10M records	10K to 10M records	<10K records
Internal data volume	HR or product design	None	None
Physical access	24/7	Office hours only	None
System access	High customer data volume	None	None

Table 4-2   Third-Party Risk Tiering

Assessing Third Parties

Assessments of third parties are used to identify specific risks in those third-party organizations. The process of assessing third parties should be thought of as just another way of performing internal risk assessments on internal processes and applications; however, the personnel that need to be contacted are not internal personnel but employees of other companies, with a variable degree of cooperation and willingness to respond. As opposed to performing risk assessments of internal processes and systems, there is a veil through which the view of information about those third-party processes and systems are obscured. Additional focus and effort are required to learn enough about the practices in a third-party organization to draw conclusions about risk. The techniques used are described in this section.

Once an organization has established its third-party risk classification and begun to identify its third parties and their respective risk tiering, third parties can be assessed. However, before assessments can be performed, a scheme by which assessments take place needs to be developed. In the preceding section, third parties are classified into three or four risk levels. The manner in which assessments are performed depends upon which risk level any particular third party is assigned. Several techniques are used to assess third parties, including the following:

- **Questionnaires**   Organizations can develop questionnaires that are sent to third parties. These questionnaires will typically include questions about a third party's IT controls and other business activity so that the organization can determine how effectively its information is being protected.

- **Questionnaire confirmation**   Upon receiving completed questionnaires from third parties, organizations can then take additional steps to confirm or validate the answers in the questionnaires. For example, the organization can request evidence in the form of process documents or samples of business records. This gives an organization added (or reduced) confidence in the answers in a returned questionnaire and, therefore, a more accurate depiction of control risk.

- **Site visit**   Sometimes an organization is not satisfied with the use of questionnaires and confirmation. In such cases, an organization can send one of its security personnel (or, ironically, outsource this activity to a third party) to conduct a site visit of the third party's work locations and information processing centers. While this is the costliest type of confirmation, organizations realize that there is sometimes no substitute for "seeing with one's own eyes" to establish confidence in a third party's controls.

- **External attestations**   Organizations can compel third parties to undergo external audits or attestations. Established standards such as SOC1, SOC2, SSAE16, ISAE3402, HITRUST, and ISO/IEC 27001 are examples of control and audit standards that can be used to better understand the effectiveness of a third party's IT controls.

- **External business intelligence**   Organizations often turn to external business intelligence services such as Dunn & Bradstreet or Lexis Nexus. Services like these collect information on the financial health of companies. This can help organizations better understand risk factors related to the health and ongoing viability of its third parties. For example, if an organization learns that a particular third party is under financial stress (perhaps because of problems with its products or services adversely affecting sales), this will raise concern that this could result in degradations in product or service quality, as well as degradations in information protection efforts and effectiveness.

- **External cyber intelligence**   Organizations are beginning to utilize the services from a growing number of companies that gather intelligence of various types on third-party companies. These services sell this information on a subscription basis. These services perform a variety of functions, including security scans and scans of the dark web for signs of an unreported breach. These cyber-intelligence services can often perform these services at lower cost than can organizations that try to conduct these activities with their own security staff.

- **Security scans and penetration tests**   Organizations can perform security scans or penetration tests on the infrastructure and/or applications of its third parties. Alternatively, organizations can require the third parties themselves to commission these activities from qualified security consulting firms and make the results available to organizations. These activities serve to bolster (or erode) confidence in a third party's ability to manage its infrastructure and applications, including running an effective vulnerability management program.

- **Intrusive monitoring**   Organizations can sometimes compel a third party to permit the organization to view or receive internal controls data in real time. For instance, an organization can provide a security system to the third party that the third party would install in its network; the system would provide some form of real-time security intelligence to the organization to give it confidence that the third party's environment is free of active threats. Or, a third party can make certain internal information available to the organization from its own internal security systems. The types of information that can be made available include security and event log data from operating systems, firewalls, intrusion detection/prevention systems; internal vulnerability scan data; network packet header capture; or network full packet capture. These activities are called *intrusive monitoring* because they represent an intrusion of the organization's visibility into the third party's environment.

These and other techniques are used to assess third parties. But as has been stated earlier, not all third parties are assessed in the same way. Instead, third parties are assessed based upon their risk level, which is discussed in the preceding section. Organizations establish schemes for assessing vendors according to their risk level. Table 4-3 depicts such a scheme.

Assessment Type	High Risk	Medium Risk	Low Risk
Questionnaire	Longest questionnaire	Medium size questionnaire	Shortest questionnaire
Questionnaire confirmation	High risk controls	Highest risk controls	Not performed
Site visits	Yes	Yes	No
External attestations	Required	Nice to have	Nice to have
External business intelligence	Yes	Yes	Yes
External cyber intelligence	Yes	Yes	No
Security scans	Yes	Yes	Yes
Penetration tests	Yes	No	No
Intrusive monitoring	In limited circumstances	No	No

Table 4-3   Assessment Activities at Different Risk Levels

Assessment Type	High Risk	Medium Risk	Low Risk
Questionnaire	Annually	Annually	Annually
Questionnaire confirmation	Annually	Every two years	Not performed
Site visits	Annual	Every three to five years	Not performed
External attestations	Annual	Annual	Annual
External business intelligence	Quarterly	Annual	Annual
External cyber intelligence	Monthly	Quarterly	None
Security scans	Monthly	Annually	Annually
Penetration tests	Annually	Not performed	Not performed
Intrusive monitoring	Continuous	Not performed	Not performed

Table 4-4   Assessment Frequency

Organizations also need to determine how frequently to perform their assessments of third parties. Table 4-4 shows a sample scheme of assessment frequency.

Organization can have hundreds to thousands of third parties that require assessments. The largest organizations can have tens of thousands of third parties. The fact that there are so many third parties is the primary reason why risk tiering is performed, as the various types of assessments are time-consuming and expensive to perform. This is why the most thorough assessments are performed only on the third parties that represent the highest risk.

Often, assessments identify issues in third-party controls that organizations find unacceptable. The topic of remediation is discussed in the next section.

Proactive Issue Remediation

The only means of exchange between a customer organization and a third party are money and reputation. In other words, the only leverage that an organization has against its third party is the withholding of payment and communicating the quality (or lack therein) of the third party to other organizations. This is especially true if the outsourcing crosses national boundaries. Therefore, an organization that is considering outsourcing must carefully consider how it will enforce contract terms so that it receives the quantity and quality goods and services that it is expecting.

Many of the risks of outsourcing to third parties can be remedied through contract provisions. These are some of the remedies:

- **Service level agreement** The contract should provide details on every avenue of work performance and communication, including escalations and problem management.

- **Quality** Depending upon the product or service, this may translate into an error or defect rate, a customer satisfaction rate, or system performance.

- **Security policy and controls** Whether the outsourcing firm is safeguarding the organization's intellectual property, keeping business secrets, or protecting information about its employees or customers, the contract should spell out the details of the security controls that it expects the outsourcing firm to perform. The organization should also require periodic third-party audits and the results of those audits. The contract should contain a "right to audit" clause that allows the outsourcing organization to examine the work premises, records, and work papers on demand.

- **Business continuity** The contract should require the outsourcing firm to have reasonable measures and safeguards in place to ensure resilience of operations and the ability to continue operations with minimum disruption in the event of a disaster.

- **Employee integrity** The contract should define how the outsourcing firm will vet its employees' backgrounds so that it is not inadvertently hiring individuals with a criminal history and so employees' claimed education and work experience are genuine.

- **Ownership of intellectual property** If the outsourcing firm is producing software or other designs, the contract must define ownership of those work products and whether the outsourcing firm may reuse any of those work products for other engagements.

- **Roles and responsibilities** The contract should specify in detail the roles and responsibilities of each party so that each will know what is expected of them.

- **Schedule** The contract must specify when and how many items of work products should be produced.

- **Regulation** The contract should require both parties to conform to all applicable laws and regulations, including but not limited to intellectual property, data protection, and workplace safety.

- **Warranty**   The contract should specify terms of warranty for the workmanship and quality of all work products so that there can be no ambiguity regarding the quality of goods or services performed.

- **Dispute and resolution**   The contract should contain provisions that define the process for handling and resolving disputes.

- **Payment**   The contract should specify how and when the outsourcing provider will be paid. Compensation should be tied not only to the quantity but also to the quality of work performed. The contract should include incentive provisions for additional payment when specific schedule, quantity, or quality targets are exceeded. The contract should also contain financial penalties that are enacted when SLA, quality, security, audit, or schedule targets are missed.

The terms of an outsourcing contract should adequately reward the outsourcing firm for a job well done, which should include the prospect of earning additional contracts as well as referrals that will help it to earn outsourcing contracts from other customers.

Responsive Issue Remediation

It's rare that a questionnaire or other bit of information about a third party comes back with absolutely no concern whatsoever on the part of the organization. Often, there are situations identified in questionnaires or during questionnaire confirmation that an organization finds undesirable. For example, a third party might specify in a questionnaire that it requires its personnel to change their passwords once per year. The organization would prefer the third party change their passwords more frequently. But in this example, what if a third party specifies that it *never* requires its personnel to change their passwords; this is something that an organization might find unacceptable. The organization initiates a discussion with the third party to discover why its personnel are never required to change their passwords, with the hopes that either the organization will find the third party's explanation acceptable (perhaps there are compensating controls such as an effective multifactor authentication system) or the parties will agree that the third party will change its systems to require its personnel to update their passwords on an acceptable frequency, perhaps quarterly.

Remediation is time-consuming, so organizations need to be careful about how often and in which situations it will undergo the process.

Onboarding

Onboarding is the process by which an organization begins a business relationship with a third party. When an organization is considering utilizing the products or services from a third party, the organization should perform up-front due diligence on the third party to better understand the level of risk. Often, an organization will establish a risk level using criteria discussed earlier in this section and then perform an assessment utilizing questionnaires and other methods according to the scheme shown in Table 4-4. These activities will uncover issues, some of which will require remediation and others that will require specific statements in the initial legal agreement between the organization and the third party.

> **NOTE** A legal agreement with a new third party should never be completed until assessments and other due diligence have been completed.

Contract Language

When an organization initially examines a new third party through the assessment process and by other means, the security manager is able to determine what the third party will be required to do, from an information security perspective. These requirements should be given to the legal department so that these requirements are present in the contract in the form of contract clauses.

There are several categories of information security–related clauses that typically appear in agreements with third parties, including the following:

- Security program
- Security controls
- Compliance
- Attestations
- Vulnerability management
- Penetration tests
- Right to audit
- Incident notification
- Cyber insurance
- Restrictions on outsourcing

Security Incidents

If a security incident occurs in a third-party organization, responding to the incident is more complex, mainly due to the fact that two or more organizations and their respective security teams are involved. This topic is explored in detail in Chapter 5 in the section "Incident Involving Third Parties."

Administrative Activities

Like virtually every other department in an organization, there is a certain amount of administrative work that must be performed by the security manager and the rest of the security team. Like other corporate departments such as human resources and finance, information security can be effective only to the extent that it has established productive relationships with many other departments in the organization. This is because the information security manager frequently acts as a catalyst to ensure that other departments and business units exercise good judgment so that their actions and decisions do not incur unnecessary risk to the organization.

The security manager also needs to forge relationships with many external entities such as law enforcement, security product vendors, security professional services vendors, professional organizations, and organizations that develop standards and frameworks used by security personnel.

The development of security staff is particularly important, considering the acute shortage of qualified security personnel. Employees who feel neglected or underutilized can quickly find other employment.

Internal Partnerships

No security manager can hope to accomplish much if she works by herself. Effective information security and information risk is a team sport, and each player on the team can help the security manager in different ways. Further, partnerships with other corporate departments and business units helps to keep the security manager informed on matters of importance. An effective way to build those partnerships while increasing the effectiveness of the program is to "deputize" team members from other groups. An example of this is to partner with the administrative assistants and have them lead the data retention program. Another example is to designate a person in another business unit (BU) as the information security liaison to both share guidance with the BU as well as report possible risk or issues that BU have that impact the date or information security of the organization. None of this is possible unless proper training is provided to the other team members and time must be allocated for them to fulfil those added duties.

Legal   In most organizations, the legal department functions as the organization's de facto business risk officer, through the negotiation of contract terms with service providers, customers, and other parties. Legal generally always attempts to tip risk in favor of the organization.

Legal and information security can collaborate on the security clauses in almost any contract with customers, suppliers, service providers, and other parties. When other parties send contracts that contain security clauses, the security manager should examine those clauses to ensure that the organization is able to meet all requirements. Similarly, when the organization is considering doing business with another party, the security manager can work with the legal department to make sure that the organization is adequately protected by requiring those other parties to take certain steps to protect the organization's information.

Sometimes an organization will enter into a business relationship without informing the security manager, who often would want to perform a risk assessment to identify any important risks that should be known. The best arrangement here is to have legal inform the security manager of every new contract that legal receives so that the security manager can take some effort to identify risks at this late stage.

Human Resources   As the steward for information and many activities regarding employees and other workers, human resources (HR) is another important ally of information security. There are many ways in which human resources can bolster the organization's security, including the following:

- **Recruiting**   Human resources works to find new employees for the organization. Through this search process, HR ensures that new personnel have the right qualifications and that they are inclined to conform to security policy and other policy. In the candidate screening process, they will perform background checks to confirm their claimed education, prior employment, and professional certifications, as well as ensure they are free of criminal history.

- **Onboarding**   For candidates who are selected for employment, HR will ensure that all new employees sign important documents including nondisclosure and that they receive their initial training, including security awareness training. In onboarding, new employees will also formally acknowledge receipt of, and pledge conformance to, security policy and other policies. HR will provision human resource information systems (HRISs), which in many organizations are integrated into organizations' identity and access management systems. HR ensures that new employees are assigned to the correct job title and responsibilities, as in some cases this automatically results in new employees receiving "birthright" access to specific information systems and applications.

- **Internal transfers**   Human resources is responsible for coordinating internal transfers, where employees change from one position to another in an organization. Internal transfers are somewhat different from promotions; in an internal transfer, an employee might be moving to an entirely different department, resulting in the need to have access to completely different information systems and applications. Notifying security and IT personnel of internal transfers is important so that employees' former roles in information systems and applications can be discontinued at the appropriate time, avoiding the phenomena known as *accumulation of privileges,* where employees with long tenure accumulate access rights to a growing number of roles in information systems and applications, thereby increasing various risks.

- **Offboarding**   HR is responsible for processing the termination, or offboarding, of employees who are leaving the organization for any reason. Human resources is responsible for ensuring that security, IT, and other departments are notified of the termination so that all access rights can be terminated at the appropriate time (this is especially important in a dismissal situation where the organization must "surgically" remove access at precisely the right moment to avoid the risk of the terminated employee—in the heat of the moment—from exacting revenge on the organization through sabotage and other acts. HR is also responsible for collecting assets issued to a departing employee such as laptop or tablet computers, mobile devices, and related peripherals; HR might also require departing employees to sign nondisclosure and/or noncompete agreements.

- **Training**   In many organizations, HR is the central focal point for most or all training that is made available to employees and for keeping records of training. Training in an organization should include security awareness training, which may be administered by HR. Human resources in many organizations is also the focal point for coordinating the use of posters, flyers, and announcements to employees on several topics including training and security reminders.

- **Investigations**   Human resources conducts investigations into matters such as employee misconduct. Where such misconduct involves any improper use of information systems or computers, HR will partner with information security, which might conduct a forensic investigation to establish a reliable history of events, and establish a chain of custody should the matter develop into legal proceedings such as a lawsuit.

- **Discipline**   Human resources is the focal point for formal disciplinary actions against employees. From an information security perspective, this includes matters of violations of security policy and other policies. Generally, the security manager will present facts and, if requested, an opinion about such matters, but human resources is responsible for selecting the manner and degree of disciplinary action, whether that includes demotion, time off without pay, reduction in compensation, forfeiture of a bonus, removal of privileges, or dismissal.

Facilities   The facilities function is the steward of workplaces used by the organization, ensuring there is adequate space and support for workers in all office locations. The partnership between facilities and information security includes the following:

- **Workplace access control**   Facilities typically manages workplace access control systems such as badge readers and door lock actuators that control which personnel are permitted to access work centers and zones within them. A well-known principle in information security states that adversaries that obtain physical access to computing assets are able to completely take them over; this reiterates the need for effective access control that prevents unauthorized personnel from accessing those assets.

- **Workplace surveillance**   Video surveillance is the companion detective control that works with preventive controls such as key card systems. Video cameras at building entrances can help corroborate the identity of personnel who enter and leave. Visible surveillance monitors can add a deterrent aspect to surveillance.

- **Equipment check-in/check-out**   Data centers and other locations with valuable assets can implement an equipment check-in and check-out function, where personnel are required to record assets coming and going in a log that resembles a visitor log.

- **Guest processing**   Facilities often assists with the identification and processing of guests and other visitors. Security guards, receptionists, or other personnel can check visitors' government IDs, issue visitor badges, contact the employees being visited, and assist in other ways.

- **Security guard**   Guards represent the human element that provides or supplements access controls and video surveillance. Guards can also assist with equipment check-in/check-out and visitor processing.

- **Asset security**   Through video surveillance, access control, and other means, facilities ensures the protection of assets including data center information-processing systems and office assets, including printers and copiers.

- **Personnel safety**   While not directly in the crosshairs of information security, many security managers are involved in personnel safety since it is closely related to asset security and because many of the same protective controls are used.

NOTE While personnel security is cited last in this list, the safety of personnel should be the highest priority in any organization.

Information Technology Information technology and information security represents perhaps the most strategic partnership that the security manager will establish and develop. There are many key functions performed by information technology that have security ramifications, requiring close coordination between these two teams. These activities include the following:

- **Access control** IT typically manages day-to-day access control, including issuing credentials to new employees, removing credentials from terminated employees, processing access requests, and resetting credentials. In some organizations, IT may also perform access reviews and recertifications.

- **Architecture** IT is responsible for the overall architecture of information systems used in the organization. This includes data architecture, network architecture, and systems architecture. In many organizations, there is also the practice of *security architecture,* which touches all other aspects of architecture. The Open Security Architecture organization defines IT security architecture as "the design artifacts that describe how the security controls (security countermeasures) are positioned, and how they relate to the overall information technology architecture. These controls serve the purpose to maintain the system's quality attributes: confidentiality, integrity, availability, accountability and assurance services." In other words, security architecture is the big-picture mission of understanding the interplay between all of the security controls and configurations that work together to protect information systems and information assets.

- **Hardening** IT owns the configuration of all operating systems for servers and end-user computing; this includes the development and implementation of *hardening standards.* Generally, hardening standards are developed by IT in accordance to policy and principles developed by information security.

- **Scanning and patching** Under the guidance of the security manager, IT often operates vulnerability scanning tools and patch management platforms to ensure that IT assets are free of exploitable vulnerabilities. It has been recognized that this is one of the most critical activities to prevent break-ins by external adversaries.

- **Security tools** In most organizations, IT operates the organization's firewalls, intrusion detection/prevention systems, spam filtering, web filtering, and others. Generally, the security manager establishes policies and principles by which these tools are used, and IT implements, maintains, and operates these tools according to those policies and principles.

- **System monitoring** IT typically performs monitoring of its IT assets to ensure all are operating normally and to manage alarms that indicate the presence of various operational issues.

- **Security monitoring**   IT may perform security monitoring of IT assets in order to be on the alert when security issues occur.
- **Third-party connections**   IT may be involved in the setup of data connections to third-party organizations. As part of an organization's third-party risk program, the security manager needs to be aware of all third-party business relationships as early in the cycle as possible, but because some vendor relationships escape the scrutiny of security managers earlier in the process, being informed of new third-party connections may sometimes be the only way that a security manager will be aware of new relationships.

Product Development   Product development is the generic term used here to represent software development, programming, integration, software engineering, and other activities all concerned with the development of software for use internally or by customers or partners.

Under guidance from the security manager, product development will manage the entire product development life cycle with security as an integral part at each stage in the process. The activities performed by product development in support of information security include the following:

- **Security by design**   This represents several activities to ensure that all new offerings, components, features, and improvements incorporate security as part of the design process. This can help the organization avoid issues later in the development process that may be more costly to remediate.
- **Secure development**   This includes secure coding to ensure that all new and changed software is free of exploitable defects that could result in security incidents.
- **Security testing**   Several activities fall under the security testing function, including code-scanning tools used by each developer's integrated development environment (IDE), unit and system testing to confirm the correct implementation of all security requirements, static application security testing (SAST) scanning tools that are run as part of a nightly build process, and dynamic application security testing (DAST) scanning tools that identify security defects in running applications.
- **Code reviews**   This includes peer reviews of security-related changes to software source code, including security-sensitive functions such as authentication, session management, data validation, and data segregation in multitenant environments. Some organizations incorporate code reviews for changes to all software modules.
- **Security review of open source software**   Some organizations perform reviews of various kinds of some or all open source modules to ensure they are not introducing unwanted security defects into the software application.
- **Developer training**   Periodic training for developers includes techniques on secure development, which helps developers avoid the otherwise common mistakes that result in security defects that must be fixed later.

- **Protection of the development process**   This includes controls to ensure that only authorized developers may access source code (and this may include restrictions on the quantity of source code that a developer can check out at any given time), security scans of source code upon check-in, and protection of all source code.

Procurement   *Procurement* is the practice of making a purchase, and in larger organizations there is a department of the same name. The procurement department is often the group that negotiates price and business terms for new purchases of hardware, software, and services, as well as renewals for subscriptions and services.

Procurement is a key relationship with the security manager when the organization is contemplating purchases. The procurement manager can be sure to notify the security manager whenever any new purchase is being considered. That way, the security manager can begin any needed due diligence related to the product or service being considered and can weigh in with messaging concerning risks and any needed controls or compensating controls to keep risk within accepted tolerances.

Finance   The primary link between information security and finance is the discovery of new vendors in the accounts payable (AP) process. An effective third-party risk program requires triggers in several parts of the business, including AP, so that security managers can be aware of all third-party vendor relationships established by the organization. AP is often considered the partnership of last resort in this regard, as a vendor relationship may already be fully established and operational by the time AP is aware of it.

Business Unit Managers   It has been said that a security manager can only protect the organization to the extent that he understands how it works. Naturally this necessitates the security manager develop relationships with business unit and department managers and leaders throughout the organization.

The objective of these partnerships is to facilitate the means through which the security manager can better understand how each business unit and department functions and who their critical personnel, processes, systems, and outside partners are. The purpose (at least not the *sole* purpose) of these partnerships is *not* for the security manager to inform business unit managers and leaders how security works. There will be times when business unit managers and leaders will ask the security manager how he does certain things; the security manager should respond with as much transparency as possible.

As these strategic relationships develop, business unit managers and leaders will begin to trust the security manager, share things with the security manager, and include the security manager in key conversations and processes. When there is adequate trust, good things can begin to happen: conversations on more sensitive topics will take place, resulting in minor and sometimes significant improvements to the business.

Affiliates and Key Business Partners   As the security manager develops strategic relationships throughout the organization, the security manager should set her sights on affiliates, business partners, and other external entities that are deeply involved in the organization's development and delivery of goods and services. With the extensive information systems integrations that are established between organizations, the security of an organization is dependent upon the security of the organization's information systems ecosystem—the interconnection of information systems, networks, and business processes. According to recent studies, about half of all security breaches have their nexus in third parties, which makes the development of strategic relationships with these third parties an essential pursuit.

External Partnerships

Successful information security is possible only when the security manager has established relationships with key external organizations. Who those organizations are depends upon the organization's industry sector, relevant regulations, information systems in use, geographic locations, and other things.

Law Enforcement   It is said that a roof is best repaired on a sunny day. Similarly, security managers should cultivate relationships with key law enforcement agencies and relevant personnel in those agencies when there is no urgent matter at hand. When organizations and law enforcement know each other, they can develop a relationship in which trusted information sharing can take place. And when an emergency such as a security breach occurs, law enforcement will already be familiar with the organization and its key personnel, and they'll be more likely to lend assistance.

Agencies that organizations might consider reaching out to include the following:

- **United States**   The FBI, Secret Service (for organizations dealing in large volumes of credit card transactions), and city and state police cybercrime units. The InfraGard organization (https://www.infragard.org/), which is a public–private partnership between the FBI and private organizations, is also noteworthy.
- **Canada**   The RCMP and city and provincial cybercrime units.
- **United Kingdom**   MI5 and city and county cybercrime units.
- **Globally**   InterPol.

Many law enforcement agencies contact a periodic "citizens' academy," which provides an insider look at these agencies and their mission and practices. The FBI Citizens' Academy (https://www.fbi.gov/about/community-outreach) is noteworthy in this regard.

Security managers will find that some of the agencies they work with do public and business outreach to inform businesses about local crime trends and methods of asset protection.

Regulators and Auditors   To the greatest extent possible, regulators and auditors should be viewed as partners and not adversaries. Developing relationships with regulators and auditors can help to improve the business relationship and the tone by which organizations and their regulators or auditors interact.

Security managers should understand regulators' ethical boundaries. In some situations, you cannot so much as buy a regulator a cup of coffee to lighten the mood and talk about work or non-work-related matters.

Standards Organizations   There are numerous standards organizations in the information security industry, and a multitude of others in all other industry sectors. In the information security industry itself, being involved in standards organizations avails the security manager with "insider" information such as "sneak previews" of emerging and updated standards, as well as learning opportunities and even conferences and conventions. These organizations include the following:

- PCI Security Standards Council (https://www.pcisecuritystandards.org/), involved with protection of credit card data for banks, issuers, processors, and merchants

- Cloud Security Alliance (https://cloudsecurityalliance.org/), which creates security standards frameworks for cloud-based service providers

- Information Security Forum (ISF), with its Standard of Good Practice publication

- International Organization for Standardization (ISO) and the International Electrotechnical Commission (IEC), which develop international standards on numerous topics including security management and IT service management

Professional Organizations   The information security profession is challenging, not only because of the consequences of ineffective security programs but also because of the high rate of innovation that takes place. Professional organizations help to fill this need for valuable information through training, professional certifications, local chapter organizations, and conferences. These organizations include the following:

- **ISACA**   Developer of the Certified Information Security Manager (CISM, the topic of this book), Certified Information Systems Auditor (CISA), and other certifications. It conducts conferences and training events worldwide. Numerous chapters have been organized around the world. See https://www.isaca/org.

- **Information Systems Security Association (ISSA)**   Conducts conferences and supports numerous local chapters worldwide. See https://www.issa.org.

- **International Information Systems Security Certification Consortium, or (ISC)²**   Developer of the Certified Information Systems Security Professional (CISSP) and other certifications. It conducts an annual conference. See https://www.isc2.org.

- **Cloud Security Alliance (CSA)**   Developer of the Cloud Controls Matrix (CCM) and the CSA Star program. It conducts conferences worldwide. See https://cloudsecurityalliance.org/.

- **International Council of Electronic Commerce Consultants (EC-Council)**   Developer of the well-known Certified Ethical Hacker (CEH) and Certified Chief Information Security Officer (CCISO) certifications. It conducts conferences worldwide. See https://www.eccouncil.org/.

- **SANS**   Developer of the GIAC family of certifications. It conducts numerous training events and conferences globally. See https://www.sans.org.

Security Professional Services Vendors   Security managers need to develop trusted relationships with one or more security professional services vendors. Because there is so much to know in the information security profession and because threats, practices, and frameworks change so often, having one or more trusted advisors can help a security manager to be continually aware of these developments.

Better security professional services vendors have senior advisors on their staff who are available for brief consultations from time to time. While these advisors may have sales responsibilities, a skilled security manager can utilize their expertise now and then to confirm ideas, plans, and strategies.

Some security professional services vendors have virtual CISOs or CISO advisors on their staff (often former CISOs) who help clients develop long-term security strategies. Often these advisors are billable resources who assist their client organizations to better understand their risks and help develop a risk-based security strategy that will make the best use of scarce resources to reduce risk. These types of services are especially useful for smaller organizations that are unable to attract and hire full-time security managers of this caliber.

Security professional services vendors can also assist with a strategy for the acquisition, implementation, and operation of security tools. Trusted advisors who are familiar with security tools can often help a security manager identify the better tools that are more likely to work in their environments.

Security Product Vendors   Security managers need to have good business relationships with each of the vendors whose security products and services are in use. Through these relationships, security managers will be better informed in a variety of ways, including product or service updates, workshops and seminars, training, and support.

Things do not always go smoothly between product vendors and their customers. It is essential that strategic relationships be established so that in times of difficulty, each party will already have familiarity with the other, enabling faster and more productive interaction and resolution.

Trusted advisors can help the security manager identify additional vendors for the purpose of relationship building. A new vendor might have a product that is a competitor of a product already used in the security manager's organization, or the vendor may have a product or service that the organization does not currently use. These relationships help the security manager understand the capabilities that she could utilize in the future.

Compliance Management

Compliance is the state of conformance to applicable policies, standards, regulations, and other requirements. *Compliance* is the process by which the security manager determines whether the organization's information systems, processes, and personnel conform to those things.

When a security manager develops or adopts a control framework and identifies applicable regulations and legal requirements, he then sees to it that controls and other measures are implemented. Then, as part of the risk management life cycle, the security manager needs to examine those controls, processes, and systems to see whether they are in compliance with all of those internal and external requirements. As discussed throughout this book, these activities include external audits, internal audits, and control self-assessments.

Compliance or Security

A frequent observation by security consultants who work with numerous client organizations is the way that organizations think about asset protection. Organizations seem to fall into one of two categories:

- **Compliance based** These are organizations that are satisfied to "check the box" on applicable standards or regulations such as PCI and HIPAA. Their interest is to do the bare minimum possible to pass audits.

- **Security and risk based** These are organizations that understand that external standards such as PCI and HIPAA are "starting points" and that periodic risk assessments and other activities are needed (in other words, all the activities discussed in this book) to help them determine what other activities and controls they must develop to be secure.

Security professionals often disagree on many topics, but generally they agree on this: being *compliant* is not the same things as being *secure*.

Applicability Security managers often find that compliance is complicated by the fact that there may be multiple, overlapping standards, regulations, and other legal requirements, each of which may be applicable to various portions of the organization. To better understand the coverage of these requirements, the security manager might develop a compliance matrix such as the one shown in Table 4-5.

Properly determining applicability helps the security manager better understand what is required of individual information systems and the processes they support. Any organization would be spending too much if it simply applied the requirements from all regulations and other legal obligations to all of its information systems. The result may be a more consistent application of controls but certainly a more expensive application as well. For most organizations, the resources required to develop the means of compliance to applicable regulations is less than the resources required to apply all required controls by all regulations to all systems. This would be an example of overspending without necessarily reducing risk.

	HIPAA	PCI	ISO27001	SOC1	SOC2
Data Centers	Yes	Yes	Yes	Yes	Yes
Electronic Medical Records (EMR) System	Yes	No	Yes	Yes	No
Payment Acceptance	No	Yes	No	Yes	Yes
Human Resources Information System (HRIS)	No	No	No	No	No
Enterprise Resource Planning (ERP) System	No	No	Yes	Yes	Yes
Payroll System	No	No	No	No	No

Table 4-5 Example Compliance Matrix Depicting Applicability of Regulations and Standards on Systems

Compliance Risk   As the security manager performs risk assessments and populates the risk ledger with risk matters requiring discussion and treatment, one form of risk that the security manager ought not overlook is compliance risk. *Compliance risk* is a risk that is associated with any general or specific consequences of the failure to be compliant with an applicable law or other legal obligation.

For example, during a risk assessment, a security manager observes that the organization stores credit card information in plaintext spreadsheets on internal file servers. There are at least two risks that the security manager can identify in this situation:

- **Sensitive data exposure**   The risk ledger calls out the fact that such sensitive data could be misused by internal personnel, and it may be discovered by a malicious outsider. The costs associated with a forensic investigation, along with potential mitigation costs such as payment for credit monitoring for victims, would be included in the total cost incurred by the organization should this information be compromised.

- **Fines and sanctions**   The risk ledger calls out the fact that the organization could face fines and other sanctions should the organization's PCI regulators learn of this. The fines and other sanctions are the potential unplanned costs that the organization might incur upon regulators' discovery of this.

Compliance Enforcement   As the security manager reviews the results of internal and external audits, control self-assessments, and other examinations of systems and processes, the security manager will need to weigh not only the direct risks associated with any negative findings but also the compliance risk. The security manager can apply both of these considerations in any discussions and proceedings during which others in the organizations are contemplating their response to these compliance items.

As a part of a metrics program, the security manager will report on the state of compliance to senior management. Matters of compliance will be reflected in metrics as areas of higher risk, whether these are risks of breach only, or also of compliance to external regulations with potentially public consequences.

Compliance, the Double-Edged Sword

My security career began before there were many laws on the topic of information security. We sometimes mused about the fact that there were no laws behind the efforts we made to get our organizations into a better security posture.

Then, laws and standards began to be developed and passed that gave us additional leverage. Laws and standards like Sarbanes–Oxley, the Federal Information Systems Management Act (FISMA), and PCI-DSS gave us a heavier bat to swing with when enforcing security controls and standards.

But it wasn't all positive. Many laws overreach or paint with too broad a brush, requiring organizations to enact certain controls that raise costs and complexity without reducing risk. And some laws don't go far enough, such as PCI-DSS still not requiring the encryption of credit card data as it traverses internal networks.

Most of us are in agreement that we're in a better place today. We appreciate the good laws and (so far) can live with the bad ones.

Personnel Management

In all but the smallest organizations where the security manager acts alone, personnel management is an important aspect of information security management. In many organizations, information security is staffed with a team ranging from two to dozens of people. The security manager is responsible for all aspects of the security team, starting with identifying and hiring candidates, assigning and supervising work, developing new skills, and developing the security team's "culture within a culture."

Finding and Retaining Talent   Security personnel are in high demand. Consequently, those in the profession command good salaries. However, because it's hard to find qualified security professionals, most organizations have trouble finding skilled, qualified persons that they can attract away from their current employment. Compensation is creeping upward faster than inflation, resulting in some organizations that cannot afford the talent they need.

Because security professionals know they are in high demand, they can choose the types of companies they want to work for, and they can live almost anywhere they want. This is so much the case today that security professionals who want to be remote workers can do so with comparative ease.

Retaining talent is a challenge in many organizations. Good technologists seem to become bored with routine and repetition, so keeping them engaged with new challenges can itself be a challenge. Security managers need to find the right balance between their security staff wanting to do "cool, new things" and aligning those desires with actual business needs.

Security managers who are looking to grow their security team or fill open positions often need look no further than their own organization: there may be one or more people in the IT department who may aspire to join the security team. Many—if not most—IT security professionals "crossed over" from corporate IT to information security, and this is still a common source for new recruits. People transferring over from IT are already familiar with the business and with IT's operations and practices. If they are looking to grow into a security career, then they're probably going to be willing to work pretty hard to succeed.

Roles and Responsibilities   As the security manager develops and begins to execute a long-term security strategy, the manager will identify all the ongoing and occasional tasks that need to be performed by members of the team. Prior to the beginning of this planning, it's important to understand the difference between roles and responsibilities.

A *role* is a designation that denotes an associated set of responsibilities, knowledge, skills, and attitudes. Example roles include *security manager, security engineer,* and *security analyst.*

A *responsibility* is a stated expectation of activities and performance. Example responsibilities include running weekly security scans, performing vendor risk assessments, and approving access requests.

As a security manager analyzes all the required activities in a security team, she may take the approach of listing all the activities, along with estimates of the number of hours per week or hours per month required to perform them. Next, the security manager will group these activities according to subject matter, skill levels, and other considerations.

As the associated workloads are tallied, the number of people required will become evident. Then, these groups of responsibilities can be given roles, followed by job titles.

Most security managers, however, do not have an opportunity to build and staff a program from scratch; instead, they are inheriting an existing program from a previous manager. Still, these activities can serve to delineate all required activities, calculate or observe levels of effort, and confirm that roles and responsibilities are assigned to the right personnel who have the required skills and experience to carry them out properly.

Job Descriptions   A *job description* is a formal description of a position in an organization and usually contains a job title, work experience requirements, knowledge requirements, and responsibilities. In most organizations, human resources is the steward of job descriptions. However, when positions become vacant or new positions are opened, HR often will consult with the hiring manager to ensure that the contents of a job description are still accurate and up-to-date.

Job descriptions are used when an organization is seeking to fill a new or vacant position. The job description will be included in online advertisements to attract potential candidates.

Job descriptions are also a tool used in professional development. Managers and leadership can develop career paths that represent a person's professional growth through a progression of promotions or transfers into other positions. Job descriptions are a primary means for a worker to understand what another position is like; interviewing people who are already in a desired position is another means for gaining insight into a position that someone aspires to. A small but effective way to drive a culture of security is to add in specific language regarding the responsibilities that each role plays in protecting the organization's data and systems used in storing, processing, and transmitting that data.

Culture   Culture is the collective set of attitudes, practices, communication, communication styles, ethics, and other behavior in an organization. Culture can be thought of as the collective consciousness of the workers in an organization. It's hard to describe an organization's culture because it has to be experienced to be understood.

Security managers seek to understand an organization's culture so that he may be a better and more effective change agent. Many organizations do not regard information security as an important activity; this compels security managers to understand the culture and then to work to make subtle changes to the culture so that there is awareness of information security in a form that most workers can understand. Security awareness training, with its attendant messaging from executives, is often regarded as a catalyst for making those subtle changes to the culture.

Security managers and their teams occasionally find they need to develop a "culture within a culture." The rest of the organization with its laissez-faire attitude toward security may still have some catching up to do, but the security team already "gets it"—the ever-conscious awareness of day-to-day activities and whether they are handling and protecting data and systems properly. With our codes of ethics from ISACA and other security professional organizations, we are obligated to conduct ourselves according to a higher standard, which is a part of the reason for the culture within a culture.

Professional Development   Dedicated and committed technologists have a built-in thirst for knowledge and for expanding their boundaries. Information security professionals should have this thirst on steroids, as it's said, because the velocity of change is higher than most other parts of information technology. Cyber-criminal organizations are innovating their malware and other attack techniques, manifested through breaches using increasingly novel methods; security tools vendors are innovating their detective and protective wares; security organizations are continually improving so many aspects of security management, including control frameworks, auditing techniques, and security awareness messaging. It's been said that information security professionals must spend four hours each week reading up on these and other new developments *just to keep from falling behind.*

Security managers need to be aware of the present knowledge and skills that each security team member possesses today, what skills are needed in the team in the future, and the professional growth aspirations that drive each team member. There are several avenues for professional development that are discussed here.

Career Paths   A *career path* is the progression of job responsibilities and job titles that a worker will attain over time. Generally, a worker who is aware of a potential career path within their organization is more likely to remain in the organization. Workers who feel trapped and unable to advance are more likely to consider a position in another organization. With the security employment market as tight as it is, any organization that neglects the topics of professional development and career paths runs the risk of losing people.

Security managers should be aware of any career paths that have been published by their organizations; however, since many organizations don't develop formal career paths, security managers will want to work one-on-one with each security staff member to determine what their individual career paths will look like.

There are many fields of specialty in information security, including the following:

- Risk management
- Risk analysis
- Information systems auditing
- Penetration testing
- Malware analysis
- Security engineering
- Secure development
- Mobile device security
- Telecommunications and network security
- Social engineering
- Security awareness training
- Forensics

- Cryptography
- Business continuity planning and disaster recovery planning
- Identity and access management
- Threat intelligence
- Third-party risk
- Privacy

Certifications   Professional certifications represent skills, knowledge, and experience among security professionals. Certifications are a badge of honor, representing thousands of hours of professional experience, as well as the drive to improve oneself. To the extent that team members value the worth of certifications, security managers should encourage their team members to earn additional certifications. Better organizations would not hesitate to reimburse their security team members' expenses to earn and maintain their certifications although, practically speaking, there may be reasonable limits on the annual spend in this regard.

Security managers should invest time in each of their security staff members to better understand their career paths and the certifications they may want to earn along the way.

The most popular non-vendor-related security certifications are, in rough order of increasing seniority, as follows:

- **Security+**   Offered by CompTIA. This is considered a popular entry-level security certification. You can find information at www.comptia.org.
- **Systems Security Certified Practitioner (SSCP)**   Offered by (ISC)². Many believe that SSCP is a "junior CISSP," but this is not the case. SSCP is more technical than the CISSP and is ideal for hands-on security professionals.
- **Global Information Assurance Certification (GIAC)**   Offered by SANS. This is a family of certifications on several different topics. Information at www.giac.org.
- **Certified Ethical Hacker (CEH)**   Offered by EC-Council. This certification is ideal for penetration testers and others who want to learn more about the world of vulnerabilities and exploits. You can find information at www.eccouncil.org.
- **Certified Cloud Security Professional (CCSP)**   Jointly offered by (ISC)² and the Cloud Security Alliance (CSA). This is a relatively new certification but one that is sure to become popular. You can find information at www.isc2.org.
- **Certified Information Systems Security Professional (CISSP)**   Perhaps the most well-known and respected information security certification. Strong, established security professionals have this certification. This is important for career growth as many organizations require this specific certification for security positions. You can find information at www.isc2.org.

- **Certified Secure Software Lifecycle Professional (CSSLP)** Offered by (ISC)². This topic of this certification is secure software development. You can find information at www.isc2.org.

- **Certified Information Security Manager (CISM)** Offered by ISACA, and the topic of this book. You can find information throughout this book and at www.isaca.org.

- **Certified Information Systems Auditor (CISA)** Also offered by ISACA. This is considered the gold-standard certification for IT auditors. You can find information at www.isaca.org.

- **Certified in Risk and Information Systems Control (CRISC)** Offered by ISACA. This is considered an essential certification for security professionals who work in risk assessments, risk managements, and the development of controls and control frameworks. You can find information at www.isaca.org.

There are many more non-vendor-related security certifications—they are too numerous to list in this book. You can find a broad list on Wikipedia at https://en.wikipedia.org/wiki/List_of_computer_security_certifications.

Many IT equipment vendors and IT security tools vendors offer security certifications that represent expertise in various categories of information security. Nearly every major security tools manufacturer has one or more certifications that can be earned. Here is a small sampling:

- Check Point Certified Security Administrator (CCSA)
- Certified Forensic Security Responder (CFSR) from Guidance Software
- Radware Certified Security Specialist (RCSS)
- Metasploit Certified Specialist from Rapid7
- WhiteHat Certified Secure Developer

Training Another important part of retaining talent is making training available to security staff. Again, because security professionals can be afflicted with boredom, they are happiest when they are learning new things. Security managers may fear that if they provide too much training, their personnel might leave for greener pastures, but what might happen if they don't provide enough training? Their personnel would almost certainly feel trapped and be compelled to leave with even more fervor.

Typical organizations provide one week of security training for its security professionals. Ideally this means that a security professional is able to attend a one-week conference of her choice. Other companies will pay for web-based training or a number of one-day training courses.

One week of training is considered the minimum required for security professionals to stay current in their chosen field. Additional training will be required for security professionals who want to move into a specialty area.

Many employers reimburse college and university tuition, often with a yearly cap. Still, this can provide a means for security personnel who want to pursue an undergraduate or graduate degree in information security and related fields.

> ### Remote Work
>
> With advances in telecommunications capabilities, remote work (also known as *telework*) is increasingly common. In several professionals such as information technology and information security, work can be performed from any location. With the shortage of qualified information security workers, security professionals will find that many organizations are willing to hire qualified professionals and arrange part-time or full-time remote work.
>
> While the details of remote work are beyond the scope of this book, management considering remote work need to understand the factors related to successful remote work.

Project and Program Management

The world of information security field is undergoing constant change. Organizations with mature risk management programs are discovering new actionable risks, attack techniques used by cybercriminals are undergoing constant innovation, security vendors make frequent improvements in their tools, and the practices of managing security are evolving. Information technology is also undergoing considerable changes, and organizations are reinventing themselves through process development and changes in the organization chart. Mergers and acquisitions in many industries inflict many broad changes in affected organizations.

The result of this phenomenon of continuous change is the fact that most organizations undertake several information security projects each year. In many organizations, information security personnel are spending more time in projects than they are in routine daily operations. For many security managers, *continuous change is the only constant*.

In addition to having a deep understanding of information technology, risk management, and most or all of the disciplines within security management, a security manager must also be skilled at both *project management* as well as *program management*—the management of several concurrent projects—to orchestrate the parade of changes being undertaken to keep the organization out of trouble.

Security managers need to keep their eye on the big picture: the strategy and objectives for the security program and alignment with the business. Every program and project in information security should align with these.

The disciplines of project management and program management are outside the scope of this book. Here is some recommended reading:

- Shina, Sammy. *Engineering Project Management for the Global High Technology Industry*. McGraw-Hill Education, 2014.

- Brown, James. *The Handbook of Program Management: How to Facilitate Project Success with Optimal Program Management, Second Edition*. McGraw-Hill Education, 2014.

Budget

Budgeting is an essential part of long-term planning for information security and arguably a more difficult undertaking than for many other departments. While the development of an information security strategy (in terms of the capabilities needed) is somewhat more straightforward, obtaining management support for the funding required to realize the strategy can be quite difficult.

When executive management does not understand the strategic value of information security, the prospect of funding activities that result in existing business capabilities or capacity seems far different from funding information security, which results in no changes in business capabilities or capacity.

The activities that the security manager needs to include in budgets include the following:

- Staff salaries and benefits
- Temporary staff for special projects and initiatives
- Training
- Equipment costs
- Software tools
- Support for equipment and software
- Space required in data centers
- Travel
- Maintenance of documents and records
- Contingencies

Often, security managers undertake a detailed analysis on the work required for each function in information security. For instance, a security manager may track time spent on routine processes as well as anticipated but unplanned activities like incident response and investigations.

Return on Security Investment

The *return on security investment (ROSI)* is a much-maligned concept familiar to many security managers. The concept is simple: in other parts of the business, management makes investment decisions that result in increased revenue or reduced costs. But the traditional means for measuring a return on investment (ROI) on security investments is not so clear. When the organization invests in security, the organization typically does not increase revenue or decrease costs—in fact, costs are increased. And the measure of success is often the absence of a potentially costly security incident or event.

Instead, investments in security need to be viewed as a means for risk reduction. Unfortunately, risk is not present on an organization's income statement or balance sheet, unless an incident does occur.

Business Case Development

ISACA defines a *business case* as "documentation of the rationale for making a business investment, used both to support a business decision on whether to proceed with the investment and as an operational tool to support management of the investment through its full economic life cycle."

In many organizations, before any information security project is permitted to begin, a business case for the project must be developed. The purpose of a business case is to explain the benefits to the business—in business terms—that will be realized as a result of the project.

The development of a business case will normally follow a feasibility study. A *feasibility study* defines the business problem and describes a number of potential solutions. However, it is possible that none of the solutions will result in a benefit for the business. For example, each potential solution may be too costly or incur excessive risk. However, the business case should go beyond the feasibility study in terms of business benefits and include actual figures for costs and benefits.

A business case is a written document that typically includes the following:

- **Business problem**   This is a description of the business problem in qualitative and quantitative terms.

- **Feasibility study results**   The business case should include results of the feasibility study if one was performed.

- **Increased revenue or efficiency analysis**   The business case should, when applicable, provide estimates of increased revenue based on the change. If a business case cannot be tied to revenue, then another approach is to determine changes in business efficiency, risk reduction, or cost savings.

- **High-level project plan**   This should include a timeline and the number of people required.

- **Budget**   This should include the cost to execute the project as well as costs associated with the solution.

- **Metrics**   The business case should include information on how business benefit will be measured, as well as expected before-and-after measurements. Estimates should be backed up by examples of the benefits of similar projects in the organization or in other organizations.

- **Risks**   The business case should include risks that may occur, as well as how those risks can be mitigated. These risks may be market risks or financial risks.

NOTE   Some organizations make the development of a business case the first phase in the actual project; however, this arrangement may be self-serving, as the project team may be taking the point of view of justifying the continuation of the project instead of focusing on whether the project will actually benefit the business. The development of a business case should be performed in an objective manner by people who do not benefit from the result.

The start of a project is not the only time to assess the project's business case and decide whether to undertake the project. At key milestones throughout the project, the business case should be reevaluated. As a project unfolds, situations often develop that could not be anticipated earlier, and these situations sometimes result in added costs, changes in risk, or other variances. For this reason, the business case should be reconsidered throughout the project so that senior management can determine whether the project should continue.

> **NOTE**   Decisions on whether to continue a project should be made not only by those people who benefit from the project but also by other stakeholders who can be more objective. Otherwise, there is a risk that projects will be continued for their own sake instead of for the good of the business.

Vendor Management

A security manager is responsible for managing business agreements and relationships with the suppliers of security tools and services used in the organization. While many of the principles of standard IT vendor management apply to information security, there is one key consideration that security managers need to keep in mind: better information security service providers are busy, and when a security manager finds himself in a situation where he needs assistance from a security services provider right away, the security manager had better have developed strategic relationships with two or more such firms. That way, the security manager has a better chance of finding a security services firm that is not only willing to help but able to help as soon as that help is needed.

Security managers need to develop a deep, trusted relationship with a security services vendor that has various capabilities that the security manager will need from time to time. A trusted relationship is critical, because the security manager needs to be able to confide some of his challenges to a vendor that can be trusted. The vendor should be customer-centric and put the customer's needs first, instead of always thinking where the next sale will come from.

Another important aspect of vendor management is the identification and management of risks that are introduced as a result of a business relationship with each vendor. This topic is addressed fully in the section "Third-Party Risk Management" earlier in this chapter.

Security Program Operations

Business activities on an organization's networks and systems, as well as reconnaissance and attack activities by adversaries, is highly dynamic and ever changing. Everything in information technology and on the Internet moves at a high velocity. For this reason, there are numerous operational activities that take place—24 hours a day, 7 days a week, and 365 days a year—that require the presence of a highly organized security operations function. This section describes typical security operations activities in modern organizations.

Larger organizations locate their security operations in a security operations center (SOC, pronounced "sock"). A SOC is frequently a 24/7/365 operation, although some organizations do not staff their SOC around the clock or on weekends.

These are the topics discussed in this section:

- Event monitoring
- Vulnerability management
- Secure engineering and development
- Network protection
- Endpoint protection and management
- Identity and access management
- Security incident management
- Security awareness training
- Managed security services providers (MSSPs)
- Data security
- Business continuity planning

Event Monitoring

Event monitoring is the practice of examining the events that are occurring on information systems, including applications, operating systems, database management systems, end-user devices, and every type and kind of network device, and being aware of what is going on throughout the entire operating environment.

Prior to the Internet, it was sufficient to review logs on a daily basis. Mainly this was a review of yesterday's events (or the weekend's events on a Monday) to ensure that there were no security incidents warranting further investigation. Those days are mostly gone.

Today, most organizations require *real-time* event monitoring. This means organizations need to have systems in place that will immediately inform them if there are events going on anyplace in the environment that warrant attention.

Log Reviews

A *log review* is an examination of an event log in an information system to see whether any security or operational incident has occurred in the system. Typically, a log review is an examination of "yesterday's" activities in a system. While still warranted in limited circumstances, most organizations conduct *continuous log review* by sending log data into a security event and incident management system, discussed later in this section.

Centralized Log Management

Centralized log management is a practice where event logs on various systems are sent over the network to a central collection and storage point, called a *log server*. There are two primary uses for a log server: the first is archival storage of events that may be used at a later date in an investigation; the second is for the review of events on a daily basis or in real time. Generally, real-time analysis is performed by a security event and incident management system, discussed next.

Security Event and Incident Management

A security information and event management system (SIEM, usually pronounced "sim" but sometimes "seem") is a system that collects and analyzes log data from many or all systems in an organization.

A SIEM has the ability to correlate events from one or more devices to provide additional detail about an incident. For instance, an attacker performing a brute-force password attack on a web server may be generating alerts on the web server itself and also on the firewall and intrusion detection system. A SIEM would portray the incident using events from these and possibly other devices to give personnel a richer depiction of the incident.

Threat Intelligence

Modern SIEMs have the ability to ingest threat intelligence feeds from various external sources. This enables the SIEM to better correlate events in an organization's systems with various threats experienced by other organizations.

For example, another organization is attacked by an adversary from a specific IP address in a foreign country. This information is included in a threat intelligence feed that arrives in the organization's SIEM. This helps the SIEM be more aware of activity of the same type or from the same IP address. This can help the organization be better alerted about incidents occurring elsewhere that could occur in the organization's network.

Orchestration

In the context of security incident and event management, *orchestration* refers to a scripted, automated response that is automatically or manually triggered when specific events occur. Orchestration systems can be stand-alone systems or may exist as part of the SIEM.

For example, an organization has developed "run books" or short procedures for personnel who manage the SIEM for actions to perform when specific types of events occur. The organization, desiring to automate some of these responses, implements an orchestration tool that has scripts that can be automatically run when specific events occur. The orchestration system can be configured to run some scripts immediately, while others can be set up and run when an analyst "approves" them.

The advantage of orchestration is twofold. First, repetitive and rote tasks are automated, relieving personnel of boredom and improving accuracy; second, response to some types of events can be performed much more quickly, thereby blunting the impact of certain incidents.

Vulnerability Management

Vulnerability management is the practice of periodically examining information systems (including but not limited to operating systems, subsystems such as database management systems, applications, and network devices) for the purpose of discovering exploitable vulnerabilities, related analysis, and decisions about remediation. Organizations employ vulnerability management as a primary activity to reduce the likelihood of successful attacks on their IT environment.

Often, one or more *scanning tools* are used to scan target systems in the search for vulnerabilities. There are a variety of scanning tools:

- Network device identification
- Open port identification
- Software version identification
- Exploitable vulnerability identification
- Web application vulnerability identification
- Source code defect identification

Security managers generally employ several of these tools for routine and nonroutine vulnerability management tasks. Routine tasks include scheduled scans of specific IT assets, while nonroutine tasks include troubleshooting and various types of investigations.

A typical vulnerability management process includes these activities:

- **Periodic scanning**   One or more tools will be used to scan assets in the organization in the search for vulnerabilities.

- **Analysis of scan results**   A security manager will examine the results of a vulnerability scan, validating the results to make sure there are no false positive results. This analysis often includes a risk analysis to better understand an identified vulnerability in the context of the asset, its role, and its criticality. Scanning tools generally include a criticality level or criticality score for an identified vulnerability so that personnel can begin to understand the severity of the vulnerability. Most tools utilize the common vulnerability scoring system (CVSS) method for scoring a vulnerability.

  After noting the CVSS score of a specific vulnerability, a security manager will analyze the vulnerability with the purpose of establishing the contextual criticality of the vulnerability. For example, a vulnerability in the service message block (SMB) service on Microsoft Windows servers may be rated as critical. A security manager may downgrade the risk in the organization if SMB services are not accessible over the Internet.

  In another example, a security manager may raise the severity of a vulnerability if the organization lacks detective controls that would alert the organization that the vulnerable component has been attacked and compromised.

- **Delivery of scan results to asset owners**   The security manager will deliver the report to the owners or custodians of affected assets so that those people can begin planning remediation activities.

- **Remediation**   Asset owners will make changes to affected assets, typically through the installation of one or more security patches or through the implementation of one or more security configuration changes. Often, risk analysis is performed to determine the risks associated with proposed remediation plans.

	CVSS Score	Internet-Facing Assets	Internal Assets
Table 4-6 Typical Vulnerability Management Remediation SLA	8.01 to 10	5 days	10 days
	4.01 to 8.0	10 days	15 days
	2.01 to 4.0	30 days	45 days
	0 to 2.0	90 days	180 days

Organizations often establish service level agreements for the maximum times required for remediation of identified vulnerabilities. Table 4-6 shows a typical SLA.

Common Vulnerability Scoring System

The *common vulnerability scoring system* (CVSS) is an open framework that is used to provide a common methodology for scoring vulnerabilities. CVSS employs a standard methodology for examining and scoring a vulnerability based on the exploitability of the vulnerability, the impact of exploitation, and the complexity of the vulnerability.

The CVSS has made it possible for organizations to adopt a consistent approach for the analysis and remediation of vulnerabilities. Specifically, organizations can develop service level agreements that determine the speed by which an organization will remediate vulnerabilities.

Vulnerability Identification Techniques

Several techniques are used for identifying vulnerabilities in target systems:

- **Security scan** A security scan is the use of one or more vulnerability scanning tools that help identify easily found vulnerabilities in target systems. A security scan will identify a vulnerability in one or two ways: first, by confirming the version of a target system or program that is known to be vulnerability; second, by making an attempt at proving the existence of a vulnerability by testing a system's response to specific stimulus.

- **Penetration test** A penetration test involves the use of a security scan, plus additional manual tests that security scanning tools do not employ. A penetration test is considered a realistic simulation of an attacker who intends to break into a target system.

  A penetration test of an organization's production environment may fall somewhat short of the techniques used by an actual attacker. In a penetration test, a tester is careful not to exploit vulnerabilities that could result in a malfunction of the target system. Often, an actual attacker will not take this precaution unless she wants to attack a system without being noticed. For this reason, it is sometimes desirable to conduct a penetration test of nonproduction infrastructure; however, nonproduction environments are often not identical to their production counterparts.

- **Social engineering assessment** This is an assessment of the judgment of personnel in the organization to see how well they are able to recognize various ruses used by attackers in an attempt to trick users into performing tasks or providing information. Several means are used, including e-mail, telephone calls, and in-person encounters. Social engineering assessments help organizations identify training and improvement opportunities.

Social engineering attacks can have a high impact on an organization. A particular form of social engineering known as *CEO fraud* or *wire transfer fraud* consists of a ruse where an attacker sends an e-mail that pretends to originate from a CEO to the chief financial officer (CFO), claiming that a secret merger or acquisition proceeding requires a wire transfer for a significant sum be sent to a specific offshore account. Aggregate losses because of CEO fraud over the past few years exceeds $2 billion.

Patch Management

Closely related to vulnerability management, the practice of *patch management* ensures that IT systems, tools, and applications have consistent version and patch levels. In all but the smallest organizations, patch management can be successful only through the use of tools that are used to automate the deployment of patches to target systems. Without automated tools, patch management is labor intensive and prone to errors that are often unnoticed, resulting in systems that remain vulnerable to exploitation even when IT and security staff believe they are protected.

Patch management is related to other IT processes including change management and configuration management, which are discussed later in this chapter.

Secure Engineering and Development

While they are not activities performed in an organization's security management program, engineering and software development are business processes that security managers will typically observe and, occasionally, influence. The primary reason for this is that most organizations do not adequately include security practices in their IT engineering and development processes, resulting in a higher-than-necessary number of security defects, inadequate security safeguards, and, occasionally, security breaches.

For decades, IT organizations employed no security personnel, nor did they include security in their design, engineering, or development processes because security involved merely the assurance that no one could enter the room where the non-networked mainframe computer resided. When networking and the global Internet emerged, many organizations continued to exclude security in its design, engineering, and development. Further, in the earlier days of Internet connectivity, security managers earned the reputation of trying to stop innovative products dead in their tracks because of security issues that often were solvable. Today, there are still numerous business executives who believe security to be a tactical activity that consists of simple, unobtrusive "overlay" functions like firewalls and antivirus. These historical phenomena largely explain why organizations still fail to include security appropriately in the design, engineering, and development phases.

Today, security managers understand the business value of security involvement as early as possible in an organization's business and software development life cycles. Security adds value when security managers understand business processes and understand how to engage in a way that demonstrates value. Security can add value at each stage of the development cycle:

- **Conceptual**   When business executives are discussing new business capabilities, lines of business, or even mergers and acquisitions, security managers can weigh in on these activities with guidance in several topics including data protection, regulations, compliance, and risk.

- **Requirements**   When requirements are being developed for the development or acquisition of a new business capability, security managers can be sure to add security, compliance, and privacy requirements to improve the likelihood that systems, applications, and other capabilities are more likely to be secure.

- **Design**   With proper input at the requirements stage, designs are more likely to be secure. Involvement in design reviews will ensure that an initiative is heading in the right direction.

- **Engineering and development**   With security involvement in requirements and design, it's more likely that engineering and development will result in secure results. Still, when engineers and developers are aware of secure engineering and development techniques, results will be improved from a security perspective.

- **Testing**   When requirements are developed in a way that makes the measurable and verifiable, then testing can include verification that requirements have been met. This will ensure that security was included properly in the engineering and development phases.

Organizations that fail to include security in their development cycles are more likely to incur additional rework as security is retrofitted into systems and applications, as opposed to being secure by design. Events such as risk assessments and vulnerability assessments can expose the lack of security by design, resulting in rework. Organizations unaware of the principle of security by design are often unaware that they could have performed their engineering and development for less cost overall, when considering the cost of rework.

Computer Science Programs Omit Security

I had wondered for most of my career why so few software developers were open to a discussion on the concept of security by design. The answer became clear when I read an article entitled "Top US Undergraduate Computer Science Programs Skip Cybersecurity Classes" (Dark Reading, April 7, 2016. http://www.dark-reading.com/vulnerabilities---threats/top-us-undergraduate-computer-science-programs-skip-cybersecurity-classes/d/d-id/1325024). The article cited a study that included an analysis of the top 121 U.S. university computer science and engineering programs, finding that none of the top ten schools required students to take a cybersecurity class. Further, three of the top ten had no cybersecurity courses at all.

Security managers need to keep this in mind. Universities are minting fresh software developers who have probably had no exposure to security in the context of software development. It is no wonder then that they may find this a foreign concept.

A recommended approach for security managers involves engaging executive management instead of developers directly, restating this in business terms, such as the increased risk of breaches and compliance violations or the added expense of rework.

Network Protection

Network protection is one of the more mature disciplines in IT and information security. Usenet, the pre-Internet dial-up protocol for transporting e-mail and other information, included user ID and password authentication as early as 1980. The first firewall was developed in 1988 as the primary means for protecting systems and data from attacks originating outside the organization. Firewalls are still considered essential, and other types of devices and design considerations are commonly used to protect organizations' internal networks from many types of unwanted activities.

Networks in organizations often grow organically, with incremental changes over time designed by a succession of network engineers or architects. In all but the most mature organizations, the details of network architecture and the reasons for various architectural features are undocumented and lost to the annals of time. This results in many organizations' networks today consisting of several characteristics and features that are poorly understood, other than knowing that they are essential to the networks' ongoing functionality.

Firewalls

Firewalls are network devices that are used to control the passage of network traffic from one network to one or more other networks. Firewalls are typically placed at the boundary of an organization's network and other, external networks. Organizations also use firewalls to logically separate internal networks from each other; examples include the following:

- A data center network is often protected from other internal networks with a firewall.
- Development and testing networks are usually protected by firewalls.
- A special network known as a demilitarized zone (DMZ) is protected by one or more firewalls, as shown in Figure 4-5.

Firewalls are managed through a user interface of some kind. At the heart of a firewall's configuration is its rules, which are a series of statements that define specific network traffic that is to be permitted or blocked. Table 4-7 contains a set of sample firewall rules. The rules in Table 4-7 are explained here, in order of appearance:

- Permit e-mail from the entire Internet to reach the e-mail server at 141.204.10.22 only.
- Permit DNS from the entire Internet to reach the DNS server at 141.204.10.24 only.
- Permit NNTP traffic from the entire Internet to reach time server at 141.204.10.22 only.
- Permit all users to access the entire Internet on ports 80 and 443 (HTTP and HTTPS protocols) only.
- Deny all other traffic from the Internet on all ports from reaching any internal system.

Figure 4-5 A firewall protects a DMZ network

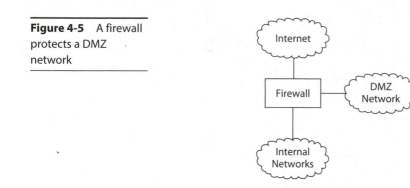

Source IP Address	Source Port	Destination IP Address	Destination Port	Permit or Deny
0.0.0.0 to 255.255.255.255	25	141.204.10.22	25	Permit
0.0.0.0 to 255.255.255.255	53	141.204.10.24	53	Permit
141.204.10.24	53	0.0.0.0 to 255.255.255.255	53	Permit
0.0.0.0 to 255.255.255.255	119	141.204.10.22	119	Permit
141.204.12.1 to 141.204.12.255	80, 443	0.0.0.0 to 255.255.255.255	80, 443	
0.0.0.0 to 255.255.255.255	0 to 65535	141.204.10.1 to 141.204.10.255 + 141.204.12.1 to 141.204.12.255	0–65535	Deny

Table 4-7 Example Firewall Rules

Application Firewalls

Application firewalls are devices used to examine and control messages being sent to an application server, primarily to block unwanted or malicious content. Most often used to protect web servers, application firewalls block attacks that may represent attempts by an attacker to gain illicit control of an application or steal data that the application server accesses.

Segmentation

Network segmentation is the practice of partitioning an organization's network into zones, with protective devices such as firewalls controlling network traffic between the zones.

The purpose of network segmentation is the protection of business functions or asset groups through network-level access control. Network segmentation is a common technique used to protect high-value assets by permitting network traffic from specific hosts, users, or applications to access other networks, while denying all others access. Figure 4-6 depicts network segmentation.

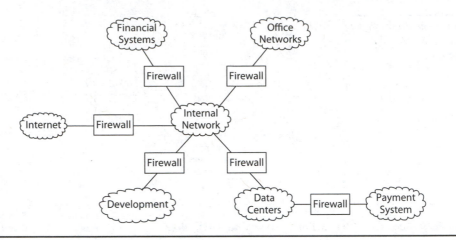

Figure 4-6 Network segmentation creates zones of trust

Common uses of network segmentation include the following:

- Protection of data center networks from networks containing end-user devices
- Isolation of systems with sensitive data as a means for reducing scope of audits
- Protection of systems on a demilitarized zone (DMZ) network from the Internet, while at the same time protecting internal networks from systems on the DMZ
- Protection of internal networks from activities taking place in a development or testing environment

Intrusion Prevention Systems

Intrusion prevention systems (IPSs) are systems that detect and block malicious network traffic that may be associated with an intrusion.

An IPS differs from a firewall in one important way: an IPS examines the content of network packets to determine whether each packet should be allowed to pass through the network or be blocked. A firewall's decision on whether to block or permit a packet is based strictly upon its origin, destination, and port.

Many IPSs also block traffic from "known malicious" IP addresses and domains, based upon network "reputation" data that is periodically sent to an IPS. The makers of several IPS products include feeds of reputation data, sometimes with several updates each day. Attackers often switch their attack origins frequently, knowing that most network engineers cannot keep up with the pace of change; however, IPSs with incoming reputation feeds help to automate this process, resulting in improved security through more effective blocking of traffic from known malicious sites.

Some IPSs can import information from a *threat intel feed,* which is a subscription service about known threats. A threat intel feed often contains IP addresses associated with known malicious sites; an IPS will automatically block traffic being transmitted to or from those IP addresses.

In addition to blocking malicious traffic, an IPS can also permit suspect traffic, log the event, and optionally create an alarm. This falls into the category of network traffic that may or may not be suspicious. This would serve to alert personnel who can investigate the event and take necessary action.

IPSs require continuous vigilance. Sometimes an IPS will block traffic that is anomalous but not actually harmful. This blocking of traffic might represent the prevention of desired business activities. In such cases, a security analyst monitoring and operating an IPS would need to "whitelist" the traffic so that the IPS will not block it in the future. Also, when an IPS sounds an alarm when it has permitted dubious traffic, a security analyst would need to investigate the matter and take needed action.

Like many security systems, IPSs initially took the form of a hardware appliance. Most IPSs are now available in the form of a virtual machine that can be installed in an organization's public or private cloud.

Network Anomaly Detection

Network anomaly detection is a common technique used to identify network traffic that may be a part of an intrusion or other unwanted event. Network anomaly detection is a strictly detective tool that does not prevent unwanted traffic. In all cases, when a network anomaly detection system identifies potentially unwanted traffic, someone must take action to identify the business nature of the traffic and take steps to block it if needed.

Network anomaly detection systems work by "learning" about all of the network "conversations" that take place between systems. Over time, the network anomaly system will easily recognize anomalous traffic, which is network traffic that is novel or unique when compared to all of the traffic that it knows about. There are a number of ways in which a network anomaly system will identify traffic as anomalous:

- Traffic between two systems that rarely, if ever, have directly communicated before
- Traffic between two systems on a network port that rarely, if ever, has been used before
- Traffic between two systems at a higher volume than has been observed before
- Traffic between two systems taking place at a different time of day than has been observed before

Network anomaly detection systems generally do not examine the contents of traffic but instead just the identity of the systems, the ports used, and the volume of traffic.

To be effective, network anomaly detection systems need to be positioned at locations in a network where large volumes of network traffic pass, such as backbone routers. But more commonly, network anomaly detection systems utilize agents on various routers and collect the traffic centrally for analysis. Figure 4-7 shows such an architecture.

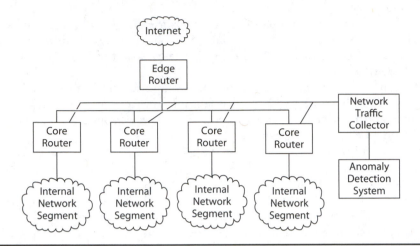

Figure 4-7   Network anomaly detection systems collect data from several sources for analysis

There are two main types of network anomaly detection systems. The first is a dedicated system (an appliance or virtual machine) that collects network traffic data from various points in the network, as depicted in Figure 4-7. The second method is the use of detailed event logging in core routers and firewalls that are sent to a SIEM where network anomaly detection rules are established. These two methods can achieve the same goal: detection of unusual network traffic that may be signs of an intrusion or other unwanted event in the network.

There are three standards used for network anomaly detection:

- **Netflow**   This is a network anomaly detection protocol developed by Cisco Systems and is available on Cisco Systems routers.

- **sFlow**   This is an industry-standard protocol for monitoring networks.

- **Remote Monitoring (RMON)**   This is an earlier protocol permitting the monitoring of network traffic.

Network Taps, aka Span Ports

Several network-based detective security systems are designed to observe all the traffic passing through one or more control points in an organization's network. These systems work by analyzing all of the organization's internal and/or external network traffic and create alarms when specific conditions are seen—generally, signs of intrusions or other unwanted events such as employee misbehavior.

A simple way to make all network traffic available for these detective systems is to place appliances in the network that are inline and receive all network traffic. However, network managers are often reluctant to place inline security tools in the network as they can impact network performance, and they would serve as an additional *single point of failure.*

A *network tap,* commonly known as a *span port,* is a special connection that is found on some network routers and switches. A copy of all the network traffic passing through the router or switch will be sent to the network tap. A network tap can be connected to an intrusion prevention system (which would be running in listen-only mode since it would not be inline in this case) or a network anomaly detection system. An advantage of a network tap is that activities there do not interfere with the network itself.

Packet Sniffers

A *packet sniffer* is a detective tool used by a security engineer or network engineer to analyze traffic on a network. Originally in the form of external appliances, packet sniffers today are in the form of software tools that can be installed on server and desktop operating systems, as well as network devices.

Packet sniffers are typically used when a network engineer is troubleshooting a network issue to better understand the precise nature of network traffic flowing between devices on a network. Because even small networks can have large volumes of traffic, packet sniffers employ rules that instruct it to display just the packets of specific interest to the engineer.

Packet sniffers can retain specific types of packets for later analysis. For instance, if a network engineer is troubleshooting a DNS problem, the engineer can capture just the DNS packets so that she can examine the contents of those packets, in the hopes that this will lead to a solution to the problem.

Because the types of problems that an engineer may be troubleshooting can vary, packet sniffers display packets in different ways, from Ethernet frames to TCP/IP packets to application messages.

Figure 4-8 shows the popular Wireshark packet-sniffing tool running on macOS Sierra.

The Cable of Fear

I once knew a network engineer who joined an organization where he played the role of network engineer and network architect. Seeking to understand the network, he used tools and physical observation to develop a first-ever comprehensive diagram of the organization's enterprise network. He proudly displayed the diagram, printed by a plotter, on the wall near his office.

I studied the diagram, and the network generally resembled a network borne out of a logical design, with various zones separated by firewalls. But I noticed a network connection that started in one network zone, bypassed all of the firewalls, and ended

(continued)

in another zone. The connection was a physical cable in a data center that directly connected two networks that should not have been directly connected to each other.

I asked the network engineer about this cable and its purpose. He replied, "This is called the Cable of Fear." I asked what that meant, and he replied that there was active network traffic on this cable, but he didn't yet know why. No documentation could be found that described the cable or its purpose. He was fearful that it existed at all, and he feared for what might happen should he unplug it.

He eventually did understand what traffic was traveling over the cable but never did understand why it was there. Finally, he succeeded in removing it, and the network continued to work properly as far as he could tell.

Wireless Network Protection

When improperly managed, wireless networks can become an avenue of attack. Older encryption protocols such as Wired Equivalent Privacy (WEP) are highly vulnerable to eavesdropping and intrusion. Employees and intruders may attempt to set up their own

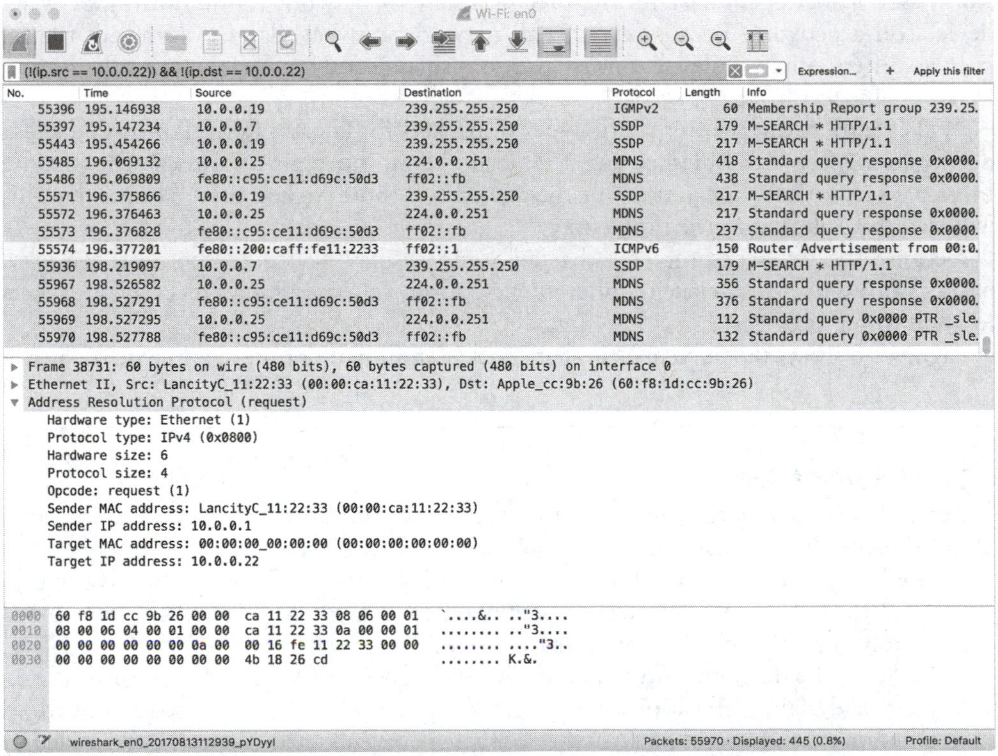

Figure 4-8   Packet-sniffing tool Wireshark capturing packets on a wireless network

wireless network access points. Weak authentication protocols may permit intruders to successfully authenticate to wireless networks. These and other types of attacks compel organizations to undertake a number of safeguards including scanning for rogue (unauthorized) access points, penetration testing of wireless networks, and monitoring of wireless access points and controllers for suspicious activity.

Web Content Filters

A *web content filter* is a central network-based system that monitors and, optionally, filters web communications. The primary purpose of a web content filter is to protect the organization from malicious content present on web sites that the organization's users might otherwise visit. Figure 4-9 shows an "access denied" window for a user attempting to access http://whitehouse.com/, which was a pornography site for many years.

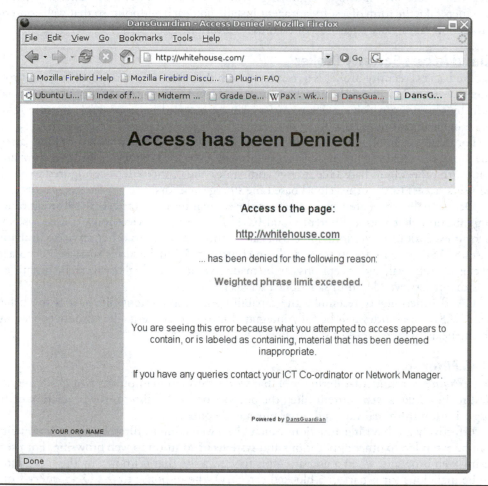

Figure 4-9 End-user "access denied" screen from web content filter (Courtesy of Bluefoxicy at en.wikipidia.org)

Web content filters closely monitor the network traffic flowing to and from users' browsers and block traffic containing malicious content as a means for protecting the organization from malware attacks. Being centrally administered by a network engineer or security engineer, web content filters are typically used to block categories of content, making web sites associated with those categories as unreachable by its users. For instance, organizations sometimes elect to block traffic not only to sites associated with malware but also for specific content categories such as gambling, pornography, weapons, or hate crimes. Sometimes organizations are put in the difficult position of web censorship when employees accuse their employers of blocking access to sites they want to visit, even if those sites are not business related.

Initial web content filtering products took the form of inline devices located in an organization's data center, thereby protecting all users connected to the internal network. But with more organizations employing remote workers, newer web content filtering products take the form of a software agent installed on each endpoint so that web content protection takes place regardless of each user's location.

Cloud Access Security Broker

A cloud access security broker is a security system that monitors and, optionally, controls users' access to Internet web sites. The purpose of a CASB is to protect sensitive information by observing which service providers can be accessed by users, and controlling or blocking access as necessary.

For example, an organization has purchased a corporate account with the cloud-based file storage company known as Box. To prevent users from storing sensitive company data with other cloud-based file storage companies, the CASB will be configured to block all users' access to the other cloud-based file storage vendors.

Occasionally, there are times where employees will need to retrieve files from another organization that uses a different cloud-based file storage service; most CASB systems permit exceptions where individual users are permitted access to other services. In many cases, CASB systems are aware of and can control individual actions such as file storage versus file retrieval, and exceptions can be made so that individual users can be permitted to store or retrieve files in unsanctioned services.

CASB functionality resembles the capabilities of web content filters. It is my belief that CASB capabilities will be fully integrated into web content filter products, leading to the near disappearance of stand-alone CASB solutions.

DNS Filter

A *DNS filter* is a content-filtering tool that works through manipulation of DNS queries and replies. Like a web content filter, the purpose of a DNS filter is the protection of an organization from malware and other unwanted content.

Effectively a DNS filter functions much like a web content filter, but its functionality can be extended to other applications and systems in addition to web browsing. For users using web browsers, when a user attempts to view a site that is known by the DNS filter to be malicious (or is part of a blocked category), the response to the DNS query from the user's workstation will direct the user's browser to a page that informs the user that access to the site has been blocked.

E-mail Protection: Spam and Phishing Filters

E-mail has been a preferred method for propagating malware for decades. More than 90 percent of successful network intrusions begin with phishing messages sent to scores of users in the hopes that one or more of those targeted users will open a malicious document or visit a compromised web site. The "trendy" schemes including CEO fraud (where a fraudster sends e-mails to company executives, requesting them to wire large amounts of money in support of a secret merger or acquisition) and ransomware (malware that encrypts users' files and then demands a ransom in exchange for file recovery). It is for these reasons that many organizations employ e-mail protection in the form of spam and phishing filters to keep those unwanted messages from ever reaching end users.

Spam and phishing e-mail filters generally have the following characteristics:

- Built-in **rules** that are used to determine whether any individual e-mail message should be blocked.

- A **quarantine** where blocked e-mails reside. End users typically can access their quarantine in order to view messages and **release** (to their e-mail inbox) messages that should not have been blocked.

- **White lists** and **black lists**, centrally configurable and generally configurable by end users, that specify which e-mail messages, as well as messages from anyone in the domain, should always be blocked or permitted.

In organizations that give users no visibility or control over spam and phishing blocking, end users have no visibility or control regarding messages that may have arrived but were blocked. In some organizations, users can contact the IT service desk and request that any messages from specific e-mail addresses be released to them.

In organizations that give users full visibility and control over the handling of spam and phishing e-mails, end users may view their quarantine, release individual messages, and manage their black lists and white lists all on their own.

There are several terms used in the topic of unwanted e-mail messages, including the following:

- **Clone phishing**   The practice of obtaining legitimate e-mail messages and subtly manipulating them for fraudulent use. The attachment or link in the legitimate message is switched for one that is malicious.

- **Phishing**   The general use of unwanted e-mails that attempt to perpetrate fraud of some kind on the recipient.

- **Smishing**   Phishing messages sent to users via SMS messages to their mobile devices and smartphones.

- **Spear phishing**   Phishing messages that are specially crafted for a target group or organization.

- **Spim**   Phishing messages that are sent to users via instant messaging.

- **Whaling**   Phishing messages sent to key executives; also known as CEO fraud when the CEO is a specific target.

In connection with their security awareness programs, some organizations acquire or develop a capability of producing test phishing messages to learn which users and user groups are more likely to click on phishing messages. Such messages are usually coded so that security personnel will know which individual persons click on the links or attachments in test phishing messages. Phishing testing can be used as a metric to see whether users are improving their skills in identifying fraudulent messages and directives to ignore them.

Phishing testing is an important activity, even in organizations that use effective phishing filters. One reason for this is to inform users that phishing filters occasionally permit phishing messages into users' e-mail. This also helps users better understand fraud of all kinds, including those for which there are no automated filters.

Network Access Control

Network access control (NAC) is an approach for network security that is used to determine the conditions wherein a device will be permitted to attach to a network. NAC is used by organizations that want to enforce specific policies or conditions in which devices will be permitted to connect to a network, including the following:

- Only company-issued devices
- Only devices with up-to-date security patches
- Only devices with up-to-date anti-malware software
- Only devices with specific security settings
- Only devices associated with authorized users

NAC is a valid approach for organizations that want to prevent unauthorized devices, such as personally owned laptops, tablets, or smartphones, from connecting to an internal network. NAC can also be a valuable front line of defense by preventing systems lacking up-to-date patches or malware prevention from connecting to a network and potentially spreading malware. Devices with these attributes are often connected to a "quarantine network" where users are directed to install security patches or other protective measures if they want to connect those devices to the network.

Endpoint Protection and Management

The term *endpoint* has come to mean the inclusivity of smartphones, tablets, laptops, and desktop computers. Endpoints are used to create, process, distribute, and store sensitive information in organizations.

Endpoints are favorite targets for cybercriminal organizations for several reasons, including the following:

- They frequently contain sensitive information targeted by criminals.
- They are more easily lost or stolen.
- Organizations struggle to ensure that anti-malware and defensive configurations exist on 100 percent of issued endpoints; therefore, a small percentage of endpoints are more vulnerable to malware attacks.

- They are often permitted to access internal corporate networks where more sensitive information resides.

- Some users are more likely to open malicious attachments in phishing messages, resulting in a favorable chance of success for a skilled attacker who targets large numbers of users and their endpoints.

- Many organizations do a marginal job of deploying security patches to all endpoints, meaning that many are vulnerable to exploitable vulnerabilities for extended periods of time.

- Some users have administrative privileges, making them more attractive targets.

- Being quite powerful and often connected to high-speed broadband networks, endpoints make attractive intermediate systems in an attack on other systems, including relaying phishing e-mail and DDoS attacks.

Because endpoints exist in relatively large numbers, cybercriminals are aware of the fact that there will always be a few endpoints that are poorly protected because of one or more of the previously listed factors.

All of these issues make corporate endpoint management a tiresome and thankless job.

Configuration Management

Most organizations manage their endpoint populations using automated tools. This makes the management of endpoints more cost effective, and the configuration of endpoints far more consistent. Organizations generally employ four main techniques for effective endpoint management:

- **Image management**   An *image* is a binary representation of a fully installed and configured operating system and applications for a computer. A typical computer support department will maintain a collection of images, with one or more images for various classes of users, as well as for various hardware makes, models, and configurations.

- **Configuration management**   A typical computer support department will utilize one or more tools to manage large numbers of endpoint systems through automation. These tools are typically used to deploy patches, change configuration settings, install software programs, and remove software programs.

- **Remote control**   A typical computer support team will use a tool that will permit them to remotely access running endpoint systems. Some of these tools permit covert remote access to a user's endpoint system without their knowledge. Most of these tools require that the end user initiate a session whereby a computer support person is granted remote access and control of an endpoint for the purpose of assistance and troubleshooting.

- **Remote destruction**   In the event of an endpoint that is lost or stolen, organizations with a remote destruct capability can direct that a lost or stolen endpoint immediately destroy any locally stored data to keep it out of the hands of a criminal who may have stolen the endpoint. This capability is often employed for laptop computers, tablet computers, and smartphones.

- **Data encryption**   Many organizations consider techniques such as *whole-disk encryption* to protect stored information on mobile devices. This helps protect sensitive data stored on mobile devices by making it more difficult for a thief to access stored data on a stolen device.

Organizations often maintain endpoint *configuration standards*, which are documents that detail the operational and security configuration for its endpoints. Occasionally the security configuration for endpoints will reside in a separate *hardening standard* document.

Malware Prevention

The nature of endpoint computing and the design of modern operating systems means that malware is a problem that is not going away any time soon. On the contrary, with the advent of *ransomware* and *destructware*, malware is getting more potent and destructive. This does not diminish the impact of older generations of malware that give attackers the ability to remotely access to victim systems (using remote access Trojan, or RAT, software), search for and exfiltrate sensitive data, steal login credentials with key loggers, relay spam and phishing messages, and participate in DDoS attacks against other organizations.

There are many types of malware. Any individual species of malware may have one or more of the following characteristics:

- **Virus**   A fragment of an executable file that is able to attach itself to other executable files. This type of malware exists almost exclusively on Windows operating systems, but with improvements in newer versions of Windows, viruses are less common.

- **Trojan**   A stand-alone program that must be executed by the end user to be activated. A Trojan typically claims to be one thing (for instance, a game), when it actually performs some malicious action.

- **Macro**   An executable file that is embedded within another file such as a document or spreadsheet file.

- **Spyware**   Malware that records one or more surveillance activities on a target system including web sites visited and keystrokes, reporting back to the spyware owner.

- **Worm**   A stand-alone program that is able to propagate itself automatically from one computer to another, typically using network communications.

- **Rootkit**   Malware that is designed to evade detection by anti-malware and even the operating system itself.

- **Fileless**   Malware that exists exclusively in a computer's memory, instead of in the file system. This type of malware is more difficult for traditional antivirus software to detect, as there is no file to examine for matching signatures.

- **Ransomware**   Malware that performs some destructive but reversible action such as encrypting files and demands a ransom be paid before the destruction can be recovered.

- **Destructware**   Malware that performs some permanent destruction, such as irreversible file encryption, on a target system. Also known as a *wiper*.

- **Remote access Trojan**   Often referred to as a RAT, this is malware that provides covert remote access visibility and control of a target system by its attacker.

- **Key logger**   Malware that records an end user's keystrokes on a target system and then sends those keystrokes to the attacker for later analysis.

Formerly known as *antivirus software*, *anti-malware* is software designed to detect the presence of malware and neutralize it before it can execute. Anti-malware utilizes a number of techniques to detect the presence of malware:

- **Signatures**   Time honored but quickly becoming obsolete, signature detection involves the matching of known bad malware with new files being introduced to the system. A match means malware has been detected.

- **Process observation**   Anti-malware observes the behavior of processes running in the operating system and generally knows the types of actions that each process will take. When anti-malware sees a process performing an action not typical of a given process, the anti-malware will terminate the process.

- **Sandbox**   Anti-malware will first install new files in a sandbox, which is a virtual container where the files will be permitted to execute. If the files behave like malware in the sandbox, they will not be permitted to execute in the system. In some products, the sandbox resides in the endpoint, but in other products the sandbox resides in the cloud.

- **Deception**   Anti-malware will use some technique to scramble the operating system's memory map so that malware will be unable to attack processes' memory images.

The Death of Antivirus Software

Antivirus software works by recognizing the "signature" of an incoming infection. When a virus spreads to another computer, the antivirus software calculates the signature of the incoming file, and if it finds a match, the antivirus software has detected a virus and will employ means to remove it.

In this regard, antivirus software has run its course. Initially developed in the mid-1980s, antivirus software initially updated its signatures a couple of times each year because of the slow emergence of computer viruses. But over the years, more and more computer viruses were discovered, resulting in signature updates multiple times each day.

The creators of malware have have won the battle. The techniques used to create malware include a process known as *packing*, where the malware program is packaged into an executable (EXE) file. Today, many species of malware repackage themselves prior to attacking each successive endpoint and employ some randomness in the process. The result: each infected endpoint's virus "signature" is unique and will never again be seen in the world. Signature-based antivirus software cannot deal with that.

Virtual Desktop Infrastructure

Organizations that are highly concerned with malware and other risks associated with endpoint computing can implement a virtual desktop infrastructure (VDI). In a VDI, end-user computing takes place on highly controlled, centralized servers, and end users' computers are essentially functioning as terminals. VDI reduces the risk of malware on endpoints, since endpoints are reduced to a simplified version of its former self with far less *attack surface* than a typical endpoint operating system. Further, no business data is stored or processed on the endpoint, but instead it resides and remains on centralized servers.

Organizations often use enterprise versions of anti-malware on their endpoints. Unlike consumer-class anti-malware programs that act as stand-alone applications, enterprise versions utilize a centralized console that permits an engineer to observe and manage anti-malware running on thousands of endpoints. Enterprise consoles can be used to reinstall anti-malware when needed, run scans of file systems on demand, and change configurations for any or all endpoints. When malware is detected, consoles can send detailed messages to security incident and event management systems, alerting personnel in a security operations center (SOC) of the incident so that action can be taken as needed.

End Users and Local Admin Rights

For decades, a thorny problem with endpoint and end user management lay in the capability of end users. In earlier versions of Microsoft Windows, end users were automatically given the role of "local administrator." This had two primary implications:

- End users were able to install programs, install drivers, and change system configuration at will, thereby relieving the IT service desk of having to do these actions themselves. While relieving the service desk of drudgery, if an end user botched an install or destroyed the system's registry, the service desk had the task of recovering the end user's system, sometimes taking hours of work.

- Malware often executes at the same privilege level as the end user to activate it. When the end user is a local administrator, malware has the run of the machine and can do anything it needs, without restriction. This can make malware attacks far more potent since the malware can alter any portion of the operating system.

Gradually, IT organizations have taken back administrative privileges from their end users, but not without a fight. In numerous cases, end users would complain and even revolt: they wanted to install their iTunes, personal income tax software, and anything else they wanted. After years of having local admin rights, end users were feeling entitled to do anything they pleased. Some even went so far as to say that the term *personal computer* meant they could do anything and everything they wanted.

Fortunately, newer versions of Windows have improved things by permitting end users without administrative privileges to perform a few "admin-like" tasks. They are still not completely happy, but the skirmishes have reduced.

Identity and Access Management

Identity and access management (IAM) represents business processes and technologies used to manage the identities of workers and systems, as well as their access to systems and information. Identity management is the activity of managing the identity and access history of each employee, contractor, temporary worker, supplier worker, and, optionally, customer. These records are then used as the basis for controlling which workplaces, applications, IT systems, and business functions each person is permitted to use.

When organizations had few business applications, organizations provisioned users' access to each separate application. As organizations began to implement additional applications, users had more credentials to use. With the mass migration to cloud-based applications, the numbers of user credentials that users had to remember spiraled out of control, leading to unsafe habits including using the same credentials across many applications and writing down credentials where they could be easily discovered. IT service desks were inundated with password reset requests from users who could not effectively manage their growing portfolio of credentials.

As a result of these developments, organizations began to centralize their identity and access management systems so that users had fewer sets of credentials to manage. Organizations implemented *reduced sign-on* and *single sign-on* to simplify access for users, which also reduced the effort required by IT to manage users' access. Another advantage came in the form of less effort required to manage user credentials. For instance, when an employee left the organization, only the user's single access credential for all applications could be locked or removed, effectively locking the terminated user out of all of the organization's business applications.

Organizations realized that the Achilles heel of reduced sign-on and single sign-on was this: if a user's sole set of credentials was compromised, the attacker would have access to all of the applications that the user had access to. As a result, organizations responded by implementing *multifactor authentication,* a mechanism whereby a user is required to provide a user ID, a password, and an additional identifier that typically resides in a smart card, mobile phone, or smartphone. Organizations can also implement *biometrics,* which is a form of multifactor authentication. The advantage of multifactor authentication is that cases of user ID and password compromise do not permit an attacker to access information unless they also have the user's mobile device in their possession.

Often, access operations are performed by the IT department, while access reviews and recertifications are performed by information security as a form of a check-and-balance system. It would not make sense for IT to perform access reviews as they will be checking their own work, and employees performing these reviews might be tempted to cover up their mistakes.

Access Operations

Identity and access management is an activity-filled discipline. Everyday activities in identity and access management include these activities:

- Provisioning access to new workers
- Adjusting access rights to workers being transferred
- Assisting workers with access issues such as forgotten passwords
- Assisting workers whose accounts have been locked out for various reasons
- Removing access from departing workers

Less routine events in identity and access management include these project-related activities:

- Integrating a new business application with a centralized authentication service
- Resetting a user's credentials in response to the loss of a laptop computer or mobile device

Access Governance

Access governance is the term that represents a number of activities used to ensure that user access conforms to policy. These activities are typically carried out by a different group than those that perform routine access operations.

Access Reviews An access review is an activity where management reviews users' access to information and information systems. The purpose of an access review is to confirm that all the workers who require access to an information system have that access and that no others have that access. Access reviews take on different forms, including the following:

- Analysis of a single user's access to all information and information systems
- Analysis of all users' access to an information system
- Analysis of all users with a particular set of access rights to one or more information systems

Access reviews are required by various regulations. This requires that personnel who perform access reviews produce a record of the review, including all of the users whose access was examined and specific actions taken as a result of the review.

Accumulation of Privileges

Users who work in an organization for many years may, during their tenure, hold a number of positions in one or more departments. When such a user moves from one department to another, the user will require access to new roles or information systems. Over many years, a user may have access to many more information systems and roles than are needed in the user's current role. This phenomenon is known as *accumulation of privileges*.

This is not an easily solved problem. When a user transfers to another department, it makes sense that the user's prior job-related access rights should be terminated right away. However, several factors make this infeasible:

- The user may still have responsibilities in their prior position.
- The user may be training a user who replaced them in their prior position.
- The user may be in the middle of a project that they will complete.

The result of this is that users' credentials often cannot be removed at the time of their transfer. Methods to remind access administrators of these weeks or months later are error prone. The result is an accumulation of access rights. Access reviews and access recertifications represent a corrective control for this phenomenon.

Segregation of Duties   In the course of managing user access schemes, security managers will recognize that there are several high-value and high-risk roles in business processes that are implemented in information systems and applications. *Segregation of duties (SOD)* is the concept that ensures that no single individual will possess privileges that could result in unauthorized activities or the manipulation or exposure of sensitive data.

For example, an accounting department allocates roles to individuals so that no single individual has the ability to create a vendor, request a payment to a vendor, and approve a payment to a vendor. Such a combination of access rights would make it tempting for an employee to set up a fictitious vendor and then have payments sent to the vendor. Another example is the request for a user account and the provisioning of a user account. The purpose of segregation of duties is to require two or more people to perform high-value and high-risk activities. Two or more individuals are far less likely to defraud the organization than would a single individual.

In a segregation of duties access review, the security manager examines user access rights to various high-risk and high-value roles to determine whether any individuals have access to more than one role within these functions. Any such findings are identified, and corrective actions are applied.

There are some situations, particularly in smaller organizations, where there are not enough personnel to break out high-value and high-risk activities among two or more persons. In such cases, security managers should recommend detailed activity reviews be performed periodically to ensure that there are no fraudulent activities taking place. In high-risk and high-value activities, activity reviews often take place anyway, but in situations where segregation of duties cannot be achieved, these reviews might take place more often.

Privileged and High-Risk Roles Information systems and applications typically have roles for ordinary users, as well as roles that are administrative in nature. These administrative roles have a number of high-risk capabilities, including the creation of user accounts, system configuration, and alteration of records. These privileged roles often warrant more frequent and more thorough reviews to ensure that the fewest possible numbers of workers have these roles.

Activity Reviews Activity reviews are an activity where an information system is examined to see which users have been active and which have not been active. Primarily, the purpose of an access review is to identify user accounts that have had no activity for an extended period of time, typically 90 days. The rationale is that if a user has not used an application in more than 90 days, the user probably does not require access to that system. Removing or locking such a user's access helps to reduce risk of compromise: if such a user's credentials were compromised, they could not be used to access the system.

An activity review is a corrective control that helps reduce accumulation of privileges.

Access Recertification Access recertification is a periodic review where information system owners review lists of users and their roles and determine for each user and role whether their access is still required. Like other reviews, personnel often create a business record showing which users and roles were examined and what corrective actions were applied.

Access recertification is a corrective control that helps reduce accumulation of privileges.

User Behavior Analytics

User behavior analytics (UBA) represents an emerging technology where individual users' behaviors are baselined and anomalous activity triggers events or alarms. UBA is one of several forms of anomaly detection that helps organizations detect unauthorized activities performed by employees or find attackers who have successfully compromised their user accounts.

Security Incident Management

Security incident management is the set of activities undertaken by an organization to ensure that it is able to quickly identify a security incident and rapidly and effectively respond and contain the incident.

Security incident management is generally broken into two parts:

- **Proactive** This is the development of policies, procedures, playbooks, and related training.
- **Responsive** This is the actual response to an incident, as well as post-incident activities.

Security incident management is covered fully in Chapter 5.

Security Awareness Training

Personnel are the primary weak point in information security. This is mainly because of lapses in judgment, inattentiveness, fatigue, work pressure, or a shortage of skills. Personnel are generally considered the largest and most vulnerable portion of an organization's attack surface.

People are sometimes tricked by social engineering attacks such as phishing e-mails that provide attackers with an entry point into an organization's network. In larger organizations, attackers who send phishing messages to hundreds or thousands of personnel are almost assured that at least one of those people will click a link or open an attachment, leading to the poten tial compromise of the user's workstation.

Many organizations conduct security awareness training so that personnel are aware of these common attacks, as well as several other topics that mainly fall into the category known as *Internet hygiene,* which is the safe use of computers and mobile devices while accessing the Internet.

Objectives

The primary objective of a security awareness program is the keen awareness, on the part of all personnel, of the reality of the different types of attacks that they may be subject to, together with knowledge of what they are expected to do in various situations. Further, personnel are to understand and comply with an organization's acceptable use policy, security policy, privacy policy, and other applicable policies.

Better security awareness training programs include opportunities to practice skills and include a test at the end of training. In computer-based training, users should be required to successfully pass the test with a minimum score—70 percent is a typical minimum score to complete the course.

The best security awareness training courses, whether in-person or online, are engaging and relevant. While some organizations conduct security awareness training for compliance purposes, many organizations do so for security persons and have a genuine interest in its personnel getting the most value out of the training. The point of security awareness training is, after all, the reduction of risk.

Business records should be created, recording when each person receives training. Many organizations are subject to information security regulations that require personnel to complete security awareness training; business records provide ample evidence of users' completion of their training.

Creating or Selecting Content

Security managers need to develop or acquire security awareness training content for personnel in the organization. The content that is selected or developed should have the following characteristics:

- **Understandable**   The content should make sense to all personnel. A common mistake security managers make is that they create content that is overly technical and difficult for many of the nontechnical personnel to understand.

- **Relevant**   The content should be applicable to the organization and its users. For example, training on the topic of cryptography would be irrelevant to the vast majority of personnel in most organizations. Irrelevant content can cause personnel to disengage from further training.

- **Actionable** The content should ensure that personnel know what to do (and not do) in common scenarios.

- **Memorable** The best content will give personnel opportunities to practice their skills at some of the basic tasks important to information security, including selecting and using passwords, reading and responding to e-mail, and interacting with people inside and outside the organization.

Audiences

When planning a security awareness program, security managers need to understand the entire worker population and their roles in the organization. This helps managers understand what training subject matter is relevant to which groups of workers. Security managers need to ensure that workers get all the training they need, as well as not over-burdening workers with training that is not relevant to their jobs.

For example, workers in a large retail organization fall into four categories:

- **Corporate workers** These people all use computers, and most of them use mobile devices.

- **Retail floor managers** These people work in retail store locations and use computers daily in their jobs.

- **Retail floor cashiers** These people work in retail store locations. They do not use computers, but they do collect payments by cash, check, and credit care.

- **Retail floor workers** These people work in retail store and warehouse locations and do not use computers.

The security manager in this example should package security awareness training so that each audience receives relevant training. Retail floor workers probably need no Internet or computer-related security awareness training at all but instead receive training on topics related to physical security and workplace safety. Cashiers need training on fraud techniques (counterfeit currency, currency counting fraud, and matters related to credit card payments such as skimming). Corporate workers and retail floor managers should probably receive full-spectrum training since they all use computers. Retail floor managers should also receive all of the training delivered to retail floor workers and cashiers since they also work at retail locations and supervise these personnel.

Technical Workers Technical workers in an organization, typically IT personnel, should be trained in security techniques that are relevant to their positions. Technical workers are responsible for architecture, system and network design, implementation, and administration. Without security training, these workers might unknowingly have lapses in judgment that could result in significant vulnerabilities that could lead to compromises.

Software Developers   Software developers typically receive little or no education on secure software development in colleges, universities, and tech schools. The art of *secure coding*, then, is new to many software developers. Training for software developers helps them to be more aware of the common mistakes made by software developers, including the following:

- Vulnerabilities that permit injection attacks
- Broken authentication and session management that can lead to attackers who can access other user sessions
- Cross-site scripting
- Broken access control
- Security misconfiguration
- Sensitive data exposure
- Insufficient attack protection
- Cross-site request forgery
- Using components with known vulnerabilities
- Underprotected APIs

The preceding list is published by the Open Web Application Security Project (OWASP, at www.owasp.org), an organization dedicated to helping software developers better understand the techniques needed for secure application development and deployment.

Security training for software developers should also include protection of the software development process itself. Topics in secure software development generally include the following:

- Protection of source code
- Source code reviews
- Care when using open source code
- Testing of source code for vulnerabilities and defects
- Archival of changes to source code
- Protection of systems used to store source code, edit and test source code, build applications, test applications, and deploy applications

Some of these aspects are related to the architecture of development and test environments and may not be needed for all software developers.

Third Parties   Security awareness training needs to be administered to all personnel who have access to an organization's data through any means. Often this includes personnel who are employees of other organizations, so this means that some of those workers need to participate in the organization's security awareness training.

In larger organizations, the curriculum for third-party personnel might be altered somewhat since there may be portions of the security awareness training content that are not applicable to outsiders.

New Hires

New employees, as well as consultants and contractors, should be required to attend security awareness training as soon as possible. There is a risk that new employees could make mistakes early in their employment and prior to their training since they would not be familiar with all the practices in the organization.

Better organizations link access control with security awareness training: new employees are not given access to systems until after they have successfully completed their security awareness training. This gives new workers added incentive to complete their training quickly since they want to be able to get access to corporate applications and get to work.

Annual Training

Most security awareness programs include annual refresher training for all workers. Required by some regulations, this is highly recommended as this helps to keep security and Internet safety as a part of every worker's day-to-day thinking process and helps them to avoid common mistakes. Further, because both protective techniques and attack techniques change quickly, annual refresher training helps workers be aware of these developments.

Training takes time, and people tend to put it off for as long as possible. This is easy to understand, since training takes time away from other important work tasks. Still, the security manager and the organization wants to make sure that as many workers as possible complete the training. Workers can be offered incentives to complete their training, through various types of rewards: for example, all workers who complete their training in the first week can be entered into a random drawing for gift cards or other prizes.

Organizations generally choose one of two options for annual training:

- **Entire organization**   The organization will develop messaging to the entire organization and conduct annual training at the same time for all workers. The advantage of this is that all-personnel messaging can be utilized in an all-out blitz to get people thinking about this training. One disadvantage is that all workers will be a little less productive all at the same time.

- **Hire month anniversary**   The organization enrolls workers for their annual training to take place on the month of their original hire date. For example, if a worker's first day is March 4, 2017, that worker (and all others hired in March) will complete annual security awareness training in the month of March. The advantage of this is that disruptions (minor as they are) are spread throughout the year. A key disadvantage is that there would probably not be an opportunity for all-personnel messaging for training.

Communication Techniques

Security awareness training programs often utilize a variety of means for imparting Internet hygiene and safe computing information to its workers. Communication techniques often include the following:

- **E-mail**   Security managers may occasionally send out advisories to affected personnel to inform them of developments, such as a new phishing attack. Occasionally, a senior executive will send a message to all personnel to impress the point of security being every workers' job and that security is to be taken seriously.

- **Internal web site**   Organizations with internal web sites or web portals may from time to time include information security messages.

- **Video monitors, posters, and bulletins**   Sometimes a security message on monitors, posters, or bulletins on various security topics keeps people thinking about information security. Typical subjects include using good passwords, being careful with e-mail, and social engineering.

- **Voice-mail**   Organizations may occasionally send voice-mail messages to all personnel or groups of affected personnel to inform them of new developments.

- **Security fairs**   Organizations can set up an annual fair or ongoing technology center where users can come and get answers or see demonstrations of some of the latest threats and exploits to the company. This assists with developing lines of communications between the security team and the users of the computing systems.

Managed Security Services Providers

There is a large number of organizations that have centralized logging, a SIEM, vulnerability scanning, and other capabilities, but these organizations are not large enough to warrant staffing a SOC 24/7/365. To ensure full coverage, including coverage for sick, vacations, holidays, and training, a minimum of 12 personnel may be required to fully staff a SOC, not counting the SOC manager or the equipment and space required. For this reason, many organizations outsource the monitoring of their SIEMs and related activities to a managed security services provider (MSSP, or commonly known as MSS).

Modern MSSPs include a variety of capabilities, including the following:

- Managed SIEM
- Managed vulnerability scanning
- Managed data loss prevention
- Managed endpoint security monitoring

MSSPs monitor events and incidents in dozens or hundreds of customer organizations and have a large staff to ensure full coverage at peak workloads. Because qualified security personnel can be difficult to attract and retain, many organizations are turning to MSSPs to offload routine tasks and free themselves of the burden of staffing and running a SOC.

Organizations that outsource parts of their security operations to an MSSP need to be mindful of several considerations, including the following:

- **Operational partnership**   An MSSP typically performs a monitoring function but in most cases does not take remedial action. Therefore, when the MSSP identifies an actionable incident, it hands off the incident to someone in the customer organization to take the required action.

- **Service level agreements**   An MSSP typically publishes a schedule of service level agreements so that customers understand how responsive the MSSP will be in various scenarios. Organizations should regularly test their MSSP to verify that events are being monitored and comply with the SLAs for alerting and response to events.

Data Security

ISACA defines *data security* as *those controls that seek to maintain confidentiality, integrity, and availability of information*. Data security is the heart of everything concerned with information security laws, standards, and practices. Several topics concerning data security are discussed here, including the following:

- Access management
- Cryptography
- Backup and recovery
- Data loss prevention
- Cloud access security brokers
- User behavior analytics

Access Management

Access management is part of the broader discipline known as *identity and access management*. This topic is described in detail earlier in this chapter in the section "Identity and Access Management."

Cryptography

Cryptography is the practice of hiding information in plain sight. Put another way, encryption is the practice of hiding information from unwanted people. The purpose of encryption is to make it difficult (*impossible* is a word to be avoided here) for someone to be able to access information. Encryption works by scrambling the characters in a message using a method known only to the sender and receiver, making the message useless to any party that intercepts the message.

Encryption plays a key role in the protection of sensitive and valuable information. There are some situations where it is not practical or feasible to prevent third parties from having logical access to data—for instance, data transmissions over public networks.

Encryption is also used as a barrier of last resort—for instance, encryption of data on backup media, should that media be lost or stolen.

Encryption can also be used to *authenticate* information that is sent from one party to another. This means that a receiving party can verify that a specific party did, in fact, originate a message and that it is authentic and unchanged. This allows a receiver to know that a message is genuine and that it has not been forged or altered in transit by any third party.

With encryption, best practices call for system designers to use well-known, robust encryption algorithms. Thus, when a third-party intercepts encrypted data, the third party can know which algorithm is being used but still not be able to read the data. What the third party does not know is the *key* that is used to encrypt and decrypt the data. How this works will be explained further in this section.

TIP   Encryption can be thought of as another layer of access protection. Like user ID and password controls that restrict access to data to everyone but those with login credentials, encryption restricts access to (plaintext) data to everyone but those with encryption keys.

Terms and Concepts Used in Cryptography   Several terms and concepts used in cryptography are not used outside of the field. Security managers must be familiar with these to be effective in understanding, managing, and auditing IT systems that use cryptography. Terms used in cryptography include the following:

- **Plaintext**   An original message, file, or stream of data that can be read by anyone who has access to it.
- **Ciphertext**   A message, file, or stream of data that has been transformed by an encryption algorithm and rendered unreadable.
- **Encryption**   The process of transforming plaintext into ciphertext. This is depicted in Figure 4-10.
- **Hash function**   A cryptographic operation on a block of data that returns a fixed-length string of characters, used to verify the integrity of a message.
- **Message digest**   The output of a cryptographic hash function.
- **Digital signature**   The result of encrypting the hash of a message with the originator's private encryption key, used to prove the authenticity and integrity of a message. This is depicted in Figure 4-11.
- **Algorithm**   A specific mathematical formula that is used to perform encryption, decryption, message digests, and digital signatures.
- **Decryption**   The process of transforming ciphertext into plaintext so that a recipient can read it.
- **Cryptanalysis**   An attack on a cryptosystem where the attacker is attempting to determine the encryption key that is used to encrypt messages.

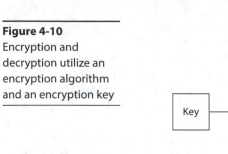

Figure 4-10
Encryption and
decryption utilize an
encryption algorithm
and an encryption key

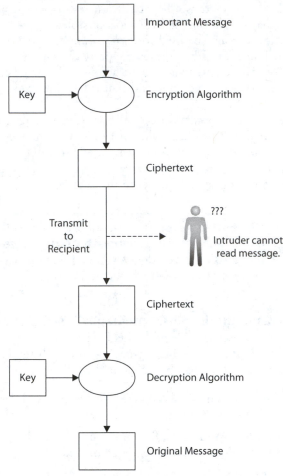

- **Encryption key**   A block of characters, used in combination with an encryption algorithm, used to encrypt or decrypt a stream or blocks of data. An encryption key is also used to create and verify a digital signature.

- **Key encrypting key**   An encryption key that is used to encrypt another encryption key.

- **Key length**   The size (measured in bits) of an encryption key. Longer encryption keys mean that it takes greater effort to successfully attack a cryptosystem.

- **Block cipher**   An encryption algorithm that operates on blocks of data.

- **Stream cipher**   A type of encryption algorithm that operates on a continuous stream of data such as a video or audio feed.

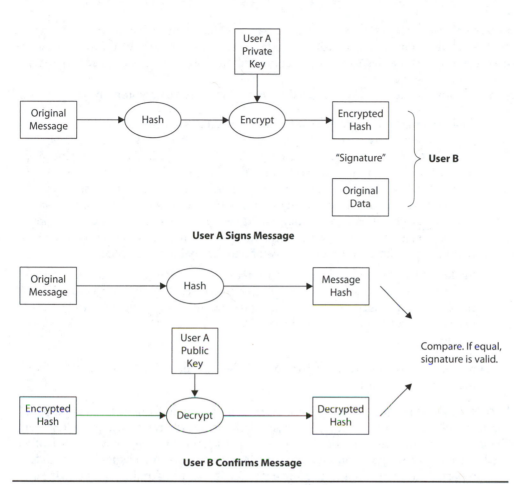

Figure 4-11   Digital signature used to verify the integrity of a message

- **Initialization vector (IV)**   A random number that is needed by some encryption algorithms to begin the encryption process.

- **Symmetric encryption**   A method for encryption and decryption where it is necessary for both parties to possess a common encryption key.

- **Asymmetric encryption**, or **public key cryptography**   A method for encryption, decryption, and digital signatures that uses pairs of encryption keys, consisting of a *public key* and a *private key*.

- **Key exchange**   A technique that is used by two parties to establish a symmetric encryption key when there is no secure channel available.

- **Nonrepudiation**   The property of encryption and digital signatures that can make it difficult or impossible for a party to later deny having sent a digitally signed message, unless they admit to having lost control of their private encryption key.

Private Key Cryptosystems A private key cryptosystem is based on a symmetric cryptographic algorithm. The primary characteristic of a private key cryptosystem is the necessity for both parties to possess a common encryption key that is used to encrypt and decrypt messages.

The following are the two main challenges with private key cryptography:

- **Key exchange** An *out-of-band* method for exchanging encryption keys is required before any encrypted messages can be transmitted. This key exchange must occur over a separate, secure channel; if the encryption keys were transmitted over the main communications channel, then anyone who intercepted the encryption key would be able to read any intercepted messages, provided they could determine the encryption algorithm used. For instance, if two parties want to exchange encrypted e-mail, they would need to exchange their encryption key first via some other means such as telephone or fax, provided they are confident that their telephone and fax transmissions are not being intercepted.

- **Scalability** Private key cryptosystems require that each sender-receiver pair exchange an encryption key. For a group of 4 parties, 6 encryption keys would need to be exchanged; for a group of 10 parties, 45 keys would need to be exchanged. For a large community of 1000 parties, many thousands of keys would need to be exchanged.

Some well-known private key algorithms in use include AES, Blowfish, DES, Triple DES, Serpent, and Twofish.

Secure Key Exchange *Secure key exchange* refers to methods used by two parties to securely establish a symmetric encryption key without actually transmitting the key over a channel. Secure key exchange is needed when two parties, previously unknown to each other, need to establish encrypted communications where no out-of-band channel is available.

Two parties can perform a secure key exchange if a third party intercepts their entire conversation. This is because algorithms used for secure key exchange utilize information known by each party but not transmitted between them.

The most popular algorithm is the Diffie–Hellman Key Exchange Protocol.

Exchanging Initial Encryption Keys

Think about a private key cryptosystem. In an established cryptosystem, two users exchange messages and encrypt/decrypt them using an encryption key.

Before they can begin exchanging encrypted messages, one of the users must first get a copy of the key to the other user. They have to do this prior to the establishment of the cryptosystem, so they cannot use the cryptosystem to transmit the key.

Secure key exchange, such as Diffie–Hellman, is used to safely transmit the key from one party to the other party. Once both parties have the key, they can begin sending encrypted messages to each other.

Without secure key exchange, the two parties would have to use some other safe, out-of-band means for getting the encryption key across to the other user.

Public Key Cryptosystems   Public key cryptosystems are based on *asymmetric,* or *public key,* cryptographic algorithms. These algorithms use two-part encryption keys that are handled differently from encryption keys in symmetric key cryptosystems.

Key Pair   The encryption keys that are used in public key cryptography are called the *public key* and the *private key.* Each user of public key cryptosystems has these two keys in their possession. Together, the public and private keys are known as a *key pair.* The two keys require different handling and are used together but for different purposes that are explained in this section.

When a user generates a key pair (the public key and the private key), the key pair will physically exist as two separate files. The user is free to publish or distribute the public key openly; it could even be posted on a public web site. This is in contrast to the private key, which must be well protected and never published or sent to any other party. Most public key cryptosystems will utilize a password mechanism to further protect the private key; without its password, the private key is inaccessible and cannot be used.

Message Security   Public key cryptography is an ideal application for securing messages—e-mail in particular. The reason for this is that users do not need to establish and communicate symmetric encryption keys through a secure channel. With public key cryptography, users who have never contacted each other can immediately send secure messages to one another. Figure 4-12 depicts public key cryptography.

Every user is free to publish a public encryption key so that it is easily retrievable. There are servers on the Internet where public keys can be published and made available to anyone in the world. Public key cryptography is designed so that open disclosure of a user's public key does not compromise the secrecy of the corresponding private key: a user's private key cannot be derived from the public key.

When User A wishes to send an encrypted message to User B, the procedure is as follows:

1. User B publishes his public key to the Internet at a convenient location.

2. User A retrieves User B's public key.

3. User A creates a message and encrypts it with User B's public key and sends the encrypted message to User B.

4. User B decrypts the message with his private key and is able to read the message.

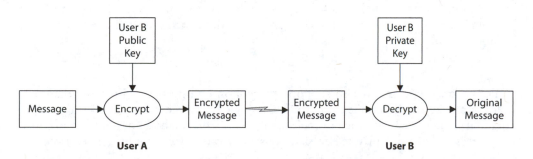

Figure 4-12   Public key cryptography used to transmit a secret message

Note that only User B's encryption key is used in this example. This method is used only to protect the message from eavesdroppers. This method is not used to verify the authenticity of the message.

Public key cryptography can also be used to verify the authenticity and integrity of a message. This is used to verify that a specific party did, in fact, create the message. The procedure is as follows:

1. User A publishes his public key to the Internet at a convenient location.

2. User B retrieves User A's public key and saves it for later use.

3. User A creates a message and digitally signs it with his private key and then sends the signed message to User B.

4. User B verifies the digital signature using User A's public key. If the message verifies correctly, User B knows that the message originated from User A and has not been altered in transit.

In this example, only the authenticity and integrity of a message are assured. The message is not encrypted, which means that any party that intercepts the message can read it.

Public key cryptography can be used to both encrypt and digitally sign a message, which will guarantee its confidentiality as well as its authenticity. The procedure is as follows:

1. User A and User B publish their public encryption keys to convenient places.

2. User A retrieves User B's public key, and User B retrieves User A's public key.

3. User A creates a message, signs it with his private key and encrypts it with User B's public key, and then sends the message to User B.

4. User B decrypts the message with his private key and verifies the digital signature with User A's public key.

Elliptic Curve Cryptography

A cryptography method called *elliptic curve cryptography (ECC)* is attracting interest for use in public key cryptography applications. ECC requires less computational power and bandwidth than other cryptographic algorithms and is thought to be more secure as well. Because of its low power requirements, it is used extensively in mobile devices.

Public key cryptography also supports encryption of a message with more than one user's public key. This permits a user to send a single encrypted message to several recipients that is encrypted with each of their public keys. This method does not compromise the secrecy of any user's private key, since a user's private key cannot be derived from the public key.

Verifying Public Keys It is possible for a fraudster to claim the identity of another person and even publish a public key that claims the identity of that person. Four methods are available for verifying a user's public key as genuine:

- **Certificate authority (CA)** A public key that has been obtained from a trusted, reputable certificate authority can be considered genuine.

- **E-mail address** Public keys used for e-mail will include the user's e-mail address. If the e-mail address is part of a corporate or government domain (for example, *apple.com* or *seattle.gov*), then some level of credence can be attributed to the successful exchange of messages with that e-mail address. However, since e-mail addresses can be spoofed, this should be considered a weak method at best.

- **Directory infrastructure** A directory services infrastructure such as Microsoft Active Directory, LDAP, or a commercial product can be used to verify a user's public key.

- **Key fingerprint** Many public key cryptosystems employ a method for verifying a key's identity, known as the key's *fingerprint*. If a user wants to verify a public key, the user retrieves the public key and calculates the key's fingerprint. The user then contacts the claimed owner of the public key, who runs a function against his private key that returns a string of numbers. The user also runs a function against the owner's public key, also returning a string of numbers. If both numbers match, the public key is genuine.

 NOTE When issuing a public key, it is essential that the requestor of the new public key be authenticated, such as by viewing a government-issued ID or by contacting the owner at a publicly listed telephone number.

Hashing and Message Digests *Hashing* is the process of applying a cryptographic algorithm on a block of information that results in a compact, fixed-length *digest*. The purpose of hashing is to provide a unique and compact "fingerprint" for the message or file—even if the file is very large. A message digest can be used to verify the integrity of a large file, thus assuring that the file has not been altered.

Some of the properties of message digests that make them ideally suited for verifying integrity include the following:

- Any change made to a file—even a single bit or character—will result in a significant change in the hash.

- It is computationally infeasible to make a change to a file without changing its hash.

- It is computationally infeasible to create a message or file that will result in a given hash.

- It is infeasible to find any two messages that will have the same hash.

One common use of message digests is on software download sites, where the computed hash for a downloadable program is available so that users can verify that the software program has not been altered (provided that the posted hash has not also been compromised).

Digital Signatures   A *digital signature* is a cryptographic operation where a sender "seals" a message or file using her identity. The purpose of a digital signature is to authenticate a message and to guarantee its integrity. Digital signatures do not protect the confidentiality of a message, however, as encryption is not one of the operations performed.

Digital signatures work by encrypting hashes of messages; recipients verify the integrity and authenticity of messages by decrypting hashes and comparing them to original messages. In detail, a digital signature works like this:

1. The sender publishes his public key to the Internet at a location that is easily accessible to recipients.

2. The recipient retrieves the sender's public key and saves it for later use.

3. The sender creates a message (or file) and computes a message digest (hash) of the message and then encrypts the hash with his private key.

4. The sender sends the original file plus the encrypted hash to the recipient.

5. The recipient receives the original file and the encrypted hash. The recipient computes a message digest (hash) of the original file and sets the result aside. She then decrypts the hash with the sender's public key. The recipient compares the hash of the original file and the decrypted hash.

6. If the two hashes are identical, the recipient knows that (a) the message in her possession is identical to the message that the sender sent, (b) the sender is the originator, and (c) the message has not been altered.

The use of digital signatures was depicted earlier in this chapter in Figure 4-11.

Digital Envelopes   One aspect of symmetric (private key) and asymmetric (public key) cryptography that has not been discussed yet is the computing requirements and performance implications of these two types of cryptosystems. It can be stated rather broadly that public key cryptography requires far more computing power than private key cryptography. The practical implication of this is that public key encryption of large sets of data can be highly compute-intensive and make its use infeasible in some occasions.

One solution to this is the use of a so-called *digital envelope* that utilizes the convenience of public key cryptography with the lower overhead of private key cryptography. This practice is known as *hybrid cryptography*. The procedure for using digital envelopes works like this:

1. The sender and recipient agree that the sender will transmit a large message to the recipient.

2. The sender selects or creates a symmetric encryption key, known as the *session key,* and encrypts the session key with the recipient's public key.

3. The sender encrypts the message with the session key.

4. The sender sends the encrypted message (encrypted with the session key) and the encrypted session key (encrypted with the recipient's public key) to the recipient.

5. The recipient decrypts the session key with his private key.

6. The recipient decrypts the message with the session key.

The now-deprecated SET (*secure electronic transaction*, a predecessor to SSL/TLS) protocol uses digital envelopes. Digital envelopes require less computing overhead than the Diffie-Hellman key exchange, which is why digital envelopes may be preferred in some circumstances.

Public Key Infrastructure   One of the issues related to public key cryptography is the safe storage of public encryption keys. While individuals are free to publish public keys online, doing so in a secure and controlled manner requires some central organization and control. A *public key infrastructure (PKI)* is designed to fulfill this and other functions.

A PKI is a centralized function that is used to store and publish public keys and other information. Some of the services provided by a PKI include the following:

- **Digital certificates**   A digital certificate is a digital credential that consists of a public key and a block of information that identifies the owner of the certificate. The identification portion of a digital certificate will follow a standard, structured format and include such data as the owner's name, organization name, and other identifying information, such as e-mail address. The public key and the identifying information will reside in a document that is itself digitally signed by a trusted party, known as a *certificate authority*.

- **Certificate authority (CA)**   A CA is a business entity that issues digital certificates and publishes them in the PKI. The CA vouches for the identity of each of the digital certificates in a PKI; the CA undergoes certain safeguards to ensure that each digital certificate is genuine and really does belong to its rightful owner.

- **Registration authority (RA)**   The RA operates within or alongside a CA to accept requests for new digital certificates. The RA vets the request, carefully examining it, and undergoes steps to verify the authenticity of the person making the request. This verification may include viewing government-issued ID cards or passports or taking other steps as needed to make sure that the request is originating from the genuine person and not an imposter. When the RA is satisfied that the requestor is indeed the person making the request, the RA will issue a digital certificate. Part of the certificate issuance will be the delivery of private encryption keys to the requesting party. This may take place in person or over a secured electronic connection.

- **Certificate revocation list (CRL)**   Some circumstances may require that a user's digital certificate be cancelled or revoked. These circumstances include termination of employment (if a person's certificate was issued expressly for employment-related purposes) or loss or compromise of a user's private key. A CRL is an electronic list of digital certificates that have been revoked prior to their expiration date. To be effective, any consumer of digital certificates needs to consult a CRL to be doubly sure that a certificate remains valid.

- **Certification practice statement (CPS)** This is a published statement that describes the practices used by the CA to issue and manage digital certificates. This helps determine the relative strength and validity of digital certificates that are issued by the CA.

Key Management The term *key management* refers to the various processes and procedures used by an organization to generate, protect, use, and dispose of encryption keys over their lifetime. Several of the major practices are described in this section.

Key Generation The start of an encryption key life cycle is its generation. While at first glance it would appear that this process should require little scrutiny, further study shows that this is a critical process that requires safeguards.

The system on which key generation takes place must be highly protected. If keys are generated on a system that has been compromised or is of questionable integrity, it would be difficult to determine whether a bystander could have electronically observed key generation. For instance, if a key logger or other process spying tool were active in the system when keys were generated, that key generation may have been observable and details about keys captured. This would mean that newly minted keys have already been compromised if an outsider knows their identities.

In many situations, it would be reasonable to require that systems used for key generation be highly protected, isolated, and used by as few people as possible. Regular integrity checks would need to take place to make sure the system continues to be free of any problems.

Furthermore, the key generation process needs to include some randomness (or, as some put it, entropy) so that the key generation process cannot be easily duplicated elsewhere. If key generation were not a random event, it could be possible to duplicate the conditions related to a specific key and then regenerate a key with the very same value. This would instantaneously compromise the integrity and uniqueness of the original key.

Key Protection Private keys used in public key cryptosystems and keys used in symmetric cryptosystems must be continuously and vigorously protected. At all times, they must be accessible to *only* the parties that are authorized to use them. If protection measures for private encryption keys are compromised (or suspected to be), it will be possible for a key compromise to take place, enabling the attacker to be able to view messages encrypted with these keys, as well as creating new encrypted messages in the name of the key's owner.

A *key compromise* is any event where a private encryption key or symmetric encryption key has been disclosed to any unauthorized third party. When a key compromise occurs, it will be necessary to reencrypt all materials encrypted by the compromised key with a new encryption key.

CAUTION In many applications, an encryption key is protected by a password. The length, complexity, distribution, and expiration of passwords protecting encryption keys must be well designed so that the strength of the cryptosystem (based on its key length and algorithm) is not compromised by a weak password scheme protecting its keys.

Key Encrypting Keys Applications that utilize encryption must obtain their encryption keys in some way. In many cases, an intruder may be able to examine the application in an attempt to discover an encryption key so that the intruder may decrypt communications used by the application. A common remedy for this is the use of encryption to protect the encryption key. This additional encryption requires a key of its own, known as a *key encrypting key*. Of course, this key also must reside someplace; often, features of the underlying operating system may be used to protect an encryption key as well as a key-encrypting key.

Key Custody *Key custody* refers to the policies, processes, and procedures regarding the management of keys. This is closely related to key protection but is focused on *who* manages keys and *where* they are kept.

Key Rotation *Key rotation* is the process of issuing a new encryption key and reencrypting data protected with the new key. Key rotation may occur when any of the following occurs:

- **Key compromise** When an encryption key has been compromised, a new key must be generated and used.
- **Key expiration** This happens in situations where encryption keys are rotated on a schedule.
- **Rotation of staff** In some organizations, if any of the persons associated with the creation or management of encryption keys transfers to another position or leaves the organization, keys must be rotated.

Key Disposal *Key disposal* refers to the process of decommissioning encryption keys. This may be done upon receipt of an order to destroy a data set that is encrypted with a specific encryption key—destroying an encryption key can be as effective (and a whole lot easier) than destroying the encrypted data itself.

However, key disposal can present some challenges. If an encryption key is backed up to tape, for instance, disposal of the key will require that backup tapes also be destroyed.

Encryption Applications Several applications utilize encryption algorithms. Many of these are well known and in common use.

Secure Sockets Layer/Transport Layer Security Secure Sockets Layer (SSL)/Transport Layer Security (TLS) are the encryption protocols used to encrypt web pages requested with the Hypertext Transfer Protocol/Secure (HTTPS) protocol. Introduced by Netscape Communications for use in its own browser, SSL and its successor, TLS, have become de facto standards for the encryption of web pages.

SSL and TLS provide several cryptographic functions, including public key encryption, private key encryption, and hash functions. These are used for server and client authentication (although in practice, client authentication is seldom used) and session encryption. SSL and TLS support several encryption algorithms, including AES, RC4, IDEA, DES, and Triple DES, and several key lengths, from 40 bits to 256 bits and beyond.

Weaknesses were discovered in all versions of SSL, as well as the first version of TLS. No versions of SSL should be used, as well as TLS 1.0.

 EXAM TIP All versions of SSL and the early version of TLS are now considered deprecated and should no longer be used.

Secure Hypertext Transfer Protocol Not to be confused with HTTPS, Secure Hypertext Transfer Protocol (*S-HTTP*) also provides encryption of web pages between web servers and web browsers. Because Netscape and Microsoft favored HTTPS, S-HTTP never caught on and is not widely supported.

The main difference between HTTPS and S-HTTP is that HTTPS secures the entire channel, regardless of the data that is transmitted through it. S-HTTP protects only individual pieces of data or messages.

Secure Multipurpose Internet Mail Extensions *Secure Multipurpose Internet Mail Extensions (S/MIME)* is an e-mail security protocol that provides sender and recipient authentication and encryption of message content and attachments. S/MIME is most often used for encryption of e-mail messages.

Secure Shell *Secure Shell (SSH)* is a multipurpose protocol that is used to create a secure channel between two systems. The most popular use of SSH is the replacement of the Telnet and r-series protocols (rsh, rlogin, etc.), but it also supports tunneling of protocols such as X-Windows and File Transfer Protocol (FTP).

Internet Protocol Security *Internet Protocol Security (IPsec)* is a protocol used to create a secure, authenticated channel between two systems. IPsec operates at the Internet layer in the TCP/IP protocol suite; hence, all IP traffic between two systems protected by IPsec are automatically encrypted.

IPsec operates in one of two modes: ESP and AH. If ESP is used, then all encapsulated traffic is encrypted. If AH is used, then only IPsec's authentication feature is used.

Secure Electronic Transaction *Secure Electronic Transaction (SET)* is a now-deprecated protocol designed to protect Internet-based financial transactions. SET never caught on because it required the installation of a separate client program. HTTPS became the standard for encrypting web pages and then became the preferred method for encryption.

SET offered greater protection of credit card transactions through the substitution of tokens for actual credit card numbers. But SET never caught on, and it is no longer used.

Backup and Recovery

Many types of events can damage information, and still other circumstances sometimes compel an organization to want to revert to earlier versions of information. It's essential that copies of stored information exist elsewhere and in a form that enables IT personnel to easily load this information into systems so that processing can resume as quickly as possible.

 CAUTION Testing backups is important; testing recoverability is critical. In other words, performing backups is valuable only to the extent that backed-up data can be recovered at a future time.

Backup to Tape and Other Media In organizations still utilizing their own IT infrastructure, tape backup is just about as ubiquitous as power cords. From a disaster recovery perspective, however, the issue probably is not whether the organization *has* tape backup but whether its current backup capabilities are adequate in the context of disaster recovery. There are times when an organization's backup capability may need to be upgraded:

- If the current backup system is difficult to manage.
- If whole-system restoration takes too long.
- If the system lacks flexibility with regard to disaster recovery (for instance, how difficult it would be to recover information onto a different type of system).
- If the technology is old or outdated.
- If confidence in the backup technology is low.

Many organizations may consider tape backup as a means for restoring files or databases when errors have occurred, and they may have confidence in their backup system for that purpose. However, the organization may have somewhat less confidence in their backup system and its ability to recover *all* of their critical systems accurately and in a timely manner.

While tape has been the default medium since the 1960s, using hard drives and solid-state drives as a backup medium is growing in popularity: hard disk transfer rates are far higher (and SSDs higher still), and disk/SSD are a random-access medium, whereas tape is a sequential-access medium. A virtual tape library (VTL) is a type of data storage technology that sets up a disk-based storage system with the appearance of tape storage, permitting existing backup software to continue to back data up to "tape," which is really just more disk storage.

E-vaulting is another viable option for system backup. E-vaulting permits organizations to back up their systems and data to an off-site location, which could be a storage system in another data center or a third-party service provider. This accomplishes two important objectives: reliable backup and off-site storage of backup data.

Backup Schemes There are three main schemes for backing up data; they are the full, incremental, and differential backups:

- **Full backup** This is a complete copy of a data set.

- **Incremental backup**   This is a copy of all data that has changed since the last full or incremental backup.
- **Differential backup**   This is a copy of all data that has changed since the last full backup.

The precise nature of the data to be backed up will determine which combination of backup schemes is appropriate for the organization. Some of the considerations for choosing an overall scheme include the following:

- Criticality of the data set
- Size of the data set
- Frequency of change of the data set
- Performance requirements and the impact of backup jobs
- Recovery requirements

An organization that is creating a backup scheme usually starts with the most common scheme, which is a full backup once per week and an incremental or differential backup every day. However, as stated previously, various factors will influence the design of the final backup scheme. Some examples include the following:

- A small data set could be backed up more than once a week, while an especially large data set might be backed up less often.
- A more rapid recovery requirement may induce the organization to perform differential backups instead of incremental backups.
- If a full backup takes a long time to complete, it should probably be performed during times of lower demand or system utilization.

Backup Media Rotation   Organizations will typically want to retain backup media for as long as possible to provide a greater array of choices for data recovery. However, the desire to maintain a large library of backup media will be countered by the high cost of media and the space required to store it. And while legal or statutory requirements may dictate that backup media be kept for some minimum period, the organization may be able to creatively find ways to comply with such requirements without retaining several generations of such media.

Some example backup media rotation schemes are discussed here.

First In, First Out   In this scheme, there is no specific requirement for retaining any backup media for long periods (e.g., one year or more). The method in the first in, first out (FIFO) rotation scheme specifies that the oldest available backup tape is the next one to be used.

The advantage of this scheme is its simplicity. However, there is a significant disadvantage: any corruption of backed-up data needs to be discovered quickly (within the period of media rotation), or else no valid set of data can be recovered. Hence, only low-criticality data without any lengthy retention requirements should be backed up using this scheme.

Grandfather-Father-Son The most common backup media rotation scheme, grandfather-father-son creates a hierarchical set of backup media that provides for greater retention of backed-up data that is still economically feasible.

In the most common form of this scheme, full backups are performed once per week, and incremental or differential backups are performed daily.

Daily backup tapes used on Monday are not used again until the following Monday. Backup tapes used on Tuesday, Wednesday, Thursday, Friday, and Saturday are handled in the same way.

Full backup tapes created on Sunday are kept longer. Tapes used on the first Sunday of the month are not used again until the first Sunday of the following month. Similarly, tapes used on the second Sunday are not reused until the second Sunday of the following month, and so on, for each week's tapes for Sunday.

For even longer retention, for example, tapes created on the first Sunday of the first month of each calendar quarter can be retained until the first Sunday of the first month of the next quarter. Backup media can be kept for even longer if needed.

Towers of Hanoi The Towers of Hanoi backup media retention scheme is complex but results in a more efficient scheme for producing a more lengthy retention of some backups. Patterned after the Towers of Hanoi puzzle, the scheme is most easily understood visually, as in Figure 4-13, which shows a five-level scheme.

Backup Media Storage Backup media that remains in the same location as backed-up systems is adequate for data recovery purposes but completely inadequate for disaster recovery purposes: any event that physically damages information systems (such as fire, smoke, flood, hazardous chemical spill, and so on) is likely to also damage backup media that is stored nearby. To provide disaster recovery protection, backup media must be stored off-site in a secure location. Selection of this storage location is as important as the selection of a primary business location: in the event of a disaster, the survival of the organization may depend upon the protection measures in place at the off-site storage location.

Day of Cycle

	1	2	3	4	5	6	7	8	9	10	11	12	13	14	15	16	17	18	19	20
		A		A		A		A		A		A		A		A		A		A
			B				B				B				B				B	
				C									C							
						D											D			
	E																			

Backup Set to Use

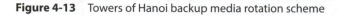

Figure 4-13 Towers of Hanoi backup media rotation scheme

EXAM TIP CISM exam questions relating to off-site backups may include details for safeguarding data during transport and storage, mechanisms for access during restoration procedures, media aging and retention, or other details that may aid you during the exam. Watch for question details involving the type of media, geolocality (distance, shared disaster spectrum such as a shared coastline, and so on) of the off-site storage area and the primary site, or access controls during transport and at the storage site, including environmental controls and security safeguards.

The criteria for selection of an off-site media storage facility are similar to the criteria for selection of a hot/warm/cold recovery site discussed in Chapter 5. If a media storage location is too close to the primary processing site, then it is more likely to be involved in the same regional disaster, which could result in damage to backup media. However, if the media storage location is too far away, then it might take too long for a delivery of backup media, which would result in a recovery operation that runs unacceptably long.

Another location consideration is the proximity of the media storage location and the hot/warm/cold recovery site. If a hot site is being used, then chances are there is some other near-real-time means (such as replication) for data to get to the hot site. But a warm or cold site may be relying on the arrival of backup media from the off-site media storage facility, so it might make sense for the off-site facility to be near the recovery site.

An important factor when considering off-site media storage is the method of delivery to and from the storage location. Chances are that the backup media is being transported by a courier or a shipping company. It is vital that the backup media arrive safely and intact and that the opportunities for interception or loss be reduced as much as possible. Not only can a lost backup tape make recovery more difficult, but it can also cause an embarrassing security incident if knowledge of the loss were to become public. From a confidentiality/integrity perspective, encryption of backup tapes is a good idea, although this digresses somewhat from disaster recovery (concerned primarily with availability).

Backup media that must be kept on-site should be stored in locked cabinets or storerooms that are separate from the rooms where backups are performed. This will help to preserve backup media if a minor flood, relatively small fire, or other event occurs in the room containing computers that are backed up.

Protecting Sensitive Backup Media with Encryption

Information security and data privacy laws are expanding data protection requirements by requiring encryption of backup media in many cases. This is a sensible safeguard, especially for organizations that utilize off-site backup media storage. There is a risk of loss of backup media when it is being transported back and forth from an organization's primary data center and the backup media offsite storage facility. If encrypted backup media were misplaced or lost, in some cases this would not be considered a security breach requiring disclosure.

Backup Media Records and Destruction   To ensure the ability of restoring data from backup media, organizations need to have meticulous records that list all backup volumes in place, where they are located, and which data elements are backed up on them. Without these records, it may prove impossible for an organization to recover data from its backup media library.

Laws and regulations may specify minimum and/or maximum periods that specific information may be retained. Organizations need to have good records management that helps them track which business records are on which backup media volumes. When it is time for an organization to stop retaining a specific set of data, those responsible for the backup media library need to identify the backup volumes that can be recycled. If the data on the backup media is sensitive, the backup volume may need to be erased prior to reuse. Any backup media that is being discarded needs to be destroyed so that no other party can possibly recover data on the volume. Records of this destruction need to be retained.

Replication   Replication is an activity where data that is written to a storage system is also copied over a network to another storage system. The result is the presence of up-to-date data that exists on two or more storage systems, each of which could be located in the same room or in different geographic regions.

Replication can be handled in several ways and at different levels in the technology stack:

- **Disk storage system**   Data-write operations that take place in a disk storage system (such as a SAN or NAS) can be transmitted over a network to another disk storage system, where the same data will be written to the other disk storage system.

- **Operating system**   The operating system can control replication so that updates to a particular file system can be transmitted to another server where those updates will be applied locally on that other server.

- **Database management system**   The database management system (DBMS) can manage replication by sending transactions to a DBMS on another server.

- **Transaction management system**   The transaction management system (TMS) can manage replication by sending transactions to a counterpart TMS located elsewhere.

- **Application**   The application can write its transactions to two different storage systems. This method is not often used.

- **Virtualization**   Virtual machine images can be replicated to recovery sites to speed the recovery of applications.

Replication can take place from one system to another system, called *primary-backup* replication. This is the typical setup when data on an application server is sent to a distant storage system for data recovery or disaster recovery purposes.

Replication can also be bidirectional, between two active servers, called *multiprimary* or *multimaster*. This method is more complicated because simultaneous transactions on different servers could conflict with one another (such as two reservation agents trying to book a passenger in the same seat on an airline flight). Some form of concurrent transaction control would be required, such as a *distributed lock manager*.

In terms of the speed and integrity of replicated information, there are two types of replication:

- **Synchronous replication**   Writing data to a local and to a remote storage system is performed as a single operation, guaranteeing that data on the remote storage system is identical to data on the local storage system. Synchronous replication incurs a performance penalty, as the speed of the entire transaction is slowed to the rate of the remote transaction.

- **Asynchronous replication**   Writing data to the remote storage system is not kept in sync with updates on the local storage system. Instead, there may be a time lag, and you have no guarantee that data on the remote system is identical to that on the local storage system. However, performance is improved, because transactions are considered complete when they have been written to the local storage system only. Bursts of local updates to data will take a finite period to replicate to the remote server, subject to the available bandwidth of the network connection between the local and remote storage systems.

 NOTE   Organizations need to consider various threat scenarios when selecting data backup and replication methods. Organizations using only replication may find that threats such as software bugs and ransomware may result in damaged data being automatically replicated to other storage systems.

Data Loss Prevention

Data loss prevention (DLP) represents a variety of capabilities where the movement and/ or storage of sensitive data can be detected and, optionally, controlled. DLP technology is considered a content-aware control that some organizations use to detect and even control the storage, transmission, and use of sensitive data.

There are two main types of DLP systems:

- **Static DLP**   These are mainly tools used to scan unstructured data storage systems for sensitive information. Static DLP tools can be effective at discovering sensitive data that personnel copy to file servers. Often, users will export sensitive data out of a business application to a spreadsheet and store that data on a file server or cloud-based file storage service. Sometimes this sensitive data is readable by most or all organization personnel and even personnel outside of the organization.

- **Dynamic DLP**   These are tools that reside in, or communicate with, file storage systems, USB-attached removable storage devices, and e-mail systems, and they are used to detect and even block the movement of sensitive data. Depending on the nature of the data being moved, users may be warned of the activity they are undertaking, or their actions may be blocked.

Implementing DLP systems is a challenging undertaking, mainly because organizations are required to thoroughly understand how sensitive and critical data are stored and used. A DLP system can inadvertently block legitimate uses of data while permitting undesired actions.

Cloud Access Security Brokers

As mentioned earlier, *cloud access security broker (CASB)* products monitor and, optionally, restrict users' access to, and use of, cloud-based resources. CASB tools are typically used to help an organization understand what Internet-based services are being used by their personnel. This visibility capability is usually considered a first step that is followed by restrictions on users' access to all but specifically sanctioned services.

CASB systems help organizations better understand how their workers use cloud-based services. Usually the objective of CASB systems is to prevent sensitive data from being uploaded to unauthorized third-party service providers. Without CASB systems, users in many organizations enroll in low-cost and zero-cost online services used to store, process, or analyze business information, resulting in the organization losing control of its sensitive information and, in many cases, not knowing where that sensitive data resides.

CASB systems are closely related to web filters in terms of functionality. It is believed that CASB functionality will soon be included in web filter systems, and that stand-alone CASB systems will cease to be used in most organizations.

Most organizations underestimate the number of cloud-based services are in use in their organizations until they initially use a CASB tool.

Digital Rights Management

Digital rights management (DRM) represents access control technologies used to control the distribution and use of electronic content. DRM is still considered an emerging technology and practice. Today, DRM exists in rather narrow usage models and has yet to be widely adopted in general ways. Current capabilities include the following:

- Software license keys
- Copy restriction of music CDs and movie DVDs
- Adobe Acrobat PDF document restriction
- Microsoft Office document restriction

These uses are proprietary and exist as islands of control, as there are no standards that work across multiple technologies or uses.

User Behavior Analytics

User behavior analytics (UBA) represents an emerging capability that enables organizations to detect anomalous or abnormal behavior of its personnel. UBA systems work by observing users' behavior over time and create events or alarms when user behavior deviates from the norm.

UBA capabilities can exist in many different contexts. For example, a cloud-based file storage service can establish baselines for each user and report on incidents where individual users are uploading or downloading copious amounts of information. Or, an application can baseline each user's behavior and report on anomalies such as large dollar value transactions and other unusual activity.

UBA capabilities are used to counter *insider threats,* which is a broad category of threats ranging from errors and poor judgment to malice (including information theft and fraud, as well as malware on a user's computer performing actions unknown to the user).

Business Continuity Planning

Business continuity planning represents the broad range of activities that enable an organization to anticipate a variety of disaster scenarios. To counter the probability and impact of those scenarios, an organization can improve its resilience and develop contingency plans to be carried out when a disaster occurs.

Business continuity planning is discussed fully in Chapter 5.

IT Service Management

IT service management (ITSM) is the set of activities that ensures the delivery of IT services is efficient and effective, through active management and the continuous improvement of processes.

ITSM consists of several distinct activities:

- Service desk
- Incident management
- Problem management
- Change management
- Configuration management
- Release management
- Service-level management
- Financial management
- Capacity management
- Service continuity management
- Availability management

Each of these activities is described in detail in this section.

ITSM is defined in the IT Infrastructure Library (ITIL) process framework, a well-recognized standard. The content of ITIL is managed by AXELOS. IT service management processes can be audited and registered to the ISO/IEC 20000:2011 standard, the international standard for ITSM.

Why ITSM Matters to Security

At first glance, IT service management and information risk may not appear to be related.

These are reasons why information risk and information security rely a great deal on effective IT service management:

- In the absence of effective change management and configuration management, the configuration of IT systems will be inconsistent, in many cases resulting in exploitable vulnerabilities that could lead to security incidents.

- In the absence of effective release management, security defects may persist in production environments, possibly resulting in vulnerabilities and incidents.

- In the absence of effective capacity management, system and application malfunctions could occur, resulting in unscheduled downtime and data corruption.

- Without effective financial management, IT organizations may have insufficient funds for important security initiatives.

Service Desk

Often known as the *help desk*, the *IT service desk* function handles incidents and service requests on behalf of customers by acting as a single point of contact. The service desk performs end-to-end management of incidents and service requests (at least from the perspective of the customer) and also is responsible for communicating status reports to the customer.

The service desk can also serve as a collection point for other ITSM processes, such as change management, configuration management, service-level management, availability management, and other ITSM functions. A typical service desk function consists of frontline analysts who take calls from users. These frontline analysists perform basic triage, and they are often trained to perform routine tasks such as password resets, troubleshoot hardware and software issues, and assist users with questions and problems with software programs. When frontline analysts are unable to assist a user, the matter is typically escalated to a subject-matter expert who can provide assistance.

Incident Management

ITIL defines an *incident* this way: "An unplanned interruption to an IT Service or reduction in the quality of an IT service. Failure of a configuration item that has not yet affected service is also an incident—for example, failure of one disk from a mirror set." ISO/IEC 20000-1:2011 defines an incident as an "unplanned interruption to a service, a reduction in the quality of a service or an event that has not yet impacted the service to the customer."

Thus, an incident may be any of the following:

- Service outage
- Service slowdown
- Software bug

IT Infrastructure Library, Not Just for the United Kingdom

While ITIL may have its roots in the United Kingdom, it has very much become an international standard. Partly this is because of ITIL being adopted by the International Organization for Standardization (ISO)/International Electrotechnical Commission (IEC), in the ISO/IEC 20000 standard and partly because IT management practices are becoming more standardized and mature.

Regardless of the cause, incidents are a result of failures or errors in any component or layer in IT infrastructure.

In ITIL terminology, if the incident has been seen before and its root cause is known, this is a *known error*. If the service desk is able to access the catalog of known errors, this may result in more rapid resolution of incidents, resulting in less downtime and inconvenience. The change management and configuration management processes are used to make modifications to the system in order to fix it temporarily or permanently.

If the root cause of the incident is not known, the incident may be escalated to a *problem*, which is discussed in the next section.

Problem Management

When several incidents have occurred that appear to have the same or a similar root cause, a *problem* is occurring. ITIL defines a *problem* as "a cause of one or more incidents." ISO/IEC 20000-1:2011 defines *problem* as the "root cause of one or more incidents" and continues by staying, "The root cause is not usually known at the time a problem record is created and the problem management process is responsible for further investigation."

The overall objective of problem management is the reduction in the number and severity of incidents.

Problem management can also include some proactive measures, including system monitoring to measure system health and capacity management that will help management to forestall capacity-related incidents.

Examples of problems include the following:

- A server that has exhausted available resources that result in similar, multiple errors (known as *incidents* in ITSM terms)
- A software bug in a service that is noticed by and affecting many users
- A chronically congested network that causes the communications between many IT components to fail

Similar to incidents, when the root cause of a problem has been identified, the change management and configuration management processes will be enacted to make temporary and permanent fixes.

Change Management

Change management is the set of processes that ensures all changes performed in an IT environment are controlled and performed consistently. ITIL defines change management as follows: "The goal of the change management process is to ensure that standardized methods and procedures are used for efficient and prompt handling of all changes, in order to minimize the impact of change-related incidents upon service quality, and consequently improve the day-to-day operations of the organization."

The main purpose of change management is to ensure that all proposed changes to an IT environment are vetted for suitability and risk and to ensure that changes will not interfere with each other or with other planned or unplanned activities. To be effective, each stakeholder should review all changes so that every perspective of each change is properly reviewed.

A typical change management process is a formal "waterfall" process that includes the following steps:

- **Proposal or request**   The person or group performing the change announces the proposed change. Typically, a change proposal contains a description of the change, the change procedure, the IT components that are expected to be affected by the change, a verification procedure to ensure that the change was applied properly, a back-out procedure in the event the change cannot be applied (or failed verification), and the results of tests that were performed in a test environment. The proposal should be distributed to all stakeholders several days prior to its review.

- **Review**   This is typically a meeting or discussion about the proposed change, where the personnel who will be performing the change can discuss the change and answer any of the stakeholders' questions. Since the change proposal was sent out earlier, each stakeholder should have had an opportunity to read about the proposed change in advance of the review. Stakeholders can discuss any aspect of the change during the review. The stakeholders may agree to approve the change, or they may request that it be deferred or that some aspect of the proposed change be altered.

- **Approval**   When a change has been formally approved in the review step, the person or group responsible for change management recordkeeping will record the approval, including the names of the individuals who consented to the change. If, however, a change has been deferred or denied, the person or group that proposed the change will need to make alterations to the proposed change so that it will be acceptable, or they can withdraw the change altogether.

- **Implementation**   The actual change is implemented per the procedure described in the change proposal. Here, the personnel identified as the change implementers perform the actual change to the IT systems identified in the approved change procedure.

- **Verification** After the implementers have completed the change, they will perform the verification procedure to make sure that the change was implemented correctly and that it produces the desired result. Generally, the verification procedure will include one or more steps that include the gathering of evidence (and directions for confirming correct versus incorrect change) that shows the change was performed correctly. This evidence will be filed with other records related to the change and may be useful in the future if there is any problem with the system where this change is suspected as part of the root cause.

- **Post-change review** Some or all changes in an IT organization will be reviewed after the change is implemented. In this activity, the personnel who made the change discuss the change with other stakeholders to learn more about the change and whether any updates to future changes may be needed.

These activities should be part of a *change control board (CCB)* or *change advisory board (CAB)*, a group of stakeholders from IT and every group that is affected by changes in IT applications and supporting infrastructure.

NOTE The change management process is similar to the software development life cycle (SDLC) in that it consists of activities that systematically enact changes to an IT environment.

Change Management Records

Most or all of the activities related to a change should include updates to business records so that all of the facts related to each change are captured for future reference. In even the smallest IT organization, there are too many changes taking place over time to expect that anyone will be able to recall facts about each change later. Records that are related to each change serve as a permanent record.

Emergency Changes

While most changes can be planned in advance using the change management process described here, there are times when IT systems need to be changed right away. Most change management processes include a process for emergency changes that details most of the steps in the nonemergency change management process, but they are performed out of order. The steps for emergency changes are as follows:

- **Emergency approval** When an emergency situation arises, the staff members attending to the emergency should still seek management approval for the proposed change. This approval may be done by phone, in person, or in writing (typically, e-mail). If the approval was by phone or in person, e-mail or other follow-up is usually performed. Certain members of management should be designated in advance who can approve these emergency changes.

- **Implementation**   The staff members perform the change.

- **Verification**   Staff members verify that the change produced the expected result. This may involve other staff members from other departments or end users.

- **Review**   The emergency change is formally reviewed. This review may be performed alongside nonemergency changes with the change control board, the same group of individuals who discuss nonemergency changes.

Like nonemergency changes, emergency changes should have a full set of records available for future reference.

Linkage to Problem and Incident Management

Often, changes are made as a result of an incident or problem. Emergency and nonemergency changes should reference specific incidents or problems so that those incidents and problems may be properly closed once verification of their resolution has been completed.

Configuration Management

Configuration management (CM) is the process of recording and maintaining the configuration of IT systems. Each configuration setting is known in ITSM parlance as a *configuration item (CI)*. CIs usually include the following:

- **Hardware complement**   This includes the hardware specifications of each system (e.g., CPU speed, amount of memory, firmware version, adapters, and peripherals).

- **Hardware configuration**   Settings at the hardware level may include boot settings, adapter configuration, and firmware settings.

- **Operating system version and configuration**   This includes versions, patches, and many operating system configuration items that have an impact on system performance and functionality.

- **Software versions and configuration**   Software components such as database management systems, application servers, and integration interfaces often have many configuration settings of their own.

Organizations that have many IT systems may automate the CM function with tools that are used to automatically record and change configuration settings. These tools help to streamline IT operations and make it easier for IT systems to be more consistent with one another. The database of system configurations is called a *configuration management database (CMDB)*.

Linkage to Problem and Incident Management

An intelligent problem and incident management system is able to access the CMDB to help IT personnel determine whether incidents and problems are related to specific configurations. This can be an invaluable aid to those who are seeking to determine a problem's root cause.

Linkage to Change Management

Many configuration management tools are able to automatically detect configuration changes that are made to a system. With some change and configuration management systems, it is possible to correlate changes detected by a configuration management system with changes approved in the change management process. Further, many changes that are approved by the change management process can be performed by configuration management tools, which can be used to push changes out to managed systems.

Release Management

Release management is the ITIL term used to describe the portion of the SDLC where changes in applications are made available to end users. Release management is used to control the changes that are made to software programs, applications, and environments.

The release process is used for several types of changes to a system, including the following:

- **Incidents and problem resolution** Casually known as *bug fixes,* these types of changes are done in response to an incident or problem, where it has been determined that a change to application software is the appropriate remedy.

- **Enhancements** New functions in an application are created and implemented. These enhancements may have been requested by customers, or they may be a part of the long-range vision on the part of the designers of the software program.

- **Subsystem patches and changes** Changes in lower layers in an application environment may require a level of testing that is similar to what is used when changes are made to the application itself. Examples of changes are patches, service packs, and version upgrades to operating systems, database management systems, application servers, and middleware.

The release process is a sequential process. That is, each change that is proposed to a software program will be taken through each step in the release management process. In many applications, changes are usually assembled into a "package" for process efficiency purposes: it is more effective to discuss and manage groups of changes than it would be to manage individual changes.

The steps in a typical release process are preceded by typical SDLC process steps, which are as follows:

- **Feasibility study** Activities that seek to determine the expected benefits of a program, project, or change to a system.

- **Requirements definition** Each software change is described in terms of a feature description and requirements. The feature description is a high-level description of a change to software that may explain the change in business terms. Requirements are the detailed statements that describe a change in enough detail for a developer to make changes and additions to application code that will provide the desired functionality. Often, end users will be involved in the development of requirements so that they may verify that the proposed software change is really what they desire.

- **Design**   After requirements have been developed, a programmer/analyst or application designer will create a formal design. For an existing software application, this will usually involve changes to existing design documents and diagrams, but for new applications, these will need to be created from scratch or copied from similar designs and modified. Regardless, the design will have a sufficient level of detail to permit a programmer or software engineer to complete development without having to discern the meaning of requirements or design.

- **Development**   When requirements and design have been completed, reviewed, and approved, programmers or software engineers begin development. This involves actual coding in the chosen computer language with approved development tools, as well as the creation or update to ancillary components, such as a database design or application programming interface (API). Developers will often perform their own *unit testing*, where they test individual modules and sections of the application code to make sure that it works properly.

- **Testing**   When the developers have finished coding and unit testing, a more formal and comprehensive test phase is performed. Here, analysts, dedicated software testers, and perhaps end users will test all of the new and changed functionality to confirm whether it is performing according to requirements. Depending on the nature of the changes, some amount of *regression testing* is also performed; this means that functions that were confirmed to be working properly in prior releases are tested again to make sure that they continue to work as expected. Testing is performed according to formal, written test plans that are designed to confirm that every requirement is fulfilled. Formal test scripts are used, and the results of all tests should be recorded and archived. The testing that users perform is usually called *user acceptance testing (UAT)*. Often, automated test tools are used, which can make testing more accurate and efficient. After testing is completed, a formal review and approval are required before the process is allowed to continue.

- **Implementation**   When testing has been completed, the software is implemented on production systems. Here, developers hand off the completed software to operations personnel, who install it according to instructions created by developers. This could also involve the use of tools to make changes to data and database design to accommodate changes in the software. When changes are completed and tested, the release itself is carried out with these last two steps:

  - **Release preparation**   When UAT and regression testing have been completed, reviewed, and approved, a release management team will begin to prepare the new or changed software for release. Depending upon the complexity of the application and of the change itself, release preparation may involve not only software installation but also the installation or change to database design, and perhaps even changes to customer data. Hence, the software release may involve the development and testing of data conversion tools and other programs that are required so that the new or changed software will operate properly. As with testing and other phases, full records of testing and implementation of release preparation details need to be captured and archived.

- **Release deployment**   When release preparation is completed (and perhaps reviewed and approved), the release is installed on the target systems. Personnel deploying the release will follow the release procedure, which may involve the use of tools that will make changes to the target system at the operating system, database, or other level; any required data manipulation or migration; and the installation of the actual software. The release procedure will also include verification steps that will be used to confirm the correct installation of all components.

- **Post-implementation**   After the software has been implemented, a post-implementation review takes place to examine matters of system adequacy, security, ROI, and any issues encountered during implementation.

Utilizing a Gate Process

Many organizations utilize a "gate process" approach in their release management process. This means that each step of the process undergoes formal review and approval before the next step is allowed to begin. For example, a formal design review will be performed and attended by end users, personnel who created requirements and feature description documents, developers, and management. If the design is approved, development may begin. But if there are questions or concerns raised in the design review, the design may need to be modified and reviewed again before development is allowed to begin.

Agile processes utilize gates as well, although the flow of Agile processes is often parallel rather than sequential. The concept of formal reviews is the same, regardless of the SDLC process in use.

Service-Level Management

Service-level management is composed of the set of activities that confirms whether IS operations is providing adequate service to its customers. This is achieved through continuous monitoring and periodic review of IT service delivery.

An IS department often plays two different roles in service-level management. As a provider of service to its own customers, the IS department will measure and manage the services that it provides directly. Also, many IT departments directly or indirectly manage services that are provided by external service providers. Thus, many IT departments are both service provider and customer, and often the two are interrelated, as depicted in Figure 4-14.

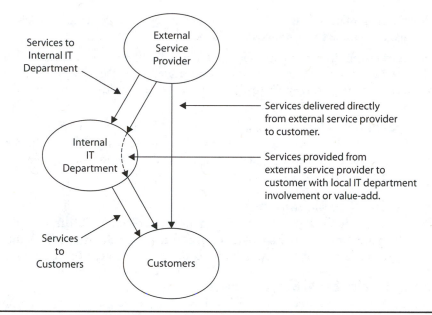

Figure 4-14 The different perspectives of the delivery of IT services

Financial Management

Financial management for IT services consists of several activities, including the following:

- Budgeting
- Capital investment
- Expense management
- Project accounting and project return on investment (ROI)

IT financial management is the portion of IT management that takes into account the financial value of IT services that support organizational objectives.

Capacity Management

Capacity management is a set of activities that confirms there is sufficient capacity in IT systems and IT processes to meet service needs. Primarily, an IT system or process has sufficient capacity if its performance falls within an acceptable range, as specified in service level agreements.

Capacity management is not just a concern for current needs; capacity management must also be concerned about meeting future needs. This is attained through several activities, including the following:

- **Periodic measurements** Systems and processes need to be regularly measured so that trends in usage can be used to predict future capacity needs.

- **Considering planned changes** Planned changes to processes and IT systems may have an impact on predicted workload.

- **Understanding long-term strategies** Changes in the organization, including IT systems, business processes, and organizational objectives, may have an impact on workloads, requiring more (or less) capacity than would be extrapolated through simpler trend analysis.

- **Changes in technology** Several factors may influence capacity plans, including the expectation that computing and network technologies will deliver better performance in the future and that trends in the usage of technology may influence how end users use technology.

Linkage to Financial Management

One of the work products of capacity management is a projection for the acquisition of additional computer or network hardware to meet future capacity needs. This information needs to be made part of budgeting and spending management processes.

Linkage to Service Level Management

If there are insufficient resources to handle workloads, capacity issues may result in violations to SLAs. Systems and processes that are overburdened will take longer to respond. In some cases, systems may stop responding altogether.

Linkage to Incident and Problem Management

Systems with severe capacity issues may take excessive time to respond to user requests. In some cases, systems may malfunction or users may give up. Often, users will call the service desk, resulting in the logging of incidents and problems.

Service Continuity Management

Service continuity management is the set of activities that is concerned with the ability of the organization to continue providing services, primarily in the event that a natural or manmade disaster has occurred. Service continuity management is ITIL parlance for the more common terms *business continuity planning* and *disaster recovery planning*.

Business continuity is discussed in Chapter 5.

Availability Management

The goal of availability management is the sustainment IT service availability in support of organizational objectives and processes. The availability of IT systems is governed by the following:

- **Effective change management** When changes to systems and infrastructure are properly vetted through a change management process, changes are less likely to result in unanticipated downtime.

- **Effective application testing** When changes to applications are made according to a set of formal requirements, review, and testing, the application is less likely to fail and become unavailable.

- **Resilient architecture**   When the overall architecture of an application environment is designed from the beginning to be highly reliable, it will be more resilient and more tolerant of individual faults and component failures.

- **Serviceable components**   When the individual components of an application environment can be effectively serviced by third-party service organizations, those components will be less likely to fail unexpectedly.

 NOTE   Organizations typically measure availability as a percentage of uptime of an application or service.

Asset Management

Asset management is the collection of activities used to manage the inventory, classification, use, and disposal of assets. Asset management is a foundational activity, without which several other activities could not be effectively managed, including vulnerability management, device hardening, incident management, data security, and some aspects of financial management.

In information security, asset management is critical to the success of vulnerability management. If assets are not known to exist, they may be excluded from processes used to identify and remediate vulnerabilities. Similarly, it will be difficult to harden assets if their existence is not known. And if an unknown asset is attacked, the organization may have no way of directly knowing this in a timely manner; instead, if an attacker compromises an unknown device, the attack may not be known until the attacker pivots and selects additional assets to compromise. This time lag could prove crucial to the impact of the incident.

Asset Identification

A security management program's main objective (whether formally stated or not) is the protection of the organization's assets. These assets may be tangible or intangible, physical, logical, or virtual. Here are some examples of assets:

- **Buildings and property**   These assets include real estate, structures, and other improvements.

- **Equipment**   This can include machinery, vehicles, and office equipment such as copiers, printers, and scanners.

- **IT equipment**   This includes computers, printers, scanners, tape libraries (the devices that create backup tapes, not the tapes themselves), storage systems, network devices, and phone systems.

- **Virtual assets**   In addition to the tangible IT equipment cited, virtual assets include virtual machines and software running on them.

- **Supplies and materials**   These can include office supplies as well as materials that are used in manufacturing.

- **Records**   These include business records, such as contracts, video surveillance tapes, visitor logs, and far more.

- **Information**   This includes data in software applications, documents, e-mail messages, and files of every kind on workstations and servers.

- **Intellectual property**   This includes an organization's designs, architectures, patents, software source code, processes, and procedures.

- **Personnel**   In a real sense, an organization's personnel *are* the organization. Without its staff, the organization cannot perform or sustain its processes.

- **Reputation**   One of the intangible characteristics of an organization, reputation is the individual and collective opinion about an organization in the eyes of its customers, competitors, shareholders, and the community.

- **Brand equity**   Similar to reputation, this is the perceived or actual market value of an individual brand of product or service that is produced by the organization.

Sources of Asset Data   An organization that is building or improving its security management program may need to build its asset inventory from scratch. Management will need to determine where this initial asset data will come from. Some sources include the following:

- **Financial system asset inventory**   An organization that keeps all of its assets on the books will have a wealth of asset inventory information. However, it may not be entirely useful: asset lists often do not include the location or purpose of the asset and whether it is still in use. Correlating a financial asset inventory to assets in actual use may consume more effort than the other methods for creating the initial asset list. However, for organizations that have a relatively small number of highly valued assets (for instance, an ore crusher in a gold mine or a mainframe computer), knowing the precise financial value of an asset is highly useful because the actual depreciated value of the asset is used in the risk analysis phase of risk management. Knowing the depreciated value of other assets is also useful, as this will figure into the risk treatment choices that will be identified later.

TIP   Financial records that indicate the value of an asset do not include the value of information stored on (or processed by) the asset.

- **Interviews**   Discussions with key personnel for purposes of identifying assets are usually the best approach. However, to be effective, several people usually need to be interviewed to be sure to include all relevant assets.

- **IT systems portfolio**   A well-managed IT organization will have formal documents and records for its major applications. While this information may not encompass every IT asset in the organization, it can provide information on the assets supporting individual applications or geographic locations.

- **Online data**   An organization with a large number of IT assets (systems, network devices, and so on) can sometimes utilize the capability of online data to identify those assets. An organization with cloud-based assets can use the asset management portion of the cloud services dashboard to determine the number and type of assets in use there. Also, a systems or network management system often includes a list of managed assets, which can be a good starting point when creating the initial asset list.

- **Security scans**   An organization that has security scanning tools can use them to identify network assets. This technique will identify authorized as well as unauthorized assets.

- **Asset management system**   Larger organizations may find it more cost effective to use an asset management application dedicated to this purpose, rather than rely on lists of assets from other sources.

None of these sources should be considered accurate or complete. Instead, as a formal asset inventory is being assembled, the security manager should continue to explore other sources of assets.

Collecting and Organizing Asset Data   It is rarely possible to take (or create) a list of assets from a single source. Rather, more than one source of information is often needed to be sure that the risk management program has identified at least the important, in-scope assets that it needs to worry about.

NOTE   As part of IT governance, management needs to determine which person or group is responsible for maintaining an asset inventory.

It is usually useful to organize or classify assets. This will help to get identified assets into smaller chunks that can be analyzed more effectively. There is no single way to organize assets, but here are a few ideas:

- **Geography**   A widely dispersed organization may want to classify its assets according to their location. This will aid risk managers during the risk analysis phase since many risks are geographic-centric, particularly natural hazards.

- **Service provider**   An organization utilizing one or more infrastructure-as-a-service (IaaS) providers can group its assets by service provider.

- **Business process**   Because some organizations rank the criticality of their individual business processes, it can be useful to group assets according to the business processes they support. This helps the risk analysis and risk treatment phases because assets supporting individual processes can be associated with business criticality and treated appropriately.

- **Organizational unit**   In larger organizations, it may be easier to classify assets according to the organizational unit they support.

- **Sensitivity**   Usually ascribed to information, sensitivity relates to the nature and content of that information. Sensitivity usually applies in two ways: to an individual, where the information is considered personal or private, and to an organization, where the information may be considered a trade secret. Sometimes sensitivity is somewhat subjective and arbitrary, but often it is defined in laws and regulations.

- **Regulation**   For organizations that are required to follow government and other legal obligations regarding the processing and protection of information, it will be useful to include data points that indicate whether specific assets are considered in scope for specific regulations. This is important because some regulations specify how assets should be protected, so it's useful to be aware of this during risk analysis and risk treatment.

There is no need to choose which of these methods will be used to classify assets. Instead, an IT analyst should collect several points of metadata about each asset (including location, process supported, and organizational unit supported). This will enable the security manager to sort and filter the list of assets in various ways to better understand which assets are in a given location or which ones support a particular process or part of the business.

 TIP   Organizations should consider managing information about assets in a fixed-assets application.

Why Asset Management Is Control #1

The well-known control framework known as the Critical Security Controls by the Center for Internet Security (known as the CIS 20) lists hardware asset inventory as the first control. I believe there is a specific purpose to this: an organization cannot protect assets that it does not know about.

Controls

The policies, procedures, mechanisms, systems, and other measures designed to reduce risk are known as *controls*. An organization develops controls to ensure that its business objectives will be met, risks will be reduced, and errors will be prevented or corrected.

Controls are used in two primary ways in an organization: they are created to ensure desired outcomes, and they are created to avoid unwanted outcomes.

Control Classification

Several types, classes, and categories of controls are discussed in this section. Figure 4-15 depicts this control classification.

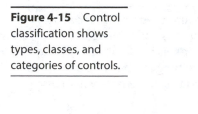

Figure 4-15 Control classification shows types, classes, and categories of controls.

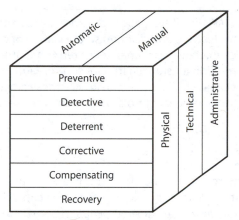

The Multidimensionality of Controls

There are many different ways to look at controls that help better understand them and how they work. In this book, controls are described using the words *types, classes,* and *categories*. These three terms are not set in stone, and there is no agreed upon standard way of modeling controls using these or other terms. The depiction of controls in this book by type, class, and category is purely arbitrary, but it is helpful to understand controls using a technique like this, as it helps security managers, IS auditors, and other security personnel understand their controls and how they contribute to the protection of assets.

Types of Controls

The three types of controls are physical, technical, and administrative:

- **Physical**   These types of controls exist in the tangible, physical world. Examples of physical controls are video surveillance, locking doors, bollards, and fences.

- **Technical**   These controls are implemented in the form of information systems and information system components and are usually intangible. Examples of technical controls include encryption, computer access controls, and audit logs. These are also referred to sometimes as *logical* controls.

- **Administrative**   These controls are the policies, procedures, and standards that require or forbid certain activities, protocols, and configurations. An example administrative control is a policy that forbids personal use of company-owned information systems. These are also referred to sometimes as *managerial* controls.

EXAM TIP ISACA does not expressly use the terms *type, class,* or *category* to describe and distinguish the variety of controls and their basic characteristics. Rather, these terms are used in this book to highlight the multidimensional nature of controls and how they can be understood and classified. Like other constructs, these are models that enable you to better imagine how controls operate and are used.

Classes of Controls

There are six classes of controls:

- **Preventive**   This type of control is used to prevent the occurrence of an unwanted event. Examples of preventive controls are computer login screens (which *prevent* unauthorized people from accessing information), keycard systems (which *prevent* unauthorized people from entering a building or workspace), and encryption (which *prevent* people lacking an encryption key from reading encrypted data).

- **Detective**   This type of control is used to record both wanted and unwanted events. A detective control cannot enforce an activity (whether it is desired or undesired), but instead it can only make sure that it is known whether, and how, the event occurred. Examples of detective controls include video surveillance and event logs.

- **Deterrent**   This type of control exists to convince someone that they should not perform some unwanted activity. Examples of deterrent controls include guard dogs, warning signs, and visible video surveillance cameras and monitors.

NOTE   Security professionals generally prefer preventive controls over detective controls because preventive controls actually *block* unwanted events. Likewise, security professionals prefer detective controls to deterrent controls because detective controls record events while deterrent controls do not. However, there are often circumstances where cost, resource, or technical limitations force an organization to accept a detective control when it would prefer a preventive control or to accept a deterrent control when it would prefer a detective control. For example, there is no practical way to build a control that would prevent criminals from entering a bank, but a detective control (security cameras) would record what they did after they arrived.

NOTE   Security managers need to understand one key difference between preventive and deterrent controls. A deterrent control requires knowledge of the control by the potential violator—it can only deter their intentions if they know the control exists. Preventive and detective controls work regardless of whether the violator is aware of them.

- **Corrective** This type of control is activated (manually or automatically) after some unwanted event has occurred. An example corrective control is the act of improving a process when it is found to be defective.

- **Compensating** This type of control is enacted because some other direct control cannot be used. For example, a guest sign-in register can be a compensating control when it is implemented to compensate for the lack of a stronger detective control, such as a video surveillance system. A compensating control addresses the risk related to the original control.

- **Recovery** This type of control is used to restore the state of a system or asset to its pre-incident state. An example recovery control is the use of a tool to remove malware from a computer. Another example is the use of backup software to recover lost or corrupted files.

 NOTE Many controls can be classified in more than one class. For example, a video surveillance camera can be thought of as both a detective control (because it is part of a system that records events) and a deterrent control (because its visibility is designed to discourage persons from committing unwanted acts). Also, an audit log can be thought of as both a detective control and a compensating control—detective because it records events and compensating because it may compensate for a lack of a stronger, preventive control, such as a user IDs and password access control. The organization of controls described in this section is not based on any published standard.

Categories of Controls

There are two categories of controls:

- **Automatic** This type of control performs its function with little or no human judgment or decision-making. Examples of automatic controls include a login page on an application that cannot be circumvented, and a security door that automatically locks after someone walks through the doorway.

- **Manual** This type of control requires a human to operate it. A manual control may be subject to a higher rate of errors than an automatic control. An example of a manual control is a monthly review of computer users.

NOTE Information security professionals generally prefer automatic controls to manual ones, as they are typically less prone to error. However, there are often circumstances where an organization must settle for a manual control because of cost or some other factor, such as the requirement for human decision and intervention, perhaps during an emergency situation or disaster, for example.

Internal Control Objectives

Internal control objectives are statements of desired states or outcomes from business operations. When building a security program, and preferably prior to selecting a control framework, it is important to establish high-level control objectives.

Example control objectives include the following:

- Protection of IT assets
- Accuracy of transactions
- Confidentiality and privacy of sensitive information
- Availability of IT systems
- Controlled changes to IT systems
- Compliance with corporate policies
- Compliance with applicable regulations and other legal obligations

Control objectives are the foundation for controls. For each control objective, one or more controls will exist to ensure the realization of the control objective. For example, the "Availability of IT Systems" control objective will be implemented via several controls, including the following:

- IT systems will be continuously monitored, and any interruptions in availability will result in alerts sent to appropriate personnel.
- IT systems will have resource-measuring capabilities.
- IT management will review capacity reports monthly and adjust resources accordingly.
- IT systems will have anti-malware controls that are monitored by appropriate staff.

Together, these four (or more) controls contribute to the overall control objective on IT system availability. Similarly, the other control objectives will have one or more controls that will ensure their realization.

After establishing control objectives, the next step is to design controls. This can be a considerable undertaking. A better approach is the selection of one of several high-quality control frameworks that are discussed later in this section.

If an organization elects to adopt a standard control framework, the next step is to perform a risk assessment to determine whether controls in the control framework adequately meet each control objective. Where there are gaps in control coverage, additional controls must be developed and put in place.

Information Systems Control Objectives

Information systems control objectives resemble ordinary control objectives but are set in the context of information systems. Examples of information systems control objectives include the following:

- Protection of information from unauthorized personnel
- Protection of information from unauthorized modification

- Integrity of operating systems
- Controlled and managed changes to information systems
- Controlled and managed development of application software

An organization will probably have several additional information systems control objectives on other basic topics such as malware, availability, and resource management.

Like ordinary control objectives, information systems control objectives will be supported by one or more controls.

General Computing Controls

An IT organization supporting many applications and services will generally have some controls that are specific to each individual application. However, IT will also have a set of controls that apply across all of its applications and services. These are usually called its *general computing controls (GCCs)*.

An organization's GCCs are general in nature and are often implemented in different ways on different information systems, based upon their individual capabilities and limitations, as well as applicability. Examples of GCCs include the following:

- Applications require unique user IDs and strong passwords.
- Passwords are encrypted while stored and transmitted and are not displayed.
- Highly sensitive information, such as bank account numbers, is encrypted when stored and transmitted.
- All administrative actions are logged, and logs are protected from tampering.

If you are familiar with information systems technology, you will quickly realize that these GCCs will be implemented differently across different types of information systems. Specific capabilities and limitations, for example, will result in somewhat different capabilities for password complexity and data encryption. Unless an organization is using really old information systems, the four GCCs shown here can probably be implemented everywhere in an IS environment. *How* they are implemented is the subject of the next section.

Control Frameworks

A *control framework* is a collection of controls that is organized into logical categories. Well-known control frameworks such as ISO/IEC 27001, NIST SP 800-53, and CIS 20 Controls are intended to address a broad set of information risks common to most organizations.

Standard control frameworks have been developed to streamline the process of control development and adoption within organizations. If there were no standard control frameworks, organizations would have to assemble their controls using other, inferior methods, including the following:

- Gut feel
- Prior experience in another organization

- From a security practitioner in another organization
- Searching the Internet
- A deficient or incomplete risk assessment

A security manager could perform a comprehensive risk assessment and develop a framework of controls based upon identified risks, and indeed this would not be considered unacceptable. However, with the variety of high-quality control frameworks that are freely available (exception: ISO/IEC 27001 must be purchased), an organization could start with a standard control framework for far less effort.

Selecting a Control Framework

Several high-quality control frameworks are available for organizations that want to start with a standard control framework as opposed to starting from scratch or other means. Table 4-8 lists commonly used control frameworks. Each is discussed in more detail in the remainder of this section.

There is ongoing debate on which control framework is best for an organization. In my opinion, the fact that there is debate on the topic reveals that many do not understand the purpose for a control framework or the risk management life cycle. The common belief is that once an organization selects a control framework, the organization is "stuck" with a set of controls and no changes will be made to the controls used in the organization. Instead, as is discussed throughout this book, selection of a control framework represents a starting point, not the perpetual commitment. Once a control framework is selected, the risk management life cycle is used to understand risk in the organization, resulting in changes to the controls used by the organization. In fact, it may be argued that, in an organization practicing effective risk management, an organization will eventually arrive at more or less the same set of controls, regardless of the starting point.

A different and valid approach to control framework selection has more to do with the structure of controls than the controls themselves. Each control framework consists of logical groupings based on categories of controls. For instance, most control frameworks have sections on identity and access management, vulnerability management, incident management, and access management. Some control frameworks' groupings are more sensible in certain organizations based on their operations or industry sector.

There is also nothing wrong with a security manager selecting a control framework based on her familiarity and experience with a specific framework. This is valid to a point, however: selecting the PCI-DSS control framework in a healthcare delivery organization might not be the best choice.

 EXAM TIP CISM candidates are not required to memorize COBIT or other frameworks, but familiarity with them will help the CISM candidate to better understand how they contribute to effective security governance and control.

Control Framework	Description	Industries Used
ISO/IEC 27001/27002	Broadly adopted international controls	All
NIST SP 800-53	Broadly adopted U.S.-based controls	Government, private industry
CIS 20 Controls	Broadly adopted U.S.-based controls	All
Payment Card Industry Data Security Standard (PCI-DSS)	Controls for protection of credit card data	Retail, banking, credit card processing
NIST Cyber Security Framework (CSF)	Emerging U.S.-based controls	All
Health Insurance Portability and Accountability Act (HIPAA)	Controls for the protection of electronic patient healthcare information (ePHI)	Medical services, including delivery, billing, and insurance
COBIT 5	Broadly adopted international controls	All
Committee of Sponsoring Organizations of the Treadway Commission (COSO)	Controls for preserving the integrity of financial information and financial statement reporting	All U.S. public companies and private companies requiring similar controls
North American Electric Reliability Corporation (NERC) Reliability Standards	Controls for the protection of electric generation and distribution infrastructure	Electric utilities
Cloud Security Alliance (CSA) Controls	Controls for use by cloud-based service providers	All
(System and Organization Controls Report) SOC1	Controls for use by financial service providers	All
(System and Organization Controls Report) SOC2	Controls for use by cloud-based service providers	All
(Standardized Information Gathering) SIG	Controls used in the assessment of third parties	All

Table 4-8 Commonly Used Control Frameworks

Mapping Control Frameworks

Frequently, organizations find themselves in a position where more than one control framework needs to be selected and adopted. The primary factors driving this are as follows:

- Multiple applicable regulatory frameworks
- Multiple operational contexts

For example, a medical clinic delivers healthcare services and accepts payments by credit card. Both the HIPAA and PCI-DSS frameworks would be applicable in the organization, as neither HIPAA nor PCI-DSS fully addresses the security and compliance needs of the business. In another example, a U.S.-based, publicly traded electric utility will need to adopt both COSO and NERC controls.

In these two examples, the respective organizations may decide to apply each control framework only to relevant parts of the organization. For example, in the medical clinic described earlier, HIPAA would apply to systems and processes that process electronic protected healthcare information (ePHI), and PCI-DSS would apply to systems and processes that process credit card data and payments. In the electric utility, NERC controls would apply to the electric generation and distribution infrastructure while COSO would apply to financial systems. The challenge with this approach is that there will be systems and infrastructure that are in scope for two (or more) frameworks. This can make IT and security operations more complex than they would be otherwise. However, applying all frameworks in use across the entire infrastructure would most likely be overly burdensome.

Organizations with multiple control frameworks often crave a simpler organization for their controls. Often, organizations will "map" their control frameworks together, resulting in a single control framework with controls from each framework present. Mapping control frameworks together is time-consuming and tedious, although in some instances the work has already been done. For instance, Appendix H in NIST SP 800-53 contains a forward and reverse mapping between NIST SP 800-53 and ISO/IEC 27001. Other controls mapping references can be found online.

The problem with mapping controls from multiple frameworks together is that, at a control-by-control level, many controls do not neatly map together. For example, in Appendix H of NIST SP 800-53, ISO/IEC 27001 control A.15.1.2 is mapped to NIST SP 800-53 CM-10. These controls read as follows:

- **NIST SP 800-53 CM-10**   "The organization: a. Uses software and associated documentation in accordance with contract agreements and copyright laws; b. Tracks the use of software and associated documentation protected by quantity licenses to control copying and distribution; and c. Controls and documents the use of peer-to-peer file sharing technology to ensure that this capability is not used for the unauthorized distribution, display, performance, or reproduction of copyrighted work."

- **ISO/IEC 27001:2013 A.18.1.2**   "Appropriate procedures shall be implemented to ensure compliance with legislative, regulatory and contractual requirements related to intellectual property rights and use of proprietary software products."

The control in NIST SP 800-53 is far more specific than the control in ISO/IEC 27001:2013. This is a good example of an imperfect mapping.

In another example, in Appendix H of NIST SP 800-53, ISO/IEC 27001:2005 control A.15.3.2 is mapped to NIST SP 800-53 AU-9. The text of each control reads as follows:

- **ISO/IEC 27001:2005 A.15.3.2**   "Access to information systems audit tools shall be protected to prevent any possible misuse or compromise."

- **NIST SP 800-53 AU-9**   "The information system protects audit information and audit tools from unauthorized access, modification, and deletion."

Here, these controls map together fairly neatly. Unfortunately, this is more of an exception.

Another issue you may have picked up in these examples is that the recent version of NIST SP 800-53 (revision 4) is mapped to an older version of ISO/IEC 27001—the 2005 version. When ISO/IEC 27001 was updated from the 2005 to the 2013 version, some of the controls were renumbered, and many were reworded. The new version of NIST SP 800-53 (revision 5) does map to the latest ISO/IEC 27001:2013 standard. However, since different control frameworks are updated at different times, organizations that rely on control framework mapping will often find their mappings out of date.

Working with Control Frameworks

Once an organization selects a control framework and multiple frameworks are mapped together (if the organization has decided to undertake that), security managers will then need to organize a framework of activities around the selected/mapped control framework.

Risk Assessment   Before a control can be designed, the security manager needs to have some idea of the nature of risks that a control is intended to address. In a running risk management program, a new risk may have been identified during a risk assessment that led to the creation of an additional control. In this case, information from the risk assessment is needed so that the control will be properly designed to handle these risks.

If an organization is implementing a control prior to a risk assessment, the organization might not design and implement the control properly. Here are some examples:

- A control might not be rigorous enough to counter a threat.

- A control might be too rigorous and costly (in the case of a moderate or low risk).

- A control might not counter all relevant threats.

In the absence of a risk assessment, the chances for one of these undesirable outcomes are quite high. If an organization is implementing a control, a risk assessment needs to be performed. If an organization-wide risk assessment is not feasible, then a risk assessment that is focused on the control area should be performed so that the organization will know what risks the control will be intended to address.

Control Design   An early step in control use is its design. In a control framework, the control language itself appears, as well as some degree of guidance. The security manager, together with personnel who have responsibility for relevant technologies and business processes, needs to determine what activity needs to take place. In other words, they need to figure out how to operationalize the control.

For instance, an organization wants to comply with NIST SP 800-53 control CM-7 ("The organization: a. Configures the information system to provide only essential capabilities; and b. Prohibits or restricts the use of the following functions, ports, protocols, and/or services."). This may require the development of one or more component hardening standards, as well as the implementation of scanning or monitoring tools to detect nonconformities. Next, one or more people will need to be assigned as the responsible parties for designing, implementing, and assessing the control. Also, the control will need to be designed in a way that makes them verifiable.

Proper control design will potentially require one or more of the following:

- New or changed policies
- New or changed business process documents
- New or changed information systems
- New or changed business records

Control Implementation   After a control has been designed, it needs to be put into service. Depending upon the nature of the control, this could involve operational impact in the form of changes to business processes and/or information systems. Changes with greater impact will require greater care so that business processes are adversely affected.

After the hardening standards are developed in the preceding example (no easy task, by the way), they will need to be tested and implemented. If a production environment is affected, this could take quite a bit of time to ensure that none of the hardening standard items adversely affects the performance, integrity, or availability of affected systems.

Control Monitoring   After an organization has implemented a control, the organization needs to monitor the control. For this to happen, the control needs to have been designed so that monitoring can take place. In the absence of monitoring, the organization will lack methodical means for observing the control to see whether it is effective.

For example, an organization identified a risk during a risk assessment that indicated that its user accounts were vulnerable to brute-force password guessing. The organization decided to change the login process on affected systems so that incorrect passwords would result in a small delay before the user could re-attempt to log on (to counter machine-driven password guessing) and that user accounts would be temporarily locked out after five unsuccessful attempts within a five-minute period. To facilitate monitoring, the organization also changed the login process to create audit log entries each time a user attempted to log in, regardless of the outcome. This provided the organization with event data that could be examined from time to time to see whether the control was performing as intended.

Some controls are not so easily monitored. For instance, a control addressing abuse of intellectual property rights includes the enactment of new acceptable use policies (AUPs) that forbid employees from violating intellectual property laws such as copyrights. There are many forms of abuse that cannot be easily monitored.

Control Assessment   Any organization that implements controls to address risks should periodically examine those controls to determine whether they are working as intended and as designed. There are several available approaches to control assessment:

- **Security review**   One or more information security staff examines the control along with any relevant business records.
- **Control self-assessment**   Control owners answer questions and include any relevant evidence.

- **Internal audit**   The organization's internal auditors (or information security staff) perform a formal examination of the control.

- **External audit**   An external auditor formally examines the control.

An organization will select one or more of these methods, guided by any applicable laws, regulations, legal obligations, and results of risk assessments.

The four approaches listed here are described in more detail elsewhere in this chapter.

Dealing with Changing Technology   Technologies change more quickly than standard control frameworks. For this reason, security managers need to keep a close eye on emerging technologies and be "plugged in" to various business processes in the organization so that he will be involved whenever new technologies or practices are being introduced into the organization.

Changes in technologies are often, by design, disruptive. This disruption starts in markets where new products, services, and practices are developed, and it continues inside organizations that adopt them. Disruption is the result of innovation—the realization of new ideas that make organizations better in some way. Here are some examples of disruptive technologies:

- **Personal computer**   Starting in the early 1980s, IBM and other companies sold PCs to organization departments that grew impatient with centralized IT organizations that were too slow to meet their business needs.

- **Cloud computing**   Starting in the early 2000s, many companies developed cloud-based services for data storage and information processing. Organization departments still waiting for corporate IT to help them instead went to the cloud because it was cheaper and faster. Corporate IT followed, as IaaS providers made server operating systems available at far less cost than before. Disruptive technologies within the realm of cloud computing include virtualization, containers, microsegmentation, software-defined networks (SDNs), software-defined security (SDS), identity-defined security (IDS), ransomware, and fileless malware.

- **Smartphones**   BlackBerry was the first widely adopted corporate smartphone, which was minimally disruptive but highly liberating for workers who could then access e-mail and other functions from anywhere. Sold mainly to consumers, Apple's iPhone proved highly disruptive, as it provided alternative means for workers to get things done.

- **Bring your own device (BYOD)**   Increasingly, company workers bring personal smartphones, tablets, laptop, and other personally owned devices and use them for business operations.

- **Shadow IT**   This is the phenomenon wherein individuals, groups, departments, and business units bypass corporate IT and procure their own computing services, typically through SaaS and IaaS services but also through BYOD.

Security managers understand that they cannot be everywhere at once, nor can they be aware of all relevant activities in the organization. Individual workers, teams, departments, and business units will adopt new services and implement new technologies without informing or consulting with information security. This underscores the need for an annual risk assessment that will reveal emerging technologies and practices so that they may be assessed for risk. While a backward look at technology adoption is not ideal (because risks may be introduced at the onset of use), because security managers are not always involved in changes in the organization, a risk assessment is sometimes the method of last resort to discover risks already present in the business.

ISO/IEC 27001

ISO/IEC 27001, "Information technology – Security techniques – Information security management systems – Requirements," is a world-renowned set of requirements and controls for building and managing an information security management system. ISO/IEC 27001 also contains a control framework in its appendix, which is explained in greater detail in ISO/IEC 27002.

The ISO/IEC 27001 appendix covers a control framework that consists of 14 control categories and 35 control objectives. Table 4-9 describes these control categories and control objectives.

The companion standard, ISO/IEC 27002, includes implementation guidance for each of the controls listed in Table 4-9. This guidance provides additional information that helps you better understand the intent of each control, as well as ideas on how it can be implemented.

In addition to its controls, the requirements section in ISO/IEC 27001 describes the necessary activities for an effective information security management system, as shown in Table 4-10.

The language in ISO/IEC 27001 requirements is written in a manner that may give the appearance of vagueness and ambiguity. However, the ISO/IEC 27001 requirements are designed to be scalable to any size organization and for organizations in any industry sector, as well as government, military, education, and nonprofit. The requirements state what must be performed, although ISO/IEC 27001 provides little implementation guidance for its requirements.

For example, ISO/IEC 27001 requirement 7.4 states that "the organization shall determine the need for internal and external communications relevant to the information security management system." The requirement does not specify the following:

- What to say
- To whom to say it
- What medium to use

These and other considerations are in the hands of the security manager and others who are building an organization's security management program. As long as the organization is following the ISO/IEC 27001 requirements in a way that works for the organization, that's all that really counts.

Control	Control Objective
A.5 Information security policies	
A.5.1 Management direction for information security	Provides management direction and support for information security per business requirements, relevant laws, and regulations
A.6 Organization of information security	
A.6.1 Internal organization	Establishes a framework to control the implementation and operation of information security in an organization
A.6.2 Mobile devices and teleworking	Ensures the security of remote workers and mobile devices
A.7 Human resource security	
A.7.1 Prior to employment	Ensures that personnel understand their responsibilities and are suitable for their roles
A.7.2 During employment	Ensures that personnel are aware of and accomplish their information security responsibilities
A.7.3 Termination and change of employment	Protects the organization as part of changing or terminating employment
A.8 Asset management	
A.8.1 Responsibility for assets	Identifies assets and define protection responsibilities
A.8.2 Information classification	Ensures that information receives appropriate protection according to its importance to the organization
A.8.3 Media handling	Prevents unauthorized misuse of information stored on media
A.9 Access control	
A.9.1 Business requirements of access control	Limits access to information and information-processing facilities
A.9.2 User access management	Ensures authorized user access and prevent unauthorized access to systems and functions
A.9.3 User responsibilities	Makes personnel accountable for protecting their authentication information
A.9.4 System and application access control	Prevents unauthorized access to systems and applications
A.10 Cryptography	
A.10.1 Cryptographic controls	Ensures use of cryptography to protect the confidentiality, authenticity, and/or integrity of information
A.11 Physical and environmental security	
A.11.1 Secure areas	Prevents unauthorized physical access, damage, and interference to the organization's information and information systems
A.11.2 Equipment	Prevents loss or compromise of assets and disruption of an organization's operations
A.12 Operations security	
A.12.1 Operational procedures and responsibilities	Ensures correct and secure operations of information-processing facilities

Table 4-9 ISO/IEC 27001 Control Objectives (*continued*)

A.12.2 Protection from malware	Ensures that information systems are protected against malware
A.12.3 Backup	Protects against accidental or deliberate loss of data
A.12.4 Logging and monitoring	Records events and create evidence
A.12.5 Control of operational software	Ensures the integrity of information systems
A.12.6 Technical vulnerability management	Prevents exploitation of vulnerabilities
A.12.7 Information systems audit considerations	Minimizes the impact of audits on operational systems
A.13 Communications security	
A.13.1 Network security management	Ensures the protection of information in networks and its supporting facilities
A.13.2 Information transfer	Maintains the security of information transferred within an organization and with external entities
A.14 System acquisition, development, and maintenance	
A.14.1 Security requirements of information systems	Ensures that information security is a key part of information systems throughout the entire life cycle
A.14.2 Security in development and support processes	Ensures that information security is designed and implemented within the life cycle of information systems
A.14.3 Test data	Ensures the protection of data used for testing
A.15 Supplier relationships	
A.15.1 Information security in supplier relationships	Ensures the protection of assets that are accessible by suppliers
A.15.2 Supplier service delivery management	Maintains an agreed level of security and service delivery
A.16 Information security incident management	
A.16.1 Management of information security incidents and improvements	Ensures an effective approach to the management of security incidents, including communication on security events and weaknesses
A.17 Information security aspects of business continuity management	
A.17.1 Information security continuity	Ensures that information security continuity is embedded in the organization's business continuity management systems
A.17.2 Redundancies	Ensures availability of information-processing facilities
A.18 Compliance	
A.18.1 Compliance with legal and contractual requirements	Avoids breaches related to information security and of any security requirements
A.18.2 Information security reviews	Ensures that information security is implemented and operated according to policies and procedures

Table 4-9   ISO/IEC 27001 Control Objectives

Section in ISO/IEC 27001	Title	Description
4	Context of the organization	The scope of the ISMS must be properly defined, based on the understanding of internal and external issues, and requirements including legal and regulatory obligations.
5	Leadership	Top management must support the development and operation of the ISMS, provide and approve policy, and define ISMS roles and responsibilities.
6	Planning	Management must develop plans to ensure that (a) the ISMS can be successful, (b) risk assessments will be performed, (c) risks will be addressed, and (d) security objectives will be developed and achieved.
7	Support	Management must support the ISMS by (a) providing adequate resources to operate the ISMS, (b) determining what competencies are required, and obtain them, (c) ensuring that all relevant personnel are aware of security policies, practices, and requirements, (d) communicating as needed, and (e) producing and maintaining required documentation and records.
8	Operation	Management must (a) develop and perform all necessary security-related processes, (b) achieve objectives (from section 6), (c) perform risk assessments, and (d) address risks through risk treatment.
9	Performance evaluation	Management must (a) establish key security and risk metrics, (b) monitor processes and controls and analyze the results of monitoring, (c) assess controls for effectiveness, and (d) review metrics, evaluations of processes and controls, and internal audit results.
10	Improvement	Management must respond to nonconformities and continually improve the ISMS through corrective action.

Table 4-10   ISO/IEC 27001 ISMS Requirements

ISO/IEC 27001 and 27002 are available from www.iso.org. These and most other ISO standards are fee-based, meaning that they must be purchased and have licensing and usage restrictions that govern their use in an organization. Generally, these standards are purchased in single quantities and are "single user" in nature, and they are not permitted to be stored on file servers for multi-user usage.

NIST SP 800-53

NIST SP 800-53, "Security and Privacy Controls for Federal Information Systems and Organizations," is published by the Computer Security Division of the U.S. National Institute for Standards and Technology. A summary of controls in NIST SP 800-53 appears in Appendix D, "Security Control Baselines," and detailed descriptions of all controls is found in Appendix F, "Security Control Catalog."

NIST SP 800-53 includes the concept of Low, Medium, and High baselines. These baselines represent collections of controls to be implemented according to the impact level of the information system. In other words, for an information system classified as high impact, the controls to be selected would come from the High baseline in Appendix D. Then, within each control, an organization would implement any stated control enhancements, again based on impact level.

Table 4-11 lists the categories of controls in NIST SP 800-53. NIST SP 800-53 is available from http://csrc.nist.gov/publications/PubsSPs.html. The standard is available without cost or registration.

Center for Internet Security 20 Controls

The Center for Internet Security (CIS) maintains a popular and respected control framework called the *CIS Controls* or commonly known as the *CIS 20*. Still referred to as the *SANS 20 Critical Security Controls*, this control framework was originally developed by the SANS Institute.

Regarded as a simpler set of security controls, the CIS Controls framework has been widely adopted by organizations seeking a control framework, while avoiding more burdensome frameworks like NIST SP 800-53 or ISO/IEC 27001 controls, which must be purchased.

Table 4-12 shows the structure of the CIS Control framework.

The CIS Control framework is structured in a way that makes it easier for security practitioners to understand and use. Within each control category, there is a section

Category	Name
AC	Access Control
AT	Awareness and Training
AU	Audit and Accountability
CA	Security Assessment and Authorization
CM	Configuration Management
CP	Contingency Planning
IA	Identification and Authentication
IR	Incident Response
MA	Maintenance
MP	Media Protection
PE	Physical and Environmental Protection
PL	Planning
PS	Personnel Security
RA	Risk Assessment
SA	System and Services Acquisition
SC	System and Communications Protection
SI	System and Information Integrity

Table 4-11 NIST SP 800-53 Control Categories

Category	Title	Control Objective
CSC1	Inventory of Authorized and Unauthorized Devices	Actively manage (inventory, track, and correct) all hardware devices on the network so that only authorized devices are given access, and unauthorized and unmanaged devices are found and prevented from gaining access.
CSC2	Inventory of Authorized and Unauthorized Software	Actively manage (inventory, track, and correct) all software on the network so that only authorized software is installed and can execute and that unauthorized and unmanaged software is found and prevented from installation or execution.
CSC3	Secure Configurations for Hardware and Software on Mobile Devices, Laptops, Workstations, and Servers	Establish, implement, and actively manage (track, report on, correct) the security configuration of laptops, servers, and workstations using a rigorous configuration management and change control process to prevent attackers from exploiting vulnerable services and settings.
CSC4	Continuous Vulnerability Assessment and Remediation	Continuously acquire, assess, and take action on new information to identify vulnerabilities, remediate, and minimize the window of opportunity for attackers.
CSC5	Controlled Use of Administrative Privileges	The processes and tools used to track/control/prevent/correct the use, assignment, and configuration of administrative privileges on computers, networks, and applications.
CSC6	Maintenance, Monitoring, and Analysis of Audit Logs	Collect, manage, and analyze audit logs of events that could help detect, understand, or recover from an attack.
CSC7	E-mail and Web Browser Protections	Minimize the attack surface and the opportunities for attackers to manipulate human behavior though their interaction with web browsers and e-mail systems.
CSC8	Malware Defenses	Control the installation, spread, and execution of malicious code at multiple points in the enterprise, while optimizing the use of automation to enable rapid updating of defense, data gathering, and corrective action.
CSC9	Limitation and Control of Network Ports, Protocols, and Services	Manage (track/control/correct) the ongoing operational use of ports, protocols, and services on networked devices to minimize windows of vulnerability available to attackers.
CSC10	Data Recovery Capability	The processes and tools used to properly back up critical information with a proven methodology for timely recovery of it.
CSC11	Secure Configurations for Network Devices such as Firewalls, Routers, and Switches	Establish, implement, and actively manage (track, report on, correct) the security configuration of network infrastructure devices using a rigorous configuration management and change control process to prevent attackers from exploiting vulnerable services and settings.
CSC12	Boundary Defense	Detect/prevent/correct the flow of information transferring networks of different trust levels with a focus on security-damaging data.
CSC13	Data Protection	The processes and tools used to prevent data exfiltration, mitigate the effects of exfiltrated data, and ensure the privacy and integrity of sensitive information.

Table 4-12   CIS Control Framework (Source: The Center for Internet Security (CIS) www.cisecurity.org) (*continued*)

CSC14	Controlled Access Based on the Need to Know	The processes and tools used to track/control/prevent/correct secure access to critical assets (e.g., information, resources, systems) according to the formal determination of which persons, computers, and applications have a need and right to access these critical assets based on an approved classification.
CSC15	Wireless Access Control	The processes and tools used to track/control/prevent/correct the security use of wireless local area networks (LANs), access points, and wireless client systems.
CSC16	Account Monitoring and Control	Actively manage the life cycle of system and application accounts—their creation, use, dormancy, deletion—to minimize opportunities for attackers to leverage them.
CSC17	Security Skills Assessment and Appropriate Training to Fill Gaps	For all functional roles in the organization (prioritizing those mission-critical to the business and its security), identify the specific knowledge, skills, and abilities needed to support defense of the enterprise; develop and execute an integrated plan to assess, identify gaps, and remediate through policy, organizational planning, training, and awareness programs.
CSC18	Application Software Security	Manage the security life cycle of all in-house developed and acquired software in order to prevent, detect, and correct security weaknesses.
CSC19	Incident Response and Management	Protect the organization's information, as well as its reputation, by developing and implementing an incident response infrastructure (e.g., plans, defined roles, training, communications, management oversight) for quickly discovering an attack and then effectively containing the damage, eradicating the attacker's presence, and restoring the integrity of the network and systems.
CSC20	Penetration Tests and Red Team Exercises	Test the overall strength of an organization's defenses (the technology, the processes, and the people) by simulating the objectives and actions of an attacker.

Table 4-12   CIS Control Framework (Source: The Center for Internet Security (CIS) www.cisecurity.org)

entitled "Why Is This Control Critical?" followed by the individual controls. This is followed by a section called "Procedures and Tools" that provides additional guidance. Finally, each control category includes a system entity relationship diagram that depicts the control's implementation in an environment. Many consider the CIS Controls as more pragmatic and less academic than NIST SP 800-53 or PCI-DSS.

The CIS Control framework includes one or more controls within each control category. Some controls are flagged as "foundational," meaning they are essential in any organization. The controls not marked as "foundational" may be considered optional.

Some controls include advanced implementation guidelines. For instance, control 8.3 ("Limit use of external devices to those with an approved, documented business need. Monitor for use and attempted use of external devices. Configure laptops, workstations, and servers so that they will not auto-run content from removable media, like USB tokens [i.e., "thumb drives"], USB hard drives, CDs/DVDs, FireWire devices, external serial advanced technology attachment devices, and mounted network shares. Configure systems so that they automatically conduct an anti-malware scan of removable media when inserted.") includes in its advanced guidance, "Actively monitor the use of external devices (in addition to logging)."

The CIS Control framework is available from www.cisecurity.org/critical-controls .cfm without cost, although registration may be required.

Cyber Security Framework

The NIST Cyber Security Framework (CSF) is a risk management methodology and control framework designed for organizations that want a single standard for identifying risk and implementing controls to protect information assets. Developed by the U.S. National Institute for Standards and Technology (NIST) and initially released in 2014, the CSF appears to be gaining acceptance in organizations lacking regulations requiring specific control frameworks (such as HIPAA for organizations in the healthcare industry).

The CSF consists of a framework core comprising five key activities in a security management program. These activities are as follows:

- **Identify**   Develop the organizational understanding to manage cybersecurity risk to systems, assets, data, and capabilities.

- **Protect**   Develop and implement the appropriate safeguards to ensure delivery of critical infrastructure services.

- **Detect**   Develop and implement the appropriate activities to identify the occurrence of a cybersecurity event.

- **Respond**   Develop and implement the appropriate activities 319 to take action regarding a detected cybersecurity event.

- **Recover**   Develop and implement the appropriate activities to maintain plans for resilience and to restore any capabilities or services that were impaired because of a cybersecurity event.

The CSF contains a methodology that an organization can use to assess the overall capability of the organization's overall information security program. The capabilities assessment resembles a maturity assessment, where the program is determined to be in one of the following tiers:

- **Partial**   Risk management is not formalized but instead is reactive and limited to few in the organization. There are no formal relationships with external entities, and supply chain risk management (SCRM) processes are not formalized.

- **Risk Informed**   Risk management is formalized but not working organization-wide. External relationships are established but not formalized. Supply chain risk management processes occur but are not formalized.

- **Repeatable** Risk management practices are formal and approved. The risk management program is integrated into the business. External parties are engaged more so that the organization can respond to events. Supply chain risk management process is governed.

- **Adaptive** Risk management practices are monitored and adapted to meet changing threats and business needs. The risk management program is fully integrated into the organization's business and process. The organization shares information with external parties on a methodical basis, and receives information as well, to prevent events. The supply chain risk management process provides high-level risk awareness to management.

These maturity ratings are similar to those used in the Software Engineering Institute Capability Maturity Model (SEI-CMM) and others.

The CSF contains a methodology for establishing or making improvements to an information security program. The steps in this methodology are similar to the structure in this book:

- **Step 1: Prioritize and Scope** Here, the organization determines which business units or business processes are part of the scope of a new or improving program.

- **Step 2: Orient** The organization identifies assets that are in scope for the program; the risk approach; and applicable laws, regulations, and other legal obligations.

- **Step 3: Create a Current Profile** The organization identifies the category and subcategory outcomes from the Framework Core (the CSF controls) that are currently in place.

- **Step 4: Conduct a Risk Assessment** Here, the organization conducts a risk assessment covering the entire scope of the program. This is an ordinary risk assessment like those described throughout this book, where threats (together with their likelihood and impact) are identified for each asset or asset group.

- **Step 5: Create a Target Profile** The organization determines the desired future states for each of the framework's categories and subcategories (the controls). This includes the desired tier level for each category and subcategory.

- **Step 6: Determine, Analyze, and Prioritize Gaps** The organization compares the current profile (developed in step 3) and the target profile (step 5) and develops a list of gaps. These gaps are analyzed and prioritized, and the necessary resources to close gaps are identified. A cost-benefit analysis is performed, which also helps with prioritization.

- **Step 7: Implement Action Plan** The organization develops plans to close gaps identified and analyzed in step 6. After action plans have been completed, controls are monitored for compliance.

Payment Card Industry Data Security Standard

The Payment Card Industry Data Security Standard (PCI-DSS) is a control framework whose main objective is the protection of *cardholder data*. PCI-DSS was developed by the PCI Security Standards Council, a nonprofit organization started by the major credit card brands in the world including Visa, MasterCard, American Express, Discover, and JCB.

Table 4-13 shows the two-tiered structure of PCI-DSS.

The PCI Security Standards Council has also defined business rules around the PCI-DSS standard. There is a tier structure based on the number of credit card transactions; organizations whose credit card volume exceeds set limits are subject to on-site annual audits, while organizations with lower volumes are permitted to complete annual self-assessments. There is also a distinction between merchants (retail and wholesale establishments that accept credit cards as a form of payment) and service providers (all other organizations that store, process, or transmit credit card data); service providers are required to comply with additional controls.

Build and Maintain a Secure Network and Systems	
Requirement 1	Install and maintain a firewall configuration to protect cardholder data
Requirement 2	Do not use vendor-supplied defaults for system passwords and other security parameters
Protect Cardholder Data	
Requirement 3	Protect stored cardholder data
Requirement 4	Encrypt transmission of cardholder data across open, public networks
Maintain a Vulnerability Management Program	
Requirement 5	Protect all systems against malware and regularly update anti-virus software or programs
Requirement 6	Develop and maintain secure systems and applications
Implement Strong Access Control Measures	
Requirement 7	Restrict access to cardholder data by business need to know
Requirement 8	Identify and authenticate access to system components
Requirement 9	Restrict physical access to cardholder data
Regularly Monitor and Test Networks	
Requirement 10	Track and monitor all access to network resources and cardholder data
Requirement 11	Regularly test security systems and processes
Maintain an Information Security Policy	
Requirement 12	Maintain a policy that addresses information security for all personnel
Appendix A	Additional PCI DSS Requirements
Appendix A1	Additional PCI DSS Requirements for Shared Hosting Providers
Appendix A2	Additional PCI DSS Requirements for Entities using SSL/early TLS
Appendix A3	Designated Entities Supplemental Validation

Table 4-13   PCI-DSS Control Framework (Source: PCI Security Standards Council, www.pcisecuritystandards.org.)

The PCI Security Standards Council also has a program of annual training and exams for personnel who can perform PCI audits and for the organizations that employ those people. The certifications are as follows:

- **Payment Card Industry Qualified Security Assessor (PCI-QSA)**   These are external auditors who perform audits of merchants and service providers that are required to undergo annual audits (as well as organizations that undertake these audits voluntarily).

- **Payment Card Industry Internal Security Assessor (PCI-ISA)**   These are employees of merchants and service providers required to be compliant with the PCI-DSS. The PCI Security Standards Council does not require any employees of merchants or service providers to be certified to PCI-ISA; however, the certification does help those so certified to better understand the PCI-DSS standard, thereby leading to better compliance.

- **Payment Card Industry Professional (PCIP)**   This is an entry-level certification for IT professionals who want to learn more about the PCI-DSS standard and earn a certification that designates them as a PCI subject-matter expert.

The PCI Security Standards Council has published additional requirements and standards, including the following:

- **Payment Application Data Security Standard (PA-DSS)**   This is a security standard for commercial credit card payment applications.

- **PCI Forensic Investigator (PFI)**   Requirements for organizations and individuals who will perform forensic investigations of credit card breaches.

- **Approved Scanning Vendors (ASV)**   Requirements for organizations that will perform security scans of merchants and service providers.

- **Qualified Integrators and Resellers (QIR)**   Requirements for organizations that sell and integrate PCI-certified payment applications.

- **Point-to-Point Encryption (P2PE)**   This is a security standard for payment applications that utilize point-to-point encryption of card data.

- **Token Service Providers (TSP)**   Physical and logical security requirements and assessment procedures for token service providers that generate and issue EMV payment tokens.

- **PIN Transaction Security (PTS)**   Requirements for the secure management, processing, and transmission of personal identification number (PIN) data during online and offline transactions at ATMs and POS terminals.

Health Insurance Portability and Accountability Act

The U.S. Health Insurance Portability and Accountability Act (HIPAA) was enacted in 2008 to address a number of issues around the processing of healthcare information, including the protection of healthcare information in electronic form, commonly known as electronic protected healthcare information (ePHI). Organizations that deliver medical care, as well as organizations with access to such information, including medical insurance companies and most employers, are required to comply with HIPAA Security Rule requirements. Table 4-14 shows the structure of the HIPAA Security Rule.

Each requirement in the HIPAA Security Rule is labeled as Required or Addressable. Requirements that are Required must be implemented. For those requirements that are Addressable, organizations are required to undergo analysis to determine whether they must be implemented.

COBIT 5

To ensure that a security program is aligned with business objectives, the COBIT 5 control framework of 5 principles and 37 processes is an industry-wide standard. The five principles are as follows:

- Meeting Stakeholder Needs
- Covering the Enterprise End-to-End
- Applying a Single, Integrated Framework
- Enabling a Holistic Approach
- Separating Governance from Management

COBIT 5 contains more than 1100 control activities to support these principles.

Established in 1996 by ISACA and the IT Governance Institute, COBIT is the result of industry-wide consensus by managers, auditors, and IT users. Today, COBIT 5 is accepted as a best-practices IT process and control framework. Starting with Version 5, COBIT has absorbed ISACA's Risk IT Framework and Val IT Framework.

Section	Description
164.302	Applicability
164.304	Definitions
164.306	Security standards: General rules
164.308	Administrative safeguards
164.310	Physical safeguards
164.312	Technical safeguards
164.314	Organizational requirements
164.316	Policies and procedures and documentation requirements
164.318	Compliance dates for the initial implementation of the security standards

Table 4-14   Requirement Sections in the HIPAA Security Rule

COSO

The Committee of Sponsoring Organizations of the Treadway Commission (COSO) is a private-sector organization that provides thought leadership through the development of frameworks and guidance on enterprise risk management, internal control, and fraud deterrence. Its control framework is used by U.S. public companies for management of their financial accounting and reporting systems.

COSO is a joint initiative of the following private-sector associations:

- American Accounting Association (AAA)
- American Institute of Certified Public Accountants (AICPA)
- Financial Executives International (FEI)
- The Association of Accountants and Financial Professionals in Business (IMA)
- The Institute of Internal Auditors (IIA)

The COSO framework is constructed through a set of 17 principles within 5 framework components, which are shown in Table 4-15. The COSO framework itself is proprietary and can be purchased from www.coso.org.

Control Environment
1. The organization demonstrates a commitment to integrity and ethical values.
2. The board of directors demonstrates independence from management and exercises oversight of the development and performance of internal control.
3. Management establishes, with board oversight, structures, reporting lines, and appropriate authorities and responsibilities in the pursuit of objectives.
4. The organization demonstrates a commitment to attract, develop, and retain competent individuals in alignment with objectives.
5. The organization holds individuals accountable for their internal control responsibilities in the pursuit of objectives.
Risk Assessment
6. The organization specifies objectives with sufficient clarity to enable the identification and assessment of risks relating to objectives.
7. The organization identifies risks to the achievement of its objectives across the entity and analyzes risks as a basis for determining how the risks should be managed.
8. The organization considers the potential for fraud in assessing risks to the achievement of objectives.
9. The organization identifies and assesses changes that could significantly impact the system of internal control.
Control Activities
10. The organization selects and develops control activities that contribute to the mitigation of risks to the achievement of objectives to acceptable levels.
11. The organization selects and develops general control activities over technology to support the achievement of objectives.
12. The organization deploys control activities through policies that establish what is expected and procedures that put policies into action.

Table 4-15   COSO Framework and Principles (*continued*)

Information and Communication

13. The organization obtains or generates and uses relevant, quality information to support the functioning of internal control.

14. The organization internally communicates information, including objectives and responsibilities for internal control, necessary to support the functioning of internal control.

15. The organization communicates with external parties regarding matters affecting the functioning of internal control.

Monitoring Activities

16. The organization selects, develops, and performs ongoing and/or separate evaluations to ascertain whether the components of internal control are present and functioning.

17. The organization evaluates and communicates internal control deficiencies in a timely manner to those parties responsible for taking corrective action, including senior management and the board of directors, as appropriate.

Table 4-15   COSO Framework and Principles

Figure 4-16 depicts the multifaceted structure of the COSO framework.

NERC Reliability Standards

The North American Electric Reliability Corporation (NERC) develops standards for use by electric utilities in most of North America. These standards encompass all aspects of power generation and distribution, including security. Table 4-16 shows the security portion of NERC standards.

Figure 4-16
COSO framework components

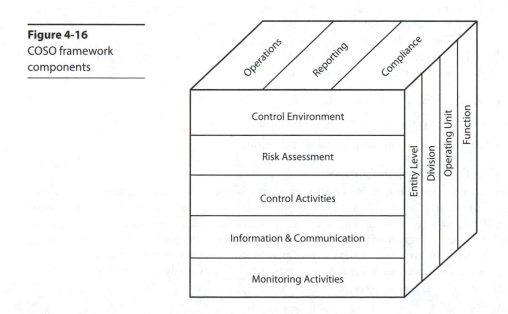

Section	Title
CIP-002-5.1a	Cyber Security – BES (Bulk Electric System) Cyber System Categorization
CIP-003-6	Cyber Security – Security Management Controls
CIP-003-7	Cyber Security – Security Management Controls
CIP-004-6	Cyber Security – Personnel & Training
CIP-005-5	Cyber Security – Electronic Security Perimeter(s)
CIP-006-6	Cyber Security – Physical Security of BES Cyber Systems
CIP-007-6	Cyber Security – System Security Management
CIP-008-5	Cyber Security – Incident Reporting and Response Planning
CIP-009-6	Cyber Security – Recovery Plans for BES Cyber Systems
CIP-010-2	Cyber Security – Configuration Change Management and Vulnerability Assessments
CIP-011-2	Cyber Security – Information Protection
CIP-014-2	Physical Security

Table 4-16 NERC Critical Infrastructure Protection Framework

Prior to the Northeast Blackout of 2003, NERC standards were voluntary. The Energy Policy Act of 2005 authorized the Federal Energy Regulatory Commission (FERC) to designate NERC standards as mandatory. NERC has the authority to enforce its standards and does so through audits and levies fines to public utilities that are noncompliant.

CSA Control Framework

The Cloud Security Alliance (CSA) has developed a control framework known as the Cloud Controls Matrix (CCM) that is designed to provide security principles to cloud vendors and to assist customers with assessments of cloud vendors.

Table 4-17 shows the structure of the CSA CCM.

The Cloud Security Alliance has developed an assurance framework known as CSA STAR that includes three assurance levels:

- Self-assessment
- Third-party assessment-based certification
- Continuous monitoring-based certification

Service Organization Controls

The trend of IT outsourcing has continued unabated and is even accelerating with so many organizations shifting to cloud-based applications and infrastructure. Obtaining assurance that IT controls exist and are effective in these third-party organizations can be cost-prohibitive: most organizations' internal IT audit functions do not have sufficient resources to audit even the topmost critical service providers. And most service providers will not permit their customers to audit their controls as this is also costly for service providers.

Domain	Description
AIS	Application & Interface Security
AAC	Audit Assurance & Compliance
BCR	Business Continuity Management & Operational Resilience
CCC	Change Control & Configuration Management
DSI	Data Security & Information Lifecycle
DCS	Datacenter Security
EKM	Encryption & Key Management
GRM	Governance and Risk Management
HRS	Human Resources
IAM	Identity & Access Management
IVS	Infrastructure & Virtualization Security
IPY	Interoperability & Portability
MOS	Mobile Security
SEF	Security Incident Management, E-Discovery, & Cloud Forensics
STA	Supply Chain Management, Transparency, and Accountability
TVM	Threat and Vulnerability Management

Table 4-17 Domains of the Cloud Security Alliance Cloud Controls Matrix

In the early 1990s, the American Institute for Certified Public Accountants (AICPA) developed the Statement on Auditing Standards No. 70 (SAS-70) standard that opened the door for audits that could be performed by public accounting firms on service providers, with audit reports made available to service providers' customers. After the Sarbanes–Oxley Act (SOX) took effect in 2003, SAS70 audits of service providers satisfied the requirements for U.S. public companies to obtain assurance of control effectiveness for outsourced IT service providers, particularly those that supported financial applications.

The SOC1, SOC2, and SOC3 audit standards are discussed next.

Service Organization Controls 1   In 2010, the SAS-70 standard was superseded by the Statement on Standards for Attestation Engagements No. 16 (SSAE16) standard in the United States and by International Standards for Assurance Engagements No. 3402 (ISAE3402) outside the United States. In 2017, SSAE16 was replaced with SSAE18. SSAE16, SSAE18, and ISAE3402 are commonly known as Service Organization Controls 1 (SOC1).

In a SOC1 audit, the service organization specifies the controls that are to be audited. While a service organization has complete latitude on which controls are in scope for a SOC1 audit, the service organization must be mindful of which controls its customers and their internal and external auditors will expect to see in a SOC1 audit report.

There are two basic types of SOC1 audits:

- **Type I**   This is a point-in-time examination of the service organization's controls and their design.
- **Type II**   This is an audit that takes place over a period of time (typically six months to one year), where the auditor examines not only the design of in-scope controls (as in the Type I) but also business records that reveal whether controls are effective.

SOC1 audits must be performed by CPA firms in good standing.

Service Organization Controls 2   The Service Organization Controls 2 (SOC2) audit standard was developed for IT service providers of all types that want to demonstrate assurance in its controls to its customers.

A SOC2 audit of a service provider is an audit of one or more of the following five trust principles:

- **Security**   The system is protected against unauthorized access.
- **Availability**   The system is available for operation and use as committed or agreed.
- **Processing integrity**   System processing is complete, valid, accurate, timely, and authorized.
- **Confidentiality**   Information designated as confidential is protected as committed or agreed.
- **Privacy**   Personal information is collected, used, retained, disclosed, and destroyed in accordance with the privacy notice commitments.

There are several controls within each trust principles. All controls within each selected trust principle are included in a SOC2 audit.

There are two basic types of SOC2 audits:

- **Type I**   This is a point-in-time examination of the service organization's controls and their design.
- **Type II**   This is an audit that takes place over a period of time (typically six months to one year), where the auditor examines not only the design of in-scope controls (as in the Type I) but also business records that reveal whether controls are effective.

SOC1 audits must be performed by CPA firms in good standing.

Service Organization Controls 3   A Service Organization Control 3 (SOC3) audit is similar to a SOC2 audit, except that a SOC3 report lacks a description of control testing or opinion of control effectiveness. Like a SOC2, a SOC3 audit includes any or all of the five trust principles: security, availability, processing integrity, confidentiality, and privacy.

Controls Development

The development of controls is a foundational part of any security program. To develop controls, a security manager must have an intimate level of knowledge of the organization's mission, goals, and objectives, as well as a good understanding of the organization's degree of risk tolerance. Figure 4-17 illustrates the relationship between an organization and the fundamentals of a security program.

As stated elsewhere in this book, the most common approach to controls development is the selection of an already-established control framework, such as any of those discussed earlier in this section. However, an organization is also free to develop a control framework from scratch. Table 4-18 illustrates the pros and cons of each approach.

Developing Controls from Scratch

For organizations that have elected to develop their controls from scratch, the first step is the development of high-level control objectives. These control objectives could be thought of as overarching principles, out of which individual controls will be developed.

Control objectives are typically similar from organization to organization. However, since each organization is different, some organizations will have one or two unique control objectives that address specific business activities or objectives.

Figure 4-17 Relationship between an organization's mission, goals, objectives, risk tolerance, policies, and controls

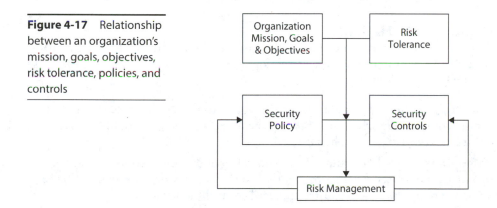

	Advantages	Disadvantages
Develop controls from scratch	Controls will address the organization's specific risks (provided a thorough and effective risk assessment and proper risk treatment are performed).	Takes more time as one or more risk assessments plus risk treatment must first be performed.
Adopt an existing control framework	Faster implementation of most controls that will address the organization's specific risks.	Controls will not address the organization's specific risks.

Table 4-18 Controls Development Comparison

Management will approve policies and activities in the security program.
All organization and worker activities will be legal and ethical.
Qualified personnel will periodically assess security and risk and make recommendations for improvement.
Only approved personnel may access organization information and work areas.
Access rules and rights will be periodically reviewed.
All workers and third parties will be vetted prior to being given access to proprietary information and work areas.
Changes to infrastructure, applications, and software will be controlled and managed.
Information will be protected and retained according to its sensitivity and value.
Only approved hardware and software will be used.
A formal incident detection and response function will be established and managed.
Security considerations will be incorporated into all business development and acquisition activities.

Table 4-19   Sample Control Objectives

Table 4-19 shows a sample set of control objectives.

Developing Control Details

Whether the organization adopts an existing control framework or develops controls from scratch, the security manager must develop several elements for each control. These elements include the following:

- **Control number**   The index number assigned to this control, according to the control numbering scheme adopted by the organization. This could be a simple number (e.g., 1, 2, 3) or a hierarchical number (e.g., 10.5.4).

- **Mapping**   Any relationships of this control to one or more controls in other control frameworks, whether those other control frameworks are specific to the organization or they are industry-standard control frameworks.

- **Title**   The title or name of the control.

- **Control objective**   In a control framework with high-level control objectives, this is a statement of a desired activity.

- **Narrative**   A detailed description of the control. Generally, this should not include implementation details (which could vary from system to system or from place to place) but instead the details needed so that a business owner, auditor, or IT worker understands the intent of the control. There should be enough detail so that IT workers and other personnel can properly implement the control.

- **Scope**   The locations, business units, departments, or systems that are affected by the control.

- **Risk**   A description of the risk that this control is intended to address.

- **Owner**   The business owner (or owners) of the control.
- **Affected and related business processes**   The business processes related to the control, as well as the business processes affected by the control.
- **Control frequency**   How often the control is performed, executed, or used.
- **Classification**   This includes whether it is automatic or manual, preventive or detective, and other classification details.
- **Testing procedure**   The steps required to evaluate the control for effectiveness. Like the control narrative, this should be a general description and not specific to any particular technology.
- **Developed by**   The name of the person who developed the control.
- **Approved by**   The name of the person who approved the control.
- **Approval date**   The date of the most recent approval of the control.
- **Version**   The version number of the control, according to whatever version numbering system is used by the organization.
- **Cross-references**   Cross-references to other controls, control frameworks, systems, documents, departments, processes, risk assessments, or risk treatment. Cross-references can help personnel better understand how controls relate to other activities or events in the organization.
- **Modification history**   A list of the changes made to the control, including a description, who made each change, who approved each change, and the date.

While organizations may prefer to document its controls in worksheets, a better approach is the development of individual documents for each control. This will lead to better outcomes as it will be easier to control versions of individual control documents.

Control Assessment

Control assessment consists of activities intended to determine whether individual controls or groups of controls are effectively functioning. Controls can be assessed in several ways, including the following:

- Internal audit
- External audit
- Control self-assessment

These techniques are discussed in detail earlier in this chapter in the "Audits" section.

Metrics and Monitoring

A *metric* is a measurement of a periodic or ongoing activity for the purpose of understanding the activity within the context of overall business operations. Metrics is the use of collecting these measurements and revealing or publishing them to various business audiences.

In the context of the overall information security program, *monitoring* is the continuous or regular evaluation of a system or control to determine its operation or effectiveness. Monitoring generally includes two activities:

- Management's review of certain qualitative aspects of an information security program or of the entire program. This may take the form of an executive briefing delivered by the security manager.
- Management's review of key metrics in the information security program to understand its effectiveness, efficiency, and performance.

Types of Metrics

There are many different activities and events in an information security program and its controls that can be measured, as well as different ways of depicting and explaining those measurements. When building and improving an information security program, security managers need to understand that there is no single framework of metrics. Instead, security managers need to determine what metrics are important for various audiences and purposes and proceed to develop those metrics.

One of the most important aspects of metrics is context. Producing raw numbers such as the number of packets dropped by an Internet firewall rarely has meaning to any audience. Security managers need to develop metrics that have appropriate context for whatever audience they are intended.

Aside from automated systems that keep records that can be examined later, there is often little point in developing metrics that have no audience. Such a pursuit would only take time away from more valuable activities.

Compliance

Compliance metrics are measures of key controls related to requirements in regulations, legal contracts, or internal objectives. Compliance metrics depict the level of conformance to these requirements.

Organizations need to understand the business context of compliance metrics, including the consequences of noncompliance. Security managers need to consider the tolerance for noncompliance with each metric, including the willingness and ability for the organization to initiate corrective action when noncompliant activities occur.

Organizational Awareness

Organizational awareness metrics help management understand the number of workers who understand security policies and requirements and how well they are known. Typical metrics in organizational awareness include the following:

- Percentage of employees who complete security training
- Percentage of employees who acknowledge awareness of, and conformance to, security policies
- Average scores on quizzes and tests of knowledge of security safeguards

Operational Productivity

Operational productivity metrics show how efficiently internal staff are used to perform essential functions. Productivity metrics can help build business cases for automation of routine tasks. Example productivity metrics include the following:

- Number of hours required to perform a segregation of duties review
- Number of hours required to perform a vulnerability assessment
- Number of hours required to perform a risk assessment

Organizational Support

Operational support metrics show the degree of support of organizational objectives. Arguably this is a subjective metric, as it can be difficult to produce meaningful measurements. While it is possible to show the achievement of key objectives, measuring the degree of support that led to their achievement may be difficult—was an achievement the result of a determined few or the whole organization?

Often, organizational support metrics take the form of project and program dashboards for projects and programs that support the achievement of organizational objectives. However, failure to complete a project on time is not necessarily an indication of support or the lack thereof but may reflect unanticipated obstacles or changes in project scope.

Technical Security Architecture

Technical security architecture metrics are typically the measures of events taking place in automated systems such as firewalls, intrusion detection and prevention systems, data loss prevention systems, spam filters, and anti-malware systems. This is generally the richest set of metrics data available to a security manager but also a category of metrics that is often presented without proper business context. For example, the number of attacks blocked by a firewall or the number of malware infections blocked by anti-malware software may have operational meaning, but these will mean nothing to management. Executives would be right to ask whether an increase in the number of blocked attacks is good, bad, or meaningless.

There are, however, some metrics available that have meaning for business executives. Examples include the following:

- Percentage of employees who responded to (clicked links or opened attachments) e-mail attacks
- Number of attacks that bypassed network controls such as firewalls, intrusion detection and prevention systems, and web filters, which resulted in unscheduled downtime
- Number of malware attacks that circumvented anti-malware controls and resulted in unscheduled downtime
- Number of brute-force password attacks that were blocked
- Number of records compromised that required disclosure

Operational Performance

Operational performance metrics generally show how well personnel are performing critical security functions. Processes measured by these metrics need to have sufficiently detailed business records so that metrics can be objectively measured. These are some examples of operational performance metrics:

- Elapsed time between onset of a security incident and incident declaration
- Elapsed time between declaration of an incident and its containment
- Elapsed time between publication of a critical vulnerability and its discovery in the organization's systems
- Percentage of critical systems not patched with critical patches within SLA
- Number of changes made without change control board approval
- Amount of unscheduled downtime of critical systems for security-related reasons

Security Cost Efficiency

Metrics related to security cost efficiency are used to measure the resources required for key controls. Security managers need to be careful with cost efficiency metrics, as demands for improvement (e.g., reduced costs) over time can result in increased risk. This is compounded by the fact that it is relatively easy to measure cost, whereas the measurement of risk is more subjective and qualitative.

Example cost efficiency metrics include the following:

- Cost of anti-malware controls per user
- Cost of anti-phishing and anti-spam controls per user
- Cost of centralized network defenses, such as firewalls, per user

Security managers should consider including staff costs in addition to tool costs to provide a more complete and accurate picture of the total costs for controls.

Audiences

When building or improving a metrics program, security managers need to consider the purpose of any particular metric and the audience to whom it is sent. A common mistake made by security managers is the publication of metrics to various audiences without first understanding whether any individual metric will have meaning to any particular person. For example, a metric showing the number of packets dropped by a firewall will have absolutely no meaning to a board of directors—nor would a trend of this metric or time have any meaning.

Some metrics will have only operational value, while other operational metrics can be successfully transformed into a management or strategic metric when portrayed in context. For example, a metric on the number of malware attacks has no business context; however, successful malware attacks that result in business disruptions have far more meaning. Or, a metric on patch management SLAs by itself has no business context, but transforming that into a metric showing critical systems not patched within SLAs depicts higher-than-desired business risk and makes sense to executive audiences.

Continuous Improvement

Continuous improvement represents the desire to increase the efficiency and effectiveness of processes and controls over time. It could be said that continuous improvement is a characteristic of an organization's culture. The pursuit of continuous improvement is a roundabout way of pursuing quality.

A requirement in ISO/IEC 27001 requires that management promote continual improvement and that security policy include a commitment to the continual improvement of the ISMS. ISO/IEC 27001 also requires that management review of the ISMS identify opportunities for continual improvement. The standard also explicitly requires organizations to "continually improve the suitability, adequacy, and effectiveness of its information security management system."

NIST SP800-53, "Security and Privacy Controls for Federal Information Systems and Organizations," similarly requires that an organization's risk management program incorporate a feedback loop for continuous improvement. Control SA-15 (6) states the following: "The organization requires the developer of the information system, system component, or information system service to implement an explicit process to continuously improve the development process."

The NIST Cyber Security Framework cites the requirement for continuous improvement throughout the standard. For instance, in the seven steps for creating an information security program, NIST CSF asserts in section 3.2 that "these steps should be repeated as necessary to continuously improve cybersecurity."

Chapter Review

An information security program is comprised of activities used to identify and treat risks. At tactical and strategic levels, all activities in a program fulfill this purpose. A security program is also outcomes-based; when a strategy is developed, the objectives of the strategy are desired end states, or outcomes. Tasks and projects carried out in the program bring the organization closer to these desired outcomes.

A charter document defines the main, long-term objectives of a security program, and it defines roles and responsibilities. The charter will typically define the scope of a program—the departments, business units, and locations that will be subject to the program. A road map is a strategic document that describes the steps to be taken to realize key objectives.

Security management frameworks are models for the overall operation of a security program. Typically, these frameworks are high level and include key activities such as risk management and governance.

Security architecture represents the overall vision as well as the details that define the role of technology and asset protection. The Open Group Architecture Framework (TOGAF) and the Zachman framework are two architecture frameworks that can be used to build a security architecture.

Security governance is the set of activities that enable management to have visibility and exert control over the security program. A key to successful governance is to establish a security steering committee or security council consisting of stakeholders from across the business.

Risk management is a life-cycle process used to identify, analyze, and treat risks. The four options for risk treatment are accept, mitigate, transfer, and avoid. These risk treatment decisions should be made by senior management or by an executive-level steering committee. Proceedings including risk decisions should be documented and maintained as part of the security program's business record.

The risk management life cycle consists of regular and ad hoc risk assessments. In a typical risk assessment, assets and threats against them are identified and evaluated. Risk analysis is a detailed activity that is used to better understand individual risks and to explore various risk mitigation and risk treatment options.

A risk assessment consists of asset identification, threat analysis, vulnerability identification, probability, and impact analysis. The risk assessment continues with qualitative, semiquantitative, or quantitative risk analysis.

Organizations undertake internal and external audits and reviews as part of its overall effort to determine the effectiveness of its controls. Like risk assessments, the organization needs to properly scope and empower audit projects so that there are sufficient resources to successfully perform and complete the audit. Control self-assessments are a form of internal audit, performed by control owners as a means for reinforcing accountability for the effectiveness of controls.

When developing security policies, the security manager needs to carefully weigh many considerations including applicable laws, risk tolerance, controls, and organizational culture. Security policy needs to align with the business and also with its controls.

Third-party risk management is a critical activity whose purpose is to identify risks in third-party organizations that have access to critical or sensitive data or that perform critical operational functions. Various techniques are needed to identify and manage risks since many third parties are less than transparent about their internal operations and risks.

Security programs include a variety of administrative activities that are vital to its success. One important success factor is the development of strategic partnerships with many internal departments in an organization, as well as external organizations and agencies. These partnerships enable the security manager to better influence internal events, learn more about external events, and obtain assistance from outside entities as needed.

Security managers need to understand how to develop business cases to secure funding for security projects. Rather than focus on return on investment (ROI), security managers need to focus on risk reduction and how each project contributes toward the fulfillment of strategic objectives.

Event monitoring is the activity whereby security events that occur in information systems will be made known to security personnel who can act on them to correct situations and avoid incidents.

Vulnerability management is the activity where tasks are carried out to identify vulnerabilities in information systems, which are followed by remediation such as installing security patches or changing security configurations.

Secure engineering and development is focused on the safe development of applications and systems that are free of exploitable security defects by design and also on the protection of systems and information related to engineering and development such as source code.

Several means are used to protect networks (and the systems and applications that reside on them) including firewalls, network segmentation, intrusion prevention systems, network anomaly detection, packet sniffers, web content filters, cloud access security brokers, DNS filters, spam and phishing filters, and network access control.

Endpoint systems, including desktop computers, laptop computers, tablet computers, and smartphones, require particular protective controls to protect them from compromise.

Identity and access management is comprised of technologies and activities to ensure that only authorized personnel have access to systems and information.

Because so many security incidents are a result of human error, security awareness training is an essential activity that helps all personnel better understand the hazards caused by poor judgment and lapses in attention.

Data security controls help to ensure that only authorized personnel are able to access, add, delete, and update business information. Several controls are often used in combination to protect information, including access controls, cryptography, backup and recovery, data loss prevention, cloud access security brokers, and user behavior analytics.

IT service management represents a collection of operational activities designed to ensure the quality of IT services. These activities include several business processes including service desk, incident management, problem management, change management, configuration management, release management, service-level management, financial management, capacity management, service continuity management, and availability management.

Controls and control frameworks are used to enforce desired outcomes. Controls need to be carefully considered, as each consumes resources. Security managers need to understand the various types of controls (e.g., preventive, detective, deterrent, manual, automatic, etc.) so that the right types of controls can be implemented.

Metrics are used to measure key activities and are used to determine whether key objectives are being met. Security managers need to select metrics carefully and consider the audience for each.

Notes

- Involving stakeholders from across the business will help ensure the success of a security program. This is because stakeholders will feel that they have a voice in how security is managed in the organization.

- In a typical security program, the security manager will select a control framework as a starting point and then add, change, or remove controls over time as a result of the risk management process. The initial control framework should be considered only a starting point and not the set of controls that the organization is required to permanently manage.

- When performing a risk assessment, the security manager will typically select assets to be assessed and will use a generic list of typical threats such as the list contained in NIST SP 800-33, "Guide for Conducting Risk Assessments." The security manager will add other relevant threats to this list.

- The outcome of risk assessments may result in one or more additions to the organization's risk register.

- While security policy should cover a wide range of topics, the security manager is free to include them in a comprehensive document or in separate documents.

- Third-party risk management is best thought of as an extension of an organization's risk management program, with special procedures for conducting risk assessments of third-party organizations that store, process, or transmit sensitive or critical data on behalf of the organization or that perform critical operations.

- Because of the worldwide shortage of qualified security personnel, it is especially important for the security manager to pay particular attention to the state and development of security staff to ensure they are engaged, challenged, and adequately compensated.

- Security managers need to avoid the return on investment or return on security investment trap and focus budget efforts instead on risk reduction.

- Security managers should resist the temptation to utilize every type of network protection technology and instead implement those in response to specific risks and threats.

- As an organization moves away from individual system and application authentication to centralized authentication, the implementation of stronger password controls as well as multifactor authentication becomes more important. This is because the consequences of compromised credentials increases since those credentials provide access to potentially many systems.

- Despite the most effective controls and the best intentions on the part of security personnel, employees who are intent on stealing internal information are usually able to do so. Rather than invest everything in preventive controls, some attention to detective controls is warranted.

- Without effective IT service management, no security manager can hope that information security will become truly effective.

- Security managers prefer preventive controls but will sometimes need to settle on detective controls.

- The selection of a control framework is less important than the risk management process that will, over time, mold it into the controls that need to exist.

- Many organizations need to implement multiple control frameworks in response to applicable regulations and other obligations. In such cases, security managers should consider mapping them into a single control framework.

- For security metrics, context and audience are critical.

- There is always room for improvement.

Questions

1. The purpose of security governance is to:
   A. Make risk treatment decisions.
   B. Enforce violations of information security policy.
   C. Provide management with visibility and control of the security program.
   D. Ensure compliance with applicable laws and regulations.

2. The purpose of risk management is to:
   A. Identify risks and make decisions about them.
   B. Control risk mitigation activities.
   C. Facilitate risk assessments and risk analysis.
   D. Facilitate the achievement of strategic program objectives.

3. The definition of risk is:
   A. Threat times impact
   B. Threat plus vulnerability
   C. Threat times vulnerability
   D. Probability times impact

4. The identification of unwanted events and their likelihood of occurrence is known as:
   A. Risk analysis
   B. Vulnerability analysis
   C. Threat analysis
   D. Probability analysis

5. A weakness in a system that makes it possible for an attacker to successfully compromise it is known as a:
   A. Threat
   B. Vulnerability
   C. Risk
   D. Patch

6. The purpose of quantitative risk analysis is to:

    A. Update financial statements with risk scenarios.

    B. Understand the potential cost of a breach.

    C. Understand the probability of a breach.

    D. Determine the most likely method of a breach.

7. The four options for risk treatment are:

    A. Mitigate, transfer, avoid, accept

    B. Accept, share, transfer, ignore

    C. Ignore, accept, share, mitigate

    D. Mitigate, ignore, share, accept

8. The best place to document new risks is:

    A. Asset ledger

    B. Risk ledger

    C. Incident log

    D. GRC system

9. The purpose of control self-assessments is to:

    A. Transfer risk to control owners.

    B. Reduce audit costs.

    C. Reduce workload in internal audit.

    D. Reinforce accountability for control effectiveness.

10. The purpose of security policy is:

    A. Comply with regulations requiring policy.

    B. Enforce accountability for all employees.

    C. Restate security controls in everyday language.

    D. Define acceptable and unacceptable behavior.

11. The best method for identifying third-party service organizations is to:

    A. Inventory all legal agreements.

    B. Examine firewall access logs.

    C. Consult with legal, procurement, and IT.

    D. Consult with accounting and legal.

12. The purpose of event monitoring to is:

    A. Identify anomalous behavior on the part of employees.

    B. Confirm that all systems and devices are performing adequately.

    C. Confirm that all systems and devices are in compliance with policy.

    D. Identify unwanted events that could be a sign of a security breach.

13. The purpose of vulnerability management is to:

    A. Identify and remediate vulnerabilities in all systems.

    B. Transfer vulnerabilities to low risk systems.

    C. Identify exploitable vulnerabilities in all systems.

    D. Transfer vulnerabilities to third parties.

14. Intrusion prevention systems are different from firewalls because:

    A. Their rules can be changed automatically.

    B. They examine the contents of headers instead of the entire payload.

    C. They examine the contents of packets instead of just the headers.

    D. They alert personnel about threats but do not stop them.

15. The purpose of web content filters is to:

    A. Permit management to track who visits which web sites.

    B. Block user access to web sites that pose a threat.

    C. Block user access to web sites that are a waste of time.

    D. Scan content for malware.

Answers

    1. C. The purpose of security governance is to create a means by which executive management is made aware of developments in the organization's security program and to enable them to control outcomes in the program.

    2. A. Risk management is the life-cycle process whereby new risks are identified, analyzed, and decisions made concerning their disposition.

    3. D. The definition of risk is probability × impact.

    4. C. Threat analysis is the examination of all reasonable threats.

    5. B. A vulnerability is a weakness in a system that could be exploited by an attacker.

    6. B. Quantitative risk analysis is used to determine the potential cost of a breach.

7. **A.** The four options for risk treatment are mitigate, transfer, avoid, and accept.

8. **B.** New risks are recorded in the organization's risk ledger.

9. **D.** Control self-assessments involve control owners and empower them to identify problems with their controls.

10. **D.** Security policy, and every other policy, defines acceptable and unacceptable behavior.

11. **C.** The best method for identifying an organization's third-party service organizations is to work with key departments including IT, legal, procurement, finance, and others.

12. **D.** Event monitoring is used to identify events that could be a sign of unwanted behavior including a security breach.

13. **A.** The purpose of vulnerability management is to identify vulnerabilities in information systems and devices and to remediate vulnerabilities on a schedule according to risk.

14. **C.** The main difference between intrusion prevention systems and firewalls is that intrusion prevention systems examine the entire contents of packets, whereas firewalls examine only packet headers.

15. **B.** The main purpose of web content filters is to block user access to web sites that pose a threat of some kind.

Information Security Incident Management

In this chapter, you will learn about

- Security incident response
- Developing security incident response plans and playbooks
- Developing and testing business continuity plans
- Developing and testing disaster recovery plans

The topics in this chapter represent 19 percent of the Certified Information Security Manager (CISM) examination. This chapter discusses CISM job practice 4, "Information Security Incident Management."

While security incident response, business continuity planning, and disaster recovery planning are often considered separate disciplines, they share a common objective: the best possible continuity of business operations during and after a threat event. There are a wide variety of threat events that, if realized, will call upon one or more of the three disciplines in response. Table 5-1 illustrates responses to threat events.

The final example in Table 5-1 is an incident where an attacker damages information or information systems. An incident of this type will necessarily require both security incident response and business continuity planning. Security incident response is enacted to discover the techniques used by the attacker to compromise systems so that any vulnerabilities can be remediated, thereby preventing similar attacks in the future. Business continuity response is required so that the organization can recover its systems and resume operations as quickly as possible. Figure 5-1 depicts the relationship between incident response, business continuity planning, and disaster recovery planning.

Event Type	Response
Natural disaster	Business continuity and/or disaster recovery
Man-made disaster	Business continuity and/or disaster recovery
Theft of information	Security incident response
Deliberate corruption of information or systems by an attacker	Security incident response, together with business continuity

Table 5-1 Event Types and Typical Response

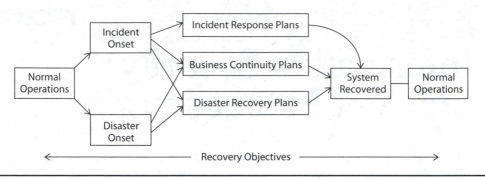

Figure 5-1 Relationship between incident response, business continuity planning, and disaster recovery planning

Security incident response, business continuity, and disaster recovery all require advance planning so that the organization will have discussed, documented, and outlined the responses required for various types of incidents in advance of their occurrence. Risk assessments are the foundation of planning for all three disciplines, as it is necessary to discover relevant risks and to establish priorities during response.

One of the byproducts of planning for security incident response, business continuity, and disaster recovery is the improvement of systems and processes. Primarily, planning efforts reveal improvement opportunities that, when implemented, will result in information systems being more secure and resilient. These improvements generally mean that incidents are either less likely to occur, or they will have less impact on the organization.

Security Incident Response Overview

A security incident is an event where the confidentiality, integrity, or availability of information (or an information system) has been or is in danger of being compromised. A security incident can also be thought of as any event that represents a violation of an organization's security policy. For instance, if an organization's security policy states that it is not permitted for one person to use another person's computer account, then such a use that results in the disclosure of information would be considered a security incident. There are several types of security incidents:

- **Computer account abuse**   Examples include willful account abuse, such as sharing user account credentials with other insiders or outsiders or one person stealing login credentials from another.

- **Computer or network trespass**   An unauthorized person accesses a computer network. The methods of trespass include malware, using stolen credentials, access bypass, or gaining physical access to the computer or network and connecting to it directly.

- **Information exposure or theft**   Information that is protected by one or more controls may still be exposed to unauthorized people through a weakness in controls or by deliberate or negligent acts or omissions. For instance, an intruder may be able to intercept e-mail messages, client-server communication, file transfers, logon credentials, and network diagnostic information. Or, a vulnerability in a system may permit an intruder to compromise the system and obtain information stored or processed there.

- **Malware**   A worm or virus outbreak may occur in an organization's network. The outbreak may disrupt normal business operations simply through the malware's spread, or the malware may also damage infected systems in other ways, including destroying or altering information. Malware can also eavesdrop on communications and send intercepted sensitive information back to its source.

- **Denial-of-service (DoS) attack**   An attacker can flood a target computer or network with a volume of traffic that overwhelms the target so that it is unable to carry out its regular functions. For example, an attacker can flood an online banking web site with so much traffic that the bank's depositors are unable to use it. Sending traffic that causes the target to malfunction or cease functioning is another form of a DoS attack.

- **Distributed denial-of-service (DDoS) attack**   Similar to a DoS attack, a DDoS attack emanates simultaneously from hundreds to thousands of computers that comprise a *botnet*. A DDoS attack can be difficult to withstand because of the volume of incoming messages, as well as the large number of attacking systems.

- **Encryption or destruction of critical information**   A ransomware or wiper attack can result in encrypted or destroyed information.

- **Disclosure of sensitive information**   This includes any sensitive information that is disclosed to any unauthorized party.

- **Information system theft**   Laptop computers, mobile devices, and other information-processing and storage equipment can be stolen, which may directly or indirectly lead to further compromises. If the stolen device contains retrievable sensitive information or the means to access sensitive information stored elsewhere, then what started out as a theft of a tangible asset may expand to become a compromise of sensitive information as well.

- **Information system damage**   A human intruder or automated malware may cause temporary or irreversible damage to information or an information system. This may result in an interruption in the availability of information, as well as permanent loss of information.

- **Information corruption**   A human intruder or automated malware such as a worm or virus may damage information stored on a system. This damage may or may not be readily noticed.

- **Sabotage**   A human intruder or automated malware attack may disrupt or damage information, information systems, or facilities in a single organization, several organizations in a market sector, or an entire nation.

The examples here should give you an idea of the nature of a security incident. Not all represent cataclysmic events. Other types of incidents may also be considered security incidents in some organizations.

Life Safety Also Included in Information Risk

The proliferation of connected devices in many industries expands the traditional confidentiality, integrity, and availability (CIA) to become confidentiality, integrity, availability, and safety (CIAS). This is because many connected devices are directly or indirectly related to life safety. When considering capabilities such as Bluetooth-equipped pacemakers, IV pumps on the network, self-driving cars, autopilots, and other technologies, it is becoming clear that a computer intrusion can have far-ranging effects that go beyond threats to data. For example, information technology is enabling autopilots, self-driving cars, GPS navigation, and robotic surgery.

 NOTE A vulnerability that is discovered in an organization is not an incident. However, the severity of the vulnerability may prompt a response that is similar to an actual incident. Critical vulnerabilities should be fixed as soon as possible to prevent an incident.

The Intrusion Kill Chain

In 2011, scientists at Lockheed-Martin developed a model that depicts a typical computer intrusion. While the model is imperfect and does not portray every type of computer intrusion, information security professionals recognize the kill chain as a valuable way to understand the phases of an attack. The phases are as follows:

- **Reconnaissance**   The intruder researches and identifies targets and learns still more about the selected target in order to choose a method of attack.

- **Weaponization**   The intruder creates or obtains malware that will be used to compromise a target system.

- **Delivery**   The intruder creates a means by which the attack will be delivered to the target system. Methods include e-mail (phishing, pharming, spear phishing, etc.), USB drop, or watering-hole attack.

- **Exploitation**   The malware exploits a weakness identified in the target system during reconnaissance.

- **Installation**   The malware installs itself on the target system.

- **Command and control**   The malware communicates back to an outside server owned or controlled by the intruder so that the intruder may begin his or her actions on the attack objective.

- **Actions on objective**   The intruder proceeds with the attack plan, which may consist of stealing data, damaging or destroying data, or disrupting the operations of one or more systems.

This model helps you to easily imagine an intruder following each of the steps in an attempt to break in to a system. The main point of the model is to help security professionals better understand a typical intrusion, as well as develop defenses to stop each phase of an intrusion.

Here is how the kill chain is used: for each phase, analysts examine their detective and preventive capabilities that are relevant to the types of activities that an intruder would be performing. This helps an organization better understand ways in which they could detect or prevent an attack in each of its phases.

Phases of Incident Response

An effective response to a security incident is organized, documented, and rehearsed. The phases of a formal incident response plan are explained in this section.

For incident response to be effective, organizations anticipate that incidents will occur and, accordingly, develop incident response plans, test those plans, and train personnel so that incident response will be effective and timely.

Briefly, the following are the phases of incident response:

- Planning
- Detection
- Initiation
- Analysis
- Containment
- Eradication
- Recovery
- Remediation
- Closure
- Post-Incident review
- Retention of evidence

These phases are described in more detail in this section.

Planning

This step involves the development of written response plans, guidelines, and procedures that are followed when an incident occurs. These procedures are created once the organization's practices, processes, and technologies are well understood. This helps to ensure that incident response procedures align with security policy, business operations, the technologies in use, and practices in place regarding its architecture, development, management, and operations. The plans, guidelines, and procedures should identify and include key external partners. The planning cannot be conducted in a vacuum since many organizations rely on partners for key business functions.

Detection

Detection represents the time when an organization is initially aware that a security incident is taking place or has taken place. Because of the variety of events that characterize a security incident, an organization can become aware of an incident in several ways, including the following:

- Application or network slowdown or malfunction
- Alerts from intrusion detection system (IDS), intrusion prevention system (IPS), data loss prevention (DLP) system, web filter, cloud access security broker (CASB), and other detective and preventive security systems
- Alerts from a security information and event management system (SIEM)
- Media outlets and their investigators and reports
- Notification from an employee or business partner
- Anonymous tips
- Notification from a regulator
- Notification from a media outlet

Initiation

This is the phase where response to the incident begins. Typically, this will include declaration of an incident, followed by notifications that are sent to response team members so that response operations may begin. Notifications are also typically sent to business executives so that they may be informed.

Analysis

In this phase, response team members analyze available data in order to understand the cause, scope, and impact of the incident. This may involve the use of forensic analysis tools that are used to understand activities on individual systems.

Containment

Here, incident responders perform or direct actions that halt the progress or advancement of an incident. The steps required to contain an incident will vary according to the means used by the attacker.

Eradication

In this phase of incident response, responders take steps to remove the source of the incident. This could involve removing malware, blocking incoming attack messages, or removing an intruder.

Recovery

When the incident has been evaluated and eradicated, often there is a need to recover systems or components to their pre-incident state. This might include restoring data or configurations, or replacing damaged or stolen equipment.

Remediation

This activity involves any necessary changes that will reduce or eliminate the possibility of a similar incident occurring in the future. This may take the form of process or technology changes.

Closure

Closure occurs when eradication, recovery, and remediation are completed. Incident response operations are officially closed.

Post-incident Review

Shortly after the incident closes, incident responders and other personnel meet to discuss the incident: its cause, impact, and the organization's response. Discussion can range from lessons learned to possible improvements in technologies and processes to further improve defense and response.

Retention of Evidence

Incident responders and other personnel direct the retention of evidence and other materials used or collected during the incident. This may include information that will be used in legal proceedings including prosecution, civil lawsuits, and internal investigations. A chain of custody may be required to ensure the integrity of evidence.

Several standards are available that guide organizations toward a structured and organized incident response, including NIST SP 800-61, "Computer Security Incident Handling Guide."

Incident Response Plan Development

The time to repair the roof is when the sun is shining.

—John F. Kennedy

Like any emergency, the best time to plan for security incident response is prior to the start of any actual incident. During an incident where there is little or no advance planning, emotions may run high, and there may be a heightened sense of urgency; this is a poor time to thoughtfully analyze the situation, conduct research, and work out the sequence of events that should take place.

Effective incident response plans take time to develop. A security manager who is developing an incident response plan must first thoroughly understand business processes and underlying information systems and then discover resource requirements, dependencies, and failure points. A security manager may first develop a high-level incident response plan, which is usually followed with the development of several incident response playbooks, which are step-by-step instructions to follow when specific types of security incidents occur.

Objectives

Like any intentional activity, organizations need to establish their objectives prior to undertaking an effort to develop security incident response plans. Otherwise, it may not be clear whether business needs are being met. Some objectives that may be applicable to many organizations may include these:

- Minimal or no interruption to customer-facing business operations
- No loss of critical information

- Recovery of lost or damaged information within disaster recovery and business continuity planning recovery targets, mainly recovery point objective (RPO)

- Least possible disclosure to affected parties

- Least possible disclosure to regulators

- Least possible disclosure to shareholders

- Incident expenses fully covered by cyber insurance and other insurance policies

Organizations may develop additional objectives that are germane to their business model, degree and type of regulation, and risk tolerance.

Maturity

When undertaking any effort to develop or improve business processes, an organization should be thinking about its current and desired levels of maturity. As a quick reminder, the levels of maturity according to the CMMi-DEV are as follows:

1. **Initial.** This represents a process that is ad hoc, inconsistent, unmeasured, and unrepeatable.

2. **Repeatable.** This represents a process that is performed consistently and with the same outcome. It may or may not be well documented.

3. **Defined.** This represents a process that is well defined and documented.

4. **Managed.** This represents a quantitatively measured process with one or more metrics.

5. **Optimizing.** This represents a measured process that is under continuous improvement.

In addition to business objectives as described previously, a security manager should seek to understand the existing level of maturity and the desired level. It is important to realize that increasing the maturity level of any process or program takes time and that hastening maturity may be unwise. For example, if an organization's current maturity for incident response is Initial and the long-term desired level is Managed, a number of improvements over one or more years may be required to effectively reach a Managed maturity level.

Resources

Security incident response requires resources; security managers keep this in mind when developing incident response plans. Each stage of incident response, from detection through to closure, requires personnel with different skill sets, as well as various tools that enable personnel to detect an incident, analyze it, contain it, and eradicate it. Various types of incidents require various tools and skills.

Personnel

Personnel are the heart of security incident response. Effective security incident response requires personnel with a variety of skills, including the following:

- **Incident detection and analysis**   Security operations center (SOC) analysts and other personnel use a variety of monitoring tools that alert them when actionable events occur. These personnel receive alerts and proceed to analyze an incident by drilling into the details. These same personnel may also undertake an activity known as *threat hunting,* where they proactively search systems and networks for signs of reconnaissance, malicious command-and-control (C&C) traffic, and intrusion. This function is often outsourced to managed security service providers (MSSPs) that run large 24/7/365 operations, monitoring hundreds or even thousands of client organizations' networks.

- **Network, system, and application SMEs**   With expertise in the network devices, systems, and applications related to alerts, these personnel understand how they work and can help SOC analysts and others better understand the meaning behind incidents and their consequences.

- **Malware analysis and reverse engineering**   These personnel use tools to identify and analyze malware to better understand what it does on a system and how it communicates with other systems. This helps the organization understand how to contain the incident and defend itself against similar attacks in the future.

- **Incident command and control**   These personnel have expertise in overall security incident response and take charge during an incident. Generally, this type of coordination is required only in high-impact incidents involving multiple parties in an organization, as well as external entities such as customers, regulators, and law enforcement.

- **Crisis communications**   These personnel are skilled in internal communications as well as communications with external parties including regulators, shareholders, customers, and the public.

- **Legal / Privacy**   One or more people in an organization's legal department will read and interpret applicable laws and make decisions related to external communications with customers, regulators, law enforcement, shareholders, and other parties.

- **Business unit leaders**   Also referred to as department heads or executives, these businesspeople will be called to make critical business decisions during an incident. Examples include decisions to take systems offline or transfer work to other processing centers.

Most of these responsibilities require training, which is discussed later in this section.

Outsourcing IR

Incident response sometimes involves the use of forensic tools and techniques used by trained and experienced incident response personnel. While larger organizations will have one or more such personnel on staff, most organizations cannot justify the expense of hiring these personnel as full-time employees. Many organizations opt to utilize forensic experts on an on-demand or contract basis. These typically come in the form of incident monitoring and incident response retainers.

Tools

Most types of security incidents, including malware and intrusions, require tools to detect an incident. Without them, organizations would be unaware of an incident in progress and might not learn of the incident until months or years later, if ever.

Tools are also used to examine and analyze an incident that has been identified. These tools help security personnel understand the events that occurred in one or more systems and/or networks. Next, there are sometimes tools used to eradicate and recover from an incident. Finally, tools are often used to chronicle all the events of an incident for later analysis during post-incident review and beyond.

These tools include the following:

- **Logging**   Events on individual systems and network devices often provide direct or indirect indications of intrusions and other types of incidents. Logs stored in a central server make this capability more powerful as events from different systems and devices can appear together, providing a more comprehensive view of events.

- **Log correlation**   Through a security information and event management system, log correlation helps security personnel realize when unwanted events are occurring.

- **Alerting**   A SIEM or other log processing system can be configured to produce alerts when specific types of incidents occur, thereby proactively notifying security personnel that something requires attention.

- **Threat hunting**   Specialized tools are available that facilitate the proactive activity known as *threat hunting*.

- **Threat intelligence**   Many organizations subscribe to one or more cyber-threat intelligence feeds. This helps personnel in the organization be aware of actionable threats, which enables them to confirm that protective and detective measures are in place. Some threat intel feeds are meant to be fed directly into a SIEM, which will correlate threats with identified vulnerabilities to direct personnel to improve defenses. Other threat intel feeds are meant to be human readable.

- **Malware prevention**   Antivirus and advanced anti-malware solutions on mobile devices, laptops, and servers detect the presence of malware and, often, are able to block or disrupt its activities. Malware detection and prevention capabilities can also be found in firewalls, intrusion prevention systems (IPSs), web filters, and spam/phishing filters.

- **Network intrusion prevention**   Intrusion prevention systems (IPSs) analyze the details and contents of network traffic passing through them. An IPS can detect—and often block—an initial intrusion or the C&C traffic generated by malware that has successfully compromised a system. A typical IPS will be configured to automatically block certain traffic but will permit certain traffic but produce alerts when it occurs.

- **Web filter**   Many organizations employ systems that provide protection from the hazards of browsing to malicious and fraudulent web sites. Web filters provide the ability to block access to known malicious sites, as well as to sites associated with various types of content. For example, an organization can block users' ability to access sites containing pornography or sites about weapons, hate crimes, or online gambling. Some web filters have the ability to examine the contents of traffic and can block malware from reaching end-user devices.

- **File integrity monitoring (FIM)**   FIM systems periodically scan file systems on servers and workstations and report on any changes that occur. While changes may be a result of periodic maintenance, they can also be indicators of compromise. A typical FIM system sends alerts to a SIEM so that SOC analysts will be notified of a potential intrusion.

- **File activity monitoring (FAM)**   File activity monitoring systems monitor directories and files on a server or workstations to detect unusual activities that may be an indicator of compromise. A typical FAM system sends alerts to a SIEM, where SOC analysts will be watching for alerts.

- **Forensic analysis**   These tools are used to study the events that have occurred on a system, examine the contents of file systems and memory, and analyze malware to understand its structure and actions. These tools require skills and experience, as forensic tools usually don't reveal "what happened" but instead show detailed information to the forensic examiner, who has to know what elements to examine in order to figure out the relevant chain of events. Forensic analysis is used to examine a malware attack, as well as chronicle the events of an employee accused of misbehavior.

- **Video surveillance**   This is needed for incidents involving human activity, generally the comings and goings of personnel and intruders, and what they may be carrying with them.

- **Record keeping**   Decisions, steps taken, and communications need to be recorded in a journal so that incident responders can understand what activities have taken place during incident response, as well as providing a backward look during post-incident review.

Incident Monitoring by MSSPs   Many organizations may choose to outsource security monitoring to a managed security services provider (MSSP). Because many types of security incidents may proceed at a rapid pace, organizations prefer to have an outside expert organization perform around-the-clock security monitoring of its critical systems to provide expert detection and rapid notification of suspected and confirmed incidents. Some MSSPs may have the capability to perform additional steps of incident response, including analysis and containment of an incident, on their customers' behalf.

Organizations that choose to outsource security monitoring do so for a number of reasons, including the following:

- **Domain expertise**   Personnel at an MSSP have expertise in security monitoring and incident detection.

- **Dedicated personnel**   The staff at an MSSP have only one job: monitoring customers' systems to identify and respond to security incidents. Unlike an organization's security staff, the personnel at an MSSP are not distracted by other activities or projects.

- **Staffing shortage**   It is difficult for many organizations to identify, recruit, and retain qualified information security personnel. By outsourcing security monitoring, organizations are relieved of the burden of staffing its security monitoring function.

- **Cost control**   In many cases, the fees charged by MSSPs are less than the salary, benefits, tools, workspace, and other costs required for in-house staff. This is mainly because of economies of scale: MSSP personnel typically perform security monitoring for numerous organizations.

Threat Hunting   The practice of *threat hunting* is used to proactively seek signs of intrusions. Rather than passively monitoring systems for signs of intrusions, threat hunters use tools to hunt for indicators of compromise (IOCs).

The objective of threat hunting is earlier detection of intrusions. When an intrusion is detected earlier, its impact on the organization may be lower, particularly if an intruder is detected prior to the intruder achieving her attack objective.

Threat hunting is considered an activity carried out by organizations that already have a mature event monitoring program in place. In other words, organizations considering threat hunting should do so only after achieving moderate to high maturity in its monitoring tools and practices.

Incident Response Retainers   An *incident response retainer (IRR)* is a legal agreement between an organization and a security professional services firm that arranges for the security firm to render assistance to the organization in the event of a security incident. The agreement may include a service level agreement that commits the security firm to quickly respond to an organization's call for assistance. The retainer agreement may include prepaid services, hourly rates for incident response, and other provisions that define roles and responsibilities.

Depending upon the nature of a security incident, the security professional services firm may need to send forensic experts to the client's business location to perform forensics on-site. However, the nature of the incident may not require on-site work; instead, the client organization may be able to send malware samples, incident logs, or other digital information to the security professional organization where analysis can be performed remotely.

In some cases, the organization experiencing an incident may need the security professional services firm to act as an incident commander. In this role, the consultant from the security services firm may fulfill the role of managing the organization's activities in response to the incident.

External Legal Counsel
Some organizations may retain outside legal counsel with expertise in the legal aspects of security incident response. Outside counsel can advise an organization on interpretation

of laws regarding cybersecurity and privacy, as well as contracts with other organizations. An outside counsel firm might also be used to assist with legal activities and logistics related to incident response. Assistance from external legal counsel can be contracted through a *retainer agreement*.

Roles and Responsibilities

A security incident response plan will contain information about specific roles and responsibilities to ensure that a security incident is handled properly and promptly. Typical defined roles and responsibilities include the following:

- **Reporting security problems**   Many organizations enact policies that require all personnel to report suspicious issues to security personnel.

- **Incident detection**   These personnel will either be dedicated security event monitoring personnel (in the case of a SOC) or be people with other responsibilities. In the latter case, these people will periodically examine event logs or be sent messages when security events occur. Also, helpdesk or service desk personnel need to be trained to recognize security incidents during their routine activities of working with end users and troubleshooting problems.

- **Incident declaration**   Some personnel will be designated as people who can formally declare a security incident. These people are usually trained so that they will be able to recognize various types of incidents and follow procedures to notify others of an incident.

- **Incident commander**   Some personnel will be designated to coordinate various activities as an incident unfolds and is managed. Organizations typically select domain experts and other personnel with technology skills and background who can direct other personnel as an incident is examined, contained, and resolved. In serious and prolonged incidents, incident commanders will take shifts.

- **Internal communications**   These people are designated to communicate information about an incident to personnel inside the organization. This helps keep other internal parties informed on the proceedings of the incident and its response.

- **External communications**   These personnel are authorized to communicate with outside parties, including law enforcement, regulators, customers, partners, suppliers, shareholders, and the public. Typically, the matter of external communications is shared with one or more people who must approve any external communications and those who do the communicating.

- **Legal counsel**   Inside or outside counsel are generally responsible for interpreting applicable laws, regulations, and legal agreements, and they advise other incident response personnel of steps that should (or should not) be taken. In many cases, incident investigations are protected by *attorney–client privilege,* which requires legal counsel to be involved in the main proceedings of the incident.

- **Scribe**   With all of the activities occurring during a security incident, one or more people are responsible for maintaining records of all the proceedings. This includes but is not limited to actions taken by all incident response personnel, decisions, communications, and the location of records such as retained logs and artifacts from forensic analysis.

- **Forensic analysis**   Many security events require one or more people with expertise in computer and/or network forensics who seek to determine the cause of an incident as well as methods that can be used to contain and eradicate it. Because some security incidents may result in subsequent legal proceedings, forensic analysts employ evidence preservation techniques and establish a *chain of custody* to ensure that evidence is not altered.

- **Containment, eradication, remediation, and recovery**   These personnel take measures to halt an incident's progress and take further steps to recover affected systems to their pre-incident state. While containment, eradication, remediation, and recovery are four distinct steps in incident response, often these are performed by the same personnel.

- **Business continuity and emergency operations**   A significant incident may result in significant downtime or other business disruption, as one or more critical systems may be affected by an incident and taken out of service. An organization may need to invoke business continuity and/or emergency operations to continue critical business operations.

Organizations need to keep in mind that despite the noise and disruption caused by a serious incident, normal business operations need to continue uninterrupted.

Gap Analysis

Prior to the development of a security incident response plan, the security manager must determine the current state of the organization's incident response capabilities, as well as the desired end state (e.g., a completed security incident response plan with specific capabilities and characteristics). A gap analysis is the best way for the security manager to understand what capabilities and resources are lacking. Once gaps are known, a strategy for developing security incident response plans will consist on the creation or acquisition of all necessary resources and personnel.

A gap analysis in the context of security incident response program development is the same gap analysis activity described in more detail in Chapter 2.

Plan Development

A security incident response plan is a document that defines policies, roles, responsibilities, and actions to be taken in the event of a security incident.

Often, a response plan also defines and describes roles, responsibilities, and actions that are related to the detection of a security incident. This portion of an incident response plan is vital, considering the high velocity and high impact experienced by certain types of security incidents.

A security incident response plan typically includes these sections:

- Policy
- Roles and responsibilities
- Incident detection capabilities
- Communications
- Record keeping

Playbooks

Recognizing that there are many types of security incidents, each with their own impacts and issues, many organizations develop a collection of incident response playbooks that provide step-by-step instructions for incidents likely to occur to them. A set of playbooks might include procedures for the following:

- Lost or stolen laptop computer
- Lost or stolen mobile device
- Extortion and wire fraud
- Sensitive data exfiltration
- Credit card data exfiltration
- Ransomware
- Malware
- Stolen user credentials
- Critical vulnerability
- Externally reported vulnerability
- Denial-of-service attack
- Unauthorized access
- Violation of information security-related law, regulation, or contract
- Business e-mail compromise

The purpose of playbooks is to guide experienced and trained personnel in the steps required to examine, contain, and recover from an incident. During a serious incident, emotions can run high, and personnel under stress may not be able to remember all of the steps required to properly handle an incident. Playbooks are commonplace in other industries: pilots and astronauts use playbooks to handle various emergency situations, and they practice them so that they will be able to effectively respond if needed.

Incidents Involving Third Parties

Organizations outsource many of their critical applications and infrastructure to third-party organizations. The fact that applications and infrastructure supporting critical processes are owned and managed by other parties does not absolve an organization from its responsibilities to detect and respond to security incidents. Often, however, this makes incident detection and response more complex. As a result, organizations need to develop incident response playbooks that are specific to various incident types at each third party to ensure that the organization will be able to effectively detect and respond to an incident.

Incident response related to a third-party application or infrastructure often requires that the organization and each third party understand their respective roles and responsibilities for incident detection and response. For example, software-as-a-service (SaaS) applications often do not make event and log data available to customers. Instead, organizations must rely on those third parties to properly develop and manage their incident detection and response capabilities, including informing affected customers of an incident in progress. Depending on the architecture of a SaaS solution, both the SaaS provider and the customer may have their own steps to take during incident response, and some of those steps may require coordination or assistance from the other party. Joint exercises between companies and critical SaaS providers helps build confidence that their incident response plans will work.

Periodic Updates

All security incident management documents need to be periodically reviewed by all of the responsible parties, subject-matter experts, and management to ensure that all agree on the policies, roles and responsibilities, and steps required to detect, contain, and recover from an incident.

Generally, organizations should review and update documents at least once per year, as well as any time a significant change is made in an organization or its supporting systems.

The Relationship of Security Incident Management to ITSM Incident Management

Rather than building a separate but similar set of procedures and business records, security incident response procedures generally utilize systems, procedures, and records used in IT departments for incident management. The IT Infrastructure Library (ITIL) defines an *incident* as "*any event* which is not part of the standard operation of a service and which causes, or may cause, an interruption to, or a reduction in, the quality of that service. The stated ITIL objective is to restore normal operations as quickly as possible with the least possible impact on either the business or the user, at a cost-effective price."

In the context of ITIL, an incident may be any of the following:

- Service outage
- Service slowdown
- Software bug

When combined with security incidents, an organization will be prepared to respond to most any type of IT or security incident.

Incident Classification

Security incidents range in severity and impact from the nearly benign to the nearly business ending. Further, an incident may or may not have an impact on sensitive information, including intellectual property and personally identifiable information (PII).

Organizations generally classify incidents according to severity, typically on a 3-, 4-, or 5-point scale. Organizations that store or process intellectual property, confidential data about their employees, or sensitive information about clients or customers often assign incident severity levels according to the level of impact on this information. Tables 5-2 and 5-3 depict two such schemes for classifying security incidents.

In Table 5-2, incidents are assigned a single numeric value of 1 to 5 based upon the impact as described. In Table 5-3, incidents are assigned a numeric value and an alphabetic value, based on impact to operations and impact to information. For example, an incident involving the loss of an encrypted laptop computer would be classified as 1A, whereas a ransomware incident where some production information has been lost would be classified as 4E or 5E.

Incident Severity	Incident Impact	Description and Examples
1	Affects a single individual	Policy violation Compromise of a function
2	Affects a workgroup	Compromise of an important function
3	Affects a department or business unit	Compromise of intellectual property of critical function
4	Affects entire organization internally	Significant compromise of intellectual property or critical function
5	Affects entire organization publicly	Significant compromise of personally identifiable information or multiple critical functions

Table 5-2 Example Single-Dimensional Incident Severity Plan

Severity Classification	Impact to Operations	Sensitivity Classification	Description
1	No impact to operations	A	No impact to information
2	Minor impact to operations	B	Compromise of small volume of critical information
3	Critical function impaired	C	Compromise of moderate volume of critical information
4	Critical function unavailable or significantly impaired	D	Compromise of large volume of critical information
5	Critical functions unavailable	E	Loss or damage to critical information

Table 5-3 Example Two-Dimensional Incident Severity Plan

Escalations

Orderly internal communication is critical to effective incident response. Communication during a security incident keeps incident responders and other affected parties informed about the proceedings of incident response.

Another aspect of internal communication that should be part of incident response plans is *escalations*. Two forms of escalations are used in many incident response plans:

- Notifying appropriate levels of upper management when an incident has been detected. It is a good practice to establish triggers or thresholds as to when and what level of the organization should be notified based on the incident type and its impact to the organization. Some organizations accomplish this by classifying different types and levels of incidents, with specific escalations for each.

- Notifying appropriate levels of management when incident response SLAs have not been met. For example, various tasks during incident response will be known to take a specific period of time. When any task takes excessive time, an escalation should take place so that appropriate management can look into the matter. Escalations in this case may trigger the use of external resources that can assist with incident response.

Rather than be an ad hoc activity, escalation should be a documented part of the incident response process. This way, incident responders know how to proceed when incident response is not progressing as expected.

Incident Response Metrics

An organization's security incident response program can be managed and improved only to the extent that key metrics are established to measure the program's performance. Metrics that can be developed and reported include the following:

- Number of incidents of each incident severity and type
- Dwell time (time from start of incident to the time the organization became aware of the incident)
- Time required to contain the incident
- Time required to resolve and close incidents
- Number of times incident response SLAs were not met
- Improvements identified and implemented based on table-top exercises and lessons learned from actual incidents
- Number or percentage of employees receiving security awareness training, as well as any correlation between this and the number of incidents
- Number of records compromised
- Number of external people affected and notified
- Total cost required to resolve each incident

Testing the Plan

Not only should security incident response plans be documented and reviewed, but they need to be periodically tested. Security incident response testing helps to improve the quality of those plans, which will help the organization to better respond when an incident occurs. A by-product of security incident plan testing is the growing familiarity of personnel with security incident response procedures.

Similar to disaster recovery and business continuity planning, various types of tests should be carried out:

- **Document review**   In this review, individual subject-matter experts (SMEs) carefully read security incident response documentation to better understand the procedures and to identify any opportunities for improvement.

- **Walk-through**   This is similar to a document review, except that it is performed by a group of subject-matter experts, who talk through the security incident response plan. Discussing each step helps to stimulate new ideas, which could lead to further improvements in the plan.

- **Simulation**   Here, a facilitator describes a realistic security incident scenario, and participants discuss how they will actually respond. A simulation usually takes half a day or longer. It is suggested that the simulation be "scripted" with new information and updates introduced throughout the scenario. A simulation can be limited to just the technology aspects of a security incident, or it can involve corporate communications, public relations, legal, and other externally facing parts of the organization that may play a part in a security incident that is known to the public.

- **Live fire**   During an annual penetration test, personnel who are monitoring systems and networks jump into action in response to the scans and probes being performed by penetration testers.

These tests should be performed once each year or even more often. In the walk-through and simulation tests, someone should be appointed as note-taker so that any improvements will be recorded and the plan can be updated. Tests should include incidents addressed in each playbook and at each classification level so that all procedures will be tested.

If the incident response plan contains the names and contact information for response personnel, the plan should be reviewed more frequently to ensure that all contact information is up-to-date.

Training Personnel

Like any procedure, incident response goes far better if incident responders have been trained prior to an actual incident. But unlike many procedures in security, emotions can run high during a security incident, and those unfamiliar with the procedures and principles of incident response can get tripped up and make mistakes. This is not unlike the emotion and stress that other types of emergency responders may experience.

Incident response training should cover all of the likely scenarios that the organization is likely to face, ranging from the not-so-dire events such as stolen mobile devices and laptop computers to the truly catastrophic events such as a prolonged DDoS attack, destructive ransomware, or the exfiltration of large amounts of sensitive data.

Incident response personnel should be trained in the use of tools used to detect, examine, and remediate an incident. This includes SOC personnel who use a SIEM and other detection and investigation tools, forensic specialists who use specialized forensic analysis tools, and all personnel who have administrative responsibilities for every type of IT equipment, application, and tool.

Professional Certifications

Security professionals specializing in incident response should consider one or more of the specialty certifications in incident response, including the following (in alphabetic order):

- **Certified Computer Examiner (CCE)**   Information at https://www.isfce.com/certification.htm
- **Certified Computer Forensics Examiner (CCFE)**   Information at http://www.iacertification.org/ccfe_certified_computer_forensics_examiner.html
- **Certified Cyber Forensics Professional (CCFP)**   Information at https://www.isc2.org/Certifications/CCFP
- **EC-Council Certified Incident Handler (ECIH)**   Information at https://www.eccouncil.org/programs/ec-council-certified-incident-handler-ecih/
- **GIAC Certified Forensic Analyst (GCFA)**   Information at https://digital-forensics.sans.org/certification/gcfa
- **GIAC Certified Incident Handler (GCIH)**   Information at https://www.giac.org/certification/certified-incident-handler-gcih
- **GIAC Network Forensic Analyst (GNFA)**   Information at https://digital-forensics.sans.org/certification/gnfa
- **GIAC Reverse Engineering Malware (GREM)**   Information at https://digital-forensics.sans.org/certification/grem
- **Professional Certified Investigator (PCI)**   Information at https://www.asisonline.org/Certification/Board-Certifications/PCI/Pages/default.aspx

There are also a number of vendor-specific certifications, including *EnCase Certified Examiner (EnCe)* for those professionals using the EnCase forensics tool, and *AccessData Certified Examiner (ACE)* for professionals who use Forensic Toolkit *(FTK)*.

Responding to Security Incidents

Response to a security incident consists of several phases, from detection to closure and a post-incident review. These phases are discussed in detail in this section.

The phases of security incident response are part of a model. As such, security managers realize that certain types of incidents don't include all of the phases in the model. For example, a stolen laptop computer may have virtually no eradication activities.

Also, some incidents may have additional phases. For instance, a security incident involving the theft of a large volume of information will have a series of post-incident proceedings that may represent greater effort and cost than the initial incident response.

Successful incident response requires considerable planning. The preceding sections in this chapter discuss the development, testing, and training of security incident response plans.

Detection

The detection phase marks the start of an organization's awareness of a security incident. In many cases, a period of time elapses between the start of the actual incident and the moment that the organization is aware of it. This period of time is known as *dwell time*.

The ability to detect an intrusion or incident requires a capability known as *event visibility*. Typically, event visibility is achieved through the use of event log collection and analysis tools (typically, a security information and event management system), together with other tools the detect activities in networks and in servers and endpoints.

There are several other ways that an organization can be made aware of an incident, besides monitoring. These include the following:

- **Reporting by an employee**   An organization's personnel can be aware of certain types of incidents, especially misbehavior by other employees.

- **Reporting by a managed security service (MSS) or security operations center analyst**   The personnel who monitor an organization's networks and systems are likely to detect activities and will initiate investigation and response.

- **Reporting by a customer or client**   An organization's customers or clients may have noticed phenomena that may be related to a breach and may report it to the organization.

- **Social media**   Clients, customers, and other parties may report observations related to a security incident via social media, particularly if they have no other means for notifying the organization.

- **Notification from law enforcement or regulator**   In the case of information theft, outside organizations and agencies may become aware through higher rates of fraud. Law enforcement investigations reveal the source of the intrusion.

- **Notification from a security researcher**   In the course of their research, security researchers sometimes discover vulnerabilities or signs of intrusion in other organizations' networks.

- **Unknown people**   Occasionally, someone not associated with the organization will contact the organization to notify them of a security problem. For example, a passer-by may notice discarded assets tossed aside by someone else who stole them.

- **IT personnel or end users** Sometimes a security incident first appears as a malfunction or error in a system or application. Only through analysis is the malfunction determined to be caused by an intruder. For this reason, IT service desk personnel need to be trained on the art of detecting security issues when users call for help.

Organizations need to keep in mind that these are example detection sources and that there may be other sources not listed here.

Shortening the Dwell Time

According to notable research organizations, in many organizations dwell time for computer intrusions often exceeds 200 days. Realizing that this is unacceptable, organizations are implementing better tools that provide earlier warnings of anomalous activities that could be the signs of an intrusion. These tools include a security information and event management system, to which the event logs of all servers, endpoints, and network devices are sent, as well as advanced anti-malware software, file integrity monitoring (FIM) tools, file activity monitoring (FAM) tools, and network and system anomaly detection tools.

Initiation

When an organization has realized that a security incident has taken place or is still taking place, an incident responder will make an incident declaration. An organization's security incident response plan should include a procedure for declaring an incident. This generally consists of notifying key personnel, including the security manager and the IT manager (whose actual titles may vary), as well as personnel on the incident response team (IRT).

Members of the IRT, together with the IT manager and security manager, need to select an incident commander. The incident commander will coordinate the use of resources and internal communications so that IRT members can work effectively to manage the incident.

When an incident has been declared, this may prompt incident response personnel to initiate and join an emergency communications conference bridge or assemble in a war room.

False Alarms

Some people are concerned with the prospect of declaring an incident when no incident is taking place—in other words, a false alarm. Organizations need to understand that a false alarm from time to time can be seen as acceptable, especially considering that the opposite problem of not recognizing and declaring an incident may be more harmful to the organization.

Evaluation

The evaluation phase of security incident response is concerned with the examination of available information that reveals the nature of the incident. This may include the use of forensic examination techniques that permit the examiner to determine how an incident was able to occur.

Incident Ranking and Rating

The types and severities of security incidents that may occur can vary significantly. A relatively minor incident such as the loss of a laptop computer with encrypted contents would be handled far differently than the theft and exploitation of a large database containing sensitive customer information. Accordingly, an organization's incident response plans should include steps to determine the scope and severity of an incident. This will help the organization determine the amount and type of resources that may be needed, as well as the need to involve and inform executive management. Using the same example, an executive on vacation should be notified of a major compromise of sensitive customer data, whereas the loss of an encrypted laptop will merely show up as a tic in security metrics.

Forensic Investigations

Forensic investigations are often required when a security incident has occurred and it is necessary to gather evidence to determine an incident's cause and effects. Because the information gathered in an investigation may later be used in a legal proceeding, a forensic investigator must follow strict *chain of custody* procedures when gathering, studying, and retaining information.

Chain of Custody   The key to an effective and successful forensic investigation is the establishment of a sound chain of custody. The major considerations that determine the effectiveness of a forensic investigation are as follows:

- **Identification**   A description of the evidence that was acquired and the tools and techniques used to acquire it. Evidence may include digital information acquired from computers, network devices, and mobile devices, as well as interviews of involved people.

- **Preservation**   A description of the tools and techniques used to retain evidence. This will include detailed records that establish the chain of custody, which may be presented and tested in legal proceedings.

- **Analysis**   A description of the examination of the evidence gathered, which may include a reconstruction of events that are a subject of the investigation.

- **Presentation**   A formal document that describes the entire investigation, evidence gathered, tools used, and findings that express the examiner's opinion of the events that occurred (or did not occur).

The entire chain of custody must be documented in precise detail and include how evidence was protected against tampering through every step of the investigation. Any "holes" in the information acquisition and analysis process will likely fail in legal proceedings, possibly resulting in the organization's failure to convince judicial authorities that the event occurred as described.

Forensic Techniques and Considerations   Computer and network forensics requires several specialized techniques that ensure the integrity of the entire forensic investigation and a sound chain of evidence. Some of these techniques are as follows:

- **Data acquisition**   This is the process of acquiring data for forensic analysis. Subject data may reside on a computer hard drive, in mobile device memory, or in an application's audit log. Several tools are used for forensic data acquisition, including media copiers, which are tools that acquire a copy of a computer's hard drive, USB memory stick, or removable media, such as an external hard drive or CD/DVD-ROM.

- **Data extraction**   If data is being acquired from a running system or from a third party, a forensics analyst must use a secure method to acquire the data and be able to demonstrate the integrity of the process used to acquire the data. This must be done in a way that proves the source of the data and that it was not altered during the extraction process.

- **Data protection**   Once data is acquired, the forensic investigator must take every step to ensure its integrity. Computers used for forensic analysis must be physically locked so that no other people have access to them. They must not be connected to any network that would allow for the introduction of malware or other agents that could alter acquired data and influence the investigation's outcome.

- **Analysis and transformation**   Often, tools are required to analyze acquired data and search for specific clues. Also, data must frequently be transformed from its native state into a state that is human- or tool-readable; in many cases, computers store information in a binary format that is not easily read and interpreted by humans. For example, the NTUSER.DAT file used in Windows is a binary representation of the HKEY_LOCAL_USER branch of the system's registry. This file cannot be directly read but requires tools to transform it into a human-readable form.

NOTE   Decisions on the use of forensic proceedings need to be made early during an incident. Employing forensic procedures can consume significant resources that may even slow down incident response. Senior executives should make the call on the use of forensic proceedings and do so as early as possible during an incident.

Triggering Business Continuity and Disaster Recovery Plans

Some incidents incur significant effects on information systems and/or sensitive information. This may necessitate initiation of business continuity and disaster recovery plans to keep critical business processes running. Examples of incidents that may require business continuity and/or disaster recovery operations include the following:

- Ransomware that makes critical production data unavailable
- Wiper malware that destroys critical production data
- Denial-of-service attack that incapacitates production systems

The best way to handle a pivot from security incident response to business continuity and/or disaster recovery is to call this out in the incident response plan. Otherwise, there is a possibility that incident responders and other IT personnel may become focused on incident response without realizing that critical services are incapacitated.

Attorney–Client Privilege

Some organizations utilize their legal counsel as a central point of communications during a security incident. Done properly, this may permit an organization to shield communications and other proceedings from discovery in the event of a lawsuit. This practice is known as *attorney–client privilege*.

While a legal tactic is discussed here, this should not be construed as legal advice. Instead, consult with legal counsel to better understand the applicability and procedures for this approach.

Eradication

The eradication phase of security incident response is concerned with the removal of the agent or factors that caused or aided the incident. Depending on the nature of the incident, this may involve the removal of physical subjects from a work center or information processing center or the removal of malware from one or more affected systems.

Modern malware and intrusion techniques can be difficult to identify and even more difficult to remove. Malware can have characteristics or employ techniques that make it more resilient, including the following:

- Hiding within legitimate processes
- Fileless malware
- Antiforensics techniques such as encryption, steganography, file wiping, and trail obfuscation
- Hiding data in memory, slack space, bad blocks, hidden partitions, or the registry
- Hiding "below" the operating system in the master boot record, in a virtual machine hypervisor, or in the system's Basic Input/Output System (BIOS) or unified extensible firmware interface (UEFI)

The personnel who examine infected systems must have up-to-date skills and experience to be able to identify and remove malware.

Recovery

The recovery phase of security incident response focuses on the restoration of affected systems and assets to their pre-incident state. Recovery is performed after eradication is completed; this means that any malware or other tools used by the intruder have been removed. The state of a system entering the recovery phase is described as free of all tools, files, and agents used by the intruder. There are two basic approaches to recovery:

- **Restoration of damaged files**   In this approach, incident responders have a high degree of certainty that all artifacts used by the intruder have been removed from the system. While this is a valid approach, it does come with some risk, as it may be difficult to positively determine that all components used by the intruder are, in fact, removed.

- **Bare-metal restore**   In this approach, all information is removed from the system, and it is recovered from backup. Typically, this involved reformatting main storage. Incident responders need to be aware of advanced techniques used by attackers, including persistence in the computer's BIOS, in UEFI, or in hidden main storage partitions. Further, if systems being restored are virtual machines, personnel need to determine that new virtual machine images themselves are free of infection.

Privacy Breaches

A breach of privacy is a unique type of security incident. In a privacy breach, there may have been a theft or compromise of sensitive or private data about customers. The steps to be taken during incident response will be largely the same as with breaches of other types of information. There are, however, two differences to keep in mind:

- Incident handlers must handle privacy data according to the organization's security and privacy policies.

- The organization may be required to notify affected people during or soon after the incident.

Organizations that store or process information in scope of privacy laws should include security incident categorization that includes privacy incidents, and security incident plans or playbooks should include specific information that direct incident responders to perform all necessary steps, including required notifications and disclosures.

Remediation

An important step in incident response is remediation of any vulnerabilities that were exploited during the incident. This includes but is not limited to technical vulnerabilities that may have permitted malware exploits to work; it also includes any supporting technologies, business processes, or personnel training that may have helped to prevent the incident from occurring if they would have been in place prior to the incident.

Incident responders need to understand that the intruder may not be satisfied that he was eradicated from target systems. If any of the same vulnerabilities still exist, the intruder may attempt to reestablish a foothold to resume the intrusion in support of its objective.

There is a broader issue of learning from the incident that is addressed later in the section "Post-incident Review."

Closure

After an incident has been identified, its causes eradicated, and any affected systems recovered, the incident can be closed. Mainly this is a "back to business as usual" declaration. However, there are some activities that need to take place.

- **Archival of forensic evidence**   All information and records obtained through forensic analysis need to be archived. The chain of custody must continue, however, should any legal proceedings take place in the future.

- **Archival of communications records**   Copies of internal communications as well as notifications sent to outside parties need to be preserved.

- **Notification to internal personnel and outside authorities**   All personnel and outside authorities who have been notified of the incident need to be informed that the incident has been closed.

Post-incident Review

When all incident response proceedings have concluded, organizations should consider performing a review of the incident that has taken place. A post-incident review should include a frank, open discussion that identifies what went well during the incident and what could have been handled or performed in a better way. A typical post-incident review should cover the following:

- **Incident awareness**   Whether the organization realized quickly enough that an incident was occurring.

- **Internal communications**   Whether internal communications were well organized, whether the right personnel were involved, and whether the right information was shared with the right parties.

- **External communications**   Whether external communications were well organized, including communications with regulators, law enforcement, customers, insurance companies, and the public.

- **Response procedures**   Whether incident response personnel acted quickly, decisively, and correctly.

- **Resilience**   Here, the organization examines its environment, including both technology and business processes, to discovery opportunities to improve the organization's resilience. This can help the organization better defend itself in the future through the reduction in incident probability as well as reduced impact.

Security organizations should operate with a culture of continuous improvement. In this regard, review of every aspect of a recent security incident should seek to identify improvements that will enable the organization to be better prepared when another incident occurs.

Business Continuity and Disaster Recovery Planning

Business continuity planning (BCP) and disaster recovery planning (DRP) are two interrelated disciplines with a common objective: keep critical business processes operating throughout a disaster scenario, while recovering/rebuilding damaged assets to restore business operations in its primary locations.

Figure 5-2 shows the relationship between BCP and DRP.

Before business continuity and disaster recovery plans can be developed, it is first necessary to deeply understand the organization's business processes, the information systems supporting them, and interdependencies. This is accomplished through a business impact analysis (BIA) and a criticality analysis (CA), which identify those business processes that are most important and how quickly they need to be recovered during and after any disaster scenario.

The primary by-product of effective BCP and DRP is improved business resilience, not only in disaster situations but on a daily basis. Close examinations of processes and systems often reveal numerous opportunities for process and system improvement that result in improved resilience and fewer unplanned outages. Thus, for many organizations, BCP and DRP benefit the organization even if a disaster never strikes.

NOTE While CISM candidates are not required to understand the details of business continuity and disaster recovery planning, they are required to understand the relationship between incident response and business continuity / disaster recovery planning. The principles, methodologies, recovery procedures, and testing techniques are so similar between the two disciplines that it is important for information security managers to understand all of these disciplines and how they relate to each other.

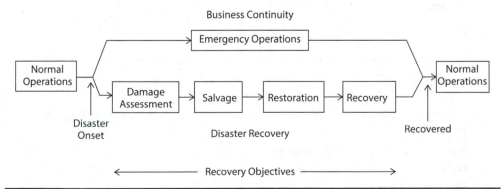

Figure 5-2   The relationship between BCP and DRP

Business Continuity Planning

Business continuity planning is undertaken to reduce risks related to the onset of disasters and other disruptive events. BCP activities identify risks and mitigate those risks through changes or enhancements in technology or business processes so that the impact of disasters is reduced and the time to recovery is lessened. The primary objective of BCP is to improve the chances that the organization will survive a disaster without incurring costly or even fatal damage to its most critical activities.

The activities of BCP development scale for any size organization. BCP has the unfortunate reputation of existing only in the stratospheric, thin air of the largest and wealthiest organizations. This misunderstanding hurts the majority of organizations that are too timid to begin any kind of BCP efforts at all because they believe that these activities are too costly and disruptive. The fact is that any size organization, from a one-person home office to a multinational conglomerate, can successfully undertake BCP projects that will bring about immediate benefits as well as take some of the sting out of disruptive events that do occur.

Organizations can benefit from BCP projects, even if a disaster never occurs. The steps in the BCP development process usually bring immediate benefit in the form of process and technology improvements that increase the resilience, integrity, and efficiency of those processes and systems.

BCP generally is managed outside of the information security function. Further, BCP is generally external to IT since BCP is focused on the continuity of business processes, not on the recovery of IT systems.

 EXAM TIP Business continuity planning is closely related to disaster recovery planning—both are concerned with the recovery of business operations after a disaster.

Disasters

In a business context, disasters are unexpected and unplanned events that result in the disruption of business operations. A disaster could be a regional event spread over a wide geographic area, or it could occur within the confines of a single room. The impact of a disaster will also vary, from a complete interruption of all company operations to merely a slowdown. (This question invariably comes up: When is a disaster a disaster? This is somewhat subjective, like asking "When is a person sick?" Is it when she is too ill to report to work or when she just has a sniffle and a scratchy throat? I'll discuss disaster declaration later in this chapter.)

Types of Disasters   BCP professionals broadly classify disasters as natural or human-made, although the origin of a disaster does not figure very much into how we respond to it. Let's examine the types of disasters.

Natural Disasters   Natural disasters are those phenomena that occur in the natural world with little or no assistance from mankind. They are a result of the natural processes that occur in, on, and above the earth.

These are examples of natural disasters:

- **Earthquakes** Sudden movements of the earth with the capacity to damage buildings, houses, roads, bridges, and dams; to precipitate landslides and avalanches; and to induce flooding and other secondary events.

- **Volcanoes** Eruptions of magma, pyroclastic flows, steam, ash, and flying rocks that can cause significant damage over wide geographic regions. Some volcanoes, such as Kilauea in Hawaii, produce a nearly continuous and predictable outpouring of lava in a limited area, whereas the Mount St. Helens eruption in 1980 caused an ash fall over thousands of square miles that brought many metropolitan areas to a standstill for days and also blocked rivers and damaged roads.

- **Landslides** These are sudden downhill movements of the earth, usually down steep slopes, can bury buildings, houses, roads, and public utilities and can cause secondary (although still disastrous) effects such as the rerouting of rivers.

- **Avalanches** These are sudden downward flows of snow, rocks, and debris on a mountainside. A slab avalanche consists of the movement of a large, stiff layer of compacted snow. A loose snow avalanche occurs when the accumulated snowpack exceeds its shear strength. A power snow avalanche is the largest type and can travel in excess of 200 miles per hour (mph) and exceed 10 million tons of material. All types can damage buildings, houses, roads, and utilities, resulting in direct or indirect damage affecting businesses.

- **Wildfires** Fires in forests, chaparral, and grasslands are part of the natural order. However, fires can also damage buildings and equipment and cause injury and death, such as the 2017 wildfires in California. Figure 5-3 shows the Sonoma County and nearby wildfires, as seen from the NASA Aqua satellite.

- **Tropical cyclones** The largest and most violent storms are known in various parts of the world as hurricanes, typhoons, tropical cyclones, tropical storms, and

Figure 5-3
Wildfires in California
(Source: NASA)

cyclones. Tropical cyclones, such as Hurricane Harvey, consist of strong winds that can reach 190 mph, heavy rains, and storm surge that can raise the level of the ocean by as much as 20 feet, all of which can result in widespread coastal flooding and damage to buildings, houses, roads, and utilities and in significant loss of life.

- **Tornadoes** These violent rotating columns of air can cause catastrophic damage to buildings, houses, roads, and utilities when they reach the ground. Most tornadoes can have wind speeds from 40 mph to 110 mph and travel along the ground for a few miles. Some tornadoes can exceed 300 mph and travel for dozens of miles.

- **Windstorms** While generally less intense than hurricanes and tornadoes, windstorms can nonetheless cause widespread damage, including damage to buildings, roads, and utilities. Widespread electric power outages are common, as windstorms can uproot trees that can fall into overhead power lines.

- **Lightning** Lightning consists of atmospheric discharges of electricity that occur during thunderstorms but also during dust storms and volcanic eruptions. Lightning can start fires and also damage buildings and power transmission systems, causing power outages.

- **Ice storms** Ice storms occur when rain falls through a layer of colder air, causing raindrops to freeze onto whatever surface they strike. They can cause widespread power outages when ice forms on power lines and the resulting weight causes those power lines to collapse. A notable example is the Great Ice Storm of 1998 in eastern Canada, which resulted in millions being without power for as long as two weeks and in the virtual immobilization of the cities of Montreal and Ottawa.

- **Hail** This form of precipitation consists of ice chunks ranging from 5 millimeters (mm) to 150 mm in diameter. An example of a damaging hailstorm is the April 1999 storm in Sydney, Australia, where hailstones up to 9.5 centimeters (cm) in diameter damaged 40,000 vehicles, 20,000 properties, and 25 airplanes and caused one direct fatality. The storm caused $1.5 billion in damage.

- **Flooding** Standing or moving water spills out of its banks and flows into and through buildings and causes significant damage to roads, buildings, and utilities. Flooding can be a result of locally heavy rains, heavy snow melt, a dam or levee break, tropical cyclone storm surge, or an avalanche or landslide that displaces lake or river water.

- **Tsunamis** A series of waves that usually result from the sudden vertical displacement of a lake bed or ocean floor but can also be caused by landslides, asteroids, or explosions. A tsunami wave can be barely noticeable in open, deep water, but as it approaches a shoreline, the wave can grow to a height of 50 feet or more. Recent notable examples are the 2004 Indian Ocean tsunami and the 2011 Japan tsunami. Figure 5-4 shows coastline damage from the Japan tsunami.

Figure 5-4
Damage to structures caused by the 2011 Japan tsunami

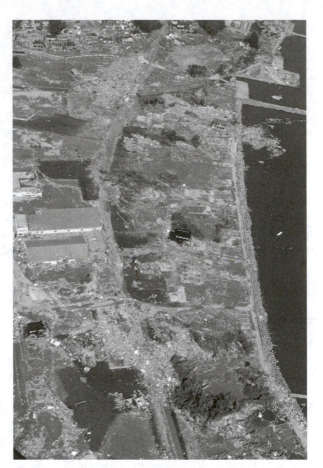

- **Pandemic** The spread of infectious disease over a wide geographic region, even worldwide. Pandemics have regularly occurred throughout history and are likely to continue occurring, despite advances in sanitation and immunology. A pandemic is the rapid spread of any type of disease, including typhoid, tuberculosis, bubonic plague, or influenza. Pandemics in the 20th century include the 1918–1920 Spanish flu, the 1956–1958 Asian flu, the 1968–1969 Hong Kong "swine" flu, and the 2009–2010 swine flu pandemics. Figure 5-5 shows an auditorium that was converted into a hospital during the 1918–1920 pandemic.

- **Extraterrestrial impacts** This category includes meteorites and other objects that may fall from the sky from way, way up. Sure, these events are extremely rare, and most organizations don't even include these events in their risk analysis, but I've included it here for the sake of rounding out the types of natural events.

Figure 5-5
An auditorium was used as a temporary hospital during the 1918 flu pandemic.

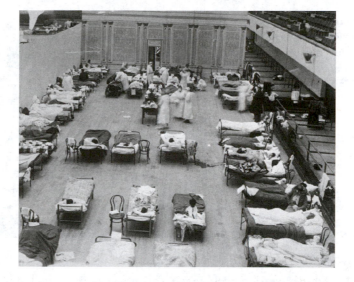

Human-Caused Disasters   Human-caused disasters are those events that are directly or indirectly caused by human activity through action or inaction. The results of human-caused disasters are similar to natural disasters: localized or widespread damage to businesses that results in potentially lengthy interruptions in operations.

These are some examples of human-caused disasters:

- **Civil disturbances**   These can take on many forms, including protests; demonstrations; riots; strikes; work slowdowns and stoppages; looting; and resulting actions such as curfews, evacuations, or lockdowns.

- **Utility outages**   These are failures in electric, natural gas, district heating, water, communications, and other utilities. These can be caused by equipment failures, sabotage, or natural events such as landslides or flooding.

- **Service outages**   These are failures in IT equipment, software programs, and online services. These can be caused by hardware failures, software bugs, or misconfiguration.

- **Materials shortages**   Interruptions in the supply of food, fuel, supplies, and materials can have a ripple effect on businesses and the services that support them. Readers who are old enough to remember the petroleum shortages of the mid-1970s know what this is all about; Figure 5-6 shows a line at a gas station during a 1970s-era gasoline shortage. Shortages can result in spikes in the price of commodities, which is almost as damaging as not having any supply at all.

- **Fires**   As contrasted to wildfires, here I mean fires that originate in or involve buildings, equipment, and materials.

- **Hazardous materials spills**   Many created or refined substances can be dangerous if they escape their confines. Examples include petroleum substances, gases, pesticides and herbicides, medical substances, and radioactive substances.

Figure 5-6 Citizens wait in long lines to buy fuel during a gas shortage.

- **Transportation accidents** This broad category includes plane crashes, railroad derailment, bridge collapse, and the like.

- **Terrorism and war** Whether they are actions of a nation, nation-state, or group, terrorism and war can have devastating but usually localized effects in cities and regions. Often, terrorism and war precipitate secondary effects such as materials shortages and utility outages.

- **Security events** The actions of a lone hacker or a team of organized cybercriminals can bring down one system, one network, or many networks, which could result in widespread interruption in services. The hackers' activities can directly result in an outage, or an organization can voluntarily (although reluctantly) shut down an affected service or network to contain the incident.

NOTE It is important to remember that real disasters are usually complex events that involve more than just one type of damaging event. For instance, an earthquake directly damages buildings and equipment but can also cause fires and utility outages. A hurricane also brings flooding, utility outages, and sometimes even hazardous materials events and civil disturbances such as looting.

How Disasters Affect Organizations Disasters have a wide variety of effects on an organization that are discussed in this section. Many disasters have direct effects, but sometimes it is the secondary effects of a disaster event that are most significant from the perspective of ongoing business operations.

A risk analysis is a part of the BCP process (discussed in the next section in this chapter) that will identify the ways in which disasters are likely to affect a particular organization. It is during the risk analysis when the primary, secondary, and downstream effects of likely disaster scenarios need to be identified and considered. Whoever is performing this risk analysis will need to have a broad understanding of the interdependencies of business processes and IT systems, as well as the ways in which a disaster will affect ongoing business operations. Similarly, those personnel who are developing contingency and recovery plans also need to be familiar with these effects so that those plans will adequately serve the organization's needs.

Disasters, by our definition, interrupt business operations in some measurable way. An event that has the appearance of a disaster may occur, but if it doesn't affect a particular organization, then you would say that no disaster occurred, at least for that particular organization.

It would be shortsighted to say that a disaster affects only operations. Rather, it is appropriate to understand the longer-term effects that a disaster has on the organization's image, brand, reputation, and ongoing financial viability. The factors affecting image, brand, and reputation have as much to do with how the organization communicates to its customers, suppliers, and shareholders, as with how the organization actually handles a disaster in progress.

These are some of the ways that a disaster affects an organization's operations:

- **Direct damage**   Events such as earthquakes, floods, and fires directly damage an organization's buildings, equipment, or records. The damage may be severe enough that no salvageable items remain, or it may be less severe, where some equipment and buildings may be salvageable or repairable.

- **Utility interruption**   Even if an organization's buildings and equipment are undamaged, a disaster may affect utilities such as power, natural gas, or water, which can incapacitate some or all business operations. Significant delays in refuse collection can result in unsanitary conditions.

- **Transportation**   A disaster may damage or render transportation systems such as roads, railroads, shipping, or air transport unusable for a period. Damaged transportation systems will interrupt supply lines and personnel.

- **Services and supplier shortage**   Even if a disaster does not have a direct effect on an organization, critical suppliers affected by a disaster can have an undesirable effect on business operations. For instance, a regional baker that cannot produce and ship bread to its corporate customers will soon result in sandwich shops without a critical resource.

- **Staff availability**   A community-wide or regional disaster that affects businesses is likely to also affect homes and families. Depending upon the nature of a disaster, employees will place a higher priority on the safety and comfort of family members. Also, workers may not be able or willing to travel to work if transportation systems are affected or if there is a significant materials shortage. Employees may also be unwilling to travel to work if they fear for their personal safety or that of their families.

- **Customer availability**   Various types of disasters may force or dissuade customers from traveling to business locations to conduct business. Many of the factors that keep employees away may also keep customers away.

CAUTION The kinds of secondary and tertiary effects that a disaster has on a particular organization depend entirely upon its unique set of circumstances that constitute its specific critical needs. A risk analysis should be performed to identify these specific factors.

The Business Continuity Planning Process

The proper way to plan for disaster preparedness is to first know what kinds of disasters are likely and their possible effects on the organization. That is, plan first, act later.

The business continuity planning process is a life-cycle process. In other words, business continuity planning (and disaster recovery planning) is not a one-time event or activity. It's a set of activities that result in the ongoing preparedness for disaster that continually adapts to changing business conditions and that continually improves.

The following are the elements of the BCP process life cycle:

- Assign ownership of the program.
- Develop BCP policy.
- Conduct business impact analysis.
- Perform criticality analysis.
- Establish recovery targets.
- Define KRIs and KPIs.
- Develop recovery and continuity strategies and plans.
- Test recovery and continuity plans and procedures.
- Test integration of BCP and DR plans.
- Train personnel.
- Maintain strategies, plans, and procedures through periodic reviews and updates.

Figure 5-7 shows the BCP life cycle. The details of this life cycle are described in detail in this chapter.

BCP Policy   A formal BCP effort must, like any strategic activity, flow from the existence of a formal policy and be included in the overall governance model that is the topic of this chapter. BCP should be an integral part of the IT control framework, not lie outside of it. Therefore, BCP policy should include or cite specific controls that ensure that key activities in the BCP life cycle are performed appropriately.

BCP policy should also define the scope of the BCP strategy. This means that the specific business processes (or departments or divisions within an organization) that are included in the BCP effort must be defined. Sometimes the scope will include a geographic boundary. In larger organizations, it is possible to "bite off more than you can chew" and define too large a scope for a BCP project, so limiting scope to a smaller, more manageable portion of the organization can be a good approach.

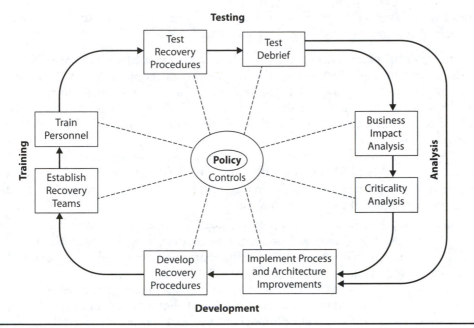

Figure 5-7 The BCP process life cycle

BCP and COBIT 5 Controls

The specific COBIT 5 controls that are involved with BCP are contained within *DSS04—Ensure continuous service*. DSS04 has eight specific controls that constitute the entire BCP life cycle:

- Define the business continuity policy, objectives, and scope.
- Maintain a continuity strategy.
- Develop and implement a business continuity response.
- Exercise, test, and review the BCP.
- Review, maintain, and improve the continuity plan.
- Conduct continuity plan training.
- Manage backup arrangements.
- Conduct post-resumption review.

These controls are discussed in this chapter and also appear in COBIT 5.

Business Impact Analysis The objective of the business impact analysis is to identify the impact that different scenarios will have on ongoing business operations. The BIA is one of several steps of critical, detailed analysis that must be carried out before the development of continuity or recovery plans and procedures.

Inventory Key Processes and Systems   The first step in a BIA is the collection of key business processes and IT systems. Within the overall scope of the BCP project, the objective here is to establish a detailed list of all identifiable processes and systems. The usual approach is the development of a questionnaire or intake form that would be circulated to key personnel in end-user departments and also within IT. Figure 5-8 shows a sample intake form.

Typically, the information that is gathered on intake forms is transferred to a multi-columned spreadsheet, where information on all of the organization's in-scope processes can be viewed together. This will become even more useful in subsequent phases of the BCP project, such as the criticality analysis.

 TIP   Use of an intake form is not the only accepted approach when gathering information about critical processes and systems. It's also acceptable to conduct one-on-one interviews or group interviews with key users and IT personnel to identify critical processes and systems. I recommend the use of an intake form (whether paper-based or electronic), even if the interviewer uses it herself as a framework for note-taking.

Process or system name	
Interviewee	
Title	
Department	
Contact info	
Date	
Process owner	
Process operator(s)	
Process description	
Customer facing (Y or N)	
IT system(s) used	
Key suppliers	
Communications needed	
Assets needed	
Process dependencies	
Other dependencies	
Documentation location	
Records location	

Figure 5-8   BIA sample intake form for gathering data about key processes

Planning Should Precede Action

IT personnel are often eager to get to the fun and meaty part of a project. Developers are anxious to begin coding before design, system administrators are eager to build systems before they are scoped and designed, and BCP personnel fervently desire to begin designing more robust system architectures and to tinker with replication and backup capabilities before key facts are known. In the case of business continuity and disaster recovery planning, completion of the BIA and other analyses is critical, as the analyses help to define the systems and processes most needed before getting to the fun part.

Statements of Impact   When processes and systems are being inventoried and cataloged, it is also vitally important to obtain one or more statements of impact for each process and system. A statement of impact is a qualitative or quantitative description of the impact on the business if the process or system were incapacitated for a time.

For IT systems, you might capture the number of users and the names of departments or functions that are affected by the unavailability of a specific IT system. Include the geography of affected users and functions if that is appropriate. Here are example statements of impact for IT systems:

- *Three thousand users in France and Italy will be unable to access customer records, resulting in degraded customer service.*
- *All users in North America will be unable to read or send e-mail, resulting in productivity slowdowns.*

Statements of impact for business processes might cite the business functions that would be affected. Here are some example statements of impact:

- *Accounts payable and accounts receivable functions will be unable to process, impacting availability of services and supplies and resulting in reduced revenue.*
- *Legal department will be unable to access contracts and addendums, resulting in lost or delayed revenue.*

Statements of impact for revenue-generating and revenue-supporting business functions could quantify financial impact per unit of time (be sure to use the same units of time for all functions so that they can be easily compared with one another). Here are some examples:

- *Inability to place orders for appliances will cost at the rate of $12,000 per hour.*
- *Delays in payments will cost $45,000 per day in interest charges.*

As statements of impact are gathered, it might make sense to create several columns in the main worksheet so that like units (names of functions, numbers of users, financial figures) can be sorted and ranked later.

When the BIA is completed, you'll have the following information about each process and system:

- Name of the process or system
- Who is responsible for its operation
- A description of its function
- Dependencies on systems
- Dependencies on suppliers
- Dependencies on key employees
- Quantified statements of impact in terms of revenue, users affected, and/or functions impacted

You're almost home.

Criticality Analysis   When all of the BIA information has been collected and charted, the criticality analysis (CA) can be performed.

The criticality analysis is a study of each system and process, a consideration of the impact on the organization if it is incapacitated, the likelihood of incapacitation, and the estimated cost of mitigating the risk or impact of incapacitation. In other words, it's a somewhat special type of a risk analysis that focuses on key processes and systems.

The criticality analysis needs to include, or reference, a threat analysis. A *threat analysis* is a risk analysis that identifies every threat that has a reasonable probability of occurrence, plus one or more mitigating controls or compensating controls, and new probabilities of occurrence with those mitigating/compensating controls in place. In case you're having a little trouble imagining what this looks like (I'm writing the book and I'm having trouble seeing this!), take a look at Table 5-4, which is a lightweight example of what I'm talking about.

In the preceding threat analysis, notice the following:

- Multiple threats are listed for a single asset. In the preceding example, I mentioned just eight threats. For all the threats but one, I listed only a single mitigating control. For the extended power outage threat, I listed two mitigating controls.

- Cost of downtime wasn't listed. For systems or processes where you have a cost per unit of time for downtime, you'll need to include it here, along with some calculations to show the payback for each control.

- Some mitigating controls can benefit more than one system. That may not have been obvious in this example, but in the case of an uninterruptible power supply (UPS) and electric generator, many systems can benefit, so the cost for these mitigating controls can be allocated across many systems, thereby lowering the cost for each system. Another example is a high-availability storage area network (SAN) located in two different geographic areas; while initially expensive, many applications can use the SAN for storage, and all will benefit from replication to the counterpart storage system.

System	Threat	Probability	Mitigating Control	Mitigation Cost	Mitigated Probability
Application Server	Denial of service	0.1%	High-performance filtering router	$60,000	0.01%
	Malware	1%	Antivirus	$200	0.1%
	Storage failure	2%	RAID 5	$20,000	0.01%
	Administrator error	15%	Configuration management tools	$10,000	1%
	Hardware CPU failure	5%	Server cluster	$15,000	1%
	Application software bug	5%	Source code reviews	$10,000	2%
	Extended power outage	25%	UPS Electric generator	$12,000 $40,000	2% 0.5%
	Flood	2%	Relocate data center	$200,000	0.1%

Table 5-4 Example Threat Analysis Identifies Threats and Controls for Critical Systems and Processes

- Threat probabilities are arbitrary. In Table 5-4, the probabilities were for a single occurrence in an entire year, so, for example, 5 percent means the threat will be realized once every 20 years.

- The length of outage was not included. You may need to include this also, particularly if you are quantifying downtime per hour or other unit of time.

It is probably becoming obvious that a threat analysis and the corresponding criticality analysis can get complicated. The rule here should be this: the complexity of the threat and criticality analyses should be proportional to the value of the assets (or revenue, or both). For example, in a company where application downtime is measured in thousands of dollars per minute, it's probably worth taking a few weeks or even months to work out all of the likely scenarios and a variety of mitigating controls and to work out which ones are the most cost-effective. On the other hand, for a system or business process where the impact of an outage is far less costly, a good deal less time might be spent on the supporting threat and criticality analysis.

EXAM TIP Test-takers should ensure that any question dealing with BIA and CA places the business impact analysis first. Without this analysis, criticality analysis is impossible to evaluate in terms of likelihood or cost-effectiveness in mitigation strategies. The BIA identifies strategic resources and provides a value to their recovery and operation, which is, in turn, consumed in the criticality analysis phase. If presented with a question identifying BCP at a particular stage, make sure that any answers you select facilitate the BIA and then the CA before moving on toward objectives and strategies.

Determine Maximum Tolerable Downtime   The next step for each critical process is the establishment of a metric called *maximum tolerable downtime (MTD)*. This is a theoretical period of time, measured from the onset of a disaster, after which the organization's very survival is at risk. Establishing MTD for each critical process is an important step that aids in the establishment of key recovery targets, discussed in the next section.

Determine Maximum Tolerable Outage   Next, the metric *maximum tolerable outage (MTO)* needs to be determined. MTO is a measure of the maximum time that an organization can tolerate operating in recovery (or alternate processing) mode. This metric comes into play in situations where systems and processes in recovery mode operate at a lower level of throughput, consistency, or integrity. MTO drives the need to reestablish normal production operations within a specific period of time.

Establishing Key Recovery Targets   When the cost or impact of downtime has been established and the cost and benefit of mitigating controls has been considered, some key targets can be established for each critical process. The two key targets are recovery time objective and recovery point objective. These objectives determine how quickly key systems and processes are made available after the onset of a disaster and the maximum tolerable data loss that results from the disaster. The key recovery targets are as follows:

- **Recovery time objective (RTO)**   This refers to the maximum period that elapses from the onset of a disaster until the resumption of service.
- **Recovery point objective (RPO)**   This refers to the maximum data loss from the onset of a disaster.
- **Recovery capacity objective (RCapO)**   This refers to the processing or storage capacity of an alternate process or system, as compared to the primary process or system.
- **Recovery consistency objective (RCO)**   This refers to the consistency and integrity of processing in a recovery system, as compared to the primary processing system.

Once these objectives are known, the disaster recovery (DR) team can begin to build system recovery capabilities and procedures that will help the organization to economically realize these targets. This is discussed in detail later in this chapter.

Developing Continuity Plans

In the previous section, I discussed the notion of establishing recovery targets and the development of architectures, processes, and procedures. The processes and procedures are related to the normal operation of those new technologies as they will be operated in normal day-to-day operations. When those processes and procedures have been completed, then the disaster recovery plans and procedures (those actions that will take place during and immediately after a disaster) can be developed.

For example, an organization has established RPO and RTO targets for its critical applications. These targets necessitated the development of server clusters and storage area networks with replication. While implementing those new technologies, the organization developed the operations processes and procedures in support of those new technologies that would be carried out every day during normal business operations. As a separate activity, the organization would then develop the procedures to be performed when a disaster strikes the primary operations center for those applications; those procedures would include all of the steps that must be taken so that the applications can continue operating in an alternate location.

The procedures for operating critical applications during a disaster are a small part of the entire body of procedures that must be developed. Several other sets of procedures must also be developed, including the following:

- Personnel safety procedures
- Disaster declaration procedures
- Responsibilities
- Contact information
- Recovery procedures
- Continuing operations
- Restoration procedures

All of these are required so that an organization will be adequately prepared in the event a disaster occurs.

Personnel Safety Procedures   When a disaster strikes, measures to ensure the safety of personnel need to be taken immediately. If the disaster has occurred or is about to occur to a building, personnel may need to be evacuated as soon as possible. Arguably, however, in some situations evacuation is exactly the wrong thing to do; for example, if a hurricane or tornado is bearing down on a facility, then the building itself may be the best shelter for personnel, even if it incurs some damage. The point here is that personnel safety procedures need to be carefully developed, and possibly more than one set of procedures will be needed, depending on the event.

NOTE   Remember, the highest priority in any disaster or emergency situation is the safety of human life.

Personnel safety procedures need to take many factors into account:

- Ensuring that all personnel are familiar with evacuation and sheltering procedures
- Ensuring that visitors will know how to evacuate the premises and the location of sheltering areas
- Posting signs and placards that indicate emergency evacuation routes and gathering areas outside of the building
- Emergency lighting to aid in evacuation or sheltering in place

- Fire extinguishment equipment (portable fire extinguishers and so on)
- The ability to communicate with public safety and law enforcement authorities, including in situations where communications and electric power have been cut off and when all personnel are outside of the building
- Care for injured personnel
- CPR and emergency first-aid training
- Safety personnel who can assist in the evacuation of injured and disabled people
- The ability to account for visitors and other nonemployees
- Emergency shelter in extreme weather conditions
- Emergency food and drinking water
- Periodic tests to ensure that evacuation procedures will be adequate in the event of a real emergency

Local emergency management organizations may have additional information available that can assist an organization with its emergency personnel safety procedures.

Disaster Declaration Procedures   Disaster response procedures are initiated when a disaster is declared. However, there needs to be a procedure for the declaration itself so that there will be little doubt as to the conditions that must be present.

Why is a disaster declaration procedure required? It's primarily because it's not always clear whether a situation is a real disaster. Sure, a 7.5 earthquake or a major fire is a disaster, but overcooking popcorn in the microwave that sets off a building's fire alarm system might not be. Many "in between" situations may or may not be disasters. A disaster declaration procedure must state some basic conditions that will help determine whether a disaster should be declared.

Further, who has the authority to declare a disaster? What if senior management personnel frequently travel and may not be around? Who else can declare a disaster? Finally, what does it mean to declare a disaster—and what happens next? The following points constitute the primary items that organizations need to consider for their disaster declaration procedure.

Form a Core Team   To be effective and workable, a core team of personnel needs to be established, all of whom will be familiar with the disaster declaration procedure, as well as the actions that must take place once a disaster has been declared. This core team should consist of middle and upper managers who are familiar with business operations, particularly those that are critical. This core team must be large enough so that a requisite few of them are on hand when a disaster strikes. In organizations that have second shifts, third shifts, and weekend work, some of the core team members should be those in supervisory positions during those off-hours times. However, some of the core team members can be personnel who work "business hours" and are not on-site all of the time.

Declaration Criteria   The declaration procedure must contain some tangible criteria that a core team member can consult to guide him down the "Is this a disaster?" decision path.

The criteria for declaring a disaster should be related to the availability and viability of ongoing critical business operations. Some example criteria include any one or more of the following:

- Forced evacuation of a building containing or supporting critical operations that is likely to last for more than four hours

- Hardware, software, or network failures that result in a critical IT system being incapacitated or unavailable for more than four hours

- Any security incident that results in a critical IT system being incapacitated for more than four hours (security incidents could involve malware, break-in, attack, sabotage, and so on)

- Any event causing employee absenteeism or supplier shortages that, in turn, results in one or more critical business processes being incapacitated for more than eight hours

- Any event causing a communications failure that results in critical IT systems being unreachable for more than four hours

The preceding examples are a mostly complete list of criteria for many organizations. The periods will vary from organization to organization. For instance, a large, pure-online business such as Salesforce.com would probably declare a disaster if its main web sites were unavailable for more than a few minutes. But in an organization where computers are far less critical, an outage of four hours might not be considered a disaster.

Pulling the Trigger   When disaster declaration criteria are met, the disaster should be declared. The procedure for disaster declaration could permit any single core team member to declare the disaster, but it may be better to have two or more core team members agree on whether a disaster should be declared. Whether an organization should use a single-person declaration or a group of two or more is each organization's choice.

All core team members empowered to declare a disaster should have the procedure on hand at all times. In most cases, the criteria should fit on a small, laminated wallet card that each team member can have with him or nearby at all times. For organizations that use the consensus method for declaring a disaster, the wallet card should include the names and contact numbers for other core team members so that each will have a way of contacting others.

Next Steps   Declaring a disaster will trigger the start of one or more other response procedures but not necessarily all of them. For instance, if a disaster is declared because of a serious computer or software malfunction, there is no need to evacuate the building. While this example may be obvious, not all instances will be this clear. Either the disaster declaration procedure itself or each of the subsequent response procedures should contain criteria that will help determine which response procedures should be enacted.

False Alarms   Probably the most common cause of personnel not declaring a disaster is the fear that a real disaster is not taking place. Core team members empowered with declaring a disaster should not necessarily hesitate. Instead, core team members could convene with additional core team members to reach a firm decision, provided this can be done quickly.

If a disaster has been declared and later it is clear that a disaster has been averted (or did not exist in the first place), the disaster can simply be called off and declared to be over. Response personnel can be contacted and told to cease response activities and return to their normal activities.

 TIP   Depending on the level of effort that takes place in the opening minutes and hours of disaster response, the consequences of declaring a disaster when none exists may be significant or not. In the spirit of continuous improvement, any organization that has had a few false alarms should seek to improve its disaster declaration criteria. Well-trained and experienced personnel can usually reduce the frequency of false alarms.

Responsibilities   During a disaster, many important tasks must be performed to evacuate or shelter personnel, assess damage, recover critical processes and systems, and carry out many other functions that are critical to the survival of the enterprise.

About 20 different responsibilities are described here. In a large organization, each responsibility may be staffed with a team of two, three, or many individuals. In small organizations, a few people may incur many responsibilities each, switching from role to role as the situation warrants.

All of these roles will be staffed by people who are available to fill them. It is important to remember that many of the "ideal" people to fill each role will be unavailable during a disaster for several reasons:

- **Injured, ill, or deceased**   Some regional disasters will inflict widespread casualties that will include some proportion of response personnel. Those who are injured, who are ill (in the case of a pandemic, for instance, or who are recovering from a sickness or surgery when the disaster occurs), or who are killed by the disaster are clearly not going to be showing up to help out.

- **Caring for family members**   Some types of disasters may cause widespread injury or require mass evacuation. In some of these situations, many personnel will be caring for family members whose immediate needs for safety will take priority over the needs of the workplace.

- **Unavailable transportation**   Some types of disasters include localized or widespread damage to transportation infrastructure, which may result in many people who are willing to be on-site to help with emergency operations being unable to travel to the work site.

- **Out of the area**   Some disaster response personnel may be away on business travel or on vacation and be unable to respond. However, some people being away may actually be opportunities in disguise; unaffected by the physical impact of the disaster, they may be able to help out in other ways, such as communications with suppliers, customers, or other personnel.

- **Communications**   Some types of disasters, particularly those that are localized (versus widespread and obvious to an observer), require that disaster response personnel be contacted and asked to help. If a disaster strikes after hours, some personnel may be unreachable if they are engaged in any activity where they do not have a mobile phone with them or are out of range.

- **Fear**   Some types of disasters (such as pandemic, terrorist attack, flood, and so on) may instill fear for safety on the part of response personnel who will disregard the call to help and stay away from the work site.

NOTE   Response personnel in all disciplines and responsibilities will need to be able to piece together whatever functionality they are called on to do, using whatever resources are available—this is part art form and part science. While response and contingency plans may make certain assumptions, personnel may find themselves with fewer resources than planned, requiring them to do the best they can with the resources available.

Each function will be working with personnel in many other functions, often working with unfamiliar people. An entire response and recovery operation may be operating almost like a new organization in unfamiliar settings and with an entirely new set of rules. In typical organizations, teams work well when team members are familiar with, and trust, one another. In a response and recovery operation, the stress level is much higher because the stakes—company survival—are higher, and often the teams are composed of people who have little experience with each other and these new roles. This will cause additional stress that will bring out the best and worst in people, as illustrated in Figure 5-9.

Figure 5-9   Stress is compounded by the pressure of disaster recovery and the formation of new teams in times of chaos.

Emergency Response   These are the "first responders" during a disaster. Top priorities include evacuation or sheltering of personnel, first aid, triage of injured personnel, and possibly firefighting.

Command and Control (Emergency Management)   During disaster response operations, someone has to be in charge. In a disaster, resources may be scarce, and many matters vie for attention. Someone needs to fill the role of decision-maker to keep disaster response activities moving and to handle situations that arise. This role may need to be rotated among various personnel, particularly in smaller organizations, to counteract fatigue.

TIP   Although the first person on the scene may be the person in charge *initially*, that will definitely change as qualified assigned personnel show up and take charge and as the nature of the disaster and response solidifies. The leadership roles may then be passed among key personnel already designated to be in charge.

Scribe   It's vital that one or more people continually document the important events during disaster response operations. From decisions to discussions to status to roll call, these events must be written down so that the details of disaster response can be pieced together afterward. This will help the organization better understand how disaster response unfolded, how decisions were made, and who performed which actions, all of which will help the organization be better prepared for future events.

Internal Communications   In many disaster scenarios, personnel may be stripped of many or all of their normal means of communication, such as desk phone, voicemail, e-mail, smartphone, and instant messaging. Yet never are communications as vital as during a disaster, when nothing is going according to plan. Internal communications are needed so that status on various activities can be sent to command and control and so that priorities and orders can be sent to disaster response personnel.

Many organizations establish means for emergency communications, including the following:

- **Broadcast alerts**   Sent via text or voice, this helps to inform large numbers of users about events affecting the organization.
- **Emergency radio communications**   When wireless and wireline communications are not functioning, emergency communication via radio helps personnel in different locations pass along important information.

External Communications   People outside of the organization need to know what's going on when a disaster strikes. There's a potentially long list of parties who want or need to know the status of business operations during and after a disaster:

- Customers
- Suppliers

- Partners
- Insurance companies
- Shareholders
- Neighbors
- Regulators
- Media
- Law enforcement and public safety authorities (first responders)

These different audiences need different messages, as well as messages in different forms. For instance, notifications to the public may be made through media outlets, whereas notifications to customers may be made through e-mail or surface mail.

Legal and Compliance   Several needs may arise during a disaster that require the attention of inside or outside legal counsel. Disasters present unique situations that need legal assistance, such as the following:

- Interpretation of regulations
- Interpretation of contracts with suppliers and customers
- Management of matters of liability to other parties

TIP   Typical legal matters need to be resolved before the onset of a disaster, with this information included in disaster response procedures since legal staff members may be unavailable during the disaster.

Damage Assessment   Whether a disaster is a physically violent event, such as an earthquake or volcano, or instead involves no physical manifestation, such as a serious security incident, one or more experts are needed who can examine affected assets and accurately assess the damage. Because most organizations own many different types of assets (from buildings to equipment to information), qualified experts are needed to assess each asset type involved. It is not necessary to call upon all available experts, only those whose expertise matches the type of event that has occurred.

Some expertise may go well beyond the skills present in an organization, such as a building structural engineer who can assess potential earthquake damage. In such cases it may be sensible to retain the services of an outside engineer who will respond and provide an assessment on whether a building is safe to occupy after a disaster. In fact, it may make sense to retain more than one in case they themselves are affected by a disaster.

Salvage   Disasters destroy assets that the organization uses to make products or perform services. When a disaster occurs, someone (either a qualified employee or an outside expert) needs to examine assets to determine which are salvageable; then a salvage team needs to perform the actual salvage operation at a pace that meets the organization's needs.

In some cases, salvage may be a critical-path activity, where critical processes are paralyzed until salvage and repairs to critically needed machinery can be performed. In other cases, the salvage operation is performed on inventory of finished goods, raw materials, and other items so that business operations can be resumed. Occasionally, when it is obvious that damaged equipment or materials are a total loss, the salvage effort is one of selling the damaged items or materials to some organization that wants them.

Assessment of damage to assets may be a high priority when an organization will be filing an insurance claim. Insurance may be a primary source of funding for the organization's recovery effort.

CAUTION   Salvage operations may be a critical-path activity or one that can be carried out well after the disaster. To the greatest extent possible, this should be decided in advance. Otherwise, the command-and-control function will need to decide the priority of salvage operations.

Physical Security   After a disaster, the organization's usual physical security controls may be compromised. For instance, fencing, walls, and barricades could be damaged, or video surveillance systems may be disabled or have no electric power. These and other failures could lead to increased risk of loss or damage to assets and personnel until those controls can be fixed. Also, security controls in temporary quarters such as hot/warm/cold sites and temporary work centers may be below those in primary locations.

Supplies   During emergency and recovery operations, personnel will require supplies of many kinds, from drinking water, writing tablets, and pens to smartphones, portable generators, and extension cords. This function may also be responsible for ordering replacement assets such as servers and network equipment for a cold site.

Transportation   When workers are operating from a temporary location, and if regional or local transportation systems have been compromised, many arrangements for all kinds of transportation may be required to support emergency operations. These can include transportation of replacement workers, equipment, or supplies by truck, car, rail, sea, or air. This function could also be responsible for arranging for temporary lodging for personnel.

Work Centers   When a disaster event results in business locations being unusable, workers may need to work in temporary locations. These work centers will need to have a variety of amenities available to permit workers to be productive until their primary work locations are again available.

Network   This technology function is responsible for damage assessment to the organization's voice and data networks, building/configuring networks for emergency operations, or both. This function may require extensive coordination with external telecommunications service providers, who, by the way, may be suffering the effects of a local or regional disaster as well.

Network Services   This function is responsible for network-centric services such as the Domain Name System (DNS), Simple Network Management Protocol (SNMP), network routing, and authentication.

Systems   This is the function that is responsible for building, loading, and configuring the servers and systems that support critical services, applications, databases, and other functions. Personnel may have other resources such as virtualization technology to enable additional flexibility.

Database Management Systems   For critical applications that rely upon database management systems, this function is responsible for building databases on recovery systems and for restoring or recovering data from backup media, replication volumes, or e-vaults onto recovery systems. Database personnel will need to work with systems, network, and applications personnel to ensure that databases are operating properly and are available as needed.

Data and Records   This function is responsible for access to and re-creation of electronic and paper business records. This is a business function that supports critical business processes and works with database management personnel and, if necessary, works with data-entry personnel to rekey lost data.

Applications   This function is responsible for recovering application functionality on application servers. This may include reloading application software; performing configuration; provisioning roles and user accounts; and connecting the application to databases, network services, and other application integration issues.

Access Management   This function is responsible for creating and managing user accounts for network, system, and application access. Personnel with this responsibility may be especially susceptible to social engineering and be tempted to create user accounts without proper authority or approval.

Information Security and Privacy   Personnel in this capacity are responsible for ensuring that proper security controls are being carried out during recovery and emergency operations. They will be expected to identify risks associated with emergency operations and to require remedies to reduce risks.

Security personnel will also be responsible for enforcing privacy controls so that employee and customer personal data will not be compromised, even as business operations are affected by the disaster.

Off-Site Storage   This function is responsible for managing the effort of retrieving backup media from off-site storage facilities and for protecting that media in transit to the scene of recovery operations. If recovery operations take place over an extended period (more than a couple of days), data at the recovery site will need to be backed up and sent to an off-site media storage facility to protect that information should a disaster occur at the hot/warm/cold site (and what bad luck that would be!).

User Hardware   In many organizations, little productive work gets done when employees don't have their workstations, printers, scanners, copiers, and other office equipment. Thus, a function is required to provide, configure, and support the variety of office equipment required by end users working in temporary or alternate locations. This function, like most others, will have to work with many others to ensure that workstations and other equipment are able to communicate with applications and services as needed to support critical processes.

Training   During emergency operations, when response personnel and users are working in new locations (and often on new or different equipment and software), some of these personnel may need training so that their productivity can be quickly restored. Training personnel will need to be familiar with many disaster response and recovery procedures so that they can help people in those roles understand what is expected of them. This function will also need to be able to dispense emergency operations procedures to these personnel.

Restoration   This function comes into play when IT is ready to migrate applications running on hot/warm/cold site systems back to the original (or replacement) processing center.

Contract Information   This function is responsible for understanding and interpreting legal contracts. Most organizations are a party to one or more legal contracts that require them to perform specific activities, provide specific services, and communicate status if service levels have changed. These contracts may or may not have provisions for activities and services during disasters, including communications regarding any changes in service levels.

This function is vital not only during the disaster planning stages but also during actual disaster response. Customers, suppliers, regulators, and other parties need to be informed according to specific contract terms.

Recovery Procedures   Recovery procedures are the instructions that key personnel use to bootstrap services (such as IT systems and other business-enabling technologies) that support the critical business functions identified in the BIA and CA. The recovery procedures should work hand in hand with the technologies that may have been added to IT systems to make them more resilient.

An example would be useful here. A fictitious company, Acme Rocket Boots, determines that its order-entry business function is highly critical to the ongoing viability of the business and sets recovery objectives to ensure that order entry would be continued within no more than 48 hours after a disaster.

Acme determines that it needs to invest in storage, backup, and replication technologies to make a 48-hour recovery possible. Without these investments, IT systems supporting order entry would be down for at least ten days until they could be rebuilt from scratch. Acme cannot justify the purchase of systems and software to facilitate an autofailover of the order-entry application to hot-site DR servers; instead, the recovery procedure would require that the database be rebuilt from replicated data on cloud-based servers. Other tasks, such as installing recent patches, would also be necessary to make recovery servers ready for production use. All of the tasks required to make the systems ready constitute the body of recovery procedures needed to support the business order-entry function.

This example is, of course, a gross oversimplification. Actual recovery procedures could take dozens of pages of documentation, and procedures would also be necessary for network components, end-user workstations, network services, and other supporting IT services required by the order-entry application. And those are the procedures needed just to get the application running again. More procedures would be needed to keep the applications running properly in the recovery environment.

Continuing Operations   Procedures for continuing operations have more to do with business processes than they do with IT systems. However, the two are related since the procedures for continuing critical business processes have to fit hand in hand with the procedures for operating supporting IT systems that may also (but not necessarily) be operating in a recovery or emergency mode.

Let me clarify that last statement. It is entirely conceivable that a disaster could strike an organization with critical business processes that operate in one city but that are supported by IT systems located in another city. A disaster could strike the city with the critical business function, which means that personnel might have to continue operating that business function in another location, on the original, fully featured IT application. It is also possible that a disaster could strike the city with the IT application, forcing it into an emergency/recovery mode in an alternate location while users of the application are operating in a business-as-usual mode. And, of course, a disaster could strike both locations (or a disaster could strike in one location where both the critical business function and its supporting IT applications reside), throwing both the critical business function and its supporting IT applications into emergency mode. Any organization's reality could be even more complex than this: just add dependencies on external application service providers, applications with custom interfaces, or critical business functions that operate in multiple cities. If you wondered why disaster recovery and business continuity planning were so complicated, perhaps your appreciation has grown just now.

Restoration Procedures   When a disaster has occurred, IT operations need to temporarily take up residence in an alternate processing site while repairs are performed on the original processing site. Once those repairs are completed, IT operations would need to be transitioned back to the main (or replacement) processing facility. You should expect that the procedures for this transition would also be documented (and tested—testing is discussed later in this chapter).

NOTE   Transitioning applications back to the original processing site is not necessarily just a second iteration of the initial move to the hot/warm/cold site. Far from it. The recovery site may have been a skeleton (in capacity, functionality, or both) of its original self. The objective is not necessarily to move the functionality at the recovery site back to the *original* site but to restore the original functionality to the original site.

Let's look at an example. To continue the Acme Rocket Boots example, the order-entry application at the DR site had only basic, not extended, functions. For instance, customers could not look at order history, and they could not place custom orders; they could only order off-the-shelf products. But when the application is moved back to the primary processing facility, the history of orders accumulated on the DR application needs to be merged into the main order history database, which was not part of the DR plan.

Considerations for Continuity and Recovery Plans   A considerable amount of detailed planning and logistics must go into continuity and recovery plans if they are to be effective.

Availability of Key Personnel An organization cannot depend upon every member of its regular expert workforce to be available in a disaster. As discussed earlier in this chapter in more detail, personnel may be unavailable for a number of reasons, including the following:

- Injury, illness, or death
- Caring for family members
- Unavailable transportation
- Damaged transportation infrastructure
- Being out of the area
- Lack of communications
- Fear, related to the disaster and its effects

 TIP An organization must develop thorough and accurate recovery and continuity documentation as well as cross-training and plan testing. When a disaster strikes, an organization has one chance to survive, and it depends upon how well the available personnel are able to follow recovery and continuity procedures and to keep critical processes functioning properly.

Emergency Supplies The onset of a disaster may cause personnel to be stranded at a work location, possibly for several days. This can be caused by a number of reasons, including inclement weather that makes travel dangerous or a transportation infrastructure that is damaged or blocked with debris.

Emergency supplies should be laid up at a work location and made available to personnel stranded there, regardless of whether they are supporting a recovery effort or not (it's also possible that severe weather or a natural or human-made event could make transportation dangerous or impossible).

A disaster can also prompt employees to report to a work location (at the primary location or at an alternate site) where they may remain for days at a time, even around the clock if necessary. A situation like this may make the need for emergency supplies less critical, but it still may be beneficial to the recovery effort to make supplies available to support recovery personnel.

An organization stocking emergency supplies at a work location should consider including the following:

- Drinking water
- Food rations
- First-aid supplies
- Blankets
- Flashlights

- Battery or crank-powered radio
- Out-of-band communications with internal and external parties (e.g., beepers, walkie-talkies, line-of-sight systems, etc.)

Local emergency response authorities may recommend other supplies be kept at a work location as well.

Communications   Communication within organizations, as well as with customers, suppliers, partners, shareholders, regulators, and others, is vital under normal business conditions. During a disaster and subsequent recovery and restoration operations, such communications are more important than ever, while many of the usual means for communications may be impaired.

Identifying Critical Personnel   A successful disaster recovery operation requires available personnel who are located near company operations centers. While the primary response personnel may consist of the individuals and teams responsible for day-to-day corporate operations, others need to be identified. In a disaster, some personnel will be unavailable for many reasons (discussed earlier in this chapter).

Key personnel, as well as multiple backup people, need to be identified. Backup personnel can consist of other employees who have familiarity with specific technologies, such as operating system, database, and network administration, and who can cover for primary personnel if needed. Sure, it would be desirable for these backup personnel also to be trained in specific recovery operations, but at the least, if these personnel have access to specific detailed recovery procedures, having them on a call list is probably better than having no available personnel during a disaster.

Identifying Critical Suppliers, Customers, and Other Parties   Besides employees, many other parties need to be notified in the event of a disaster. Outside parties need to be aware of the disaster, as well as of basic changes in business conditions.

In a regional disaster such as a hurricane or earthquake, nearby parties will certainly be aware of the disaster and that your organization is involved in it somehow. However, those parties may not be aware of the status of business operations immediately after the disaster: a regional event's effects can range from complete destruction of buildings and equipment to no damage at all and business-as-usual conditions. Unless key parties are notified of the status, they may have no other way to know for sure.

Parties that need to be contacted may include the following:

- **Key suppliers**   This may include electric and gas utilities, fuel delivery, and materials delivery. In a disaster, an organization will often need to impart special instructions to one or more suppliers, requesting delivery of extra supplies or temporary cessation of deliveries.

- **Key customers**   Many organizations have key customers whose relationships are valued above most others. These customers may depend on a steady delivery of products and services that are critical to their own operations; in a disaster, those customers may have a dire need to know whether such deliveries will be able to continue or not and under what circumstances.

- **Public safety**   Police, fire, and other public safety authorities may need to be contacted, not only for emergency operations such as firefighting but also for any required inspections or other services. It is important that "business office" telephone numbers for these agencies be included on contact lists, as 911 and other emergency lines may be flooded by calls from others.

- **Insurance adjusters**   Most organizations rely on insurance companies to protect their assets from damage or loss in a disaster. Because insurance adjustment funds are often a key part of continuing business operations in an emergency, it's important to be able to reach insurers as soon as possible after a disaster has occurred.

- **Regulators**   In some industries, organizations are required to notify regulators of certain types of disasters. While regulators obviously may be aware of noteworthy regional disasters, they may not immediately know an event's specific effects on an organization. Further, some types of disasters are highly localized and may not be newsworthy, even in a local city.

- **Media**   Media outlets such as newspapers and television stations may need to be notified as a means of quickly reaching the community or region with information about the effects of a disaster on organizations.

- **Shareholders**   Organizations are usually obliged to notify their shareholders of any disastrous event that affects business operations. This may be the case whether the organization is publicly or privately held.

- **Stakeholders**   Organizations will need to notify other parties, including employees, competitors, and other tenants if the organization uses one or more multitenant facilities.

The people or teams responsible for communicating with these outside parties will need to have all of the individuals and organizations included in a list of parties to contact. This information should all be included in emergency response procedures.

Setting Up Call Trees   Disaster response procedures need to include a call tree. This is a method where the first personnel involved in a disaster begin notifying others in the organization, informing them of the developing disaster and enlisting their assistance.

Just as the branches of a tree originate at the trunk and are repeatedly subdivided, a call tree is most effective when each person in the tree can make just a few phone calls. Not only will the notification of important personnel proceed more quickly, but each person will not be overburdened with many calls.

Remember, in a disaster a significant portion of personnel may be unavailable or unreachable. Therefore, a call tree should be structured so that there is sufficient flexibility as well as assurance that all critical personnel will be contacted. Figure 5-10 shows an example call tree.

An organization can also use an automated outcalling system to notify critical personnel of a disaster. Such a system can play a prerecorded message or request that personnel call an information number to hear a prerecorded message. Most outcalling systems keep a log of which personnel have been successfully reached.

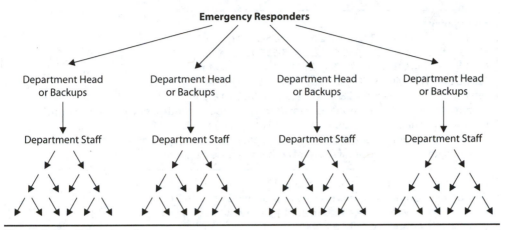

Figure 5-10   Example call tree structure

An automated calling system should not be located in the same geographic region. If it were, a regional disaster could damage the system or make it unavailable during a disaster. The system should be Internet accessible so that response personnel can access it to determine which personnel have been notified and to make any needed changes before or during a disaster.

Wallet Cards   Wallet cards containing emergency contact information should be prepared for core team personnel for the organization, as well as for members in each department who would be actively involved in disaster response. Wallet cards are advantageous, because most personnel will have their wallet, pocketbook, or purse nearby at all times, even when away from home, running errands, traveling, or on vacation. Not everyone carries their mobile devices with them every minute of the day. Information on the wallet card should include contact information for fellow team members, a few of the key disaster response personnel, and any conference bridges or emergency call-in numbers that are set up. Figure 5-11 shows an example wallet card.

Organizations may also issue digital versions of wallet cards for people to store on mobile devices.

Electronic Contact Lists   Arguably, most IT personnel and business leaders have smartphones and other mobile devices with onboard storage that is available even when cellular carriers are experiencing outages. Copies of contact lists and even disaster response procedures can be stored in smartphones as an additional means for having this information handy during a disaster.

Transportation   Some types of disasters may make certain modes of transportation unavailable or unsafe. Widespread natural disasters, such as earthquakes, volcanoes, hurricanes, and floods, can immobilize virtually every form of transportation, including highways, railroads, boats, and airplanes. Other types of disasters may impede one or more types of transportation, which could result in overwhelming demand for the

Emergency Contacts
Joe Phillips, VP Ops: 213-555-1212 h, 415-555-1212 m
Marie Peterson, CFO: 206-555-1212 h, 425-555-1212 m
Mark Woodward, IT Ops: 360-555-1212 h, 253-555-1212 m
Gary Doan, VP Facilities: 509-555-1212 h, 702-555-1212 m
Jeff Patterson, IT Networks: 760-555-1212 h, 310-555-1212 m
Documentation at briefcase.yahoo.com: Userid = wunderground, password = L0c43Dupt1te
Emergency conference bridge: 1-800-555-1212, host code 443322, PIN 0748
Disaster declaration criteria: 8-hr outage anticipated on critical systems, 2 core members vote, then initiate call tree procedure to notify other response personnel

Off-site media storage vendor: 719-555-1212
Telecommunications and network service provider: 312-555-1212
Local emergency response authorities: 714-555-1212
Local health authorities: 702-555-1212
Local law enforcement authorities: 512-555-1212
Local hospitals: 808-555-1212, 913-555-1212
National weather service hotline: 602-555-1212
Regional transportation authority hotline: 312-555-1212
Local building inspectors: 414-555-1212

Figure 5-11 Example laminated wallet card for core team participants with emergency contact information and disaster declaration criteria

available modes. High volumes of emergency supplies may be needed during and after a disaster, but damaged transportation infrastructure often makes the delivery of those supplies difficult.

Components of a Business Continuity Plan The complete set of business continuity plan documents will include the following:

- **Supporting project documents** These will include the documents created at the beginning of the business continuity project, including the project charter, project plan, statement of scope, and statement of support from executives.

- **Analysis documents** These include the following:
  - Business impact analysis
  - Threat assessment and risk assessment
  - Criticality analysis
  - Documents defining recovery targets such as recovery time objective, recovery point objective, recovery capacity objective, and recovery consistency objective

- **Response documents** These are all the documents that describe the required action of personnel when a disaster strikes, plus documents containing information required by those same personnel. Examples of these documents include the following:

- **Business recovery (or resumption) plan**   This describes the activities required to recover and resume critical business processes and activities.

- **Occupant emergency plan (OEP)**   This describes activities required to safely care for occupants in a business location during a disaster. This will include both evacuation procedures and sheltering procedures, each of which might be required, depending upon the type of disaster that occurs.

- **Emergency communications plan**   This describes the types of communications imparted to many parties, including emergency response personnel, employees in general, customers, suppliers, regulators, public safety organizations, shareholders, and the public.

- **Contact lists**   These contain names and contact information for emergency response personnel as well as for critical suppliers, customers, and other parties.

- **Disaster recovery plan**   This describes the activities required to restore critical IT systems and other critical assets, whether in alternate or primary locations.

- **Continuity of operations plan (COOP)**   This describes the activities required to continue critical and strategic business functions at an alternate site.

- **Security incident response plan (SIRP)**   This describes the steps required to deal with a security incident that could reach disaster-like proportions.

- **Test and review documents**   This is the entire collection of documents related to tests of all of the different types of business continuity plans, as well as reviews and revisions to documents.

Training Personnel

The value and usefulness of a high-quality set of disaster response and continuity plans and procedures will be greatly diminished if those responsible for carrying out the procedures are unfamiliar with them.

A person cannot learn to ride a bicycle by reading even the most detailed how-to instructions on the subject, so it's equally unrealistic to expect personnel to be able to properly carry out disaster response procedures if they are inexperienced in those procedures.

Several forms of training can be made available for the personnel who are expected to be available if a disaster strikes, including the following:

- **Document review**   Personnel can carefully read through procedure documents to become familiar with the nature of the recovery procedures. But as mentioned earlier, this alone may be insufficient.

- **Participation in walk-throughs**   People who are familiar with specific processes and systems that are the subject of walk-throughs should participate in them. Exposing personnel to the walk-through process will not only help to improve the walk-through and recovery procedures but will also be a learning experience for participants.

- **Participation in simulations**   Taking part in simulations will similarly benefit the participants by giving them the experience of thinking through a disaster.

- **Participation in parallel and cutover tests**   Other than experiencing an actual disaster and its recovery operations, no experience is quite like participating in parallel and cutover tests. Here, participants will gain actual hands-on experience with critical business processes and IT environments by performing the actual procedures that they would in the event of a disaster. When a disaster strikes, those participants can draw upon their memory of having performed those procedures in the past, instead of just the memory of having read the procedures.

You can see that all of the levels of tests that need to be performed to verify the quality of response plans are also training opportunities for personnel. The development and testing of disaster-related plans and procedures provide a continuous learning experience for all of the personnel involved.

Making Plans Available to Personnel When Needed

When a disaster strikes, often one of the effects is no access to even the most critical IT systems. Given a 40-hour workweek, there is roughly a 25 percent likelihood that critical personnel will be at the business location when a disaster strikes (at least the violent type of disaster that strikes with no warning, such as an earthquake—other types of disasters, such as hurricanes, may afford the organization a little bit of time to anticipate the disaster's impact). The point is that chances are good that the personnel who are available to respond may be unable to access the procedures and other information that they will need, unless special measures are taken.

 CAUTION   Complete BCP documentation often contains details of key systems, operating procedures, recovery strategies, and even vendor and model identification of in-place equipment. This information can be misused if available to unauthorized personnel, so the mechanism selected for ensuring availability must include planning to exclude inadvertent disclosure.

Response and recovery procedures can be made available in several ways to personnel during a disaster, including the following:

- **Hard copy**   While many have grown accustomed to the paperless office, disaster recovery and response documentation is one type of information that should be available in hard-copy form. Copies, even multiple copies, should be available for each responder, with a copy at the workplace and another at home, and possibly even a set in the responder's vehicle.

- **Soft copy**   Traditionally, soft-copy documentation is kept on file servers, but as you might expect, those file servers might be unavailable in a disaster. Soft copies should be available on responders' portable devices (laptops, tablets, and smartphones). An organization can also consider issuing documentation on memory sticks and cards. Depending upon the type of disaster, it can be difficult to know what resources will be available to access documentation, so making it available in more than one form will ensure that at least one copy of it will be available to the personnel who need access to it.

- **Alternate work/processing site**   Organizations that utilize a hot/warm/cold site for the recovery of critical operations can maintain hard copies and/or soft copies of recovery documentation there. This makes perfect sense; personnel working at an alternate processing or work site will need to know what to do, and having those procedures on-site will facilitate their work.

- **Online**   Soft copies of recovery documentation can be archived on an Internet-based site that includes the ability to store data. Almost any type of online service that includes authentication and the ability to upload documents could be suitable for this purpose.

- **Wallet cards**   It's unreasonable to expect to publish recovery documentation on a laminated wallet card, but those cards could be used to store the contact information for core response team members as well as a few other pieces of information, such as conference bridge codes, passwords to online repositories of documentation, and so on. An example wallet card appears earlier in this chapter, in Figure 5-11.

Maintaining Recovery and Continuity Plans

Business processes and technology undergo almost continuous change in most organizations. A business continuity plan that is developed and tested is liable to be outdated within months and obsolete within a year. If much more than a year passes, a DR plan in some organizations may approach uselessness. This section discusses how organizations need to keep their DR plans up-to-date and relevant.

A typical organization needs to establish a schedule whereby the principal DR documents will be reviewed. Depending on the rate of change, this could be as frequently as quarterly or as seldom as every two years.

Further, every change, however insignificant, in business processes and information systems should include a step to review, and possibly update, relevant DR documents. That is, a review of, and possibly changes to, relevant DR documents should be a required step in every business process engineering or information systems change process and a key component of the organization's information system development life cycle (SDLC). If this is done faithfully, then you would expect that the annual review of DR documents would conclude that few (if any) changes were required, although it is still a good practice to perform a periodic review, just to be sure.

Periodic testing of DR documents and plans, discussed in detail in the preceding section, is another vital activity. Testing validates the accuracy and relevance of DR documents, and any issues or exceptions in the testing process should precipitate updates to appropriate documents.

Sources for Best Practices

It is unnecessary to begin business continuity planning and disaster recovery planning by first inventing a practice or methodology. Business continuity planning and disaster recovery planning are advanced professions with several professional associations, professional certifications, international standards, and publications. Any or all of these are, or can lead to, sources of practices, processes, and methodologies:

- **U.S. National Institute of Standards and Technology (NIST)** This is a branch of the U.S. Department of Commerce that is responsible for developing business and technology standards for the federal government. The standards developed by NIST are exceedingly high, and as a result, many private organizations all over the world are adopting them. The NIST web site is at www.nist.gov.

- **Business Continuity Institute (BCI)** This is a membership organization dedicated to the advancement of business continuity management. BCI has more than 8,000 members in almost 100 countries. Its web site is at www.thebci.org. BCI holds several events around the world, prints a professional journal, and has developed a professional certification, the Certificate of the BCI (CBCI).

- **U.S. National Fire Protection Agency (NFPA)** NFPA has developed a pre-incident planning standard, NFPA 1620, which addresses the protection, construction, and features of buildings and other structures. It also requires the development of pre-incident plans that emergency responders can use to deal with fires and other emergencies. The NFPA web site is at www.nfpa.org.

- **U.S. Federal Emergency Management Agency (FEMA)** FEMA is part of the Department of Homeland Security (DHS) and is responsible for emergency disaster relief planning information and services. FEMA's most visible activities are its relief operations in the wake of hurricanes and floods in the United States. Its web site is at www.fema.gov.

- **Disaster Recovery Institute International (DRI International)** This is a professional membership organization that provides education and professional certifications for disaster recovery planning professionals. Its web site is at www .drii.org. Its certifications include the following:
  - Associate Business Continuity Professional (ABCP)
  - Certified Business Continuity Vendor (CBCV)
  - Certified Functional Continuity Professional (CFCP)
  - Certified Business Continuity Professional (CBCP)
  - Master Business Continuity Professional (MBCP)

- **Business Continuity Management Institute (BCM Institute)** This is a professional association that specializes in education and professional certification. BCM Institute is a co-organizer of the World Continuity Congress, an annual conference that is dedicated to business continuity and disaster recovery planning. Its web site is at www.bcm-institute.org. Certifications offered by BCM Institute include the following:
  - Business Continuity Certified Expert (BCCE)
  - Business Continuity Certified Specialist (BCCS)

- Business Continuity Certified Planner (BCCP)
- Disaster Recovery Certified Expert (DRCE)
- Disaster Recovery Certified Specialist (DRCS)

Disaster Recovery Planning

Disaster recovery planning is undertaken to reduce risks related to the onset of disasters and other events. DRP is mainly an IT function to ensure that key IT systems are available to support critical business processes.

Disaster recovery planning is closely related to business continuity planning. The groundwork for DRP begins in BCP activities such as the business impact analysis, criticality analysis, establishment of recovery objectives, and testing. The outputs from these activities are the key inputs to DRP:

- The business impact analysis and criticality analysis help to prioritize which business processes (and, therefore, which IT systems) are the most important.

- Key recovery targets specify how quickly specific IT applications are to be recovered. This guides DRP personnel as they develop new IT architectures that make IT systems compliant with those objectives.

- Testing of DRP plans can be performed in coordination with tests of BCP plans to more accurately simulate real disasters and disaster response.

The relationships between business continuity planning and disaster recovery planning was discussed in detail earlier in this chapter and depicted in Figure 5-2.

Disaster Response Teams' Roles and Responsibilities

Disaster recovery plans need to specify the teams that are required for disaster response, as well as each team's roles and responsibilities. Table 5-5 describes several teams and their roles. Because of variations in organizations' disaster response plans, some of these teams will not be needed in some organizations.

 NOTE Some of the roles in Table 5-5 may overlap with responsibilities defined in the organization's business continuity plan. DR and BC planners will need to work together to ensure that the organization's overall response to disaster is appropriate and does not overlook vital functions.

Recovery Objectives

During the business impact analysis and criticality analysis phases of a business continuity and disaster recovery (BCDR) project, the speed with which each business activity (with its underlying IT systems) needs to be restored after a disaster is determined.

Team	Responsibilities
Emergency management	Coordinates activities of all other response teams.
First responders	Usually outside personnel such as police, fire, and rescue who help to extinguish fires, evacuate personnel, and provide emergency medical aid.
Communications	Coordinates communication among teams, as well as between teams and outside entities.
Damage assessment	Examines equipment, supplies, furnishing, and assets to determine what can be used immediately in support of critical processes and what will need to be handed off to salvage teams.
Salvage	Examines equipment, supplies, furnishings, and other assets to determine what can be salvaged for immediate or long-term reuse.
Network engineering	Establishes and maintains electronic (voice and data) communications in support of critical services during a disaster.
Systems engineering	Establishes and maintains systems as needed to support critical applications and services.
Database engineering	Establishes and maintains database management systems as needed to support critical applications. Performs data recovery, using local or remotely stored media as needed.
Application support	Establishes and maintains critical applications in support of critical business processes.
Application development	Makes changes to critical applications as needed during the recovery effort.
End-user computing	Establishes and maintains end-user computing facilities (desktop computers, laptop computers, mobile devices, etc.) as needed in support of critical applications and services.
Systems operations	Performs routine and nonroutine tasks such as backups to keep critical applications running.
Transportation	Coordinates transportation of personnel to recovery sites.
Relocation	Acquires housing and other resources needed by personnel who are working at remote operations centers.
Security	Coordinates physical and logical security activities to ensure the continuous protection of staff, assets, and information.
Finance	Facilitates the availability of financial resources as needed to commence and continue emergency response operations.

Table 5-5   Disaster Response Teams' Roles and Responsibilities

Recovery Time Objective   A *recovery time objective* is the period from the onset of an outage until the resumption of service. RTO is usually measured in hours or days. Each process and system in the BIA should have an RTO value.

RTO does not mean that the system (or process) has been recovered to 100 percent of its former capacity. Far from it—in an emergency situation, management may determine that a DR server in another city with, say, 60 percent of the capacity of the original server is adequate. That said, an organization could establish two RTO targets, one for partial capacity and one for full capacity.

NOTE   For a given organization, it's probably best to use one unit of measure for recovery objectives for all systems. That will help to avoid any errors that would occur during a rank-ordering of systems so that two days does not appear to be a shorter period than four hours.

Further, a system that has been recovered in a disaster situation might not have 100 percent of its functionality. For instance, an application that lets users view transactions that are more than two years old may, in a recovery situation, contain only 30 days' worth of data. Again, such a decision is usually the result of a careful analysis of the cost of recovering different features and functions in an application environment. In a larger, complex environment, some features might be considered critical, while others are less so.

CAUTION   Senior management should be involved in any discussion related to recovery system specifications in terms of capacity, integrity, or functionality.

Recovery Point Objective   A *recovery point objective* is the period for which recent data will be irretrievably lost in a disaster. Like RTO, RPO is usually measured in hours or days. However, for critical transaction systems, RPO could even be measured in minutes.

RPO is usually expressed as a worst-case figure; for instance, the transaction processing system RPO will be two hours or less.

The value of a system's RPO is usually a direct result of the frequency of data backup or replication. For example, if an application server is backed up once per day, the RPO is going to be at least 24 hours (or one day, whichever way you like to express it). Maybe it will take three days to rebuild the server, but once data is restored from backup tape, no more than the last 24 hours of transactions are lost. In this case, the RTO is three days, and the RPO is one day.

Recovery Consistency Objective   The *recovery consistency objective* of a recovery site is defined as the degree to which a recovery site's calculations or features are measured as compared to the primary processing site. RCO is calculated as

1–(number of inconsistent objects) / (number of objects)

For example, an organization's online application is used to calculate the current and future costs of a household budget. While the primary site uses inputs and performs calculations based upon twelve external data sources, the recovery site performs calculations based on only eight external data sources. Economic considerations compelled management to accept the fact that the recovery site will calculate results based upon fewer inputs, and that this is an acceptable tradeoff between higher licensing fees for use of some external sources and small variations in the results shown to users of the site.

Recovery Capacity Objective   The *recovery capacity objective* is the processing and/or storage capacity of a recovery site, as compared to the primary processing site. RCapO is generally expressed as a percentage.

For economic reasons, an organization may elect to build a recovery site that has less processing or storage capacity than the primary site. Management may agree that a recovery site with reduced processing capacity is an acceptable trade-off, given the relatively low likelihood that a failover to a recovery site would occur. For instance, an online service may choose to operate its recovery site at 80 percent of the processing capacity of the primary site. In management's opinion, the relatively low decrease in capacity is worth the cost savings.

Publishing Recovery Targets   If the storage system for an application takes a snapshot every hour, the RPO could be one hour, unless the storage system itself was damaged in a disaster. If the snapshot is replicated to another storage system four times per day, then the RPO might be better expressed as six to eight hours.

The last example brings up an interesting point. There might not be one golden RPO figure for a given system. Instead, the severity of a disrupting event or a disaster will dictate the time to get systems running again (RTO) with a certain amount of data loss (RPO). Here are some examples:

- A server's CPU or memory fails and is replaced and restarted in two hours. No data is lost. The RTO is two hours, and the RPO is zero.

- The storage system supporting an application suffers a hardware failure that results in the loss of all data. Data is recovered from a snapshot on another server taken every six hours. The RPO is six hours in this case.

- The database in a transaction application is corrupted and must be recovered. Backups are taken twice per day. The RPO is 12 hours. However, it takes 10 hours to rebuild indexes on the database, so the RTO is closer to 22 to 24 hours since the application cannot be returned to service until indexes are available.

 NOTE   When publishing RTO and RPO figures to customers, it's best to publish the worst-case figures: "If our data center burns to the ground, our RTO is X hours and the RPO is Y hours." Saying it that way would be simpler than publishing a chart that shows RPO and RTO figures for various types of disasters.

Organizations that publish RCO and RCapO targets will need to also explain the practical meaning of these targets, whether these targets represent an exact match of capacity and integrity or some reduction. For example, if an organization's recovery site is engineered to process 80 percent of the transaction volume of the primary site, then an organization should consider stating that processing capacity at a recovery site may be reduced.

Pricing RTO and RPO Capabilities   Generally speaking, the shorter the RTO or RPO for a given system, the more expensive it will be to achieve the target. Table 5-6 depicts a range of RTOs along with the technologies needed to achieve them and their relative cost.

The BCP project team needs to understand the relationship between the time required to recover an application and the cost required to recover the application within that time. A shorter recovery time is more expensive, and this relationship is not linear. This means that reducing RPO from three days to six hours may mean that the equipment and software investment might double, or it might increase eightfold. There are so many factors involved in the supporting infrastructure for a given application that the BCP project team has to just knuckle down and develop the cost for a few different RTO and RPO figures.

The business value of the application itself is the primary driver in determining the amount of investment that senior management is willing to make to reach any arbitrary RTO and RPO figures. This business value may be measured in local currency if the application supports revenue. However, the loss of an application during a disaster may harm the organization's reputation. Again, management will have to make a decision on how much it will be willing to invest in DR capabilities that bring RTO and RPO figures down to a certain level. Figure 5-12 illustrates these relationships.

RTO/RPO	Technologies Needed	Cost
2 weeks	Backup tapes; buy a server when the original server has burned or floated away	$
1 week	Backup tapes; replacement server on hand	$$
2 days	Backup tapes; application software installed on replacement server	$$
12 hours	Backup tapes or replication; application server installed and running on replacement server	$$$
1 hour	Server cluster with auto or manual failover; near-real-time replication	$$$$
5 minutes	Load balancing or rapid failover server cluster; real-time replication	$$$$$

Table 5-6   The Lower the Recovery Time Objective, the Higher the Cost to Achieve It

Figure 5-12
Aim for the sweet spot and balance the costs of downtime and recovery.

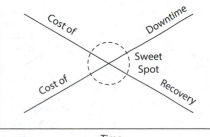

Developing Recovery Strategies

When management has chosen specific RPO and RTO targets for a given system or process, the BCP project team can now roll up its sleeves and devise some ways to meet these targets. This section discusses the technologies and logistics associated with various recovery strategies. This will help the project team to decide which types of strategies are best suited for their organization.

NOTE Developing recovery strategies to meet specific recovery targets is an iterative process. The project team will develop a strategy to reach specific targets for a specific cost; senior management could well decide that the cost is too high and that they are willing to increase RPO and/or RTO targets accordingly. Similarly, the project team could also discover that it is less costly to achieve specific RPO and RTO targets, and management could respond by lowering those targets. This is illustrated in Figure 5-13.

Figure 5-13
Recovery objective
development flowchart

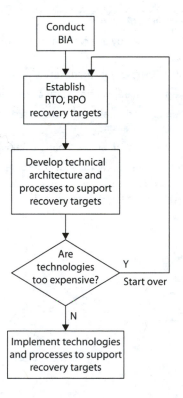

Contingencies for Contingencies

When developing contingency plans, DR planners need to keep in mind that contingency plans won't always work out. This is especially true in disaster situations that are more regional in nature. For instance, in a region impacted by a widespread natural disaster, recalling backup tapes by courier may be problematic as transportation infrastructure may be impacted. After the September 11, 2001, attacks, shipping anything by air was out of the question as the airspace in North America was closed for several days.

Site Recovery Options   In a worst-case disaster scenario, the site where information systems reside is partially or completely destroyed. In most cases, the organization cannot afford to wait for the damaged or destroyed facility to be restored, as this could take weeks or months. If an organization can take *that* long to recover an application, you'd have to wonder whether it is needed at all. The assumption has got to be that in a disaster scenario, critical applications will be recovered in another location. This other location is called a *recovery site.* There are two dimensions to the process of choosing a recovery site: the first is the speed at which the application will be recovered at the recovery site; the second is the location of the recovery site itself. Both are discussed here.

As you might expect, speed costs: developing the ability to recover more quickly costs more money and resources. If a system is to be recovered within a few minutes or hours, the costs will be much higher than if the system can be recovered in five days.

Various types of facilities are available for rapid or not-too-rapid recovery. These facilities are called *hot sites, warm sites*, and *cold sites.* As the names might suggest, hot sites permit rapid recovery, while cold sites provide a much slower recovery. The costs associated with these are somewhat proportional as well, as illustrated in Table 5-7.

The details about each type of site are discussed in the remainder of this section.

Hot Sites   A *hot site* is an alternate processing center where backup systems are already running and in some state of near-readiness to assume production workload. The systems at a hot site most likely have application software and database management software already loaded and running, perhaps even at the same patch levels as the systems in the primary processing center.

Site Type	Speed to Recovery	Cost
Hot	0 to 24 hours	$$$$
Warm	24 hours to 7 days	$$$
Cold	More than 7 days	$$
Mobile	2 to 7 days	$$$ to $$$$
Cloud	0 to 7 days	$$
Reciprocal	0 to 7 days	$$ to $$$$

Table 5-7

Relative Costs of Recovery Sites

A hot site is the best choice for systems whose RTO targets range from zero to several hours, perhaps as long as 24 hours.

A hot site may consist of leased rack space (or even a cage for larger installations) at a colocation center. If the organization has its own processing centers, then a hot site for a given system would consist of the required rack space to house the recovery systems. Recovery servers will be installed and running, with the same version and patch level for the operating system, database management system (if used), and application software.

Systems at a hot site require the same level of administration and maintenance as the primary systems. When patches or configuration changes are made to primary systems, they should be made to hot-site systems at the same time or very shortly afterward.

Because systems at a hot site need to be at or very near a state of readiness, a strategy needs to be developed regarding a method for keeping the data on hot standby systems current. This is discussed in detail in the later section "Recovery and Resilience Technologies."

Systems at a hot site should have full network connectivity. A method for quickly directing network traffic toward the recovery servers needs to be worked out in advance so that a switchover can be accomplished. This is also discussed in the "Recovery and Resilience Technologies" section.

When setting up a hot site, the organization will need to send one or more technical staff members to the site to set up systems. But once the systems are operating, much or all of the system- and database-level administration can be performed remotely. However, in a disaster scenario, the organization may need to send the administrative staff to the site for day-to-day management of the systems. This means that workspace for these personnel needs to be identified so that they can perform their duties during the recovery operation.

NOTE Hot-site planning needs to consider work (desk) space for on-site personnel. Some colocation centers provide limited work areas, but these areas are often shared and have little privacy for phone discussions. Also, transportation, hotel, and dining accommodations need to be arranged, possibly in advance, if the hot site is in a different city from the primary site.

Warm Sites A *warm site* is an alternate processing center where recovery systems are present but at a lower state of readiness than recovery systems at a hot site. For example, while the same version of the operating system may be running on the warm site system, it may be a few patch levels behind primary systems. The same could be said about the versions and patch levels of database management systems (if used) and application software: they may be present, but they're not as up-to-date.

A warm site is appropriate for an organization whose RTO figures range from roughly one to seven days. In a disaster scenario, recovery teams would travel to the warm site and work to get the recovery systems to a state of production readiness and to get systems up-to-date with patches and configuration changes to bring the systems into a state of complete readiness.

A warm site is also used when the organization is willing to take the time necessary to recover data from tape or other backup media. Depending upon the size of the databases, this recovery task can take several hours to a few days.

The primary advantage of a warm site is that its costs are lower than for a hot site, particularly in the effort required to keep the recovery system up-to-date. The site may not require expensive data replication technology but instead data can be recovered from backup media.

Cold Sites   A *cold site* is an alternate processing center where the degree of readiness for recovery systems is low. At the least, a cold site is nothing more than an empty rack or just allocated space on a computer room floor. It's just an address in someone's data center or colocation site where computers can be set up and used at some future date.

Often, there is little or no equipment at a cold site. When a disaster or other highly disruptive event occurs in which the outage is expected to exceed 7 to 14 days, the organization will order computers from a manufacturer, or perhaps have computers shipped from some other business location, so that they can arrive at the cold site soon after the disaster event has begun. Then personnel would travel to the site and set up the computers, operating systems, databases, network equipment, and so on, and get applications running within several days.

The advantage of a cold site is its low cost. The main disadvantage is time and effort required to bring it to operational readiness in a short period which can be costly. But for some organizations, a cold site is exactly what is needed.

Table 5-8 shows a comparison of hot, warm, cold, and cloud-based recovery sites and a few characteristics of each.

Mobile Sites   A *mobile site* is a portable recovery center that can be delivered to almost any location in the world. A viable alternative to a fixed-location recovery site, a mobile site can be transported by semitruck and may even have its own generator, communications, and cooling capabilities.

APC and SunGuard have mobile sites installed in semitruck trailers. Oracle has mobile sites that can include a configurable selection of servers and workstations, all housed in shipping containers that can be shipped by truck, rail, ship, or air to any location in the world.

Cloud Sites   Organizations are increasingly using cloud hosting services as their recovery sites. Such sites charge for the utilization of servers and devices in virtual environments.

	Cold	Warm	Hot	Cloud (IaaS)
Computers	Ship to site	On-site	Running	On site
Application Software	To be installed	Installed	Running	Any desired state
Data	To be recovered	To be recovered	Continuously updated	To be recovered
Connectivity	To be established	Ready to go	Already connected	Already connected
Support Staff	Travel to site	Travel to site	On site or remotely managed	Remotely managed
Cost	Lowest	Moderate	Highest	Moderate

Table 5-8   Detailed Comparison of Cold, Warm, Hot, and Cloud Sites

Hence, capital costs for recovery sites is near-zero, and operational costs come into play as recovery sites are used.

As organizations become accustomed to building recovery sites in the cloud, they are with increasing frequency moving their primary processing sites to the cloud as well.

Reciprocal Sites   A *reciprocal recovery site* is a data center that is operated by another company. Two or more organizations with similar processing needs will draw up a legal contract that obligates one or more of the organizations to temporarily house another party's systems in the event of a disaster.

Often, a reciprocal agreement pledges not only floor space in a data center but also the use of the reciprocal partner's computer system. This type of arrangement is less common but is still used by organizations that use mainframe computers and other high-cost systems.

 NOTE   With the wide use of Internet colocation centers, reciprocal sites have fallen out of favor. Still, they may be ideal for organizations with mainframe computers that are otherwise too expensive to deploy to a cold or warm site.

Geographic Site Selection   An important factor in the process of recovery site selection is the location of the recovery site. The distance between the main processing site and the recovery site is vital and may figure heavily into the viability and success of a recovery operation.

A recovery site should not be located in the same geographic region as the primary site. A recovery site in the same region may be involved in the same regional disaster as the primary site and may be unavailable for use or be suffering from the same problems present at the primary site.

By "geographic region," I mean a location that will likely experience the effects of the same regional disaster that affects the primary site. No arbitrarily chosen distance (such as 100 miles) guarantees sufficient separation. In some locales, 50 miles is plenty of distance; in other places, 300 miles is too close—it all depends on the nature of disasters that are likely to occur in these areas. Information on regional disasters should be available from local disaster preparedness authorities or from local disaster recovery experts.

Considerations When Using Third-Party Disaster Recovery Sites   Since most organizations cannot afford to implement their own secondary processing site, the only other option is to use a disaster recovery site that is owned by a third party, including cloud-based sites. This could be a colocation center, a disaster services center, or a cloud-based infrastructure service provider. An organization considering such a site needs to ensure that its services contract addresses the following:

- **Disaster definition**   The definition of disaster needs to be broad enough to meet the organization's requirements.
- **Equipment configuration**   IT equipment must be configured as needed to support critical applications during a disaster.
- **Availability of equipment during a disaster**   IT equipment needs to actually be available during a disaster. The organization needs to know how the disaster

service provider will allocate equipment if many of its customers suffer a disaster simultaneously.

- **Customer priorities**   The organization needs to know whether the disaster services provider has any customers (government or military, for example) whose priorities may exceed their own.

- **Data communications**   There must be sufficient bandwidth and capacity for the organization plus other customers who may be operating at the disaster provider's center at the same time.

- **Data sovereignty**   The organization needs to take into account the geographic locations of stored data, particularly when that data involves private citizens. The locations of primary and recovery processing sites, together with the location of data subjects, may bring various privacy regulations into play.

- **Testing**   The organization needs to know what testing it is permitted to perform on the service provider's systems so that the ability to recover from a disaster can be tested in advance.

- **Right to audit**   The organization should have a "right to audit" clause in its contract so that it can verity the presence and effectiveness of all key controls in place at the recovery facility.

- **Security and environmental controls**   The organization needs to know what security and environmental controls are in place at the disaster recovery facility.

Acquiring Additional Hardware   Many organizations elect to acquire their own server, storage, and network hardware for disaster recovery purposes. The way that an organization will need to go about acquiring hardware will depend on its high-level recovery strategy:

- **Cold site**   An organization will need to be able to purchase hardware as soon as the disaster occurs.

- **Warm site**   An organization will need to purchase hardware in advance of the disaster, or it may be able to purchase hardware when the disaster occurs. The choice taken will depend on the recovery time objective.

- **Hot site**   An organization will need to purchase its recovery hardware in advance of the disaster.

- **Cloud**   An organization will not need to purchase hardware, as this is provided by the cloud infrastructure provider.

Table 5-9 lists pros and cons to these strategies. Warm site strategy is not listed since an organization could purchase hardware either in advance of the disaster or when it occurs. But because cold, hot, and cloud sites are deterministic, they are included in the table.

The main reason for choosing a cloud hosting provider is the elimination of capital costs. The cloud hosting provider provides all hardware and charges organizations when the hardware is used.

The primary business reason for not choosing a hot site is the high capital cost required to purchase disaster recovery equipment that may never be used. One way around this

Strategy	Advantages	Disadvantages
Hot	Hardware already purchased and ready for use.	Capital is tied up in equipment that may never be used. Higher cost to continue maintaining recovery systems.
Cold	Capital is spent only if needed. Lower costs (until a disaster occurs).	The right equipment may be difficult to find and purchase. Difficult to test recovery strategy unless hardware is purchased, leased, or borrowed.
Cloud	Capital costs are zero. Operational costs only as cloud-based infrastructure is used.	Infrastructure is owned by a third party.

Table 5-9 Hardware Acquisition Pros and Cons for Cold, Hot, and Cloud Recovery Sites

obstacle is to put those recovery systems to work every day. For example, recovery systems could be used for development or testing of the same applications that are used in production. This way, systems that are purchased for recovery purposes are being well utilized for other purposes, and they'll be ready in case a disaster occurs.

When a disaster occurs, the organization will be less concerned about development and testing and more concerned about keeping critical production applications running. It will be a small sacrifice to forgo development or testing (or whatever low-criticality functions are using the DR hardware) during a disaster.

Recovery and Resilience Technologies   Once recovery targets have been established, the next major task is the survey and selection of technologies to enable recovery time and recovery point objectives to be met. The following are important factors when considering each technology:

- Does the technology help the information system achieve the RTO, RPO, and RCapO targets?
- Does the cost of the technology meet or exceed budget constraints?
- Can the technology be used to benefit other information systems (thereby lowering the cost for each system)?
- Does the technology fit well into the organization's current IT operations?
- Will operations staff require specialized training on the technology used for recovery?
- Does the technology contribute to the simplicity of the overall IT architecture, or does it complicate it unnecessarily?

These questions are designed to help determine whether a specific technology is a good fit, from a technology as well as from process and operational perspectives.

RAID   Redundant Array of Independent Disks (RAID) is a family of technologies that is used to improve the reliability, performance, or size of disk-based storage systems. From a disaster recovery or systems resilience perspective, the feature of RAID that is of particular interest is the reliability. RAID is used to create virtual disk volumes over an array (pun intended) of disk storage devices and can be configured so that the failure of any individual disk drive in the array will not affect the availability of data on the disk array.

RAID is usually implemented on a hardware device called a *disk array*, which is a chassis in which several hard disks can be installed and connected to a server. The individual disk drives can usually be "hot swapped" in the chassis while the array is still operating. When the array is configured with RAID, a failure of a single disk drive will have no effect on the disk array's availability to the server to which it is connected. A system operator can be alerted to the disk's failure, and the defective disk drive can be removed and replaced while the array is still fully operational.

There are several options for RAID configuration, called *levels*:

- **RAID 0**   This is known as a striped volume, where a disk volume splits data evenly across two or more disks to improve performance.

- **RAID 1**   This creates a mirror, where data written to one disk in the array is also written to a second disk in the array. RAID 1 makes the volume more reliable, through the preservation of data, even when one disk in the array fails.

- **RAID 4**   This level of RAID employs data striping at the block level by adding a dedicated parity disk. The parity disk permits the rebuilding of data in the event one of the other disks fails.

- **RAID 5**   This is similar to RAID 4 block-level striping, except that the parity data is distributed evenly across all of the disks instead of dedicated on one disk. Like RAID 4, RAID 5 allows for the failure of one disk without losing information.

- **RAID 6**   This is an extension of RAID 5, where two parity blocks are used instead of a single parity block. The advantage of RAID 6 is that it can withstand the failure of any two disk drives in the array, instead of a single disk, as is the case with RAID 5.

 NOTE   Several nonstandard RAID levels have been developed by various hardware and software companies. Some of these are extensions of RAID standards, while others are entirely different.

Storage systems are hardware devices that are entirely separate from servers—their only purpose is to store a large amount of data and to be highly reliable through the use of redundant components and the use of one or more RAID levels. Storage systems generally come in two forms:

- **Storage area network (SAN)**   This is a stand-alone storage system that can be configured to contain several virtual volumes and connected to several servers through fiber optic cables. The servers' operating systems will often consider this storage to be "local," as though it consisted of one or more hard disks present in the server's own chassis.

- **Network attached storage (NAS)**   This is a stand-alone storage system that contains one or more virtual volumes. Servers access these volumes over the network using the Network File System (NFS) or Server Message Block/Common Internet File System (SMB/CIFS) protocols, common on Unix and Windows operating systems, respectively.

Replication   Replication is an activity where data that is written to a storage system is also copied over a network to another storage system. The result is the presence of up-to-date data that exists on two or more storage systems, each of which could be located in a different geographic region.

Replication can be handled in several ways and at different levels in the technology stack:

- **Disk storage system**   Data-write operations that take place in a disk storage system (such as a SAN or NAS) can be transmitted over a network to another disk storage system, where the same data will be written to the other disk storage system.

- **Operating system**   The operating system can control replication so that updates to a particular file system can be transmitted to another server where those updates will be applied locally on that other server.

- **Database management system**   The database management system (DBMS) can manage replication by sending transactions to a DBMS on another server.

- **Transaction management system**   The transaction management system (TMS) can manage replication by sending transactions to a counterpart TMS located elsewhere.

- **Application**   The application can write its transactions to two different storage systems. This method is not often used.

- **Virtualization**   Virtual machine images can be replicated to recovery sites to speed the recovery of applications.

Replication can take place from one system to another system, called *primary-backup* replication. This is the typical setup when data on an application server is sent to a distant storage system for data recovery or disaster recovery purposes.

Replication can also be bidirectional, between two active servers, called *multiprimary* or *multimaster*. This method is more complicated because simultaneous transactions on different servers could conflict with one another (such as two reservation agents trying to book a passenger in the same seat on an airline flight). Some form of concurrent transaction control would be required, such as a *distributed lock manager*.

In terms of the speed and integrity of replicated information, there are two types of replication:

- **Synchronous replication**   Here, writing data to a local and to a remote storage system are performed as a single operation, guaranteeing that data on the remote storage system is identical to data on the local storage system. Synchronous replication incurs a performance penalty, as the speed of the entire transaction is slowed to the rate of the remote transaction.

- **Asynchronous replication** Writing data to the remote storage system is not kept in sync with updates on the local storage system. Instead, there may be a time lag, and you have no guarantee that data on the remote system is identical to that on the local storage system. However, performance is improved, because transactions are considered complete when they have been written to the local storage system only. Bursts of local updates to data will take a finite period to replicate to the remote server, subject to the available bandwidth of the network connection between the local and remote storage systems.

NOTE Replication is often used for applications where the RTO is smaller than the time necessary to recover data from backup media. For example, if a critical application's RTO is established to be two hours, then recovery from backup tape is probably not a viable option, unless backups are performed every two hours. While more expensive than recovery from backup media, replication ensures that up-to-date information is present on a remote storage system that can be put online in a short period.

Server Clusters A *cluster* is a collection of two or more servers that appear as a single server resource. Clusters are often the technology of choice for applications that require a high degree of availability and a very small RTO, measured in minutes.

When an application is implemented on a cluster, even if one of the servers in the cluster fails, the other server (or servers) in the cluster will continue to run the application, usually with no user awareness that such a failure occurred.

There are two typical configurations for clusters, *active/active* and *active/passive*. In active/active mode, all servers in the cluster are running and servicing application requests. This is often used in high-volume applications where many servers are required to service the application workload.

In active/passive mode, one or more servers in the cluster are active and servicing application requests, while one or more servers in the cluster are in a "standby" mode; they can service application requests but won't do so unless one of the active servers fails or goes offline for any reason. When an active server goes offline and a standby server takes over, this event is called a *failover*.

Figure 5-14 shows a typical server cluster architecture.

A server cluster is typically implemented in a single physical location such as a data center. However, a cluster can also be implemented where great distances separate the servers in the cluster. This type of cluster is called a *geographic cluster*, or geocluster. Servers in a geocluster are connected through a WAN connection. Figure 5-15 shows a typical geographic cluster architecture.

Network Connectivity and Services An overall application environment that is required to be resilient and have recoverability must have those characteristics present within the network that supports it. A highly resilient application architecture that

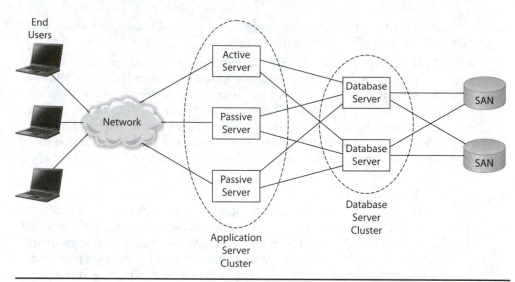

Figure 5-14 Application and database server clusters

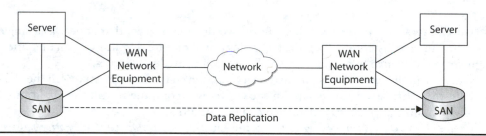

Figure 5-15 Geographic cluster with data replication

includes clustering and replication would be of little value if it had only a single network connection that was a single point of failure.

An application that requires high availability and resilience may require one or more of the following in the supporting network:

- **Redundant network connections** These may include multiple network adapters on a server but also a fully redundant network architecture with multiple switches, routers, load balancers, and firewalls. This could also include physically diverse network provider connections, where network service provider feeds enter the building from two different directions.

- **Redundant network services** Certain network services are vital to the continued operation of applications, such as DNS (the function of translating server names like www.mheducation.com into an IP address), NTP (used to synchronize computer time clocks), SMTP, SNMP, authentication services, and perhaps others. These services are usually operated on servers, which may require clustering and/or replication of their own, so that the application will be able to continue functioning in the event of a disaster.

Developing Recovery Plans

A disaster recovery planning effort starts with the initial phases of the business continuity planning project: the business impact analysis and criticality analysis lead to the establishment of recovery objectives that determine how quickly critical business processes need to be back up and running.

With this information, the DR team can determine what additional data processing equipment is needed (if any) and establish a road map for acquiring that equipment.

The other major component in the DR project is the development of recovery plans. These are the process and procedure documents that will be triggered when a disaster has been declared. These processes and procedures will instruct response personnel how to establish and operate business processes and IT systems after a disaster has occurred. It's not enough to have all of the technology ready if personnel don't know what to do.

Most DR plans are going to have common components, which are as follows:

- **Disaster declaration procedure**   This needs to include criteria for how a disaster is determined and who has the authority to declare a disaster.

- **Roles and responsibilities**   DR plans need to specify what activities need to be performed and specify which people or teams are best equipped to perform them.

- **Emergency contact lists**   Response personnel need contact information for other personnel so that they may establish and maintain communications as the disaster unfolds and recovery operations begin. These contact lists should contain several different ways of contacting personnel since some disasters have an adverse impact on regional telecommunications infrastructure.

- **System recovery procedures**   These are the detailed steps for getting recovery systems up and running. These procedures will include a lot of detail describing obtaining data, configuring servers and network devices, confirming that the application and business information is healthy, and starting business applications.

- **System operations procedures**   These are detailed steps for operating critical IT systems while they are in recovery mode. These detailed procedures are needed because the systems in recovery mode may need to be operated differently than their production counterparts; further, they may need to be operated by personnel who have not been doing this before.

- **System restoration procedures**   These are the detailed steps to restore IT operations to the original production systems.

NOTE   Business continuity and disaster recovery plans work together to get critical business functions operating again after a disaster. Because of this, BC and DR teams need to work closely when developing their respective response procedures to make sure that all activities are covered, but without unnecessary overlap.

DR plans need to take into account the likely disaster scenarios that may occur to an organization. Understanding these scenarios can help the DR team take a more pragmatic approach when creating response procedures. The added benefit is that not all disasters result in the entire loss of a computing facility. Most are more limited in their scope, although all of them can still result in a complete inability to continue operations. Some of these scenarios are as follows:

- Complete loss of network connectivity
- Sustained electric power outage
- Loss of a key system (this could be a server, storage system, or network device)
- Extensive data corruption or data loss

These scenarios are probably more likely to occur than a catastrophe such as a major earthquake or hurricane (depending on where your data center is located).

Data Backup and Recovery

Disasters and other disruptive events can damage information and information systems. It's essential that fresh copies of this information exist elsewhere and in a form that enables IT personnel to easily load this information into alternative systems so that processing can resume as quickly as possible.

CAUTION Testing backups is important; testing recoverability is critical. In other words, performing backups is only valuable to the extent that backed-up data can be recovered at a future time.

Backup to Tape and Other Media In organizations still utilizing their own IT infrastructure, tape backup is just about as ubiquitous as power cords. From a disaster recovery perspective, however, the issue probably is not whether the organization *has* tape backup but whether its current backup capabilities are adequate in the context of disaster recovery. An organization's backup capability may need to be upgraded if:

- The current backup system is difficult to manage.
- Whole-system restoration takes too long.
- The system lacks flexibility with regard to disaster recovery (for instance, how difficult it would be to recover information onto a different type of system).
- The technology is old or outdated.
- Confidence in the backup technology is low.

Many organizations may consider tape backup as a means for restoring files or databases when errors have occurred, and they may have confidence in their backup system for that purpose. However, the organization may have somewhat less confidence in their backup system and its ability to recover *all* of their critical systems accurately and in a timely manner.

While tape has been the default medium since the 1960s, using hard drives as a backup medium is growing in popularity: hard disk transfer rates are far higher, and disk is a random-access medium, whereas tape is a sequential-access medium. A virtual tape library (VTL) is a type of data storage technology that sets up a disk-based storage system with the appearance of tape storage, permitting existing backup software to continue to back data up to "tape," which is really just more disk storage.

E-vaulting is another viable option for system backup. E-vaulting permits organizations to back up their systems and data to an off-site location, which could be a storage system in another data center or a third-party service provider. This accomplishes two important objectives: reliable backup and off-site storage of backup data.

Backup Schemes   There are three main schemes for backing up data; they are the full, incremental, and differential backups:

- **Full backup**   This is a complete copy of a data set.
- **Incremental backup**   This is a copy of all data that has changed since the last full or incremental backup.
- **Differential backup**   This is a copy of all data that has changed since the last full backup.

The precise nature of the data to be backed up will determine which combination of backup schemes is appropriate for the organization. Here are some considerations for choosing an overall scheme:

- Criticality of the data set
- Size of the data set
- Frequency of change of the data set
- Performance requirements and the impact of backup jobs
- Recovery requirements

An organization that is creating a backup scheme usually starts with the most common scheme, which is a full backup once per week and an incremental or differential backup every day. However, as stated previously, various factors will influence the design of the final backup scheme. Here are some examples:

- A small data set could be backed up more than once a week, while an especially large data set might be backed up less often.
- A more rapid recovery requirement may induce the organization to perform differential backups instead of incremental backups.
- If a full backup takes a long time to complete, it should probably be performed during times of lower demand or system utilization.

Backup Media Rotation   Organizations will typically want to retain backup media for as long as possible to provide a greater array of choices for data recovery. However, the desire to maintain a large library of backup media will be countered by the high cost of media and the space required to store it. And while legal or statutory requirements may dictate that backup media be kept for some minimum period, the organization may be able to creatively find ways to comply with such requirements without retaining several generations of such media.

Some example backup media rotation schemes are discussed here.

First In, First Out   In the first in, first out (FIFO) scheme, there is no specific requirement for retaining any backup media for long periods (e.g., one year or more). The method in the FIFO rotation scheme specifies that the oldest available backup tape is the next one to be used.

The advantage of this scheme is its simplicity. However, there is a significant disadvantage: any corruption of backed-up data needs to be discovered quickly (within the period of media rotation), or else no valid set of data can be recovered. Hence, only low-criticality data without any lengthy retention requirements should be backed up using this scheme.

Grandfather-Father-Son   The most common backup media rotation scheme, grandfather-father-son creates a hierarchical set of backup media that provides for greater retention of backed-up data that is still economically feasible.

In the most common form of this scheme, full backups are performed once per week, and incremental or differential backups are performed daily.

Daily backup tapes used on Monday are not used again until the following Monday. Backup tapes used on Tuesday, Wednesday, Thursday, Friday, and Saturday are handled in the same way.

Full backup tapes created on Sunday are kept longer. Tapes used on the first Sunday of the month are not used again until the first Sunday of the following month. Similarly, tapes used on the second Sunday are not reused until the second Sunday of the following month, and so on, for each week's tapes for Sunday.

For even longer retention, for example, tapes created on the first Sunday of the first month of each calendar quarter can be retained until the first Sunday of the first month of the next quarter. Backup media can be kept for even longer if needed.

Towers of Hanoi   The Towers of Hanoi backup media retention scheme is complex but results in a more efficient scheme for producing a longer retention of some backups. Patterned after the Towers of Hanoi puzzle, the scheme is most easily understood visually, as in Figure 5-16 in a five-level scheme.

Backup Media Storage   Backup media that remains in the same location as backed-up systems is adequate for data recovery purposes but completely inadequate for disaster recovery purposes: any event that physically damages information systems (such as fire, smoke, flood, hazardous chemical spill, and so on) is likely to also damage backup media. To provide disaster recovery protection, backup media must be stored off-site in a secure location. Selection of this storage location is as important as the

Day of Cycle

	1	2	3	4	5	6	7	8	9	10	11	12	13	14	15	16	17	18	19	20
Backup Set to Use		A		A		A		A		A		A		A		A		A		A
			B			B			B			B			B			B		
				C									C							
						D											D			
	E																			

Figure 5-16   Towers of Hanoi backup media rotation scheme

selection of a primary business location: in the event of a disaster, the survival of the organization may depend upon the protection measures in place at the off-site storage location.

The criteria for selection of an off-site media storage facility are similar to the criteria for selection of a hot/warm/cold recovery site discussed earlier in this chapter. If a media storage location is too close to the primary processing site, then it is more likely to be involved in the same regional disaster, which could result in damage to backup media. However, if the media storage location is too far away, then it might take too long for a delivery of backup media, which would result in a recovery operation that runs unacceptably long.

Another location consideration is the proximity of the media storage location and the hot/warm/cold recovery site. If a hot site is being used, then chances are there is some other near-real-time means (such as replication) for data to get to the hot site. But a warm or cold site may be relying on the arrival of backup media from the off-site media storage facility, so it might make sense for the off-site facility to be near the recovery site.

An important factor when considering off-site media storage is the method of delivery to and from the storage location. Chances are that the backup media is being transported by a courier or a shipping company. It is vital that the backup media arrive safely and intact and that the opportunities for interception or loss be reduced as much as possible. Not only can a lost backup tape make recovery more difficult, but it can also cause an embarrassing security incident if knowledge of the loss were to become public. From a confidentiality/integrity perspective, encryption of backup tapes is a good idea, although this digresses somewhat from disaster recovery (concerned primarily with availability). Backup media encryption is discussed later in this section.

NOTE The requirements for off-site storage are a little less critical than for a hot/warm/cold recovery site. All you have to do is be able to get your backup media out of that facility. This can occur even if there is a regional power outage, for instance.

Backup media that must be kept on-site should be stored in locked cabinets or storerooms that are separate from the rooms where backups are performed. This will help to preserve backup media if a relatively small fire breaks out in the room containing computers that are backed up.

Protecting Sensitive Backup Media with Encryption

Information security and data privacy laws are expanding data protection requirements by requiring encryption of backup media in many cases. This is a sensible safeguard, especially for organizations that utilize off-site backup media storage. There is a risk of loss of backup media when it is being transported back and forth from an organization's primary data center and the backup media's off-site storage facility.

Backup Media Records and Destruction　To ensure the ability of restoring data from backup media, organizations need to have meticulous records that list all backup volumes in place, where they are located, and which data elements are backed up on them. Without these records, it may prove impossible for an organization to recover data from its backup media library.

Laws and regulations may specify maximum periods that specific information may be retained. Organizations need to have good records management that helps them track which business records are on which backup media volumes. When it is time for an organization to stop retaining a specific set of data, those responsible for the backup media library need to identify the backup volumes that can be recycled. If the data on the backup media is sensitive, the backup volume may need to be erased prior to use. Any backup media that is being discarded needs to be destroyed so that no other party can possibly recover data on the volume. Records of this destruction need to be kept.

Testing BC and DR Plans

It's surprising what you can accomplish when no one is concerned about who gets the credit.
—Ronald Reagan

Business continuity and disaster recovery plans may look elegant and even ingenious on paper, but their true business value is unknown until their worth is proven through testing.

The process of testing DR and BC plans uncovers flaws not only in the plans but also in the systems and processes that they are designed to protect. For example, testing a system recovery procedure might point out the absence of a critically needed hardware component, or a recovery procedure might contain a syntax or grammatical error that misleads the recovery team member and results in recovery delays. Testing is designed to uncover these types of issues.

Testing Recovery and Continuity Plans

Recovery and continuity plans need to be tested to prove their viability. Without testing, an organization has no way of really knowing whether its plans are effective. With ineffective plans, an organization has a far smaller chance of surviving a disaster.

Recovery and continuity plans have built-in obsolescence—not by design but by virtue of the fact that technology and business processes in most organizations are undergoing constant change and improvement. Thus, it is imperative that newly developed or updated plans be tested as soon as possible to ensure their effectiveness.

Types of tests range from lightweight and unobtrusive to intense and disruptive:

- Walk-through
- Simulation
- Parallel test
- Cutover test

These tests are described in more detail in this section.

 TIP   Usually, an organization will perform the less intensive tests first to identify the most obvious flaws and follow with tests that require more effort.

Test Preparation

Each type of test requires advance preparation and record keeping. Preparation will consist of several activities:

- **Participants**   The organization needs to identify personnel who will participate in an upcoming test. It is important to identify all relevant skill groups and department stakeholders so that the test will include a full slate of contributors. This would also include key vendors/partners to support their systems.
- **Schedule**   The availability of each participant needs to be confirmed so that the test will include participation from all stakeholders.
- **Facilities**   For all but the document review test, proper facilities need to be identified and set up. This might consist of a large conference room or training room. If the test will take place over several hours, one or more meals and refreshments may be needed as well.
- **Scripting**   The simulation test requires some scripting, usually in the form of one or more documents that describe a developing scenario and related

circumstances. Scenario scripting can make parallel and cutover tests more interesting and valuable, but this can be considered optional.

- **Recordkeeping**   For all of the tests except the document review, one or more people need to take good notes that can be collected and organized after the test is completed.
- **Contingency plan**   The cutover test involves the cessation of processing on primary systems and the resumption of processing on recovery systems. This is the highest-risk plan, and things can go wrong. A contingency plan to get primary systems running again in case something goes wrong during the test needs to be developed.

Table 5-10 shows these preparation activities.

The various types of tests are discussed next.

Document Review   A *document review* test is a review of some or all disaster recovery and business continuity plans, procedures, and other documentation. Individuals typically review these documents on their own, at their own pace, but within whatever time constraints or deadlines that may have been established.

The purpose of a document review test is to review the accuracy and completeness of document content. Reviewers should read each document with a critical eye, point out any errors, and annotate the document with questions or comments that can be sent back to the document's author (or authors), who can make any necessary changes.

If significant changes are needed in one or more documents, the project team may want to include a second round of document review before moving on to more resource-intensive tests.

The owner or document manager for the organization's business continuity and disaster recovery planning project should document which people review which documents and perhaps even include the review copies or annotations. This practice will create a more complete record of the activities related to the development and testing of important BCP planning and response documents. It will also help to capture the true cost and effort of the development and testing of BCP capabilities in the organization.

	Document Review	Walk-through	Simulation	Parallel Test	Cutover Test
Participants	Yes	Yes	Yes	Yes	Yes
Schedule	Yes	Yes	Yes	Yes	Yes
Facilities		Yes	Yes	Yes	Yes
Scripting			Yes	Optional	Optional
Record keeping	Yes	Yes	Yes	Yes	Yes
Contingency plan					Yes

Table 5-10   Preparation Activities Required for Each Type of DR/BC Test

Walk-Through   A *walk-through* is similar to a document review: it's a review of just the BCP documents. However, where a document review is carried out by individuals working on their own, a walk-through is performed by an entire group of individuals in a live discussion.

A walk-through is usually facilitated by a leader who guides the participants page by page through each document. The leader may read sections of the document aloud, describe various scenarios where information in a section might be relevant, and take comments and questions from participants.

A walk-through is likely to take considerably more time than a document review. One participant's question on some minor point in the document could spark a worthwhile and lively discussion that could last a few minutes to an hour. The group leader or another person will need to take careful notes in the event that any deficiencies are found in any of the documents, as well as issues to be handled after the walk-through. The leader will also need to be able to control the pace of the review so that the group does not get unnecessarily hung up on minor points. Some discussions will need to be cut short or tabled for a later time or for an offline conversation among interested parties.

Even if major revisions are needed in recovery documents, it probably will be infeasible to conduct another walk-through with updated documents. However, follow-up document reviews are probably warranted to ensure that they were updated appropriately, at least in the opinion of the walk-through participants.

CAUTION   Participants in the walk-through should carefully consider that the potential audience for recovery procedures may be people who are not as familiar as they are with systems and processes. They need to remember that the ideal personnel may not be available during a real disaster. Participants also need to realize that the skill level of recovery personnel might be a little below that of the experts who operate systems and processes in normal circumstances. Finally, walk-through participants need to remember that systems and processes undergo almost continuous change, which could render some parts of the recovery documentation obsolete or incorrect all too soon.

Simulation   A simulation is a test of disaster recovery and business continuity procedures where the participants take part in a "mock disaster" to add some realism to the process of thinking their way through procedures in emergency response documents.

A simulation could be an elaborate and choreographed walk-through test where a facilitator reads from a script and describes a series of unfolding events in a disaster such as a hurricane or an earthquake. This type of simulation might almost be viewed as "playacting," where the script is the set of emergency response documentation. By stimulating the imagination of simulation participants, it's possible for participants to really imagine that a disaster is taking place, which may help them to better understand what real disaster conditions might be like. It will help tremendously if the facilitator has actually experienced one or more disaster scenarios so that he can add more realism when describing events.

To make the simulation more credible and valuable, the scenario that is chosen should be one that has a reasonable chance of actually occurring in the local area. Good choices would include an earthquake in San Francisco or Los Angeles, a volcanic eruption in Seattle, or an avalanche in Switzerland. A poor choice would be a hurricane or tsunami in central Asia, because these events would not ever occur there.

A simulation can also go a few steps further. For instance, the simulation can take place at an established emergency operations center, the same place where emergency command and control would operate in a real disaster. Also, the facilitator could change some of the participants' roles to simulate the real absence of certain key personnel to see how remaining personnel might conduct themselves in a real emergency.

TIP   The facilitator of a simulation is limited only by his own imagination when organizing a simulation. One important fact to remember, though, is that a simulation does not actually affect any live or DR systems—it's all as pretend as the make-believe cardboard television sets and computers found in furniture stores.

Parallel Test   A parallel test is an actual test of disaster recovery and/or business continuity response plans and their supporting IT systems. The purpose of a parallel test is to evaluate the ability of personnel to follow directives in emergency response plans—to actually set up the DR business processing or data processing capability. In a parallel test, personnel are actually setting up the IT systems that would be used in an actual disaster and operating those IT systems with real business transactions to find out if the IT systems perform the processing correctly.

The outcome of a parallel test is threefold:

- It evaluates the accuracy of emergency response procedures.
- It evaluates the ability of personnel to correctly follow the emergency response procedures.
- It evaluates the ability of IT systems and other supporting apparatus to process real business transactions properly.

A parallel test is called a parallel test because live production systems continue to operate and the backup IT systems are processing business transactions in parallel to see if they process them the same as the live production systems do.

Setting up a valid parallel test is complicated in many cases. In effect, you need to insert a logical "Y cable" into the business process flow so that the information flow will split and flow both to production systems (without interfering with their operation) and to the backup systems. Results of transactions need to be compared. Personnel need to be able to determine whether the backup systems would be able to output correct data without actually having them do so. In many complex environments, you would not want the DR system to actually feed information back into a live environment because that might cause duplicate events to occur someplace else in the organization (or with customers, suppliers, or other parties). For instance, in a travel reservations system, you would not want a DR system to actually book travel because that would cost real money and consume available space on an airline or other mode of transportation. But it would be important to know whether the DR system would be *able* to perform those functions. Somewhere along the line, it will be necessary to "unplug" the DR system from the rest of the environment and manually examine results to see if they appear to be correct.

Organizations that do want to see whether their backup/DR systems can manage a real workload can perform a cutover test, which is discussed next.

Cutover Test   A cutover test is the most intrusive type of disaster recovery test. It will also provide the most reliable results in terms of answering the question of whether backup systems have the capacity and correct functionality to shoulder the real workload properly.

The consequences of a failed cutover test, however, might resemble an actual disaster: if any part of the cutover test fails, then real, live business processes will be going without the support of IT applications as though a real outage or disaster were in progress. But even a failure like this would show you that "no, the backup systems won't work in the event a real disaster were to happen later today."

In some respects, a cutover test is easier to perform than a parallel test. A parallel test is a little trickier, since business information is required to flow to the production system and to the backup system, which means that some artificial component has been somehow inserted into the environment. However, with a cutover test, business processing does take place on the backup systems only, which can often be achieved through a simple configuration someplace in the network or the systems layer of the environment.

TIP   Not all organizations perform cutover tests because they take a lot of resources to set up and are risky. Many organizations find that a parallel test is sufficient to tell whether backup systems are accurate, and the risk of an embarrassing incident is almost zero with a parallel test.

Documenting Test Results

Every type and every iteration of DR plan testing needs to be documented. It's not enough to say, "We did the test on September 10, 2015, and it worked." First of all, no test goes perfectly—opportunities for improvement are always identified. But the most important part of testing is to discover what parts of the test still need work so that those parts of the plan can be fixed before the next test (or a real disaster).

As with any well-organized project, success is in the details. The road to success is littered with big and little mistakes, and all of the things that are identified in every sort of DR test need to be detailed so that the next iteration of the test will give better results. Here are some key metrics that can be reported:

- Time required to perform key tasks
- Accuracy of tasks performed (or, number of retries needed)
- Amount of data recovered
- Performance against recovery targets including RTO, RPO, RCO, and RCapO

Recording and comparing detailed test results from one test to the next will also help the organization to measure progress. By this I mean that the quality of emergency response plans should steadily improve from year to year. Simple mistakes of the past should not be repeated, and the only failures in future tests should be in new and novel parts of the environment that weren't well thought out to begin with. And even these should diminish over time.

Improving Recovery and Continuity Plans

Every test of recovery and response plans should include a debrief or review so that participants can discuss the outcome of the test: what went well, what went wrong, and how things should be done differently next time. All of this information should be collected by someone who will be responsible for making changes to relevant documents. The updated documents should be circulated among the test participants who can confirm whether their discussion and ideas are properly reflected in the document.

Chapter Review

Security incident management, disaster recovery planning, and business continuity planning all support a central objective: resilience and rapid recovery when disruptive events occur.

A security incident is an event where the confidentiality, integrity, or availability of information or information systems has been or is in danger of being compromised. The proliferation of connected devices makes life safety an additional consideration in many organizations.

The phases of incident response are planning, detection, initiation, analysis, containment, eradication, recovery, remediation, closure, and post-incident review. Planning consists of the development of incident response policies, roles and responsibilities, procedures, as well as testing and training.

An organization that is developing security incident response plans needs to determine high-level objectives. This is necessary so that response plans will meet the objectives.

Security incident response requires incident detection capabilities that enable an organization to be aware of an incident as it occurs. Without incident detection capabilities, organizations may not know about an intrusion for many months, if ever. A primary capability in incident response is event visibility, which is usually provided through a security information and event management system.

Many organizations choose to outsource security event monitoring to a third-party managed security services provider. Organizations also often outsource incident response to security professional services firms by purchasing an incident response retainer, which is a prepaid arrangement. Remember that outsourcing the activity does not mean the company is transferring the risk or responsibility of the program or its impact on the business.

With the proliferation of outsourcing to cloud-based service providers, many security incidents now take place in a third-party organization. This requires additional planning and coordination so that incident response involving a third party is effective.

Business continuity planning and disaster recovery planning work together to ensure survival of an organization during and after a natural or man-made disaster.

The business impact analysis is an activity used to identify the impact of various disaster scenarios and to determine the most critical processes and systems in an organization. The BIA helps an organization focus its BCP and DRP planning on the business functions that are most critical to the organization.

The development of recovery targets, including recovery time objective, recovery point objective, and recovery capacity objective, help an organization understand how quickly various business processes should be recovered after a disaster. Recovery speed is an important factor as the cost of recovery varies widely.

Business continuity plans define the methods that an organization will use to continue critical business operations after a disaster has occurred. Disaster recovery plans define the steps that an organization will use to salvage and recover systems damaged by a disaster. Both BCP and DRP activities work toward the restoration of capabilities in their original (or replacement) facilities.

The safety of personnel is the most important consideration in any disaster recovery plan.

Disaster recovery planning is concerned with system resilience matters including data backup and replication, the establishment of alternate processing sites (hot, warm, cold, cloud, mobile, or reciprocal), and the recovery of applications and data. The complexity of DR plans necessitates reviews and tests to ensure that DR plans are effective and will work during an actual disaster.

Notes

- Understanding the computer intrusion kill chain can help an organization identify opportunities to make their systems more resilient to intruders.

- The development of custom playbooks that address specific types of security incidents will ensure a more rapid and effective response to a security incident. High-velocity incidents such as data wipers and ransomware require rapid, almost-automated, response.

- Organizations need to carefully understand all of the terms and exclusions in any cyber-incident insurance policy to make sure there are no exclusions that would result in a denial of benefits after an incident.

- With so many organizations using cloud-based services, it's especially important that organizations understand, in detail, their own roles and responsibilities, as well as that of each cloud service provider. This is necessary so that the organization can build effective incident response should an incident occur at a cloud-based service provider.

- Threat hunting and cyber-threat intelligence can help an organization more effectively anticipate and detect an incident as it unfolds. This helps reduce potentially damaging effects through prevention.

- Many organizations choose to outsource the forensic examination and analysis portion of security incident response because personnel with these skills are difficult to find and the tools used are expensive.

- When responding to a security incident, organizations should consider establishing a chain of custody early on, in the event that disciplinary or legal proceedings may follow.

Questions

1. The purpose of a SIEM is:

    A. centrally log event data

    B. correlate events and generate alerts

    C. track remediation of known vulnerabilities

    D. scan systems and devices for new vulnerabilities

2. An organization lacks personnel and tools to conduct forensic analysis. What is the best way for the organization to acquire this capability?

    A. Purchase advanced anti-malware tools.

    B. Purchase a security information and event management system (SIEM).

    C. Purchase an incident response retainer.

    D. Post a position for a computer forensics specialist.

3. A large organization operates hundreds of business applications. How should the security manager prioritize applications for protection from a disaster?

    A. Conduct a business impact analysis.

    B. Conduct a risk assessment.

    C. Conduct a business process analysis.

    D. Rank the applications in order of criticality.

4. An organization wants to protect itself from the effects of a ransomware attack. What is the best data protection approach?

    A. Periodically scan data for malware.

    B. Replicate data to a cloud-based storage provider.

    C. Replicate data to a secondary storage system.

    D. Back up data to offline media.

5. The types of incident response plan testing are:

    A. Document review, walk-through, and simulation

    B. Document review and simulation

    C. Document review, walk-through, simulation, parallel test, and cutover test

    D. Document review, walk-through, and cutover test

6. The length of time between incident occurrence and incident detection is known as:

   A. Dwell time

   B. Lag time

   C. Lead time

   D. Propagation

7. The purpose of attorney–client privilege during an investigation is:

   A. To improve the results of the investigation

   B. To obtain better forensic examination services

   C. To protect investigation proceedings from a discovery order

   D. To improve the integrity of investigation proceedings

8. The purpose of chain of custody procedures is:

   A. To prove the ownership of investigation data

   B. To determine the cause of an incident

   C. To prove the integrity of investigation data

   D. To determine who is responsible for an incident

9. An organization has developed its first-ever business continuity plan. What is the first test of the continuity plan that the business should perform?

   A. Walk-through

   B. Simulation

   C. Parallel test

   D. Cutover test

10. An organization is experiencing a ransomware attack that is damaging critical data. What is the best course of action?

   A. Security incident response

   B. Security incident response followed by business continuity plan

   C. Concurrent security incident response and business continuity plan

   D. Business continuity plan

11. What is the most important consideration when selecting a hot site?

   A. Time zone

   B. Geographic location in relation to the primary site

   C. Proximity to major transportation

   D. Natural hazards

12. An organization has established a recovery point objective of 14 days for its most critical business applications. Which recovery strategy would be the best choice?

    A. Mobile site

    B. Warm site

    C. Hot site

    D. Cold site

13. What technology should an organization use for its application servers to provide continuous service to users?

    A. Dual power supplies

    B. Server clustering

    C. Dual network feeds

    D. Transaction monitoring

14. An organization currently stores its backup media in a cabinet next to the computers being backed up. A consultant told the organization to store backup media at an off-site storage facility. What risk did the consultant most likely have in mind when he made this recommendation?

    A. A disaster that damages computer systems can also damage backup media.

    B. Backup media rotation may result in loss of data backed up several weeks in the past.

    C. Corruption of online data will require rapid data recovery from off-site storage.

    D. Physical controls at the data processing site are insufficient.

15. An organization has just experienced a major earthquake at its operations center. Which should be the organization's top priority?

    A. Ensuring that an automatic failure to the recovery site will occur as personnel may be slow to respond

    B. Ensuring that visitors will know how to evacuate the premises and the location of sheltering areas

    C. Ensuring that data replication to a recovery site has been working properly

    D. Ensuring that backup media will be available at the recovery site

Answers

1. **B**. A security information and event management system (SIEM) is used as a central event log processing system that correlates events among various devices and produces alerts that may represent intrusions and other types of security incidents.

2. C. An organization that lacks personnel and tools to conduct computer forensics should purchase an incident response retainer. With a retainer, forensics experts are available on-call to respond to an incident. While an organization can consider hiring one or more people with these skills, a job search can take several months, and people with these skills command high salaries.

3. A. A business impact analysis (BIA) is used to identify the business processes and, hence, the information systems that are most critical for the organization's ongoing operations.

4. D. The best approach for protecting data from a high-velocity attack such as ransomware is to back up the data to offline media that cannot be accessed by end users. Replicating data to another storage system may only serve to replicate damaged data to the secondary storage system, making recovery more difficult or expensive.

5. A. The types of security incident response plan testing are a document review, a walk-through, and a simulation. Parallel and cutover tests are not part of security incident response planning or testing but instead are tests used for disaster recovery planning.

6. A. Dwell time is the term used to define the period of time between the occurrence of a security incident and the organization's awareness of the incident.

7. C. The purpose of attorney–client privilege is the protection of correspondence and exhibits, including those in an investigation. If an organization that has experienced a security incident believes it may be defending itself in a lawsuit, the organization can choose to protect its investigation (including actions performed by a third-party firm) and its proceedings so that the organization will not be required to turn over that information during the lawsuit.

8. C. The purpose of chain of custody procedures is to demonstrate the integrity of the investigation, namely, that no information has been altered, including the contents of any computer memory and hard drives.

9. A. The best choice of tests for a first-time business continuity plan is a document review or a walk-through. Since this is a first-time plan, other tests are not the best first choice.

10. C. If an organization's critical data has been damaged by a ransomware incident, the organization should invoke its business continuity plan alongside its security incident response plan. This may help the organization restore services to its customers more quickly.

11. B. An important selection criterion for a hot site is the geographic location in relation to the primary site. If they are too close together, then a single disaster event may involve both locations.

12. D. An organization that has a 14-day recovery time objective (RTO) can use a cold site for its recovery strategy. Fourteen days is enough time for most organizations to acquire hardware and recover applications.

13. **B**. An organization that wants its application servers to be continuously available to its users needs to employ server clustering. This enables at least one server to always be available to service user requests.

14. **A**. The primary reason for employing off-site backup media storage is to mitigate the effects of a disaster that could otherwise destroy computer systems and their backup media.

15. **B**. The safety of personnel is always the top priority when any disaster event has occurred. While important, the condition of information systems is a secondary concern.

About the CD-ROM

The CD-ROM included with this book comes complete with Total Tester customizable practice exam software with 400 practice exam questions and a secured PDF copy of the book.

NOTE If you do not have a CD-ROM drive you may download the Total Tester by simply going to the following URL:

http://www.totalsem.com/126002704Xd/

Also, to access the PDF ebook, visit McGraw-Hill Professional's Media Center by going to the URL below and entering the 13-digit ISBN 978-1-260-02704-4 and your email address. You will then receive an e-mail message with a download link for the ebook.

https://www.mhprofessionalresources.com/mediacenter/

System Requirements

The software requires Windows Vista or higher and 30MB of hard disk space for full installation, in addition to a current or prior major release of Chrome, Firefox, Internet Explorer, or Safari. To run, the screen resolution must be set to 1024 × 768 or higher. The secured book PDF requires Adobe Acrobat, Adobe Reader, or Adobe Digital Editions to view.

Installing and Running Total Tester Premium Practice Exam Software

From the main screen you may install the Total Tester by clicking the Total Tester Practice Exams button. This will begin the installation process and place an icon on your desktop and in your Start menu. To run Total Tester, navigate to Start | (All) Programs | Total Seminars, or double-click the icon on your desktop.

To uninstall the Total Tester software, go to Start | Control Panel | Programs And Features, and then select the Total Tester program. Select Remove, and Windows will completely uninstall the software.

Total Tester Premium Practice Exam Software

Total Tester provides you with a simulation of the CISM exam. Exams can be taken in Practice Mode, Exam Mode, or Custom Mode. Practice Mode provides an assistance window with hints, references to the book, explanations of the correct and incorrect answers, and the option to check your answer as you take the test. Exam Mode provides a simulation of the actual exam. The number of questions, the types of questions, and the time allowed are intended to be an accurate representation of the exam environment. Custom Mode allows you to create custom exams from selected domains or chapters, and you can further customize the number of questions and time allowed.

To take a test, launch the program and select CISM from the Installed Question Packs list. You can then select Practice Mode, Exam Mode, or Custom Mode. All exams provide an overall grade and a grade broken down by domain.

Secured Book PDF

The entire contents of the book are provided in secured PDF format on the CD-ROM. This file is viewable on your computer and many portable devices.

- **To view the PDF on a computer,** Adobe Acrobat, Adobe Reader, or Adobe Digital Editions is required to view the file. A link to Adobe's website, where you can download and install Adobe Reader, has been included on the CD-ROM.

 NOTE: For more information on Adobe Reader and to check for the most recent version of the software, visit Adobe's website at www.adobe.com and search for the free Adobe Reader or look for Adobe Reader on the product page. Adobe Digital Editions can also be downloaded from the Adobe website.

- **To view the book PDF on a portable device,** copy the PDF file to your computer from the CD-ROM and then copy the file to your portable device using a USB or other connection. Adobe offers a mobile version of Adobe Reader, the Adobe Reader mobile app, which currently supports iOS and Android. For customers using Adobe Digital Editions and an iPad, you may have to download and install a separate reader program on your device. The Adobe website has a list of recommended applications, and McGraw-Hill Education recommends the Bluefire Reader.

Technical Support

For questions regarding the Total Tester software or operation of the CD-ROM, visit **www.totalsem.com** or e-mail **support@totalsem.com**.

For questions regarding the secured book PDF, e-mail **techsolutions@mhedu.com** or visit **http://mhp.softwareassist.com**.

For questions regarding book content, e-mail **hep_customer-service@mheducation .com**. For customers outside the United States, e-mail **international_cs@mheducation .com**.

802.1X   A standard for network authentication and access control used to determine whether a device will be permitted to attach to a LAN or wireless LAN. *See also* network access control (NAC).

A-123   A U.S. Office of Management and Budget (OMB) government circular that defines the management responsibilities for internal controls in U.S. federal agencies.

acceptable interruption window (AIW)   *See* maximum tolerable downtime (MTD).

acceptable use policy   Security policy that defines the types of activities that are acceptable and those that are not acceptable. An acceptable use policy is generally written for general audiences, applying to all personnel in an organization.

access bypass   Any attempt by an intruder to bypass access controls to gain entry into a system.

access control   Any means that detects or prevents unauthorized access and that permits authorized access.

access control policy   Statement that defines the policy for the granting, review, and revocation of access to systems and work areas.

access governance   Policies, procedures, and activities that enforce access policy and management control.

access management   A formal business process that is used to control access to networks and information systems.

access recertification   The process of reconfirming subjects' access to objects in an organization.

access review   A review of the users, systems, or other subjects that are permitted to access protected objects. The purpose of a review is to ensure that all subjects should still be authorized to have access.

account lockout   An administrative lock that is placed on a user account when a predetermined event occurs, such as reaching an expiration date or when there have been several unsuccessful attempts to access the user account.

accumulation of privileges   A situation where an employee accumulates computer system access privileges over a long period of time because of internal transfers or other privilege changes and old access privileges not being removed.

administrative audit   An audit of operational efficiency.

administrative control   Controls in the form of policies, processes, procedures, and standards.

advanced persistent threat (APT)   A class of threat actor that uses an array of reconnaissance and attack techniques to establish a long-term presence within a target organization.

algorithm   In cryptography, a specific mathematical formula that is used to perform encryption, decryption, message digests, and digital signatures.

allowable interruption window (AIW)   *See* maximum tolerable downtime (MTD).

annualized loss expectancy (ALE)   The expected loss of asset value due to threat realization. ALE is defined as SLE × ARO.

annualized rate of occurrence (ARO)   An estimate of the number of times that a threat will occur every year.

antiforensics   Any of several techniques whose objective is to make it more difficult for a forensic examiner to identify and understand a computer intrusion.

anti-malware   Software that uses various means to detect and block or prevent malware from carrying out its purpose. *See also* antivirus software.

antivirus software   Software that is designed to detect and remove computer viruses.

appliance   A type of computer with preinstalled software that requires little or no maintenance.

application firewall   A device used to control packets being sent to an application server, primarily to block unwanted or malicious content.

APT   *See* advanced persistent threat.

architecture standard   A standard that defines technology architecture at the database, system, or network level.

assessment   An examination of a business process or information system to determine its state and effectiveness.

asset inventory   The process of confirming the existence, location, and condition of assets; also, the results of such a process.

asset management   The processes used to manage the inventory, classification, use, and disposal of assets.

asset value (AV)   The value of an IT asset, which is usually (but not necessarily) the asset's replacement value.

assets   The collection of property that is owned by an organization.

asymmetric encryption   A method for encryption, decryption, and digital signatures that uses pairs of encryption keys, consisting of a public key and a private key.

asynchronous replication   A type of replication where writing data to the remote storage system is not kept in sync with updates on the local storage system. Instead, there may be a time lag, and there is no guarantee that data on the remote system is identical to that on the local storage system. *See also* replication.

attack surface   A metaphor often used to depict a greater or lesser extent of attackable systems, services, and personnel in an organization, or the attackable programs, services, and features in a running operating system.

attestation of compliance   A written statement that serves as an assertion of compliance to a requirement, standard, or law. An attestation of compliance is often signed by a high-ranking official or executive.

attorney–client privilege   As defined by Black's Law Dictionary, "a client's right privilege to refuse to disclose and to prevent any other person from disclosing confidential communications between the client and the attorney." In the context of information security, certain business proceedings can be protected with attorney–client privilege as a means for preventing those proceedings from being made available during legal discovery.

audit   A formal review of one or more processes, controls, or systems to determine their state against a standard.

audit logging   A feature in an application, operating system, or database management system where events are recorded in a separate log.

audit methodology   A set of audit procedures that is used to accomplish a set of audit objectives.

audit objective   The purpose or goals of an audit. Generally, the objective of an audit is to determine whether controls exist and are effective in some specific aspect of business operations in an organization.

audit plan   A formal document that guides the control and execution of an audit. An audit plan should align with audit objectives and specify audit procedures to be used.

audit procedures   The step-by-step instructions and checklists required to perform specific audit activities. Procedures may include a list of people to interview and questions to ask them, evidence to request, audit tools to use, sampling rates, where and how evidence will be archived, and how evidence will be evaluated.

audit program   The plan for conducting audits over a long period.

audit report   The final, written product of an audit. An audit report will include a description of the purpose, scope, and type of audit performed; people interviewed; evidence collected; rates and methods of sampling; and findings on the existence and effectiveness of each control.

audit scope   The process, procedures, systems, and applications that are the subject of an audit.

authentication   The process of asserting one's identity and providing proof of that identity. Typically, authentication requires a user ID (the assertion) and a password (the proof). However, authentication can also require stronger means of proof, such as a digital certificate, token, smart card, or biometric.

automatic control   A control that is enacted through some automatic mechanism that requires little or no human intervention.

availability management   The IT function that consists of activities concerned with the availability of IT applications and services. *See also* IT service management (ITSM).

background check   The process of verifying an employment candidate's employment history, education records, professional licenses and certifications, criminal background, and financial background.

background verification   *See* background check.

back-out plan   A procedure used to reverse the effect of a change that was not successful.

backup   The process of copying important data to another media device in the event of a hardware failure, error, or software bug that causes damage to data.

backup media rotation   Any scheme used to determine how backup media is to be reused.

basic input/output system (BIOS)   The firmware on a computer that tests the computer's hardware and initiates the bootup sequence. Superseded by unified extensible firmware interface (UEFI). *See also* unified extensible firmware interface (UEFI).

bare metal restore   The process of recovering a system by reformatting main storage, re-installing the operating system, and restoring files.

biometrics   Any use of a machine-readable characteristic of a user's body that uniquely identifies the user. Biometrics can be used for multifactor authentication. Types of biometrics include voice recognition, fingerprint, hand scan, palm vein scan, iris scan, retina scan, facial scan, and handwriting. *See also* authentication, multifactor authentication.

block cipher   An encryption algorithm that operates on blocks of data.

board of directors   A body of elected or appointed people who oversee the activities of an organization.

bot   A type of malware in which agents are implanted by other forms of malware and are programmed to obey remotely issued instructions. *See also* botnet.

botnet   A collection of bots that are under the control of an individual. *See also* bot.

bring your own app   A practice whereby workers use personally owned applications and use them for company business.

bring your own device (BYOD)   A practice whereby workers use personally owned devices (typically laptop computers and mobile devices) for company business.

budget   A plan for allocating resources over a certain time period.

bug   *See* software defect.

business case   An explanation of the expected benefits to the business that will be realized as a result of a program or project.

business continuity planning (BCP)   The activities required to ensure the continuation of critical business processes.

business e-mail compromise   *See* CEO fraud.

business functional requirements   Formal statements that describe required business functions that a system must support.

business impact analysis (BIA)   A study that is used to identify the impact that different disaster scenarios will have on ongoing business operations.

business recovery plan   The activities required to recover and resume critical business processes and activities. *See also* response document.

call tree   A method for ensuring the timely notification of key personnel, such as after a disaster.

capability maturity model   A model that is used to measure the relative maturity of an organization or of its processes.

Capability Maturity Model Integration for Development (CMMi-DEV)   A maturity model that is used to measure the maturity of a software development process.

capacity management   The IT function that consists of activities that confirm there is sufficient capacity in IT systems and IT processes to meet service needs. Primarily, an IT system or process has sufficient capacity if its performance falls within an acceptable range, as specified in service level agreements (SLAs). *See also* IT service management (ITSM), service level agreement (SLA).

cardholder data   As defined by the PCI Security Standards Council: "At a minimum, cardholder data consists of the full PAN (Primary Account Number, also known as a credit card number). Cardholder data may also appear in the form of the full PAN plus any of the following: cardholder name, expiration date and/or service code." *See also* Payment Card Industry Data Security Standard (PCI-DSS).

career path   The progression of responsibilities and job titles that a worker will attain over time.

CEO fraud   A type of fraud where a perpetrator, impersonating an organization's CEO, sends phishing e-mails to other company executives and directs them to wire large amounts of money to a bank account, typically in support of a secret merger or acquisition. *See also* phishing, spear phishing, *and* whaling.

certificate authority (CA)   A trusted party that stores digital certificates and public encryption keys.

certificate revocation list (CRL)   An electronic list of digital certificates that have been revoked prior to their expiration date.

certification practice statement (CPS)   A published statement that describes the practices used by the CA to issue and manage digital certificates.

chain of custody   Documentation that shows the acquisition, storage, control, and analysis of evidence. The chain of custody may be needed if the evidence is to be used in a legal proceeding.

change advisory board (CAB)   *See* change control board (CCB).

change control   *See* change management.

change control board (CCB)   The group of stakeholders from IT and business who propose, discuss, and approve changes to IT systems. Also known as a *change advisory board*.

change management   The IT function that is used to control changes made to an IT environment. *See also* IT service management (ITSM).

change request   A formal request for a change to be made in an environment. *See also* change management.

change review   A formal review of a requested change. *See also* change request, change management.

charter   *See* program charter.

chief information risk officer (CIRO)   The typical job title for the topmost information security executive in an organization.

chief information security officer (CISO)   The typical job title for the topmost information security executive in an organization.

chief risk officer (CRO)   The typical job title for the topmost risk officer in an organization.

chief security officer (CSO)   The typical job title for the topmost security officer in an organization.

ciphertext   A message, file, or stream of data that has been transformed by an encryption algorithm and rendered unreadable.

CIS Controls A control framework maintained by the Center for Internet Security (CIS).

clone phishing The practice of obtaining legitimate e-mail messages, exchanging attachments or URLs for those that are malicious, and sending the altered e-mail messages to target users in the hopes the messages will trick users on account of their genuine appearance.

cloud Internet-based computing resources.

cloud access security broker (CASB) A system that monitors and, optionally, controls users' access to, or use of, cloud-based resources.

cloud computing A technique of providing a dynamically scalable and usually virtualized computing resource as a service.

cluster A tightly coupled collection of computers that is used to solve a common task. In a cluster, one or more servers actively perform tasks, while zero or more computers may be in a "standby" state, ready to assume active duty should the need arise.

COBIT A control framework for managing information systems and security. COBIT is published by ISACA.

code of ethics A statement that defines acceptable and unacceptable professional conduct.

cold site An alternate processing center where the degree of readiness for recovery systems is low. At the least, a cold site is nothing more than an empty rack or just allocated space on a computer room floor.

command and control (C&C) Network traffic associated with a system compromised with malware. Command-and-control traffic represents communication between the malware and a central controlling entity.

Committee of Sponsoring Organizations of the Treadway Commission (COSO) A private sector organization that provides thought leadership, control frameworks, and guidance on enterprise risk management.

common vulnerability scoring system (CVSS) An open framework for communicating the quantitative characteristics and impacts of IT vulnerabilities.

compensating control A control that is implemented because another control cannot be implemented or is ineffective.

compliance Activities related to the examination of systems and processes to ensure they conform to applicable policies, standards, controls, requirements, and regulations; also, the state of conformance to applicable policies, standards, controls, requirements, and regulations.

compliance audit An audit to determine the level and degree of compliance to a law, regulation, standard, contract provision, or internal control. *See also* audit.

compliance risk   Risk associated with any general or specific consequences of not being compliant with a law, regulation, or private legal obligation.

configuration item   A configuration setting in an IT asset. *See also* configuration management.

configuration management   The IT function where the configuration of components in an IT environment is independently recorded. Configuration management is usually supported by the use of automated tools used to inventory and control system configurations. *See also* IT service management (ITSM).

configuration management database (CMDB)   A repository for every component in an environment that contains information on every configuration change made on those components.

configuration standard   A standard that defines the detailed configurations that are used in servers, workstations, operating systems, database management systems, applications, network devices, and other systems.

contact list   A list of key personnel and various methods used to contact them. *See also* response document.

containerization   A form of virtualization where an operating system permits the existence of multiple isolated user spaces, called containers. *See also* virtualization.

continuity of operations plan (COOP)   The activities required to continue critical and strategic business functions at an alternate site. *See also* response document.

continuous log review   A process where the event log for one or more systems is being continuously reviewed in real time to determine whether a security or operational event warranting attention is taking place. *See also* security information and event management system (SIEM).

continuous improvement   The cultural desire to increase the efficiency and effectiveness of processes and controls over time.

content delivery network (CDN)   Also known as a content distribution network, a globally distributed network of servers in multiple data centers designed to optimize the speed and cost of delivery of content from centralized servers to end users.

content distribution network (CDN)   *See* content delivery network (CDN).

contract   A binding legal agreement between two or more parties that may be enforceable in a court of law.

control   Policy, process, or procedure that is created to ensure desired outcomes or to avoid unwanted outcomes.

control existence   An activity that takes place in an audit where the auditor seeks to determine whether an expected control is in place.

control framework   A collection of controls, organized into logical categories.

control objective   A foundational statement that describes desired states or outcomes from business operations.

control risk   The risk that a significant or material error exists that will not be prevented or detected by a control.

control self-assessment (CSA)   A methodology used by an organization to review key business objectives, risks, and controls. Control self-assessment is a self-regulation activity that may or may not be required by applicable laws or regulations.

corrective action   An action that is initiated to correct an undesired condition.

corrective control   A control that is used after an unwanted event has occurred.

countermeasure   Any activity or mechanism that is designed to reduce risk.

covered entity   Any organization that stores or processes electronic protected health information (ePHI). *See also* Health Insurance Portability and Accountability Act (HIPAA).

critical path methodology (CPM)   A technique that is used to identify the most critical path in a project to understand which tasks are most likely to affect the project schedule.

criticality analysis (CA)   A study of each system and process, a consideration of the impact on the organization if it is incapacitated, the likelihood of incapacitation, and the estimated cost of mitigating the risk or impact of incapacitation.

cryptanalysis   An attack on a cryptosystem where the attacker is attempting to determine the encryption key that is used to encrypt messages.

cryptography   The practice of hiding information from unwanted people.

culture   The collective attitudes, practices, communication, communication styles, ethics, and other behavior in an organization.

custodian   A person or group delegated to operate or maintain an asset.

cutover   The step in the software development life cycle where an old replaced system is shut down and a new replacement system is started.

cutover test   An actual test of disaster recovery and/or business continuity response plans. The purpose of a parallel test is to evaluate the ability of personnel to follow directives in emergency response plans—to actually set up the DR business processing or data processing capability. In a cutover test, personnel shut down production systems and operate recovery systems to assume actual business workload. *See also* disaster recovery plan.

cyber risk insurance   An insurance policy designed to compensate an organization for unexpected costs related to a security breach.

cybersecurity framework (CSF)   *See* NIST CSF.

cyclical controls testing   A life cycle process in which selected controls are examined for effectiveness.

damage assessment   The process of examining assets after a disaster to determine the extent of damage.

data acquisition   The act of obtaining data for later use in a forensic investigation.

data classification policy   Policy that defines sensitivity levels and handling procedures for information.

data loss prevention (DLP) system   A hardware or software system that detects and, optionally, blocks the movement or storage of sensitive data.

data restore   The process of copying data from backup media to a target system for the purpose of restoring lost or damaged data.

data security   Those controls that seek to maintain confidentiality, integrity, and availability of information.

decryption   The process of transforming ciphertext into plaintext so that a recipient can read it.

denial of service (DoS)   An attack on a computer or network with the intention of causing disruption or malfunction of the target.

desktop computer   A nonportable computer used by an individual end user and located at the user's workspace.

desktop virtualization   Software technology that separates the physical computing environment from the software that runs on an endpoint, effectively transforming an endpoint into a display terminal. *See also* virtualization.

destructware   *See* wiper.

detective control   A control that is used to detect events.

deterrent control   A control that is designed to deter people from performing unwanted activities.

Diffie–Hellman   A popular key exchange algorithm. *See also* key exchange.

digital certificate   An electronic document that contains an identity that is signed with the public key of a certificate authority (CA).

digital envelope   A method that uses two layers of encryption. A symmetric key is used to encrypt a message; then a public or private key is used to encrypt the symmetric key.

digital rights management (DRM)   Any technology used to control the distribution and use of electronic content.

digital signature   The result of encrypting the hash of a message with the originator's private encryption key, used to prove the authenticity and integrity of a message.

directory   A centralized service that provides information for a particular function.

disaster   An unexpected and unplanned event that results in the disruption of business operations.

disaster declaration criteria   The conditions that must be present to declare a disaster, triggering response and recovery operations.

disaster declaration procedure   Instructions to determine whether to declare a disaster and trigger response and recovery operations. *See also* disaster declaration criteria.

disaster recovery and business continuity requirements   Formal statements that describe required recoverability and continuity characteristics that a system must support.

disaster recovery plan   The activities required to restore critical IT systems and other critical assets, whether in alternate or primary locations. *See also* response document.

disaster recovery planning (DRP)   Activities related to the assessment, salvage, repair, and restoration of facilities and assets.

disaster recovery-as-a-service (DRaaS)   A cloud-based set of tools and services that streamline the planning and execution of data backup and data replication for disaster recovery purposes.

discovery sampling   A sampling technique where at least one exception is sought in a population. *See also* sampling.

disk array   A chassis in which several hard disks can be installed and connected to a server. The individual disk drives can be "hot swapped" in the chassis while the array is still operating.

distributed denial of service (DDoS)   A denial-of-service (DoS) attack that originates from many computers. *See also* denial of service (DoS).

DNS filter   A network system or device used to protect systems from malicious content through manipulation of the results of DNS queries. *See also* web content filter.

document review   A review of some or all disaster recovery and business continuity plans, procedures, and other documentation. Individuals typically review these documents on their own, at their own pace, but within whatever time constraints or deadlines that may have been established.

documentation   The inclusive term that describes charters, processes, procedures, standards, requirements, and other written documents.

Domain Name System (DNS)   A TCP/IP application layer protocol used to translate domain names (such as www.isecbooks.com) into IP addresses.

dwell time   The period of time that elapses from the start of a security incident to the organization's awareness of the incident.

dynamic application security testing (DAST)   Tools used to identify security defects in a running software application.

eavesdropping   The act of secretly intercepting and, optionally, recording a voice or data transmission.

elasticity   The property of infrastructure-as-a-service whereby additional virtual assets can be created or withdrawn in response to rising and falling workloads.

electric generator   A system consisting of an internal combustion engine powered by gasoline, diesel fuel, or natural gas that spins an electric generator. A generator can supply electricity for as long as several days, depending upon the size of its fuel supply and whether it can be refueled.

electronic protected health information (ePHI)   Any information—in electronic form—about the health, health status, and medical treatment of a human patient.

elliptic curve   A public key cryptography algorithm.

e-mail   A network-based service used to transmit messages between individuals and groups.

emergency communications plan   The communications that are required during a disaster. *See also* response document.

emergency response   The urgent activities that immediately follow a disaster, including evacuation of personnel, first aid, triage of injured personnel, and possibly firefighting.

employee handbook   *See* employee policy manual.

employee policy manual   A formal statement of the terms of employment, facts about the organization, benefits, compensation, conduct, and policies.

employment agreement   A legal contract between an organization and an employee, which may include a description of duties, roles and responsibilities, confidentiality, compliance, and termination.

encryption   The act of hiding sensitive information in plain sight. Encryption works by scrambling the characters in a message using a method known only to the sender and receiver, making the message useless to anyone who intercepts the message.

encryption key   A block of characters, used in combination with an encryption algorithm, to encrypt or decrypt a stream or block of data.

endpoint   A general term used to describe any of the types of devices used by end users, including mobile phones, smartphones, terminals, tablet computers, laptop computers, and desktop computers.

enterprise architecture   Activities that ensure important business needs are met by IT systems; the model that is used to map business functions into the IT environment and IT systems in increasing levels of detail.

enterprise risk management (ERM)   The methods and processes used by an organization to identify and manage business risks.

evacuation procedure   Instructions to safely evacuate a work facility in the event of a fire, earthquake, or other disaster.

e-vaulting   The practice of backing up information to an off-site location, often a third-party service provider.

event   An occurrence of relevance to a business or system.

event monitoring   The practice of examining the events that occur on information systems, including operating systems, subsystems such as database management systems, applications, network devices, and end-user devices.

event visibility   A capability that permits an organization to be aware of activities that may be a sign of a security incident.

evidence   Information gathered by the auditor that provides proof that a control exists and is being operated.

exploitation   The process of exploiting a vulnerability in a target system in order to take control of the system.

exposure factor (EF)   The financial loss that results from the realization of a threat, expressed as a percentage of the asset's total value.

facilities classification   A method for assigning classification or risk levels to work centers and processing centers, based on their operational criticality or other risk factors.

feasibility study   An activity that seeks to determine the expected benefits of a program or project.

fiduciary   A person who has a legal trust relationship with another party.

fiduciary duty   The highest standard of care that a fiduciary renders to a beneficiary.

file   A sequence of zero or more characters that is stored as a whole in a file system. A file may be a document, spreadsheet, image, sound file, computer program, or data that is used by a program.

file activity monitoring (FAM)   A program that monitors the use of files on a server or endpoint as a means for detecting indicators of compromise.

file integrity monitoring (FIM)   A program that periodically scans file systems on servers and workstations, as a means of detecting changes to file contents or permissions that may be indicators of compromise.

file server   A server that is used to store files in a central location, usually to make them available to many users.

fileless malware   Malware that resides in a computer's memory instead of the file system.

financial audit   An audit of an accounting system, accounting department processes, and procedures to determine whether business controls are sufficient to ensure the integrity of financial statements. *See also* audit.

financial management   Management for IT services that consists of several activities, including budgeting, capital investment, expense management, project accounting, and project ROI. *See also* IT service management (ITSM), return on investment (ROI).

fingerprint   *See* biometrics, key fingerprint.

firewall   A device that controls the flow of network messages between networks. Placed at the boundary between the Internet and an organization's internal network, firewalls enforce security policy by prohibiting all inbound traffic except for the specific few types of traffic that are permitted to a select few systems.

first in, first out (FIFO)   A backup media rotation scheme where the oldest backup volumes are used next. *See also* backup media rotation.

forensic audit   An audit that is performed in support of an anticipated or active legal proceeding. *See also* audit.

forensics   The application of procedures and tools during an investigation of a computer or network-related event.

fraud   The intentional deception made for personal gain or for damage to another party.

gap analysis   An examination of a process or system to determine differences between its existing state and a desired future state.

general computing controls (GCCs)   Controls that are general in nature and implemented across most or all information systems and applications.

general data protection regulation (GDPR)   The European law, which takes effect in 2018, that protects the privacy of European residents.

governance   Management's control over policy and processes.

governance, risk, and compliance (GRC) tool   A software program used to track key aspects of an organization's information risk program.

grandfather-father-son   A hierarchical backup media rotation scheme that provides for longer retention of some backups. *See also* backup media rotation.

hacker   Someone who interferes with or accesses another's computer without authorization.

hard disk drive (HDD)   A storage device using magnetic storage on rapidly rotating disks.

hardening   The technique of configuring a system so that only its essential services and features are active and all others are deactivated. This helps to reduce the "attack surface" of a system to only its essential components.

hardening standard   A document that describes the security configuration details of a system, or class of systems. *See also* configuration standard, hardening.

hardware monitoring   Tools and processes used to continuously observe the health, performance, and capacity of one or more computers.

hash function   A cryptographic operation on a block of data that returns a fixed-length string of characters, used to verify the integrity of a message.

Health Insurance Portability and Accountability Act (HIPAA)   A U.S. law requiring the enactment of controls to protect electronic protected health information (EPHI).

HITRUST   A healthcare control framework and certification that serves as an external attestation of an organization's IT controls.

host-based intrusion detection system (HIDS)   An intrusion detection system (IDS) that is installed on a system and watches for anomalies that could be signs of intrusion. *See also* intrusion detection system (IDS).

hot site   An alternate processing center where backup systems are already running and in some state of near-readiness to assume production workload. The systems at a hot site most likely have application software and database management software already loaded and running, perhaps even at the same patch levels as the systems in the primary processing center.

human resources (HR)   The department in most organizations that is responsible for employee onboarding, offboarding, internal transfers, training, and signing important documents such as security policy.

human resource information system (HRIS)   An information system used to manage information about an organization's workforce.

human resource management (HRM or HR)   Activities regarding the acquisition, onboarding, support, and termination of workers in an organization.

hybrid cryptography   A cryptosystem that employs two or more iterations or types of cryptography.

Hypertext Transfer Protocol (HTTP)   A TCP/IP application layer protocol used to transmit web page contents from web servers to users who are using web browsers.

Hypertext Transfer Protocol Secure (HTTPS)   A TCP/IP application layer protocol that is similar to HTTP in its use for transporting data between web servers and browsers.

HTTPS is not a separate protocol but instead is the instance where HTTP is encrypted with SSL or TLS. *See also* Hypertext Transfer Protocol (HTTP), Secure Sockets Layer (SSL), Transport Layer Security (TLS).

hypervisor Virtualization software that facilitates the operation of one or more virtual machines.

identity and access management (IAM) The activities and supporting systems that are used to manage workers' identities and their access to information systems and data.

identity management The activity of managing the identity of each employee, contractor, temporary worker, and, optionally, customer, for use in a single environment or multiple environments.

image A binary representation of a fully installed and configured operating system and applications for a server or an end user's computer.

impact The actual or expected result from some action such as a threat or disaster.

impact analysis The analysis of a threat and the impact it would have if it were realized.

incident Any event that is not part of the standard operation of a service and that causes, or may cause, interruption to or a reduction in the quality of that service.

incident declaration The process of determining that a security incident is taking place so that incident responders can begin the task of managing it.

incident management (ITSM) The IT function that analyzes service outages, service slowdowns, security incidents, and software bugs, and seeks to resolve them to restore normal service. *See also* IT service management (ITSM), security incident management.

incident prevention Proactive steps taken to reduce the probability or impact of security incidents.

incident responder A worker in an organization who has responsibility for responding to a security incident.

incident response retainer A legal agreement between an organization and a security professional services firm that arranges for the security firm to render assistance to the organization in the event of a security incident.

incident response team (IRT) Personnel who are trained in incident response techniques.

indicator of compromise (IoC) An observation on a network or in an operating system that indicates evidence of a network or computer intrusion.

industrial control system (ICS) A control system used to monitor and manage physical machinery in an industrial environment. *See also* supervisory control and data acquisition (SCADA).

information classification The process of assigning a sensitivity classification to an information asset.

information risk   Paraphrased from the ISACA Risk IT Framework: the business risk associated with the use, ownership, operation, involvement, influence, and adoption of information within an enterprise.

information security management   The aggregation of policies, processes, procedures, and activities to ensure that an organization's security policy is effective.

Information Security Management System (ISMS)   The collection of activities for managing information security in an organization, as defined by ISO/IEC 27001.

information security policy   A statement that defines how an organization will classify and protect its important assets.

infrastructure   The collection of networks, network services, devices, facilities, and system software that facilitates access to, communications with, and protection of business applications.

infrastructure-as-a-service (IaaS)   A cloud computing model where a service provider makes computers and other infrastructure components available to subscribers. *See also* cloud computing.

inherent risk   The risk that there are material weaknesses in existing business processes and no compensating controls to detect or prevent them.

initialization vector (IV)   A random number that is needed by some encryption algorithms to begin the encryption process.

insider threat   Any scenario where an employee or contractor knowingly, or unknowingly, commits acts that result in security incidents or breaches.

integrated audit   An audit that combines an operational audit and a financial audit. *See also* operational audit, financial audit.

integrated development environment (IDE)   A software application that facilitates the writing, updating, testing, and debugging of application source code.

intellectual property   A class of assets owned by an organization; includes an organization's designs, architectures, software source code, processes, and procedures.

internal audit   A formal audit of an organization's controls, processes, or systems, which is carried out by personnel who are part of the organization. *See also* audit.

internal audit (IA)   The name of an organization's internal department that performs audits.

Internet   The interconnection of the world's TCP/IP networks.

Internet hygiene   The practice of security awareness while accessing the Internet with a computer or mobile device to reduce the possibility of attack.

intrusion detection system (IDS)   A hardware or software system that detects anomalies that may be signs of an intrusion.

intrusion kill chain   The computer intrusion model developed by Lockheed-Martin that depicts a typical computer intrusion. The phases of the kill chain are reconnaissance, weaponization, delivery, exploitation, installation, command and control, and actions on objective.

intrusion prevention system (IPS)   A hardware or software system that detects and blocks malicious network traffic that may be signs of an intrusion.

intrusive monitoring   Any technique used by an organization to actively monitor activities within a third party's IT environment.

IS audit   An audit of an IS department's operations and systems. *See also* audit.

ISACA   Formerly the Information Systems Audit and Control Association, now just ISACA. Global organization the develops and administers numerous certifications including Certified Information Security Manager (CISM), Certified Information Systems Auditor (CISA), Certified in Risk, Information Security, and Control (CRISC), and Certified in the Governance of Enterprise IT (CGEIT).

ISACA audit standards   The minimum standards of performance related to security, audits, and the actions that result from audits. The standards are published by ISACA and updated periodically. ISACA audit standards are considered mandatory.

ISAE 3402 (International Standard on Assurance Engagement)   An external audit of a service provider. An ISAE 3402 audit is performed according to rules established by the International Auditing and Assurance Standards Board (IAASB).

ISO/IEC 20000   An ISO/IEC standard for IT service management (ITSM).

ISO/IEC 27001   An ISO/IEC standard for IT security management.

ISO/IEC 27002   An ISO/IEC standard for IT security controls.

IT Infrastructure Library (ITIL)   *See* IT service management (ITSM).

IT service management (ITSM)   The set of activities that ensures the delivery of IT services is efficient and effective, through active management and the continuous improvement of processes.

job description   A written description of a job in an organization. A job description usually contains a job title, work experience requirements, knowledge requirements, and responsibilities.

job title   See *position title*.

judgmental sampling   A sampling technique where items are chosen based upon the auditor's judgment, usually based on risk or materiality. *See also* sampling.

key   *See* encryption key.

key compromise   Any unauthorized disclosure or damage to an encryption key. *See also* key management.

key custody   The policies, processes, and procedures regarding the management of keys. *See also* key management.

key disposal   The process of decommissioning encryption keys. *See also* key management.

key encrypting key   An encryption key that is used to encrypt another encryption key.

key exchange   A technique that is used by two parties to establish a symmetric encryption key when no secure channel is available.

key fingerprint   A short sequence of characters that is used to authenticate a public key.

key generation   The initial generation of an encryption key. *See also* key management.

key goal indicator (KGI)   Measure of progress in the attainment of strategic goals in the organization.

key length   The size (measured in bits) of an encryption key. Longer encryption keys mean that it takes greater effort to successfully attack a cryptosystem.

key logger   A hardware device or a type of malware that records a user's keystrokes and, optionally, mouse movements and clicks, and sends this data to the key logger's owner.

key management   The various processes and procedures used by an organization to generate, protect, use, and dispose of encryption keys over their lifetime.

key performance indicator (KPI)   Measure of business processes' performance and quality, used to reveal trends related to efficiency and effectiveness of key processes in the organization.

key protection   All means used to protect encryption keys from unauthorized disclosure and harm. *See also* key management.

key risk indicator (KRI)   Measure of information risk, used to reveal trends related to levels of risk of security incidents in the organization.

key rotation   The process of issuing a new encryption key and reencrypting data protected with the new key. *See also* key management.

kill chain   *See* intrusion kill chain.

laptop computer   A portable computer used by an individual user.

last in, first out (LIFO)   A backup media rotation scheme where the newest backup volumes are used next. *See also* backup media rotation.

learning management system (LMS)   An on-premise or cloud-based system that makes online training and testing facilities available to an organization's personnel. Some LMSs automatically maintain records of training enrollment, test scores, and training completion.

least privilege   The concept where an individual user should have the lowest privilege possible that will still enable them to perform their tasks.

Lightweight Directory Access Protocol (LDAP)   A TCP/IP application layer protocol used as a directory service for people and computing resources.

log correlation   The process of combining log data from many devices in order to discern patterns that may be indicators of operational problems or compromise.

log review   An examination of the event log in an information system, typically to see whether any security events or incidents have occurred. *See also* continuous log review.

log server   A system or device to which event logs from other systems are sent for processing and storage. *See also* security information and event management (SIEM).

macro virus   Malicious software that is embedded within another file such as a document or spreadsheet.

malware   The broad class of programs that are designed to inflict harm on computers, networks, or information. Types of malware include viruses, worms, Trojan horses, spyware, and rootkits.

man-made disaster   A disaster that is directly or indirectly caused by human activity, through action or inaction. *See also* disaster.

managed security service provider (MSSP)   An organization that provides security monitoring and/or management services for customers.

manual control   A control that requires a human to operate it.

maximum acceptable outage (MAO)   *See* maximum tolerable outage (MTO).

maximum tolerable downtime (MTD)   A theoretical time period, measured from the onset of a disaster, after which the organization's ongoing viability would be at risk.

maximum tolerable outage (MTO)   The maximum period of time that an organization can tolerate operating in recovery (or alternate processing) mode.

message digest   The result of a cryptographic hash function.

methodology standard   A standard that specifies the practices used by the IT organization.

metric   A measurement of a periodic or ongoing activity, for the purpose of understanding the activity within the context of overall business operations.

microsegmentation   A design characteristic of a network where each network node resides on its own segment, resulting in improved network security and efficiency.

mitigating control   *See* compensating control.

mobile device   A portable computer in the form of a smartphone, tablet computer, or wearable device.

mobile site   A portable recovery center that can be delivered to almost any location in the world.

monitoring   The continuous or regular evaluation of a system or control to determine its operation or effectiveness.

multifactor authentication   Any means used to authenticate a user that is stronger than the use of a user ID and password. Examples of multifactor authentication include digital certificate, token, smart card, or biometric.

natural disaster   A disaster that occurs in the natural world with little or no assistance from mankind. *See also* disaster.

netflow   A network diagnostic tool that collects all network metadata, which can be used for network diagnostic or security purposes.

network access control (NAC)   An approach for network authentication and access control that determines whether devices will be permitted to attach to a LAN or wireless LAN.

network anomaly detection   A technique used to identify network traffic that may be a part of an intrusion or other unwanted event.

network attached storage (NAS)   A stand-alone storage system that contains one or more virtual volumes. Servers access these volumes over the network using the Network File System (NFS) or Server Message Block/Common Internet File System (SMB/CIFS) protocols, common on Unix and Windows operating systems, respectively.

network segmentation   The practice of dividing a network into two or more zones, with protective measures such as firewalls between the zones.

network tap   A connection on a network router or network switch. A copy of all of the network traffic passing through the router or switch is also sent to the network tap. Also known as a *span port*.

NIST CSF   A risk management methodology and controls framework developed by the U.S. National Institute for Standards and Technology (NIST).

NIST 800 Series   A collection of documents published by the U.S. National Institute for Standards and Technology (NIST).

nonrepudiation   The property of encryption and digital signatures that can make it difficult or impossible for a party to later deny having sent a digitally signed message—unless they admit to having lost control of their private encryption key.

North American Reliability Corporation (NERC)   The organization that maintains resilience and security controls for use by public utilities.

North American Reliability Council Critical Infrastructure Protection (NERC CIP)   The standards and requirements defined by the North American Reliability Council for protection of the electric power generation and distribution grid.

occupant emergency plan (OEP) Activities required to safely care for occupants in a business location during a disaster. *See also* response document.

off-site media storage The practice of storing media such as backup tapes at an off-site facility located away from the primary computing facility.

onboarding The process undertaken when an organization hires a new worker or when it begins a business relationship with a third party.

operational audit An audit of IS controls, security controls, or business controls to determine control existence and effectiveness. *See also* audit.

operational risk The risk of loss resulting from failed controls, processes, and systems; internal and external events; and other occurrences that impact business operations and threaten an organization's survival.

Operationally Critical Threat Asset and Vulnerability Evaluation (OCTAVE) A qualitative risk analysis methodology developed at Carnegie Mellon University.

orchestration In the context of security information and event management (SIEM), this is the scripted, automated response that is automatically or manually triggered when specific events occur. *See also* security information and event management (SIEM).

organization chart A diagram that depicts the manager-subordinate relationships in an organization or in part of an organization.

out of band Communications that takes place separately from the main communications method.

outsourcing A form of sourcing where an employer will use contract employees to perform a function. The contract employees may be located on-site or off-site.

owner A person or group responsible for the management and/or operation of an asset.

packet sniffer A device, or a program that can be installed on a network-attached system, to capture network traffic.

parallel test An actual test of disaster recovery (DR) or business continuity response plans. The purpose of a parallel test is to evaluate the ability of personnel to follow directives in emergency response plans—to actually set up the DR business processing or data processing capability. In a parallel test, personnel operate recovery systems in parallel with production systems to compare the results between the two to determine the actual capabilities of recovery systems.

password An identifier that is created by a system manager or a user; a secret combination of letters, numbers, and other symbols that is known only to the user who uses it.

password complexity The characteristics required of user account passwords. For example, a password may not contain dictionary words and must contain uppercase letters, lowercase letters, numbers, and symbols.

password length   The minimum and maximum number of characters permitted for a password that is associated with a computer account.

password reset   The process of changing a user account password and unlocking the user account so that the user's use of the account may resume.

password reuse   The act of reusing a prior password for a user account. Some information systems can prevent the use of prior passwords in case any were compromised with or without the user's knowledge.

patch management   The process of identifying, analyzing, and applying patches (including security patches) to systems.

Payment Card Industry Data Security Standard (PCI-DSS)   A security standard whose objective is the protection of credit card numbers in storage, while processed, and while transmitted. The standard was developed by the PCI Security Standards Council, a consortium of credit card companies, including Visa, MasterCard, American Express, Discover, and JCB.

personally identifiable information (PII)   Information that can be used on its own, or combined with other information, to identify a specific person.

phishing   A social engineering attack on unsuspecting individuals where e-mail messages that resemble official communications entice victims to visit imposter web sites that contain malware or request credentials to sensitive or valuable assets. *See also* CEO fraud, spear phishing, whaling.

physical control   Controls that employ physical means.

plaintext   An original message, file, or stream of data that can be read by anyone who has access to it.

platform-as-a-service (PaaS)   A cloud computing delivery model where the service provider supplies the platform on which an organization can build and run software.

playbook   A procedure to be performed to accomplish some purpose.

policy   A statement that specifies what must be done (or not done) in an organization. A policy usually defines who is responsible for monitoring and enforcing the policy.

population   A complete set of entities, transactions, or events that are the subject of an audit.

position title   A label that designates a person's place or role in an organization.

pre-audit   An examination of business processes, controls, and records in anticipation of an upcoming audit. *See also* audit.

preventive control   A control that is used to prevent unwanted events from happening.

privacy   The protection of personal information from unauthorized disclosure, use, and distribution.

privacy policy   A policy statement that defines how an organization will protect, manage, and handle private information.

private cloud   A cloud infrastructure that is dedicated to a single organization.

private key cryptosystem   A cryptosystem that is based on a symmetric cryptographic algorithm.

procurement   The process of making a purchase of hardware, software, and services; also, the name of the department that performs this activity.

probability   The chances that an event may occur.

probability analysis   The analysis of a threat and the probability of its realization.

problem   An incident—often multiple incidents—that exhibits common symptoms and whose root cause is not known.

problem management   The IT function that analyzes chronic incidents and seeks to resolve them and also enacts proactive measures in an effort to avoid problems. *See also* IT service management (ITSM).

procedure   A written sequence of instructions used to complete a task.

process   A collection of one or more procedures used to perform a business function. *See also* procedure.

process   A logical container in an operating system in which a program executes.

program   An organization of many large, complex activities; it can be thought of as a set of projects that work to fulfill one or more key business objectives or goals.

program charter   A formal definition of the objectives of a program, its main timelines, sources of funding, the names of its principal leaders and managers, and the business executives who are sponsoring the program.

program management   The management of a group of projects that exist to fulfill a business goal or objective.

project   A coordinated and managed sequence of tasks that results in the realization of an objective or goal.

project management   The activities that are used to control, measure, and manage the activities in a project.

project plan   The chart of tasks in a project, which also includes start and completion dates, resources required, and dependencies and relationships between tasks.

project planning   The activities that are related to the development and management of a project.

protocol analyzer   A device that is connected to a network in order to view network communications at a detailed level.

public cloud   A cloud infrastructure used by multiple organizations.

public key cryptography   *See* asymmetric encryption.

public key infrastructure (PKI)   A centralized function that is used to store and publish public keys and other information.

questionnaire   A list of questions sent to a third party, used to assess control effectiveness and risk.

qualitative risk analysis   A risk analysis methodology where risks are classified on a nonquantified scale, for example, from High to Medium to Low.

quantitative risk analysis   A risk analysis methodology where risks are estimated in the form of actual costs and/or probabilities of occurrence.

quarantine   A holding place for e-mail messages that have been blocked by a spam or phishing filter.

Responsible, Accountable, Consulted, Informed (RACI) Chart   A tool used to assign roles to individuals and groups according to their responsibilities.

rank   A part of a person's position title that denotes seniority or span of control in an organization.

ransomware   Malware that performs some malicious action, requiring payment from the victim to reverse the action. Such actions include data erasure, data encryption, and system damage.

reciprocal site   A data center that is operated by another company. Two or more organizations with similar processing needs will draw up a legal contract that obligates one or more of the organizations to temporarily house another party's systems in the event of a disaster.

reconnaissance   Any activity in which a would-be intruder or researcher explores a potential target system or network, generally to learn of its makeup, to determine a potentially successful attack strategy.

records   Documents describing business events such as meeting minutes, contracts, financial transactions, decisions, purchase orders, logs, and reports.

recovery capacity objective (RCapO)   The processing and/or storage capacity of an alternate process or system, as compared to the normal process or site. RCO is usually expressed as a percentage, as compared to the primary processing site.

recovery consistency objective (RCO)   A measure of the consistency and integrity of processing at a recovery site, as compared to the primary processing site. RCO is calculated as 1 − (number of inconsistent objects) / (number of objects).

recovery control   A control that is used after an unwanted event to restore a system or process to its pre-event state.

recovery point objective (RPO)   The period of acceptable data loss due to an incident or disaster. RPO is usually measured in hours or days.

recovery procedure   Instructions that key personnel use to bootstrap services that support critical business functions identified in the business impact assessment (BIA).

recovery strategy   A high-level plan for resuming business operations after a disaster.

recovery time objective (RTO)   The period from the onset of an outage until the resumption of service. RTO is usually measured in hours or days.

Redundant Array of Independent Disks (RAID)   A family of technologies that is used to improve the reliability, performance, or size of disk-based storage systems.

registration authority (RA)   An entity that works within or alongside a certificate authority (CA) to accept requests for new digital certificates.

release management   The IT function that controls the release of software programs, applications, and environments. *See also* IT service management (ITSM).

release process   The IT process whereby changes to software programs, applications, and environments are requested, reviewed, approved, and implemented.

remote access   A service that permits a user to establish a network connection from a remote location so that the user can access network resources remotely.

remote access Trojan (RAT)   Malware that permits the attacker to remotely access and control a target system.

remote destruct   The act of commanding a device, such as a laptop computer or mobile device, to destroy stored data. Remote destruct is sometimes used when a device is lost or stolen to prevent anyone from being able to read data stored on the device.

remote work   The practice of employees working in locations other than their organizations' work premises.

reperformance   An audit technique where an IS auditor repeats actual tasks performed by auditees in order to confirm they were performed properly.

replication   An activity where data that is written to a storage system is also copied over a network to another storage system and written. The result is the presence of up-to-date data that exists on two or more storage systems, each of which could be located in a different geographic region.

request for change (RFC)   *See* change request.

request for information (RFI)   A formal process where an organization solicits information regarding solution proposals from one or more vendors. This is usually used to gather official information about products or services that may be considered in the future.

request for proposal (RFP)   A formal process where an organization solicits solution proposals from one or more vendors. The process usually includes formal requirements and desired terms and conditions. It is used to formally evaluate vendor proposals to make a selection.

requirements   Formal statements that describe required (and desired) characteristics of a system that is to be changed, developed, or acquired.

residual risk   The risk that remains after being reduced through other risk treatment options.

response document   Required action of personnel after a disaster strikes. It includes the business recovery plan, occupant emergency plan, emergency communication plan, contact lists, disaster recovery plan, continuity of operations plan (COOP), and security incident response plan (SIRP).

responsibility   A stated expectation of activities and performance.

retainer agreement   A contract in which an organization pays in advance for professional services. Examples include external legal counsel and security incident response.

return on investment (ROI)   The ratio of money gained or lost as compared to an original investment.

return on security investment (ROSI)   The return on investment (ROI) based on the reduction of security-related losses compared to the cost of related controls.

right to audit   A clause in a contract where one party has the right to conduct an audit of the other party's operations.

risk   Generally, the fact that undesired events can happen that may damage property or disrupt operations; specifically, an event scenario that can result in property damage or disruption.

risk acceptance   The risk treatment option where management chooses to accept the risk as is.

risk analysis   The process of identifying and studying risks in an organization.

risk appetite   The level of risk that an organization is willing to accept while in pursuit of its mission, strategy, and objectives, and before action is needed to treat the risk.

risk assessment   A process where risks, in the form of threats and vulnerabilities, are identified for each asset.

risk avoidance   The risk treatment option involving a cessation of the activity that introduces identified risk.

risk awareness   Programmatic activities whose objective is to make business leaders, stakeholders, and other personnel aware of the organization's information risk management program. *See also* security awareness.

risk capacity   The objective amount of loss that an organization can tolerate without its continued existence being called into question.

risk ledger   *See* risk register.

risk management   The management activities used to identify, analyze, and treat risks.

risk mitigation   The risk treatment option involving implementation of a solution that will reduce an identified risk.

risk monitoring   Ongoing activities including control effectiveness assessments and risk assessments to observe changes in risk.

risk register   A business record containing business risks and information about their origin, potential impact, affected assets, probability of occurrence, and treatment.

risk tolerance   *See* risk appetite.

risk transfer   The risk treatment option involving the act of transferring risk to another party, such as an insurance company.

risk treatment   The decision to manage an identified risk. The available choices are mitigate the risk, avoid the risk, transfer the risk, or accept the risk.

roadmap   The list of steps required to achieve a strategic objective.

role   A set of user privileges in an application; also, a formal designation assigned to an individual by virtue of a job title or other label.

rollback   A step in the software development life cycle where system changes need to be reversed, returning the system to its previous state.

root cause analysis (RCA)   Analysis of a problem to identify the underlying origins, not merely factors or symptoms. *See also* problem management.

sabotage   Deliberate damage of an organization's asset.

salvage   The process of recovering components or assets that still have value after a disaster.

sample   A portion of a population of records that is selected for auditing.

sample mean   The sum of all samples divided by the number of samples.

sample standard deviation   A computation of the variance of sample values from the sample mean. This is a measurement of the "spread" of values in the sample.

sampling   A technique that is used to select a portion of a population when it is not feasible to test an entire population.

sampling risk   The probability that a sample selected does not represent the entire population. This is usually expressed as a percentage, as the numeric inverse of the confidence coefficient.

sandbox   A security mechanism, often used by antimalware programs, for separating running programs. *See also* anti-malware.

SANS 20 Critical Security Controls *See* CIS Controls.

Sarbanes–Oxley A U.S. law requiring public corporations to enact business and technical controls, perform internal audits of those controls, and undergo external audits.

SAS 70 (Statement of Accounting Standards No. 70) An external audit of a service provider. An SAS 70 audit is performed according to rules established by the American Institute of Certified Public Accountants (AICPA). This has been deprecated by SSAE 18. *See also* Statements on Standards for Attestation Engagements No. 18 (SSAE 18).

scanning tool A security tool that is used to scan files, processes, network addresses, systems, or other objects, often for the purpose of identifying assets or vulnerabilities that may be present in assets.

screening router A network device that filters network traffic based on source and destination IP addresses and ports. *See also* firewall.

secure coding The practice of developing program source code that is free of security defects. *See also* secure development training.

secure development training Training for software developers on the techniques of writing secure code and avoiding security defects that could be exploited by adversaries.

secure electronic transaction (SET) A protocol used to protect credit card transactions that uses a digital envelope. SET has been deprecated by Secure Sockets Layer (SSL) and Transport Layer Security (TLS). *See also* digital envelope, Secure Sockets Layer (SSL), Transport Layer Security (TLS).

Secure Multipurpose Internet Mail Extensions (S/MIME) An e-mail security protocol that provides sender and recipient authentication and encryption of message content and attachments.

Secure Shell (SSH) A TCP/IP application layer protocol that provides a secure channel between two computers whereby all communications between them are encrypted. SSH can also be used as a tunnel to encapsulate and thereby protect other protocols.

Secure Sockets Layer (SSL) An encryption protocol used to encrypt web pages requested with the HTTPS URL. This has been deprecated by Transport Layer Security (TLS). *See also* Transport Layer Security (TLS), Hypertext Transfer Protocol Secure (HTTPS).

security architecture The mission of understanding the interplay between all of the security controls and configurations that work together to protect information systems and information assets.

security audit A formal review of security controls, processes, or systems to determine their state. *See also* audit.

security awareness A formal program used to educate employees, users, customers, or constituents on required, acceptable, and unacceptable security-related behaviors. *See also* risk awareness.

security by design   The concept of product and software development that incorporates security into the design of the software rather than as an afterthought.

security governance   Management's control over an organization's security program.

security incident   An event where the confidentiality, integrity, or availability of information (or an information system) has been compromised.

security information and event management (SIEM)   A system that collects logs from systems, correlates log data, and produces alerts that require attention.

security incident log   A business record consisting of security incidents that have occurred.

security incident management   The overall program and activities to ensure that an organization is able to quickly detect, respond, and contain a security incident.

security incident response   The formal, planned response that is enacted when a security incident has occurred. *See also* security incident.

security operations center (SOC)   An IT function wherein personnel centrally monitor and manage security functions and devices, watch for security anomalies and incidents, and take actions as warranted.

security policy   *See* information security policy.

security review   An examination of a process, procedure, system, program, or other object to determine the state of security.

semiquantitative risk analysis   A risk analysis methodology where risks are classified on a simple numeric scale, such as 1 to 5.

segregation of duties (SOD)   The concept that ensures single individuals do not possess excess privileges that could result in unauthorized activities such as fraud or the manipulation or exposure of sensitive data.

separation of duties   *See* segregation of duties (SOD).

server   A centralized computer used to perform a specific task.

service continuity management   The IT function that consists of activities concerned with the organization's ability to continue providing services, primarily in the event that a natural or man-made disaster has occurred. *See also* IT service management (ITSM), business continuity planning (BCP), disaster recovery planning (DRP).

service delivery objective (SDO)   The level or quality of service that is required after an event, as compared to business normal operations.

service desk   The IT function that handles incidents and service requests on behalf of customers by acting as a single point of contact. *See also* IT service management (ITSM).

service level agreement (SLA)   An agreement that specifies service levels in terms of the quantity of work, quality, timeliness, and remedies for shortfalls in quality or quantity.

service level management   The IT function that confirms whether IT is providing adequate service to its customers. This is accomplished through continuous monitoring and periodic review of IT service delivery. *See also* IT service management (ITSM).

shadow IT   The phenomenon wherein individuals, groups, departments, and business units bypass corporate IT and procure their own computing services, typically through SaaS and IaaS services. *See also* cloud, infrastructure-as-a-service (IaaS), software-as-a-service (IaaS).

shared responsibility model   A model that depicts responsibilities between service providers and customers, typically in a cloud environment.

simulation   A test of disaster recovery, business continuity, or security incident response procedures where the participants take part in a "mock disaster" or incident to add some realism to the process of thinking their way through emergency response documents.

single loss expectancy (SLE)   The financial loss when a threat is realized one time. SLE is defined as AV × EF. *See also* asset value (AV), exposure factor (EF).

single point of failure   An element or device in a system or network lacking redundancy, and when it fails for any reason, the entire network or system will experience an outage.

smart card   A small, credit-card–sized device that contains electronic memory and is accessed with a smart card reader and used in two-factor authentication.

smartphone   A mobile phone equipped with an operating system and software applications.

smishing   Phishing in the context of SMS messaging. *See also* phishing.

snapshot   A continuous auditing technique that involves the use of special audit modules embedded in online applications that sample specific transactions. The module copies key database records that can be examined later.

sniffer   *See* packet sniffer.

social engineering   The act of using deception to trick an individual into revealing secrets or performing actions.

software defect   A defect introduced into a program that results in unexpected behavior. Commonly known as a bug.

Software Engineering Institute Capability Maturity Model (SEI-CMM)   A model used to determine the maturity of security processes. *See also* Capability Maturity Model Integration for Development (CMMi-DEV).

software-as-a-service (SaaS)   A software delivery model where an organization obtains a software application for use by its employees and the software application is hosted by the software provider, as opposed to the customer organization.

software-defined networking (SDN)   A class of capabilities where network infrastructure devices such as routers, switches, and firewalls are created, configured, and managed as virtual devices in virtualization environments.

solid-state drive (SSD)   A solid-state device used for persistent data storage, generally a replacement for a hard-disk drive. *See also* hard disk drive (HDD).

SOX   *See* Sarbanes–Oxley.

spam   Unsolicited and unwanted e-mail.

spam filter   A central program or device that examines incoming e-mail and removes all messages identified as spam.

span port   *See* network tap.

spear phishing   Phishing that is specially crafted for a specific target organization or group. *See also* CEO fraud, phishing, whaling.

spim   Spam or phishing in the context of instant messaging. *See also* phishing, smishing, spam.

spyware   A type of malware where software performs one or more surveillance-type actions on a computer, reporting back to the spyware owner. *See also* malware.

standard   A statement that defines the technologies, protocols, suppliers, and methods used by an IT organization.

statement of impact   A description of the impact a disaster scenario will have on a business or business process.

Statements on Standards for Attestation Engagements No. 16 (SSAE 16)   An audit standard superseded by Statements on Standards for Attestation Engagements No. 18. *See also* Statements on Standards for Attestation Engagements No. 18 (SSAE 18).

Statements on Standards for Attestation Engagements No. 18 (SSAE 18)   A standard for audits performed on a financial service provider. An SSAE 18 audit is performed according to rules established by the American Institute of Certified Public Accountants (AICPA). *See also* System and Organization Controls 1 (SOC1).

static application security testing (SAST)   Tools that are used to scan software source code to identify security defects.

statistical sampling   A sampling technique where items are chosen at random; each item has a statistically equal probability of being chosen. *See also* sampling.

steganography   Any technique where data is hidden within another data file.

System and Organization Controls 1 (SOC1)   An external audit of a service provider. A SOC1 audit is performed according to the SSAE18 standard established by the American Institute of Certified Public Accountants (AICPA). *See also* Statements on Standards for Attestation Engagements No. 18 (SSAE 18).

System and Organization Controls 2 (SOC2)   An external audit of a service provider on one or more of the following trust principles: security, availability, processing integrity, confidentiality, and privacy. A SOC2 audit is performed according to audit standards established by the American Institute of Certified Public Accountants (AICPA).

System and Organization Controls 3 (SOC3)   An external audit of a service provider on one or more of the following trust principles: security, availability, processing integrity, confidentiality, and privacy.

stop-or-go sampling   A sampling technique used to permit sampling to stop at the earliest possible time. This technique is used when the auditor thinks there is low risk or a low rate of exceptions in the population. *See also* sampling.

storage area network (SAN)   A stand-alone storage system that can be configured to contain several virtual volumes and connected to many servers through fiber-optic cables.

strategic objective   A corporate objective that is a part of a high-level strategy.

strategic planning   Activities used to develop and refine long-term plans and objectives.

strategy   The plan required to achieve an objective.

stratified sampling   A sampling technique where a population is divided into classes or strata, based upon the value of one of the attributes. Samples are then selected from each class. *See also* sampling.

stream cipher   A type of encryption algorithm that operates on a continuous stream of data, such as a video or audio feed.

strong authentication   *See* multifactor authentication.

supervisory control and data acquisition (SCADA)   A control system used to monitor and manage physical machinery in an industrial environment. *See also* industrial control system (ICS).

symmetric encryption   A method for encryption and decryption where it is necessary for both parties to possess a common encryption key.

synchronous replication   A type of replication where writing data to a local and to a remote storage system is performed as a single operation, guaranteeing that data on the remote storage system is identical to data on the local storage system. *See also* replication.

tablet   A mobile device with a touchscreen interface. *See also* mobile device.

technical control   A control that is implemented in IT systems and applications.

technology standard A standard that specifies the software and hardware technologies that are used by the IT organization.

telework *See* remote work.

termination The process of discontinuing employment of an employee or contractor.

terrorist A person or group who perpetrates violence for political or religious reasons.

The Open Group Architecture Framework (TOGAF) A life-cycle enterprise architecture framework used for the design, plan, implementation, and governance of an enterprise security architecture.

third party An external organization providing goods or services to an organization.

third-party risk management (TPRM) The practice of identifying risks associated with the use of outsourced organizations to perform business processes.

threat An event that, if realized, would bring harm to an asset.

threat assessment An examination of threats and the likelihood and impact of their occurrence.

threat hunting The proactive search for intrusions, intruders, and indicators of compromise.

threat intel feed A subscription service containing information about known threats. A threat intel feed can come in the form of human-readable or machine-readable information.

threat intelligence Information about security tools, tactics, and trends of intrusions that can help an organization know how to better protect itself from intrusion.

threat management Activities undertaken by an organization to learn of relevant security threats so that the organization can take appropriate action to counter the threats.

threat modeling The activity of looking for potential threats in a business process, information system, or software application.

Towers of Hanoi A complex backup media rotation scheme that provides for more lengthy retention of some backup media. It is based on the Towers of Hanoi puzzle. *See also* backup media rotation.

Towers of Sauron A collection of towers, including Dol Guldur, Orthanc, Cirith Ungol, Minas Tirith, Minas Morgul, and Barad-dûr, all located in Middle-earth.

total cost of ownership (TCO) A financial estimate of all of the costs associated with a process or system.

training The process of educating personnel; to impart information or provide an environment where they can practice a new skill.

Transport Layer Security (TLS)   An encryption protocol used to encrypt web pages requested with the HTTPS URL. This is a replacement for Secure Sockets Layer (SSL). *See also* Secure Sockets Layer (SSL), Hypertext Transfer Protocol Secure (HTTPS).

unified extensible firmware interface (UEFI)   The firmware on a computer that tests the computer's hardware and initiates the bootup sequence. UEFI is considered a successor to BIOS. *See also* basic input/output system (BIOS).

uninterruptible power supply (UPS)   A system that filters the incoming power of spikes and other noise and supplies power for short periods through a bank of batteries.

user   A business or customer who uses an information system.

user behavior analytics (UBA)   A capability where user behavior is baselined and anomalous activities trigger events or alarms.

user ID   An identifier that is created by a system manager and issued to a user for the purpose of identification or authentication.

variable sampling   A sampling technique used to study the characteristics of a population to determine the numeric total of a specific attribute from the entire population. *See also* sampling.

vendor standard   A standard that specifies which suppliers and vendors are used for various types of products and services.

virtual machine   A software implementation of a computer, usually an operating system or other program running within a hypervisor. *See also* hypervisor.

virtualization   Software technology that separates the physical computing environment from the software that runs on a system, permitting several instances of operating systems to operate concurrently and independently on a single system.

virus   A type of malware where fragments of code attach themselves to executable programs and are activated when the program they are attached to is run.

vulnerability   A weakness that may be present in a system that can be exploited by a threat.

vulnerability assessment   An assessment whose objective is to identify vulnerabilities in target assets.

vulnerability management   A formal business process that is used to identify and mitigate vulnerabilities in an IT environment.

walk-through   A review of some or all disaster recovery and business continuity plans, procedures, and other documentation. A walk-through is performed by an entire group of individuals in a live discussion.

war room   A meeting room or other place where incident responders will gather to coordinate incident response activities.

warm site   An alternate processing center where recovery systems are present but at a lower state of readiness than recovery systems at a hot site. For example, while the same version of the operating system may be running on the warm site system, it may be a few patch levels behind primary systems.

watering hole attack   An attack on one more organizations that is performed by introducing malicious code on a web site that personnel in target organizations are thought to frequent.

weaponization   The process of creating or obtaining malware that is to be delivered to a target as a part of a computer intrusion.

web application firewall (WAF)   A firewall that examines the contents of information in transit between a web server and its users, for the purpose of identifying and blocking malicious content that could represent an attack on the web server.

web content filter   A central program or device that monitors and, optionally, filters web communications. A web content filter is often used to control the sites (or categories of sites) that users are permitted to access from the workplace. Some web content filters can also protect an organization from malware.

web proxy filter   *See* web content filter.

web server   A server that runs specialized software that makes static and dynamic HTML pages available to users.

web-based application   An application design where the database and all business logic are stored on central servers and where user workstations use only web browsers to access the application.

whaling   Spear phishing that targets executives and other high-value and high-privilege individuals in an organization. *See also* CEO fraud, phishing, spear phishing.

white list   In a security system, a list of identifiers that should always be permitted, regardless of their other characteristics.

whole-disk encryption   The practice of encrypting the main storage on a server, workstation, or mobile device.

wiper   Malware designed to wipe the hard drive of a system.

wired equivalent privacy (WEP)   A now deprecated encryption protocol used by WiFi networks.

worm   A type of malware containing stand-alone programs capable of human-assisted and automatic propagation.

Zachman framework   An enterprise architecture framework used to describe an IT architecture in increasing levels of detail.

INDEX

Numbers

360 feedback, monitoring, 38

A

A-123, internal audit cycle, 229
acceptable interruption window (AIW), MTD, 160
acceptable risk. *See* risk acceptance
acceptable use policy, 83
access bypass, security incidents, 380
access control
    balanced scorecard, 45
    computer, 337
    managing IT, 255
    managing workplace, 254
    network access control, 288
    network segmentation and, 279–280
    security awareness training linked to, 300
access control policy, 136
access governance, IAM, 294–296
access grants, 30
access management, continuity plans, 429
access operations, IAM, 294
access owners, 30–31
access recertification, 295
access reviews, 31, 294
access revocation, 31
AccessData Certified Examiner (ACE), 398
accountability, organizational culture, 74
accounts payable, identifying third parties via, 242
accumulation of privileges, access, 295
accuracy, information classification, 129
ACE (AccessData Certified Examiner), 398
active/active mode, server clusters, 455–456
active/passive mode, server clusters, 455–456
activities, security governance, 21–22, 200–201
activity reviews, IAM, 296
actors. *See* threat actors (or actors)
Addressable controls, HIPAA, 59
administrative activities
    budgeting, 268–269
    business case development, 270–271
    compliance management, 260–262
    external partnerships, 258–260
    internal partnerships. *See* internal partnerships
    overview of, 251–252

personnel management, 263–268
project and program management, 268
vendor management, 271
administrative audits, 221
administrative control, 337
advanced persistent threats (APTs), 138–140
advisory services, risk management, 114
affiliates, internal partnerships with, 257–258
AH mode, IPSec, 314
AIW (acceptable interruption window), MTD, 160
ALE (annualized loss expectancy), 148–149, 212
alerts
    detection phase of incident response, 384
    emergency communications plan, 426
    to incident response personnel, 387
    incident response tools for, 388
algorithms, encryption, 303, 313–314
allowable interruption window (AIW), MTD, 160
analysis phase, incident response, 384
annual training, security awareness, 300
annualized loss expectancy (ALE), 148–149, 212
annualized rate of occurrence (ARO),
    148–149, 212–213
ANSI (American National Standards Institute), 2–3
anti-malware
    attack innovations evading, 140, 290
    detecting malware, 290
    endpoint protection with, 209
    metrics, 38
    risk management with, 105
antiforensics, incident response, 403
antivirus software, death of, 290, 291. *See also*
    anti-malware
appliances
    network anomaly detection systems as, 282
    vulnerability assessment of, 69
application, CISM certification, 4, 8, 12
application firewalls, 279
applications
    developing continuity plan, 429
    managing replication, 319, 454
    penetration testing, 173
    requiring high availability/resilience, 456–457
    scanning, 173
    testing, 332
Approved Scanning Vendors (ASV), PCI, 358
APTs (advanced persistent threats), 138–140